THE ARCHITECTURE
OF ANCIENT GREECE

THE ARCHITECTURE
OF ANCIENT GREECE

AN ACCOUNT OF ITS HISTORIC DEVELOPMENT

William Bell Dinsmoor

W · W · Norton & Company
New York · London

W. W. Norton & Company, Inc., 500 Fifth Avenue, New York, N.Y. 10110
W. W. Norton & Company Ltd., 37 Great Russell Street, London WC1B 3NU

Copyright © 1975 by W. W. Norton & Company, Inc.

Library of Congress Cataloging in Publication Data
Dinsmoor, William Bell, 1886–
    The architecture of ancient Greece.
    Reprint of the 1950 3d ed. rev., published by
B. T. Batsford, London, with a new pref. and new
photos.
    First published in 1902 under title: The archi-
tecture of ancient Greece and Rome.
    Bibliography: p.
    Includes index.
    1. Architecture—Greece—History. I. Title.
NA270.D5   1975   722'.8   75–6960

ISBN 0-393-00781-2

Printed in the United States of America
     5 6 7 8 9

PREFACE

"TO the late William J. Anderson, of Glasgow, is due the conception of this work. The course of lectures which, on the invitation of the Governors of the School of Art in that city, he delivered in 1893–1894 on the Architecture of the Renaissance in Italy (published in 1896), was followed in 1896–1897 by a course on the History and Development of Greek Architecture. To this subject he devoted his studies for three years, repeating his course with various revisions, and adding to it in 1897 three additional lectures on Roman Architecture, which, with those on Greek, he intended to publish as his second work. Immediately following these Roman lectures, he continued, in 1898, with a course which included the various styles down to the present day, and in the winter of 1898–1899 a further special course dealing with the Renaissance in France."

With these words R. Phené Spiers began his preface to the original edition of *The Architecture of Greece and Rome* in 1902. Therein he explained how the preparation of courses dealing with later periods of architectural history, and Mr. Anderson's own failing health and death, had greatly interfered with the completion of the book, and how it had been finally terminated by himself with the addition of a seventh chapter on Greek secular architecture and the composition of those on Roman architecture. This first edition of 1902, published at the very moment when I was listening to my first lectures on Greek and Roman architecture from the late H. Langford Warren, had formed the textbook of my youthful years. A second and slightly revised impression was published in 1907.

The preparation of another revision of *The Architecture of Greece and Rome* had been considered before the outbreak of the First World War; at that time the plan was to republish the book merely with verbal emendations and corrections, leaving it as a whole essentially unaltered. But when the project was taken up again after the delay caused by the war, the outlook had changed; it seemed preferable to make the revision as thorough as might be necessary in order to make the book more useful and attractive to students, and to embody more of the latest results of excavation and research. To that end the book was divided into its two component parts, each half being entrusted by Mr. Harry Batsford to a specialist in the field concerned. My acceptance of the task of re-writing the Greek portion, while I was still resident in Greece, was followed by my unforeseen return to the United States, where other work awaited me; the ensuing delay permitted me, however, to take account of the important discoveries of the next few years and of observations made during my subsequent visits to Greece in 1924–1926. The result was the revised edition of 1927.

Though the final decision had been to revise the work so thoroughly that it was practically a new book, nevertheless it seemed desirable to retain, to as great an extent as was possible, the arrangement and the language of the second impression of 1907. The method then followed in the revision, therefore, requires brief explanation.

The stress laid upon the idea of evolution by the original authors precluded any other scheme of arrangement; the evolutionary scheme seems, furthermore, all the more desirable, because it is the opposite or analytical viewpoint that underlies most of the recent surveys of Greek architecture. For this reason the material was freely rearranged in order that it might be perfectly consistent with the chronological framework; the most obvious change was the disintegration of the original chapter (VII) on secular architecture, and the discussion of all the secular monuments in the chapters dealing with the periods concerned where, in fact, a few works such as the monument of Lysicrates and the Tower of the Winds had already been described. By drawing a sharp distinction between the fourth century and the Hellenistic period, however, the original number of chapters (seven) was retained. Within each period, moreover, I attempted to restrict myself to the examples selected by the original authors and to refrain from introducing new ideas or following out lines of investigation other than those indicated by Messrs. Anderson and Spiers, lest I depart too radically from their work. With this in mind, I excluded from the final draft much of the material which I should have wished to include if I had assumed the entire responsibility. But I gave, whenever possible, the most recent versions of the theories which they discussed and, wherever their conclusions did not bear the test of later research, I exercised the power of suppressing them or relegating them to footnotes. The one exception to this treatment was the first chapter, which, on account of the rapid advance in our knowledge of the pre-classical epoch, was perforce almost totally new. Some general material was separated from the original first chapter to form, what it was in fact, an introduction to the whole subject.

The number of illustrations was increased by eighty, but as only fifty-four of the original illustrations of the second edition were retained (and even these in part revised), the number of new illustrations was actually one hundred and forty-nine. The chronological memoranda at the beginning were somewhat amplified, and the chronological table of Greek temples at the end of the book was entirely recomposed, with changes not only in the dates but also, in practically every case, in the dimensions and proportions, the measurements being in all cases taken either directly from the buildings themselves or from the detailed monographs. The bibliography was brought up to date and rearranged in accordance with the chapters of the book.

Now, amid the struggle for survival in this Second World War, has come the word that a new edition should be prepared. I have taken from my shelves, therefore, the materials that I omitted from the edition of 1927, as well as the notes made during the seventeen intervening years, particularly in the course of sojourns in Greece in 1927–1928, 1937, and 1939, and during a survey of

South Italy and Sicily in 1932. I have added to the Bibliography the important new publications of these years, and their results have been incorporated in my text. The additional material thus accumulated has been almost overwhelming, in spite of the constant effort to exclude what is non-essential. The explanation of this increase must be sought in the extraordinary activity in architectural research since 1927. In that very year, for instance, and hence not utilised in the previous edition of this work, appeared fundamental monographs on the Erechtheum and on Eleusis and Calydon; and in the same year began my own studies at Bassae which resulted in the alteration of nearly everything hitherto written about this temple. Since 1927, furthermore, entire sites have been excavated or re-excavated: the Athenian Agora and Ceramicus, Eleusis, Olympia, Paestum, Olynthus, Cyprus, and Troy, to name only a few. Since 1927, also, have begun to appear definitive publications of older excavations, such as Corinth, Sparta, Corcyra, Cos, and Larisa; and similar publications previously begun have acquired invaluable supplementary volumes, as in the case of Cnossus, Delos, and Delphi. Well-known buildings have formed the subjects of new revisionary studies, such as the Erechtheum and temple at Bassae mentioned above, and also the Parthenon, the so-called "Theseum," and the temple at Didyma. There have been notable synthetic studies of special classes of material, such as theatres, city walls, roof terra-cottas, and profiles of mouldings.

In order to take account of these new developments without undue expansion, it has seemed imperative to economise in space by deleting all doubtful conjectures from this new edition, and also by omitting various observations of a general nature which, having appeared in the original text of 1902, had been faithfully preserved in the succeeding editions. In the present edition, moreover, I have adhered more closely to historical continuity by removing from the text itself all allusions to present condition of the ruins, modern investigations, correction of erroneous theories, and even evidence for the solutions adopted. Some of these will now be found in the footnotes, in which I have also included, in more consistent fashion than heretofore, considerable information as to the locations of such architectural and decorative members as have been removed from their original sites to the various European and American museums.

In view of the careful revision of the illustrations for the edition of 1927, and of the difficulties in transmission of additional illustrative material between two continents at the present moment, it has been decided to retain the illustrations of the preceding edition, with alterations in a few cases and with only fifty-five additions (forming a total of two hundred and sixty illustrations, including the two maps). Apart from emendations made in a few borrowed from other sources (Figs. 4, 7, 10, 14, 39, 44, 74, Pl. XXXVII), nineteen others are from my own drawings (Figs. 18, 20, 22, 40, 50, 56–57, 65–67, 70–71, 75–76, 81, 99, Pl. LXIII top) or photographs (Pls. XVI top, LXVII top). It is obvious that no comprehensive set of illustrations can be correct in all details; drawings and restorations are necessarily subjective, and it would be hopeless

PREFACE

to attempt to revise all the minor faults of interpretation wherein drawings have been shown by later research to be in error. Features wherein the illustrations seem to be at variance with the statements in the text are indicated in the footnotes.

For the opinions and interpretations in the present edition, therefore, I assume the responsibility. Many of them are the results of my personal experience and observations, even of unpublished studies which I had once intended to hold in reserve until they could be given more detailed consideration in monographs. With the consciousness that time is passing, however, and that the possibilities of further study in the immediate future may be limited, I feel that a presentation of the chief results in connected form is appropriate at this moment when the Doric columns of Syracuse, Acragas, and Paestum are witnesses of the innate kinship, in arms as in letters, of the English-speaking peoples.

WILLIAM BELL DINSMOOR.

LONDON,
July, 1944

Five years have elapsed since the foregoing words were written during nights of aerial bombardment in London, so that a few additional words seem necessary. The page proof as printed from my manuscript of 1944 has been revised, so far as space restrictions have permitted, to accommodate the later discoveries of the last five years. The selection of illustrations originally made, however, has been retained; I can only regret that certain publications such as those of Knackfuss on Didyma (of which I was able to utilise one plate from an advance prospectus) and of Robinson on Olynthus (vol. XII), and the restored models and drawings of the Athenian Acropolis by Stevens and of the Athenian Agora by Travlos, were not available in time. An appendix has been added, giving the principal dimensions of the buildings analysed in the Chronological Table, but in the metric system for the use of archaeologists who prefer this system, thus avoiding the danger of inaccuracies through conversion from English feet and inches. The bibliography has been greatly enlarged (including publications during and since the war), and has been carefully classified by subjects and sites, in the hope that it will be of greater service in stimulating further studies. Similarly the indexes have been subdivided and amplified, especially that of subjects, through which, by starting with the key words "Construction" and "Design," an analytical survey of Greek architecture may be obtained.

W. B. D.

NEW YORK,
August, 1949

PREFACE TO THE PRESENT EDITION

DURING the quarter century since the last authorized edition of this book was published (a pirated edition has since had some circulation), tremendous strides forward have been made in all branches of Greek archaeology. Numerous new excavations and continued study of older ones have contributed extensively to our knowledge of ancient architecture, sculpture, epigraphy, numismatics, pottery, etc., and through these to better understanding of life and the history of the past. In some of the new excavations archaeologists have discovered and uncovered, for instance, the important Minoan palace at Kato Zakro on Crete, parts of the Minoan city on Thera with its magnificent and informative frescoes, the Mycenaean palace of Nestor at Messenian Pylos, the apsidal temples at Eretria, the entire sanctuary of Poseidon at Isthmia with its early archaic and its classical temples, the Venerable Royal Stoa in Athens, well known from epigraphical evidence—the list is lengthy. In addition, new technological advances and more extensive knowledge of the placing of pottery and coins in the framework of time have helped to date more accurately the finds that are made.

In this present posthumous reprinting of Professor Dinsmoor's classic and unparalleled work on ancient Greek architecture serious thought was given to making select changes and additions to the text in note form. It was decided, however, that such necessarily limited and incomplete notations would be unworthy of the book and completely unsatisfactory. Professor Dinsmoor himself thought along these same lines. Ten years ago he started to prepare a slightly modified new edition of his work, but he soon despaired of accomplishing any desirable results by this method. He then began to revise the book completely by bringing it up to date to include the more recently discovered sites and important buildings. He incorporated as well the results of later scholarly studies that have revised many of the earlier ideas published in his third edition. He expanded at great length his discussions of the various buildings. The cumulative effect was the approximate doubling in length of the present text, a size which is not economically feasible to publish. Also a great deal of work would still be required to assemble, research, and complete the various parts and to edit the work in general. Instead, it is the hope of the undersigned to be able eventually to put together both from the wealth of material in his manuscript and from more recent studies a comprehensive fourth edition of the book which will be as wieldy and serviceable to students and scholars as is this present work. In the meantime, to meet current demand, W. W. Norton & Company has reprinted the third edition with fifty-five fresh photographic illustrations.

ATHENS,
August, 1974

WILLIAM BELL DINSMOOR, JR.

ACKNOWLEDGMENT

Many of the subjects included among the illustrations are from various foreign sources, and the author must acknowledge his debt to a number of Works and Transactions of Learned Societies in which these appear. Thanks are due to the Authorities of the British Museum for permission to include the subjects illustrated on Plate XVI (bottom two), Plate XXX, Plate LV (centre) and Plate LVI (top). He must also thank Mr. A. E. Henderson, F.S.A., and the Royal Institute of British Architects for permission to reproduce the reconstruction of the Later Temple of Artemis at Ephesus, appearing on Plate LIV, in the galleries of the Institute. A large number of reproductions have been made from original drawings and reconstructions in which the names of the responsible authorities appear on the titles to the illustrations, and grateful acknowledgment must be made for the use of these subjects, which must be considered indispensable to a general survey of Greek Architecture. Useful comments on the earlier edition have been received from several and have been carefully considered; particularly valuable were those of the late Professor W. S. Purchon of Cardiff, whose insistence that the restoration of the Lesser Propylaea at Eleusis, as published by the Society of Dilettanti, should not be too lightly rejected, led to fruitful reconsideration of this building. The author is particularly indebted to Miss G. R. Levy and the Library of the Societies for the Promotion of Hellenic and Roman Studies for invaluable facilities afforded under somewhat trying conditions during the last stages of revision. Finally, the author can only inadequately express his gratitude for the unflagging encouragement, assistance, and patience of Mr. Harry Batsford and his colleagues, Messrs. W. Hanneford-Smith and Charles D. Fry.

W. B. D.

Thanks are due to the following sources for fresh illustrations:
Alison Frantz: Plates IV (left), VII (top), VIII, XV, XVI (top), XXII (top), XXVII (both), XXIX (right), XXXV (bottom), XXXVIII, XLV, XLVI (top), XLVIII (top), LIII (top), LX (right); Hirmer Fotoarchiv: Plates XVIII (bottom), XXIII (bottom), XXXV (top), XXXVI (bottom), XXXIX (right), LXIX (top); Warder Collection: Plates XL (bottom), LVIII (left); W. B. Dinsmoor, Jr.: Plates XXVI, XXXIII (bottom right), XXXVI (bottom); Robert E. Farlow: Plates II, XXII (bottom), XXV (both), XLII (top), XLVI (bottom), LX (left), LXX (top); G. P. Brockway: Plates I, III (left), IX (bottom), XI (both), XII, XIV (left), XVII (bottom), XXII (bottom), XXIV (top), XLI, XLIII (top), XLIV (right), XLVIII (bottom), L (top), LII, LVII (bottom), LXI, LXII (top), LXIV, LXVIII (right).

CHRONOLOGICAL MEMORANDA

c. 5000 B.C.	Beginning of the Neolithic Age in Crete.
c. 3000 ,,	Beginning of the Bronze Age in Crete.
c. 2000 ,,	Minyan invasion of Greece.
c. 1500 ,,	Achaean invasion of Greece.
1184 ,,	Fall of Troy, traditional date.
1104 ,,	Dorian invasion of Greece, traditional date.
776 ,,	First Olympiad, the earliest recorded date.
c. 760 ,,	Foundation of Cumae, the first western colony, by Chalcis.
c. 750 ,,	Age of Homer.
733 ,,	Foundation of Corcyra and Syracuse by Corinth.
627 ,,	Foundation of Selinus.
580 ,,	Foundation of Acragas.
569 ,,	Accession of Aahmes (Amasis) II of Egypt.
566 ,,	Organisation of the Panathenaic Festival at Athens.
561 ,,	Accession of Peisistratus of Athens.
560 ,,	Accession of Croesus of Lydia.
548 ,,	Burning of the temple of Apollo at Delphi.
546 ,,	Conquest of Lydia by Cyrus of Persia.
527 ,,	Death of Peisistratus.
510 ,,	Fall of the tyranny at Athens.
499 ,,	Beginning of the Ionian Revolt.
494 ,,	Miletus taken by Darius of Persia.
490 ,,	First Persian invasion of Greece; battle of Marathon.
485 ,,	Accession of Gelon at Syracuse.
480 ,,	Second Persian invasion of Greece; battles of Thermopylae and Salamis; destruction of Athens. First Carthaginian invasion of Sicily; battle of Himera.
479 ,,	Expulsion of the Persians from Greece; battle of Plataea.
477 ,,	Foundation of the Delian Confederacy under Athens.
461 ,,	Assumption of leadership at Athens by Pericles.
454 ,,	Transfer of the Delian Treasury to Athens.
449 ,,	Peace signed between Athens and Persia; abortive effort to hold Panhellenic Congress at Athens.
448 ,,	Dedication of the Zeus Olympius by Phidias.
447 ,,	Beginning of the Parthenon at Athens.
438 ,,	Dedication of the Athena Parthenos by Phidias.
437 ,,	Beginning of the Propylaea at Athens.
431 ,,	Outbreak of the Peloponnesian War.
429 ,,	Death of Pericles at Athens.
425 ,,	Organisation of the Delian Festival at Delos.
423 ,,	Burning of the temple of Hera near Argos.
421 ,,	Peace of Nicias between Athens and Sparta.

CHRONOLOGICAL MEMORANDA

413 B.C.	Defeat of the Athenians at Syracuse.
409 ,,	Second Carthaginian invasion of Sicily; destruction of Selinus.
404 ,,	Fall of Athens; end of the Peloponnesian War.
394 ,,	Burning of the temple of Athena Alea at Tegea.
377 ,,	Foundation of the second Delian Confederacy under Athens.
373 ,,	Destruction of the temple of Apollo at Delphi by earthquake.
356 ,,	Burning of the temple of Artemis at Ephesus; birth of Alexander the Great.
353 ,,	Death of Mausolus at Halicarnassus.
338 ,,	Conquest of Greece by Philip of Macedon; battle of Chaeronea.
334 ,,	Invasion of Persia by Alexander.
331 ,,	Foundation of Alexandria in Egypt.
323 ,,	Death of Alexander the Great at Babylon.
315 ,,	Demetrius of Phalerum enacts sumptuary laws at Athens.
307 ,,	Demetrius Poliorcetes occupies Piraeus and Athens; he and his father proclaimed "kings" by the Athenians.
306 ,,	Ptolemy Soter assumes royal title in Egypt.
301 ,,	Foundation of Antioch by Seleucus.
286 ,,	Athens revolts against the Macedonians.
279 ,,	Gallic raid on Delphi; second battle of Thermopylae.
264 ,,	Athens recaptured by the Macedonians.
229 ,,	Athens throws off the Macedonian yoke.
174 ,,	Beginning of the temples of Zeus at Athens and Lebadea by Antiochus IV of Syria.
166 ,,	Delos awarded to Athens by Rome.
146 ,,	Destruction of Corinth by the Romans.
86 ,,	Capture of Athens by Sulla.
45 ,,	Refoundation of Corinth by Julius Caesar.
31 ,,	Battle of Actium.
27 ,,	Establishment of the Roman Empire under Augustus.
132 A.D.	Emperor Hadrian at Athens; dedication of the Olympieum.
c. 150–180 A.D.	Pausanias writes his description of Greece.
c. 170 A.D.	Invasion of Attica by the Sarmatian Costobocs.
267 ,,	Invasion of Attica by the Herulian Goths.
324 ,,	Transfer of the Roman capital to Byzantium (Constantinople).
393 ,,	Last Olympiad, suppression of the games by Theodosius the Great.
395 ,,	Invasion of Greece by Alaric and the Goths; destruction of Eleusis.

CONTENTS

★

PREFACE *page* v

PREFACE TO THE PRESENT EDITION *page* ix

ACKNOWLEDGMENT *page* x

CHRONOLOGICAL MEMORANDA *page* xi

INTRODUCTION *page* xv

I

THE AEGEAN AGE *page* 1

Island houses (4), Mainland houses (5), Island palaces (8), Mainland palaces (16), Fortifications (22), Temples (24), Tombs (25).

II

THE ORIGINS OF GREEK ARCHITECTURE *page* 36

Nondescript temples (39), Doric temples (50), Ionic temples (58), Altars (65), Secular buildings (65), Houses (65), Tombs (65).

III

THE RISE OF THE DORIC STYLE *page* 69

Doric temples (70), Telesteria (113), Propylaea (114), Treasuries (115), Tholoi (117), Altars (117), Stoas (118), Fountain-houses (118), Bouleuteria (118), Theatres (119), Palaces (121), Votive monuments (121), Tombs (121).

IV

THE RISE OF THE IONIC STYLE *page* 123

Ionic temples (124), Treasuries (138), Altars (140), Stoas (142), Special types (142), Votive monuments (143), Tombs (144).

V

THE CULMINATION IN ATTICA AND THE PELOPONNESUS *page* 147

Doric temples (149), Ionic temples (184), Telesteria (195), Propylaea (198), Treasuries (205), Tholoi (205), Club-houses (206), Stoas (206), Bouleuteria (206), Theatres (207), Houses (211), Votive monuments (211), Tombs (212), City plans (212).

VI

THE BEGINNING OF THE DECADENCE *page* 216

Doric temples (217), Ionic temples (221), Telesteria (233), Treasuries (233), Tholoi (234), Choragic monuments (236), Stoas (240), Market-halls (241), Arsenals (241), Ship-sheds (242), Bouleuteria (242), Theatres (244), Stadia (250),

CONTENTS

Hippodromes (251), Gymnasia (251), Hotels (251), Houses (252), Votive monuments (253), Tombs (254), City plans (262), Agoras (263).

VII

THE HELLENISTIC AND GRAECO-ROMAN PHASES *page* 265

Doric temples (267), Ionic temples (271), Corinthian temples (279), Tholoi (284), Propylaea (284), Altars (287), Choragic monuments (288), Fountain-houses (288), Lighthouses (289), Clock-towers (289), Ship-sheds (290), Arsenals (290), Stoas (290), Market-halls (293), Bouleuteria (295), Theatres (297), Odeums (319), Amphitheatres (319), Stadia (319), Hippodromes (320), Gymnasia (320), Baths (321), Guildhalls (322), Houses (322), Palaces (325), Votive monuments (326), Tombs (327), City plans (330), Agoras (333), Colonnaded streets (334).

PLATES *between pages* 198-199

MAPS OF GREECE, ASIA MINOR AND ITALY *facing page* 336

APPENDIX: METRIC MEASUREMENTS OF TEMPLES *page* 337

CHRONOLOGICAL LIST OF GREEK TEMPLES *facing page* 340

BIBLIOGRAPHY *page* 341

GLOSSARY *page* 387

INDEX TO TEXT AND ILLUSTRATIONS

A, Places *page* 398
B, Persons *page* 407
C, Subjects *page* 410

INTRODUCTION

THAT works of architecture as things of man's creating are inferior in interest, in excellence of design, and in perfection of workmanship, to the humblest of Nature's works outside humanity, has often been the burden of the moralising of theologian, naturalist, and astronomer. But in this reflection lies a fallacy which is fully exposed to those who can discern in the successive intellectual works of man the path of the human spirit, and who regard them as manifestations of Nature, of which he forms a part. A spiritual element marks off the work of man from that of animals: it is here that architecture begins. Building, whose end and aim is the fulfilment of material wants, remains building, and, whatever be the nature of the material want, differs in no essential from the work of the lower animals; but if to this be added an element of aspiration involving the exercise of a higher kind of design, there is the distinction that makes the difference.

Works of architecture in themselves are material, perishable, incomplete; but a style of architecture is one of the higher manifestations of Nature, reaching in through the human spirit. Should we try to grasp as a whole one great period of architecture, one great style of art, like that of Greece, our study is simplified in finding that it presents all the features of a natural growth. Art is a flower, and, like the flower of the field, is sown in obscurity, nourished by the decay of pre-existing organisms, and, though refined and perfected by high culture, buds and blooms at its own time. It is in a large measure what the soil and the atmosphere and the sunshine make it; it repays the care and toil that human hands bestow upon it; yet its form and its colour are its own. And so we may not know all the causes which produce the phenomenon, but we may at least watch it grow, enjoy its full beauty, and follow it in its withering; for, like the plant, it is beautiful not only when in full flower, but at every stage of progress, and even in decline.

Like other simpler natural manifestations, Greek architecture, while the fruit of all the civilisations which preceded the great period of Greek culture, did not live for itself alone; for it has sown the seed of European architecture, and has determined the future form and growth of most subsequent European art. Behind and beyond the fountain-head which it makes for Western art, the tributary arts of Egypt, Mesopotamia and Phœnicia shrink into their narrower channels, their sources lost in obscurity. From it flows the main stream of European culture, the arts of Rome and the Middle Ages, the rejuvenescence of Roman tradition in the fifteenth century, not to say the prevailing architecture of the cities in which we dwell. The influence of the past upon the present is part of the nature of things in which we live and move; but rarely, if ever, in the world's history have past forms and principles and ideals exercised so potent an influence on subsequent art as those of the vigorous, rarely dowered race which settled, perhaps more than two thousand years before Christ, on the coasts and islands of the Eastern Mediterranean.

The higher flights of literature and architecture present an almost perfect

INTRODUCTION

parallel. Both have more of art than science, and show little progress within themselves all down the ages, while they clearly reflect the progress of the soul of man. It may be that the greatness of the Greeks is not demonstrated most of all in their architecture; but it is by their architecture, using the word in its widest sense, that we may now most readily comprehend their civilisation in all its bearings. A masterpiece turned out in the workshop where Phidias and Ictinus perfected their marvellous designs is in itself a document, for those who have eyes to read it, more precious by far than any single work of Greek literature. To the mythologist, sculptor, architect, philologist, and historian it has opened separate fields of investigation, and from each quarter a beam of light has been shed on the whole subject of Greek civilisation. What is true of the Parthenon in this connection, for instance, is much more true of the whole architectural development from the time of Agamemnon to that of Alexander, as illustrated by the monuments, and by all that is comprehended in them—inscriptions, sculpture, and religious, civic, or domestic furniture. In this sense architecture might be called the sheet-anchor of history, which without the everlasting testimony of the monuments would certainly become fluid and unstable.

But let us not make the mistake of depreciating in return the literary side of the study. We need them both; for how much more is open to the student who examines architectural works with full mythological knowledge, or from the point of view of the trained philologist or historian! No exposition of any of these subjects will appear satisfactory to one whose education has fitted him to view it solely from another standpoint; inevitably the subject must appear as if presented in false perspective, or as if badly lighted, or carelessly drawn. Yet, even at the risk of such distortion, the scope of this sketch must be limited to that which is comprehended in the architect's point of view, though this need not mean the abandonment of all historic narration, the rejection of all mythological explanation, nor the divorce of sculpture from its architectural setting. It involves rather the subservience of our programme to an architect's needs and ideals. But so rooted was the architectural purpose in the motives of the social and religious life of the Hellenes that, it is believed, this point of view will give to others, who may not be specialists, a broader and swifter view of the whole subject of Greek civilisation and history than is possible by any other simple method in the same limited space. For what can tell of the Greeks more worthily than the actual buildings which the wants and ideals of their civilisation determined?

Yet this wider historic view is only a subsidiary purpose. Our business is to impart the lessons of architectural history in such a light as to give the architectural student a clear apprehension of the historic significance of style. Nothing is more likely to wean him from the misuse or feeble copyism of its characteristics than a grasp of their relation to surrounding circumstances. To this end, buildings will be studied in their plan and design, rather than in their details or furnishings.

The reason why it is essential, in studying architecture, to have some regard for the broad views of history, religion, and society is that the purpose for which the building is erected is the greatest controlling factor in shaping that building. For example, it is really of greater importance in the evolution of

Greek architecture that the Greeks devised shrines to house their gods and goddesses and for the needs of their particular ceremonies, than that marble was the building material which lay close at hand. Material is, of course, another influence, but a decidedly minor one. Temples were built of marble at Athens, and of limestone at Paestum and Corinth, the only effect upon the design being a greater refinement of detail at Athens: the type is one and the same, and the type was determined by tradition.

In what way to use tradition is the problem of modern architecture. In earlier days an architect's retrospect was bounded by the works of his grandfather, or at most by the primitive arts of his own district. But now there is this difference, that it ranges over the larger traditions of all architectural history, choosing the good and refusing the bad, and doubtless out of this selective use will come in the fullness of time a living art as noble as Greek, more cosmopolitan than Roman, and perfectly characteristic of the age we live in.

Progress in every department is attained only by making good use of the experience of the past; and it is more to the point that we should select and profit by the true and everlasting principles of Greek art than that we should desire to know where the Greeks came from, and who they were—matters that can never concern us practically as architects or citizens. Yet this sketch would be strangely incomplete if in summarising the controlling factors of Greek art we did not take into account the origins of the Greek race and the environment which influenced the development of its civilisation.

The territory of Greece itself was, in ancient times, much as it was defined on the maps of Europe before the Balkan Wars of 1912–1913, that is, with a northern frontier including Acarnania and Thessaly. But this territory, the part of Europe nearest to Asia Minor and Egypt, is, of all the lands bordering on the Mediterranean, more profusely indented in its configuration than any other. Thus, while in area Greece was smaller than Scotland, its coast line was much longer than that of all Great Britain. The whole country, furthermore, is a vast assemblage of high mountain peaks, much recalling, though on a grander scale, the steeper and rockier parts of the Western Highlands and Islands of Scotland. A labyrinth of land-locked bays and harbours, of wild mountain tracts and ravines, it was divided and isolated one part from the other, save for the means of communication that the sea afforded. The natural harbours lie open to the east and south, stretching out their long arms as if to invite and welcome the sailor; and the island stepping-stones fill in the great geographical design, placed as if to lure the caiques from Crete and the coasts of Asia Minor. But on the other hand we have Crete and the numerous Aegean islands, at one time the source from which came colonists to the Greek mainland, and subsequently the destination of counter-currents returning from the Greek mainland, including both fugitives seeking refuge and conquerors seeking expansion. This eastward movement gradually engulfed the shores of Asia Minor, and from that time Greece was to plant colonies around the greater part of the Mediterranean and the Black Sea. Hemeroscopion in Spain, Massilia in France, Sybaris in South Italy, Syracuse in Sicily, Cyrene in North Africa, Naucratis in Egypt, Sinope in Pontus, and Olbia in South Russia, are but a few of the more important settlements of this wonderful people, who, while often at enmity with one another, and divided in dialect, laws, and manners, yet spoke

INTRODUCTION

one language, worshipped the same gods, and mingled in the same games and festivals.

Now it is not difficult for us to trace some relation between the environment of the Greek race and their expression in art. Their separation into small communities, and their more or less independent development; the necessities which drove them to a seafaring life; circumstances, also, such as the extreme brilliancy, the lightness and bracing properties of their atmosphere; the clay, fine limestone, and marble in which the soil abounded; the want of metal and other commodities which led to traffic with other lands; these and other similar causes, it is easy now to say, affected the types of Greek art. But there was a good deal more than this; the "Glory that was Greece" was *in the race*, an instinct, a tendency, an aspiration, an inspiration. Not that the Greeks any more than others were "a nation of artists"; rather was the instinct in the select few revealed and matured largely because the nation prepared an atmosphere favourable to the culture of art.

No study of Greek architecture would now be possible solely on the basis of the writings of ancient authors. Historians and geographers of antiquity generally made only passing allusion to buildings with which their readers were assumed to be so familiar as not to require description. And when, to emphasise peculiarities or size, details or dimensions were given, these in turn were often mere approximations or guesses, usually so garbled in transmission by the mediaeval copyists of ancient manuscripts that they are nearly useless to us. The writings by professional architects and art historians, which would have been of extreme importance for our subject, have been totally lost apart from a few distorted reflections through Roman eyes, such as the abstracts from the art historians in Pliny's encyclopaedia (*Historia Naturalis*) and the allusions to Greek buildings and methods of design in the manual by Vitruvius (*De Architectura*). Valuable as the latter work was in its effects upon the Renaissance of the fifteenth and sixteenth centuries, yet its limitations as an independent basis for the study of Greek architecture are demonstrated by the fantastic illustrations supplied by Fra Giocondo (1511) and Cesare Cesariano (1521), or even by the restorations made two centuries later by Fischer von Erlach (1721).

Long before this, however, travellers with antiquarian inclinations had begun to bring personal notes and sketches back to western Europe. The first to examine and draw the ruins of Greece and the Aegean was Ciriaco of Ancona (1424–1447), but even his faithful sketches were woefully misinterpreted in the copies made by Giuliano da Sangallo (1465). A century passed before the next traveller of importance, Pierre Belon (1546–1550), collected his notes in the Greek islands, Asia Minor, and Macedonia. Nearly a century later, again, King Charles I and the Earl of Arundel (1621–1642) undertook, as the latter expressed it, "to transplant old Greece into England" by bringing home actual marbles rather than mere drawings, and thus anticipated the Earl of Elgin by importing, among other things, architectural marbles from Delos and Paros. A great step was taken in the establishment of French Capuchin monks at Athens in 1658; they, from their monastery (which included the monument of Lysicrates), and the French consul Giraud, transmitted information about the ruins to the Western world. The Marquis de Nointel, ambassador at Constantinople, came to Athens with a staff of draftsmen and antiquarians (1674)—just as the Earl of

Elgin did long afterwards—and to him we owe valuable drawings of the Parthenon sculptures. Greece and Asia Minor were next traversed by the first archaeologist worthy of the name, Jacques Spon of Lyons, together with four Englishmen, Sir George Wheler, Giles Eastcourt, Francis Vernon, and Bernard Randolph (1675–1676), all of them embodying their observations in letters or books. Even the Venetian expedition of 1686–1688, destructive as it was to the Athenian Acropolis, resulted in the dissemination of much architectural information to all parts of Europe. For some time after this, Greece was closed to foreigners by the Turks, apart from the portion of the Peloponnesus held by the Venetians until 1715; but Asia Minor was explored by Paul Lucas (1699), and the botanist Tournefort left invaluable records of the Aegean Islands (1700). The Abbé Montfaucon profited by the lull to systematise our knowledge in his *Antiquité expliquée* (1719–1724), and even proposed the excavation of Olympia. The Greek ruins of Sicily were explored by D'Orville in 1724, but publication was delayed for forty years. The Abbé Fourmont and his nephew succeeded in obtaining permission to explore Greece (1729–1730), but their results again remained unpublished. The Earl of Sandwich studied the monuments of Athens in 1738, but his book was not published until sixty years later. Richard Pococke, however, rendered invaluable service through the prompt publication of his careful observations in Greece and Asia Minor (1740). Lord Charlemont and Richard Dalton recorded the monuments of Sicily, Greece, and Asia Minor in 1749. And during this period the monuments of Acragas were being studied by Pancrazi, and were afterwards published with British assistance (1751–1752).

All this, as far as it was then known, formed the sketchy background for the epoch-making studies of James Stuart and Nicholas Revett in Greece (1751–1754), with the support of the Society of Dilettanti. Their great publication, the *Antiquities of Athens*, which for a long period was the basis of our knowledge of Greek architecture, appeared at irregular intervals, only Vol. I being published by "Athenian Stuart" himself (1762), Vol. II being edited by Newton (1788), Vol. III by Reveley (1797), and Vol. IV by Joseph Woods (1816). Supplementary volumes were published by Gell, Bedford, and Gandy-Deering (*Unedited Antiquities of Attica*, 1817), and by Cockerell, Donaldson, Jenkins, and Kinnard (1830). A second edition with invaluable footnotes was published by Kinnard (1825–1830), and translations appeared in French (1808) and German (1829–1833), with gradually accumulating footnotes which constituted a *corpus* of information. Despite the vehement opposition of Sir William Chambers (1791), the popularity of Greek architecture was now firmly established.

Meanwhile, Wood and Dawkins of Palmyra-Baalbek fame had traversed Asia Minor (1750) and found Athens in the capable hands of their compatriots. Less welcome was the intervention of David LeRoy, who came to Athens just as Stuart and Revett left (1754), and anticipated them with his publication of *Les Ruines de la Grèce* (1758). Slightly earlier the conspicuous but unknown temples of Paestum, discovered by Antonini in 1745, were studied by the first French visitor (Soufflot, 1750), by the first German (Winckelmann, 1758), then were drawn in greater detail by Gazola (1764), visited by the first American (the painter Copley, 1775), and engraved by the great Piranesi (1778). Winckelmann had arrived in Rome in 1755, concerning himself primarily

INTRODUCTION

with ancient sculpture, but wrote essays on Greek architecture, based upon Paestum and Acragas, in 1759 and 1762. The Society of Dilettanti initiated a second great *corpus* of drawings with its Ionian expedition of 1764–1766, consisting of Chandler, Revett, and Pars; their works, Vols. I and II of the *Antiquities of Ionia*, first appeared in 1769 (revised 1821) and 1797. The Duc de Choiseul-Gouffier began his *Voyage pittoresque* in 1776, and from that date one of his staff, the draftsman Fauvel, remained intermittently at Athens, eventually as French consul, until 1822, serving as the focus of architectural investigation for forty years. During the first part of this period came, among others, Sir Richard Worsley (1785).

The next epoch-making step was the suggestion made to the Earl of Elgin, by his architect Thomas Harrison, on the eve of the Earl's departure for his post in Constantinople in 1799, that he bring home actual specimens of Greek architecture. Acting upon this suggestion, and failing to secure the services of the painter Turner, Elgin recruited a large staff in Rome, headed by the painter Lusieri and the architect Ittar. The result was the accumulation of the vast collection of originals, both of architecture and of decorative sculpture, that eventually came into the possession of the British Museum (1816) and established its international reputation. While these were being collected, the insecurity of Europe during the Napoleonic wars caused Greece to become a centre of research; the five years 1801–1806, alone, were marked by the topographical and architectural work of Clarke, Gell, Dodwell, Leake, Wilkins (who studied also in South Italy and Sicily), and the Earl of Aberdeen, as well as the first American, Nicholas Biddle. A similar period of surprising activity, but less exclusively British, was that between 1810 and 1817, dominated by the self-styled "Society" composed of Cockerell and Foster, Haller von Hallerstein and Linckh, Stackelberg of Estonia and Bröndsted of Denmark. Their projected *corpus* of architectural material broke down into individual publications, Stackelberg's *Bassae*, Bröndsted's incomplete *Grèce*, and Cockerell's contributions to Leake's *Athens*, the British Museum's *Ancient Marbles*, the supplementary volume of the *Antiquities of Athens*, and the eventual publication of *Aegina and Bassae* (1860). Of vital importance, too, was the second Ionian expedition of the Society of Dilettanti, including, as noted above, Gell, Bedford, and Gandy-Deering (1812), to whom we owe the *Unedited Antiquities of Attica* (1817), Vol. III of the *Antiquities of Ionia* (1840) and the material so dramatically discovered and published in Vol. V (1915). Valuable contributions were made through the studies of Williams (1817), Woods and Sharpe (1818), Inwood (1819), and Wolfe and Donaldson (1820). And throughout this activity centred at Athens the work of Fauvel was indefatigable but fruitless. But as Greece in turn became untenable during the War of Independence, attention shifted to South Italy and Sicily, where the work of Wilkins and Cockerell was carried forward by Leo von Klenze (Acragas, 1821), Harris and Angell (Selinus, 1822–1823), Hittorff and Zanth (Selinus and Segesta, 1824–1825), Labrouste (Paestum and Acragas, 1826–1828), the Duc de Luynes and Debacq (Metapontum, 1828), and the Duca di Serradifalco and Cavallari (all of Sicily, 1831–1839). Nor should we omit the synthetic studies of Greek architecture during this period by Hirt, Quatremère de Quincy, Hübsch, Schinkel, and Canina.

The closing stage of the Greek War of Independence was marked by two events of outstanding archaeological importance, the sending of the French expeditionary force to Greece (*Expédition de Morée*) in 1829, with its architectural section under the leadership of Abel Blouet, and the foundation, in the same year, of the international Instituto di Corrispondenza Archeologica at Rome (transferred to Berlin as the Deutsches Archäologisches Institut in 1871, though the famous library remained in Rome, as part of the Roman branch of the German Institute, until 1944). The great publication of the *Expédition de Morée* covers the Peloponnesus (especially Olympia and Bassae) and the Aegean islands. The liberation of Greece resulted in the first active studies by the Greeks themselves, under Pittakis and Rangabé, and the establishment of the Greek Archaeological Society in 1837. The selection of a German prince as king, furthermore, resulted in a considerable activity of German scholars, including Friedrich Thiersch, Ludwig Ross, Schaubert, von Klenze, and Hoffer, as well as the Danish Christian Hansen. Now were undertaken the first serious excavations, such as those of Pittakis and Ross on the Athenian Acropolis (as contrasted with earlier clearing of the ground merely to obtain measurements), and also the beginnings of a new activity, the restoration of buildings with the ancient pieces (first exemplified in the Parthenon and the Nike temple). British architectural studies in Greece were now restricted to special problems, such as the work of Pennethorne in 1837, and of Penrose in 1846, on optical refinements. The French sent Grand Prix de Rome architects in 1845, Paccard, Tétaz, and Titeux, who chose as their subjects the Parthenon, Erechtheum, and the Propylaea, respectively; and as a result of their success the French School at Athens, the first of the foreign schools, was founded in 1846. One of its most spectacular successes was the opening of the west entrance to the Acropolis by Beulé in 1850–1852. But Asia Minor proved more and more attractive. Texier was entrusted by the French Ministry with a complete architectural survey of Asia Minor in 1833–1837. Sir Charles Fellows made his spectacular journeys in 1838–1842, acquiring the Xanthian monuments for the British Museum. Lebas and Landron, in 1843–1844, made records of Asia Minor as well as of Athens and the Peloponnesus. Sir Stratford Canning obtained some sculptures of the Mausoleum at Halicarnassus in 1846, and thereby revived interest in that monument, leading to the excavations undertaken for the British Museum in 1856–1859 by Sir Charles Newton, aided by Smith and Pullan. Smith and Porcher explored Cyrene in 1860. Pullan remained in Asia Minor to excavate at Teos and Priene in 1862–1869, shipping more marbles to the British Museum and publishing the results as Vol. IV of the *Antiquities of Ionia* (1881). John Turtle Wood was sent out by the British Museum to excavate at Ephesus (1863–1874), his efforts to discover the temple of Artemis being finally crowned by success. Meanwhile the French resumed their interest in the outlying sites, Heuzey and Daumet exploring Acarnania and Macedonia in 1859–1861, Perrot and Guillaume recording Bithynia and Galatia in 1860–1861, while Rayet and Thomas covered the region of Miletus in 1872–1873. The American consul Cesnola excavated in Cyprus during 1867–1876. The Austrians worked at Samothrace in 1873–1875.

The year 1875 formed a new landmark in the evolution of the study. Excavation had hitherto been purely for the purpose of discovering the

INTRODUCTION

remains or recording the measurements of a given building, or to obtain specimens for the enrichment of collections and museums. Now, in drawing up the programme for the German excavations at Olympia, a five-year plan was worked out whereby the entire area was to be uncovered, minor as well as major monuments, all being studied and published in such a way as to reveal all aspects of the history of a great international sanctuary, but the actual remains to stay at Olympia instead of being transported to Germany. The work was done under the supervision of the historian Ernst Curtius and the architect Friedrich Adler, aided by a younger generation of architects such as Wilhelm Dörpfeld and Richard Borrmann, and also by archaeologists such as Adolf Furtwängler and Georg Treu. At the same time, however, the discovery of fragments of the Great Altar of Pergamum built into mediaeval walls of that citadel led to the systematic excavation of Pergamum by Conze and Humann, from 1878 to 1886 and again after 1900, the most important remains in this instance being taken to Berlin. The Germans likewise excavated the sanctuaries at Cos (1902–1904) and Samos (1910–1933), and renewed work at Olympia during 1936–1943. The French undertook the clearing of the sanctuary of Apollo at Delos in 1877–1894, and again after 1902, while during 1893–1901 they concentrated at Delphi. The Greek Archaeological Society undertook the excavation of several sanctuaries, Epidaurus in 1881–1903, Eleusis in 1882–1890, and the Athenian Acropolis in 1885–1891. The Greeks likewise excavated at Thermum (1897–1899, 1912–1924), renewed work at Eleusis (1917–1940), and collaborated with the Danes at Calydon (1926–1935). The Danes worked also at Lindos in Rhodes (1902–1911), the Swedes at Larisa in Asia Minor (1902–1934), the Americans at the Argive Heraeum (1892–1893), the British at Naucratis (1884–1886) and Megalopolis (1890–1891) and in the sanctuary at Perachora opposite Corinth (1930–1933), and the Italians in the sanctuary on the Silaris near Paestum (1934–1940).

In the latter part of the nineteenth century began the excavation of entire cities for the purpose of disclosing not only the religious buildings, known either from literature or from prominent ruins, but also the civic structures as well as the private houses and all the other architectural appurtenances of ancient life. The earliest excavation of a city site was an American venture, resulting from the visit of Bacon and Clarke to Assos in Asia Minor in 1879; the excavation was carried out in 1881–1883, for the Archaeological Institute of America, and it was in this connection that Robert Koldewey received his initial training. Next came the German excavations at Magnesia (1891–1893), Priene (1895–1899), Thera (1896–1901), Miletus (1899–1938), and Pergamum (1900–1938), as well as the clearing of the Cerameicus cemetery at Athens (1914–1943). Similarly the Austrians excavated at Ephesus (1895–1935); the Americans worked at Corinth (1896–1949), at Nemea (1924–1927), at Olynthus (1928–1938), and uncovered the Agora of Athens (1931–1949). The British likewise undertook comprehensive work at Sparta (1907–1928), the Italians at Cyrene (1914–1942), and the Swedes at various sites in Cyprus (1927–1931). A large proportion of this detailed work has been carried out by the various foreign archaeological schools which, following the example set by the French, have gradually been established at Athens, the German School in 1874, the American in 1882, the British in 1886, the Austrian in 1897, and the Italian in

1909, and also by the Greek Archaeological Society and the Archaeological Section of the Greek Ministry of Education.

The investigation of individual temples and monuments, nevertheless, was pursued even throughout the most recent years. Haussoullier studied Didyma (1895–1896) and was followed by Wiegand and Knackfuss (1906–1938); Hogarth resumed work on the sister temple at Ephesus (1906), while Butler investigated a third of these huge temples at Sardis (1910–1914). Other important studies of this nature were those of Furtwängler at Aegina (1901–1903), of Dugas and Clemmensen at Tegea (1900–1910), of Dörpfeld and Rhomaios at Corcyra (1911–1920), of Marconi at Acragas and Himera (1924–1941), and of Schede and Krencker at Ancyra and Aezani (1926–1928).

Specialised surveys of types of buildings or of their parts have also characterised the last few decades. Koldewey and Puchstein surveyed the temples of South Italy and Sicily; Wiegand the archaic temples on the Athenian Acropolis, with studies of the poros limestone decorative sculpture by Heberdey and of the marble decorative sculpture by Schrader and by Payne. Theatres have been studied comprehensively, from the architectural standpoint, by Dörpfeld and by Fiechter, gravestones by Conze and Möbius and Miss Richter, sima ornament by Schede, roof terracottas by Koch and Buschor and Mrs. Van Buren, and profiles of mouldings by Miss Shoe.

Of special importance in the facilitating of architectural studies during the last decades has been the scientific reconstruction of ancient buildings for the purpose of replacing fallen stones in their original places and thus reconstituting the ancient appearance of the monuments, so far as the material is preserved. This process was begun by the French at Delphi (the Athenian Treasury, 1904–1906), and was followed by the Greeks on the Athenian Acropolis (Parthenon, 1897–1903, 1922–1929; Erechtheum, 1904–1909; Propylaea, 1909–1917; temple of Athena Nike, 1936–1941) as well as at Sunium and Bassae, and by the Italians at Acragas (temple of Heracles) and Selinus (temple 'C'). These processes of reconstruction have in many instances led to specialised studies of the individual buildings in course of reconstruction, not only by those in charge of the work, but also by others, as by the Americans in the case of the Erechtheum, Propylaea, Parthenon, temple of Athena Nike, and temple at Bassae.

Greek architecture, as we now know it through all these investigations, might be treated from either one of two points of view, the analytical or the historical. We might, for instance, investigate first the materials and methods of construction, then the orders and other elements of design, and finally examine one by one the various classes of buildings—temples, commemorative and sepulchral monuments, administrative buildings, porticoes and markets, gymnasia and baths, theatres, private houses, and the like.[1] Or we might, on the other hand, adopt a chronological treatment, dividing the field into successive epochs, examining the general characteristics of the civilisation of each period and the ways in which these gradually modified the ideals and forms of architectural expression. The latter method is more in keeping with

[1] This analytical method is followed, for instance, by Borrmann, Choisy, Durm, Marquand, Stevens, and Benoit.

INTRODUCTION

our purpose, which is that of studying the fundamental principles of the style through the influences that shaped its evolution and growth.

As for the subdivision into the successive periods, it happens that every style of art shows a gradual evolution, the rise, the brief culmination, and the decline. So also we may view Greek architecture in such a way as to emphasise this principle, taking as the central or culminating period that of the greatness of Athens under Pericles (about 450–400 B.C.). Before it lies the archaic period, the beginning of Greek political power and art, closing with a transitional stage at the epoch of the Persian Wars (600–450 B.C.); and after the culmination, on the other hand, we have the fourth century with its change of ideals, the beginning of the decline (400–300 B.C.). Then we have the beginning and the end, the primitive period in which the first germs of classical Greek architecture appeared (1000–600 B.C.), and the Hellenistic and Graeco-Roman periods during which Greek culture was spread over, and contaminated by, the entire eastern Mediterranean, and so finally extinguished (300 B.C. to A.D. 300). Each of these stages will be considered in a single chapter, with the exception of the archaic period, wherein, because of the distinct cleavage of the styles in accordance with two racial types, it is preferable to treat separately the west and the east.

But before this development lies a prelude, a separate civilisation, that of the Aegean age. For it is now but seventy years since the history of Greek architecture entered upon a new phase by reason of the discoveries of Heinrich Schliemann at Troy, Mycenae, and Tiryns. This phase was carried even further back during the opening years of the present century, by the researches of Sir Arthur Evans on the island of Crete, bringing to light the remains of a palace at Cnossus, several centuries older than that which Schliemann discovered at Tiryns, and containing revelations of so early a civilisation that, as Evans says, one might imagine a new record had risen from the earth. The principal discoveries here belong to the sixteenth century B.C., but they show so high a degree of civilisation as to suggest many centuries of earlier development; while at lower levels are strata through which this development can actually be traced back to about 5000 B.C. In the field of Aegean studies, after the epic campaigns of Schliemann and Evans, with less spectacular results attained by the French, Italian, British, American, and Greek investigators, came a resumption of activity on the main sites with the consequent revaluation and republication. Thus the Germans began again at Tiryns (1905–1914), the British at Mycenae (1920–1939), and the Americans at the Argive Heraeum (1925–1928), Troy (1932–1939), and Pylos (1939). To the drama of the history of Greece, which not so long ago opened with the scenes of the Iliad, there has thus been unfolded a background and a prologue. The Cretan excavations have shown that the legend of Minos and his maritime power had a solid foundation in fact. The richness of this prehistoric period in every kind of decorative art, to which the treasures in the Mycenaean and Minoan rooms of the Museums of Athens and Candia (Herakleion) bear the most striking testimony, has been such as almost to overshadow, for the time, the glories of the Periclean age. It will be our aim in the following chapter to select out of the mass of material published on the subject some of the matters which give fuller significance to the later developments, and appear to have influenced profoundly the course of Greek architecture.

THE ARCHITECTURE
OF ANCIENT GREECE

CHAPTER ONE

THE AEGEAN AGE

THE district round Mycenae was formerly regarded as the centre of a prehistoric civilisation called, for convenience, Mycenaean; but the later discoveries in Crete proved that Mycenaean art was only a local development of a much older one, extending over Crete and the whole of the area about the Aegean Sea. The broader title of Aegean may, therefore, be regarded as more suitable for the entire epoch.[1]

The Aegean civilisation, however, concerns itself with two distinct races at least, the islanders and the mainlanders. The islanders were non-Greek, of neolithic "Mediterranean" stock of southern origin, on which was superposed an Asiatic or Anatolian copper-using culture. The original mainlanders, on the other hand, were gradually overrun by newcomers, Greeks, a branch of those "Aryan" peoples who were migrating westward through central Europe, sending offshoots at intervals toward the south. The stronghold of the islanders was Crete, while the mainlanders occupied continental Greece and Troy. Certain ethnological changes, and the contemporary changes of style, permit a subdivision into periods which correspond, from the standpoint of evolution, to those into which we shall subdivide historical Greek architecture. These periods may be summarised here, though the brevity with which we must consider Aegean architecture will not permit us to discuss the stylistic variations of each phase.[2]

We meet first a primitive period characterised by the neolithic civilisation,[3] of which the beginnings go back, in Crete at least, to 5000 B.C., while the lower limit may be placed, in Crete, the Troad, and part of the mainland, at about 3000 B.C.; among the smaller Aegean islands, only those bordering the Asiatic coast (Chios, Lemnos, Lesbos, Samos) show traces of such a period. This was followed by an archaic period, of which the initiation, at about 3000 B.C. in Crete and the other islands (which now for the first time began to play a part), was doubtless due to the infusion of a new stock from Asia Minor, bringing with it copper from Syria or Cyprus, and mingling with

---

[1] The term Minoan is generally applied to the civilisation of Crete, Cycladic to that of the smaller Aegean islands, and more recently the corresponding development on the mainland has been described as Helladic: in all these classifications, the epoch is minutely and somewhat mechanically divided into three periods and eight or nine sub-periods. The Minoan classification proposed by Evans follows that of Egypt, and so is necessarily artificial as far as the internal history of Crete is concerned; but at least it has the advantage of being comprehensible in terms of absolute chronology. The Thessalian culture of northern Greece is divided into only four periods. I have followed a more general classification based rather on the recognised stages of artistic evolution.

[2] A detailed study of Aegean architecture is much to be desired.

[3] Palaeolithic remains have now been discovered in Boeotia. Even of the neolithic period (except in northern Greece) the architectural remains are very scanty; particularly notable is the entire absence of megalithic architecture of the kind found in western Europe.

the earlier neolithic inhabitants. This period, marked by the introduction of copper and the gradual evolution of bronze, lasted in all areas until about 2000 B.C.[1] On the mainland the period clearly falls into two halves, in the first of which the civilisation continued to be purely neolithic, developed from that which preceded it, though we meet in East Thessaly an infusion of new blood in the form of a migration of a Danube culture by way of Macedonia from its trans-Carpathian home; while in the second half the neolithic civilisation of southern and central Greece was partly overwhelmed by an invasion of the bronze-using islanders; Troy remained purely northern, but adopted the use of bronze. Fresh arrivals from the north, the "Minyan" invasion of about 2000 B.C., regained the Peloponnesus for the mainlanders, backed by a fresh wave of the Danube culture in Thessaly; the early settlements of the mainland, at least of central Greece, Attica, and the eastern Peloponnesus, were destroyed by the hostile invaders and in some cases were never again occupied, while in others the new settlements rose above the charred strata covering the old. The northern origin of the invaders is demonstrated by their distinctive pottery, the soapy grey "Minyan," as well as by new house and burial types, and also, apparently, by the introduction of the Greek language. This change ushered in the transitional period (2000-1600 B.C.);[2] the islanders, on the other hand, retained supreme control of the sea, and in the security of Crete and the other islands developed their art to a surprising degree. The result was a period of culmination, the golden age of the Aegean civilisation (1600-1400 B.C.),[3] in which the power of Crete was at its highest, and her artistic supremacy (though probably not her political suzerainty) was accepted by the "Minyan" rulers of Mycenae and Tiryns; these northerners, however, were already beginning to undermine the Cretan empire by seizing some of the islands, such as Melos and Paros. Later, at about 1500 B.C., came another wave of northerners, the Achaeans, whose advent begins a period (1500-1100 B.C.) characterised by a gradual decline in taste, the silver age of the Aegean civilisation, corresponding to the fourth century in classical architecture;[4] they, more venturesome than their predecessors, plundered and destroyed the Cretan cities (about 1400 B.C.), and even raided the coasts of Asia (Troy, about 1250 and 1193-1184 B.C.; Cyprus, 1225 B.C.) and Africa (Egypt, ninth year of Rameses III, 1171 B.C.). The Achaeans thus established their political supremacy and their language, and brought the island culture to an end; but they adopted the arts of the people whom they displaced; and their reflection of Cretan art continued to develop until they in turn were overwhelmed by their own brethren, a final and ruder wave of Greek invaders, the Dorians (1104 B.C., according to the traditional dating).[5] But for this catastrophe the evolution would have continued through further stages of decline; and indeed we have suggestions of such a decline in the (sub-Mycenaean) survivals of the Aegean culture in island fastnesses on

[1] This is Early Minoan (Cycladic) I-III of the island systems, Thessalian II-III and Early Helladic I-III of the mainland systems of chronology.
[2] This is Middle Minoan (Cycladic) I-III, and Middle Helladic I-II.
[3] This is Late Minoan (Cycladic) I-II with Late Helladic I.
[4] This is Late Helladic II-III, with Late Minoan (Cycladic) III.
[5] Chiefly Eratosthenes; others gave 1209 (Parian marble), 1182 (Eusebius), or 1172 (Syncellus) for the fall of Troy, 1098 B.C. (Eusebius) for the Dorian invasion.

Aegina and Crete (Karphi), and in the cities wherein the fleeing Achaeans sought refuge, as at Troy, Miletus, and on the islands of Rhodes and Cyprus.[1]

The centres of the Cretan civilisation were Phaestus on the south coast and its rival Cnossus on the north. At first, during the archaic period, owing to affiliations with Egypt, Phaestus seems to have been the stronger; but during the transitional period the two cities were on equal terms, Cnossus having found a means of building up an empire over the Aegean islands toward the north; and so strong did this Empire of Minos become that in the period of the culmination Cnossus was supreme. The other Cretan cities and towns, Gournia, Mallia, Mochlos, Palaikastro, Pseira, Sitia, Tylissos, and Zakro, were subject to these two main centres. Among the Aegean islands, Melos (Phylakopi) was of the greatest importance because it was the centre of the obsidian trade, and hence it was one of the first outposts to be wrested from Cnossus by the mainlanders; of less importance were Naxos and Paros (which then shared a monopoly in marble), Seriphos and Siphnos (the centres for various minerals), Syra and Thera. The distant island of Cyprus, southeast of Asia Minor, on the fringe of the Aegean area, was one of the richest districts because of its control of the copper market. Likewise Troy (Hissarlik), at the northwest corner of Asia Minor, though lying at the very edge of the Aegean area, rose to special prominence because of its commanding position at the entrance to the Black Sea, in a region of silver mines; nine successive settlements ranging in date from the primitive village of about 3000 B.C. at the bottom to the Hellenistic-Roman city of Ilium at the top—six of them destroyed during the Aegean period—bear witness to the jealousies and struggles of its neighbours to secure this lucrative position. On the Greek mainland, held partly by the uncultured northerners and partly by weak outposts of the islanders, many centuries elapsed before any site was able to rival the splendours of Crete, Cyprus, and Troy. The Thessalian settlements (Dimini, Rakhmani, Rini, Sesklo, Tsangli), those of central Greece (Chalia opposite Chalcis, Hagia Marina in Phocis, Lianokladi, Orchomenus, Thebes), of Attica (Athens, Eleusis, Menidi, Spata, Thoricus), Thermum in the far west, the Argive group (Argos, the Argive Heraeum, Asine, Midea, Mycenae, Nauplia, Tiryns, Dendra, Zygouries, Korakou and its neighbours near Corinth), the other Peloponnesian centres (Sparta, Messenian Pylos, Triphylian Pylos or Kakovatos, Olympia), and the Ionian islands (Cephallenia, Leucas), were, in comparison, mere villages. But from their number developed the centres of the last phase, the silver age, of the Aegean civilisation: the twin rulers of the Argive plain, Mycenae and Tiryns; the twin guardians of the Copaic lake, Gla and Orchomenus; Thebes, the city of Cadmus; and, last and least important, the city of Theseus, Athens.

Before we begin the study of the monumental structures, we may well take account of certain valuable evidence presented by remains of a more humble and elementary character, the houses of the people. For it was always from the

[1] The chronology of the Aegean age is still in a state of fluctuation, since every new excavation affords fresh evidence and alters the perspective. See, in general, Bury, *History of Greece* (new ed. 1924), pp. 5–84; Hall (H. R.), *Ancient History of the Near East* (3rd ed. 1916), pp. 31–72; Wace (A. J. B.) and others in the *Cambridge Ancient History*, I (1923), especially pp. 92–93, 103–106, 136–142, 173–180, 589–615; II (1924), pp. 26–31, 285–290, 431–517.

private houses that was developed the dominant architectural type in which the history of each epoch can be most easily traced.

The private houses differed according to the racial characteristics of the inhabitants, that is, "Mediterranean" Cretans or "Aryan" Greeks. Among the former we find the southern type of house, rectangular, shallow and wide, with a terraced flat roof. On the Greek mainland we find the northern type, originally of circular or horse-shoe plan, eventually rectangular but always deep and narrow, with a sloping roof. The differing elements later intermingled to a slight extent, as the Cretan civilisation was imported or imitated on the mainland, or when the Achaean Greeks subsequently invaded Crete; but in general they may be regarded as fundamentally separate architectural styles.

The Cretans, at a period long antedating the earliest remains of their houses, had lost all recollection of a nomadic state and of the circular nomadic hut, unless we are to suppose that the few early circular tombs (dated between 2700 and 2000 B.C.) dimly reflect such a tradition, a reflection due to religious conservatism. Possibly the decomposed remains in the lowest strata at Cnossus may have come from wattle-and-daub huts of circular form, but this is purely conjectural.[1] The earliest existing houses, and most of the tombs (which reflect house forms), were already of rectangular plan (Fig. 1);[2] a typical form is the so-called "but and ben" scheme of two rooms, an outer living room and an inner bedroom. As civilisation advanced, the houses began to contain additional rooms, spreading over larger areas; and since in such complex plans it was impossible to provide outside light in all cases, central courts and even additional light-wells made their appearance. The tendency was to use wide but shallow units, with two or more doorways in the longer wall of the rectangle. In the more pretentious houses, even as early as 2000 B.C., wooden columns were employed to permit deeper rooms; and when these occurred in an upper storey, they were supported on square stone piers in the lower storey. Such complicated and irregular plans could not have originated unless the roofs had been flat, as was generally the case among the southern peoples; and the flat roof, in turn, suggested the superposition of an additional storey, and the insertion of stairways. In the towns, where the areas were more restricted, the houses seem to have compensated for this in height; the small faience plaques found at Cnossus (Plate IV) show houses in two or even three storeys with flat terrace

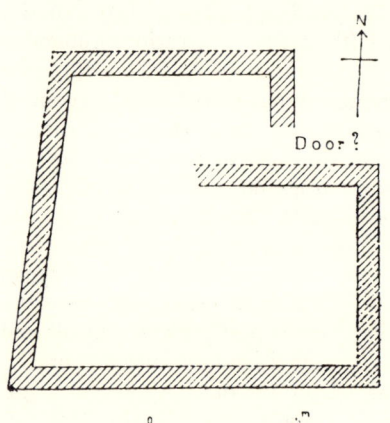

FIG. 1.—NEOLITHIC HOUSE AT MAGASA, CRETE.

[1] The situation in Crete was probably parallel to that in Egypt, where the earliest cultures are represented by circular houses, though long before the dynastic period, presumably at about 4700 B.C. ("sequence date 40"), the curved plans were beginning to be abandoned in favour of the rectangular. See Smith (E. B.), *Egyptian Architecture as Cultural Expression* (New York and London, 1938, p. 21).

[2] Possible neolithic examples occur at Magasa and Trypiti.

roofs and small roof attics or pent-houses above the stairways to the terraces, all dating from before 1700 B.C. The ground storey is blank except for one or two doorways symmetrically placed; the upper storeys show windows framed in timber, containing two, four, or six panes subdivided by mullions and transoms. The lower portions of the walls were of rubble, the upper parts of sun-dried bricks framed in wooden beams set both horizontally and vertically, the whole covered with rough lime plaster; the latter, in turn, might be coated with red wash, or the decorations might emphasise the form of the half-timbered construction of the walls, with horizontal tie-beams and the round ends of floor and roof beams.

The type of rectangular house, with local variations, migrated with the Cretans to the other islands and even to parts of the mainland. Thus we find it in the first settlement at Phylakopi (Melos), before 2000 B.C. A little later, before the volcanic eruption of about 1500 B.C., the houses of Thera were being erected of irregular blocks of lava, bonded with branches and logs of olive wood, roofed with a layer of earth and stones one foot in thickness, supported on wooden beams; wooden columns or stone piers were employed when intermediate supports were necessary; doorways and windows were spanned, not by wooden

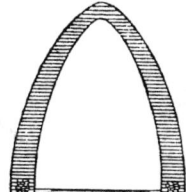 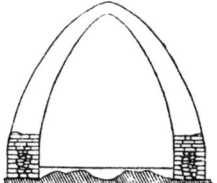

FIG. 2.—SECTIONS OF CIRCULAR HUTS AT ORCHOMENUS.
(Restored by Bulle.)

lintels, but by corbelled stones. Such island forms came to the mainland after 2500 B.C.; at Zygouries, south of Corinth, are small rectangular houses with flat roofs and very irregular plans, though generally there was one main chamber of square plan in each house, either with or without a fixed hearth, and usually with a smaller anteroom entered from the long side of the house rather than opposite the door to the main room. Rectangular rooms characterise also the Early Aegean houses at Eutresis and the Argive Heraeum. A more inexplicable instance of the spread of the southern type on the mainland occurs at Tsangli (Thessaly), where the houses are square, each wall with two internal buttresses, while one house has also a row of four interior columns in the centre, dating from the primitive (neolithic) period; the construction consisted of low stone foundations or sills, on which the walls were carried up in sun-dried brick.

On the Greek mainland, however, the normal form of the earliest houses was the circular hut common to all nomadic peoples; the most developed forms, with circular sills composed of flat stones on which were reared beehive domes, first of wattle-and-daub and then of sun-dried brick, are to be found at Orchomenus in Boeotia (Fig. 2)[1] and at Sesklo in Thessaly.[2] On account of

[1] The two examples shown are about 25–26 feet in external diameter.
[2] A village of such houses must have superficially resembled the Kurdish villages of the Mosul-Diarbekr region in Mesopotamia and the "trulli" of Alberobello in Apulia in South Italy.

the difficulties of domical construction and the inconvenience of living in such houses, the walls were sometimes made vertical, and were covered by a low conical roof made of reeds, leaves and mud, as we see it represented in an urn or model of green marble from Amorgos. Such a house might be enlarged by the juxtaposition of two or more circular huts, as in another marble model from Melos (Plate IV);[1] and when these were connected the result was the elliptical plan like that at Rini. Such elliptical huts might in turn be joined together, for example, two at right angles in the form of a letter L, as at Thermum (Fig. 14); and it is interesting to note that in these examples the curving vaulted roofs were still retained. But it was more usual to obtain separate rooms by subdividing the ellipse, using internal partitions as at Rini in Thessaly, and at Chamaizi (Sitiá) in Crete (under northern influence).[2] On the other hand, it had been found that an entrance cut through the wall of a beehive hut exposed part of the interior to the weather; therefore the entrance was sometimes protected by a slight hood or porch. The next step was the opening of the entrance, giving the horseshoe or hairpin plan, short or long, as at Olympia (Fig. 44), Orchomenus, and elsewhere. The gradual straightening of the walls until the sides became parallel, with a façade wall at right angles containing the doorway, marks the beginning of the rectangular plan; the entrance, as determined by the open mouth of the horseshoe, remained at the square end opposite the apse. Interior cross-walls, parallel to the façade, in effect form a rectangular plan with the apse attached, as in examples at Paros, Rakhmani (Thessaly), Thermum (Fig. 14), and Korakou (Corinth, Fig. 3). The apse then formed a sleeping chamber, the thalamus; and gradually the front portion was cut off to form a porch or prodomus. As the plans became elongated, we must suppose that the roof, retaining its traditional pitched form—or, as at Thermum,[3] pointed vaulted section—acquired a horizontal ridge, shedding rainwater toward either side and probably also toward the back;[4]

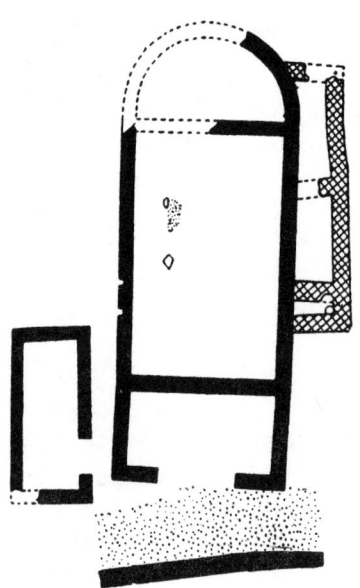

FIG. 3.—APSIDAL HOUSE AT KORAKOU, CORINTH.

[1] The model from Melos is a representation of seven of these circular huts (or, as it has been suggested, granaries) grouped round three sides of a central court, of which the fourth side is closed by a wall with an entrance porch with a gable roof. This is now in the Munich Museum; the urn from Amorgos is in the Athens Museum.

[2] The example at Sitiá, apart from its elliptical outline, is thoroughly Cretan, with a central light court; it is of great size (46 by 74 feet in plan), and dates from about 2000 B.C.

[3] Building 'A' at Thermum (Fig. 14), a megaron with an apsidal end and an entrance on the south between antae, was certainly a dwelling of prehistoric times.

[4] A flat terrace roof would hardly be logical with the circular or even with the apsidal plan.

the open porch on the façade undoubtedly had a horizontal lintel resting on the antae or thickened ends of the lateral walls; and above it we are probably to restore a triangular gable.

The next step was the straightening of the apse, which became segmental at Rakhmani, polygonal at Lianokladi, until eventually it was made perfectly straight, so that the rear room, and with it the entire plan, became wholly rectangular; the entrance remained, however, at one of the narrow ends. The resulting plan (unless, as sometimes happened, the thalamus was in a separate building) was a rectangle of three compartments, the central one being the largest; in the middle of this main compartment was the hearth,[1] which was the centre of social intercourse and hospitality; our traditions of the fireside, the hearth and the home, thus go back to the beginning of European civilisation in Greece.[2] Such plans appear, for instance, at Thermi in Lesbos, in the First, Second, and Sixth Citadels of Troy (the walls in the last being of hewn stone), and in the Second and Third Citadels at Melos (which after 1400 B.C. seems to have been a mainland outpost). Probably at this time the ridge roof began to be terminated by gables at both ends.[3] Further developments consisted in the widening of the plan, which necessitated the introduction of intermediate supports, a row of columns or posts along the central axis of the rectangle (Fig. 4),[4] sustaining, not the ridge-pole,[5] but the horizontal ceiling beams running from side to side. The posts were of wood, resting on stone bases; there might be two or more in the great hall, and sometimes also one at the centre of the façade of the prodomus between the antae or in-antis, as at Korakou (Corinth), Asine, and in the Sixth Citadel of Troy (where the main chamber measures $27\frac{1}{2}$ by 50 feet).[6] When even greater width was desired, two rows of intermediate supports were used, but never more than two; and with two columns in the width it was even more obviously a question of supporting a transverse

[1] At Thermi in Lesbos the hearths were sometimes outside as well as inside the houses.

[2] The fixed hearth was such a distinctive northern feature that only a few examples (probably imitations) are found in Crete during the Early Aegean period, and they had entirely disappeared by the Late Aegean period.

[3] It is often assumed that the roofs of these buildings were flat or, as Dörpfeld suggested, slightly convex or domical with greater thickness at the middle to shed water; though it has been pointed out that the modern flat roofs of Crete are slightly concave rather than convex. But apart from the racial characteristics of this northern people, we have certain specific evidence, such as the model from Melos (Plate IV), an intaglio from Mycenae, the roof sections of rock-cut tombs at Mycenae, Nauplia, Dendra, and Spata, to show that they sloped to a central ridge. Masses of clay with roof-pole impressions from several sites are non-committal; but Vitruvius (II, 1, 5) specifically mentioned sloping roofs of mud kneaded with straw at Massilia and Athens. Several actual clay roof-tiles of the Aegean period, with turned-up edges as if to guide the water towards the eaves (unless all can be interpreted as drain tiles in pavements) may be decisive, since these could hardly have developed on flat roofs. And Homer's allusion (*Iliad*, XXIII, 712) to sloping rafters meeting at the ridge, as an illustration of the attitude of two wrestlers braced against each other, shows that he (though some would regard this as later interpolation) was acquainted with ridge roofs.

[4] A house at Asine, and another at Phylakopi, have longitudinal partitions instead of a central row of columns, dividing the main room into halves.

[5] The opinion that such single lines of supports rose to the ridge-pole is controverted by a later structure, the temple at Neandria (Fig. 22).

[6] This example at Troy (VI C) is sometimes dubiously explained as a temple, as was formerly the case also at Asine, where the structure in question is now known to have been the main room of a complex house (G).

ceiling girder rather than a longitudinal ridge-pole; such forms, showing on the façade two columns between antae, occur at Dimini and Sesklo (Thessaly).[1] This stage gives us the fully developed megaron type of the Greek mainland.[2]

We are now prepared to investigate the more monumental structures for which the private houses served as models, namely, the palaces. The latter are, as it happens, the most important works of the Aegean civilisation. Just as the course of historic Greek architecture is most apparent in the development of one type of building, the temple, so that of prehistoric Greece is best examined in the characteristic structure of the period, the palace. The Aegean king, furthermore, was the predecessor of the Greek god. Not only were the palace and the temple, respectively, the supreme productions of the two epochs, but we have abundant literary and monumental evidence that the Greek temple, if not the lineal descendant of the Mycenaean palace, at least had an ancestry in common.

Of the palaces there are, again, two leading types, corresponding to the two phases of the Aegean civilisation, the Cretan (island) and the Mycenaean (mainland). In Crete we have two important examples, the palace at Cnossus already mentioned, and a second but smaller palace at Phaestus. On the Greek mainland, again, there are two examples of exceptional importance, the palaces of Mycenae and Tiryns. These types are easily distinguishable in the planning and arrangement of their component parts.

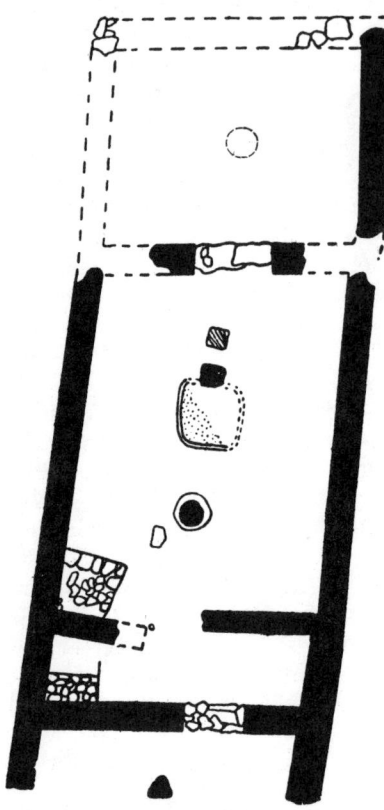

FIG. 4.—RECTANGULAR HOUSE AT KORAKOU, CORINTH.

[1] A curious structure at Troy (VI F), measuring internally 28 by 38½ feet, has two rows each of five column bases, and two additional column bases along the central axis. This seems, however, to have been the basement of a house (entered only from above), and the columns seem to be of two periods; first were erected the two rows of columns dividing it into three aisles, and later, perhaps because additional support was required for the upper storey, the central post in each row was removed and four more carefully built posts were inserted at the centre forming a diamond pattern.

[2] On account of the successive waves of northern tribes, each arriving with traditions of the nomadic hut which their predecessors had forgotten, we find the evolution from circular to rectangular house several times repeated. Thus in the period before 2000 B.C. we can trace the complete evolution from circle to rectangle, while between 2000 and 1500 B.C. we retrace the evolution from ellipse to rectangle in the hands of the "Minyans"; the Achaeans undoubtedly brought the same traditions, reflected in their beehive tombs; and when Greece fell into the hands of the Dorians we once more revert to elliptical and horseshoe plans.

THE PALACE AT CNOSSUS

The palace at Cnossus (Plate VI) measured about 400 feet each way, and was built on an eminence round a court 200 feet long by 86 feet wide, running nearly north and south; the total area is more than six acres. On the south and west sides were the principal Halls of State and the King's Entrance; on the east side was the private residence of the king and queen, which, built on the slope of the hill, occupied a lower level; and at the north end was the chief entrance to the court and the offices. The entrance from the open space on the west, which may be regarded as the Agora, seems to have been left quite unprotected; whilst on the east side the private residence opened on gardens or terraces, probably sheltered and made more private by trees, but enclosed by little more than a garden wall, with a single bastion. Almost the only means of defence at Cnossus would appear to have been a tower or bastion at the north, commanding the main road from the city and port. At the south descended a great stairway to a stone platform, whence a bridge crossed the ravine and led to the road southward to Phaestus.

Although at first sight the plan with its great central court and main entrance at the north end, and the walls all built at right angles to one another, would suggest its having been set out symmetrically or on a well-considered programme, yet further study shows that it departs widely from the principles of symmetry and axial planning. The walls of the west front jut out into the western court to varying distances; in the central court there are projecting blocks at the northeast and southwest corners. The northern entrance passage is not quite on the axis of the central court; the great corridor of the east wing is very nearly on the transverse axis of the court, but there is no corresponding feature at the west.

The walls of the western wing of the palace, as now existing, consist only of a basement about 8 feet in height, the floor of which is a little below the level of the central court. With the exception of one hall, to which the title of "throne room" has been given, there are no architectural features in this basement storey which it is necessary here to discuss. The wing consists chiefly of a long series of storerooms and magazines, which in their solid masonry and general construction were far superior to that of the ephemeral materials of which the upper storeys were built, and therefore permit a conjectural restoration of the main storey.

The secondary state entrance was in the southeast corner of the west court, through a portico of one column in-antis; the Cretan architects generally preferred to use one column as an intermediate support (if the span were not too great), rather than to encumber the entrance with two columns. From this, at one side of a guard room, opened a corridor 10 feet wide, its walls decorated with paintings representing a state procession. This corridor led southward to meet at right angles a continuation extending along the southern edge of the palace for a distance of 185 feet; and parallel to the latter was a covered portico, overlooking the ground outside, at this point about 10 or 12 feet below the level of the terrace. From the east end of the corridor a passage led north to the central court; but greater emphasis was laid on a monumental entrance leading north from the exact middle of the long corridor, passing through two walls each pierced with three doorways (Plate V). Beyond these again was a propylon, from which, still on the same axis, a flight of stone steps led up to a portico. The great halls on this upper level can only be conjecturally restored. Immediately behind the portico was apparently an inner vestibule, its ceiling supported by rows of columns, approached at right angles also by a corridor and a flight of steps from the central court. The audience hall was a great compartment about 42 feet deep and 48 feet wide overlooking the west court, its roof supported by two columns, for which heavy piers were carried down through the basement magazines. In these Cretan halls, placed in upper storeys, there was no fixed hearth such as we shall find in those placed on the ground level in the mainland palaces.

The only other hall in the west wing which it is necessary here to describe is that known as the "throne room" on the lower floor (Plate VII). Through four doorways between piers facing the central court, near the northern end of its western side, one descends five steps to an anteroom, and thence through two doorways enters a room measuring 20 by $12\frac{1}{2}$ feet, in the centre of which, against the wall on the right-hand side, is a seat of gypsum with a high back of very unusual design; flanking this seat on either side is a low bench running along the wall and returning at one end, while the wall above was frescoed with reclining griffins guarding the seat of honour. Opposite the throne is an open court or light-well, the floor sunk about two feet below the level of the throne room and approached by six steps; this area was divided from the throne room by a low parapet with columns in timber, for which sockets were sunk into the parapet and into the stone bench before it.[1]

Coming now to the eastern wing of the palace, the floor of the north half, about $13\frac{1}{2}$ feet below that of the central court, must be regarded as a basement, there being no halls or residential rooms in it. Over it was a great hall at a level slightly below that of the central court; one evidently descended from the central court to a portico, behind which lay an anteroom and a great hall with a row of columns across the centre. This hall nearly balanced the audience hall in the upper storey of the west wing, and its rear wall likewise formed, at this high level, part of the outer wall of the palace.

The most interesting portion of the whole palace, however, is the southeast block, because here we find the actual living rooms of the Minoan king and queen (Fig. 5): Its lowest floor was built at a level of about $27\frac{1}{2}$ feet below that of the central court, and the identical plan of the main group of apartments was reproduced on two, and in part on three superposed storeys, all having the same monumental character. The main "hall of the double axes"—about 26 feet wide and 19 feet deep—is lighted from a court at its inner end, while the outer end, in the two lower storeys at least, opens through four doorways into a second chamber of the same width but only $17\frac{1}{2}$ feet in depth. The latter room had no fewer than eleven doorways, the four mentioned above and seven others leading out to a peristyle which surrounded two adjacent sides of the room; thus three sides of the outer room were composed solely of doorways

[1] The exact purpose of the sunken area has been disputed, and it is sometimes regarded as a tank for a bath, though no outlet is provided, so that it could only have been used in connection with a terracotta tub; it is, furthermore, only one of several examples scattered through the palace, and others occur at Phaestus. The plan of the "throne room," with its throne, bench, and tank, resembles a hall of initiation dedicated to Men Ascaenus and a Mother Goddess near Antioch in Pisidia, so that likewise at Cnossus it may have been a hall of religious ceremonial.

and their intervening jambs (the doors being hung on pivots which revolved in sockets in threshold and lintel, so that they could be folded back into the reveals), and thus could be thrown entirely open either to the inner room or to the peristyle outside. Beyond the peristyle, in turn, lay a terrace about 49 feet long, overlooking the valley; and other narrow terraces projected at lower levels until the natural slope of the hill was reached at a point fifty feet below the level of the central court.

Other rooms of similar character but on a smaller scale lie south of those

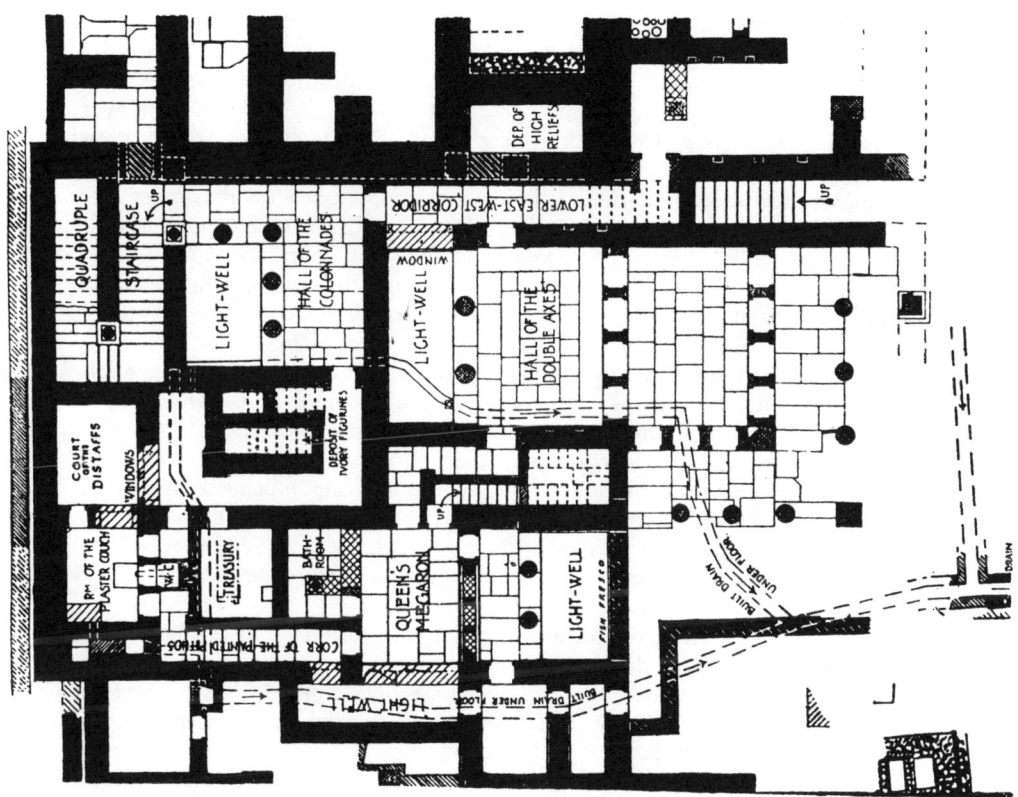

Fig. 5.—Detail Plan of the Domestic Quarter at Cnossus.

described above, and in immediate connection with them by means of circuitous corridors and winding stairways; these smaller rooms therefore probably formed the queen's suite, a suggestion which is confirmed by their strict isolation. The main room (misnamed "megaron") is only 19½ feet wide and 14½ feet deep; it opens eastward, by means of a doorway and three windows, to a shallow portico, and this in turn, though it might have opened directly upon the above-mentioned broad terrace, is nevertheless shut off from the outer world by a solid wall enclosing a light-court with a frescoed landscape to alleviate confinement. The walls of the main room consist, as in the king's suite, almost entirely of openings; there are five doorways and seven windows.

At the east is the portico with the light-court, at the south is another light-well, at the north are doorways to a corridor and a stairway, and at the west is a bathroom which borrows light through a window and a doorway, and a corridor which leads to a retiring room containing a plastered stone couch, with a toilet room adjoining. The suite likewise was reproduced almost without change in the upper storeys.

On the north side of the king's suite is a straight corridor running across the entire east wing, its inner end, toward the central court, being lighted by a court surrounded by columns 11 feet 2 inches in height (Plate VIII), and giving access to a stone staircase, with return flights leading up through three storeys and reaching above the level of the central court. The flights are 6 feet wide, with a central wall newel 3 feet thick, which allows of three steps on the return between the landings; each run contains twelve steps, so that there were twenty-seven steps in each storey—eighty-one in all—besides an additional landing at the very bottom. The steps have a rise of $5\frac{1}{2}$ inches and a tread of 18 inches, and consist of solid slabs of gypsum, finished on the under sides where they formed the roof of the flight below, and built seven inches into the wall at both ends. Light is borrowed from the small court, the wall enclosing the staircase on this side consisting almost entirely of open colonnades rising parallel to the steps, so that the masonry is carried by wooden columns and lintels (Plate VIII).[1]

One of the most interesting adjuncts of the palace is the theatral area at the northwest, with low step-like seats enframing a rectangular area which apparently served for ceremonies, pageants, or sports. An attempt has even been made to bring it into connection with the bull-fights which are so frequently represented on the wall paintings of the Aegean age, and which may have been the source of the legendary Minotaur supposed to have inhabited the labyrinth —the palace of Cnossus.[2] But we must assume that the bull-fights were held elsewhere; the theatral area was not designed to protect spectators of this dangerous sport.

The existing portions of the walls consist of gypsum or limestone blocks, forming merely a dado; the upper parts were built of unburnt brick[3] or rubble masonry with clay mortar and enclosed in timber framing; this ephemeral construction was protected by stucco on which painted patterns repeated the structure of the wall behind, the painted representations of timbers even imitating the wood graining with all its knots. Other paintings and tablets (Plate IV) suggest that the crowning feature of each storey, a row of circular disks, may have symbolised the ends of logs of wood serving as floor joists or supporting the roof. Among other architectural details are the stone column bases, flat disks like truncated cones, the earlier examples fairly high (up to

---

[1] The alternating construction of stone and wood materially increased the difficulty of its preservation. The recovery of this staircase, as Sir Arthur Evans remarks, "is probably unparalleled in the history of excavation, flights of stairs one above another being unknown even in Pompeii."

[2] It may be noted that labyrinths or mazes figure among the designs on the frescoes of Cnossus.

[3] Baked bricks have been reported from Gournia, Palaikastro, and Zakro; but it seems probable that the baking was merely the result of the conflagration which destroyed the houses.

18 inches), carved in party-coloured stones and resembling Egyptian models, the later very low (about 2 or 3 inches). The column shafts were of cypress wood (Plate VIII). For the capitals, which must likewise have been of wood, it is necessary to depend upon the representations of columns in small objects, such as carved ivories, and especially on the "Temple fresco," a painting which adorned one of the walls (Plate IX).[1]

The capital thus restored includes several members: at the bottom is an astragal between two fillets, above which comes a necking in the form of a hollow, then a full spreading echinus, sometimes terminated by another hollow to separate it more distinctly from the square abacus at the top (compare Plates VIII, IX, XII).[2] The abacus had a great projection; in the staircase court, where it had to carry the superstructure and the cross beams of the upper floor, it was 3 feet 5 inches square. The shaft of the column, furthermore, tapered downward, the diminution being about one-seventh. It would seem that the Cretan architects recognised that the trunk of a tree was equally capable of carrying weight in its natural position or inverted, and that when employed in the latter position the rain would more readily fall off it and thus preserve it better; it had the further advantage that, with its greater diameter at the top, an increased support was given to the abacus.[3] But other columns (Plate VII), known only from representations on stone vases and wall paintings,[4] tapered in the opposite direction, diminishing upward, and hence were probably constructed of bricks or stone. They were crowned by rectangular bracket-shaped capitals, which might be regarded as the forerunners of the Ionic capital; but the Aegean peoples seem never to have taken the next step, the adornment of these brackets with spiral scrolls or volutes, despite the fact that Egyptian ornaments, identical with those which afterwards formed the prototypes of the Ionic capital, were even then being imported into Crete and Mycenae.[5] And as the most interesting decorative feature may be noted the so-called "triglyph frieze" (Plate VII), similar to examples found at Mycenae and Tiryns (Plate X), frequently used to adorn the faces of benches.[6]

[1] See also the mainland representations, mentioned on p. 23, note 3, and p. 33.

[2] The button-like metal projections from the hollows, shown in the paintings and sometimes interpreted as double axes, were intended for the attachment of hangings or awnings.

[3] Such downward tapering columns were independently evolved in the megalithic architecture of the west. Thus in an elliptical grotto at Talati de Dalt, in the Balearic Islands, the roof slabs are supported on a central column of which the capital, a cushion-shaped block $1\frac{1}{4}$ feet high and 5 feet in diameter, rests upon a shaft only 4 feet high, 2 feet 1 inch in diameter at the top and only 1 foot 7 inches at the bottom. These columns or piers in the talayots of Minorca and Mallorca were generally constructed by piling up flat boulders with the smallest at the bottom and the largest at the top. There is a bare possibility that these were influenced by Cretan prototypes, a relationship suggested also by the bull ceremonies in these islands. Downward tapering columns were frequent also in the wooden architecture of Egypt, where they also appear once in monumental form, in the festival hall of Thothmes III (1482–1428 B.C.) at Karnak.

[4] Outside the Aegean area, however, some limestone examples, with cubical capitals decorated with disks and double-axes, have recently been found at Baeza in Spain, used as second-hand building material in a Roman bathing establishment. (*Rev. Arch.*, XXIII, 1926, p. 260.) A single column of masonry, though of mud brick, was actually found in an Early Aegean house at Eutresis near Thebes.

[5] Cf. the carved ivory tusk from Mycenae (Athens Museum, No. 2916).

[6] The assumption that this motive is the ancestor of the Greek Doric triglyph frieze is hardly tenable.

The palace at Phaestus (Fig. 6) resembles that at Cnossus in the orientation with the long axis of the court running north and south, in the grouping of the rooms round this central court, in the details of the planning of the rooms themselves, in the presence of an open west court with the theatral area, and in the secondary entrance, through a small propylon with a single column between antae, at the southern end of the west court. Probably the main approach was at the south. The outer limits of the palace are not very well defined, except on the west, but its greatest dimensions would seem to have been about 350 by 400 feet, so that it was practically as large as its rival at

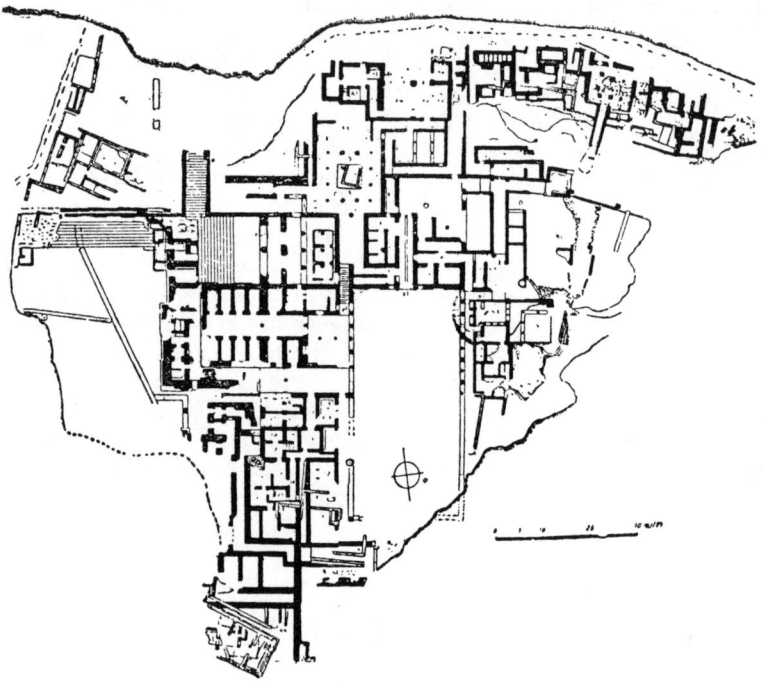

FIG. 6.—PLAN OF THE PALACE AT PHAESTUS.

Cnossus. The dimensions of the central court, 73 by 153 feet, are slightly smaller; but on the other hand the use of open porticoes on both long sides, columns alternating with square piers, gives it a more monumental appearance. At Phaestus, furthermore, the arrangements of the public rooms are more easily discerned. A flight of twelve steps (Plate IX), 46 feet wide, leads up from a terrace overlooking the theatral area to a great propylon or propylaeum, of which the outer portico has one column in-antis, while the inner portico has three, facing upon a light-court. From this inner portico lateral doorways gave access, on the one hand, to a stairway leading to an upper storey, and on the other to the audience hall which, as at Cnossus, was above the level of the main court, with its back overlooking the west court. A small stairway beyond the small light-court descends to the portico of the great central court. Under the

OTHER CRETAN PALACES

audience hall were magazines, not as at Cnossus all on one side of a long corridor, but short and symmetrically placed on either side of a central corridor. This symmetrical arrangement facilitates the restoration of the great rooms above, the portico, the anteroom, and the audience hall. The private quarters, which at Cnossus are found on the lower levels to the east, are here built on the higher levels toward the north. But, apart from this variation to fit the site, we have the same general arrangement of the rooms, such as the hall with four sets of folding doors in each of two adjoining walls, giving access on one side to a small portico facing upon a light-court, and on the other to a larger portico facing the exterior. A different feature, however, is the greater prevalence of peristyle courts; not only is the central court lined with porticoes on two sides, but there is a smaller square peristyle court at the north, and there are remains of another at the east.

The palaces described above, however, were those of the period of culmination, about 1600-1400 B.C.; both were preceded by more rudimentary structures, of which we can trace several stages, dating from their foundation at the beginning of the transitional period, about 2000 B.C. Thus the great court then occupied its present position, though at Cnossus the area was slightly greater; and it was entirely surrounded by isolated blocks of buildings (at Cnossus ten or eleven) devoted to various purposes: public offices, private quarters, workshops, shrines and magazines, with narrow streets leading between them to the court or public square. It was the gradual linking together of these separate blocks, the roofing of the passages to form corridors, and the various alterations of the internal arrangements of the blocks, that gave us the palaces which we see to-day. This consolidation took place at about 1800 B.C., but the internal alterations were more gradual. Thus at Cnossus, the great cutting for the domestic quarters on the east, replacing the graded terraces by a sudden descent of two storeys from the great court, dates from about 1800 B.C., as do the grand stairway and the very elaborate drainage system; but the other rooms of this quarter were remodelled at about 1600 B.C.; and the so-called "throne room" in the west wing is an alteration of even later date. At Phaestus the same process can be traced, though here the differences between the transitional plan and the final structure are even greater, some of the older rooms, such as those buried in the west terrace (overlooking the theatral area), being quite outside the area of the final palace.

But there are, both at Phaestus and at Cnossus, relics of even earlier date, fragments of walls now unintelligible, belonging to palaces of about 2250 B.C. With these, at Cnossus, are associated subterranean chambers of uncertain purpose. One is circular, domed and somewhat bottle-shaped, the diameter at the bottom being 27 feet, while higher up it is 34 feet, and the height from floor to crown of vault is $46\frac{1}{2}$ feet. To it descends a curved stairway in a vaulted tunnel, winding about half of the circumference of the chamber, with arched openings through which artificial light in the chamber itself would illuminate the stairway.

Similar traits are displayed in the less pretentious Cretan palaces at Tylissos, Mallia, and Gournia. The small summer palace near Phaestus, at the spot called Hagia Triada, follows a less formal plan, the scheme being that of two wings at right angles. Of special interest on account of their unusual details are the "little palace" at Cnossus, connected with the great palace by a paved walk, and the "royal villa" to the northwest, with a reception hall of basilican plan, and wooden columns of which the shafts are reeded rather than fluted, tapering downward.

When we turn to the Greek mainland, and to the other areas which came under the sway of the northerners, we find very different characteristics, corresponding to the fundamental differences between the two types of private houses.

The citadel of Tiryns is described in Greek literature as "the elder sister of Mycenae," and it is from the ruins of its citadel palace that we best learn the character of the fortifications and royal dwellings of the Heroic Age in Achaean Greece. But before we describe the final form of the palace which crowned its acropolis, we may note the traces of a much earlier building on the same site, though at a lower level.[1] It is a great circular structure built on a platform 91 feet in diameter; the walls are constructed in two shells connected by ribs, with a total thickness of 13 feet, and are strengthened externally by a series of buttresses arranged like the cogs of a wheel; the clear diameter of the interior was thus only 46 feet. The lower portion of the construction was of stone, the upper part of sun-dried brick. It would seem as if this were a magnified beehive hut, one suited to the dignity of the chief of a newly arrived nomadic people; and all round it the crest of the hill was covered with the less imposing houses of his followers, in three distinct strata, and ranging through all the types from circular to rectangular.

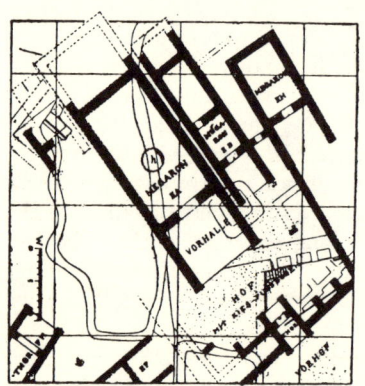

Fig. 7.—Plan of the Palace in the Second Citadel of Troy.

A much later stage of development appears at Troy,[2] where already in the Second Citadel, destroyed at about 2000 B.C., we find that the rulers built imposing halls of the developed northern type, long, narrow, and rectangular (Fig. 7). Three such megara stand side by side, independent of each other but parallel, forming three suites of apartments without the party walls characteristic of Crete, the intervals between them apparently having been left for the drainage of the roofs. The most important contains an open porch 33 feet square, and behind it a megaron of twice this depth, with a central circular hearth; behind this the walls may have been prolonged to form a shallow rear room. The walls are $4\frac{3}{4}$ feet in thickness, the lower parts of stone, while the upper parts

[1] The circular palace at Tiryns was discovered during the German supplementary excavations in 1912.
[2] The excavations at Troy were conducted by Schliemann in 1870–90, by Dörpfeld in 1893–94, and by Blegen in 1932–38. Schliemann distinguished six successive cities (I–V, and VII which really included VII–IX), while Dörpfeld distinguished nine (I–IX); Blegen follows Dörpfeld's classification in general but distinguishes many sub-periods and makes some important corrections in the dating. For the distinction between "city" and "citadel" see p. 22.

are of mud brick (the bricks 18 by 27 by 4¾ inches), strengthened by wooden beams laid lengthwise every four courses and connected by cross-beams at intervals of 13 feet. The ends of the walls, the antae, had special stone socles on which rose a protective facing of vertical planks 10 inches thick. In view of the great span, 33 feet, we must assume either that there were interior columns (of which no traces exist) or that the transverse beams supporting the roof were braced by diagonal struts; in any case there probably was a ridge roof, terminating in a gable over the entrance.[1] The two buildings at the right are narrower and therefore without columns, but similar in plan; one has an extra room before the megaron. Before the palace is a propylon, consisting of a gate wall with an open porch before and behind, likewise without columns; and the structure at the left was probably a similar rear gateway or propylon.[2]

Of the Sixth Citadel, the most impressive of the prehistoric settlements,[3] the central portion had been cut away in levelling operations by the Hellenistic Greeks. The palace, which stood on the higher part, is therefore missing; but from the plans of the private houses on the lower terraces it is clear that the palace must have been of the type which we see finally developed at Tiryns and Mycenae, to which we may therefore turn.

At Tiryns the primitive beehive palace was eventually succeeded, at about 1750 B.C., by a great structure rivalling in dignity those of Crete; simultaneously was erected the earlier palace at Mycenae. In neither case is it possible to make out the plan, since both were completely rebuilt in later times, leaving only disconnected foundations and floor levels. Among the remains of these earlier palaces are numerous fragments of magnificent wall paintings, very similar in style to those at Cnossus.

Also the later palace at Mycenae, dating from about 1400–1200 B.C., is in poor preservation (Fig. 8).[4] The steep and winding ascent from the main gate of the citadel led to a small vestibule at the foot of a double stairway 8 feet wide, which ascended to a reception room corresponding to the "throne room" at Cnossus, and also gave access to the southwest corner of the main court, here only 38 feet square. At the northwest was, however, a propylon of the Cretan type, with one column between antae. At the northeast corner of this court was the megaron, of the long, narrow type of plan characteristic of the mainlanders, with the portico distyle in-antis, giving access through one doorway

---

[1] Holland suggests rather pointed barrel vaults ("hoop roofs"), and Dörpfeld restored heavy flat or slightly convex masses of mud; both seem contrary to structural analogy and to traditional precedent. The absence of the flat shapeless stone bases for interior columns or posts, if such once existed, need not surprise us, since in many other instances such bases were removed by marauders or overlooked by excavators.

[2] In the official plan this is restored as a megaron, but facing in the opposite direction. Other dubious features of the official restoration are the useless rear porches, analogous to the opisthodomus of a Greek temple; these seem too sophisticated for the Aegean period. All these elements of the plan at Troy are now obscured through the destruction wrought by Schliemann's great exploratory trench.

[3] The traces of the Sixth City were missed by Schliemann and were first identified by Dörpfeld, who regarded this stratum as the Troy of which Homer wrote; but Blegen thinks that it is slightly too early, and that stratum VIIA was that with which the Homeric siege of 1194–1184 B.C. should be associated.

[4] The palace at Mycenae was excavated by the Greeks in 1886–1888, and restudied by the British School in 1920–23.

to the antechamber, whence another central doorway opened into a megaron 27¾ feet wide and 42½ feet long, with four central columns enclosing a circular hearth raised on two steps, covered with ten layers of painted stucco. The floors had borders of gypsum slabs imported from Crete, and the central portions were stuccoed and painted; in the antechamber, for instance, there were three panels with dark red borders, filled with zig-zags of red, pink, white and blue. Several other rooms exist, including storerooms and a magazine with great jars, a shrine with two offering tables, and a "tank" with descending steps. There were at least two storeys in places; a stairway ascended in two flights from a doorway at one side of the portico of the megaron. Some important room must have been at the upper level, where large Mycenaean

FIG. 8.—NORTHWEST CORNER OF PALACE COURT AT MYCENAE.
(Restored by Holland.)

column bases were employed in the foundations of the Greek temple built on this height. In all this work at Mycenae we may observe a close imitation of the Cretan style, yet containing elements which are characteristic of the mainland, especially the deep narrow megaron with its fixed central hearth; we may suppose that the Achaeans imported artisans and designers from Crete, insisting, however, upon results suited to their more northern climate and to their ancestral customs. But for the study of details we must turn to the later palace at Tiryns.

In the rival stronghold of Tiryns[1] we find the most perfectly preserved of all the mainland palaces (Fig. 9). The ascent through the two successive gateways of the fortification (Plate XI) leads up to a third entrance, the outer propylon which is worthy of attention as the model of all the great gateways of the Greeks, including even the Propylaea on the Athenian Acropolis; its disposition

[1] The palace at Tiryns was excavated by Schliemann in 1884, and restudied by the German School in 1912–1915.

is that of a portico distyle in-antis, 46 feet wide, the doorway in the cross-wall admitting one to a similar portico facing in the opposite direction. This inner portico opens upon a great court surrounded by columns; thence we pass through a second propylon, similar to the first but only 36 feet wide, and so into the second court of the palace, again surrounded by columns. The bases of the columns consist of irregular blocks of limestone, with a circular die in the centre of each, raised about 1½ inches above the ground in order to protect the lower ends of the wooden shafts. In the light of the discoveries at Cnossus there can be no doubt that these columns tapered downward toward the base,[1] like their imitations in stone; the capitals were likewise of the Cretan echinus type, which was imported to the mainland without change.

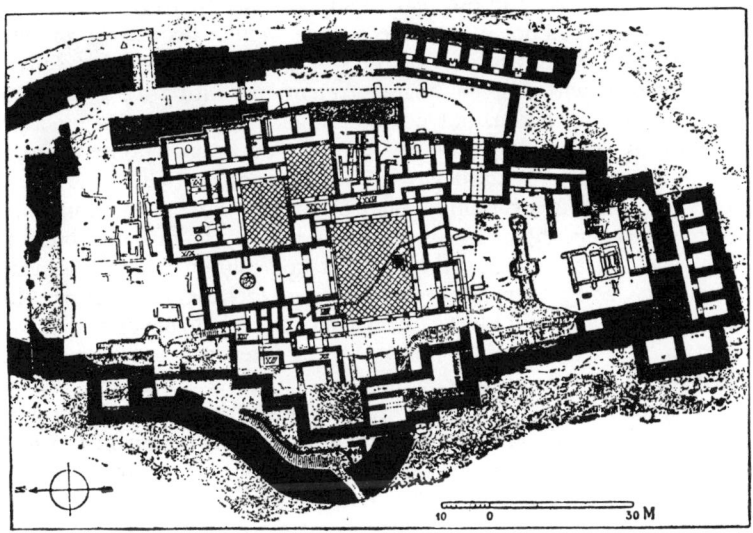

FIG. 9.—PLAN OF THE PALACE AT TIRYNS.

The second court possesses as its chief features the open altar on one side, originally circular but afterwards rebuilt on a rectangular plan, and opposite this the entrance to the men's apartment, or megaron, of which the plan is almost identical with that at Mycenae. Everything indicates the predominance of this, the largest covered apartment in the building (Plate X). Its façade, placed centrally on the court, presents the same arrangement as the porticoes of the propyla, viz., two columns in-antis, the bases of the columns and the plinths or socles of the antae being of stone. It has been disputed whether the crowning feature was a horizontal cornice or a pediment; but in view of the longitudinal plan, the avoidance of party walls, and the racial characteristics of the people, the ridge roof ending in a pediment seems to be more probable

[1] Dörpfeld assumed that they tapered upward; the credit of insisting upon the reversed taper is due to Perrot and Chipiez. Durm's assumption of a uniform diameter from bottom to top was based upon erroneous measurements.

(Plate X).¹. On the other hand, the triglyph frieze of alabaster, inlaid with blue glass paste, is now known to have formed, not a part of the entablature, but a bench lining the lower parts of the side walls of the portico, in a position somewhat analogous to the "triglyph friezes" of Crete.² Beyond is an antechamber, approached from the portico through three doorways (rather than one as at Mycenae); and the doors could be folded back into the thickness of the wall, thus virtually throwing the two rooms together into one, as was usually done in Crete. Thence a large central doorway (without pivot holes and so closed only by a curtain) led to the megaron itself, a large room about 32 by 39 feet, the roof carried upon four wooden columns; within the oblong formed inside these was the round hearth, and at one side, facing the hearth, was the dais for the throne. The arrangement of the four columns suggests a clerestorey above; but probably their sole purpose was to support the transverse beams of the roof construction. The floor was of stucco, painted in a chequer design with the alternative squares filled with the octopus or pairs of dolphins; the plastered walls were painted with conventional ornament and with a frieze representing a hunt. Beside the megaron, but not accessible therefrom, is an inner court, approached only by winding passages from the outer propylon and from the inner propylon, and by a third passage which is carried all round the great megaron, thus ensuring a certain amount of privacy. For off this court opened the private apartment, the thalamus, similar in plan to the megaron but simpler and of smaller dimensions; thus the porch lacked columns, there was no intervening vestibule, and on account of the short span (20 feet) the interior columns were omitted, though the hearth remained in the centre. Beyond, and parallel to this again, lay a third unit consisting of an anteroom and main chamber, even smaller in scale; the series reminds us of the group of three parallel buildings in the Second Citadel of Troy. On the opposite side of the megaron is the bathroom, with a floor consisting of a single black stone 11 by 13 feet in plan. The rest of the area was occupied by smaller rooms, some in two storeys; but a noticeable characteristic of this plan is the disposition of all the important rooms on the ground floor, and the absence of the numerous small light-wells of the Cretan palaces implies that the whole was kept low, permitting the introduction of light through windows in the upper parts of the main rooms. The corridors surrounding the megaron and thalamus may have been for the use of slaves, serving to connect the two sides of the palace without making use of the peristyles; they were in communication also with a small flight of steps leading down to what may have been the service courts of the palace, and to the postern gate.

The palace at Tiryns, besides giving the clue to the distribution of the Homeric house as described in the *Odyssey*, betrays the origin of many features which we find reproduced in stone or marble in the perfected types of Greek

---

¹ The internal evidence adduced from the whole plan of the palace, by the supporters of the two opposing views, seems particularly weak. But Reber's restoration seems more justifiable than that of Perrot and Chipiez, for instance, which shows the flat roofs characteristic of the islands. In the recent official German publication, to be sure, the roofs are again restored as flat; but this seems very improbable.

² Thus Plate X should probably be corrected by removing the "triglyph frieze" from the entablature, though it is not entirely unsuitable for this position in view of the fact that it was located above the columns on the façade of the tomb of Agamemnon.

architecture. Thus the propyla, with their porticoes in-antis, developed into such entrance gateways as those to the Acropolis of Athens, and to the sacred enclosures of Olympia, Epidaurus, and elsewhere. The portico in-antis of the megaron also is the elementary form which is to be found in almost every Greek temple, for although in later times single or double peristyles were built round the cella to give greater importance to the latter and to protect its walls, nevertheless the pronaos or entrance to the cella remained virtually of the Mycenaean plan. Even the grouping of the portico and of the megaron behind, on the same longitudinal axis, is the same which was afterwards revived by the Greeks for their temples. Perhaps the most interesting feature is that of the antae or parastades. In consequence of the ephemeral nature of the materials used in the walls (rubble stone bedded in clay as a base to the mud-brick wall), a reinforcement of timber was employed to protect the ends of the flank walls and to assist in supporting the architrave carried by the columns; this facing, at Tiryns, was raised on stone plinths, being secured to the stone by wood pins. It was the same practice of placing the baulks of timber or posts side by side to encase the ends of walls that gave rise to the antae of the Greek temples, which finally had no longer a constructive but only an artistic function. In the partition walls such wooden casing, forming the door jambs, was even more prominent, and likewise left its mark on subsequent architecture in stone; and, although there is no internal evidence to prove that the jambs inclined inward to lessen the bearing of the lintel, yet this inclination is found reproduced in the tomb façades, suggesting, therefore, its wooden origin.

This later palace at Tiryns was destroyed by fire, probably shortly before the Dorian invasion; and on the ruins of its chief megaron rose a smaller megaron, poorly constructed, utilising the foundations of one of the earlier flank walls, and so locating the other flank wall as to leave one of the column bases of the earlier façade exactly on the axis of the new structure. One of the cross-walls likewise utilised the older foundations, and the portico was lined with rude benches, the whole forming an anticlimax to the splendid Achaean megaron.[1]

A nameless fortress in the Copaic lake in Central Greece, now known as Gla but sometimes identified as the Homeric Arne, contains a palace of unusual plan, with two wings at right angles,[2] each about 250 feet in length; a great corridor extends along the inner face of each wing, serving as the means of communication between the great megaron, at the extreme end of the north wing, and the more private megaron at the opposite end of the east wing. Each megaron has an antechamber, the latter entered from the corridor at one side; the plan is thus distinctly northern in type, so that we must imagine the roofs of the megara as sloping to a ridge and overtopping the rest of the palace. No columns were employed. The interval between the two megara is filled with smaller rooms, in both wings, with a special service corridor just behind the main public corridor.

Traces of other mainland palaces have been found at Orchomenus (opposite Gla), at Thebes, at Athens, and at Pylos in Messenia, but in such a fragmentary state that they add little to our knowledge. The palace at Athens lay beneath

[1] These ruins had always been regarded as those of a Greek temple, until Blegen demonstrated their immediate connection with the Mycenaean epoch.
[2] Thus recalling the Cretan summer palace at Hagia Triada.

the Old Temple of Athena destroyed by the Persians, where even now there are Mycenaean column bases and foundation walls, while the entire circuit of the Acropolis is enclosed by a Cyclopean wall of the same date. But the Acropolis was a site continuously occupied and frequently remodelled, and, like every city that has retained her population instead of being suddenly deserted, has to some extent submerged her earlier history so far as that was written in stone. Thus it has come to pass that we can read the story of the Mycenaean period, all important in the evolution of Greek art, chiefly in the buried cities of the Peloponnesus.

These megara of the northerners are also found in regions which were strongholds of the islanders. Melos, as we have seen, came under mainland influence in the period of the culmination (the second city); and in the third city, belonging to the period of decline, we see not only houses but also a palace of the megaron type. The megaron has the position for the hearth marked in the centre, but it must have been a portable hearth such as was used in Crete, since there is no trace of ashes; before the megaron was a portico $19\frac{1}{2}$ feet wide and 15 feet deep, with great anta bases on each side but with no central column base. On either side of this megaron are long corridors, that at the right giving access to parallel magazines. This northern plan was even introduced into Crete after the Achaean invasion of 1400 B.C., when all the great palaces were destroyed by fire;[1] later palaces, of the megaron type, have left their traces at Hagia Triada and at Gournia.

No discussion of the Aegean palace would be complete without some allusion to its latest phase, the literary tradition of such a palace as it descended to Homer and was by him transmitted to us. The palace of Odysseus at Ithaca was described by the poet in such detail that it has frequently been the subject of restorations. The classical Greek house by no means fits the action of the story. But the Aegean palaces at Mycenae, Tiryns, and Gla agree better with Homer's description, so that there can be little doubt that his ancestors, the Ionians who migrated from the mainland to Asia Minor, carried with them the tradition or memory, at least, of the northern or mainland type of palace.

In glancing at the plans of the island and mainland palaces we are struck, not only by the differences in their elements, but also by a difference in their surroundings. In all the Cretan palaces and towns, and also in the first settlement at Phylakopi (Melos), we note an entire absence of those walls of defence which in the northern settlements were deemed to be of the greatest importance. It is not as if the Cretan architects were unacquainted with the art of fortification; in the "town mosaic" from Cnossus appear towers and gates of regular ashlar masonry, and similar representations occur on a silver rhyton of Cretan workmanship from Mycenae; but it is evident that the bulwarks of the Minoans were rather in the wooden walls of their navy.

The northern method was very different. The palace itself formed a citadel, placed on a low hill, and surrounded by strong walls; generally the houses of

---

[1] Alternative suggestions, that the destruction of the Cretan palaces was not due to an Achaean invasion but rather to a great earthquake or a tidal wave (of the time of the volcanic eruption at Thera), seem less probable. Certainly the invasion occurred at this time and was followed, if not by total destruction of the palaces, at least by new palaces of megaron form and by tholos tombs.

CITADEL WALLS AND GATES

the nobles and retainers were likewise included within the walls; but the agricultural classes were scattered in unwalled villages, and only assembled within the walls in time of war. Thus the citadel of Troy was too small to form an actual city; Tiryns was in a large part bare of houses, some of the area within the walls forming merely an emergency shelter; the lower city at Mycenae was unwalled in Mycenaean times.[1]

While the consideration of citadel and city walls, and of military architecture in general, must be left outside the limits of this discussion,[2] there are a few special adjuncts of some of these works that have a broader interest. The first of these, at Mycenae, lies in the main gate, the so-called "Lion Gate," which is in a fine state of preservation even though it has been known since antiquity and was never buried (Plate XI). The ascending ramp approaching it is 48 feet long and 30 feet wide, with, as usual, a heavy wall on the right side, though in this case it was formed by a special bastion, the main wall being on the left or shielded side of the assailants. Advantage was taken of this utilitarian requirement to place the gate at the end of a deep court. The illustration shows the stone jambs of the doorway, and the still greater lintel, which is 8 feet broad, $3\frac{1}{2}$ feet high at the middle, and has a length of $16\frac{1}{2}$ feet, with a clear span of 9 feet. Such a lintel would assuredly bear any superincumbent weight that the builders of these fortifications were likely to put upon it; but either from caution or custom a triangular void was left by means of corbelling, so as to relieve the lintel. It was to fill this void that a limestone slab, 12 feet wide and at present 10 feet high (Plate XII), was carved in relief with a heraldic religious composition, the sacred pillar representing the protecting divinity of the citadel. The central pillar is, perhaps, the most interesting part of the composition to an architect; it stands on a kind of twin pedestal or altar, with the shaft tapering downward,[3] and a capital with echinus and abacus foreshadowing to a certain extent the Greek Doric; and this in turn is surmounted apparently by a fragment of entablature, which, like the ornament over the tomb doorways, suggests the wood log ceilings of the primitive house. The sculpture, the oldest on a large scale yet revealed on the Greek mainland, shows a technical skill in outline and modelling and even a nobility of expression (as in the resolute fore-legs and paws) that give it a high place; the heads were carved separately (probably in steatite) in order to obtain a greater relief. It does not seem possible to date this work earlier than 1250 B.C., for it is clearly not as old as the greater part of the fortification walls, which had originally been of the Cyclopean type.[4]

[1] The existing city walls are Hellenistic.
[2] Thus we pass over such notable works of military architecture as the walls of the Second and Sixth Citadels of Troy, of the Second and Third Cities of Phylakopi (Melos), of Gla and Midea, and, with the exception of a few details, those of Mycenae and Tiryns.
[3] Durm's theory that this shaft is cylindrical is erroneous; the diameter is $12\frac{1}{4}$ inches at the top and $10\frac{3}{4}$ inches at the bottom. Such columns with downward tapering shafts and echinus capitals are represented also in ivory reliefs from the tholos tomb at Menidi, at Delos, and in a basalt house or palace model with three columns, now in the Berlin Museum.
[4] That the ashlar facing about the Lion Gate and the main postern gate are later insertions is shown by the similar ashlar masonry of the southeast bastion of the citadel, which is clearly an addition. The so-called intermediate or third class into which the masonry of the Aegean period has been divided, that of polygonal type, seems really to be later Greek; for it is represented by three repairs in the walls of Mycenae which are apparently subsequent to the destruction of the town in 468 B.C.

The second detail of special importance for architects is to be found at Tiryns, in the high wall of enormous thickness, 24 to 57 feet, constructed of great unhewn stones with the joints filled with small stones and yellow clay (believed by later generations to be the work of a race of giants known as the Cyclopes, whose name is therefore given to this kind of masonry). At two points, in the new portions of the outer wall, are contrived galleries each with five or six lateral chambers, serving as store-rooms; like the domed tombs to be described later, these passages and chambers (the latter $10\frac{3}{4}$ feet wide) are roofed by courses of stone in horizontal beds, projecting one over the other, and cut on the under side to the contour of a pointed arch (Plate XIV).

* * * * *

A noteworthy characteristic of the Aegean civilisation is the subordinate part played by religious architecture. Traces of the Aegean religions exist, to be sure; we have evidence of the worship of a supreme mother-goddess (Rhea, the mother of Zeus), and perhaps of other divinities, as well as of pillar worship; and we also possess considerable illustrative material with regard to the forms of ritual. But this worship seems to have been conducted in rustic shrines or in small chapels in the palaces, of little architectural importance; the most imposing structures are those represented on gold plaques from Mycenae and Volo, in a fresco from Tiryns, and in the so-called "Temple fresco" of Cnossus; the last (Plate IX) represents three shrines, the middle one distyle in-antis and raised above the others, which have but one column in-antis (a peculiarity which is proved to be no mere painter's convention by the single bases found in the propylaea at Cnossus and Phaestus). Among larger structures may be cited the hill-top shrines of Petsofa and Mount Juktas in Crete, originally mere open sanctuaries in which the rocky peak itself was worshipped, later provided with rectangular buildings resembling the simplest house plans, with an outer and an inner room, and a magazine. At Eleusis there is a small temple (under the Telesterion) with two columns on the central axis and a porch with a single column between the antae, approached by two parallel flights of steps separated by a central bema or ceremonial platform (Fig. 10). Less important for our purposes are the cave sanctuaries, such as the Dictaean cave at Psychro, the Kamares cave on Mount Ida, and the Skoteino cave above Cnossus.[1]

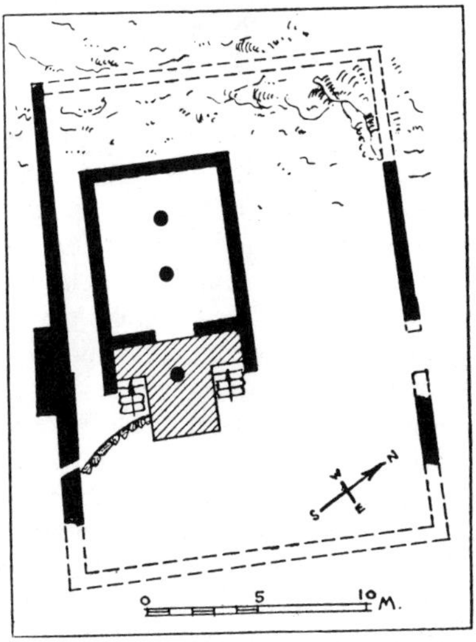

FIG. 10.—PLAN OF THE TEMPLE AT ELEUSIS.

[1] The "primitive" cave-temple at Delos, sometimes regarded as Aegean, is undoubtedly later Greek. Its construction is so sophisticated, and the manner in which boulders have been rolled down upon its gabled ceiling is so artificial, as to suggest that it is a Hellenistic structure purporting to be prehistoric.

PIT AND SHAFT GRAVES

Rock-cut tombs, memorial cairns, barrows, and other forms of graves are among the most frequent traces of a prehistoric race, and often the earliest attempts in architectural expression or sculptural art that have survived. And so it is from its tombs, as well as from the palaces, that the story of the age of Aegean culture is being gradually reconstructed.

There are seven distinct classes of tombs in the Aegean region. (A) *Pit graves* were those in which, as to-day, the great majority were no doubt interred. Those of rectangular plan, like the rectangular house, seem to have been at first characteristic of the islanders. The simplest form, apart from mere cavities or pits hollowed in the earth, was the *cist grave*, consisting of slabs of stone, forming the floor (though this might be merely of earth), the four walls, and the cover resting on the walls; the whole was then covered with earth so as to leave no outward indication. These are found especially in the Cyclades (where they form the earliest architectural remains) and in Crete. Sometimes the sides were lined with rubble walls rather than with single slabs; and the roof was sometimes of reeds and clay, or of timber, or of overlapping slabs corbelled toward the centre. A development from these was the *shaft grave*, sunk much deeper below the surface (7 to 14 feet), the lower part either lined with rubble walls or provided with a rock-cut ledge on which the cover slab might rest. For ease in reopening these graves, for subsequent interments, it was sometimes preferred to place the body, not in the bottom of the shaft itself, but in a chamber excavated at one side of the bottom of the shaft, and afterwards closed with a vertical wall. But such forms were by no means confined to the islands; due to island influence, early cist graves occur at Tiryns, shaft graves with lateral chambers at Corinth, simple shaft graves at Pylos (Messenia) and, most important of all, on the Acropolis of Mycenae.

Here the shaft graves, in the period 1600–1500 B.C., covered a large area on the east slope of the hill, outside the older and even outside the present walls; six of them, containing seventeen bodies (eleven men and six women) were apparently royal; the bodies were covered with gold ornaments and jewelry, and surrounded by all manner of arms and vessels. These graves were cut in the solid rock, in the form of rectangular shafts sunk from the natural surface of the hill, with the result that they are on very different levels; the floors were covered with pebbled pavements, the sides lined with battering walls which supported wooden beams with the ends encased in bronze, and on these in turn were laid stone slabs, the upper portion of the shaft being filled in with earth. The largest of these graves is about $18\frac{1}{2}$ by 24 feet in plan. They were marked by stelae or upright slabs, eleven of them (those for the men in the royal group) rudely sculptured; and in the centre of the group was built a circular altar for the offerings to the deified kings.[1]

Long afterwards, when the new fortifications at Mycenae were laid out at about 1250 B.C., their line was carried right through the old cemetery, and then all the graves were emptied except six of the most important, those of the kings.

---

[1] It has sometimes been suggested that the royal shaft graves at Mycenae contain the material taken in antiquity from the tholos tombs, which were found practically empty. But this seems impossible on account of the chronological discrepancies, the material in the shaft graves being two centuries earlier (on the average) than the potsherds found under and behind the structure of the great tholoi such as that of Agamemnon.

The latter were protected by a semicircular retaining wall (Fig. 11), battering at about 75 degrees; and the fortification wall was made to deviate from the line it would normally have followed, making a curve concentric with the terrace wall, with the result that the graves, contrary to custom, were now included within the Acropolis. They now formed a sacred precinct, the slope being terraced up with earth, in places to a height of 13 feet, forming a uniform level to which the old stelae were now elevated. Most important is the surrounding wall, a slab circle 95 feet in diameter, the slabs 8 inches thick being set up on edge in two concentric circles 4 feet apart, filled in between with earth, connected by wooden braces, and covered with cross-slabs, thus forming a

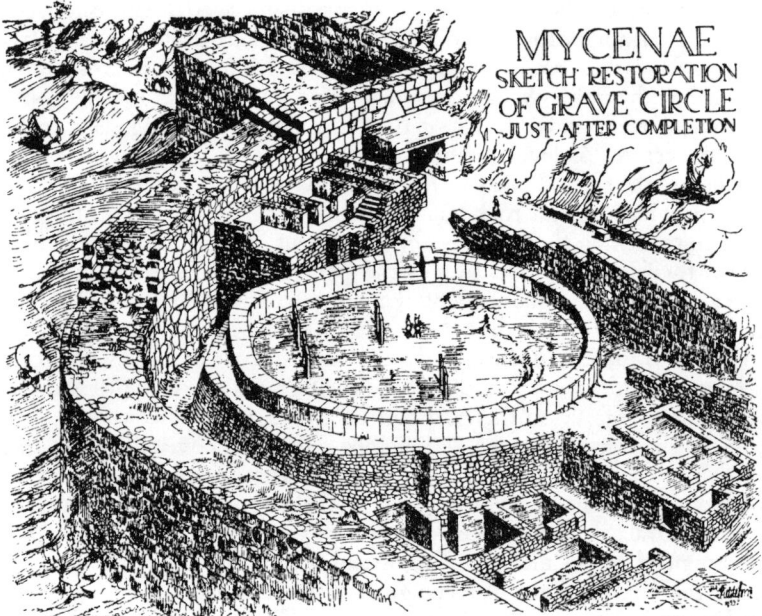

Fig. 11.—The Grave Circle at Mycenae. (Restored by De Jong.)

heavy parapet from 3 to 5 feet in height; at one side, toward the Lion Gate, was left an entrance 8 feet in width.[1] Such was the sepulchral precinct which survived through classical times, and was described by Pausanias in the second century of our era; the Greeks attributed the graves to Agamemnon and his associates;[2] but now we know that they antedated the family of Agamemnon by two centuries.[3]

(B) *Rock (or chamber) tombs*, of which vast numbers exist at Mycenae, Argos,

[1] The existence of this entrance is one of many indications that the whole was not, as some have assumed, covered with a tumulus of earth.

[2] This tradition was accepted by Schliemann, who even identified one of the skeletons as that of Agamemnon himself.

[3] The only analogous monuments yet discovered are the circles of stones built round cist graves at Leucas, earlier in date and more primitive in form than the grave circle at Mycenae.

the Argive Heraeum, in Attica (as at Athens and Spata), and elsewhere, are particularly characteristic of the Late Aegean period and are of greater architectural importance. These tombs are generally carved out of the soft stone or hardpan underlying rocky ledges in the hillside, having a narrow passage (*dromos*), sometimes horizontal but usually sloping more or less steeply downward (even with steps to accelerate the descent if it be short).[1] The scarps forming the sides of the dromos usually lean toward each other; and sometimes, when the dromos is narrow, they incline inward so sharply that they nearly meet, leaving merely a narrow slot in the surface above (Fig. 12). The dromos is terminated by an entrance doorway, usually merely hewn in the rock with inclined jambs and a horizontal or arched top. This admits to a tomb chamber, usually roughly oval or rectangular but sometimes of irregular plan. Very often a smaller chamber adjoins, entered from the greater one; the latter was

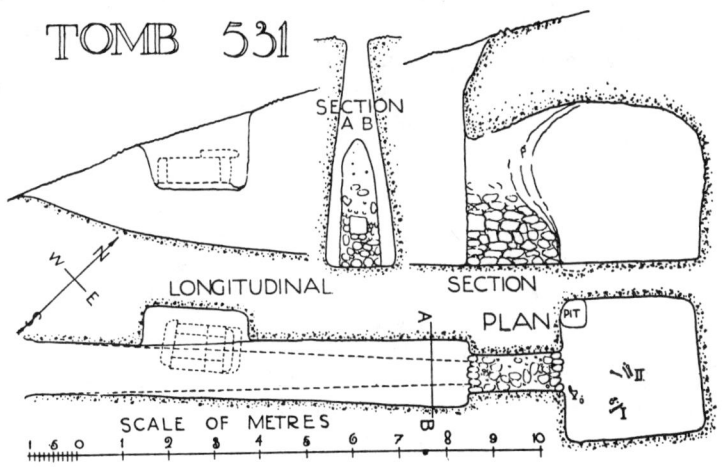

FIG. 12.—PLAN AND SECTIONS OF CHAMBER TOMB, MYCENAE.

sometimes provided with a bench and served as a vestibule, the inner chamber being filled with bodies. The roofs of the chambers might be hewn in the form of a vault or of a gable roof.[2] Instead of actual doors, the entrances were filled with rubble walls, which had to be taken down and rebuilt for each interment. Also the dromos itself was kept filled with earth, which was repeatedly emptied out and thrown back again. The enframement of the doorway, however, might be stuccoed and painted, with stripes, wave patterns, running spirals, or a series of rosettes. One of the largest of these tombs, at Mycenae, is about 20 feet square and 20 feet in height, with a dromos more than 90 feet in length.

[1] There are instances of dromoi which were abandoned without excavating the tomb chamber, because they unexpectedly encountered rock formations too hard for the simple tools employed.

[2] A chamber tomb at Dendra in Argolis is the exact negative of a house with a ridge roof, the eaves being strongly marked and the roof slopes themselves somewhat convex and thus giving the effect of a pointed vault, like that which in a later model from Perachora (see p. 41) seems to be due to thatched construction.

The royal Temple Tomb at Cnossus is really a special variant of a chamber tomb, with only the chamber itself cut back into the face of the cliff, about 12 feet square, with a central square pier and corresponding pilasters at the corners and middle of each side (the entrance being near a corner), framing thinner panels of gypsum lining the walls. Heavy wooden beams crossing on the central pier held the pilasters upright, and the rough rock ceiling above was painted blue. Instead of the usual dromos, the tomb is preceded by several compartments built of masonry: immediately in front is a crypt with two square piers, and before this a covered passage with a door which was locked from within, opening upon a court. Beyond the court, and facing the entrance to the tomb, was a pavilion with two columns between antae; a stairway at one side of the pavilion ascended to the outer ground level. Another stairway, beside the covered passage but outside the locked door, gave access to a terrace with an upper columnar sanctuary built directly above the crypt, its back against the ledge; there must have been a trap-door to give access to the crypt when the door was locked. The whole arrangement recalls the tomb of Minos at Heraclea Minoa on the south shore of Sicily (between Selinus and Acragas), as described by Diodorus, with an underground tomb below and a temple of Aphrodite above.

Another variant is the royal tomb at Isopata (1500–1400 B.C.), just north of Cnossus, approached by a dromos of the usual form, leading, however, to a vestibule about 22 feet long, through which in turn is entered the rectangular tomb chamber, 20 by 26 feet in plan. The walls are of ashlar masonry; the end walls are vertical, while the side walls of the tomb chamber curve inward until the interval between them could be covered with a single row of slabs, giving the appearance of a pointed barrel vault, probably 20 feet in height.

(C) *Tholos tombs,* or beehive domed chambers, in general form very much resemble the rock tombs, though their construction was usually very different. For while they, too, were cut in the side of a hill, and approached by an open horizontal avenue or dromos, yet instead of being rock-cut they were lined artificially with masonry; and the tomb chamber, instead of being excavated from the entrance passage, was formed by sinking from above a well of the desired diameter, within which the pointed dome was then built up in horizontal courses, which were backed with earth as they rose. The well was not sunk so deeply but that the top of the dome projected slightly above the surface of the ground, and was therefore covered with a slight artificial tumulus, sometimes even with a low surrounding wall. It is notable that this form reproduces, with the conservatism characteristic of funerary architecture, the most primitive form of the circular hut. Many of them, of large dimensions, carefully dressed masonry (breccia), peculiar construction, and with highly decorative façades, are to be classed among the most important remains of the Mycenaean era. About forty of them are known on the Greek mainland and in the adjoining islands, one in Asia Minor (at Colophon), and three in Crete, all of the latter being Late Aegean and later than the Achaean invasion.[1]

[1] One at Cnossus is certainly no earlier than 1500 B.C., while a second at Cnossus and that at Hagios Theodoros belong to the latest stage of Late Aegean III. A circular water-basin at Arkhanes near Cnossus, dated as early as 1580 B.C. by the pottery, has been regarded as the lower part of a beehive vault; but the lower courses step outward, and there is no real evidence that the missing upper courses curved inward.

GRAVE CIRCLES AND THOLOI

The earliest suggestions of this form of tomb are to be found in the Mesara plain of southern Crete, where, between 2700 and 2000 B.C., great community circles were constructed with stone walls up to 8 feet in thickness, provided with doorways and leaning slightly inward, the largest 43 feet in diameter internally and containing about two hundred bodies.[1] Probably, however, they were mere enclosures, not carried up high enough to form domes, thus foreshadowing the grave circle at Mycenae. By a coincidence, this circular type was abandoned only to be revived again on the Greek mainland by the Achaean invaders, after 1500 B.C. There we find a lengthy series which shows a gradual structural advance. First we have those in which the construction is rather primitive, the walls of small pieces of undressed limestone bedded in clay, the entrances showing no knowledge of the principle of the triangular relieving opening above the lintel, which is of harder limestone; the walls of the dromos are sometimes merely excavated in the rock, without linings. Three of the nine tholos tombs at Mycenae, among them the tomb of Aegisthus (about 40 feet in diameter), belong to this stage, of about 1500–1425 B.C., as well as the three at Triphylian Pylos, and one at Thoricus in Attica. The second stage, of about 1425–1350 B.C., is characterised by the adoption of more regular architectural lines; but since the harder material could not yet be readily cut to such forms, the façade formed a mere screen of light poros limestone laid up as ashlar masonry, with the heavier construction behind it. Such a screen was added in later times to the tomb of Aegisthus, independently of the older façade behind; and three other tombs at Mycenae, together with one at the Argive Heraeum, were actually designed with double façades, bonded together. For the lining of the doorway, behind the poros façade, larger and harder stones were selected, conglomerate or breccia, dressed as yet without the aid of the saw; and the same hard breccia was used for the lintel even on the façade itself, where poros would have been unsuitable for the great span. In these more developed examples which follow the tomb of Aegisthus we find a new feature, the triangular relieving opening constructed by corbelling above the lintels, filled with a screen of light poros ashlar. The interiors were still of rubble except immediately around the doorway; and the dromoi, lined partly with rubble and partly with poros ashlar in the earlier examples of this group, were lined wholly with poros ashlar in the later examples. In the latest of these, the Lion Tomb at Mycenae, the rubble wall hitherto used for closing the door was replaced by actual doors, with a stone threshold, placed however practically flush with the façade as was the case with the earlier rubble walls. In the third group, of about 1350–1275 B.C., we see the height of technical skill, all the work, not only on the façade but also the lining of the dromos and tholos, being in regular ashlar masonry of hard breccia blocks, frequently of tremendous size, but now conquered by means of the saw. As in the Lion Tomb, the entrances were closed by double doors resting on stone thresholds, but now set back at the middle of the passage in order to protect them from the weather. To this latest stage, which in workmanship is comparable to the Lion Gate and

[1] At Platanos; others exist at Hagia Triada, Hagios Onouphrios, Koumasa, and Siva near Phaestus. There is no proof that they were domical, apart from the heaps of stones which had fallen into the interior. Xanthoudidis and Sir Arthur Evans assumed that they were domical; but Marinatos seems to have conclusively proved that they were not.

the latest portions of the palaces at Mycenae and Tiryns, we may assign the three other tholos tombs at Mycenae (including the tomb of the Genii and those popularly assigned to Agamemnon and Clytemnestra) and the great tomb at Orchomenus. Of these, the largest and most perfect of the tombs at Mycenae, that which is variously called the "Tomb of Agamemnon" or the "Treasury of Atreus," dating from just about 1325 B.C.,[1] may be taken as representative of the type, and described in detail (Fig. 13).

The domed part is about 47½ feet in diameter, and 44 feet in extreme height. Directly upon the floor, which is formed of rammed clay, is laid, without other foundation, the lowest course of the masonry. The curve of the pointed dome begins at the floor and is carried up through thirty-four courses. The dome is not constructed on the arcuated or vault principle; the courses simply project one over another, uncemented, until by the lessening diameter of the concentric circles the top could be covered by a single stone, hollowed on the under side to continue the curve to a rounded point.[2] In plan, however, the blocks of stone approach more nearly the shape of voussoirs, their inner parts being chamfered to form radiating joints, though the outer portions retain their previous rectangular forms leaving wide gaps at the back which were filled in with small stones and clay. The inner face of the masonry appears to have been dressed down after the construction was complete. The masonry as it exists to-day shows a great number of holes over its entire surface, those in the upper part being single and containing pins which apparently fastened rosettes of bronze, while in the third, fourth, and fifth courses the holes are larger and grouped in pairs, evidently for securing friezes of metallic plates, producing on the whole a stately and impressive interior.[3] A very similar appearance was presented by the "Treasury of Minyas" at Orchomenus, which has been famous since antiquity, Pausanias claiming that it was not less wonderful than the pyramids; the dome is of practically the same dimensions (46 feet in diameter), with the same construction in smoothed masonry, and with the same holes for the attachment of rosettes above the fifth course that we found in the "Tomb of Agamemnon." In the "Tomb of Clytemnestra," 44 feet in diameter, the masonry of the interior is not so regular and is composed of smaller courses, in startling contrast with which is the high course containing the lintel, carried round like a belt course (Plate XIV).

In two of these examples there is a smaller rectangular chamber at one side of the tholos and entered from it; the doorway which appears in the section (A-B) of the "Tomb of Agamemnon" is that which leads to the small secondary chamber. In this case the chamber is about 27 feet square and 19 feet high, with a base for a central pier to support the ceiling. Far more imposing, however, was the comparatively small side chamber at Orchomenus, only 9 by 12¼ feet in plan; the ceiling was formed by four great slabs of green schist

[1] Considerably earlier dates are assigned to all these tholos tombs at Mycenae by Sir Arthur Evans, on account of his assumption that the early material found in the shaft graves had been transported from the tholos tombs; see, however, p. 25, note 1.

[2] This hollowing of the cap stone is not represented in Fig. 13. Actually the hollow does not quite fit the rest of the curve, but forms a slight horizontal offset, as if it had been cut separately.

[3] From such evidence of metal attachments it is now possible to understand how Homer came to speak of brazen walls and bases, silver columns and lintels.

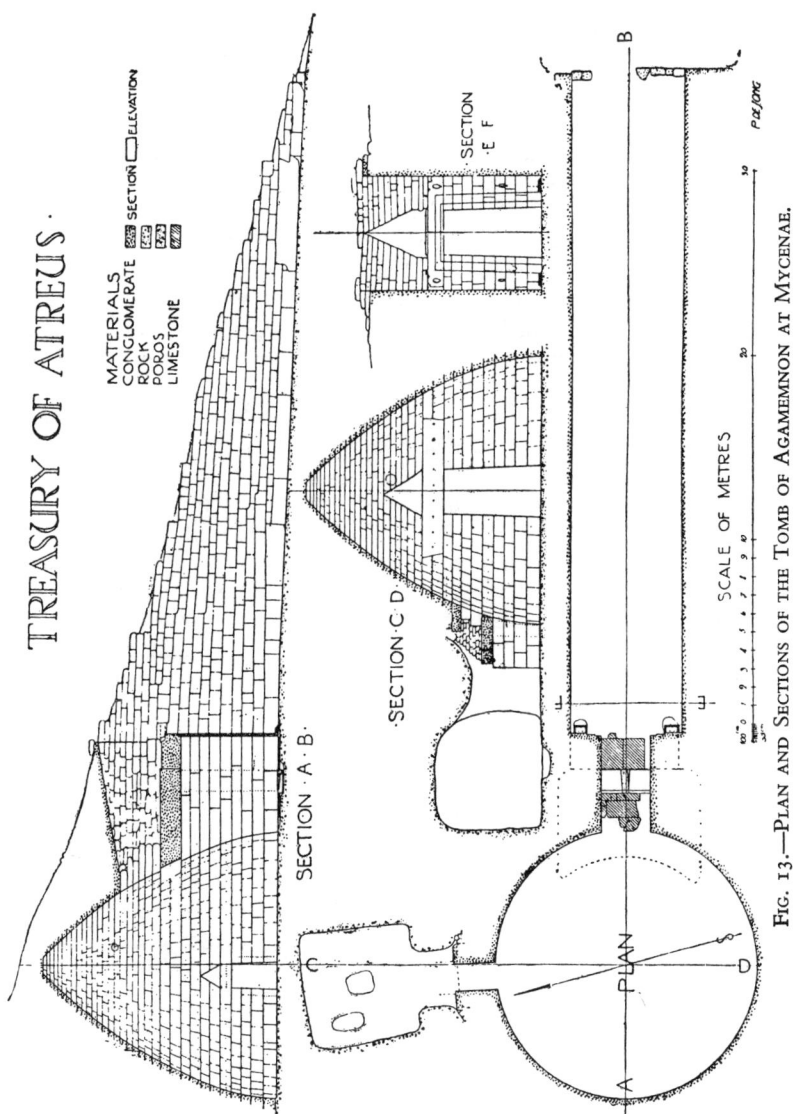

Fig. 13.—Plan and Sections of the Tomb of Agamemnon at Mycenae.

16 inches thick, the lower surface carved with a pattern of rosettes and spirals which was clearly derived from Egypt (Plate XVI); the walls were lined with thin slabs covered with a similar pattern.[1] Many of the tholos tombs, however, lack the side chamber, as in the great "Tomb of Clytemnestra" at Mycenae; sometimes as a substitute there were pit graves sunk in the floor of the tholos, as at Vaphio and the Argive Heraeum;[2] or there might even be a sort of sarcophagus built up in rude masonry at one side of the tholos, as at Thoricus.

The dromos, or entrance passage, by which the remains of the dead would be conducted to their final resting-place, is about 21 feet wide and 115 feet long in the "Tomb of Agamemnon" (Fig. 13), 20 feet wide and 125 feet long in the "Tomb of Clytemnestra," but only $16\frac{3}{4}$ feet wide in the "Treasury of Minyas." The walls are built of ashlar masonry, apparently finished with a special coping and rising gradually from the entrance to the façade, where the height is 45 feet in the "Tomb of Agamemnon." In this example the conglomerate construction varies from 7 to 10 feet in thickness on each side, and behind this in turn is a thick wall of yellow mud brick to render the ashlar impervious to the infiltration of water; the total thickness from side to side is thus about 61 feet, including the 21 feet of the dromos.

This led to a splendid portal, which, in the case of the "Tomb of Agamemnon," is in even greater degree than the dome itself the glory of the edifice. The present state of this doorway is shown in Plate XV; the façade is 20 feet 8 inches wide and 46 feet high, with a doorway 18 feet 2 inches in height, varying in width from 9 feet 1 inch (exactly half of the height) at the bottom to 8 feet 1 inch at the top, with a reveal of 17 feet 6 inches (at the bottom). The lintel is composed of two colossal stones, the inner one $29\frac{1}{2}$ feet in length, $16\frac{1}{2}$ feet in width, and 3 feet 4 inches in height, weighing more than 100 tons; above the lintel is the characteristic relieving opening. Similar treatments and dimensions appear in the "Tomb of Clytemnestra" and the "Treasury of Minyas."[3] The thresholds in each case are composed of two blocks with a wedge between to thrust them tightly against the side walls. Pivot holes in the thresholds and lintels show that there were double doors. The thresholds and the immediate jambs of the doors were sheathed with bronze, fastened by bronze nails. In the richest tombs the façades were revetted with slabs of coloured stones, red, green, and white, instead of the painted stucco of the rock tombs; and the doorways were surrounded with architectural enframements of columns and architrave. In the "Tomb of Clytemnestra" there were engaged columns with vertical fluting (thirteen flutes in the semi-circumference); part of one shaft remains in place (Plate XIII), with a downward taper of $\frac{3}{4}$ inch in this piece alone; while dressed surfaces show that in a height of $10\frac{1}{2}$ feet the taper was more than $2\frac{1}{2}$ inches. The architrave was faced with two projecting courses of grey stone, the lower carved with disks in low relief, the upper with spirals; and above this were carved slabs of red porphyry, enframed between two pilasters which carried up the lines of the fluted columns. More detailed informa-

---

[1] The fallen ceiling blocks of the lateral chamber at Orchomenus were reconstructed in 1914.

[2] Two shallow pit graves occur even in the "Tomb of Agamemnon" at Mycenae.

[3] The stones, however, are smaller, the inner lintel at Orchomenus weighing only 26 tons.

tion is to be obtained from the "Tomb of Agamemnon." The immediate enframement of the doorway consists of receding fascias cut on the ashlar masonry of the jambs and on the lintel. Outside this are the bases of the engaged columns, of breccia with a stepped profile.[1] The total height of the green alabaster columns was 20 feet $6\frac{1}{4}$ inches, with the capitals, about 12 lower diameters. The lower diameter is $20\frac{1}{2}$ inches, and the upper 22 inches, making the diminution about one-fifteenth, with the same reversed taper that we saw in the shaft on the Lion Gate and in that at the "Tomb of Clytemnestra";[2] but instead of the smooth shaft of the former, or the simple vertical fluting of the latter, the surface of each shaft is covered with nine chevron bands of alternate spiral ornament and plain (slightly concave) surfaces (Plate XIII), perhaps imitated from a metal sheathing applied to wooden columns. The capital consists of a necking in the form of a cavetto, vertically fluted, an echinus with the same chevrons that appear on the shaft, and another cavetto forming the transition to the plain abacus; an incision below the necking may have been intended for an astragal of bronze, or more probably a special collar with a beaded astragal was interposed, giving the profile found on the Lion Gate. Above the capitals were plinths or dies bonded into the wall and projecting from it; these were probably connected by the band of greenish stone like the columns (Plate XVI), resting directly on the architrave of the doorway, the lower fascia carved with discs to represent beam ends and the upper fascia carved with spirals, like the courses still *in situ* on the "Tomb of Clytemnestra." On the dies rested pilasters faced by smaller engaged columns, which carried up the lines of the lower columns and enframed the upper portion of the façade; the upper shafts had the same decorative motives that appear in the lower, but winding in continuous spirals instead of zigzags; and below their capitals were special collars of astragal profile with vertical incisions giving the appearance of beads. Between the pilasters were two sizes of red marble friezes carved with the so-called triglyph motive, 7 inches and $9\frac{3}{8}$ to $11\frac{1}{4}$ inches in height, also bands of rosettes, and white marble slabs showing a band of spirals along one edge. The triangular relieving opening was filled by a screen, evidently set back slightly behind the wall plane, and composed of horizontal red marble slabs (Plate XVI), carved with triple bands of spirals, alternating with plain horizontal bands of red stone or pinkish conglomerate, rather than by any such heraldic design as that over the Lion Gate. Two gypsum slabs carved with lions in relief may perhaps have flanked the triangular panel on either side.[3]

[1] The decorative elements of the façade are distributed in fragmentary form in various museums, at Nauplia near Mycenae itself, at Athens, Munich, Berlin, Carlsruhe, and the British Museum. This last material came in part from the collection of the Earl of Elgin, and in part from the Marquis of Sligo (1904) whose ancestor brought them from Greece in 1810.

[2] Durm's assertions to the contrary were again based on erroneous measurements.

[3] The restoration by Chipiez, reproduced in the first edition of this work, is now, like Reber's, impossible. It shows the columns with a diminution of one-sixth and with thirteen chevrons. There is no foundation whatever for his elaborately carved lintel, and he fails to take note of the plain projecting course crowning the wall (part of which still exists, and can be seen in Plate XV), which was specially provided to protect the ornamental facing below. On the other hand, Chipiez is certainly correct in filling the triangular panel with rows of spirals. Because of the erroneous treatment of this panel, restoring a heraldic design following the tradition set by Ittar (Lord Elgin's architect), Donaldson, Blouet, Adler, and

The last phase in the development of the tholos tombs is represented by the rude example at Menidi in Attica, though its rudeness may be due merely to its provincial character. The construction is of rubble throughout; its chief interest lies in the fact that there are four horizontal lintels above the main lintel, instead of the usual triangular relieving opening, though the latter form is discernible on the interior of the domed chamber.

(D) *House tombs*, more specifically imitating house types, formed the Cretan counterpart of the tholos tombs. These were built chambers of squared stones, miniature houses of rectangular plan, with roofs of reeds and clay, and doorways blocked by slabs. Such were the community tombs of Mochlos, Gournia and Palaikastro; at Palaikastro we find square buildings divided by partitions into long narrow compartments; among the examples at Mochlos are some with outer and inner rooms, in one case the inner room being placed beside rather than behind the outer one, because of the rocky slope behind, and so giving a plan like a maeander pattern.

(E) Terracotta coffins (*larnakes*) are particularly rare on the mainland but are numerous in Crete, where even stone sarcophagi occur. As for (F) burials in jars and (G) the tumuli of Asia Minor, these are not of sufficient architectural interest to delay us at this point.

In all these tombs it was deemed advisable to surround the occupant with the necessities and luxuries of life; but scepticism as to their practical utility, coupled with regard for the resources of the living generation, led to the manufacture of a class of light gold-leaf ornaments, utensils, and masks, which are the most prolific product of these graves, now violated by the hand of man. In the case of the tholos tombs, however, it is only in the outlying districts that they are found with their contents intact, as at Menidi and Thoricus in Attica, at Vaphio near Sparta, and at Triphylian Pylos near Olympia. Elsewhere they are usually empty; some were undoubtedly cleared out by the Mycenaean people themselves, while others, perhaps plundered only in later times, were open in the historic period, the "Treasury of Minyas" containing pedestals and other traces of Hellenistic and Roman times, while a tholos tomb at Tiryns contains a Roman oil mill.[1]

*   *   *   *   *

How this early civilisation, so far on the right track, was cut short and scattered by the Dorian invasion, to begin its life over again, and to work out its destiny, permeating with its artistic instinct the country from which it was now expelled, has yet to be considered. Five barren centuries at least elapsed before the conditions favoured what may be called the reappearance of Achaean, henceforward to be named Ionian art. The more we dwell on the earliest periods of Greek art, the more shall we discover what it owed to the Aegean civilisation; and it is astonishing to find how many Aegean principles and motifs survived.

Reber, we must likewise reject the restoration by Spiers, reproduced in the second edition of this work; the latter restoration, furthermore, was made before the discovery of the pilasters and upper columns above the lower, and so is of value only because of its correct representation of the portion below the column capitals. Further study is necessary before an accurate restoration can be offered.

[1] The tomb of Clytemnestra, however, was exactly covered by the Hellenistic Theatre of Mycenae.

But the chief importance of the Aegean culture to a student of classical architecture is, not that the one was the direct ancestor of the other—for such an interpretation is not supported by the most recent discoveries—but the light that it throws on the origins of Greek architecture, as evolved by kindred tribes in the same environment, on the basis of the same fundamental traditions. It enables us to fill out the hazy background of the primitive period of Greek architecture, to retrace the development of the megaron plan, of the dadoes and antae of walls, of the inclined jambs of doorways. And even though we may admit that certain details, the bracket capital, the Doric echinus, the fluting of the shafts, the rosette, and the spiral, seem to have been direct survivals from the Aegean age, yet it remained for the later Hellene to exercise on them his refining genius and hand them down ennobled to future generations. In short, Aegean architecture was an earlier parallel development, rather than the immediate source of Greek architecture; the true fountain-head lay rather in the earlier northern home from which came the successive "Aryan" invaders of Greece.[1]

[1] Among some noteworthy reflections of the Cretan civilisation which was dispersed by the Achaean invaders of their island about 1400 B.C. are the so-called royal tombs of Ugarit (Ras Shamra) in Syria, where many of the Cretans found refuge. In date (just after 1400), style, and construction these tombs are direct successors of the royal tomb at Isopata near Cnossus (p. 28), though considerably smaller. Each is preceded by a dromos with a steep flight of stone steps descending to one end of the tomb, where is a doorway spanned by a corbelled arch, either polygonal or semicircular. The rectangular chambers themselves, of perfect ashlar masonry, vary from $6\frac{1}{2}$ by 10 feet to $12\frac{1}{2}$ by $14\frac{3}{4}$ feet in plan; the flank walls curve inward towards each other, the horizontal courses carefully trimmed to form bent or continuous arcs, meeting at the top in sharp ridges (ogival barrel vaults) or slightly truncated by horizontal spanning slabs; the heights of the vaults vary from $6\frac{1}{2}$ to $10\frac{1}{4}$ feet. The end walls are usually vertical; but sometimes they likewise slope or curve inward, giving almost the effect of rectangular domes or cloister vaults.

CHAPTER TWO

THE ORIGINS OF GREEK ARCHITECTURE

THE dispersion of the Aegean tribes at about 1100 B.C., which was the beginning of the making of the living Greece of history, appears to have been brought about by disturbances in Epirus and Thessaly, from which regions numerous armed bands periodically invaded central Greece and the Peloponnesus, driving the earlier inhabitants, Ionians, Aeolians, or Achaeans, to Attica and the island of Euboea and the central uplands of Arcadia, where they soon became subject to Doric influence, or across the sea to Asia Minor. The chief motive of these invasions of central and southern Greece may safely be set down to plunder, the great repute of the wealth of Mycenae and kindred cities sufficiently accounting for the enterprise, which in many respects presents an analogy with the invasion of Roman Italy by the northern hordes. The "Return of the Heracleidae" was the fanciful term which the Dorian tribe afterwards gave to their occupation of southern Greece and subjugation of the real owners of the soil. In overturning the Achaean civilisation these invaders, being by nature rude and unskilled, interrupted the progress of the arts and threw back every development in this direction. But this stoppage was only temporary; it was as if a fire which blazed brightly in the open had been smothered by a bundle of damp twigs; the flame was quenched temporarily, only to burst forth again more warmly and clearly. So from the mingling of the conquered and the conquering races, after a lapse of three or four centuries, issued the Dorian Greek race of history, destined, on subsequently meeting again the Ionian element which meanwhile had been taking a different direction, to produce in Athens the highest results in art which the world has yet witnessed. It will be one of the objects of this chapter to trace the origins of the Dorian type, which characterised the architecture of European Hellas and the West.

The majority of those whom the Dorians had displaced, the Ionians and Aeolians, fled across the Aegean Sea to the Asiatic coasts and islands. Asia Minor, the threshold of Asia and the gate of the west, was then dominated successively by the Hittites and Phrygians, the star of empire setting ever farther westward; it was not until 687 B.C. that Lydia as a kingdom began to play a part. But prior to this time the tribes thrust out of the Peloponnesus and central Greece had fringed Asia Minor with their colonies, seizing the shore land and the islands held of little account by the powers of the interior, or expanding what had formerly been trading outposts of their own Aegean ancestors. Greek tradition records migrations of the Aeolians in 1124 and of the Ionians in 1044 B.C.; and by the eighth century Ephesus, Miletus, Smyrna, Erythrae, Phocaea, were already great cities, and were rivalling Tyre and Sidon, whose civilisation they were so largely to displace. It was in Cyprus that fugitives from the Peloponnesus and Crete came into direct contact with the Phoenicians, collaborating in the foundation of a new civilisation on the ruins of the Aegean culture. The swift rise of these Ionian centres is one of the most striking things in the history of the Aegean; it was in great measure from them that the fine arts and philosophy, modified yet invigorated by fresh contact with the Oriental types of civilisation, passed back again into European Hellas.

To a slightly later moment in the historical period belongs the epoch of colonisation. From the new cities of Asia Minor bands moved toward the north, where the Black Sea was soon fringed with Ionian colonies, sent especially from Miletus and Phocaea; Miletus alone sent out ninety colonies. The Euboeans of central Greece devoted special attention to Macedonia. Other bands turned in the opposite direction; Eretrians of Euboea established a half-way station at Corcyra, and from Chalcis in Euboea went colonists to Cumae in southern Italy as early as about 760 B.C., and afterwards to neighbouring sites, Naples, Pompeii, and Rhegium. There is no mention of the Greeks in Sicily earlier than about 734 B.C., when Naxos was founded by another Ionian colony from Chalcis; others came to Syracuse; from Cumae was settled Zancle (Messina), from Naxos spread Catana and Leontini; and Ionians predominated in the settlement of Himera as late as 625 B.C. The Phocaeans were even more adventurous: not only did they settle Hemeroscopion and Maenace in Spain, about 620–600 B.C., and Massilia (Marseilles) in France shortly afterward, but also Alalia in Corsica (560) and Velia (Elea) in Italy, south of Paestum. In Egypt, too, the various Ionian cities established commercial outposts, beginning in the reign of Psammetichus I (664–610 B.C.).

Whatever may have been the impulse that brought the Dorians and the associated tribes into the Peloponnesus, it was land-hunger doubtless that soon sent them swarming out of it. From every part of Greece they followed their fleeing Mycenaean predecessors, and passed into Crete, the southern Cyclades such as Thera, also Cos and Rhodes, and even settled in one or two cities on the Asiatic mainland, such as Halicarnassus. Dorians from Megara (near Athens) settled Byzantium (Constantinople) and Chalcedon perhaps even before the Ionians had thought of seizing the entrance to the Black Sea. Bands of Dorians likewise, in the last third of the eighth century, followed the other Ionian remnants who had passed westward. Dorians of Corinth wrested Corcyra and Syracuse from the Eretrians and Chalcidians in 733; others from Megara settled Megara Hyblaea in 727; the Laconians appeared at Tarentum in 705; and the Rhodians and Cretans established Gela in 688 B.C. The Dorians of Thera crossed to Cyrene in Africa in 632 B.C. The Doricised Achaeans confined their efforts to Italy, settling Sybaris and Croton about 720 and 710 B.C.; the Locrians founded Epizephyrian Locri about 676 B.C. Other colonies in turn hived off from these, the Sybarites establishing Metapontum and Poseidonia (Paestum), the Megarians of Sicily founding Selinus in 627, the Syracusans settling Acrae and Camarina, while the last of the important colonies was that planted by the Geloans at Acragas in 580 B.C. These Greek colonists of Sicily succeeded in placing under subjection the earlier inhabitants of the eastern part, the Sicels, from whom the island derives its name; and the Phoenician trading posts which had previously occupied this part of the coast were forced to withdraw to the territory of the Sicans and Elymians to the west. But the colonists who occupied the heel of Italy were constantly at war with the inland barbarians, especially the Illyrian tribes (Calabrians, Messapians, and Japygians).

The period with which we are concerned falls into four cultural stages, characterised by their ornament and sometimes overlapping in time: sub-Mycenaean (1100–1000), proto-geometric (1000–900), geometric (925–650), and orientalising (725–600 B.C.). But strict observance of these periods in our discussion of the architecture would be impractical.

* * * * *

When we speak of Greek architecture we refer, as a rule, to their public buildings; for, in contrast to their Aegean predecessors, the Greeks of the historical periods devoted less attention to their private dwellings, whether houses and palaces for the living or tombs for the dead. And of their public buildings those of religious character occupy the most prominent place, first of all their temples and altars, to which were subsequently added the treasuries, propylaea, votive monuments, stoas, theatres, and other adjuncts of the sacred temenos. Public buildings of secular character were of later development. It was long before the agora or market-place, with its fortuitous assemblage of administrative and commercial buildings, took on the monumental character of the Roman forum, with formal colonnades and peristyles. Likewise buildings for educational or athletic purposes, such as the gymnasium and palaestra and stadium, were at first unpretentious or temporary structures.

Before considering the development of Greek religious architecture, it may be noted that the religion was a combination of the worship of personified natural phenomena with that of deified heroes or ancestor worship. The Aegean tribes, especially the Cretan, seem to have worshipped a supreme goddess (Rhea); and when they went over to Ionia in Asia Minor they found that there, too, the Phrygian religion was that of a great goddess, Cybele, the mother of the gods, the patroness of all fertility. But the earliest records of the primitive European Greek religion point to a worship of Zeus, the supreme god. These two beliefs appear to have mingled, and the number of Greek gods rapidly multiplied; they married and begot offspring innumerable, and in the different localities the ingenuity of the priesthood soon determined the special worship of a certain god or gods without regard to the worship of the same god or gods as practised elsewhere in the Greek world. In some such way it came to pass that the favourite dwelling-places of Zeus were supposed to be at Olympia and Dodona, of Hera at Samos and Argos, of Athena at Athens, of Demeter at Eleusis, and of Apollo at Delos and Delphi, while the Asiatic mother-goddess was nationalised as Artemis (Cybele) at Ephesus and near-by Sardis, and as Aphrodite (Astarte) at Paphos in Cyprus. Zeus, Athena, and Apollo may be instanced as constituting the greatest triad of the Greek gods, each embodying to the Greek mind one of the forces of nature: Zeus was ruler of earth and heaven, the god producing storms, darkness, and rain; Apollo was the "shining one," the sun god; Athena was the queen of the air, worshipped in a variety of aspects and especially at Athens as Pallas-Athena, the goddess of wisdom and handicrafts. Then there were Demeter, the goddess of agriculture; Dionysus, the patron of wine and of the drama; Poseidon, god of the sea and earthquakes; Hephaestus, the god of fire and metal-working; Asclepius, the god of medicine; Hermes, the messenger and herald of the gods. Temples and sanctuaries were devoted even to nymphs and lesser mythological individuals such as Aphaea. These examples will be sufficient, for it would be impossible to do more than give a general idea of the nature of Greek mythology, which was largely the idealisation of God's mysterious workings by people who in spite of, or because of, their healthy animation were full of sensitive and earnest imagination. Beautiful scenery affected the Greeks in a religious way, for they were keenly susceptible to the permanence of spirit-life in Nature, and to them the mountain, the water, and the wood were peopled with divinities. If landscape touched them at all artistically, at least it did not lead them to pictorial representation, but solely to this personification and deification. Numbers of cults, in addition, were created out of the admiration for the prowess displayed by heroes of the same clay as themselves, such as Heràcles and Theseus, and, as in modern days, honours were paid to these deified mortals and pilgrimages were made to their shrines.

The artistic feelings of the Greeks led them not only to express the symbolic meaning, attributes, and achievements of their countless gods in sculpture, but also to surround their sacred statues with quantities of votive offerings of every description—in this way the buildings dedicated to their divinities were decorated and furnished, and a wide field was opened to the artist and a magnificent opportunity given to the development of art. Earth and sea and sky, mountains and rivers, which the Pantheism of the Greeks personified and idealised, had to be represented in sculptural form. The earlier statues were rude and primitive images (xoana) carved in wood, and even down to a later day, when buildings were of marble, many great chryselephantine images of Zeus, Athena, and Poseidon were in wood, albeit overlaid with gold and ivory. The beautiful material which Naxos, Paros, and Mount Pentelicus yielded could not, however, long be ignored; and the introduction of hollow-casting from Egypt opened another field for art. As far back as we can trace the primitive temple, so far we can trace its accompaniment of votive offerings and marble or bronze statues of the god.

The primitive Greek religion required at first, however, only altars in open areas, such as those of Zeus and Hera at Olympia, of Artemis Orthia at Sparta, and of Aphaea at Aegina. An excellent illustration of this stage exists at Karphi in Crete, a lofty city of refuge to which the Minoan and Achaean remnants fled at the time of the Dorian invasion. In a precinct dating from between 1000 and 900 B.C., with an entrance in the east wall, there is an altar at the north side of the court and a shelf along the south side for cult statuettes and votive offerings; a flight of steps ascends through a doorway on the west side to a group of subordinate rooms. In the sanctuary of Hera at Samos is a stratified series of altars, seven of them belonging to the primitive period with which we are concerned. The earliest, apparently of about 950 B.C., consisted of no more than a low enclosure of flat stones forming a rectangle about 5 by 8 feet to contain the ashes, and was built on a curving terrace facing toward the southeast, so that it was unrelated to the easterly direction of the later temples. Other forms of this altar, dating from about 850, 775, 750, 725, 675, and 625 B.C.,[1]

---

[1] For our purpose the most important result obtained from these dates is the determination of the chronology of the accompanying temples.

retained the same orientation and consisted of concentric enlargements with more formal casings, attaining in the time of the sixth altar (675 B.C.) the maximum dimensions of 19½ by 43 feet—the seventh was built directly above with the same dimensions—besides a step or platform added on the northwest side. At Ephesus, where our literary evidence carries the foundation of the sanctuary of Artemis so far back into the mists of time that it was attributed to the age of the Amazons, and the destruction of the first sanctuary was even dated by Eusebius as early as 1146 B.C., the material remains on the contrary suggest an origin more recent than at Samos, though again with merely an altar ('A') in an open precinct, with a stairway toward the east, dated by votive offerings as of about 700 B.C.[1]

It was not until the gods had become personified and embodied in statues of considerable size that they would have required specially built shelters. Homer, living apparently in the eighth century, belongs to a period of transition; he knows the open-air altars, but he speaks also of temples of Apollo at Delphi and Troy, of temples of Athena at Troy and Athens (though the last, at any rate, may be a sixth-century interpolation); and in the temple of Athena at Troy seems to have been a seated image. There is nothing in Homer to disagree with the archaeological evidence that the beginnings of Greek temple design were several centuries later than the Dorian invasion.[2] Perhaps the concept of an enclosed and roofed space, forming the actual temple or home of the god, originated in the more highly organised east. Thus at Samos, in the time of the second altar, soon after 850 B.C., a path leading westward can only be explained as a connection between the altar and a modest chapel of which no remains have survived, unless we can suppose that a circular limestone pedestal, 2 feet high and 3 feet 2 inches in diameter with a rectangular socket, supported the rude log image of the goddess. At Olympia there seems to have been no temple until about 700 B.C., by which time the scheme was well on the road of evolution. At Ephesus there are no traces of anything more than the simple altar until after the Cimmerian invasion of 652 B.C., when the primitive altar seems to have been embellished with some sort of niche or tabernacle, placed on a special podium or basement and facing toward the stairway to the altar, explaining the unusual westward orientation that ever afterwards obtained at Ephesus and was reproduced in several other temples of Asia Minor (Neandria, Larisa, Magnesia). Not many years later, perhaps about 625 B.C., the entire complex structure at Ephesus was encased within a simple rectangular platform ('B') with a surrounding wall.[3]

[1] The letters 'A' to 'C' assigned by Hogarth to the three earliest temples are here retained, 'D' being the "Croesus temple" and 'E' the "Alexander temple." Likewise with regard to the chronology we may follow Hogarth (except with regard to 'B,' see note 3). There has been a more recent tendency to lower these dates, Gjerstad assigning 'A' to about 650, 'B' to about 600, and 'C' to about 575 B.C., while Loewy regarded 'A,' 'B,' 'C,' and 'D' as all of one date, about 550 B.C.

[2] For this reason we must discard such traditional dates as the burning of the first temple at Ephesus in 1146 B.C. as given by Eusebius, or that of 1096 B.C. (eight years after the Dorian invasion) assigned by Pausanias to the Heraeum at Olympia.

[3] Hogarth had regarded both the "green schist base" at the east and the T-shaped yellow limestone structure at the west as contemporary, forming temple 'A.' But the green schist base rests on the stem of the T (the stairway ascending to the altar), and also is of more developed masonry, and thus is later; this separation of 'A' into two stages is due to

BEGINNINGS OF THE TEMPLE PLAN

It is extremely probable that the earliest covering provided for the Greek cult image, or xoanon, was little more than a hut which served the material purpose of shelter. The Greeks themselves retained vague traditions of the crude forms and ephemeral materials of their earliest temples; thus they recorded that the first temple of Apollo at Delphi was constructed of laurel boughs, and the second of wax and feathers. But it was not in the nature of the Greeks to be satisfied with this, and it was necessary to give the tabernacle the character and spiritual significance of a god's house. Such a motive lies behind the fable that the third temple at Delphi was of bronze.[1] Mere advances in construction do not account for the development of the shrine; it is of the aspiration of humanity toward something fulfilling their ideal of a house of God that the Greek temples speak.

It was long, however, before such a complex organism as the peripteral temple with all its parts, and the formal columnar orders, came into being. The earliest temples of the gods, in all parts of the Greek world, were merely the houses of men, enlarged and embellished. And in them, therefore, we may trace the various stages corresponding to the development of the house plan, retracing the very cycle from circle to rectangle which had run its course during the Aegean period. To the circular hut, for instance, corresponds a circular rustic temple at Gasi (four miles from Candia) in Crete.[2] The stage of the elliptical houses is represented in domestic architecture by a foundation of the geometric period buried beneath the Athenian market-place, and in temple architecture by a limestone votive model from the island of Samos. A horseshoe temple survived until late times at Gonnos in Thessaly, dedicated to Athena Polias, and rebuilt with two Doric columns in-antis.[3] As the plan was thus elongated, cross-walls were introduced to mark off a pronaos and sometimes an inner room or adytum. The development of the straight front and the elongation of the ridged roof at the same time tended to form a gable on the front, leading to the pedimental façade. The hairpin plan appears in the apsidal foundations of a temple about 25 feet long dedicated to Hera Acraea at Perachora (the peninsula opposite Corinth), and others underlying the temples of Aphaea at Aegina and of Apollo Daphnephorus at Eretria.[4] More detailed impressions of the actual appearance of such structures may be obtained from three terracotta votive models of temples, dedicated at Perachora in the first half of the eighth century B.C. One, about 14 inches long, has a hairpin plan with the flank walls converg-

Lethaby and Weickert. Also Hogarth's assumption that 'B' was the temple built by Theodorus of Samos, who would then have to be regarded as the grandfather of the famous Theodorus, seems untenable.

[1] More authentic examples of bronze temples are that of Athena of the Brazen House (Chalkioikos) at Sparta and the shrines dedicated by Myron of Sicyon at Olympia (Pausanias, III, 17, 3; VI, 19, 2).

[2] The circular tholoi of archaic and later times probably have no relation to this primitive stage of development.   [3] A horseshoe peristyle at Thermum will be noted later.

[4] The same apsidal scheme was repeated in more monumental form in several structures of the archaic and later periods, such as the oracle temple at Corinth, temple 'B' on the Athenian Acropolis, and the Bouleuterion at Olympia. There are also more sophisticated apsidal forms, in which the flank walls do not continue the circumference of the circle but break out beyond it, as in a little shrine buried before 513 B.C. at Delphi and a small marble shrine of the fourth century in the castle at Paros (see p. 233). Compare also the internal apses of the later temples at Samothrace and Lebadea.

ing toward the apsidal rear; the doorway has three small square windows above, and an anta on either side; and in front of each anta was a small rectangular base supporting a pair of slender columns or posts. The capitals of the posts (if there were such distinct members) have been lost, together with their architrave and the porch roof; but enough remains of the main roof to indicate the steep angle at which it rose. Another of these models had a very steep ridged roof, slightly curved in an ogival section, with a cylindrical ridge-pole and an open gable at the front; all the details suggest thatched construction.

As the temple plan, under the continued influence of domestic architecture, was squared and the atrophied remnant of the circular hut disappeared, the elongated rectangle developed under northern influence normally presented a long ridged roof with gables at both ends, sometimes with a front porch either closed with a doorway or open with corner posts. One of the earliest of such plans, and perhaps not originally a temple at all (because of its early date) but rather a chieftain's house, is the so-called megaron 'B' at Thermum in Aetolia (Fig. 14), built in imitation of the Aegean megaron 'A' (which, in this distant corner of the Greek world, may have survived the Dorian invasion). The outer walls of this rectangular plan are curved, convex to the exterior, and seem to have been curved also in section, like an ogival vault constructed in mud brick; the entrance is at the south, thus determining the peculiar orientation of the later temple, and two cross-walls divide the main room (cella) from the prodomus and a rear room.[1] To a later period belongs a terracotta votive model of a temple (or possibly a mere house) found at the Argive Heraeum, of which the decoration shows that it belongs to the very end of the geometric period with some intrusion of orientalizing elements (Fig. 15). This again is about $14\frac{1}{2}$ inches long; and the walls support a very steep ridged roof with a large rectangular opening in the front gable, which is located, however, above the

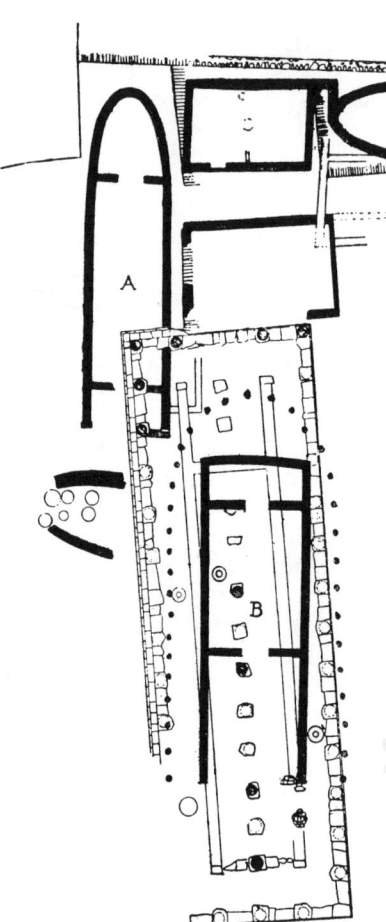

Fig. 14.—Megara 'A' and 'B' at Thermum.

[1] The excavators assumed that 'B,' like 'A,' was of Aegean date; but such a long existence (down to about 620 B.C.) seems incredible.

cross-wall with the doorway; the projecting porch was regarded as an addition with a flat roof resting on two corner posts.[1] Actual foundations of such simple temples, either early in date or in such rustic surroundings as to retain their primitive construction, with low socles of irregular stone supporting walls of mud brick or even, in mountainous and stony districts, built up with small stones to the roof, are very numerous; thus we have, among others, the temple of Dionysus-in-the-Marshes at Athens, that of Apollo on the hill at Asine, those of Aphrodite and Artemis high on the mountain at Bassae and probably also the early temple of Apollo a little lower down, that of Hera Limenia (with a central hearth or internal altar) at Perachora opposite Corinth, and a temple (which at this period was a simple rectangle) at Larisa in Asia Minor.

FIG. 15.—TERRACOTTA HOUSE MODEL FROM THE ARGIVE HERAEUM.

The ridge roofs of these early structures were probably at first constructed of wattle-and-daub covered with mud and, externally, with thatch.[2] At the front, and eventually at both ends, they terminated in rude gables of very steep pitch. Gradually, however, roof tiles of terracotta were substituted, whereupon the pitch was lowered and the fronts assumed the characteristic pedimental form. Greek tradition reported that tiles and pediments were invented at Corinth; and since Corinth was always the centre of the roof-tile industry the story is likely enough, with the understanding that the term "pediment" applies, not to the high primitive gable, but only to the low triangular type faced with terracotta and eventually constructed of stone.[3] Terracotta tiles were of three general categories (Fig. 16): the Laconian (Spartan) system had concave pantiles with the joints protected by convex cover-tiles (semicircular in section),

[1] The restoration published in 1923, when it was thought that there were parts of two models, was considerably modified in 1931 when all the fragments were combined in one.
[2] The theory that these northern temples were roofed with a thick mass of mud, resting on horizontal timbers and slightly convex to shed the rain, is devoid of foundation and contrary to the evidence. It has been pointed out that where flat mud roofs are still used in Greece, as in Crete, they are concave rather than convex so that the central pool evaporates instead of draining off. The northern roofs, on the other hand, were too steep for solid mud construction. And there is no evidence for wooden shingles such as were used in Rome in the third century B.C.
[3] For the tradition see Pindar, *Olymp.* XIII, 21; Pliny, XXXV, 152. Assuming that true pediments had been used previously by the Mycenaean builders, we might better say that they were revived at Corinth.

while the Corinthian system had flat pan-tiles (with raised rims) and triangular or saddle-shaped cover-tiles; the Ionians in general followed the Corinthian scheme, but the Aeolians further north and the Sicilian system of the west compromised with flat pan-tiles and semicircular cover-tiles. To accompany these were gradually developed the special forms used in exceptional positions, eaves tiles, antefixes, simas, ridge tiles, ridge cover-tiles, and acroteria. Of the decorative members edging the roof, the Laconian raking simas are vertical, with elaborate patterns and with triangular dentellation along the top; the antefixes and acroteria are semicircular like the cover- or ridge tiles that they terminate, the acroteria in particular being huge disks with dentellated edges; manufactured at Sparta, these were exported to all the cities of the Peloponnesus and even, in one instance, to Sicily. The earliest Corinthian simas, likewise with the vertical surface predominating, curve forward slightly at the top like the Egyptian concave throat moulding, and from the same source they likewise derived their painted decoration with upright rectangular petals, the Doric leaf; examples occur at Corinth, Eleusis, Athens, Delphi, and Corcyra. The antefixes generally preserve some relation to the triangular form of the cover-tile, sometimes with a palmette decoration. The Sicilian sima, with its greater flare, resembles even more closely the Egyptian throat moulding, and is decorated on its concave surface with a Sicilian variant of the Doric leaf, more triangular than rectangular; and the Sicilians preferred to carry such a sima along the flanks, with very numerous trumpet-like spouts, instead of antefixes. The characteristic frieze- or parapet-simas of the Asia Minor coast, often with dentellation on top like the Laconian, will be discussed later. Such roof terracottas often formed the sole decoration of the primitive temples.[1]

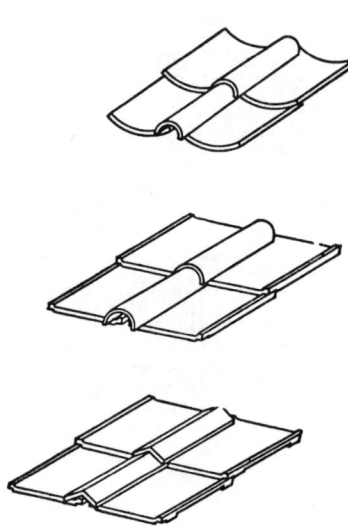

FIG. 16.—ROOF TILES, LACONIAN, SICILIAN, AND CORINTHIAN.

As an example of one of the latest of the primitive temples, depending for its effect almost entirely upon the richness of its fictile revetment, we may note the temple of Athena at Syracuse in Sicily, built as we are told by a tyrant named Agathocles, who was reputed to have selected the best of the stone for his own house and, even though he paid into the treasury the monetary equivalent, to have been killed for his impiety by a thunderbolt. Only a portion of the stone sill now remains; but two periods, the original construction and a later repair, are fully represented in the roof terracottas. In both stages the facing slabs applied to the wooden cornice are painted with a double guilloche; and the sima, with its lower fascia decorated with chequers or intertwined stems (from which project trumpet spouts on the flanks), its concave throat moulding painted with a Sicilian leaf pattern, and its crowning fascia with a maeander,

[1] Often, too, these terracottas are the sole relics of early temples.

was carried not only along the flanks and up the slopes of the pediments, but also across horizontally under the pediments where the presence of a sima is absurd. In the later period, apart from minor variations of pattern, a fringe of pendant palmettes was suspended from the cornice casing, and there were elaborate acroteria, a youth on horseback at the apex and sphinxes at the outer corners, and a running-flying Gorgon in the tympanum.

Apart from the few instances in which corner posts were employed in front porches, the earliest temples were quite without posts or columns. But as temples were increased in width, and as the walls were located too far apart to permit the use of simple transverse beams, such posts were introduced within (Figs. 17, 22) to assist in supporting the ceiling and roof. The first stage was marked by the use of posts in a single line along the main axis of the temple, directly under the ridge beam, though instead of supporting the ridge beam directly they sustained the transverse beams at mid-span; these in turn carried the horizontal ceiling and also struts under the ridge beam. When a temple

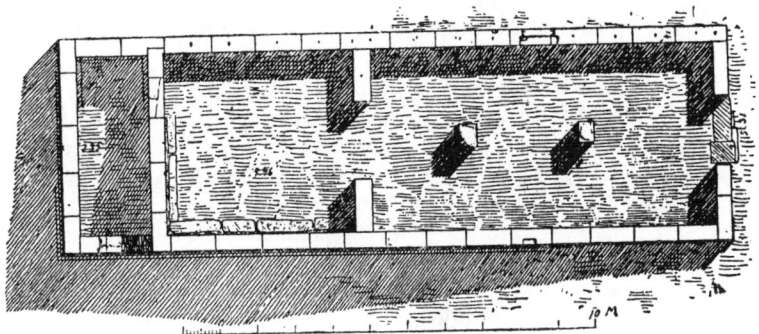

FIG. 17.—THE MEGARON ON THE ACROPOLIS AT SELINUS.

containing an inner row of columns had likewise a pronaos enclosed with antae, the inner row was usually recalled in the pronaos by a single post in-antis, as at Locri Epizephyrii and Prinias. The posts inside the cella sometimes were set far apart, only two in the length of the cella, as in an archaic temple in the Heracleum at Thasos and in the megaron on the acropolis of Selinus in Sicily (Fig. 17); compare also the temples at Dreros and Prinias in Crete as described below. Or the posts in this single row might be set closer together, forming a series of five in the cella of the early temple at Locri Epizephyrii in South Italy, of seven in the temple at Neandria in Asia Minor as described below (Fig. 22). In the temple of Artemis Orthia at Sparta, of which the front portion was destroyed in building the later temple, the number of wooden posts in the median line must have been more considerable; and exactly opposite these were corresponding vertical timbers imbedded in the mud-brick flank walls, forming a half-timbered construction to assist in supporting the ceiling and roof beams. At Samos, while the second altar was still in use and so shortly before 775 B.C., the hypothetical original temple was rebuilt in the most pretentious form known up to that time, a rectangular building with mud-brick walls resting on a socle of flat stones, 21 feet wide and 108 feet long, open at the east front with three wooden posts in-antis, and with twelve additional posts spaced about 8 feet on centres forming a single line down the main axis. Against the rear wall stands the rectangular pedestal of the xoanon statue, thrust slightly toward the right so that it would not be directly behind a column.

Among the primitive temples of Crete, though we find conflicting influences in plan, the flat roof of the south seems to have been characteristic of most,[1] as in a terracotta model from Cnossus. Some were planned as broad and shallow rectangles, with the entrance on the broad side rather than the narrow end, a survival of native Cretan influence. Such were the temples of Rhea at Phaestus and of Apollo Pythius at Gortyna, the latter (with curious panelled walls and corner frames) so large, 57 feet wide and 51 feet deep, that there must have been internal supports of which those inserted in Roman times were the successors.[2] Other rectangular temples followed the northern plan with the entrance at one end. Such was the temple of Apollo Delphinius at Dreros in eastern Crete, consisting of a single room about 19 feet wide and $30\frac{1}{2}$ feet deep internally, perhaps preceded by an open porch with corner posts. Along the main axis were two cylindrical posts about 11 inches in diameter, spaced nearly 11 feet on centres, resting merely on flat stones and supporting the main cross-beams; and we may infer that the three compartments into which the depth was thus divided, unequal because of the position of the central hearth, were spanned by horizontal joists supporting the flat mud roof (no traces of tiles having been discovered). Against the rear wall at the right corner was built a high bench supporting votive jars and terracottas of about 750 B.C. Beside the bench, on the floor against the rear wall, were heaped up the horns cut from sacrificial kids; and about fifty years later the pile was enclosed by a parapet, probably with a plank cover with a hole through which additions could be dropped, forming an offering table on which were set three bronze statues, one 28 inches and the others 17 inches high.[3] A similar plan appears in temple 'A' at Prinias, with the cella $19\frac{1}{2}$ feet wide internally (increasing by 1 foot toward the rear) and 32 feet deep and a pronaos enframed by antae; the two bases on the axis of the cella are low discs of Aegean form, and between them is a rectangular hearth. The doorway had a central post supporting a stone transom of which the soffit is carved with female figures in relief, and the faces of the transom have animal friezes (a prototype of the sculptured lintels of Assos, Xanthus, and Trysa); the transom in turn supports two seated goddesses who seem to carry the true lintel on their heads. A single post stood in-antis on the front, and the roof, as may be judged from the absence of terracotta tiles, was flat. Somewhere in connection with this temple was set up a limestone frieze (an idea suggestive of Oriental influence) 2 feet 9 inches in height, carved in relief with primitive figures of horsemen; but, the concept of a sculptured frieze in the conventional position between architrave and cornice

[1] An exception is the temple of Dictaean Zeus at Palaikastro, of which the terracotta simas belong to pediments as well as horizontal eaves.

[2] The pronaos of this temple, with six engaged Doric columns, is an addition of the Hellenistic period, while the apse at the rear is a Roman alteration.

[3] In publishing this temple Marinatos first restored, above the main flat roof, a tent-like roof over the hearth, with the ends of its ridge beam supported on two very tall posts. But in his revised restoration the two posts are shortened to act as normal supports of two of the assumed seven cross-beams, leaving the tent-like roof over the hearth with even less corroboration. Probably, therefore, a simple flat roof with a central opening is the solution.

CRETE, OLYMPIA, AND EPHESUS

not having been attained at this early period, and the peculiar flange protruding backward at the bottom (as in the letter L) being inexplicable if this were a mere revetment or dado at the foot of a wall, it seems preferable to restore it as a parapet bordering the edge of the flat mud roof, the prototype of the parapet-simas moulded or carved in relief. In any case, this elaborately carved temple at Prinias may be assigned to the middle of the seventh century.[1]

As temples increased in size, the problem of spanning the cella demanded the substitution of two internal colonnades for one, thus forming a nave with aisles and leaving an unobstructed view of the cult statue at the back. A transitional example is the [older Heraeum at Olympia] apparently erected long after the beginning of the recorded Olympiads (776 B.C.) and rather toward the end of the century.[2] In this structure, however, the width was insufficient for three distinct aisles; hence alternate columns were attached to the flank walls by means of buttresses, forming niches each with an isolated column at its centre, a scheme of special interest in that it was the prototype of the later Heraeum and so of the temple at Bassae. In the niches votive offerings might conveniently have been exhibited (Fig. 19).[3] Later still was the [third temple of Artemis ('C') at Ephesus,] erected at about 600 B.C. with projecting antae and apparently with columns in-antis, to which the Ephesians tied the town walls by a rope when seeking protection during the siege by Croesus.[4]

The temple plan, as yet, consisted only of the pronaos and cella, perhaps with an adytum behind; the walls, generally of mud-brick, were exposed to the weather on three sides of the building, very inadequately protected by the slightly overhanging eaves. Partly to protect the mud-brick walls, and partly, no doubt, to increase the impressiveness of the temple, the architecture of the façade was extended to the flanks and rear. The result was a colonnaded portico surrounding the temple, giving the peripteral plan. In this way the Greek temple gradually assumed its characteristic columnar form and embodied the fundamental principle of Greek architecture, the post-and-lintel system. Perhaps the earliest instance of its use was the peristyle added round the chieftain's house [(megaron 'B') at Thermum] which was now transformed into a

---

[1] The published restoration of the façade is unsatisfactory not only because the hypothetical central square pier is certainly too heavy, but also because the sculptured frieze is placed between the architrave and cornice.

[2] This date raises the question of the chronology of the Heraeum, which Pausanias mentions as having been founded eight years after the Dorian invasion, i.e. in 1096 B.C. Before any earlier remains were known, this preposterous date was applied by Dörpfeld to the existing temple, which belongs rather to about 600 B.C. (see p. 53). After the discovery of earlier foundations under the existing temple, it was assumed by Dörpfeld that the date 1096 B.C. applied rather to the first temple. But this again is impossible if we are to judge either from the debris found below the floor of the first temple (including fragments of pottery and a bronze statuette later than the middle of the eighth century), or from the general course of Greek architectural development.

[3] Since the plan of the older Heraeum was almost identical with that of the present temple, with the omission of the peristyle, the plan of the inner part of the later Heraeum (Fig. 19) will adequately illustrate the scheme.

[4] Hogarth assigns 'C' to Chersiphron and Metagenes, a theory which Picard rightly discards because their temple certainly had a peristyle; furthermore, they would hardly have composed an architectural book on the subject as early as the seventh century. The story of the columns is given by Polyaenus (VI, 50) and Aelian (*V.H.* III, 26), though Herodotus (I, 26) merely mentions the temple.

primitive temple of Apollo, consisting merely of wooden posts resting on isolated flat stone bases (Fig. 14). Here, with the same archaism that had dictated the segmental walls of the earlier cella building, the peristyle was straight only across the south front and formed a continuous ellipse round the three other sides, preserving the old tradition of the horseshoe plan. The roof construction is uncertain in view of the absence of remains; apparently the long ridge ended in a gable at the south front and in a conical roof at the rear, the wooden rafters carrying merely the mud slope covered with thatch, without terracotta tiles.[1]

More regular was the peristyle added to the temple at Samos; the fronts recalling the three posts in-antis and the flank walls, as well as the flank colonnades, and thus becoming heptastyle with a spacing of about 5 feet on centres, the total width of the stylobate being 31 feet. The length was about 121 feet, giving room for twenty-five posts on each flank (counting the corner ones twice).[2] The posts may have been square, and seem to have been supported on truncated conical bases of somewhat Aegean form, 8 inches high and $15\frac{1}{2}$ inches in diameter at the bottom. The fact that the peristyle was an addition is shown by the level, 10 inches higher than that for which the walls were constructed; and the date may have been about 725 B.C. Later still, at the time of the sixth altar (about 675 B.C.), this temple was rebuilt at a slightly higher level, the central row of columns being omitted so that the statue pedestal could be placed against the middle of the rear wall and yet be visible from the entrance. Thus the need of a central column on the front disappeared; the stylobate being about $38\frac{1}{2}$ by 124 feet, with hexastyle fronts, the posts were spaced about 7 feet 2 inches all round the temple and so required eighteen on the flanks. The depth of the pteroma, 8 feet on the flanks and rear, seems to have been increased to 15 feet on the east front;[3] and the entrance to the cella was now partially closed by three gates separated by two wooden posts between the antae. The interior of the cella has a bench 16 inches wide along the flank walls and 28 inches wide along the rear wall; and it is possible that wooden posts rested on this for the purpose of supporting the roof, projecting like buttresses opposite each of the outer columns,[4] instead of being imbedded like the half-timbered construction

[1] The flat stone slabs serving as bases lie directly on, and are apparently later than, the original pavement surrounding the cella, though they are earlier than a higher accumulation of debris containing geometric bronzes. The older vault-like walls must have been retained, since they still survive to a height of 3 feet; in the absence of any traces of central posts, presumably the ogival vault supported the ridge of a gable roof of reeds and clay, of which masses were found. A flat roof, as in primitive Crete, would be unthinkable in this northern environment.

[2] The excavators restore seven posts at the east but only six at the west where there was no need of correspondence with the axial colonnade; yet such unnecessary difference in the fronts seems improbable. Likewise they assume only seventeen posts on the flanks with a wider spacing, coinciding in part with that of the interior posts; but since the outer posts formed an addition, and the coincidence in any case is not perfect, the closer spacing seems preferable and would agree equally well with the single weathered trace of a base on the south flank.

[3] The excavators restore a second (or inner) row of posts across the east front, as a rudimentary dipteral arrangement; this is possible, though no foundations exist.

[4] The excavators restore such buttresses only opposite alternate posts of the flank peristyle, on the analogy of the Heraeum at Olympia; but the construction at Samos is so much lighter that more numerous supports should have been employed.

at Sparta. Similarly, at Locri Epizephyrii in Italy, a peristyle of six by twelve columns was added round the old temple, very widely spaced, 10 feet 7 inches on the façades and 4 inches less on the flanks, and so probably of wood.

Early in the primitive period, therefore, the main lines of the Greek temple had begun to assume their final shape. The altar, which had usually formed the original element of any sanctuary, was sometimes incorporated within the temple, forming a hearth at the middle or back of the cella; but more frequently it remained in the open air, before the main front of the temple, with a more or less formal relationship between them. In some cases the temple was first built without much relation to the altar, and the latter was afterwards revised to conform to the temple; in other cases, where altar and temple were originally in line, the temple might be moved to a new site while the altar was left behind in its old position. And even when altar and temple were in line, with the step or platform located on the west side of the altar so that the officiating priest could face toward the east, he rarely at the same time looked toward the temple; usually his back was toward the temple front and the statue within, as these likewise faced eastward toward the rising sun—"Gods who face the rising sun . . . with gleaming eyes."[1] A temple at Artemisium in Euboea was actually named that of Artemis Prosoea ("who faces east.") From this custom arises the term "orientation," primarily applied to the direction of the axis of a temple. In actual fact, the axes of Greek temples box the entire compass; but more than 80 per cent run, if not exactly east-and-west, at least within the arc formed on the horizon between the sunrise directions at the summer and winter solstices. It seems that most temples were laid out to face the sunrise on the actual day of their foundation, presumably the festival day of the divinity; a minority faced in other directions for special reasons of site, tradition, or relation to other buildings.[2] All the great temples had a vestibule (pronaos), a large habitation (cella or naos) for the idol which was so placed as to face the entrance, and sometimes a chamber in the rear used as a treasury, inner sanctum, or oracle chamber (adytum), as well as the rear porch (opisthodomus, posticum). The whole was frequently surrounded by a portico or peristyle, so that it became a peripteral temple. The pronaos and opisthodomus frequently housed valuable offerings, serving as a treasury, and so were enclosed by metal railings and gates. It is possible that the interior of the temple was open to privileged persons only, and that the one view which most of the people had of the god (except perhaps at festivals) was from the open doorway to the east; and one can under such circumstances have some idea of the awe and sense of mystery inspired among them by such a view of the image of Zeus or Athena.

Up to this point the temples considered have been of nondescript character, so far as the columnar supports are concerned. But with the next step, the advent of the column, it became necessary to evolve the order; and from the different manners in which this was accomplished simultaneously, on the

[1] Aeschylus, *Agamemnon*, 519–520; this is the earliest allusion to the custom mentioned by several later writers: for temples, Vitruvius (IV, 5), Frontinus (in *Gromatici veteres*, p. 27), Hyginus (*ibid.*, p. 169), Plutarch (*Numa*, 14, 4), Lucian (*House*, 6), Clement of Alexandria (*Strom.* VII, p. 724); for towns, Pliny (XVIII, 34), Frontinus (*loc. cit.*, pp. 31, 108), Hyginus (*ibid.*, pp. 170, 182, 183), Isidore of Seville (*Orig.* XV, 4, 7).

[2] There is no authority for the oft-repeated statement that the temples of heroes, on the other hand, faced westward.

opposite shores of the Aegean Sea, developed the two great styles of Greek architecture. In the lands occupied by Dorians the Doric order was the first to make its appearance, and was almost exclusively used, while on the coasts occupied by the Ionians and kindred tribes Doric buildings only occasionally appear, the Ionic always predominating. Thus the Ionic order, although placed after the Doric in our scheme of treatment, should not on that account be regarded as later; we wish to emphasise the fact that its development was co-extensive in time, and that it was not in any sense a form which replaced the Dorian style. Rather, as we shall afterwards see, they may both have come out of the same root in the soil of Mycenae. Hence the differing treatments became not only symbolic of the two greatest divisions of the Greek race, whose rivalry makes the history of Greece, but also they most expressively represent, on the one hand, the grave, severe Dorian of Hellas and, on the other, the lighter, more versatile and luxurious emigrant to Asia who stands for the type of the Ionian race farthest removed from the Dorian.[1]

*   *   *   *   *

It is possible that, just as the cornice had been the first portion of the temple to be decoratively treated, so it was in this member that distinctively Doric traits first appeared. The ends of the rafters protruding under the eaves on the flanks were treated as decorative elements, the mutules, and were adorned with rows of wooden pegs or guttae (Fig. 20).[2] Properly speaking, these sloping mutules or rafter ends could appear only on the flanks of a ridge-roofed building, or on all four sides only if the building were hip-roofed, as in a stone reproduction of a building in an archaic Athenian pedimental sculpture of about 570 B.C., wherein, under the hip roof, mutules appear on all sides without any frieze or architrave below them. But it is evident that because of their decorative character the mutules were soon applied even to the horizontal cornice under a façade pediment, where, in the absence of rafters, they were illogical. The next step was further embellishment by means of the triglyph frieze: the ends of the ceiling beams of the pronaos and of those traversing the cella were permitted to appear on the exterior, and were even emphasised to form a decorative motive, recalling, where such existed, the supports below them. The exposed grain of the wood in these beam ends was protected from the weather by a grooved facing known as the triglyph. It is probable that these triglyphs were at first widely spaced, appearing only above columns and antae (but not above the centres of intervals) and at corresponding distances on flank walls, leaving between them horizontal oblong metope panels of which we see later reflections particularly in Syracuse. It is barely possible that a primitive temple erected at Mycenae in the second half of the seventh century

---

[1] Vitruvius (IV, 1, 6–7) has a different simile: "The Doric column, as used in buildings, began to exhibit the proportions, strength, and beauty of the body of a man. Just so afterward, when they desired to construct a temple to Diana in a new style of beauty, they translated the footprints (lower diameters) into terms characteristic of the slenderness of women. . . . Thus in the invention of the two different kinds of columns, they borrowed manly beauty, naked and unadorned, for the one, and for the other the delicacy, adornment, and proportions characteristic of women."

[2] It must be remembered that Greek rafters were always large squared timbers, frequently laid flatwise, not like the planks set on edge in modern American frame houses.

was of this character; it was constructed of stone to the very top, and the curiously irregular stone cornice was faced with terracotta slabs nailed on. The sculptured metopes (if such they are), the earliest on the Greek mainland, were of elongated form and suggest a wide spacing of the triglyphs.[1]

On the Greek mainland, one of the earliest peripteral temples of definitely Doric style is that which succeeded the primitive temple of Apollo (megaron 'B') at Thermum in Aetolia (Figs. 14, 18), with five columns on the fronts, fifteen columns on the flanks. The extremely long and narrow cella was open at the front, without pronaos or cross-wall; thresholds for gates occupy the two intervals between the antae and a central column, the first of a single row of ten down the centre of the cella, with two others in the opisthodomus (which now appears almost for the first time), to assist the mud-brick walls in carrying the ceiling and roof. It is clear that the plan was evolved by carrying the lines of the flank walls and of the central line of columns through to the ends, adding colonnades on the flanks, and thus producing the pentastyle façade. The spacing of the columns, 9 feet 3 inches on the fronts and 8 feet $9\frac{1}{4}$ inches on the flanks, was very great in proportion to the diameter; and it is evident that contraction of the endmost intervals had not yet been introduced. Only the isolated footings of the columns, with raised circular beds in the Mycenaean manner, were of stone, the original columns, being of wood, as well as the entablature, have not survived; but of the latter, fortunately, much of the terracotta revetment is preserved, including the great painted metopes which prove that the temple was Doric in style (Plate XVII).

We must suppose that two beams side by side formed the architrave, tied by cross-straps of which the ends formed regulae on the front, and capped by a plank floor appearing as the taenia. The triglyphs are not preserved; but smaller triglyphs from a neighbouring temple show that they formed terracotta facings for the ends of heavy wooden ceiling beams. The intervals between these beams, above the architrave, were filled with mud-brick and faced with the terracotta metopes, 2 feet $10\frac{1}{2}$ inches high and 2 feet 9 inches to 3 feet 3 inches wide, showing that there were two metopes to each intercolumniation in contrast to the primitive system with single horizontal oblong metopes over each interval. The metopes are gaily painted (rather than sculptured) with Gorgons and mythological scenes, surrounded with borders of rosettes and with red frames. On their tops are pairs of lugs about $2\frac{1}{2}$ inches high, extending up into mortises in the soffit of the wall plate; and the latter in turn supported the sloping rafters, of which the ends, forming mutules, carried a terracotta cornice of considerable projection, the soffit being decorated for a width of 11 inches.[2] The temple thus described is of about 620 B.C.; but the roof terracottas belong to two periods, the original construction and a sixth-century renovation. Thus the roof seems originally to have had a pediment only at the front, with a hip roof at the back (reflecting the conical roof of its predecessor;[3]

[1] The fragments were discarded at the time of building a Hellenistic temple and their exact purpose is not clear; a sculptured frieze or an altar would not be impossible, but these seem less plausible than the interpretation as metopes.

[2] In this respect the illustration (Plate XVII) should be corrected, in that it lacks the mutules.

[3] At Sparta has been found an early model of a temple with a similar combination of a gable at one end and a hip roof at the other.

later a pediment was erected likewise at the back. The simas are of these two periods, with various sorts of antefixes and spouts, moulded as lion heads and as male and female masks. In the Hellenistic period the column footings were connected to form a stylobate, and the columns themselves were replaced in stone in three instalments (with differences in style) as the necessary funds were acquired; but the entablature must always have remained of wood, there being not a fragment of stone entablature.

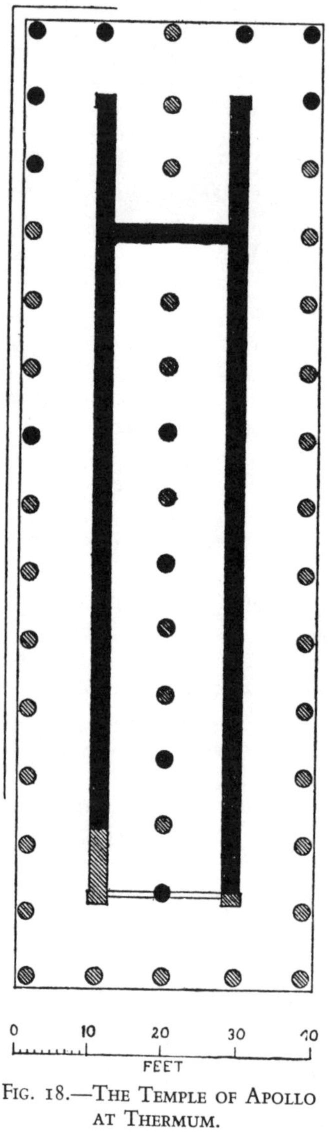

Slightly later than the temple at Thermum was the distyle in-antis temple of Apollo Laphrius at neighbouring Calydon, with terracotta metopes painted with mythological scenes, and with drooping antefixes moulded in the form of female heads, prototypes of those used in the sixth-century renovation at Thermum; the apex acroterion was a terracotta shield nearly 3 feet in diameter with a painted Gorgon head. Beside it was built a temple of Artemis Laphria, again with painted terracotta metopes, now surrounded by rosette borders; the acroteria were Sphinxes at the lower corners and a figure of a Gorgon at the apex. At about 530 B.C. the temple of Apollo was renovated with a third series of painted metopes; its most remarkable feature was the terracotta roofing ordered ready-made from Corinth and assembled on the temple at Calydon, with each piece already numbered for its place. The profile is the characteristic Corinthian ovolo of the second half of the century, decorated with pendant rectangular Doric leaves with midribs, above a high fascia painted with a double guilloche. The flank simas are marked "east" and "west," showing that the factory had received instructions that the temple faced more nearly south than east.[1]

Other temples with wood and terracotta construction existed at Thermum (with smaller terracotta metopes and triglyphs), at

Fig. 18.—The Temple of Apollo at Thermum.

[1] The foundations of the older temple of Artemis are buried under the terrace of the fourth century. Even of a rebuilding at about 500 B.C., abandoning the wooden entablature and using poros stone metopes and late archaic terracotta roof tiles, there are only loose step blocks used as second-hand material in the fourth-century foundations (p. 218). But temple 'A' (here assigned to Apollo, though Dyggve prefers Dionysus) seems to have retained its second roof, with the numbered simas, until the Roman period. Dyggve employs "Chinese roofs" with all these terracottas (see note on p. 82).

Homolium in Thessaly (with terracotta metopes), at Elis (with terracotta triglyphs), and at Tegea and Pallantium in Arcadia (both with wooden columns). Pliny refers to the wooden columns of a temple of Hera at Metapontum, and Pausanias mentions also the oak columns supporting the roof of the tomb of Oxylus at Elis, and a single surviving wooden column of the "house of Oenomaus" at Olympia, as well as the single surviving oak column in the opisthodomus of the Heraeum as noted below.

In temple plans with two rows of interior columns, forming aisles and a nave with the cult statue at the end, these two inner rows, together with the walls and the flank colonnades, required a hexastyle façade instead of the more elementary pentastyle form. Such was the plan of the archaic temple of Hera near Argos;[1] but of this exists only the stylobate or continuous step supporting part of the south flank colonnade, important however on account of the weathered traces of the wooden columns, 2 feet $7\frac{1}{2}$ inches in diameter. An accidental fire in 423 B.C. caused the destruction of the temple, which was replaced by that designed by Eupolemus, later to be described.

The most notable of all the early Doric peripteral temples is the Heraeum at Olympia (Figs. 19, 44 at H; Plate XVII), originally a temple of Zeus and Hera together, but relegated, after the completion of the new temple of Zeus in 460 or 456 B.C., to the worship of Hera alone. The date of its foundation was attributed by Pausanias to 1096 B.C., but certainly on fallacious grounds; at that early epoch no temples were as yet being erected, and the existing Heraeum, furthermore, is the second of two successive temples on the same site, so that its date must have been considerably later; we should prefer rather about (or just after) 600 B.C.[2] Such a date is more in harmony with certain well-developed features of the plan, in particular the contracted intercolumniation at the corners, a feature which was still unknown at Thermum and did not make its appearance in the western colonies until the very end of the sixth century. The general proportions of the plan, however, are still very long, the relation of width to length being about 2 to $5\frac{1}{2}$, whereas in more developed Greek temples it was about 3 to 7; there are six columns on the front and sixteen on the sides, as compared with thirteen in the normal hexastyle temple of the best period; and it stands on a crepidoma of only two steps (the stylobate and one below)

---

[1] The position of the statue basis on axis determines the width of the temple as hexastyle, but the length is unknown. The date is uncertain; potsherds discovered under the foundations show merely that it is later than about 700 B.C.

[2] Dörpfeld, who at first gave 1096 B.C. as the date of the present temple, would now apply this to the earlier of two (as he assumes) predecessors lying at lower levels; this theory has been discussed above, and we have noted that the first (non-peripteral) temple dates rather from the end of the eighth century. The so-called second temple (which Dörpfeld assigns to the end of the tenth century) seems never to have existed, not even as an idea; for the plan is admittedly identical with that of the present temple, and there is no appreciable difference or line of demarcation in the foundation courses or filling strata below the present floor; furthermore a Corinthian vase, found under the so-called earlier peristyle foundation, is nearly if not quite as late as 600 B.C. and thus would show that the very idea of a peristyle did not exist until that date, leaving practically no time interval between the laying of the so-called earlier peristyle foundations and the erection of the present temple. We must assume that there were only two temples, the non-peripteral structure of the end of the eighth century and the present peripteral temple of which the date (now given by Dörpfeld as about 900 B.C. and so three centuries too early) should be about 600 B.C. according to the sherds found below it and the style of its roof terracottas.

instead of the usual three. The wide intercolumniation shows that the architrave was of wood; that the columns were originally of the same material is suggested, firstly, by the existence of one oak column in the rear porch, the opisthodomus, as related by Pausanias (who was here in A.D. 173), and, secondly, by the fact that the present columns vary considerably in their diameter and their character (Plate XVII). Some of the shafts are monolithic, others built of drums; the lower diameters vary in adjacent columns from 3 feet $3\frac{1}{2}$ inches to 4 feet $2\frac{1}{2}$ inches; one has only sixteen flutes, while the others have twenty; and the echinus of the various capitals differs in contour and projection, ranging from the bulging archaic echinus to the straight or quarter-circle echinus of Hellenistic and Graeco-Roman times. All these facts point to the conclusion now generally accepted, that the original wooden columns were replaced gradually by those in stone.[1] The use of wood, however, was due not so much to the early date (for at this epoch stone temples were already being erected elsewhere) as to some peculiar local tradition, or, more probably, to expense. In fact, since the earliest stone columns are stylistically about as early as the erection of the temple, we may assume that the substitution began almost immediately and was continued at intervals as subscriptions came in, over a period of eight hundred years; some of the tablets let into the column shafts may have recorded these contributions.[2] The form of the original wooden columns can only be surmised; their lower diameter is suggested by crescent-shaped cuttings in the stylobate (utilised while setting up the original wooden shafts, but completely hidden under those of stone) as 3 Doric feet (or 3 feet $2\frac{1}{2}$ inches);[3] their height was necessarily identical with that of the stone columns which gradually replaced them, 16 Doric feet of $12\frac{7}{8}$ inches,[4] the axial spacing on the flanks being

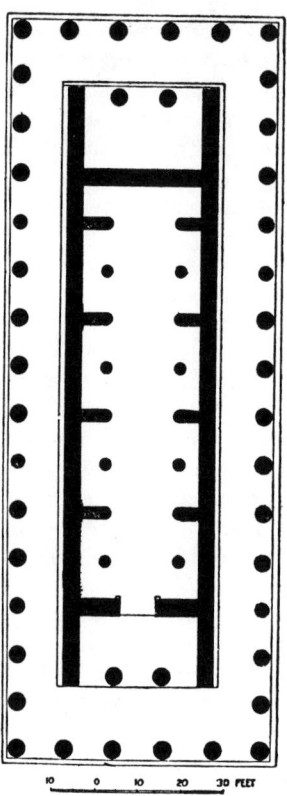

Fig. 19.—The Heraeum at Olympia.

[1] Probably the first to be replaced was the second column from the west, on the south flank, which has the only capital showing the hollow scotia cutting back into the line of the shaft.

[2] It was formerly assumed that the replacement was due to the gradual decay of the oak columns, and that if the first one decayed after about five hundred years and was replaced by a stone substitute of about 600 B.C., this very fact would confirm the Pausanias date of 1096 B.C. But this sort of argument must now be abandoned.

[3] The crescent cuttings are $7\frac{1}{2}$ inches from the face of the stylobate, the column centres $26\frac{3}{4}$ inches from the stylobate face, leaving a radius of $19\frac{1}{4}$ inches.

[4] These are commonly designated as Aeginetan-Attic feet, the length being $12\frac{7}{8}$ inches (see p. 161, note 1; p. 195, note 1; p. 199, note 3); but my studies of the temples of the Greek mainland and of the west have shown that this unit was so widely employed, wherever the Doric style penetrated, in fact, that I propose the more general designation of "Doric

five-eighths as much or 10 Doric feet (and more on the fronts). A ring of pendant bronze leaves, apparently nailed on under the echinus,[1] suggests that the capitals were of the form later executed in stone at Corcyra. The absence of any remains of a stone entablature as well as the wide intercolumniation at this early date shows that the architrave must have been of wood, and the closer intercolumniation of the columns at each angle suggests the presence of a frieze, with triglyphs and metopes; for the only explanation of such a contraction is that it was introduced in order to bring the triglyph to the corner. The walls of the cella were of great thickness, the base consisting of four narrow courses of masonry to the height of $3\frac{1}{2}$ feet, their exterior face toward the peristyle being protected by vertical slabs of stone known as orthostates (*cf.* Plate XXXIX), with the function of the primitive rubble base; for on this base rested a superstructure of crude or unburnt mud-brick.[2] Here also, as in the Mycenaean buildings, the ends of the side walls of the pronaos and opisthodomus were encased with timber (the prototype of the anta) in order to carry, in conjunction with the columns in-antis, the architrave and superstructure; and the jambs of the doorway leading to the cella were similarly encased. In the interior of the cella, on either side, was a range of eight columns to lessen the bearing of the main beams carrying the horizontal ceiling and the sloping roof over the cella,[3] aligning exactly with the outer columns on the flanks in such a way as to divide the total width of the temple into three parts (a more scientific procedure than at Thermum), thus dispensing entirely with the support of the crude brick walls. Alternate columns were originally attached by spur walls to the cella wall to give further strength to the latter, though at a later date the spur walls were cut away, The roof was covered with terracotta tiles of the Laconian type, with cornice revetments, acroteria crowning the pediments, and semicircular antefixes terminating the cover-tiles, all richly painted in dark colours; particularly impressive were the huge central acroteria, forming circles 7 feet 7 inches in diameter with the lower portion cut out to fit the apex of the pediment.

At this point we may terminate our survey of the primitive Doric or Proto-Doric temples, by calling attention to some disputed questions relating to this subject, and the manner in which they should now be viewed.

(A) We have sufficient evidence to show that the column, in its earliest stages, was of wood like those of the Aegean period; and in at least two examples (Olympia and the Argive Heraeum) we can compare diameter and spacing,

foot." This must not be taken to mean that every Doric temple was constructed with such a foot; geographical and racial factors must be taken into consideration, and it appears that in some areas Doric temples were constructed with the shorter "Ionic foot" (see p. 222, note 2; p. 229, note 2), while in others, as at Athens, Ionic temples were built with Doric feet.

[1] Two pieces of these bronze leaf garlands have been found at Olympia, sixty years apart.

[2] It is to the latter that we owe the preservation of the statue of Hermes by Praxiteles, which was found buried in the clay of the disintegrated walls at the foot of its pedestal.

[3] The existence of a ceiling under the sloping roof is suggested by a story told by Pausanias, in which he says that "when the Eleans were repairing the dilapidated roof of the Heraeum the corpse of a foot-soldier was found between the ceiling and the roof." And likewise in other Greek temples, though the wooden ceilings themselves have perished, their existence is attested by the horizontal cuttings for them, as in the temple of Concord at Acragas and the Propylaea at Athens, and by allusions in literature and inscriptions, as in the Artemisium at Ephesus and the Erechtheum at Athens.

obtaining proportions of $3\frac{1}{3}$ and $4\frac{3}{8}$ diameters on centres, respectively. And, while it must be admitted that our knowledge of the forms of their wooden capitals is indefinite, yet we may reasonably conjecture that they had, like those of stone which followed them, the characteristic abacus and echinus, obviously a derivation from the Aegean type, which must have been well known to the Dorians through the stone copies on the Lion Gate (Plate XII) and the Tomb of Agamemnon (Plate XIII). Perhaps the cavetto above the echinus was omitted at an early date, for we see no trace of it in the earliest existing Doric capitals; the scotia and astragal below the echinus, on the other hand, survived until a later period and prove the relationship between such capitals as those at Paestum (Fig. 37) and their Aegean prototypes. It has been suggested, however, that the wooden columns of primitive Greek architecture had no relationship to the Doric column, and that the latter was imitated rather from certain Egyptian stone columns, to which, to be sure, it bears a superficial resemblance. But the heavy proportions of the earliest known Greek Doric columns of stone, little more than four diameters high in buildings of monumental size (Fig. 27),[1] also the pronounced upward taper of the shaft and the fact that from the very beginning the echinus formed an essential feature between the shaft and the abacus, while the abacus was of much greater width that the upper diameter of the shaft, militate seriously against the theory that there was any connection between the Greek Doric column and the so-called "Proto-Doric" examples at Beni-Hasan or at Karnak and Der-el-Bahari in Thebes. It is hard to find a wider dissimilarity than that between the earliest Greek Doric columns and the Egyptian fluted columns, where the proportion in height varies from $5\frac{1}{2}$ to 6 diameters, where there is no echinus and where the abacus slightly, if at all, exceeds the upper diameter of the shaft.[2] On the other hand, the well-known timidity of the Greeks in stone construction would be enough to account for the sudden thickening of the proportions, in all but the smallest examples, when translating from a prototype hitherto of wood.

(B) The entablatures of these early temples having almost entirely disappeared, we are forced to trust to a few fragments of their terracotta trimmings (especially those of Thermum), to the archaic reproductions in stone of what were originally wooden features, and to the description of the primitive entablature as given by Vitruvius. And though the same controversy that we noted in the case of the columns, for an origin in wood or in stone, is being waged also with regard to the entablature, yet we may unhesitatingly affirm that the triglyphs in the frieze reproduce the ends of beams (Fig. 20) or rather the decorative grooved facing of the ends of such beams, secured in position by

---

[1] Of course a few early examples of Doric columns on a small scale, as those of the earliest temple of Athena Pronaea at Delphi (Fig. 24), are exceedingly slender, $6\frac{1}{2}$ diameters high, evidently imitating the proportions of wooden prototypes; but here again the emphatic taper and the widely spreading capitals are very un-Egyptian.

[2] There comes a further reflection, that if the Greeks copied one type of Egyptian column, why should they not have adopted others? At Beni-Hasan the lotus bud capital exists in the interior of many tombs, and at Thebes both the bud and the bell-shaped capitals are found in great profusion, yet the former never appeared in Greece, while the Greek examples of the bell type formed an independent movement. Furthermore, the so-called "Proto-Doric" column ceased to be employed in Egypt after the eighteenth dynasty, more than six hundred years before the earliest Greek stone columns.

pins or pegs passing through the projecting taenia or fascia surmounting the architrave and through the regula or short strip under the taenia, below each triglyph; the pins became the trunnels or guttae, still detached from the architrave in the earlier stone temples, and even sloping (as in temple 'D' at Selinus) as if driven in diagonally from below. The mutules or projecting blocks on the soffit of the cornice are as clearly the ends of the rafters of the roof, likewise with pegs or guttae, and all the other details are easily interpreted as translations of wood or terracotta members into stone, the metopes being the terracotta

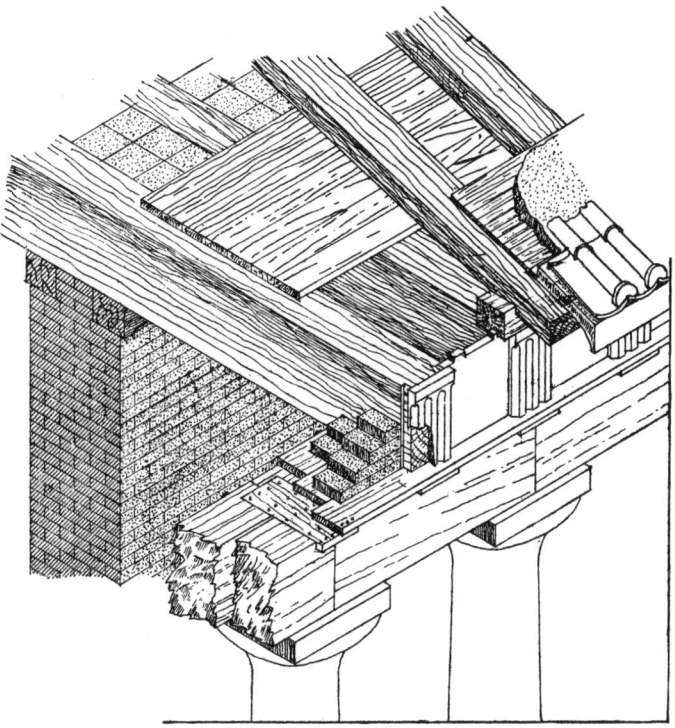

Fig. 20.—Conjectural restoration of Proto-Doric Entablature.

facing of the brick walls between the triglyph beam ends. Whilst the mutules and their interspaces always continued to represent the approximate slope of the roof in the peristylar temple, the triglyphs gradually came to be employed only in a decorative sense, as they did not correspond to the cross-beams of the peristyle ceiling, which were at a much higher level. This, however, was merely the result of the translation of the entablature into stone; the primitive wooden form was probably quite consistent, the beams coinciding with the triglyphs; and even in later stone architecture we have examples of such coincidence, as in the eastern portico of the Propylaea of the Athenian Acropolis (Plate L).

(C) Finally, with regard to the plan as a whole, we must refer to the popular theory that the structure within the peristyle, that is, the cella and pronaos, is a direct derivation from the Mycenaean megaron (Plate X). This theory was seemingly corroborated by the ancient traditions that the palace of Erechtheus at Athens was succeeded by the temple of Athena Polias, the palace of Cadmus at Thebes by the temple of Demeter Thesmophorus, and also by the actual existence of temples above the palaces at Mycenae and Athens, and perhaps also at Tiryns. So long as the Heraeum at Olympia was our earliest example of primitive Doric architecture, such an explanation was the best method of bridging the gap; but now that the Heraeum has been assigned rather to the end of the seventh century, while on the other hand numbers of temples intermediate between the Mycenaean megaron and the Olympian Heraeum have come to light, we see that the farther we recede toward the darkness of the Dorian invasion, the more elemental the plan becomes (Fig. 17), resembling more the primitive ancestor of the Mycenaean megaron (Fig. 4) than the developed product. The long rectangular plan, the use of a base of rubble masonry (eventually replaced by orthostates of stone), in order to raise the mud-brick walls above the foot-worn or rain-washed ground, the timber casing of the antae and door jambs where the mud-brick alone would have been too weak—all these were merely the logical development of the ideas which the Dorians, like the Achaeans before them, had brought from their northern homes. The colonnaded pronaos of the Greek temple, the most "Mycenaean" feature, did not appear in Greek architecture until long after all memory of the Mycenaean palaces had died away. The house of the Greek god was an independent growth, related to that of the Mycenaean king only in its common ancestry.

*   *   *   *   *

In order to trace the origins of the other order, the Ionic, we must change our vantage ground from Europe to Asia, thus following the footsteps of the Mycenaeans, the Ionian and Aeolian tribes, whom the migration of the Dorians at about 1100 B.C. drove out of the Peloponnesus and part of central Greece. In the period with which we are concerned, the mastery of the seas had passed from the Cretans and the Aegean mainlanders to the Carians or Lycians and finally to the Phoenicians; and at the dawn of historic times Phoenician traders were exporting to all parts of the Mediterranean, and particularly to the rich new colonies on the coast of Asia Minor, the metal bowls and other products of their imitative craftsmen, decorated with motives adopted impartially from Egypt and Assyria, the lotus-and-bud and the palmette, the spiral and the guilloche and rosette, and, most significant of all, the lily capital.

The characteristics of the Ionic order are by no means summed up in the capital, nor even in the column itself; but it is natural to deal first with the member that has always been regarded as the index mark of the style. The obviously reasonable position to take is that not one cause, but many, contributed to produce this graceful and ornamental form. Few, if any, architectural features can be attributed to one cause alone; practically all can be traced back to a combination of impulses. So in the case of the Greek Ionic capital various technical processes may have influenced the form. One possibility is the theory of a wooden origin, the spirals being originally merely painted or scratched on the surface of the block which served as a bracket capital to diminish the span

ORIGINS OF THE IONIC CAPITAL

of the lintels; wooden bracket capitals are native to all Asia Minor, Mesopotamia, and Persia, sometimes closely approximating Ionic forms. Such scratched spirals, though of later date and executed on marble, have actually been found at Athens (Fig. 53); and we have noted that such bracket capitals, though decorated with disks rather than spirals, had been employed in Aegean Crete. Another factor that may have been influential is the probability that some of the pre-Hellenic examples (e.g., in Mesopotamia) were executed in bronze, the metal coil thus giving a special character to the volute. Behind either of these technical factors, however, lay the source of the ornamental form itself, which we must now investigate.

The forerunner of the scheme which found ultimate expression in the Ionic capital is to be sought in Egypt; for Egyptian decorative capitals frequently represented the papyrus superposed on the fleur-de-lys, from the time of the XVIIIth Dynasty (1555–1296 B.C.). Some of these Egyptian lily designs with pairs of volutes carved on ivory were even imported into Aegean Greece; part of an ivory tusk from a grave outside the Acropolis of Mycenae even has an almost perfect representation of a Proto-Ionic capital carved in relief. The readiness of the Aegean world to accept such imported forms, the post-Aegean survival of the influence of Crete—where the old language and writing continued to be used in some districts, in close contact with the offshoot culture of Cyprus—are factors which cannot be ignored in a consideration of the origins of the Ionic style. Crete had long before employed the bracket capital, and through association with Egypt had imported such decorative motives as the spiral, guilloche, and rosette, all of which survived through the dark ages. To these were added, apparently through commercial relations with Cyprus, other motives contained on imported Oriental artifacts, palmettes and lotus borders. As early as the eighth century the Cretans began to incorporate these motives in silver bowls and bronze shields of local manufacture which were exported to Greece (as to Olympia) in rivalry with Phoenician wares; and in such Cretan work appears the first combination of the lotus and palmette into an alternating design. The bell-shaped capital with upright overhanging petals or lobes, which became an integral part of the Proto-Ionic capital, had been used for lampstands and other minor works during the Aegean period in Crete, perhaps in imitation of the palm capital of Egypt; and in the first half of the seventh century it reappeared at least once in Crete as an architectural member, carved in stone at Arcades. Unfortunately the bell and abacus in this case were found separately in later tombs, used as second-hand material, and so cannot be associated with any building; the bell has twenty-six lobes tied at the bottom with an astragal in rope pattern, and the abacus is double, the lower carved with guilloche patterns on the faces and with rosettes in the four corners of the soffit; a square hole passing vertically through both members perhaps contained a wooden post round which the entablature was mortised. And, while no actual Proto-Ionic capitals have yet been found in Crete, we must recall that here the characteristic Ionic frieze first attained monumental form (as at Prinias), at an earlier date than on the Asiatic shore, and also that, in the sixth century, two Cretans from Cnossus, Chersiphron and Metagenes, were foremost among Ionic architects.

It was likewise from Egypt that similar influences reached the territories of

THE ORIGINS OF GREEK ARCHITECTURE

other nations with which she maintained commercial relations, the Canaanites and Hittites, so that we have to take into account the remains in Palestine, Phoenicia, Cyprus, and Anatolia. The lily capital with vertical volutes, and with the calyx conventionalised in equilateral triangular form, appears on a Hittite royal seal from Boghazkeuy with the names of kings of about 1350 B.C. Even more sophisticated, from our standpoint, are the horizontal volutes of the capitals crowning pillars supporting winged sun-disks in the so-called "royal cartouche" motive on Anatolian cylinder seals, and those on rock reliefs of the fourteenth or thirteenth century at Yasili-kaya. In these regions the volute capital was particularly employed in the design known as the "sacred tree," as on a Syro-Hittite cylinder seal of the eleventh century B.C., the sarcophagus of King Ahiram of Byblus dating from the same period, ivory reliefs from the palace of King Ahab (875–851 B.C.) at Samaria known as the "ivory house" (I Kings xxii. 39), others from Arslan Tash associated with Hazael (II Kings viii. 8–15) who became king of Damascus (c. 842 B.C.), and others again forming part of the loot carried off by Assyrian kings (the Nimrud collection). Such forms appeared also on stone reliefs, such as many of the dado reliefs of the tenth century from Tell Halaf on one of the branches of the Euphrates,[1] one of the ninth century from Ramath Rahel with a girdle of pendant leaves below the paired volutes, a throne relief of the eighth century from Tell Tainat with superposed pairs of volutes above the pendant leaves, or the multiple form of the "sacred tree" appearing on Hittite reliefs of the eighth century at Sakje-Gozu and on such later monuments as the sarcophagus of the sixth century from Amathus in Cyprus.

It was in this region that the scheme first found architectural expression, with the pair of vertical volutes springing from a triangular calyx appearing as the first stage of the Proto-Ionic capital. Such capitals were employed in this region for piers and door jambs, or for rectangular stelae, rather than for true columns; the earliest of these stone capitals known are two series at Megiddo (respectively 8 feet and 3½ feet long), others at Samaria, and an example at Medeibiyeh in Transjordan, all of the tenth and ninth centuries B.C.;[2] and such, too, were probably the contemporary capitals of "open flowers" on the door jambs (I Kings vi. 32) and of "lily work" on the pillars (I Kings vii. 19, 22) in Solomon's temple at Jerusalem. It is only among the most orientalised of the Hellenes, those of Cyprus, that this form, with two volutes springing vertically from a triangular kernel (Plate XVIII), sometimes with a palmette filling the angle between the volutes, survived without change into classical times. In Cyprus, again, the type seems to have been confined to square piers or stelae (such as a sixth century sepulchral stele from Golgoi, Plate XVIII, and others from Idalium and Atheniu), or to the jambs of doorways (such as that of a tomb at Tamassos, Plate XVIII). Another variety of capital which played a part in the development, similar to one already mentioned in Crete, is a trophy apparently of Canaanite origin but carried off to Assur, with sixteen shallow flutes in the shaft, and a bell to which were bolted ten upright lobes of metal,

---

[1] These reliefs are sometimes dated fantastically as early as 3000 B.C., an anachronism which none of the ornamental details would permit.

[2] Identical but miniature capitals in ivory relief were found at Samaria (7 inches long) and Nimrud (5 inches long).

curving forward with heavy voluted ends which were set into sockets at the top.[1] Still another was the bowl form, usually decorated with lotus patterns or with interlaced or scalloped designs, and frequently with one or more girdles of actual columns on the sun-god tablet of Nabu-apal-iddina (885–852 B.C.) from below the bowl, is a limestone incense-stand from Megiddo, contemporary with those made for Solomon's temple (I Kings vii. 41–42).

Neither the Aegean nor western Asia formed the sole channels of influence. For the volute capital had also passed from Egypt to Mesopotamia, either directly or through Syria as intermediary, and thus is found in representations of actual columns on the sun-god tablet of Nabu-apaliddina (885–852 B.C.) from Sippara and on dado reliefs from the palace of Sargon II (722–705 B.C.) at Khorsabad. In some instances the volutes spring vertically from the shaft; in others they are already horizontal, sometimes in superposed pairs. The decorated bowl type was frequently employed in Assyria for column bases, as at Khorsabad. The girdles of pendant leaves, single or superposed, decorated all sorts of architectural accessories, such as window grilles and the legs of Assyrian thrones. Combinations of all these, with the vertical volutes, appear in the "sacred tree" motive on the glazed brick walls of the sixth century throne room of the palace of Nebuchadnezzar at Babylon.[2] From such sources there were direct contacts with the Greek cities; for there were Ionians in the service of Sennacherib (705–681 B.C.), and the brother of the poet Alcaeus was similarly attached to Nebuchadnezzar (605–562 B.C.). Thus it would be difficult to say whether the form which the Ionians ultimately evolved owed most to coastwise Phoenician-Cypriote influence or to the caravan trade through Mesopotamia and Anatolia.

FIG. 21.—PROTO-IONIC CAPITAL FROM NEANDRIA. (Istanbul Museum.)

True examples of Proto-Ionic capitals are found in temples at Neandria in the Troad (Fig. 21) and at Nape (Klomidado or Klopede) in the island of Lesbos, and also at Mytilene in Lesbos and at Larisa near Smyrna (Plate XVIII).[3] In all these, the spirals of the volute rise vertically from the shaft and spring

---

[1] Another monument at Assur, antedating the re-use of its broken stump by Samsi-Adad IV (1054–1050 B.C.), is sometimes regarded as the forerunner of the Mesopotamian capitals of this form; but the cluster of petals is so far below the top of the octagonal shaft that they cannot be said to form a capital, and they are not in any sense volutes.

[2] Thus the later compound capitals of Persepolis and Susa were, in a sense, part of the normal Mesopotamian tradition, though in them we may also trace the effects of a return wave of influence from Ionian Greece.

[3] It has been suggested that this type of capital should in reality be called "Aeolic," since most of the extant examples of purely Greek workmanship happen to come from Aeolian territory. The related Phoenician type, however, could not under any circumstances be called "Aeolic"; and a general term applicable to the entire group seems desirable. I prefer, therefore, to employ the term "Proto-Ionic" which was applied by the discoverer of the first example at Neandria in 1882, reserving the name "Aeolic" for the bell-shaped capital (pp. 140, 157) which is, in fact, restricted to Aeolian territory or origins.

THE ORIGINS OF GREEK ARCHITECTURE

outward, the angle between the volutes being occupied by a great palmette; the eyes of the volutes are bored through at Neandria and Mytilene and are sunk to receive inserted eyes at Nape, while at Larisa the volutes wind up tightly to their points of origin. The spiral is usually a convex member (with marginal borders, at least on the front of the capital); but at Larisa it is flat, divided by four grooves into five strands. The equilateral triangle, forming the source of the volutes in the Phoenician version, is omitted; instead, below the volutes and binding them together, is a great torus decorated with an interlaced leaf pattern—a relic of the above-mentioned bowl capital—though in some examples at Neandria this is replaced by a group of smaller mouldings, and at Nape and Larisa there is instead a large torus enframed by astragals, in the latter case carved with an archaic bead-and-reel.[1] Lower still is usually a third member, though no traces of such have yet been found at Nape or Mytilene; this was a pendant girdle of overhanging leaves, the serrated lower edge sometimes isolated from the shaft by means of a deep cavetto. The capitals were usually built with three blocks corresponding to these three members, and attained heights of 4 feet both at Neandria and at Larisa. The top of the palmette formed the actual bed for the architrave at Neandria, while at Larisa the volutes participated in this supporting function and for this reason were strengthened by brackets in the form of paired S-scrolls. Thus we are more fortunate than in the case of the other order, of which the primitive capital, the Proto-Doric, seems to have been executed solely in wood and is hopelessly lost. It must be admitted, however, that all the known examples of the Proto-Ionic capitals are as late as the first half of the sixth century, no earlier than 580 B.C. in the case of Neandria.[2]

By the middle of the sixth century B.C. the Proto-Ionic capital seems to have been replaced by the classical form. We find the girdle of pendant leaves surviving only in the Persian imitations of Greek work at Persepolis[3] and Susa. For as the Ionic capital developed the hanging leaves were transformed into the egg-and-dart ovolo, which thereupon became the characteristic lower member and likewise, because of its Oriental origins, the most typical Ionic moulding.

---

[1] This bead-and-reel, 5½ inches high, was discovered after the capital had been set up in the Istanbul Museum and so does not appear in Plate XVIII.

[2] The examples at Neandria were dated much too early (seventh century) by Koldewey; as he rightly observed, they should be later than the Heraeum at Olympia (on account of the roof terracottas), so that, with our revised date for the Heraeum, an earlier date than 580 B.C. seems impossible. The Swedish excavators of Larisa, though influenced by Koldewey's early date for Neandria, rightly date their own capital in the period of the richest roof terracottas (600–560 B.C.), preferring 570 B.C. for Larisa. Such a date would accord also with a volute from a poros limestone stele capital found at Athens, the only example yet known of a true Proto-Ionic capital on the Greek mainland (found in the Cerameicus cemetery in 1938). More problematical is an example of the pendant leaf member found at Aegae in Asia Minor, among miscellaneous blocks of various periods; a Hellenistic column base was associated with it, but probably wrongly, so that we may perhaps accept the capital as a surviving relic of the archaic period.

[3] The great halls at Persepolis, in which the columns were decorated with the Ionic volutes placed vertically, above the calyx with pendant leaves, were not built until 520–485 B.C., so that these features, which might otherwise seem to have been models for the Greek Ionic capitals, were in reality imitated from them. The architects of the great halls of Darius and Xerxes would seem to have utilised in their design architectural features derived from the Greek coast cities.

The intervening feature, the bowl-shaped element, had been almost suppressed even in the capital from Larisa, and thereafter entirely disappeared. The vertically springing volutes, too, outside of Cyprus, survived only in the above-mentioned Persian imitations and in 'some fanciful Ionic capitals of archaic votive offerings; but in Cyprus the vertical volutes, which here seem to date no earlier than the sixth century, long continued to form the characteristic capitals.

Already, in these primitive examples, others of the chief characteristics of the Ionic column have become apparent. One of the most distinctive marks of the Ionic style is the individual base; for, while the Doric column rose directly from the continuous stylobate, the more slender Ionic column required a base of its own, for a greater effect of stability, and it also admitted of a projecting base because of the wider intercolumniation. Such bases, though lacking at Neandria, already have the characteristic torus in the temple at Nape. The Ionic shaft appears always to have been very slender, even when translated from wood to stone; at Neandria the diameter diminishes from 21 to 15¾ inches. Of fluting there is at first no trace.

FIG. 22.—THE TEMPLE AT NEANDRIA.

Of actual temples in which Proto-Ionic columns were used, the typical example is that at Neandria, a simple cella with a central row of columns but none on the exterior (Fig. 22).[1] Thus the plan falls into the primitive class which we have described among the nondescript temples; and it shows other characteristics of this class, in the internal hearth built against the left-hand wall and the presumable location of the statue of the god at the end of the right-hand aisle. The seven capitals, of which the main forms have been described, vary as to details and thus are of four varieties; also they are less finished on the backs in such a way as to show that they all faced the entrance, being crosswise with respect to the main axis so that they supported, not the main ridge beam, but the individual transverse girders.[2] In other instances, however, such columns were employed externally, appearing in a stone model of a temple from Larisa at the four outer corners of the cella as if in prostyle porches. And the actual temple at Larisa was enlarged from the primitive rectangle (only 10 feet 8 inches wide in the clear and so not requiring internal columns) by the addition of a peristyle platform on all sides, of double width on the west front. The columns, of the form illustrated in Plate XVIII, may have numbered four on the fronts and six on the flanks, or six and nine respectively, perhaps even with

[1] Dörpfeld, followed by Perrot and Chipiez and also by Schefold, suggested that these capitals be dissected and the lower portions assigned to a hypothetical outer peristyle, of which there are no remains, standing on the edge of the surrounding terrace. Koldewey's restoration, however, is perfectly trustworthy, and is confirmed both by the finds at Larisa and by the absence of proper peristyle foundations at Neandria.

[2] This is very important, since it constitutes our only contemporary evidence that the central row of columns in such temples did not, as is so frequently stated on the basis of a rapid glance at the plans, support the ridge beam directly.

an inner row (dipteral) on the west front. At Nape there was not only a central row inside the cella but also a peristyle, with eight columns on the fronts and seventeen on the flanks. It would be interesting to know how, with such an awkward form of capital, the designers met one of the most difficult problems of the Ionic order, that of turning the corner of an external peristyle. Probably it was by means of two intersecting capitals forming a cruciform plan, such as the Persians later imitated at Susa and Persepolis.

Though the entablatures, having been constructed of wood, no longer exist, we may infer that both the transverse ceiling beams of the interior, especially when resting on column capitals, and also, in the case of an outer peristyle, the architrave, instead of having the plain face of the Doric, were triply divided and stepped into fascias, like later copies in the tomb and palace of Darius and other Persian examples or in the native tombs of western Asia (Plate XIX). It apparently was built up in several courses of timbers, each corbelled or projecting forward to secure a wider bearing for the smaller ceiling beams or joists at right angles. The ends of these smaller beams, not only in Asia Minor but also in Persia, were allowed to appear on the exterior to give support to the projecting cornice, and constituted as dentils one of the most important decorative characteristics of the Ionian and Persian styles; but they were gradually reduced in dimensions (Fig. 23, Plate XIX). With these two motives combined, the dentils and cornice resting directly on the architrave, there resulted the friezeless entablature which characterised the native Ionic style of Asia Minor.

Even though the frieze was not properly a member of the true Ionic entablature, the continuous horizontal band or frieze of decoration was a characteristic Ionic feature and had reached this area by way of the same three routes that the capital and other decorative elements had followed. We see such friezes on Phoenician bowls, Assyrian palaces, and Hittite rock sanctuaries; and it was this Oriental use of the frieze, for the decoration of the bottoms or tops of walls or even of the parapet or sima of the roof, that the Ionian Greeks at first adopted. The most available position was the roof, which on the Asiatic coast was of the ridge form with pediments; and the terracotta simas which here crowned the pediments, and sometimes the eaves as well, were made with high but simple vertical profiles, well adapted to decoration with relief. One of the earliest known instances—though, if our interpretation be correct, employed with a flat roof—is the stone parapet-frieze at Prinias in Crete, of the middle of the seventh century. Later, and likewise from Crete, are the terracotta parapet-simas of Praesus and of the temple of Dictaean Zeus at Palaikastro, in the latter used for the pediments of a ridge roof as well as for the eaves. Others come from Thasos and from Apollonia in Thrace. But by far the greatest number are to be found in Asia Minor, in the terracotta simas of Neandria, Larisa, and Smyrna, of Sardis in Lydia, of Gordium and Pazarli in Phrygia, and of Ak-Alan in Pontus, the areas in which the Ionic style was to develop, so that they may justly be regarded as the prototypes of the sculptured Ionic friezes of Periclean Athens.

* * * * *

Apart from temples, the monumental requirements of the Greeks of primitive times were limited to a few types of structures of simple form and cheap material. Thus the altars of the early sanctuaries, sometimes inside but more frequently outside the temples, are usually too primitive in form to require analysis; some of these, and particularly the seven successive primitive altars at Samos, have been mentioned above because of their chronological importance. Likewise gateways or propyla forming the entrances to precincts were of simple form; and in such instances as the Athenian Acropolis the fortified Mycenaean gate must have continued to serve, presumably with slight alteration of the actual doors. At Samos, in the time of the seventh altar (about 625 B.C.), there was a propylon even wider than the older temple to which it gave access, heralding the stately dimensions of the sixth-century temple.

The secular buildings of this primitive period are almost entirely unknown. A very primitive structure of two rooms on the Athenian Agora seems to have served as a Bouleuterion. And at Olympia it is probable that there was a primitive Bouleuterion with an elongated horseshoe plan (the flank walls being convex) and a central row of columns, and that to it belong fragments of terracotta roofing with Laconian disk acroteria.[1] Some curious terracotta models found at Lemnos, with a tripartite division as in an Etruscan temple, and with flat roofs, are perhaps to be interpreted as fountain-houses.

Even of private houses we possess only slight traces. These traces are sufficient, however, to indicate that the Dorians, arriving from the same environment and descended from the same stock as their Achaean predecessors, must have begun with the same element, the circular nomadic hut. The foundations of an elliptical house of the Geometric period exist under what later became the Athenian Agora; and near by, on the slope of the Areopagus, a primitive mud-roofed house still existed in the time of Vitruvius. A series of small models, illustrating the development from the elliptical structure at Samos through the horseshoe or hairpin plans at Perachora to the rectangular plan at the Argive Heraeum, has been described in connection with temples,[2] though these may represent houses. Foundations of Geometric houses exist at Asine in Argolis, at Miletus (Kalabak-tepe) in Asia Minor, and at Praesus in Crete.

Among sepulchral monuments (usually outside the towns), apart from a few rude miniature tholos tombs at Praesus and Kavousi in Crete, and large artificial earth mounds or tumuli, the most interesting are the so-called Dipylon graves outside the Dipylon gate of Athens. They are small individual shaft graves of rectangular plan, about 6 or 7 feet in depth, with a ledge at about half of the depth to support a ceiling of planks or stone slabs. On this ceiling in turn rested the monument, a great terracotta vase as much as 6 feet in height, painted with geometric patterns and funerary scenes; round it the shaft was filled with earth, so that only half of the vase protruded above the surface, forming a basin into which libations could be poured. A similar method of marking graves with colossal funerary vases, but with moulded rather than painted decoration, was in vogue in Boeotia. The stele or upright slab of stone or marble was sometimes used in primitive Attica, though as yet without decoration; but in Sparta such marble stelae were beginning to be carved with

---

[1] This would be the south wing (rebuilt in the fifth century) of the complex structure forming the later Bouleuterion (see p. 119, and Fig. 44 at B).
[2] See pp. 41, 42.

representations of the deceased, seated as if at a funeral feast, crudely cut in silhouette with flat receding planes.

* * * * *

Of the earlier kingdoms in Asia Minor which were bordered by the Greek colonies, those of Phrygia, Lydia, and Lycia are the most important so far as their architectural remains, chiefly sepulchral monuments, are concerned. For our present purposes, however, the Lydian tombs are of the least importance, because, of the two classes of which they are composed, the most monumental examples are of the tumulus form in which there was little to influence the development of Greek detail. The best is the tomb of Tantalus near Smyrna, with a vertical podium of polygonal masonry with base and crowning mouldings, enclosing a circle 110 feet in diameter and supporting a cone likewise faced with polygonal masonry, surmounted by a finial, the whole attaining a height of about 100 feet. There is no passage or dromos leading to the interior; but in the centre is a rectangular tomb chamber, its side walls curving inward to form a pointed barrel vault of corbelled masonry (as in the Aegean tomb at Isopata in Crete), and from it radiate masonry ribs intersecting concentric circular walls and forming a skeleton for the mound of earth. There are also more than a hundred tumuli at the capital of Sardis, such as that of Alyattes, 1165 feet in diameter and about 200 feet high, surrounded by a stone retaining wall 60 feet high and inclined 189 feet; on the saucer-like mound of earth above was a burnt brick platform supporting five stone balls as finials, the central one more than 9 feet in diameter. Here the tomb chamber, with a flat roof of great slabs, was placed 160 feet away from the centre of the circle in order to deceive possible tomb robbers, and to it led a vaulted passage of which the outer end was concealed; similar expedients were practised in the other tumuli at Sardis, of which some are only 80 feet in diameter. As for the second class, the Lydian rock-cut tombs are crudely worked and gave little opportunity for refinements of design. The cliffs along the Pactolus River near Sardis are honeycombed with them, each consisting of a narrow horizontal dromos leading to a doorway closed by stone slabs; within is a rectangular chamber with the roof hewn roughly into gable form. A couch is usually hewn on either side of the chamber, while at the rear may be a pair of couches in a niche, or a doorway leading to an inner room with couches on three sides; the couches may be flat to receive bodies on stretchers, or hollowed to receive sarcophagi.

In Phrygia, on the other hand, the rock-cut tombs assume greater importance, and some are of special interest because they repeat the symbol of the Lion Gate at Mycenae; these rock-cut tombs show it to have been a common design in these parts, and as the examples discovered are of later date than that of Mycenae they probably represent the influence of the Ionic immigrants. Another class of Phrygian rock-cut tombs is that which has a square front in one plane (such as the tomb of Midas), decorated with patterns suitable for a woven fabric, and believed to be a reminiscence of the movable tent—the house of the nomadic tribes. There was thus a tendency in primitive architecture to perpetuate forms which were matured in phases of life preceding those of the erection of durable architectural works.

In Lycia we meet with a parallel class of rock-cut tombs, that of the wooden

LYCIAN TOMBS

hut sculptured in the rock, with all its beams and poles, its mortises and pegs—an imitation so close as to be unmistakable. It is from such tombs that we obtain, as noted above, the best evidence for the form of the Proto-Ionic entablature; though in actual date these tombs are by no means all primitive, since in this inaccessible territory the traditional forms prevailed until Hellenistic times. At Myra, the ancient capital, there is an imposing group of these cliff dwellings of the dead on the mountain side; and others exist in hundreds in this southwestern corner of Asia Minor, as at Phellus, Antiphellus, Telmessus,

FIG. 23.—TOMB OF PAYAVA FROM XANTHUS.
(British Museum.)

Pinara, Limyra, Trysa, Arycanda, and Cyaneae, as a rule cut in the sides of cliffs. Broadly speaking, there are three types. The oldest are those forming direct copies of framed timber houses, generally having horizontal cornices (Plate XIX). The entablature is composed of the double or triple fascias of the architrave, representing two or three tiers of beams; there is no frieze; the horizontal cornice is supported by round discs, representing the ends of roof poles or unsquared logs laid side by side, such as are shown above the pillar of the Lion Gate at Mycenae; in the original hut they carried the flat mud roof, and in the rock-cut tombs of Lycia they are of the same dimensions as the original wood beams that they represent. Later we find the ends of squared logs occupying this position, and these squared timber ends were carried over into monumental architecture in stone, retained probably to give support to the projecting cornice, but reduced in dimensions and constituting as dentils one of the most important decorative characteristics of the Ionic style. The third type of tomb consists of those in which the design was largely influenced by the stone architecture of the neighbouring Greek cities; this influence is clearly shown in the Lycian Ionic tombs, in which the front of the tomb carved in the rock is copied from a portico in-antis with Ionic columns, but with some details reproduced from the earlier wood structures native to the country (Plate XIX).

Yet a fourth class of monuments is met with in Lycia, those of the sarcophagus type (Fig. 23);[1] and these are not less wooden in their origin—at least, so far as regards their upper parts—though they are probably of later date. Some are rock-cut and some are constructed, but in general they consist of a sarcophagus with a pointed curvilinear roof, apparently copied from a portable ark or shrine, the staves or beams for carrying it being carved in full relief. The latter type rests on a podium of colossal stones, sometimes double, with the upper portion carved with a continuous frieze of figures; a fine example is the tomb of Payava (375–362 B.C.) from Xanthus. The upright posts and framing, the end pieces fixed by a wood key, the mortising of the cross beams, the ceiling joists appearing at the sides but not at the ends, the planking of the roof—every detail represents wood construction perfectly, and the whole effect is that of a wooden cover to a sculptured stone sarcophagus; yet it is all of stone. It is worth noting, too, that it seems to represent ship rather than hut construction; and this not unnaturally, for Lycia fringed the south coast of Asia Minor, and the Lycians were a sea-faring people; a boat turned upside down on the beach might have suggested the upper part. The opening was doubtless for the introduction of the body. The reliefs and the inscriptions are of doubtful interpretation. Here again is a suggestion of the origin of the Greek dentils, and it will be seen how similar in many ways was the treatment of the cornice in the island of Cyprus (Plate XVIII), which lies right off the coast of Asia Minor.

[1] The same ogival roof motive appears also in the Aegean disk inscribed with hieroglyphs from Phaestus in Crete, and in the so-called Lycian sarcophagus of the fifth century from Sidon in Phoenicia.

CHAPTER THREE

THE RISE OF THE DORIC STYLE

WE have outlined in the preceding chapter the story of the foundation of the Greek states in European Hellas and of their colonies in the east and west; and it is now the further development of these cities, and of their architecture, that we have to discuss, particularly with reference to the monumental achievements of the sixth century B.C. A most astounding feature of this period is the comparative insignificance, in an architectural sense, of the mother country, as contrasted with the almost unexampled prosperity of these colonies. In many ways they outstripped the mother country in the race, and their reactive influence on Greece proper is very clearly traceable. It was much as it is to-day with Europe and America; America, the offshoot of Europe, outrunning the mother countries in many things, but awakening them by its reactive influence to fuller life, and enriching them with the fruits of its rapid and brilliant development. The art of Athens in the fifth century would have been impossible but for the earlier developments of the Peloponnesus and of Dorian colonies in Magna Graecia and Sicily on the one hand, and of the Ionian cities of Ephesus and Miletus on the other. Of these earlier developments, we shall first examine those of the Doric style, leaving the Ionic for the following chapter.

Each of the great cities of this time was a separate commonwealth, and in some, though the general tendency was democratic, the power during the sixth century at least was in the hands of kings or "tyrants," often merchant princes or captains of industry who assumed dictatorial power. Not only traditional kingdoms such as Sparta, but also democratic cities such as Athens, Corinth, Syracuse, and Acragas were under the sway of such men, in whose hands accumulated the wealth drawn from subject cities within the sphere of influence of the various capitals. The early architectural monuments were largely the work of these men, structures through which they strove to be ostentatious or to conciliate the people to their rule. This tendency prevailed throughout the sixth century, the archaic period pure and simple.

After 490 B.C. we have a period of preparation, a transition toward the culmination. The chief impulses which led to the great constructions of the early part of the fifth century were due not so much to the pride of rulers as to public patriotism. The defeat of the Persians at Marathon in 490 B.C., the second series of defeats at Salamis and Plataea a decade later, simultaneously with the defeat of the Carthaginians at Himera, greatly enheartened the Greeks both of the mainland and of the west; for in this respect the Persian and Carthaginian wars were beneficial, in that they aided the development of race feeling, and led the Greeks of the Sicilian cities, as well as those of Greece proper, to act together in the face of a common danger as they had never done before. Besides the wealth and influence which these victories brought them, the desire to commemorate their great achievements by monumental buildings and elaborate votive offerings had no small share in the subsequent artistic developments. To these transitional monuments we shall return later on; for the present we must review the earlier examples of the Doric order and endeavour to follow their gradual evolution.

* * * * *

The Doric temples now to be described differ from the primitive examples considered in the preceding chapter in being of more monumental construction in stone, illustrating the gradual standardisation of the order. They were usually built of soft limestone (*poros*) taken from various local quarries, on account of the scarcity of marble in these districts; the limestone was covered with a fine coating of stucco, firstly, to fill in the crevices in the limestone; secondly, to permit a greater smoothness and refinement to be given to flat surfaces and mouldings; and thirdly, to provide a suitable ground for enrichment in colour. Not only the columns, but also the entablatures and cella walls were now executed in this permanent material, though with many survivals from primitive wood and mud-brick construction: thus the walls, though now of coursed masonry, still have the bottom course in the form of slightly projecting orthostates two or three times the height of the upper courses, a reminiscence of the old stone dado; and the antae or terminations of the flank walls, forming responds to the columns in-antis, are thickened in imitation of the primitive wooden casing of the ends of mud-brick walls, while in door jambs even the wooden casing itself continued to be used. Marble, imported from considerable distances, was used in the west and in Greece proper only for a few decorative accessories, and even for these the builders in Italy usually resorted to friable sandstone; the general use of marble for all parts of the temple was, in the archaic period, practically confined to the Ionic temples of Asia Minor and the Aegean islands. Wood was employed for the ceilings and roofs, the latter being covered with terracotta (rarely stone or marble) tiles; and we find some instances of the continued use of terracotta revetment over wood and stone.

So numerous are the temples of the archaic period, and so varied are their characteristics in different localities, that exact determination of their relative sequence becomes very difficult; an example may be more archaic in one respect, more advanced in another. Historical evidence is very scanty for these early times; and for the archaic period there are few contemporary inscribed records pertaining to the temples themselves. The best that can be done is to arrange the buildings on each site in a sequence based on all the evidence at our disposal, and then to interrelate these series with reference to their resemblances and the few known contacts between the sites. We may divide the period approximately into two halves, with the separation at about 540 B.C.

On the Greek mainland the tendency was always toward greater strictness of form. The scale was generally modest, and the plan was comparatively simple; in the earlier archaic temples, even of the most important divinities, there was merely a cella preceded and sometimes backed by a simple porch distyle in-antis. Because of their early dates and unpretentious design most were either accidentally destroyed or intentionally dismantled in the course of time.

EARLY TEMPLES: DELPHI, AEGINA, ATHENS

Thus only scattered fragments of these earlier structures, usually employed as sanctified second-hand material in the foundations or terrace fill of their successors, now remain for examination. Such is the case with the first stone temple of Apollo at Delphi, destroyed by fire in 548 B.C. but evidently erected only during the preceding half-century, according to tradition from the designs of Trophonius and Agamedes. It certainly stood on the sacred site now occupied by the fourth-century temple; but the sole relics are fragments of large columns with wide-spreading capitals, and of wall blocks, so that it is only by inference that we restore a distyle in-antis plan. Similar plans were employed for the earlier temple of Aphaea at Aegina and for the tiny temple 'Aa' on the Athenian Acropolis.[1] More elaborate was temple 'A' on the Acropolis, with a tetrastyle in-antis façade. In these temples may be seen the characteristic Greek practice of using a different type of anta capital (with the Doric hawksbeak, which was now being developed from the Egyptian cavetto, always a prominent feature) from that of the column (Plate XX). In the entablatures, while the mainland tendency was to leave the metopes uncarved, they were frequently accented by the use of thin slabs of white marble, contrasting with the dark blue or black of the triglyphs and the blues and reds of the taenia below and cornice above. The metopes, furthermore, were so narrow as to require particularly narrow mutules above them, alternating with the wider mutules above the triglyphs in the restless manner characteristic of the first half of the century; thus at Aegina the mutules had alternately three and four guttae in each row, in temple 'A' four and five guttae. Temple 'Aa' is of special interest because the pediment had a composition of animals executed, not in sculptured relief, but merely in painting, the animals being light on a dark ground like the red-figured vases of later times. The "Hydra gable" (belonging to an unknown building on the Acropolis) illustrates the growing Athenian tendency to use sculptured pediments, though here the amount of relief is only 1 inch. The sculptured pediments of temple 'A' have a relief of 10 inches; that from the main front (the so-called "olive-tree pediment") represents a mythological scene of architectural importance because of the meticulously detailed representation of a building, with pseudo-isodomic coursing of the wall masonry, a mutular cornice, and a tiled hip roof, occupying the centre;[2] the rear pediment illustrated the combat of Heracles with Triton.

Another fragmentary example, to be restored in tristyle in-antis form, was the Hecatompedon or "hundred-foot temple" of Athena on the Athenian Acropolis, which according to its style should be associated, either as to its foundation or more probably its dedication, with the date of the establishment of the quadrennial Panathenaic festival in 566 B.C. The exact site of this temple

---

[1] The small early temples on the Athenian Acropolis (like those at Selinus in Sicily) are designated by letters, since their positions and dedications are alike uncertain. Wiegand distinguished five of these buildings, 'A,' 'B,' 'C,' 'D,' and 'E'; Heberdey separated the members of 'A' into three buildings, but obviously wrongly, there being actually two which we may distinguish as 'A' and 'Aa.' Probably 'B,' 'C,' and 'E' were treasuries (pp. 89, 91).

[2] This is sometimes identified as a representation of a "pre-Erechtheum," on the assumption that the tree appearing behind the garden wall is the sacred olive tree of Athena. But such exact representation of a definite building in sculpture seems foreign to Greek ideas; nor does its form appear suitable for that of a fountain-house, as suggested in the theory that the pediment depicts the myth of Troilus.

has not been discovered;[1] but by elimination it must have been directly beneath the Parthenon which inherited the name of Hecatompedon. Thus we cannot now see the plan; but in any case we should restore porches of four bays at both ends, tristyle in-antis according to the jointing of the corner architraves. The spacing of the flank triglyphs was closer than on the fronts. The blank marble metopes on the flanks and rear had upright Doric leaves, alternately red and blue, just below the crowning fascia (Plate XX). The east front had poros metopes to which were affixed reclining marble leopards and lions in relief. The mutules of the cornice had only two rows of guttae (as in temple 'A'), and the number in each row was alternately four and six. The soffit of the raking cornice was curiously decorated with designs of flying birds (seen from below) and tremendous lotus flowers, all incised and gaily coloured. The pediment sculptures are of poros limestone, the depth of the relief being 22 inches; on the front pediment was a triple-bodied snaky-tailed monster at the right, balanced by Heracles wrestling with Triton at the left, enframing a central symmetrical composition of two lions tearing at a fallen bull; the rear pediment is somewhat less advanced in skill, both angles being filled by colossal serpents, while at the right of the centre was a lioness devouring a calf, balanced by another lion group. The simas and roof tiles are of local Hymettian marble; the simas have the vertical Ionic profile with, instead of friezes, a lotus-and-palmette pattern, varied by the addition of a chevron border on the front pediment and a chequer border on the rear; the flank sima was surmounted by false antefixes, alternately lotuses and palmettes, attached by dowels directly above waterspouts which were cut in the form of pipes. The chevron and chequer borders curl up to form volute acroteria at the lower extremities, while at the apex of each pediment was a running-flying Gorgon likewise carved in marble. As will be seen, this temple was intentionally demolished about seventy-eight years after its dedication, in order to make room for the Older Parthenon.

The few peripteral temples of this period on the Greek mainland were far less imposing. Thus at Delphi the first temple of Athena Pronaea, of which the exact plan is unknown, had stone columns only 20 and $20\frac{1}{2}$ inches in lower diameter and 11 feet 1 inch or $6\frac{1}{2}$ diameters in height (Fig. 24). The shafts contain sixteen flutes; the echinus is almost horizontal, the spread of the abacus

[1] The erroneous attribution of the remains of the Hecatompedon, by Wiegand in 1904, to the comparatively narrow inner tetrastyle prostyle rectangle of the Peisistratid foundations (shown in Fig. 74 at A) at the middle of the Acropolis—on the assumption that the surrounding peristyle was a later addition—was made possible only by the omission of the central portions of the sculptured pediments and the failure to take account of all the existing pieces of the raking simas, which are so numerous as to demand a much wider structure. An alternative theory of Schuchhardt is that the Hecatompedon, with a hexastyle peripteral plan, originally occupied the entire width of the Peisistratid peristyle foundation, being subsequently dismantled to make way for the Peisistratid colonnade itself; but this is eliminated not only by evidence that the flank entablatures rested on solid walls rather than open colonnades, but also by the late workmanship of the foundations throughout—much more advanced than the technique of the architecture supposed to have rested on them, in which the claw or toothed chisel was as yet unknown—and by the date of the destruction of the Hecatompedon (as indicated by the circumstances in which the remains have been found), which must have been after 490 B.C. and so nearly forty years after the erection of the Peisistratid peristyle. The name "Hecatompedon" probably means that the length was exactly 100 Doric feet or 107 feet 4 inches (32.71 m.), exactly fitting the flank triglyph spacing; the width was half as much, 50 Doric feet and so in the ratio 1 : 2.

being more than two and a half times the upper diameter (32 inches as contrasted with 12½ inches), the widest proportions known. These columns were probably widely spaced to support a wooden entablature, giving proportions somewhat like those depicted on the François Vase in Florence; and the special interest of the temple is the very fact that at a time when contemporary columns on a larger scale were erected with very sturdy proportions, only four diameters in height (*cf.* Fig. 27), these columns on a very small scale were proportionately more than half again as high, becoming almost literal copies of their wooden prototypes.

Another feature which must be mentioned before we leave the early archaic Doric of the mainland is the sporadic infiltration of Ionic influence. This usually appears in minor details of the capitals. At Tiryns, for example, each of the sixteen flutes is treated at the top as a single petal curling forward and terminating in the annulet; the early date of this example may be judged by the great width of the abacus, 33½ inches, as contrasted with the upper diameter of only 14½ inches in the shaft.[1] Many other instances of such Ionic influence may be found in Doric columns used as votive or sepulchral monuments.

Intermediate between the Greek mainland and the western colonies, and partaking of the qualities of both, lay the Corinthian colony of Corcyra (Corfu), with a more elaborate peripteral archaic temple than any hitherto considered. This was a temple of Artemis (the so-called "Gorgon temple"), apparently dating from about 580 B.C., as we may infer from the style of the pediment sculpture.[2] Unfortunately almost nothing remains in place apart from the foundation trenches and a bit of the foundation itself at the southwest corner, together with some of the stones once serving as pavement supports; but from these we learn that the total measurements were about 77 by 161 feet. From the scale of the columns, 36¾ and 37¾ inches in upper diameter, and from the widths of the triglyphs, 23 and 24½ inches (the wider in both cases presumably being on the fronts), it is clear that the temple was octastyle, with seventeen columns on the flanks.[3] It is unfortunate that in this early but closely datable

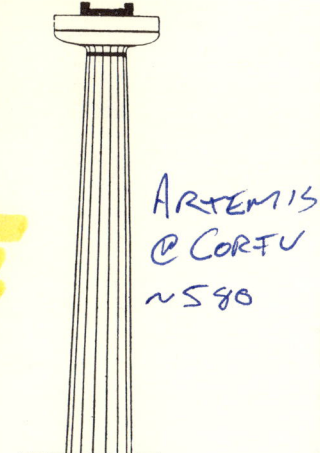

FIG. 24.—COLUMN OF THE TEMPLE OF ATHENA PRONAEA AT DELPHI.

---

[1] The form of the temple at Tiryns is quite unknown; the attribution of the capital to one of the front columns of the Mycenaean megaron, on the assumption that it was rebuilt in temple form, is now untenable (see p. 21).

[2] Dörpfeld assigned this temple to the end of the eighth century, soon after the Corinthian occupation in 733 B.C., but this is far too early; Darsow's date of 550 B.C. is too late.

[3] Exact equality of spacing on front and flank being impossible, the German publication leaves it uncertain whether there were sixteen or seventeen flank columns, with a spacing either greater (as in some of the western temples) or less than on the fronts. But it fails to observe that the examples with greater flank spacings do not have the columns thinner on the flanks than on the fronts (for the exceptional circumstances in the temple of Poseidon at Paestum, see p. 111); we may conclude that the spacing on the flanks at Corcyra was the narrower. Incidentally, we must be on our guard against restorations, such as this, which with very little evidence strive to obtain specious accuracy on the erroneous assumption that all dimensions must be whole numbers of ancient feet without fractions, particularly when the "foot" is one of 12·09 inches such as never existed.

example we cannot be certain whether there was contraction at the corners. The long cella was just as narrow as if the fronts had been hexastyle, the walls being aligned with the third column from each corner; thus we have here the oldest pseudo-dipteral plan, anticipating by four hundred years the story of its "invention" as related by Vitruvius. Two long rows of columns divided the interior into three aisles. The twenty-four flutes of the peristyle columns are cut at the necking by five wide and two narrow reeds or astragals, instead of

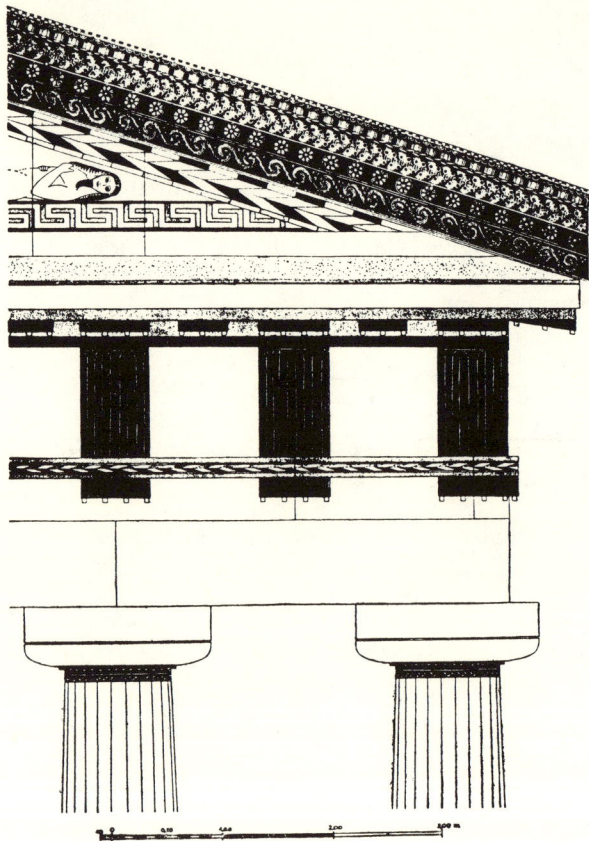

FIG. 25.—ENTABLATURE OF THE GORGON TEMPLE AT CORCYRA. (W. PEDIMENT)

the usual incisions; and above each flute are three petals curling forward, replacing the annulets (Fig. 25). The taenia crowning the architrave is enriched with a countersunk astragal, and the regulae below it had only four guttae on each. The most imposing part of the temple is the sculptured west pediment (the east pediment being almost entirely lost), carved in high relief on twenty-one limestone slabs (besides the angle pieces); the field of the tympanum is bordered above and below by projecting bands, the upper decorated with a chevron and the lower with a maeander. In the centre appears the Gorgon, twice life size, with her two offspring Pegasus and Chrysaor, flanked by two leopards, while at either end are unrelated scenes of combat. The cornice was crowned by a terracotta sima; but this was replaced, toward the end of the sixth century, by marble tiles at the edge of the roof on all sides, with eaves tiles and palmette antefixes on the flanks, while the raking sima was particularly elaborate, a cyma recta (of which this is one of the earliest examples, developed from the Egyptian cavetto merely by curving the bottom inward) carved with a Doric leaf pattern (which gives the hollowing effect of a Doric hawksbeak) with a beaded astragal below, surmounted by an anthemion cresting attached by pins.[1]

As we proceed westward among the colonies we find even more emphasis on the tendency toward ostentation, accompanied however by a certain amount of provincialism or "cultural lag" and also, especially on the Italian mainland, by barbaric distortions resulting from the intermixture not only of colonists of various origins but also of native taste. For examples of provincialism we turn first to the most important of the Dorian colonies, Syracuse, the largest city in Sicily or in the whole Greek world, so powerful that on one occasion (413 B.C.) it shattered the navy and army of Athens, which never afterwards recovered its former prestige. It is here, in the temples of Apollo on the island of Ortygia (sometimes, though less probably, attributed to Artemis)[2] and of Zeus Olympius across the great harbour, outside the city, that we find some of the most primitive examples of Doric peristyles in stone, the former dating perhaps from about 565 B.C., the latter from about a decade later. Of the temple of Zeus Olympius, only two stumps of monolithic columns are still upright, without their capitals; but of the former more remains, and on the face of the east stylobate is a most unusual feature, an inscription recording the dedication of the temple to Apollo by Cleo[sthen]es, apparently a tyrant of Syracuse, Epicles being the architect. The proportions of the plans (Fig. 26) show the characteristic extreme length of the early peristyles; with hexastyle façades, there are seventeen columns on the flanks.[3] In these examples, however, the unusual length is partly accounted for by the additional portico two columns in depth which was added on the main front, the double façades exemplifying on a more economical scale the grandiose spirit found in the dipteral peristyles of the great Ionic temples of Asia Minor. In fact, it seems probable that the temple of Apollo may have been directly inspired by one of the Asiatic temples, presumably that at Samos begun about ten years earlier; for not only do we have the double front (the colonnades are too far apart to permit use of the term dipteral) but also the Ionic habit of terminating the flank walls without anta projections, as well as another peculiar feature, the widening of the central intercolumniation, a variation which has nothing in common with angle contraction—the other façade intervals, and also those on the flanks, being evenly spaced—but is directly imitated from the Ionic system. As for the mode of transmission, we have another coincidence that Pollis, uncle of the Syracusan tyrant . . . . es (apparently our very Cleosthenes), was the dedicator of

---

[1] Certain fragments of relief sculpture are sometimes assigned to metopes or a frieze; but their source is so doubtful that it is better to leave them out of account.

[2] There was an early temple of Artemis on the island, but probably elsewhere.

[3] The temple of Apollo was completely excavated in 1937–1939, showing definitely that there were seventeen flank columns and not nineteen, as has sometimes been assumed.

"Daedalid" archaic statues at Lindus in Rhodes[1] and so may well have visited Samos. This peculiarity did not recur in the Olympieum, where the spacings were uniform across the fronts and also uniform, though somewhat closer, along the flanks; the endmost intervals were just as wide as the others, there being no angle contraction such as already existed on the Greek mainland. Also may be noted the proportions of the cella, which, in the Olympieum at least, was very narrow compared with its length. The inner building, as we

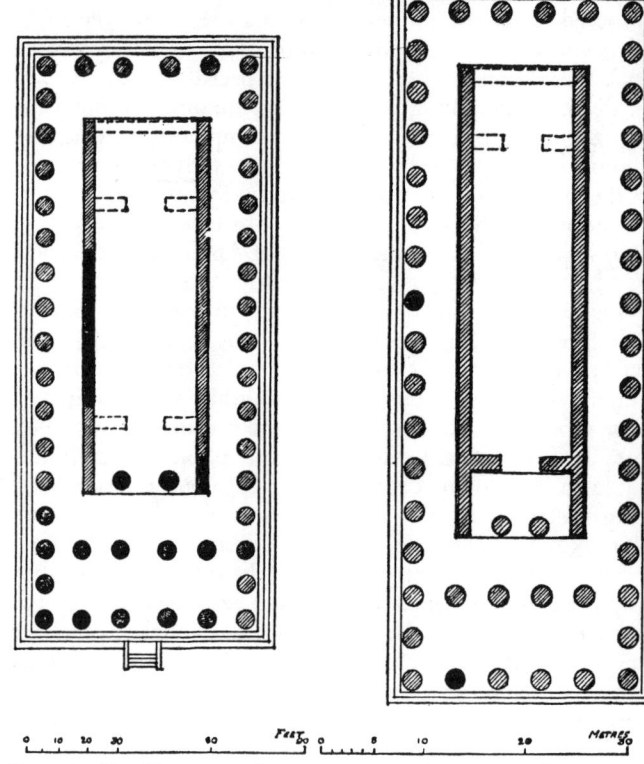

FIG. 26.—THE TEMPLE OF APOLLO AND THE OLYMPIEUM, SYRACUSE.

learn from the temple of Apollo, had a pronaos distyle in-antis; and probably at the rear end of the long cella was the characteristic Sicilian closed adytum.

In both of these Syracusan temples stone was employed for the columns and entablatures, the columns being only a little over four diameters high, with monolithic shafts, and the capitals with a wide-spreading abacus above the echinus, so much so that in the temple of Apollo they are nearly contiguous (Fig. 27). And while it is not easy at first glance to account for the enormous diameter of the columns and their close intercolumniation, if, as we must believe, they were copies of wooden originals, yet it is obvious that the new

[1] According to the Lindian Chronicle, xxxi.

circumstances demanded a different treatment; the Greeks, who were always timid as to the bearing value of stone, preferred to err in the direction of excessive strength than of too little, and seem at first to have considered that in the case of large buildings the immense weight of the entablature required columns set close together, even, as in the temple of Apollo, less than a diameter apart. The shafts have only sixteen flutes in both temples; and in some of the columns (the northeast angle column of the temple of Apollo, and both of those surviving in the Olympieum) the flutes were not carried down to the stylobate but stop above a smooth band 11 or 12 inches high.[1] The capitals, in the temple of Apollo, show a characteristic western feature, the deep hollow scotia separating the fluting from the annulets of the echinus. The architrave is

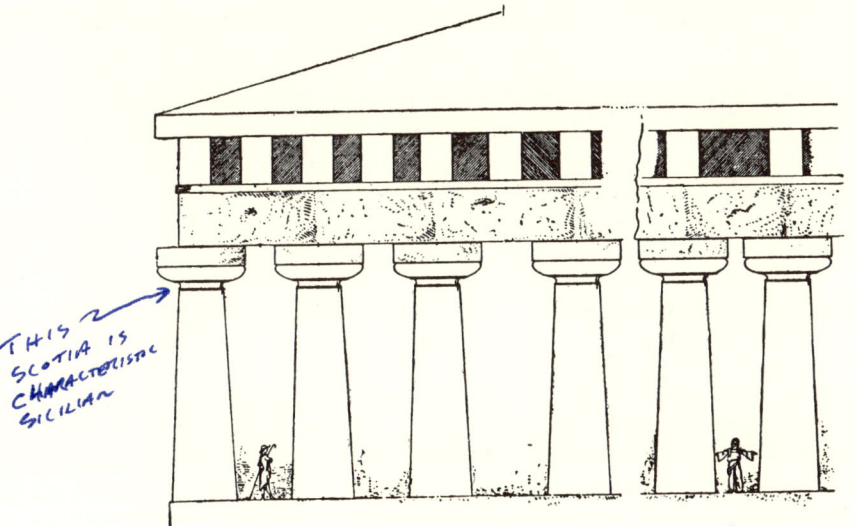

FIG. 27.—COLUMN SPACING IN THE TEMPLE OF APOLLO, SYRACUSE.
(Restored by Durm.)

of a peculiar L-shaped section, adopted probably with the idea of reducing the weight of the span between the columns; presumably a wooden beam rested along the inner face and formed the support of the ceiling beams. The crowning details of the outer face of the architrave are missing, and may have been carved mouldings; in any case, we have no indication as to the arrangement of the missing frieze and so are reduced to conjecture. It seems clear, however, that the closely spaced flank columns would not have permitted triglyphs to be centred over the intervals, and that the variant spacings on the fronts would be equally unsuitable for intermediate triglyphs,[2] so that we must restore the

[1] Similar "bases" are found in the so-called temple of Hephaestus at Acragas and on one column of the Heraeum at Olympia; they are merely signs of incompletion; the fluting at the bottoms of archaic Doric limestone columns never being executed before erection, as contrasted with the Periclean practice in marble, was sometimes left for final attention which in these cases it never received.

[2] In Fig. 27 the triglyphs on the front (shown at the left) should be wider, with those over the intervals between the columns omitted so as to leave horizontally oblong metopes

horizontal oblong metopes which we now know to have been peculiarly Syracusan, though such limitation of triglyphs to positions above the columns may also have been a survival from the primitive period. The missing cornice was probably extremely heavy, like that at Selinus described below; there are fragments of the terracotta casing of the cornice, following the precedent of earlier construction in wood, and of the flank sima with the closely spaced trumpet spouts and gaily decorated collars, as well as pieces of the strange Sicilian horizontal sima of the pediment floor, tapering to a feather edge at each angle (cf. Fig. 45), without any escape for rain water caught behind the sima. At the Olympieum were found so many kinds of terracottas that we must assume frequent repairs; in those of the fifth century, while the members were the same as before, new forms began to intrude, the cornice casing, for instance, having a complicated maeander in relief instead of the painted double guilloche, while above and below are beaded astragals instead of mere half rounds.

Next in importance was Selinus, the most westerly of the true Greek cities of Sicily. Here, in addition to the fragments of many others, we find six hexastyle temples, known as 'A,' 'C,' 'D,' 'O,' 'ER,' and 'FS'; the magnificent octastyle example 'GT'; and a small distyle in-antis temple 'B,' the last being of a later date.[1] The plans of all these temples are shown in Fig. 28. Those with the single letters lie on the Acropolis; those with the double letters are on the plateau about a thousand yards to the northeast. The megaron discussed in the preceding chapter lies south of temple 'C' and west of 'B.' Also not shown on the plan is the sanctuary of Demeter Malophorus with two small temples, at Gaggera beyond the river valley toward the west. The temples are all in absolute ruin, having been thrown down by earthquakes (Plate XX). They were built in limestone from quarries about seven miles from Selinus, and the whole of the stone work was covered with a fine coat of stucco.

Preceding the temples of which the platforms still exist in place, however, there are fragments of others of even earlier date, but demolished in antiquity so that their plans are unknown. One of these ('X') must have been of colossal scale, since the two tiers of terracotta encasing the upper part of the cornice and forming the sima were together 4 feet 5 inches high. Another of these

as on the flank. The triglyphs must have been partially supported on filling blocks placed directly over the columns (another argument for the absence of intermediate triglyphs), since the face of the architrave would have been insufficient. The peculiar section of the architrave has been regarded as an exceptional repair; but the slight possibility that of forty-two architraves the only surviving example would have been the exceptional one is now eliminated by the Syracusan treasury at Delphi, where the same construction obtained throughout.

[1] The dedications of these temples being in most cases unknown, they are usually described according to the letters assigned them by Hittorff and Zanth, or according to those used by Serradifalco and preferred by Koldewey and Puchstein. The two series being respectively 'A,' 'B,' 'C,' 'D,' 'R,' 'S,' 'T' and 'A,' 'B,' 'C,' 'D,' 'E,' 'F,' 'G' (using 'O,' 'X,' and 'Y' for remains later discovered on the Acropolis), I have compromised in the manner indicated in the text. In addition to the works by these authors we obtain valuable information from the later studies by Hulot and Fougeres and by Gabrici. It may be mentioned, however, that the gradual removal of débris during the present century has not been accompanied by adequate architectural study; many of the Koldewey-Puchstein measurements, generally accepted as final, were taken under such difficult conditions that I had to make considerable revisions during my survey of the western colonial temples in 1932.

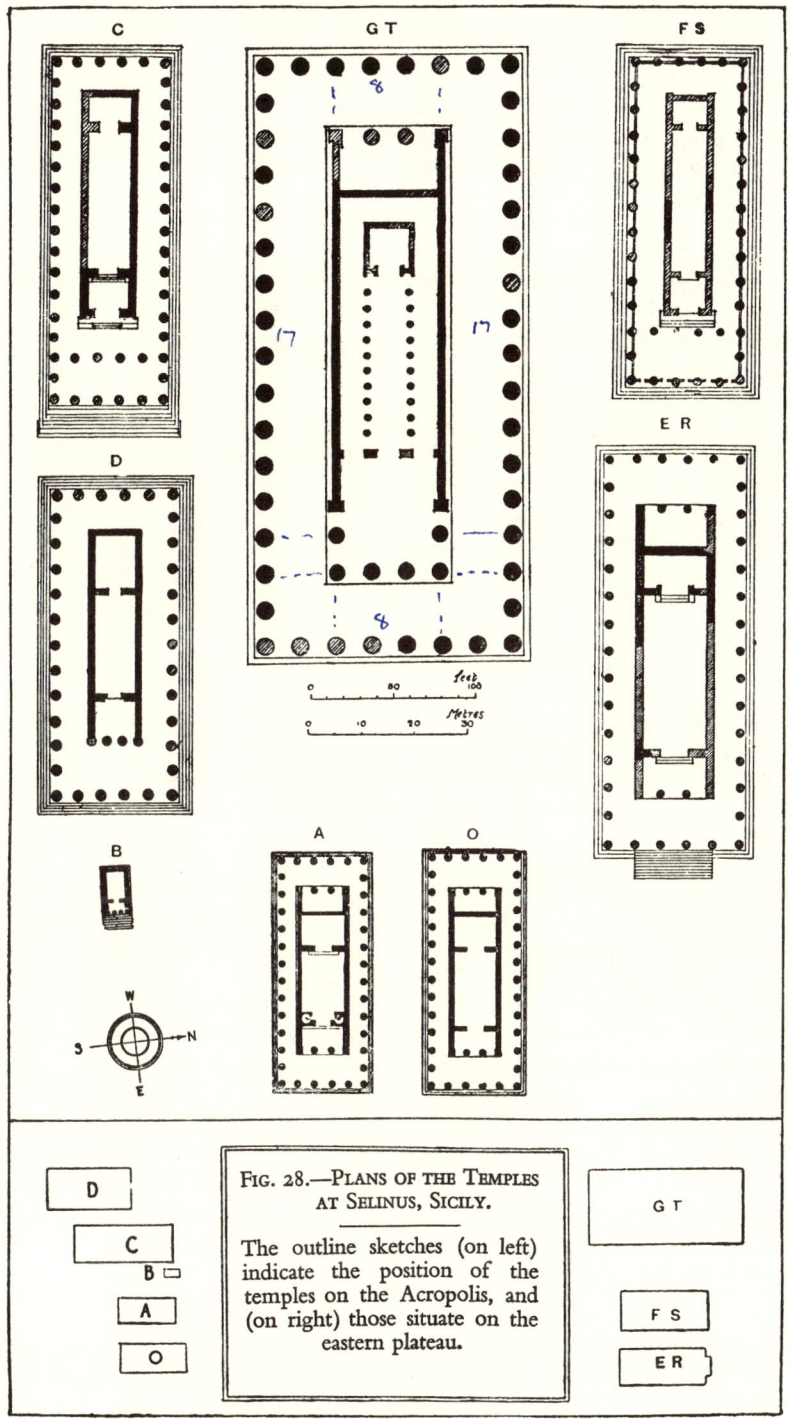

FIG. 28.—PLANS OF THE TEMPLES AT SELINUS, SICILY.

The outline sketches (on left) indicate the position of the temples on the Acropolis, and (on right) those situate on the eastern plateau.

dismembered temples ('Y') was small but elaborately decorated with sculptured metopes, unlike any later examples in the row of pendant leaves carved (and painted alternately red and blue) just under the crowning fascia (recalling the upright leaves of the Athenian Hecatompedon) and in the delicate incised patterns of interlaced semicircles (double in the case of the Sphinx metope), once relieved by painting, on the fascia itself. The metopes and their accompanying triglyphs and column capitals were found immured in the fortifications built at the north end of the Acropolis for defence against the Carthaginians in 409 B.C.; it was presumably to this emergency that the temple was sacrificed. The narrow metopes and close spacing of the triglyphs mark the stage following that of the horizontal oblong metopes of Syracuse; by the insertion of intermediate triglyphs each horizontal oblong was subdivided into two vertical oblongs.

The earliest of the existing examples at Selinus is temple 'C,'[1] of which the architectural design seems to be of the middle of the sixth century (Plate XXI). The plan is hexastyle, with seventeen columns on the flanks, and with the double colonnade across the front, as in the two temples at Syracuse. The cella is extremely narrow in proportion to its length, even more so than at Syracuse, and the pteroma or passage behind the peristyle is very deep, the cella walls not corresponding as in most later hexastyle examples with the line of the second column from each corner of the façade. The pronaos lacks the usual columns in-antis and has instead a wide doorway. Another special peculiarity of this and of several other Selinuntine temples is the use of an enclosed room or adytum behind the cella, instead of the normal opisthodomus. As at Syracuse, the column spacing is less on the flanks than on the façades, though both dimensions are relatively more open than at Syracuse; and a new principle is the reduction of the column diameters on the flanks in sympathy with the spacings, one of the rare colonial instances of a trait prevalent among archaic temples of the Greek mainland. Yet we find neither the angle contraction of Greece proper nor the widened central interval of the temple of Apollo at Syracuse; on each side the spacings were intended to be perfectly uniform from corner to corner, though there was some carelessness in execution.[2] The columns were monoliths on the east front and in the seven adjoining positions on the south flank, while all the rest were built up in drums;[3] and, while they normally agree as to the number of sixteen flutes, three on the east front and two on the west front have twenty. The greater openness of the spacing is accompanied by an increase in the proportionate height or slenderness of the columns as a whole. In the capitals, not only was the hollow scotia retained below the echinus, but the scotia in turn seems to have been separated from the shaft, at least in some examples, by an astragal, a Mycenaean survival; long afterward, however, these astragals were chiselled off and replaced by groups of three rudely cut incisions, while the flutes were carried up through the scotia in stucco, in an effort to modernise the temple.

The entablature is proportionately of enormous height, almost half of the

---

[1] There are no definite traces, as has sometimes been assumed, of an earlier temple under 'C,' though some little shrines were demolished to make space for it.

[2] The gradation of spacing shown on the fronts by Hittorff and Zanth is erroneous.

[3] A large portion of the north flank peristyle has recently been reconstructed with the original pieces.

column height. The wide taenia crowning the architrave has a countersunk astragal as at Corcyra; also some of the triglyphs, at least at the corners, have special borders enframing the glyphs with ogival tops. The architrave soffit is so narrow that the distortion in the frieze, due to the absence of angle contraction in the peristyle, was very slight and was wholly taken up, not by widening the endmost metope, but by enlarging the corner triglyph itself by 4 to 7 inches. As in temple 'Y,' there were two vertical oblong metopes in each bay, hardly wider than the triglyphs themselves (Fig. 29; Plate XXI); the metopes of the east façade were sculptured in high relief, extremely vigorous in execution but lacking the dignity of the nearly contemporary Ionian sculptures of the archaic temple of Artemis at Ephesus.[1] Their chief interest lies in their primitive composition: on all four edges the original surface is retained in the form of a frame, within which the background is sunk to a depth of 6 inches, and the relief projects only to the plane of the original surface with the result that, since the frame was set directly against the chamfered triglyphs, the sculpture was entirely recessed behind the triglyph faces. The relief which represents a chariot and four horses (quadriga) in front view is most remarkable, because the foreshortening was so difficult, and to give the sculptor more scope this particular metope has been sunk to twice the depth of the others, which represent Perseus beheading Medusa, Heracles with the Cercopes, etc. On account of the narrowness of the metopes, the mutules above them are also narrow, showing only three guttae in elevation, in order to give room for intervals (*viae*), alternating with the wide mutules above the triglyphs, a characteristic feature of these early cornices. The cornice itself is extremely heavy, about as high as the architrave or frieze, and consists of two courses of stone, the lower representing the stone translation of the wooden cornice with its underlying mutules, while the upper is an actual survival of the primitive cornice with its terracotta casing, though in this case nailed to stone rather than to wood. Particularly interesting also is the third course, the terracotta gutter or sima, that on the flanks being unique in Sicily in that it is silhouetted as a cresting, with the interstices of the anthemion ornament pierced to allow the escape of rain water (Fig. 29)[2] while on the fronts a solid sima was carried along the pediment floor in the senseless Sicilian manner, tapering off to a feather edge in each angle. The two tiers of polychrome terracotta on the flanks occupy a height of 3 feet $4\frac{1}{4}$ inches, and on the horizontal front cornice a height of 3 feet $6\frac{1}{4}$ inches; the similar treatment on the raking cornice is 3 feet $3\frac{1}{2}$ inches high.[3] Each pediment enframed a huge moulded terracotta

[1] These sculptured metopes, like those of temples 'Y,' 'ER,' and 'FS,' are now in the Palermo Museum.

[2] Such pierced simas occur also in Italy at Locri, Caulonia, Croton and Metaurum, at Olympia in Greece proper, and in Periclean work at Athens (Propylaea and Erechtheum).

[3] The restorations of the roof terracottas of temple 'C' are very confusing. The correct arrangement illustrated for the flanks (Fig. 29), with the cornice casing below and the cresting above, was due to Dörpfeld (1881). An attempt by Cavallari (1882) to make the cornice even heavier, by interpolating a sima between the cornice casing and cresting (both schemes illustrated by Durm, *Baukunst*, pp. 200–201), is to be rejected because the sima thus used on the flank is really the raking sima of the pediments, and the restored trumpet-like spouts never existed. Another fallacy appears on the façades, as restored by Koldewey and Puchstein (1899), in that they interpreted the notched slots on the top of the flank revetted course as attachments for the second row of tiles, which would then have descended

Fig. 29.—Entablature of Temple 'C' at Selinus.
(Restored by Koldewey.)

mask of Medusa, about 9 feet high. Primitive as these forms may be, the decoration in itself belongs to a period of high development, as shown by its anthemion designs and (on the front horizontal sima) the moulded globular

as low as the bottoms of the eaves tiles (cresting); if the latter had horizontal beds, as this restoration would require, the raking simas of the pediments must likewise have been horizontal at their lower extremities. This "Chinese roof" effect (cf. Fig. 38) was favoured by Gabrici (1933), Darsow (1938), and Dyggve (1948), and was supposed to have been reproduced at Calydon (see p. 52), at Paestum (see p. 96), at Eretria (see p. 91), and at Ephesus (see p. 132). But the entire hypothesis appears to be without foundation; it is illogical at Selinus, and has now been proved to be erroneous at Paestum, while the two other instances are conjectural. On the other hand, Hulot and Fougères (1910), who rightly protested against it, are in error with respect to the façades in that they omit the horizontal sima under the pediments and also the raking cornice casing (except for a narrow casing with a single guilloche which really belongs to a much smaller building). Thus there is as yet no available correct drawing of the façade arrangement.

beads and sharp reels; the only method of reconciling the terracottas with the early style of the architecture and the intermediate stage of the sculptured drapery in the metopes is to assume that the erection of the temple occupied a rather long period, from about 550 to about 530 B.C.[1]

At this point may be mentioned the unique Megaron of Demeter Malophorus at Selinus (in the suburb called Gaggera), a simple rectangular structure measuring 31¼ by 67 feet, with a closed pronaos and an adytum behind the cella, but with no columns whatever. Apart from the careful ashlar construction, the interest of the structure lies in its curious cornices, a great cavetto toward the interior, while the higher external cornice has a smaller cavetto with a torus

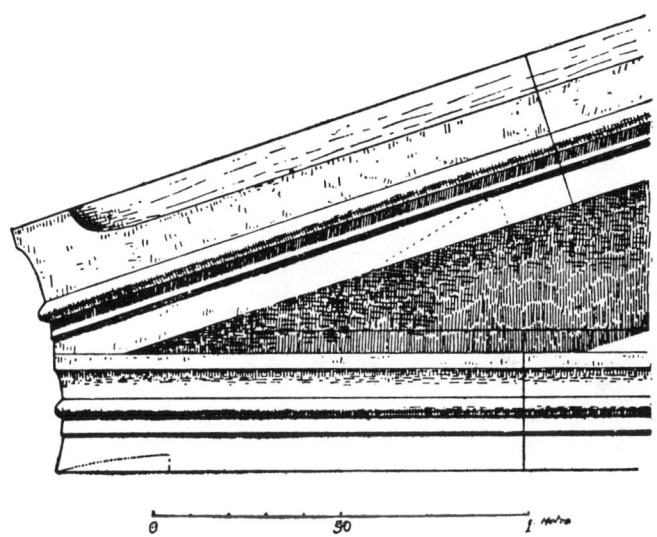

Fig. 30.—Cornice of the Megaron of Demeter at Selinus (Gaggera).

and two fascias below, forming the sima and cornice in a single member (Fig. 30). Most curious is the repetition of the same profile for the raking cornice,

[1] This chronology is of some importance in that temple 'C' forms the beginning of the rapidly developing series at Selinus, a series which with temple 'A' reaches the stage corresponding to temples dated just after 480 B.C. on other sites such as Syracuse and Himera. It was formerly thought that this development must have required a very long period, and that temple 'C' in consequence must be older (about 580 or 570 B.C.) and the temple of Athena at Syracuse much later (about 440-420 B.C.). The latter of these will be discussed below. As for temple 'C,' the very early date to which some attribute the architecture is in part contradicted by the sculptured metopes, though recent attempts to date these as late as 520-510 or 500 B.C. seems fantastic. As for the terracotta revetment, it has usually been supposed that this belongs to two periods, which might have solved our difficulties if it could have been shown that the late elements among these terracottas belonged to a period of replacement. Such a solution is excluded, however, by Gabrici's proof that all the terracottas belong to a single consistent scheme, with the sole exception that parts of the delicate cresting of the flanks were broken and repaired in a slightly later style. Darsow's dating of the terracottas in the last quarter of the century is too late. We may assume that the work on the temple almost covered the third quarter of the century, yielding a span of only seventy years (550-480 B.C.) for a very rapid evolution of the Sicilian temple plan.

not mitred at all on the main front (so that the tympanum triangle fills the entire length of the horizontal cornice) and only slightly mitred toward the rear; this raking cornice is in reality a coping, rising above the level of the tile roof behind. In the Hellenistic period the adytum was opened and the walls were reinforced to form an exedra with a barrel vault $19\frac{1}{2}$ feet in span, with an arched niche at the back.

On the Italian mainland the art of design was far more backward than in Sicily, so that temples which correspond closely to certain stages of the Sicilian development were often considerably later in date. An early temple of Apollo Alius at Punta Alice (the Crimisa promontory) near Ciro in South Italy has a very primitive plan with the cella open at the front, as at Thermum, with a central row of columns; at the rear is a closed adytum with four columns arranged in a square, a forerunner of the scheme in the Parthenon. These columns were probably of wood, perhaps mere posts of nondescript form; and there was as yet no peristyle. Most remarkable was the terracotta revetment,

Fig. 31.—Cornice of the Temple of Apollo at Crimisa.

nailed on the wooden cornice and moulded in the form of two superposed architrave taenias with the regulae and guttae staggered in most barbaric fashion, appearing with special inappropriateness even on the raking cornice (Fig. 31). The terracotta sima is the Egyptian cavetto moulded with vertical petals; and on its top, contrary to usual procedure, appear antefixes decorated not only with the ubiquitous regulae but also with moulded masks, and not only on the flanks but even on the pediments, normal to the slopes. A more garbled interpretation of Doric architectural forms is hardly conceivable.

Across the gulf from Punta Alice, at Tarentum, are two columns of another early temple, in this case peripteral. The lower diameter was as great as 6 feet 9 inches and the height only $4\frac{1}{8}$ diameters.[1] The shafts, with twenty-four flutes as at Corcyra, are built up with numerous drums; a deep scotia separates the fluting from the widely spreading echinus; and the abaci so nearly touch that we are probably, as in the temple of Apollo at Syracuse, to assume that triglyphs occurred only above the columns and not midway between.

An archaic peripteral Doric temple at Pompeii, in the triangular forum, was altered in later times so that much of its original character is lost. It was peculiar, however, in having seven columns on each front, the columns having eighteen

[1] The smaller diameter hitherto published was measured within the flutes.

flutes and widely spreading capitals. The roof terracottas were several times renewed, the original sima having at the top a roll moulding which occasionally rears up in the forms of serpents.

FIG. 32.—ANTA CAPITALS OF THE OLDER TEMPLE OF HERA ON THE SILARIS.

Five miles from the famous site of Paestum (Poseidonia) lies the sanctuary of Hera on the River Silaris (Sele). In this sanctuary the older temple of Hera, now existing only in foundations, was a simple rectangular cella faced by a tetrastyle portico, of which the four Doric columns rested on separate blocks rather than a continuous stylobate. The decorative details, as in most of these

South Italian temples, were cut in friable sandstone; these include the Doric capitals with hollow throat moulding and widely spreading echinus, and two anta capitals of a peculiar flaring form which might almost be called "Egyptian" were it not that they seem to have been derived from Proto-Ionic stele or anta capitals such as those of Cyprus and Phoenicia, the peculiar little cylinders suspended under the ends of the abacus replacing the volutes of their prototypes (Fig. 32). The abacus is richly decorated with rosettes on one anta and with a lotus-and-palmette on the other; the mouldings crowning the abacus likewise differ, as do the borders at the bottom of the flaring throat (a serpentine motive in one, a maeander in the other). The most notable portions of the sandstone decoration are the triglyphs and thirty-six sculptured metopes completely surrounding the building (six on each end, twelve on each side, widened toward the corners because of the absence of angle contraction), depicting the adventures of Heracles and a great variety of other mythological scenes in a somewhat crude and naïve style that gives an impression of greater antiquity—heightened by the fact that many were left unfinished in the form of flat silhouettes—than the architectural forms could justify. For the temple can hardly be earlier than the middle of the sixth century; and because of the resemblance of the metopes to those of temple 'C' at Selinus (*cf.* that of Heracles and the Cercopes) it seems preferable to assume that the Heraeum was in this respect an imitation and thus datable about 540 B.C.[1] A peculiarity is the strongly marked upward taper of the triglyphs, amounting to $1\frac{3}{8}$ inches or about one-fifteenth of the width, with a corresponding upward widening of the metopes. The stone sima, as in so many of these examples, is profiled as an Egyptian cavetto.

The temple of Apollo at Cyrene in North Africa was built with a technique recalling the Heraeum at Olympia and the temple designed by Trophonius and Agamedes at Delphi, particularly as regards its wall construction with the outer orthostates backed by three horizontal courses (with cuttings for rope loops near the ends of the blocks), and presumably with mud-brick construction above. The cella building lacked a pronaos, the doorway in the front wall leading directly into the cella, which had two rows each of five columns, supporting upper tiers of columns; behind was a closed adytum with four columns as at Crimisa. The surrounding peristyle, hexastyle and with only eleven columns on the flanks, may have been contemporary with the cella or slightly later. And it is possible that large marble acroteria, each with a Medusa mask enclosed within a lyre-shaped pattern of scrolls and palmettes, were added toward the beginning of the fifth century.

Somewhat later was erected at Cyrene a great limestone octastyle temple of Zeus, with seventeen columns on the flanks. The stylobate measures $99\frac{3}{4}$ by 224 feet, and the columns are uniformly 6 feet $4\frac{3}{8}$ inches in diameter, spaced 13 feet $8\frac{1}{2}$ inches on centres on the flanks, $1\frac{1}{8}$ inches less on the fronts; angle contraction of 15 and 16 inches, respectively, shows a closer connection with the Greek mainland than with the western colonies at this early date. For the temple can hardly be later than 540 B.C.[2]; not only the proportions of the

[1] The date of the metopes was first reported as about 600 or within ten years thereafter, and later as about 560–550 B.C.
[2] Excavations were conducted in 1861 by Smith and Porcher, in 1926 and 1939–1942 by the Italians, who strangely date the temple as late as 460–450 B.C.

columns, 29 feet 4 inches high with extremely heavy capitals 8 feet 10¼ inches wide (1⅞ times the upper diameter of the shaft), but also the heavy entablature 13 feet 9¼ inches high, nearly half of the height of the columns, demonstrate

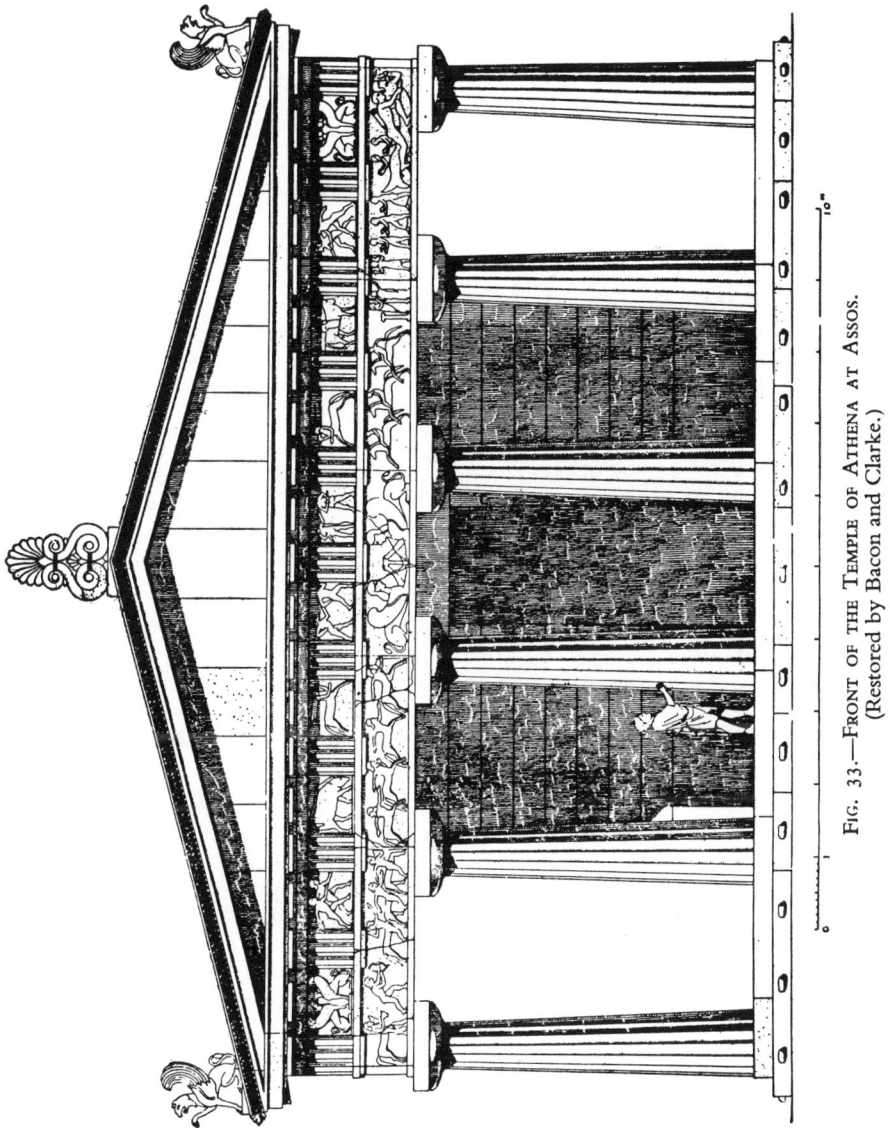

FIG. 33.—FRONT OF THE TEMPLE OF ATHENA AT ASSOS. (Restored by Bacon and Clarke.)

its early date. Even more definite are the alternating mutules, narrow (with 3 × 3 guttae) over the metopes and wider (with 5 × 3 guttae) over the triglyphs, the five guttae of the latter contrasting with six guttae under the regulae. The peristyle columns have twenty-four flutes, those of the inner porches twenty. The pronaos had two columns between elbow-shaped antae, while the opisthodomus was tristyle in-antis. The interior was remodelled with Roman marble Corinthian columns; and here were found remains of a colossal marble copy of the Zeus by Phidias at Olympia.

Having reached the approximate point of demarcation between the halves of the archaic period, shortly after the middle of the sixth century, we find that then was inaugurated what may be known as the strict archaic style, when the Doric members tended to assume the canonical forms that were retained with little change until the decay of Greek architecture. Among the significant details is the fact that the metopes had become sufficiently widened to permit the mutules of the cornice to be of uniform width throughout, avoiding the restless alternation characteristic of the earlier period.

We may turn, for a moment, to the coast of Asia Minor, the Ionian homeland, where Vitruvius, as a matter of fact, pretends that the first temple constructed by the Ionians to Apollo Panionius was in the Doric order. The only known archaic Doric temple in Asia Minor, however, is that dedicated to Athena at Assos in the Troad (Fig. 33), which, as might be expected from its Oriental location, is a peculiar example showing Ionic influence. The plan is hexastyle peripteral, with only thirteen columns on the flanks; but the cella is of great length as compared with its width, and there is no opisthodomus or adytum. The plan shows an unusual sense of co-ordination, more Ionic than Doric, in the alignment of the front of the pronaos with the third flank column on either side; another Ionic trait is the absence of anta returns. The reduction of the column spacing on the flanks, the absence of angle contraction (the distortion being taken up solely by the end metope), the use of sixteen flutes (eighteen in the pronaos) with an arris at the front, the widely spreading capitals, and the style of the sculpture, all indicate an archaic stage of development; on the other hand the use of mutules of equal width above triglyphs and metopes would make a date earlier than 540 B.C. improbable.[1] A curious detail is the omission of guttae, both in the cornice and on the architrave, and the use of a projecting taenia at the bottom of the architrave as a frame for the sculpture. For the sculptured decoration is not limited to the metopes; the chief interest of the temple lies in the sculptured architrave,[2] the only Doric example of such a departure from precedent (apart from a late imitation at Lesbos), a concession to Ionic taste, apparently derived from the archaic temple at Didyma.[3]

FIG. 34.—
OLD TEMPLE
OF NEMESIS,
RHAMNUS.

On the Greek mainland, during this second half of the century, many of the temples continued to be of simple plan, and in the outlying districts they might even be nondescript as to style. Thus a temple at Taxiarchi in Aetolia, about 24½ by 37 feet in plan, consists merely of a square cella and a pronaos, the walls built of

---

[1] A later date, in the fifth century, has sometimes been suggested, on the erroneous assumption that the distance from Athens would be enough to account for its archaic characteristics both in plan and decorative sculpture.

[2] Portions are now exhibited in the Louvre and in the museums of Istanbul and Boston.

[3] For the archaic temple at Didyma, see p. 133; for a later analogy in an Ionic building, the Nereid Tomb at Xanthus, see p. 257; for the Doric temple of Apollo Bresaeus at Lesbos, see p. 271.

irregular masonry with an entrance 7 feet high and 14 feet wide on the front; two slender intermediate piers, only 10¾ inches wide and 29½ inches deep, with nondescript bases and capitals, help to support the lintel. More formal, but equally modest in plan, are some of the minor distyle in-antis temples of Attica, the older temples of Dionysus Eleuthereus at Athens (Fig. 77) and of Nemesis at Rhamnus—the latter (Fig. 34) unusual in its reversal of the materials, soft poros being employed for the carved detail and marble in the form of polygonal masonry for the cella walls, but dating apparently from the early fifth century[1]—and probably also temple 'C' on the Athenian Acropolis. The last of these, and also temple 'B' on the Acropolis, seem to have been treasuries erected west of the Hecatompedon. Temple 'B' had a more pretentious portico, tristyle in-antis; in this example, too, we meet an unusual feature in the treatment of the back of the cella as a segmental apse, round which the triglyph frieze and cornice were carried, a reminiscence of the primitive horseshoe plan. Somewhat similar was the plan of an oracle temple at Corinth, where the apse was a full semicircle; but in this case there was no pronaos, the front having had merely a doorway to the cella.[2]

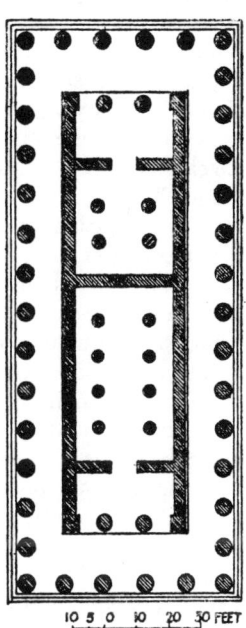

FIG. 35.—THE TEMPLE OF APOLLO AT CORINTH.

Just as the Corinthian colony of Corcyra produced the most imposing peripteral temple of Hellas during the first half of the century, so Corinth itself initiated the great series of large peripteral Doric temples during the second half. In this rich commercial city stands one of the most notable examples, the well-known temple of Apollo (Fig. 35; Plate XXII); erected soon after the middle of the sixth century.[3] Of this temple but seven columns now remain, but the entire plan survives in the rock-cut foundation trenches. Thus we see that it was hexastyle, with fifteen columns on the flanks, and that it presented the unusual feature of a double cella, one facing east, the other west, giving very long proportions in the plan. The shafts are monoliths, 20 feet 11 inches high, absolutely without entasis; the capitals above these are cut in separate blocks, the echinus with less bulging and showing greater refinement than in earlier examples. The diameters and spacings are reduced on the flanks, in accordance with archaic practice on the mainland, the differences amounting to 4 inches for the columns and 11 inches for the axial spacings. Here too, as in the Olympian Heraeum, the angle spacings are contracted to overcome the distortion occasioned by the angle triglyph, to the extent of 10 inches on the fronts and 9½ inches on the flanks. There still remained enough of the distortion, however, to require the

[1] The probable date is 487 B.C., contemporary with the Older Parthenon (p. 149).
[2] Compare also the Bouleuterion at Olympia (p. 118).
[3] The date of about 540 B.C. is now confirmed by potsherds found in the masons' chip dump of the temple.

THE RISE OF THE DORIC STYLE

widening of the two metopes nearest each corner by 2 inches each. Another sign of advance was the appearance, for the first time, of the optical refinement of upward curvature in the stylobate, on both front and flank.[1] Of the portion above the architrave we have only a few fragments of triglyphs and a few mutular guttae. It is probable that the sima was of terracotta, with the new profile which had just been invented at Corinth, a prominent ovolo rising from a wide fascia and crowned by a little astragal (or small ovolo), and painted with the lotus-and-palmette.[2]

On the Acropolis at Athens, shortly after the erection of the temple at Corinth, Peisistratus and his sons rebuilt the Ancient Temple of Athena, with a peristyle of stone (Fig. 74 at A). Only the foundations, with one block of stylobate resting directly on them, remain in place; the stylobate, of pink Kara limestone, curved upward. Everything above this was of poros limestone except the following details: the metopes, pediment sculptures, raking cornice, simas and roof tiles, acroteria, and an inner frieze, were all of imported island marble, an indication of the close relations of the Peisistratids with the Ionic tyrants. The peristyle had six columns on the fronts and twelve on the flanks, with similar variations in the diameters and spacings, and the same employment of angle contraction that we observed at Corinth. The Doric profiles are a little more refined than at Corinth; the echinus of the capitals shows a stiff curve at a steeper angle, and the necking is separated from the shaft by four incisions. Most unusual is the difference of material in the marble raking cornice, with its hawksbeak bed moulding and a crowning moulding which, though an ovolo, is also painted with a Doric leaf. The sima is likewise of marble, and on the pediments has the ovolo imitated from Corinthian terracotta simas, but on the flanks it retains the old Ionic vertical face with pipe-like spouts at intervals, while the water-spouts carved on the four angle acroterion bases were lion heads at one end, ram heads at the other. Here for the first time great pedimental groups were carved in marble, and consequently in the round rather than relief, for the technical reason that it was cheaper to construct the tympanium background separately in local limestone; the subjects were, at the east the battle of the gods and giants, and at the rear a combat of animals. The inner plan again was that of a double temple: the east cella of Athena Polias had two rows of interior columns; but the rear porch gave access to three special rooms, an anteroom and two inner rooms side by side, apparently consecrated to Poseidon-Erechtheus, Hephaestus, and Butes.[3] Ionic influence, to which the Peisistratids were addicted, seems to have caused the use of poros limestone Ionic columns in the inner porches, which we may restore as prostyle (cf. Fig. 71), though the distyle in-antis form is possible; above the architrave was a continuous Ionic frieze of marble 3 feet $11\frac{5}{8}$ inches high, carved in low relief, the prototype of the Panathenaic frieze of the Parthenon. The temple was injured to such an extent by the Persians in 480 B.C. that the peristyle was demolished and built

---

[1] It is sometimes stated that the curvature at Corinth appears only on the front.

[2] Remains of an even larger temple at Corinth, probably fifth-century, were roughly hewn into disk form by the Venetians and thus rolled to the line of their fortifications.

[3] In other words, this was the predecessor of the Erechtheum. It will be noted that the interior is here described in accordance with the new evidence that it was erected simultaneously with the Peisistratid peristyle, and that it was not the mere relic of an older temple around which the peristyle was supposed to have been wrapped (see p. 72, note 1).

PEISISTRATID TEMPLE, OLYMPIEUM, AND DELPHI

into Themistocles's north wall of the Acropolis; the ruined cella survived, however, and its western portion was eventually reroofed for use as the state treasury, the Opisthodomus (Fig. 70).[1]

Other Athenian temples of this period were the miniature temple 'E' on the Acropolis, unknown as to location (possibly one of three treasuries, including temples 'B' and 'C,' west of the Hecatompedon) though its details obviously imitate those of the Peisistratid temple of Athena, and also its direct antithesis, the huge but frustrated beginning of the great Olympieum by the sons of Peisistratus, abandoned when Hippias was driven into exile in 510 B.C. The idea of the colossal octastyle dipteral plan, designed by Antistates, Callaeschrus, Antimachides, and Porinus, was undoubtedly derived from the great Ionic temples of Asia Minor; but it was to have been translated into Doric terms. The two lower steps were actually built, as well as the foundations of the second or inner rows of columns, so that we may determine its exact dimensions, $134\frac{1}{2}$ by $353\frac{1}{2}$ feet on the stylobate, as well as the arrangement of the columns, the outer rows having eight on the fronts and twenty-one on the flanks, with a diameter of 7 feet $11\frac{1}{4}$ inches. The undertaking was so colossal, vying with the huge temples at Ephesus and Samos, Selinus and Acragas, that work was stopped upon the dissolution of the tyranny, not to be resumed until an Oriental despot more than three centuries later adopted the project and substituted Corinthian columns for Doric (Figs. 101–102; Plate LXIV).[2]

To the series initiated by the temples of Apollo at Corinth and Athena Polias at Athens belong also the temples of Apollo at Eretria and Delphi. The former, dedicated to Apollo Daphnephorus, is known chiefly because of its wonderful pediment sculptures in marble.[3] The second stone temple of Apollo at Delphi was undertaken in the last quarter of the century to replace the structure burnt in 548 B.C., and was begun at the west end, the rear, using poros limestone throughout even to the pediment sculptures in high relief. But after the military defeat of the exiled Athenian democrats in 513 B.C., Cleisthenes assumed the contract in an effort to win the support of the priesthood to his cause, and carried out the east end in Parian marble from stylobate to roof, including the pediment sculptures at the east end and the upper portions of the entablature on the flanks.[4] The plan was almost identical with that of the later temple

---

[1] The problem of *the* Opisthodomus (*par excellence*) on the Acropolis is chiefly of topographical interest; but the allusion of Herodotus to the "megaron facing west" with smoke-blackened walls, and the inventories of its contents, would point to the survival of the cella of the Peisistratid temple through three incendiary or accidental fires in 480, 406, and 377 B.C., until final abandonment at the middle of the fourth century.

[2] The dipteral arrangement of the older plan was demonstrated in minor excavations by a German investigator, who miscounted the more closely spaced flank columns and assumed that they would have been twenty as in the Corinthian temple. He also restored Ionic bases for the older temple, assuming that it would have been a reproduction of one of the great structures of Asia Minor; but this is contradicted by the great diameter of the columns as compared with the spacing, and also by the technical treatment of the bottom drums (now built into later foundations) which show that they were to rest directly on the stylobate without bases.

[3] Very little has been published about the architecture, beyond the most improbable suggestion that the raking cornice had a "Chinese roof" effect (see p. 82, note).

[4] With regard to the distribution of the marble portions the results of my studies are in agreement with Herodotus but somewhat at variance with the French publication.

which took its place after the destructive earthquake of 373 B.C., hexastyle and peripteral, with fifteen columns on the flanks; the long proportions, which at Corinth were due to the double cella, were here the result of the introduction of the adytum between the cella and opisthodomus. To the same period belongs the second temple of Athena Pronaea at Delphi, erected wholly in poros limestone, with an unusual orientation facing toward the south; on account of this position, athwart a narrow terrace, the opisthodomus was omitted and the hexastyle peristyle contained only twelve columns on the flanks. The second temple of Hera Acraea at Perachora, built to the west of the apsidal temple, is another work of this school, though not peripteral; the missing façade was apparently distyle in-antis. As at Corinth, there was a cross-wall dividing the cella into two parts, of which the inner was perhaps an adytum since this was an oracle temple; but unlike Corinth was the abnormal treatment with two longitudinal parapets on which rested the interior columns dividing the cella into three aisles. The pediment tympanum was recessed $3\frac{3}{4}$ inches as if for pediment sculpture which seems never to have been applied.

Returning towards the western colonies, we examine another Doric temple on the island of Corcyra (Corfu), that at Kardaki (Cadacchio).[1] The plan was hexastyle and peripteral, with only eleven columns on the flanks because of the absence of opisthodomus or adytum. The columns are widely spaced, with intervals of nearly $2\frac{2}{3}$ diameters; and the spacing is uniform on both front and flank, with a contraction of only $1\frac{3}{4}$ inches at the corners which was apparently imitated from the mainland and serves no useful purpose, in the absence of a triglyph frieze. For the most striking portion of the temple, the entablature, consists merely of an architrave crowned by a heavy ovolo moulding, upon which rests directly a strange cornice, a great cyma recta (with a rudimentary profile clearly suggesting its Doric hawksbeak origin) with an astragal below and fillets above. The raking cornice is equally strange, with archaic beaded astragals below and above a large carved egg-and-dart moulding. These profiles, and particularly the absence of the frieze, with the resulting diminution of the entablature to a mere quarter of the column height, suggest direct imitation of Ionic architecture.[2]

For examples of the South Italian mixture of provincialism with Ionic and barbaric influences we turn to the famous series of temples at Paestum (Poseidonia). Of the three standing temples the earliest is the so-called Basilica (Fig. 36; Plate XXIII), shown to be a temple by the large altar at the east end, probably to be associated with an archaic inscription honouring Poseidon. It has nine columns on the east and west fronts, with eighteen on the flanks, and a row of eight columns down the centre of the cella; one of the intercolumniations inside the cella was slightly wider than the others; the pronaos is tristyle in-antis, and at the rear was probably an adytum. The plan reflects the temple of Artemis at Corcyra in being nearly, though not quite, pseudo-

[1] The date of the temple at Kardaki has been considerably debated, its peculiar forms having led even to the inference that it is Hellenistic; but the late sixth century is unquestionably its true date.

[2] In the older publications a blank frieze was restored, since a friezeless entablature was formerly inconceivable; also the architrave was turned inside out. The columns, too, were formerly restored as much too slender, 5·6 instead of the actual 4·8 lower diameters in height.

dipteral, the flank walls being slightly outside the lines of the corresponding columns. The neighbouring though slightly later temple popularly attributed to Demeter (Ceres) is of the ordinary hexastyle type (Fig. 36); the pronaos has an unusual prostyle portico,[1] and there is no opisthodomus or adytum. Both temples lack angle contraction; but in the temple of Demeter the spacing is uniform on all sides, while in the Basilica, somewhat perversely, the flanks show a wider spacing throughout as in contemporary temples at Selinus. Some uncertainty in the designing of the Basilica is illustrated by two matters affecting the levels of the floors and ceilings. The interior columns of the cella are of the same height as those of the pronaos, 20 feet $8\frac{1}{4}$ inches, but the cella pavement

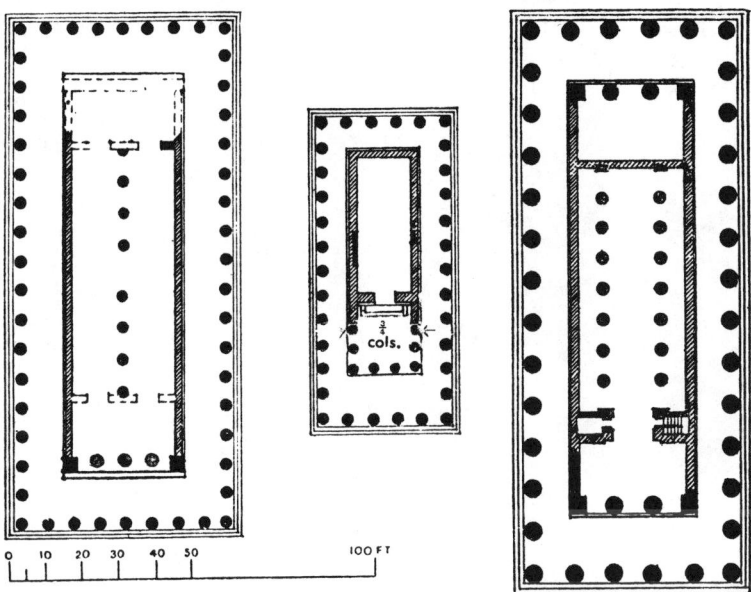

FIG. 36.—BASILICA, TEMPLE OF DEMETER, AND TEMPLE OF POSEIDON AT PAESTUM.

level was decided afterwards by fitting slabs round the columns 1 foot $8\frac{3}{4}$ inches above their bottoms, so that when they were fluted the imbedded lower portions were left in cylindrical form. For the ceiling of the pteroma, on the other hand, beam cuttings were prepared on the inner face of the architrave, just under the sandstone crowning moulding, including sockets at 45 degrees in the corners; but the corresponding sockets for the opposite ends of the beams (which should have been, for instance, in the face of the pronaos architrave) were never cut, and even those of the peristyle were plugged with small blocks of stone showing that they were not used in the final design.[2]

[1] Perhaps imitated from the great temple 'GT' at Selinus.
[2] The diagonal beam cuttings in the corners, moreover, would have required enlargement if they had ever been used, since the diagonal beams must have been heavier in order to support the ordinary beams (above the second column from each corner) which would have been framed into them. Possibly a hip roof was originally proposed.

In both temples the capitals surpass any other known examples in the decorative treatment of the neck and echinus, the fluting terminating in Ionic semicircles below a fillet or even (as in the original form of temple 'C' at Selinus) an astragal which in the temple of Demeter is carved with a bead-and-reel; between the semicircular flute terminations in the latter are also tiny petals. The necking above this is a deep scotia filled with drooping petals, two to three corresponding to each flute; the bottom of the echinus has mouldings in relief instead of the usual annulets. Of special interest are the nine capitals on the west front of the Basilica (the rear, though facing on the main street), with at least seven different designs unsymmetrically arranged: the four at the left show various combinations of half-rounds, the middle one a rosette-and-lotus motif (Fig. 37), the next a guilloche, the seventh an Ionic design of the lotus-and-palmette resembling that in the Siphnian Treasury at Delphi (Plate XXXI),[1] while the two at the right show a row of tiny petals, six to each flute. In a few of the other capitals of the Basilica, the southeast corner capital of the peristyle, the three of the pronaos, and the two easternmost of the interior, the echinus is a separate block of sandstone; the easternmost capital of the cella, though a quarter imbedded in the pronaos cross-wall, is completely carved, while the shaft, being fluted afterward, is finished for only three-quarters of the circumference. In both temples there is a remarkable diminution in the upper diameter, and the swelling curve of the entasis is more emphasised than that of any other temples. The prostyle inner columns of the temple of Demeter were completely Ionic, with twenty-eight flutes meeting in sharp arrises. The bases have a circular disk below with a torus above, resembling those later used at Locri. The shafts are terminated by a simple fillet at the bottom (above the torus) and by a fillet and astragal at the top. The sandstone capitals of the columns, with the upper portion of the shaft cut in the same block, are of the elongated archaic form, and the cushion is convex, with a single bordering astragal. Unlike the earliest Ionic capitals, however, the inner portion of the volute is replaced by a very large convex eye. Below the cushion is an ovolo carved with the egg-and-dart, the shells of the eggs being rounded astragals in the archaic manner; and above is a pronounced abacus.[2] The capitals of the antae in the Basilica at Paestum are also of unusual form, flaring and with tiny volutes resembling

Fig. 37.—Doric Capital of Basilica, Paestum, with Lotus and Rosettes. (Durm.)

---

[1] Even the foot unit employed in these temples was Ionic, 11·568 to 11·578 inches.

[2] One complete capital, found in 1948, serves as the model for this description and confirms the assumption that the inner order was Ionic; portions of the bases and shafts had long been known. The idea of an Ionic pronaos inside a Doric peristyle had previously been tested in the Peisistratid temple of Athena at Athens.

those of Proto-Ionic type in the neighbouring sanctuary of Hera on the River Silaris.

The architraves of the above-mentioned temples at Paestum are crowned by elaborate Ionic continuous mouldings carved in sandstone, without regulae or guttae; in the Basilica an ovolo is surmounted by a concave range of drooping petals, while in the temple of Demeter a carved egg-and-dart appears in this position. The details of the frieze in the Basilica are uncertain; in spite of the loss of the outer face, however, from the marks of joints on the top of the architrave moulding, with lesser intervals alternating with greater, we may conclude that it had triglyphs and metopes. The frieze of the temple of Demeter is very peculiarly constructed; the triglyphs are of sandstone with all the prismatic faces slightly concave to give greater sharpness at the edges, and they are merely inlaid in the limestone frieze blocks, of which the exposed intervening portions form the metopes. Because of the absence of angle contraction in the

Fig. 38.—Temple of Demeter at Paestum. Partly restored. (Koldewey.)

peristyle, a wider metope was required to allow the triglyph to be placed at the angle (Fig. 38).[1] In the case of the Basilica the exact form of the cornice is

---

[1] It happens that all the four corners of the entablature of the two fronts are gone, and Labrouste in his restoration placed a half-metope at the corner, and the last triglyph over the axis of the angle column. A metope, however, measuring 3 feet 8 inches instead of 2 feet 9 inches (the average dimension of the others) was later found, proving that the triglyph was in its proper place, viz., at the corner.

unknown, though the roofing terracottas indicate that it was revetted in primitive fashion and had a terracotta sima. The cornice of the temple of Demeter, on the other hand, is fully known and constitutes the most unusual feature in these temples. Directly on the triglyph frieze rest two courses of sandstone, the lower elaborately carved with a serpentine pattern, the upper with the egg-and-dart; these are carried horizontally all round the temple, and on the façades these alone form the cornice below the pediments. But on the flanks, instead of the usual mutular cornice, there are overhanging eaves of limestone, the soffit coffered in a manner reminiscent of woodwork; and on the façades the coffered eaves are bent and carried up the slopes. The bend appears, however, only in the soffit and is insufficient to affect the upper outline, where the raking cornice forms the usual unbroken continuous slope.[1] The panel of each coffer was filled with a sandstone plaque, carved with a star in relief and fastened into place with lead. The crowning sima of the temple is the earliest known example of the cyma recta used in this position; and this, too, is carved in sandstone with an anthemion design in relief, nine-petal palmettes alternating with lotus flowers of Egyptian style, resting on connecting spiral stems (reproduced long afterwards in more developed style at Bassae and Delos), with lion-head spouts on the flanks.

Five miles away, on the River Silaris (Sele), were discovered the foundations of a later temple of Hera, octastyle and peripteral, with seventeen columns on the flanks, surrounding a fairly long cella with a pronaos and, at the back, an adytum. It is interesting as a pseudo-dipteral plan on three sides, while the front portico was even deeper, equivalent to three intercolumniations; but in spite of the complicated plan the scale is even smaller than in the older temple, the stylobate measuring only about 56 by 123 feet. Whether this plan was a development from that of the Basilica, or whether, like the older temple of Hera, it was influenced by contact with Selinus (compare the plan of temple 'GT'), it is now difficult to say; the stylistic dates would permit the latter assumption. Though the column capitals still show archaic characteristics such as eighteen flutes terminating in semicircles with tiny petals between (the echinus being separately carved in sandstone in some instances), yet the hollow scotia has disappeared; also the richly carved Ionic mouldings in sandstone crowning the architrave show the later and more oval form of egg-and-dart. The triglyph frieze above the non-Doric architrave perpetuates the provincial hybrid tradition; the friable sandstone metopes contain well-developed sculpture of about 500 B.C., and from the fact that some are about $4\frac{1}{2}$ inches wider than others, apparently having been located near corners, it is clear that angle contraction had not yet been introduced. The cornice was crowned by a sandstone gutter consisting of a hollow "Egyptian" profile with lion-head spouts. The erection of the larger temple, apparently for the same cult, not many years after its predecessor, may perhaps have been due to a feeling that the rapidly growing importance of the sanctuary required a more expert design which would not shame Hera in comparison with the developed workmanship of other cities.

[1] The "Chinese roof" effect shown in Fig. 38, therefore, is imaginary and erroneous. This disposes of the only positive argument ever adduced for the "Chinese roof" theory, so that Paestum now becomes an argument in the opposite sense.

METAPONTUM AND LOCRI

This Ionic influence appears also in another Achaean colony of South Italy, at Metapontum, where we find two temples of which one, at least, again used sandstone for the finer details. The earlier of the two, known as the *Chiesa di Sansone* but probably the temple of Apollo, is now represented merely by a rectangular excavation, while the later, the so-called *Tavole Paladine* ("Knights' Tables"), retains ten columns on the north flank and five on the south (Plate XXIII). The foundations of the *Chiesa* indicate that the plan was of the unusual type with a single colonnade on the long axis of the cella, as in the Basilica at Paestum, suggesting that there was an odd number of columns on the front; and since the total dimensions and also the scale of the columns are practically

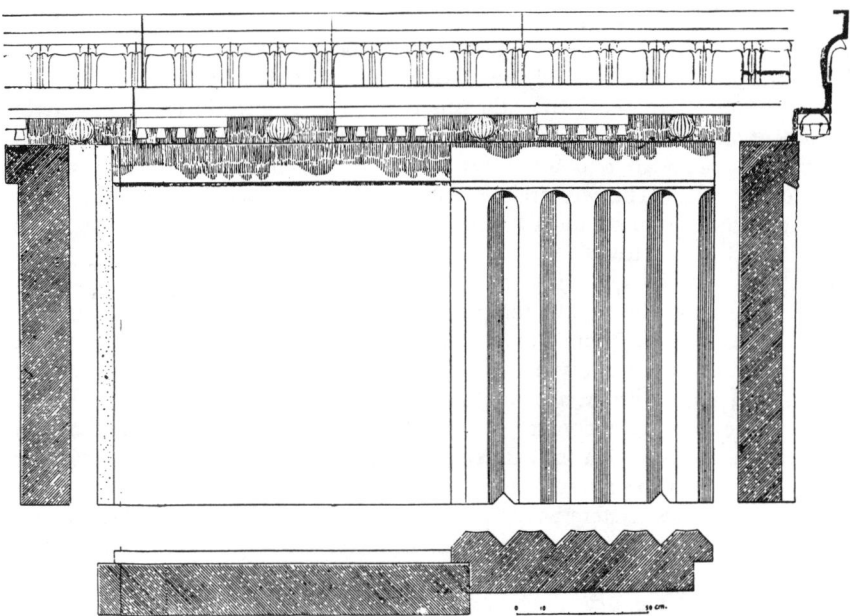

FIG. 39.—ENTABLATURE OF THE DORIC TEMPLE AT LOCRI.

the same as in the Basilica, it is natural to assume that there were nine columns on the fronts and eighteen on the flanks, the latter again showing a wider spacing. The *Tavole* was of the ordinary hexastyle type, and the columns were intended to be uniformly spaced on all sides, as in the temple of Demeter at Paestum; the pronaos was in-antis, but at the back was an adytum rather than an opisthodomus. In both examples the echinus is heavy and bulging, and the scotia, though not yet abandoned, merely undercuts the echinus and does not cut into the line of the shaft. The architrave of the *Chiesa* was crowned by heavy mouldings rather than by regulae and guttae; the triglyphs were of sandstone, the glyphs semicircular with a decorative central groove rather than triangular in plan, and the intervals between them concave with projecting fillets; but the cornice was of ordinary mutular form. The lower course of the architrave of the *Tavole* remains in place, but we have very inadequate information as to its crowning members and the upper parts of the entablature. Each of these two temples seems to be about a decade later than its counterpart at Paestum.

The most peculiar example was a Doric temple in the Ionicising colony of Locri Epizephyrii, of which the plan was apparently tristyle in-antis; there was, at least, no peristyle. The members of the entablature (Fig. 39) were all cut on thin slabs, perhaps because of the scarcity of material.[1] The triglyphs were of very wide proportions, really pentaglyphs divided into five parts; some have concave intervals between the glyphs as at Paestum and Metapontum, and the angle triglyphs were curiously decorated with astragals at every vertical edge, as at Selinus and Metapontum. Above these came a very decorative cornice, the lower course carved with an elaborate leaf ornament and with miniature mutules of slight projection (with two rows of guttae) alternating with full-sized pomegranates 3¾ inches in diameter; the upper course was of coarse limestone to which was nailed a terracotta revetment. The simas, roof tiles, and acroteria are all of terracotta; the simas have a delicate lotus-and-palmette ornament in relief, that on the flanks with pierced triangular interstices to permit the escape of rain water (as at Selinus), while false lion-head spouts covered the joints. The acroteria represent youths on horseback, each supported by a crouching sphinx, the forerunners of the marble acroteria of the Ionic temple in the same town.

Returning to Sicily, we first consider two of the temples at Selinus, 'D' on the acropolis and the middle temple ('FS') on the eastern plateau, apparently begun respectively at about 535 and 525 B.C., both resembling 'C' in the width of the pteroma and narrowness of the cella as compared with the tremendous length, and both with an adytum instead of the opisthodomus (Fig. 28). But the peristyles are proportionately shorter, there being only thirteen and fourteen columns, respectively, on the flanks; yet, as if to counteract this shortening, the spacings on the flanks are uniformly greater rather than less than on the fronts, initiating a perverse system which was destined to run through several examples. The column diameters are uniform on all sides, and angle contraction is still absent. To permit the shortened peristyle, in temple 'D' the inner row of columns behind the façade was omitted and, in compensation, the front of the pronaos was opened, with two engaged columns terminating the walls and two standing between, a transition to the distyle in-antis plan; but temple 'FS' retains the inner row of columns at the front, together with the enclosed pronaos which is found in 'C,' thrust close against the inner row of columns on account of the shortened peristyle. While temple 'D' is more advanced as to its plan, and 'FS' seemingly a reversion, the opposite is the case with the entablatures: here temple 'D' retains the older traits, such as the alternating

[1] The difficult combination of frieze and cornice requires some discussion, since, though found together, it has hitherto been impossible to make them fit each other. The mutules, which project only 5 inches, are only 13⅝ inches wide as contrasted with 39 inches for the pentaglyphs. The mutule spacing seems to be one-third of the pentaglyph spacing, rather than half as usual; and presumably mutules were centred above pentaglyphs, the pomegranates helping to mitigate the discrepancy in width. In the known width of 65½ feet over the foundations there is room for nine pentaglyphs and eight metopes. Presumably the east front (now concealed under the Casa Marafioti) may have had three columns between antae, and the west end (which alone could be examined) may have formed a closed adytum. With a central column on the east front, we are probably to restore a single internal row of columns on the main axis.

system with narrow mutules over the metopes, whereas in temple 'FS' the mutules of the cornice are uniform throughout. Also the sculptured metopes on the façade of temple 'FS' (which in this respect also resembles 'C'), peculiarly constructed in two courses, descend nearly to 500 B.C., as if the temple were a long time in building. Among individual details, the raking cornice soffit of temple 'D' requires mention because of its division by means of offsets into four longitudinal bands, painted alternately white and dark blue; and the mutules of 'FS' are exceptional in having four rows each of six guttae. A special peculiarity of 'FS' was the use of a screen wall, 15 inches thick and 10 feet 5 inches high, to fill the lower parts of the intervals between the columns, evidently with the purpose of veiling ceremonial processions which took place in the pteroma, so that their lower parts seem engaged.

The largest temple ('GT') at Selinus, begun on the eastern plateau shortly after 'FS' and dedicated to Apollo, measured no less than about $164\frac{1}{4}$ by $361\frac{1}{4}$ feet, the first of the colossal structures of the west, vying with the Ionic temples of Asia Minor. Like them, too, it was octastyle; the flanks had seventeen columns (Fig. 28). It is now such a massive heap of ruins, overturned by earthquake (Plate XX), that exact measurement and analysis are as yet impossible. It is clear, however, that work started at the main east front, and that angle contraction had not yet been introduced, uniform spacing being employed across the east front and also down the flanks, though the flank spacing shows the same perverse increase that we met in the more justifiable cases of 'D' and 'FS'; the axial spacings exhibit the vast dimensions of 21 feet 5 inches (20 Doric feet) and 21 feet $8\frac{1}{4}$ inches ($20\frac{1}{4}$ Doric feet) on front and flanks, respectively. The west front, on account of the length of time required for the erection of the temple, was carried out in the style of the fifth century; and here angle contraction appears, to the extent of $12\frac{1}{2}$ inches, the normal axial spacings being increased to 21 feet $8\frac{1}{4}$ inches as on the flanks. The lower diameters were intended to be uniformly 9 feet $7\frac{3}{4}$ inches (9 Doric feet) on all sides; but the later columns of the west front were increased to 10 feet $8\frac{1}{2}$ inches (10 Doric feet). As the work proceeded slowly from east to west, even with the uniform lower diameters of the older columns (9 feet $7\frac{3}{4}$ inches), the upper diameters were successively increased from 5 feet $9\frac{1}{4}$ inches to 6 feet $3\frac{1}{2}$ inches and to 7 feet, while those of the heavier west columns were increased to 7 feet $7\frac{1}{2}$ inches. The height of the columns, assumed to have been 48 feet $2\frac{1}{2}$ inches,[1] would have been almost 5 diameters in the three earlier periods and only $4\frac{1}{2}$ diameters in the later work of the fifth century, yielding the curious anomaly of more slender columns in the earlier periods. The enormous capitals, still with the hollow scotia at the necking, have a spread of 12 feet $10\frac{1}{2}$ inches in the first two periods and of $2\frac{1}{4}$ inches more in the third; the developed fifth-century capitals of the west front have a spread of 13 feet $3\frac{1}{2}$ inches. The shafts are of various stages of workmanship, some merely blocked out in round drums, others trimmed to form twenty facets, while the southeast angle column and the second from the north show the preliminary fluting with wide fillets

---

[1] The preposterous heights of 58 feet as estimated by Cavallari, or of $53\frac{1}{2}$ feet as estimated by Hittorff and Koldewey, are not based on actual reconstruction of the fallen drums and are quite at variance with the permissible proportions in these periods. The height of 48 feet $2\frac{1}{2}$ inches is based on a study of the principles followed in Sicily at this time.

between as in Ionic columns, and the northeast angle column was completely finished with true Doric fluting. In the neighbouring quarries at Campobello are huge drums in the living rock, up to 12 feet in diameter and 14 feet in height, standing only 12 to 16 inches apart. The temple was never completed on account of the subjugation of the city by the Carthaginians in 409 B.C.; but the discouraging task must have been tentatively abandoned at an even earlier date, since traces of stucco finish survive even on cylindrical undressed column shafts. The entablature follows the precedent of 'FS', with wide mutules throughout.

The plan of the inner building repeats the general narrow proportions of the earlier temples at Selinus, the flank walls here aligning with the third column from each corner of the façade, leaving a pteroma of such depth that we have another example of the plan known as pseudo-dipteral. The clear span of the wooden ceiling beams between architrave and wall became about 38 feet. The tetrastyle pronaos of temple 'D' here reappears, with the difference that the columns are all free-standing, having on either flank an additional column and so two open bays as in the temple of Demeter at Paestum; the heavy square antae have capitals recalling those of the concave "Proto-Ionic" profile in the Basilica at Paestum, though here the Ionic volutes are combined with palmettes in the relief decoration of the surface. The result was a deep prostyle portico, with a clear area of about 59 by 65 feet which, unless there were interior columns, there could have been no intention of roofing; it may have formed an open court. From this, three doorways gave access to the cella, which was so wide that, alone among all the Sicilian temples,[1] it was subdivided by inner rows of columns, not merely by a central row of large columns as in some of the temples on the Italian mainland, but by two rows of smaller columns, probably fifteen on either side and arranged in three storeys, ninety interior columns in all. For these cella columns were so small in scale that even the lowest were only 3 feet $9\frac{1}{2}$ inches in diameter, with monolithic shafts and sixteen flutes. At the beginning, the rear compartment of the plan was probably intended to form a closed adytum; its transformation into an opisthodomus, and the transference of the adytum to the nave, probably represent fifth-century alterations.

About sixty miles to the east of Selinus along the coast lies the city of Acragas (Agrigentum or Girgenti), one of the most remarkable examples of the way in which the Greeks availed themselves of the peculiarities of the site to give grandeur and emphasis to their temples. A higher ridge on the north became the acropolis, surrounded with walls and crowned with the principal temple of Athena, of which only six columns remain, embedded under the church of S. Maria dei Greci; this acropolis is now the modern town of Agrigento. On the crest of the southern range, which lies parallel to the seaboard, and for the length of half a mile, are the remains of six temples. It is the magnificent treatment of the southern range which suggests one of the lessons that we may learn from Greek architecture. The Greeks did not think of cutting down the hills, or even of levelling the rock; they rather made the most of their natural character (Plate XXIV), wedded art to nature, and so united their work with the everlasting hills that it seems to be part of the same design. At the eastern, the highest,

[1] Apart from the primitive megaron on the Acropolis at Selinus. It is not probable that a hypaethral roof should be restored in temple 'GT.'

point of the range is the so-called temple of Hera Lacinia, raised on a platform to give it greater prominence. Then follow in succession the temples popularly ascribed to Concord, Heracles, Zeus Olympius, Castor and Pollux, and Hephaestus, of which, however, only that of Zeus Olympius is definitely named.

Though there are traces of earlier temples of moderate size at Acragas, it was not until the arrival of news of the huge undertaking in temple 'GT' at Selinus that the Acragantines bethought themselves of erecting monumental structures.[1] It was then that they began, out of rivalry with the Selinuntines, the most colossal temple ever created in Sicily, that of Zeus Olympius, its stylobate measuring about 173 feet by 361 feet, nearly three times the dimensions of the neighbouring temples of Concord and Hera Lacinia. The temple had seven columns on the main fronts, fourteen on the flanks, and is technically described as heptastyle pseudo-peripteral, that is, a peripteral temple of which the columns are engaged to the walls of the cella (Fig. 40). For the order was on so gigantic a scale that the intercolumniations were filled with screen walls, to assist in supporting the entablature; possibly the suggestion came from the screens of the mystery temple ('FS') at Selinus. It is as if, not satisfied with having copied the exact length of the stylobate of temple 'GT' and having exceeded the width by nearly 9 feet, the builders boastfully set out even to surpass the scale at Selinus, claiming that they could erect a wider façade with one column less. The results of their calculations were the huge axial spacings of 26 feet $4\frac{1}{2}$ inches on the fronts and of 26 feet $10\frac{1}{4}$ inches on the flanks (the greatest of all Doric axial spacings), showing the curious flank enlargement found also at Selinus. The column diameters, moreover, are as great as 13 feet $3\frac{1}{2}$ inches,[2] the largest ever constructed, exceeding by $3\frac{2}{3}$ feet the rival diameters at Selinus. It was obvious that such columns could not be built up in the usual manner with circular drums; the alternative was ashlar construction with the circumference divided into sectors by radial joints, the core being circular or polygonal in alternate courses. The capitals likewise were constructed in several pieces, the necking and echinus forming one course with a vertical joint, while the abacus made a separate course with two vertical joints, five blocks in all. Furthermore, even though the proportions were such

---

[1] Since this interpretation of the date and relationships of the temple of Zeus Olympius is contrary to the generally accepted theory, a word of explanation is advisable. Diodorus tells us that Carthaginian captives taken at the battle of Himera in 480 B.C. were set to work, not only on municipal projects at Acragas, but also on great temples for the gods. It has been inferred by our modern authorities that the temple of Zeus, being the largest of the temples of Acragas, was in consequence one of those to which Diodorus refers as constructed by Carthaginian prisoners, and that, as a further consequence, it dates from after 480 B.C., a great thankoffering for the victory at Himera. But it must be recalled that these great temples, like mediaeval cathedrals, required a long time for erection. The facial traits of the telamones are characteristic of sculpture of about 470 B.C.; but the foundations, as much as 87 feet below, were laid out for a plan still archaic in conception, based on temple 'GT' at Selinus, at a time when the idea of angle contraction, though as yet quite misunderstood (there being none on the fronts, while the flanks had two equally but inadequately contracted bays towards each corner), was beginning to percolate from the Greek mainland, at about 510 B.C.

[2] The terrific diameter of 14 feet $1\frac{1}{4}$ inches given by Koldewey and later writers is an error, resulting from confusion with the more easily measurable ring of the base.

that the intervals were reduced approximately to the size of the diameters themselves (barely less on the fronts, barely more on the flanks), the impossibility of securing architraves of such size made it necessary to build them up in three courses, with three blocks to each span and a joint exactly at midspan,

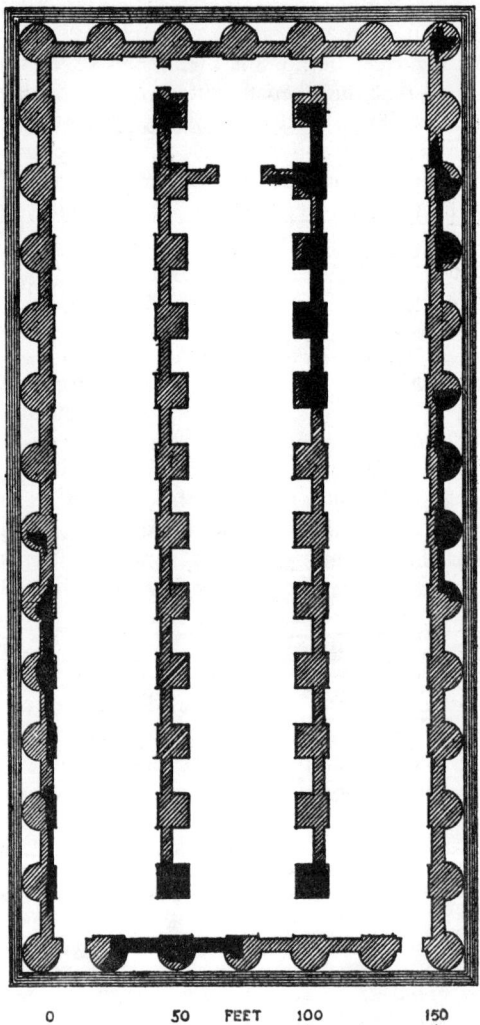

FIG. 40.—THE TEMPLE OF ZEUS OLYMPIUS AT ACRAGAS.

thus requiring intercolumnar support. The above-mentioned screen wall, by means of which the problem was solved, lies 5 inches behind the column centres; and from its inner face project pilasters, with their faces exactly tangent to the theoretical column circumferences as projected from the exterior. With a central column on each front, an axial entrance became impossible; and the preserved portions of the screen wall are just sufficient to prove, by elimination, that the only possible positions for entrances are the two angle intervals of the front, probably only at the east (Fig. 40).[1] The cella walls were composed of square piers corresponding to the pilasters, again with screen walls between; thus the entire plan is a compromise between a normal pseudo-dipteral temple with a one-aisled cella and a non-peripteral temple with a three-aisled cella (both the pseudo-dipteral idea and the three-aisled cella occurring in temple 'GT'). Just how the ceiling and roof would have been carried across the cella proper, with its clear span of 42 feet, is uncertain; possibly the Greeks themselves never solved the problem, since there is evidence that the roof was never built.

The height of the outer columns was probably 56 feet 7 inches (Fig. 41), that is, twenty-one wall courses besides the six corresponding to the bases and capitals, overtopping the huge columns at Selinus by nearly $8\frac{1}{2}$ feet.[2] The bases given to the columns, which are suggestive of Ionian influence, and the stylobate raised on a base with four steps below, are all innovations peculiar to this temple, which is just as remarkable for the unusual qualities of its design as for its size. In the column capitals, the echinus is of the developed stiff form and the necking lacks the scotia, suggesting that this level was not attained until well into the fifth century. The colossal telamones (atlantes), male figures used as architectural supports, 25 feet 2 inches high, were placed on the external screen walls, midway between the Doric columns, to assist in carrying the entablature. These are the figures from which is derived the popular name, "Temple of the Giants."[3] To give space for them, the screen wall was recessed still more at the top, the stilting of the column axes being increased to $17\frac{1}{4}$ inches; and the shelf of $12\frac{1}{4}$ inches thus formed was broadened by the use of a "belt course" three courses high, with a Doric hawksbeak moulding in the upper course and a carved Ionic egg-and-dart in the middle.[4] The style of the sculptured heads agrees with that

[1] An analogy for these two doorways in the corners may be found in the later temple of Apollo at Didyma near Miletus (see p. 231). It has recently been suggested that the entrance was at the middle of the south flank (with no corresponding entrance at the north); this rather illogical arrangement would be permissible in view of the absence of remains of the screen wall at this point, but the only positive argument, the fact that no remains of an intercolumnar telamon happened to be discovered at this spot, is in reality no argument at all since telamones were required in every interval and any door lintels would have been below the level of their feet.

[2] As in the case of temple 'GT,' the height at Acragas is usually exaggerated; that shown in Fig. 41, for instance, 63 feet or thirty wall courses, should be diminished by the omission of three wall courses. Krischen even suggests a height of $71\frac{1}{2}$ feet or thirty-four courses, using Koldewey's excessive diameter and a proportion dubiously based on the golden section.

[3] The location of the telamones is still disputed. The fragments of one of them were collected and pieced together by Cockerell, who, in his restoration, assumed that they were raised on the square piers of the interior of the cella and carried the timber roof; and some still adhere to this view. But Koldewey rightly placed them on the external screen walls between the columns, such being the relative positions in which they were found lying on the ground.

[4] Thus the form of the belt course shown in Fig. 41, while properly three courses high (the bottom course should project more and cast a pronounced shadow), is imaginary as to profile and requires correction. In spite of its errors, however, Koldewey's restoration is much better than others more recently published. Pace and Pierce wrongly assume that the engaged columns were exact semicircles from bottom to top (without stilting); and, having no shelf, they decided that the telamones must be inside the cella where Cockerell had put

103

of the column capitals in that they should be dated about 470 B.C.; so that we may infer that the temple had reached nearly this level when the Carthaginian captives taken at the battle of Himera in 480 B.C. were put to work on it, as Diodorus relates.[1] Even the support afforded by the heads and forearms of the

FIG. 41.—EXTERIOR ORDER OF THE OLYMPIEUM AT ACRAGAS.
(Restored by Koldewey.)

telamones was regarded as insufficient, however, so that iron beams 14 or 15 feet long and as much as 5 inches wide and 12 inches high were let into the

them. Marconi and Leporini likewise adopted the shelfless wall; but, realising that the telamones were outside, they restored a single corbel under each, in a way that is structurally impossible and aesthetically makes the telamones resemble gigantic tassels suspended from the architrave which they purport to sustain.

[1] To say that the unusual device of employing engaged columns was due to Carthaginian inspiration, as suggested by Drerup, is absurd; they had been planned long before, by ingenious Greek architects overcoming hitherto unsolved problems, and were destined to influence much later work, as the engaged columns of the temples of Asclepius at Acragas and of Serapis at Taormina, and even as far afield as the west wall of the Erechtheum at Athens, the stoa at Epidaurus, the Lion Tomb at Cnidus, the magazine hall in the south market at Delos, and the Bouleuterion at Miletus.

TEMPLE OF HERACLES AT ACRAGAS

soffits of the architraves, resting on the edges of the column capitals. The metopes were uncarved, but sculpture in relief exists on the tympanum blocks of the pediments, of which the subject was, according to Diodorus, the battle of the gods and giants on the east, the fall of Troy on the west. Diodorus also tells us, as does Polybius before him, that the temple was roofless and unfinished, because of the Carthaginian invasion in 406 B.C.; and this seems to be borne out by the condition of the upper member of the cornice, of which the unfinished top on the flanks was apparently to have been carved in the form of tiles.[1]

Of the numerous other temples at Acragas, only that ascribed to Heracles is of our period, dating from the last years of the sixth century. This is of the ordinary hexastyle peripteral type; and in it appears, for the first time in Sicily, a column spacing uniform on all sides, apart from the corners, where a partially misunderstood angle contraction is applied to the fronts but not to the flanks. We must emphasise the curious fact that angle contraction, a century older on the Greek mainland, did not reach any of the western colonies until 480 B.C., except in these two partial applications of the preceding decades, the temples of Zeus and Heracles at Acragas. In the latter temple the stiff echinus of the Greek mainland capitals for the first time appears in the west, combined with a last effort to retain the hollow scotia cutting back into the shaft; at a later period (as in temple 'C' at Selinus) the fluting was carried up through the scotia in stucco, and three shallow grooves in the stucco now defined the necking in a manner more agreeable to the taste of later times. The mutules of the cornice, as in temple 'FS,' have twenty-four guttae arranged in four rows. Particularly imposing is the great vertical sima of limestone, 2 feet $8\frac{1}{2}$ inches high, with groups of mouldings in the upper half and a painted fascia with lion heads in the lower. The problem of roofing the great width of the cella, 38 feet 10 inches, must have required considerable ingenuity (probably involving the use of braced beams), and bears witness to the pertinacity of Sicilian architects in avoiding interior columns. Evidence of the destruction of the temple by the Carthaginians in 406 B.C. appears in the cracked and flaked surfaces of the stone, reddened by fire to a depth of 2 inches, and in the eventual Roman repairs.[2]

We return for a moment to the Greek mainland to examine the temple of Aphaea at Aegina, the most perfectly developed of the late archaic temples in European Hellas, though it really belongs to the beginning of the fifth century (Fig. 42; Plate XXIV). It is still fairly well preserved, and was built in the limestone of the district, coated with a thin layer of stucco, and richly painted; the pediment sculptures, and the tiles on the pediments and eaves, were of Parian marble, the other tiles being of terracotta. The temple was hexastyle,

---

[1] Disregarding the carved tympanum blocks, Pace and Pierce assumed that the metopes contained the sculpture and that the temple was planned without pediments, with a flat or truncated hip roof and with the cella hypaethral or open to the sky. Needless to say, this restoration is quite contrary to the facts. On the other hand, efforts to assign to the roof a few fragments of archaic terracotta tiles found during excavation seem to be contradicted by the date of the fragments and the improbability that there was a roof.

[2] Several of the columns on the south flank have now been reconstructed; the south wall of the cella lies flat on the floor, with the blocks in their proper relative positions, just as it was upset during an earthquake.

THE RISE OF THE DORIC STYLE

with only twelve columns on the flanks. Access to the east façade was provided by a sloping ramp of the height of the three steps. Here was made one of those rare efforts to execute a design with simple dimensions; the columns are 3 Doric feet in diameter, and their axial spacing, at least on the fronts, 8 Doric feet (slightly less on the flanks), the width of the stylobate being $42\frac{1}{12}$ Doric feet. The columns being of uniform diameter on all sides, a new method of emphasis was adopted by slightly thickening the corner columns.[1] A detail of special interest is the fact that, while all other shafts of the peristyle are monolithic, three adjacent columns of the north flank were built up with drums, obviously for the purpose of leaving a gap until the last possible moment to facilitate the erection of the interior, after which the limited space demanded the use of smaller units for the remaining columns. The existence within the cella of superposed rows of columns on each side has sometimes been regarded as evidence that the centre was open to the sky, forming a hypaethron or opaion. But the primary object of such columns was to carry a flat ceiling and to assist in supporting the beams of the roof; for although there were undoubtedly some exceptional instances of hypaethral temples, such as two unfinished colossal archaic temples (that of Zeus Olympius at Acragas and the Heraeum at Samos), the later temple of Apollo at Didyma near Miletus, and the temple of Zeus Olympius at Athens at the time that it was mentioned by Vitruvius, they were probably extremely rare. The roof was normally unbroken throughout its length, though some of the tiles may have been pierced to admit light to the attic space.[2] With regard to another assumed function of such interior rows of columns in two storeys, the theory that they supported a gallery floor resting on the intervening architrave, this is incorrect in the case of most temples; but it so happens that this temple at Aegina, though originally so constructed that a visitor standing on the aisle floor could look directly up to the main ceiling, eventually received extemporised gallery floors to which access was had by ladders. The taper of the lower columns was continuous with that of the upper columns, which in consequence have a lower diameter slightly less than that at the necking of the lower columns, on account of the

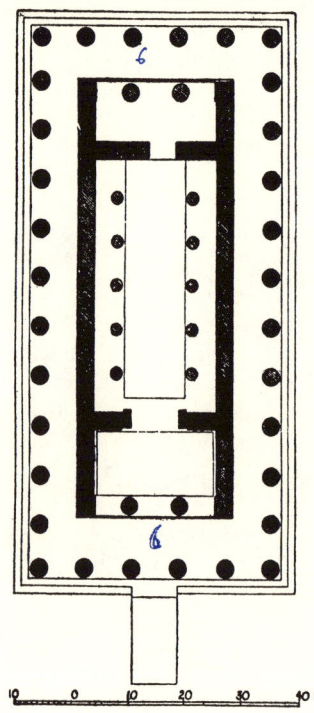

Fig. 42.—The Temple of Aphaea at Aegina.

---

[1] This enlargement, noted by Cockerell, was wrongly denied in the German publication.
[2] See below, with reference to Olympia and Bassae. Cockerell found at Aegina a block which he had the appearance of being a coping-stone to an opening of some sort, and hence employed it for an opaion in the roof. But it has since been proved that this was part of an acroterion base at the apex of the pediment.

interruption caused by the architrave. As in other temples, the inner architrave is decorated with regulae and guttae even though the triglyph frieze is omitted; and the ends are merely bonded into the cross-walls, there being no antae responding to the inner colonnades. A curious feature is the doorway from the cella to the opisthodomus, off axis, and obviously an afterthought; it was pierced after the lower courses of the cross-wall had been laid.

To the pediments of this temple belong elaborate marble sculptures, carved in the round and representing in almost identical fashion two combats before Troy in the presence of Athena.[1] Each apex was crowned by a great floral acroterion flanked by female figures, and at the lower angles were griffins. But the problem is complicated by the fact that we possess the remains of three sets of pediment sculptures, and three great floral acroteria once crowning the pediments, whereas only two positions were available. We may perhaps conclude that the more archaic west pediment was completed before 490 B.C., along with the temple architecture, and the east pediment a little after 490 B.C.; the latter may then have been injured during some raid, perhaps by the Persians at the time of the battle of Salamis, and have been replaced by the final east pediment sculptures (which seem to date from just after 480), their damaged predecessors being set up opposite the east front as a memorial of the war.[2] Other pediment sculptures were employed in a second temple of this period at Aegina, that of Apollo in the port.[3]

Another temple erected so shortly before 490 B.C. that it was not quite finished at the time of the Persian invasion in that year, when it apparently suffered from a raid, was the older temple of Poseidon at Sunium. Only parts of the platform under the later marble temple, and scattered pieces of columns and entablature used in later structures, survive at the present day; but from these we learn that, even more than at Aegina, the temple was intended to embody new and definite principles of design. Not only were the columns 3 Doric feet in diameter on all sides, but the axial spacings were likewise uniform, $7\frac{1}{2}$ Doric feet or $2\frac{1}{2}$ diameters except at the contracted corners; the peristyle had the characteristic fifth-century plan with one more than twice the number of front columns on the flanks, six by thirteen, and the stylobate, if finished, would have had the simple dimensions of 40 by $92\frac{1}{2}$ Doric feet.

* * * * *

Strictly speaking, we should terminate our consideration of the archaic Doric style at this point, having attained the historical and cultural limit marked by the year 490 B.C. But it seems advisable to continue with Sicily and South Italy,

[1] These sculptures, now in Munich, were discovered by Cockerell, Foster, Haller von Hallerstein, and Linckh in 1811, and were sold at auction to the Crown Prince of Bavaria, who had them restored by Thorwaldsen; other pieces were discovered by a German expedition in 1903.

[2] For such war memorials see the instances at Athens, pp. 91, 150. This explanation seems preferable to the alternative that the "non-pedimental" sculptures were set up east of the temple by the loser in a sculptural competition; for in a competition the medium would have been clay, and it is hardly likely that the loser would have perpetuated his design in marble at full size, even to the acroterion.

[3] Of this temple, formerly attributed to Aphrodite, only the stump of one opisthodomus column now stands, where there were two with their architrave in 1814. In that year a fragment of sculpture was excavated by Cockerell, and others have been found recently.

examining some of the colonial temples of the fifth century which cannot properly be regarded as representative of the culmination on the Greek mainland.

Besides the two very early examples at Syracuse, we must refer to one later temple, in the island of Ortygia—the temple of Athena, apparently begun by Gelon (who, having made himself master of Gela, obtained possession of Syracuse in 485 B.C.) after the battle of Himera in 480 B.C., though it must have been finished by his brother Hieron I who began to reign two years later.[1] The temple was hexastyle (Fig. 43), with fourteen columns on the flanks, but differs from the ordinary plan because of an innovation which must be traced back to Ionic influence, though the old temple of Apollo at Syracuse was the vicarious agent. In other words, the graduated spacing of the front columns, suggested in the temple of Apollo, was here more systematically applied, even to the flanks, where the two spacings nearest each corner were narrowed like those on the fronts. Thus originated the system of double contraction which became characteristic of many of the fifth-century Doric temples of the west; it formed a subtle method of distributing the distortion caused by angle contraction, so that it is somewhat astonishing not to find it in other parts of the Greek world.[2] Among the notable features of the temple of Athena were its splendid doors of gold and ivory, and the statue of Athena on the summit of a pediment with a golden shield visible from far at sea. Another trophy of the battle of Himera was the temple of Victory at Himera itself, with an almost identical plan, though very little now stands above the stylobate level. Analysis of the plan yields the very curious fact that it was originally designed with double contraction on the fronts only, with single contraction on the flanks; yet, before the stylobate blocks were actually cut to fit the column spacing, it was decided

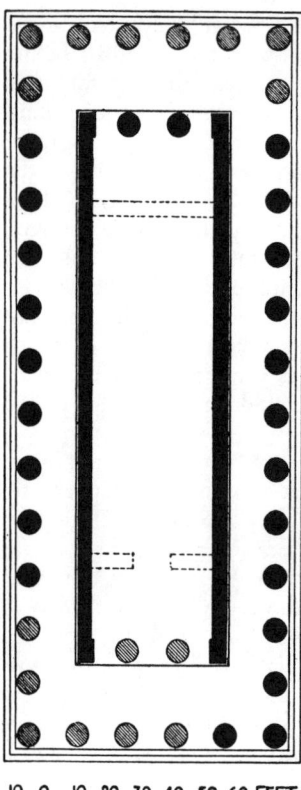

FIG. 43.—TEMPLE OF ATHENA AT SYRACUSE.

---

[1] The temple owes its partial preservation to the fact that it was converted into the cathedral of the city; the cella became the nave, and the cutting of large arched openings through the ashlar flank walls (but lined with true arches) into the peristyle on either side, and the filling of the intercolumniations with walls, permitted the use of the flank colonnades as lateral aisles, while the rear end was eventually rebuilt as a baroque church façade. Restorations were conducted in 1927, removing the plaster from the walls to reveal the ancient jointed masonry, and clearing away as many obstructions as possible.

[2] The absence of double contraction in the Parthenon and other temples of the mainland must here be emphasised in view of recurring but careless statements that such gradation exists among them.

to employ double contraction on the flanks as well, and in order to effect this, with the total length of the stylobate already fixed by the lower steps, it became necessary to widen all the intervening axial spacings on the flanks by $\frac{7}{8}$ inch. Another strange feature pertains to the marvellously carved lion-head spouts of the flank sima; for they are spaced 3 feet $8\frac{3}{8}$ inches on centres, quite without relation to the triglyph spacing of 6 feet $10\frac{5}{8}$ inches, and examination reveals that the total length of the flank sima had been divided into a number of intervals deficient by one.[1] Two stone staircases, on either side of the cella doorway, gave access to the attic or roof space above the ceiling, a habit which became prevalent during this period among the western colonies.

Not all of the Sicilian temples dating after 480 B.C. exhibit double contraction, which, apart from the two above-mentioned examples by Syracusan architects, seems to have been unknown elsewhere for about twenty years longer. For single contraction itself was such a recent idea that it had not yet run its course. Thus the southernmost of the three great temples on the eastern plateau at Selinus, 'ER' (Fig. 28; Plate XX), was apparently begun at about the same time as the temples at Syracuse and Himera, just after 480 B.C. In scale it is enormous, the largest of the temples in the west apart from the two colossi at Selinus and Acragas; the columns are 7 feet $5\frac{1}{2}$ inches in diameter, and the angle contraction is uniformly 12 inches at each corner. The great length of the flank, with fifteen columns, is due to the fact that the plan of the inner building is a compromise between the traditional Selinuntine type and the opisthodomus of the Greek mainland, yielding a succession of four rooms, pronaos, cella, adytum, and opisthodomus; the antae are of developed form with narrow outer returns, and both porches have two columns in-antis. Above the porches were sculptured metopes such as in earlier examples ('C' and 'FS') had been applied to the façades; the reliefs as usual were executed in limestone, but in this instance with white marble inserts for the faces, hands, and feet of the feminine figures; and the top of the pronaos architrave taenia was bevelled to permit a better view of the lower portions. At about the same time was carried out the west front of the great temple 'GT,' likewise with single contraction and with an opisthodomus instead of the presumably originally intended adytum.

In Acragas at this same time, as we have seen, work was being prosecuted on the huge Olympieum. Under the latter's influence, apparently, was now begun a smaller temple on the northern hill, dedicated to Athena, hexastyle but of unknown length; single contraction appeared on the fronts and probably also on the flanks.[2] The influence of the Olympieum consists in the remarkably close spacing of the columns, which could have had no structural reason at this small scale; the intervals are hardly, if at all, greater than the column diameters. At about the same time, also, was erected at Acragas a small but beautiful temple of Demeter consisting merely of a cella and pronaos, the latter distyle in-antis; the style of the lion heads of the sima is of the decade 480-470 B.C.[3]

---

[1] The discrepancy in spacing had led Koldewey to doubt the attribution of the lion heads to this temple; but no doubt is now permissible since simas and cornice blocks have been found lying in their original relationship.

[2] The remains of this temple are visible beneath the church of S. Maria dei Greci.

[3] This temple is partly incorporated into the little Norman church of S. Biagio.

Slightly later is a normal peripteral temple in the same city, popularly attributed to Hera Lacinia (Plate XXIV), hexastyle and with the usual number of thirteen columns on the flanks. Unusual, however, is the reduction of the column diameters on the flanks (the only other Sicilian example being temple 'C' at Selinus), accompanied by a similar reduction of the axial spacing so that the columnar intervals are identical on all sides.[1]

The true temple of Hera Lacinia, out on the tip of Capo Colonna at Croton, was formerly the most splendid temple of South Italy, with rich treasures of sculpture and painting. Now only one column survives; but three centuries ago there were two, and it was then evident that there had once been forty-eight. From this number, as compared with the trenches for the foundations, it seems clear that the peristyle was hexastyle with sixteen columns on the flanks, and with a second colonnade across the front in the old Sicilian manner; the porches would have been distyle in-antis. The few known details of the architecture, with the columns inclined inward, and of the fragments of Parian marble pedimental sculpture, show that this was not an archaic temple but one rather of the second quarter of the fifth century, so that the double façade was a revival.[2] Its marble roof tiles were famous in antiquity.

Gradually the theory of double contraction, as evolved by Gelon's architects at Syracuse and Himera, began to penetrate to other western colonies. At Selinus, perhaps at about 460 B.C., was begun temple 'A' (Fig. 28), hexastyle and with fourteen columns on the flanks; the fronts had double contraction, while single contraction appeared on the flanks, so that it was of the hybrid class to which the original design of the temple at Himera had belonged.[3] In this, as well as in temple 'O' which seems to have been similar, both the adytum and opisthodomus appear as in temple 'ER.' Another and more notable example of this hybrid class is the largest of the temples at Paestum, that of Poseidon (Neptune), one of the best preserved of all ancient temples (Fig. 36; Plate XXV). It seems to have replaced the older temple known as the "Basilica" which stood beside it in the same precinct. The relative proportion of the diameter to the height of the columns, 1 to 4.21 and 1 to 4.36, might seem at first glance to suggest an earlier date, but these heavy proportions are due only to the great size of the columns (the diameters being 6 feet 11 inches and 6 feet 8 inches), the Greeks always observing the practice of making large Doric columns heavier in proportions than small ones. On the other hand, the mere fact that the temple follows, at least in part, the principle of double contraction is not to be taken as evidence of lateness.[4] The true date must be about 460 B.C. It

[1] This difference in the column diameters has not been hitherto noticed. On the other hand, the upward curvature of the platform assumed to appear in this temple is fictitious, having been created by the lens of a camera.

[2] Most of the temple was removed by Bishop Lucifero to obtain material for building his palace in the sixteenth century. American excavations, prematurely interrupted, took place in 1886 and revealed what little we know of the plan; additional excavation in 1910 yielded only fragments of details.

[3] The presence of double contraction on the fronts of temple 'A' has not been previously recognised.

[4] Thus Koldewey and Puchstein employ the fallacious argument that the temple must be later than the Parthenon merely because double contraction does not appear in the latter; but the same argument would prove that Paestum was also later than all the temples of the fourth century and of all the subsequent periods on the Greek mainland!

would seem that the peristyle was planned to have uniform axial spacings on all sides, with single contraction, and with the diameters of the flank columns reduced as in the contemporary temple of Hera Lacinia at Acragas.[1] As at Himera, however, the flanks were revised to permit the use of double contraction, but at the cost of widening all the intervening axial spacings by $1\frac{3}{8}$ inches, resulting in the anomaly of smaller flank diameters associated with wider spacings. The columns are unusual in having twenty-four flutes, as at Corcyra and Tarentum; though for the interior columns of the cella the number of flutes was reduced to twenty in the lower and to sixteen in the upper storey. For the cella, for the first time in Italy, contains double ranges of superposed columns (Plate XXV), the sole object of which would appear to have been the support of the ceiling and roof, as there is no trace of any gallery, and the steps behind the pronaos led only to the roof. The steps, furthermore, occur only on the right hand of one entering; the corresponding compartment on the left was merely a closet and never contained stairs, so that a gallery over the left aisle, had such existed, would have been inaccessible.[2] The two storeys of columns are separated merely by an architrave with a continuous crowning moulding instead of regulae and guttae; and the lower diameters of the upper columns are considerably less than the upper diameters of those below, in order that the lines of diminution might be continuous. This temple at Paestum is the only one that preserves intact this characteristic interior treatment.

The final stage of the fifth-century development in the western colonies is represented by the adoption of double contraction on all sides of the peristyle. This uniform treatment seems to have appeared at about 430 B.C.[3] in another of the best preserved of Greek temples, that popularly attributed to Concord at Acragas (Plate XXVI).[4] This temple is very similar, in its main dimensions and arrangements, to that of Hera Lacinia near by; but the proportions and details belong to a later phase. The interior is so complete as still to show the cornice running round above the cella, with a sinking to receive a flat ceiling, while above, in the cross-walls of the pronaos and opisthodomus, are openings to allow of a free passage through the attic space from one end to the other, with very inclined jambs and ogee enframements. Here we have our best examples of stone stairways leading directly to the attic space and provided for that sole purpose, there having been no galleries or interior columns.[5] Two other Doric temples at Acragas seem to date from about the same time, both being peripteral with six by thirteen columns, attributed in one case to Hephaestus and in the other to Castor and Pollux. The former is unfinished, the columns having received only the preliminary fluting, perhaps as a con-

[1] This difference in the column diameters at Paestum again has escaped attention.

[2] It has been customary to restore stairways symmetrically on both sides.

[3] The date may be fairly accurately fixed by the fact that the bed moulding of the cornice seems to be later than the Propylaea at Athens (437-432 B.C.); yet the temple must be earlier than that at Segesta.

[4] Like the temple of Athena at Syracuse, it owes its preservation to the fact that it was at one time converted into a church by walling up the flank columns and piercing arches through the flank walls to form aisle arcades.

[5] Besides the rectangular stair-wells just mentioned at Himera and Paestum and in the temple of Concord at Acragas, others occur in the temples of Heracles, Hera Lacinia, and Asclepius at Acragas, while circular stair-wells occur in temple 'A' at Selinus, all of these (except the temple at Paestum) lacking interior columns.

sequence of the Carthaginian invasion in 406 B.C.; and in the latter may be noted the Hellenistic cornice (due either to damage or incompletion of the original structure) with its unusually heavy bed mouldings (a carved egg-and-dart and astragal below the cyma reversa) and the weighty sima carried on iron cantilevers to relieve the cornice.[1]

The latest and at the same time the most impressive of these temples, owing to its isolated position in the hills and its perfect preservation, is the one at Segesta, in the northwest of Sicily (Plate XXVII). This non-Greek city of the native Elymian race, lying west of the true Greek cities, had been at odds with its powerful neighbour Selinus ever since 580 B.C. Because of these political differences Segesta had been allied with the Carthaginians in 509 B.C., and both in 453 and 426 B.C. it was cultivated by the Athenians in opposition to Syracuse; and finally, after the Athenian defeat at Syracuse in 413 B.C., Segesta again called in the Carthaginians and was responsible for the disastrous invasions of 409-405 B.C. which destroyed Selinus, Acragas, Gela, Himera, and Camarina. The temple is a silent witness to these last events, having apparently been begun during the alliance with Athens after 426 B.C., and the cause of its incompletion was evidently the stagnation resulting from the subjugation of the island by the Carthaginians in 409 B.C. Hexastyle and with fourteen columns on the flanks, the peristyle has columns of uniform diameter throughout (6 Doric feet), without the angle enlargement customary during the fifth century in Greece; the normal spacing is also uniform on fronts and flanks, and the amount of the angle contraction was carefully divided into thirds, one-third being assigned to the second interval and two-thirds to the endmost interval at each corner. It has also other points of interest in that, never having been completed, the columns retain their cylindrical mantles, the fluting not being worked; also the stones of the stylobate are only drafted, retaining their rough surfaces and the ancones or bosses by which the blocks were hoisted, since even the lowest stones of the visible structure were carefully handled by derricks. The cella, furthermore, was apparently never built (Plate XXVII); and this fact not only illustrates the complete independence of the peristyle, but suggests that in these peripteral temples the first part executed was not the cella but the peristyle.[2]

A glance at the table of Doric temples arranged in chronological order, given at the end of this book, will show that the proportions of the columns and entablatures do not by any means vary directly in accordance with the dates of the temples, as is sometimes lightly remarked. Only in the broadest sense may we trace a general tendency from heaviness toward lightness; but this tendency was so confused by geographical considerations, by the relative sizes of the temples (contrast Figs. 24 and 27, columns of the same date), and by the archaic custom of using different diameters and spacings on the fronts and

[1] The picturesque artificial ruin well known to all visitors as the temple of Castor and Pollux was erected in 1836-1871, not even in its correct position, and composed of elements which may come from different buildings. Of the temple of Hephaestus there are only two surviving columns. Koldewey and Puchstein assigned both temples to the third century, but Marconi's arguments for a fifth-century date seem reasonable.

[2] Other Greek Doric temples of the sixth and fifth centuries in the western colonies, as at Velia, Hipponium, Caulonia, Gela, Camarina, Megara Hyblaea, etc., do not contain peculiarities that require special examination.

flanks, that careful analysis is required before we can discern the principles upon which the architects worked. But such problems of proportion, like matters of construction and technique, would carry us far beyond the allowable limits of this book, and must in general be passed over.

* * * * *

Very different in plan from the ordinary Greek temple was the type erected at Eleusis in honour of Demeter; for this was rather a Hall of the Mysteries, a hall of initiation, than an ordinary temple intended to serve as the dwelling of a divinity. This type, after the experimental forms employed in the Aegean period and again during the primitive stage of the sanctuary,[1] was defined as a square in plan, with its roof supported internally by a forest of columns, recalling an Egyptian hypostyle hall. The sixth-century "temple," only a quarter of the size of the great structure designed in the Periclean period, was erected by Peisistratus and destroyed by Xerxes. It contained five rows each of five columns, the central column showing that there was as yet no central lantern or opaion but rather that it was lighted from windows high in the external walls; against the walls on three sides (but not on the front) were nine tiers of stone steps, too narrow for use as seats. On the southeast front was a portico of nine Doric columns; the construction was entirely of poros limestone, apart from the marble raking cornice and simas of the pediment (with false spouts in the form of ram's heads at the corners), roof tiles, and a floral apex acroterion.

Up to the present our references to the temples have treated them as isolated buildings irrespective of their surrounding dependencies and enclosures. But the most important temples of Greece were invariably surrounded by a wall forming a sacred enclosure or temenos (hieron), in which the principal shrine and other subsidiary buildings connected with it were erected. In some cases, as on the Acropolis at Athens, an entire rocky hill was girdled with walls and formed the sacred enclosure (Fig. 44; Plate LI); in other cases, as at Olympia (Fig. 4), where the site was a fertile valley, or as at Delphi, on the slope of a great hill (Plate XXVIII), an area of arbitrary shape was laid out and enclosed. These precincts contained not only the great temple of the presiding deity, and minor temples dedicated to other deities, but treasuries erected by various cities to contain their offerings and the regalia of their processions; also, stoas or covered colonnades, on the walls of which were painted episodes of history or mythology; altars; and votive columns and statues, set up in memory of victors in the games, of heroes, or of munificent donors. In addition, the enclosures were often planted with trees and sacred groves, and provided with colonnades and exedras (semicircular seats or shallow walled recesses) given by wealthy devotees. The conjectural restorations of Olympia, Epidaurus, Delphi, Delos, and Eleusis, based on the actual foundations and on the architectural remains so far as the buildings are concerned, and supplemented by the addition of the groves of sacred trees with which the sanctuaries were planted, have suggested a magnificence, a combination of nature and art, which it is now difficult to realise to its fullest extent, and of which the only parallel is to be found in some

---

[1] For the oblong Aegean megaron at Eleusis, see p. 24. That of the primitive period is now represented only by two walls meeting at right angles; but from the contours of the ground it is evident that we must restore, not a square, but an oblong facing northeast.

of the Buddhist sanctuaries in India, China, and Japan, where, in consequence of a somewhat similar cult, temples, tombs, and other monuments exist up to the present day. Researches on many of the mainland sites have been greatly facilitated by the writings of Pausanias, who may be looked upon as the

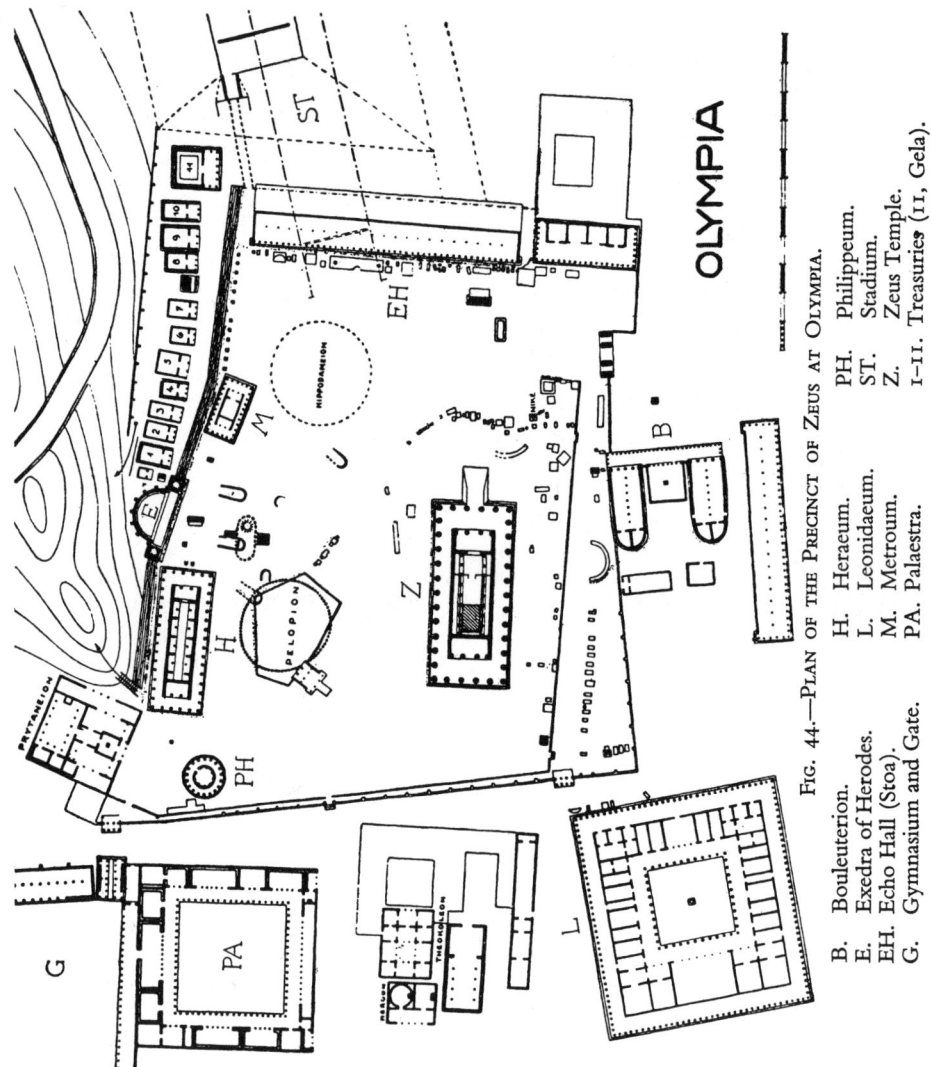

FIG. 44.—PLAN OF THE PRECINCT OF ZEUS AT OLYMPIA.

B. Bouleuterion.
E. Exedra of Herodes.
EH. Echo Hall (Stoa).
G. Gymnasium and Gate.
H. Heraeum.
L. Leonidaeum.
M. Metroum.
PA. Palaestra.
PH. Philippeum.
ST. Stadium.
Z. Zeus Temple.
1–11. Treasuries (11, Gela).

"Baedeker" or "Murray" of ancient Greece, and with whose descriptions it has been possible to walk through the sacred precincts and to locate the principal monuments, giving them their true names and dates—a course which has been made easier by the numerous inscriptions on all the sites.

Most of the entrance gateways or propylaea of the archaic precincts were subsequently demolished and rebuilt, and so need not detain us. But one example, at Aegina, continued to stand through ancient times, so that its simple elements are available for examination. The width was only 24 feet, the depth 20½ feet, with a cross-wall exactly midway between the outer and inner fronts. These, both distyle in-antis, had interesting slender octagonal columns only 20¼ inches in diameter at the bottom, 13½ inches at the top, and spaced 8 feet 5 inches on centres. With such proportions, the architrave must have been of wood; and probably the ridge of the roof coincided with the cross-wall, the rafters descending toward front and back in a practical though not monumental fashion.

Akin to the temples, and situated within the sacred enclosure of the Altis of Olympia, were buildings known as Treasuries, which were built by the various

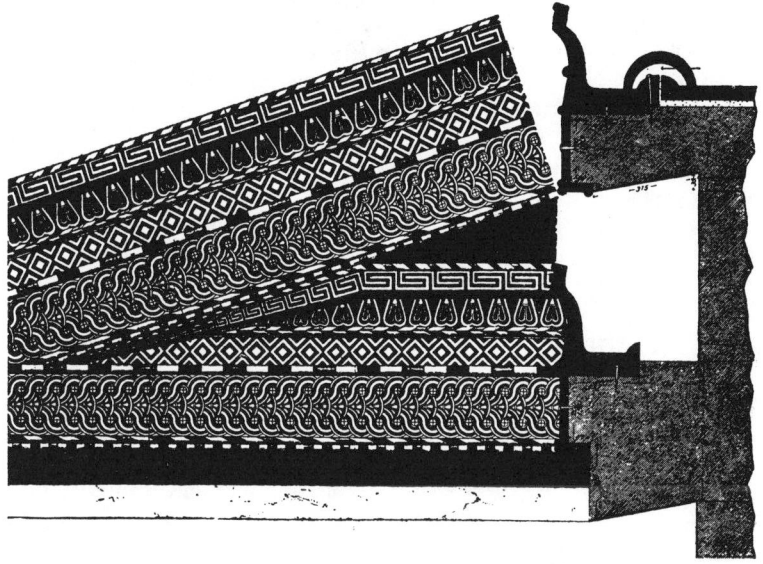

Fig. 45.—Terracotta Facing of Cornices, Treasury of Gela at Olympia.
(Colours: Light yellow, red, and black.)

cities taking part in the Olympic games, for the reception of their most valuable offerings, arms, and other properties. Similar treasuries existed at Delphi, Delos and other sacred shrines to which pilgrimages were made. The plans of eleven of these treasuries have been laid bare at Olympia, on a terrace at the foot of Mount Cronus (Fig. 44, at nos. 1–11). Each of these buildings normally consists of a chamber about 16 to 20 feet square, preceded by a portico in-antis; and all of those at Olympia are of the Doric order. One of the treasuries, that of Gela (Fig. 44, at no. 11), is of nondescript character and of more imposing size than usual; the chamber measures about 42 feet by 35 feet, and at a later date a hexastyle Doric portico was added to it. Among the most notable features of the original building are the profile of the cornice without mutules, and the presence of nails which showed that the cornices were protected or sheathed with terracotta slabs. And of the slabs themselves numerous bright-coloured examples were found (Fig. 45), illustrating the peculiar use of the sima on the horizontal cornice under the pediment as well as on the flanks, and the manner in which all the decorative patterns on this sima taper in order to fit into the angles of the pediment. Such evidence has shown that this treasury was built by Sicilian architects and that the terracottas themselves were imported from Gela in the south of Sicily. The protection of timber cornices by terracotta plaques was universal in Greece, but this is one of the transitional instances in which the tradition was extended to the sheathing of stone. The date of this treasury is probably about 540 B.C.,[1] the portico having been added half a century later.

Less abnormal are the other treasuries at Olympia, of which the Syracusan shows the peculiar architrave taenia with the sunken astragal, sometimes found in Sicily; the columns, too, have a similar treatment of countersunk astragals in sixteen of the arrises, while the alternating sixteen are sharp; and a sunken astragal encircles the echinus just above the range of overhanging leaves on the necking. The cornice also is peculiar in the cavetto substituted for the usual vertical face; and the mutules, like the regulae, have only four guttae in each row. In the case of the Metapontine treasury the triglyph frieze is peculiar in the offsets below the pointed arched tops of the glyphs, and in the extra fascia crowning the frieze. The Selinuntine and Megarian treasuries are regular examples of the last quarter of the sixth century. Of the former, the Doric capitals lack carved annulets and the mutules lack guttae. In the Megarian treasury an interesting feature is the transition, or lack of it, between the entablature on the façade and the bare walls on the flanks, each architrave return showing a half regula, while the triglyph does not even turn the corner, and the cornice abruptly changes to a curved soffit without mutules. Particularly important is the sculptured pediment of the Megarian treasury, a battle of the gods and giants in high relief. The latest of the archaic treasuries is that of the Sicyonians, a normal structure of good proportions, with a little astragal introduced as the crowning feature of triglyphs and metopes, and with marble simas and tiling in which the cover-tiles (or antefixes) and pan-tiles are all in one piece, as later at Bassae.[2]

Among the Doric treasuries at Delphi the earliest of interest, apart from the somewhat nondescript Corinthian treasury, is that of the Syracusans, dating from the middle of the sixth century and demolished after 413 B.C. to make way for a successor commemorating the Athenian defeat. The older building had an unusual plan, prostyle tetrastyle,[3] with very slender and proportionately

[1] The Geloan terracottas have usually been dated much too early, while Darsow has recently preferred the excessively late date of 500 B.C. because of the circumscribed palmette ornament appearing on the flanks (not shown in Fig. 45). But circumscribed palmettes appear just after the middle of the sixth century on Rhodian and Samian pottery, and also on one of the Larisa terracotta friezes, so that a date of about 540 B.C. is possible.

[2] The date contemporary with the Parthenon sometimes assigned to the Sicyonian treasury, merely because of the little astragal at the top of the frieze, is certainly much too late.

[3] My identification of the treasury as Syracusan has not been uniformly accepted, some still preferring to retain the Sicyonian attribution because the materials were later used at second hand in the Sicyonian foundations. Also the plan is sometimes restored as a simple columned pavilion of four by five columns without walls, an improbable interpretation. A terracotta sima of typical Sicilian profile found at Delphi may perhaps come from this treasury.

widely spaced columns, though only 4 feet 2¼ inches on centres. The frieze of the façade had triglyphs only above the columns, exactly as in the earliest temples at Syracuse, omitting those midway between so that the metopes were oblong, 33½ to 34½ inches in length but only 22 inches high; and this same wide spacing was carried all round the building. The metopes were filled with sculpture in accordance with the Sicilian custom. The regulae below and the mutules above the triglyphs have five guttae in each row, while the alternating mutules above the metopes have only four, as in the early archaic system. Contrasting with this is the marvellous Athenian treasury (Plate XXIX), erected wholly in island marble just after the establishment of the democracy at Athens in 507 B.C. The story told by Pausanias, that it was a memorial of the battle of Marathon (490 B.C.), is an error due to an inscribed base later fitted against the south flank of the building.[1] A curious feature of this and other Delphian treasuries is the absence of steps, though the stylobate is 2 feet 11½ inches above the platform and thus almost inaccessible; it was not, in fact, intended to be entered by the general public. The plan is of the usual distyle in-antis form. In the entablature a curious detail is the use of five guttae on the regulae of the architrave (as in the Syracusan treasury opposite) while the mutules directly above them have the usual six guttae in each row. The metopes, thirty in all, were filled with sculpture, again probably under the influence of the Syracusan treasury; for this was the first Athenian building to receive such decoration. Sculpture appeared also in the pediments, besides the acroteria crowning the three angles.

A very unusual type of structure at Delphi was the old Tholos (Plate XXIX), the predecessor of the imposing circular structures of the fourth century. This again was demolished and used for second-hand material in the Sicyonian treasury foundations; but the original position and purpose are unknown. The structure consisted of a circular cella with a surrounding peristyle of thirteen slender Doric columns (about 6½ diameters in height), the total diameter on the stylobate being only 20 feet 8 inches. In the entablature, however, the frieze contained twenty triglyphs, spaced with absolute disregard of the columns and of the architrave joints (a circumstance unique in all Greek architecture), apparently for the purpose of securing approximately square metopes. An additional peculiarity is the absence of guttae both below the regulae of the architrave and the mutules of the cornice, as at Assos; but the mutules themselves, unlike Assos, are alternately wide and narrow, following the early archaic system.

Among the structures erected in the sacred enclosures the most important, apart from the temples, were the altars, some of which were of considerable size, though they might be composed chiefly of mounds of ashes, like that of Zeus at Olympia. Generally they were long narrow oblongs, parallel to the temple façades and so facing approximately eastward, like that of the Olympieum at Acragas which corresponds to the entire width of this enormous temple, and those at Paestum. Sometimes these altars were decorated with triglyph friezes resting merely on a sill or step, such as that before the "Gorgon

---

[1] The whole building was completely reconstructed with the original pieces at the cost of the city of Athens in 1903–1906. The original date of erection is still contested, the French officially preferring 490 B.C. or later as given by Pausanias, though this seems far too late for the sculpture, the painted ornament, and the non-Athenian imported material.

THE RISE OF THE DORIC STYLE

temple" at Corcyra and another beside the temple of Athena at Syracuse; in the latter the triglyphs were painted red (rather than the usual blue) and the metopes are the horizontal oblongs (here 41½ inches long and 20¾ inches high) found in so many structures of Syracusan origin. At Olympia is a small circular altar with triglyph decoration. A more primitive circular altar occurs at Acragas.

Another type of structure characteristic of sanctuaries, and also of public places such as the agora, was the colonnade or stoa, affording protection from sun and rain. Only a few simple examples date from the archaic period, however; more important are those to be described in later chapters.

Among the imposing works of public utility were the city fountains, with their porticoes providing shade for the gossip of women gathering to fill their amphorae or hydriae, as the stoa did for the transactions of men. The earliest form of the great fountain of Pirene at Corinth consisted of four parallel vaulted reservoirs hewn in a substratum of clay, supplied by long galleries into which water filtered through a conglomerate stratum above; at the front of each reservoir is a decorative screen of stone, separating it from the draw-basins sheltered under the overhanging ledge. The fountain of Glauce, in the same city, was hewn rather in solid rock, again with four parallel reservoirs separated by partitions from the draw-basins; in this example, however, those drawing water were sheltered by a portico of three square piers between antae, supporting a segmental vault, wholly cut in the living rock. At Megara the tyrant Theagenes erected a fountain-house of masonry, with the ceiling of the reservoirs supported on rows of octagonal piers. Megara was the home of the engineer Eupalinus, who was called by the tyrant Polycrates to Samos to pierce a mountain with the great tunnel or aqueduct which still continues to excite admiration. The terracotta water-pipes laid in the floor of the subterranean aqueduct of Peisistratus at Athens closely resemble those at Samos, and perhaps Eupalinus was the author of this work as well. The most famous of the Athenian fountains was the Enneacrunus (the "nine-mouthed"), depicted on Athenian painted vases, and named because of the nine lion heads through which water spouted to fill hydriae set on the pavement below, apparently arranged to form three sides of a court; there are remains of great reservoirs, and parapet slabs of draw-basins, their ends cut to fit between slender wooden columns.[1] A less pretentious fountain in the middle of the Agora at Corinth is of special interest because its two bronze lion heads have survived in place, and also because, as the ground level gradually rose around it, the area was enclosed to form a sunken chamber, decorated externally with a low triglyph frieze as in the case of the above-mentioned altars.

The normal type of administrative building was the Bouleuterion or Council-house. The earliest extant example, the north wing of the complex known as the Bouleuterion at Olympia (Fig. 44 at B), was erected in the sixth century just to the north of what was presumably its predecessor, and likewise was a long hall like an apsidal temple with a central row of columns, the porch at

---

[1] The much disputed question of the identification of Enneacrunus, which Dörpfeld placed west of the Acropolis, is complicated by the discovery of another fountain-house to the north, facing on the Agora. But the latter seems technically (treatment of unfinished poros Doric columns, form of dowels, etc.), however, to belong to the fifth century, too late for the Enneacrunus of Peisistratus.

the open rectangular end being Doric tristyle in-antis, with metal grilles extending from the antae to the outer columns and swinging grilles in the two central intercolumniations. The apse is cut off by a cross-wall and is in itself divided by a central wall into two rooms like quadrants of a circle. The lateral walls are straight; and along them were probably ranged tiers of wooden seats, as in Pausanias's description of the Phocicon on the road from Daulis to Delphi. The triglyph frieze of the porch was carried round the entire building. Somewhat later, in the fifth century, the primitive south wing was rebuilt, curiously preserving the more archaic convex flank walls and the more pointed apse; otherwise it shows developed Doric details. Still later was built a connecting link in the form of a square court, and the whole complex was fronted by a portico along the east façade.

The Bouleuterion at Delphi was much smaller than either of the halls at Olympia and lacked the internal columns and the apse; wooden seats perhaps were arranged crosswise, the highest at the rear end.[1] A totally new scheme appeared in the Old Bouleuterion at Athens, a square plan with one side walled off to form an entrance corridor while wooden seats were arranged along the three other walls of the main room. With the larger spans here encountered it was necessary not only to employ interior columns, but also to arrange them in such a way that the central rectangular "orchestra" would not be encumbered, in other words, with five columns forming a ⊓-shape. As for the plan of the assembly-hall or Scias at Sparta, designed by the Ionian architect Theodorus of Samos, we are quite without information, except that it was obviously not a circle.[2]

For the popular assembly at Athens, Cleisthenes erected, presumably just after 507 B.C., an open theatral area known as the Pnyx (the earliest of three structures on this site), cut on the northeast rocky slope of the hill, with the bema or orator's platform placed against a straight back wall, low on the slope so that the natural rock could be used as the seating space. The upper edge had the outline of a circular arc; and the area thus enclosed was about 25,000 square feet, accommodating about 5,000 citizens.

It was during the sixth century that the art of theatre design originated, beginning with the performance of choral dances pertaining to the worship of Dionysus in the rural districts outside Athens, as at Icaria. It was after they had been introduced into the city that Thespis, in 534 B.C., combined an actor with the chorus. Henceforth tragedies and satyr plays became an integral part of the Dionysiac festivals, with comedies added later. Such performances, at the beginning, were given in the open circular area of stamped earth known as the "Orchestra" (dancing-place) in the Agora.[3] But eventually the site was transferred to the precinct of Dionysus Eleuthereus on the south slope of the Acropolis, where, on account of the advantages offered spectators by the Acropolis slope, there were more possibilities of accommodation. In fact, the reason for the transfer to the precinct of Dionysus appears to have been the

[1] This is suggested by the rising rock within the structure.
[2] Pausanias mentions a circular building beside the Scias, which in itself, therefore, was not circular; the supposition that it was synonymous with Tholos is erroneous.
[3] The Orchestra in the Agora (wrongly located by Dörpfeld on the Areopagus) has not yet been discovered, though it was probably beneath the Odeum of Agrippa in the middle of the Agora.

collapse of the wooden scaffolding or bleachers (*ikria*) which had been erected round the orchestra in the Agora, during a performance at about 498 B.C.[1]

The earliest theatre construction in the precinct of Dionysus, dating presumably from 498 B.C.,[2] lies just to the northeast of the little temple of Dionysus mentioned above (Fig. 77). This consists of part of the retaining wall of the original orchestra, a perfect circle perhaps about $83\frac{1}{2}$ feet in diameter,[3] the scene of the dance which was conducted round the altar of Dionysus in the centre. There was at first no scene building, and the seating space was the bare hillside, which formed a natural auditorium or "viewing-place" (*theatron*). Eventually a temporary booth or tent (*skene*) appears to have been set up behind or at one side of the orchestra, where the single actor could make his changes; but, apart from the orchestra, there was as yet no permanent construction in stone.[4]

Consideration of structures intended for relaxation and exercise, such as the

[1] The collapse of the *ikria*, mentioned by so many late lexicographers, is recorded for some performance during the 70th Olympiad (500–496 B.C.), when Aeschylus first competed with the older dramatists Choerilus and Pratinas. Through some confusion by Suidas, this event is associated with Aeschylus again just before his second departure to Sicily in 458 B.C.; and some modern writers have compromised by dating it at the time of the first departure of Aeschylus in 476 B.C.; but these later dates are probably fictitious. Modern writers, furthermore, have generally assumed that the collapse occurred in the theatre of Dionysus, whereas the ancient authors are unanimously opposed to such a view. Both Photius and Eustathius state emphatically that the accident occurred in the Agora before the building of the theatre of Dionysus; and Hesychius and Suidas, while not mentioning the Agora, to be sure, assert that the event occurred before the building of the theatre, and that the erection of the theatre of Dionysus was the direct consequence of the accident.

[2] Improbably early dates have sometimes been assigned to this construction, such as about 600 B.C., or 534 B.C. (the date of Thespis). But, though the temple of Dionysus is approximately of the latter date, the curved retaining wall (though of polygonal masonry) is not necessarily as early as the sixth century. Furthermore, if any performances took place in this precinct during the sixth century—a most improbable assumption—they must have been of modest character, like those recorded for the Lenaean precinct where no theatre building has yet been found, perhaps because the separate performances of comedies in the Lenaeum were abandoned when the Lycurgan theatre was erected.

[3] Dörpfeld believed that he could distinguish three points on the circumference of a circle, thus permitting an estimate of the diameter as about 87 feet. But one of these points (a rock cutting in the present east parodos) seems to be imaginary, or at least cannot be detected by later observers. Of the two others (short pieces of wall), a 14-foot stretch of polygonal masonry forming a curved retaining wall is the most convincing evidence, and is more probably to be assigned to the orchestra itself (forming the drop of $6\frac{1}{2}$ feet from the orchestra level to the temple precinct just to the south) than to a curved ramp leading up to it, as has sometimes been suggested. But one point is insufficient for accurate measurement of the radius, though the short arc suggests about 40 feet; if, however, we bring this into connection with the other piece of wall (which in spite of the inclusion of some poros stone seems to belong to the same construction), we can define the circle more closely as $83\frac{1}{2}$ feet in diameter, locating the first orchestra centre about 41 feet south and $9\frac{1}{2}$ feet east of the present (third) orchestra centre. We may, therefore, reject Fiechter's restoration of a small orchestra only 67 feet in diameter, with a concentric ramp $16\frac{1}{2}$ feet outside it. We may also reject Anti's theory, based on the gutter at Syracuse (p. 210) and on other inadequate evidence, that the orchestras at Athens and in all other theatres before 350 B.C. were trapezoidal or rectangular, together with his argument that the circular orchestra was first used by Polycleitus at Epidaurus.

[4] It was suggested by Bulle that actual traces of a stone foundation of a scene building about $11\frac{1}{2}$ feet by 59 feet, of about 534 B.C., still exist; but later investigators dispute this imaginative restoration of the dubious patch of masonry in question. Even more fantastic is Fiechter's attribution of the breccia stoa foundations to a date as early as 534 B.C. (his so-called *skenotheke*).

stadium and gymnasium, may be deferred until we reach the later periods yielding more intelligible remains. It is interesting to note, however, that public baths with hot water are known to have existed at Sybaris before its destruction in 510 B.C., though we are ignorant of their plan and appointments.

As for private houses of the archaic period, there is little that can yet be said. Palaces, on the other hand, are represented by two examples which, though on the oriental fringe of Greek civilisation, deserve mention here. At Larisa near Smyrna is a palace of which the plan imitates the Hittite pavilion or *hilani* type of Syria, with two square towers symmetrically enframing a central receding portico of four Proto-Doric columns in-antis. The main palace apartments correspond to the length of the portico, and the isolated tower rooms were entered only from the ends of the portico. Quite different is a palace at Vouni in Cyprus, dating from about 500 B.C. but subsequently greatly enlarged. In its original form it was 165 feet wide and 200 feet deep, with the main elements arranged on a central axis: entrance porch, large anteroom, and inner porch—each porch with a central column between antae—and seven steps forming a flight 55 feet wide descending to a peristyle court, upon which faced, at the back, three identical rooms. At the left of the court was a large room 24 feet deep and 39 feet wide, its width completely open to the court like a pastas; and smaller rooms, hot and cold baths, latrines, and stairways filled the remainder of the area.

Among the smaller monuments, votive or commemorative, with which the precincts were filled, it is to be noted that the pedestals supporting statues or groups of sculpture were generally low, with their tops below eye level so that the inscriptions were frequently carved on their tops rather than on the faces. In other cases more lofty pedestals were preferred, rectangular or cylindrical with moulded and painted capitals, or even in the form of single columns. One of the strangest of the latter was a large limestone Doric column on the Athenian Acropolis, with the fluting twisted spirally; this and a smaller example at Delphi are the only forerunners of the spirally fluted columns of Roman times. Many of these Doric votive columns were of special interest because of their rich detail, which in part is the result of Ionic influence. Thus a marble capital from the sanctuary of Apollo Corynthius at Corone (Longa) in Messenia has more than fifty flutes terminating in petals under the necking, and the abacus is crowned by a row of small vertical leaves curling forward and resting on a beaded astragal.[1] Often the deep hollow under the necking was decorated with plastic leaves; in an example found near Sparta these are tall narrow leaves separated by tiny petals, while at Tegea there are two pointed and two horseshoe leaves corresponding to each flute; in an example from Mantinea there are plastic leaves not only in the hollow but also in a second tier above, five to each flute. Of special importance in this connection is the vast series of votive supports of the archaic period from the Athenian Acropolis, both columns and more conventional pedestals, many of them with ovolos painted with varied ornament, scale patterns, long leaves, inverted palmettes in scrolls, inverted palmettes between scrolls, etc.

The types of votive monuments merge insensibly with those of sepulchral

[1] This capital at Corone, found in a local church, has been conjecturally attributed to a temple which it hardly fits, and of which all the details, though attributed to the sixth century, are at least two centuries later.

monuments, likewise commemorative, but erected outside the cities rather than within the precincts. Where there was plenty of space, as in the open country, large mounds of earth (tumuli as in Asia Minor) continued to be employed, as at Velanideza and Vourva in Attica. But in restricted areas closer to the cities these were reduced in size, like that of Menecrates at Corcyra (faced with masonry and with a lion on the saucer-domed top) or like the miniature egg-shaped mounds covered with stucco in the Athenian cemeteries. There might also be large rectangular offering tables with stuccoed mud-brick walls and tiled tops. Statues of youths or maidens (*kouroi* or *korai*) might serve as monuments, on simple or stepped pedestals; the "Apollo" of Tenea formed such a grave monument, and the feet of a maiden carved by Phaedimus are imbedded in the top of a stepped pedestal from Velanideza. As among the votive monuments, columns served also to commemorate the dead, one of the most beautiful being the Doric marble column of Xenvares at Corcyra, with elaborately carved and painted leaves drooping below the echinus. But in view of limited space the form specially favoured, particularly in Attica, was the tall slender shaft or stele, either painted or carved in relief with a standing figure of the deceased, and usually crowned by some sort of capital or acroterion. The earlier examples, in poros limestone, are of heavier proportions because of the material; but with the introduction of marble they became more graceful. During the first half of the sixth century the crowning feature of these Attic stelae was often a great cavetto reminiscent of the Egyptian cornice, which it might resemble also in the decoration with vertical petals, as in that from Lapmtrae; in other examples the decoration is a huge lotus flower; and above the abacus (usually adorned with rosettes) might be a seated sphinx, symbolic of death. In the second half of the century, under Ionic influence, the preferred forms were the double or lyre-shaped volutes likewise supporting an abacus and a sphinx, as in the stele associated with Megacles, or more frequently a severe palmette rising from volutes (like the antefixes employed on temples), either carved in relief or merely painted, as on the monument of Antiphanes (Fig. 46).[1]

Fig. 46.—
Painted Grave
Stele of
Antiphanes.
(Athens Museum.)

The plans of cities, at this early period, seem to have been purely haphazard, the development of the formal plan being a concept of the following century.[2]

[1] A particularly important and representative series of these archaic stelae is to be found in the Metropolitan Museum of Art in New York; other notable examples are in the Boston Museum.

[2] See p. 212. It has been suggested by Dunbabin that the gridiron plan of the Acropolis of Selinus is as early as the erection of temple 'D' and so of about 535 B.C., "the first piece of regular Greek town-planning which has survived." But Gabrici, upon whose results he relies, dates it only in the first half of the fifth century, while Gerkan, with more probability, dates it after 409 B.C. Admittedly all the houses facing on these streets are later than the Carthaginian destruction; and the assumed parallelism with temple 'D,' cited by Dunbabin, is illusory, since the west front of this temple forms a marked angle with the north-south street which it borders. It seems clear that the gridiron plan was inserted between the temples at a later date, presumably when the houses had to be rebuilt after 409 B.C. (see p. 330).

CHAPTER FOUR

THE RISE OF THE IONIC STYLE

A SLIGHT sketch of the history of Asia Minor during the archaic period may help us in understanding the relationship of the kingdoms and colonies whose architectural expression, as distinct from that of the Greek mainland and the western colonies, forms our present subject. We have traced the story of the foundation of the Ionian colonies by the fleeing remnants of the Mycenaean populations, of their early contacts with the native peoples of Phrygia, Mysia, Lydia, and Lycia, and of the colonies which they in turn, as they increased in power, sent off to other parts of the Greek world. The result of this dispersion is that our knowledge of the Ionic style has to be gathered, not only from the great cities of Asia Minor, but also from trading colonies such as Naucratis in Egypt (probably dating from the seventh century, but subsequently enlarged by Aahmes II, 569–526 B.C.), and from outposts established to receive surplus populations, such as Rhegium (Reggio) in southern Italy and Massilia (Marseilles) in France.

Like the Dorian cities, the wealthy Ionian cities became in this period the prey of "tyrants"; and to their love of display we owe some of the most important monuments of the time. Ephesus, "the first city of Asia," may be taken as the type. One of the earliest of the Ionian settlements, it came to be the leader of the confederacy, and was famous for its poets and philosophers, while it possessed great schools of architecture, sculpture, painting, and metal work. Another important centre was the island of Samos, which had a famous school of statuary, to which is accorded the invention of casting in metal. The influence of these cities upon the interior of Asia seems to have been of little account for some centuries: it was the narrow strip of shore that was magnetised by the greater mass of the interior, and the Achaeans parted with many of their characteristics under the new conditions. Lydia's greatest period, about 560 B.C., is connected with the name of its king, Croesus, who extended his territory to incorporate the Ionian cities, and tried to ally himself with Egypt and Babylon; but no party was ripe for such a conjunction of aims and resources. For want of this united front the district was conquered (in 546 B.C.) and Sardis captured by Persia, which was henceforth supreme for more than two hundred years. Yet the fringe of Greek cities retained many of their privileges and still prospered. The proverbial jealousy, and consequent disunion, of the Greeks was the necessary weakness of their independent polity; even in the Ionian revolt of the beginning of the fifth century, these Asiatic Greeks failed to meet the Persians as a compact and united force, and the rivalry of Miletus and Samos handed them a prey to Darius. It was left to their hardier European kinsmen to throw back the wave of Persian aggression at Marathon and Salamis. And it was as a direct result of the battle of Salamis that the Ionian cities were induced to form a part of the Delian League under Athens, and so, throughout the fifth century, temporarily lost their power

THE RISE OF THE IONIC STYLE

of independent artistic expression and were subordinated to the leader of the hegemony.

With some slight idea before us of the racial, historic, and social relationships of the Ionian Greeks, we may now turn to the more technical side of the development of the material fabric.

* * * * *

A special characteristic of the archaic period in Asia Minor was the erection of colossal dipteral temples (i.e. with a double peristyle of columns all round), the Ionians thus revealing a desire for magnificence which in Sicily was expressed by the double colonnade across the façade alone. The earliest of these was designed for the sanctuary of Hera at Samos by Rhoecus and Theodorus of that island, inspired by the great columned halls of Egyptian temples such as the so-called Labyrinth near Lake Moeris described by Herodotus and Strabo; the Samian temple was likewise on that account called the Labyrinth. Almost every vestige of the temple was removed about fifty years later, leaving only scraps of foundation and the pieces built into the foundations of its successor; but its fame was so great, because of the dipteral innovation and the book written about it by Theodorus,[1] that it requires detailed consideration. The date was earlier than the middle of the sixth century (preceding the rival plan at Ephesus), and so probably about 575 B.C.;[2] and it must have been the fourth temple on this site. To give more space before the rebuilt altar (the eighth on this sacred site) the façade was thrust back some distance toward the west, so that the rear of the temple had to be erected on ground created by diverting a stream westward and filling up the marshy surroundings. The entire rectangle measured about 174 by 314 feet; and, there being only two steps, the stylobate was about 171 by 311 feet. But the columns were not located close to the stylobate edge as was done in later times; instead, a passage about 10 feet wide was left round the outer peristyle, so that the axial rectangle was about 146 by 286 feet.[3] On the octastyle east front the two outer spacings on either side were about $17\frac{1}{2}$ feet each on centres, the next 24 feet, leaving about 28 feet for the central spacing, a system of gradation which may likewise have been derived from the great

---

[1] The book by Theodorus (the earliest architectural treatise of which the title has come down to us), cited by Vitruvius, was evidently the source of garbled statements by Pliny, as when he located the Labyrinth once in Samos and once again in Lemnos (the latter apparently being a misinterpretation of the Greek term *en-limnais* or "in the marshes" which characterised the location of the temple of Hera at Samos). Egyptian influence on Rhoecus and Theodorus is evident also in the story of the upper and lower halves of an archaic bronze statue of Apollo, cast by them independently but so closely following Egyptian models that they fitted. Besides the two Samian architects, a third name is mentioned, that of Smilis of Aegina, sometimes as architect though he was more probably the sculptor of the new cult statue.

[2] Buschor's analysis of the remains, which in general we follow, would place the date between 560 and 550 B.C.; but a slightly earlier date (there being no contrary evidence) seems desirable in view of the probability that Samos was the inspiration for the double façade colonnades at Syracuse and Selinus (see p. 75).

[3] In obtaining these dimensions, it has been necessary to judge from the scale of the plans, no accurate measurements having been published. The restored dimensions in "Samian ells," as given by the excavators, fail to inspire confidence because they are suspiciously "round numbers."

hypostyle halls of Egyptian temples, the difference in a Greek temple being that the central columns were no higher than those on either side. The rear would undoubtedly have had nine columns;[1] and the length, in view of the much closer spacing on the flanks of the later temple, probably had as many as twenty-one columns spaced 14 feet 2 inches or, toward the east front, 15 feet 6 inches on centres.[2] Being dipteral throughout, the exterior had one hundred and two columns, besides two rows of five each in the deep pronaos, which seems to have been inspired by the central aisles of the Egyptian hypostyle halls; there was no opisthodomus. In addition, the cella contained two rows each of ten columns; their presence and that of the cella flooring indicates that the temple was not hypaethral or open to the sky, and exactly in the centre was a special pavement forming a rectangular enclosure for the cult statue. The hundred and thirty-two column bases, of which most are built into the foundations of the later temple, are of soft limestone and show clear traces of having been turned out by lathes, so that they confirm Pliny's mention of the "hundred and fifty columns of the Labyrinth" turned in a lathe invented by Theodorus. The varying sizes of the bases show that the column diameters differed in accordance with their spacings. Some of the poros shafts had forty flutes with sharp arrises between, while others are still unfluted as if the temple had not been quite completed. The column and anta capitals are not preserved and must be restored from other examples. For neither their absence nor that of any remains of the entablature can signify that the work failed to reach this level; many terracotta roof tiles of Corinthian style exist, with antefixes containing stunted palmettes rising from addorsed volutes, and even part of what seems to be a poros limestone acroterion. We must conclude, therefore, that the temple was roofed and thus nearly finished, and that its entablature was of wood, the only practicable material for such great spans in view of the fact that marble was nowhere employed. This great temple was destroyed by fire, as the remains indicate, though probably not by the Persians as Pausanias reports; for Herodotus says nothing of such vandalism, and the sequence of the remains would suggest that the fire occurred considerably before the Persian Wars, perhaps accidentally.

Slightly later in date is the temple of Apollo in the Greek trading colony at Naucratis in Egypt, a daughter city of Miletus; the date probably goes back to about 566 B.C., when Aahmes (Amasis) II allied himself with the Greeks and gave them special religious and commercial privileges. Here, where we meet for the first time what has always been regarded as the index mark of the style, the capital, it is apparent that now a marked change transformed the order. The volutes, instead of springing vertically from the shaft as in the Proto-Ionic examples, now lie horizontally, and are connected by the cushion, and below them the girdle of hanging leaves has become the egg-and-dart, the ovolo or echinus. The volute cushion in this case was carved separately; a restoration is

---

[1] The excavators restore ten columns on the rear; but the fact that the later temple (and presumably also Ephesus) had nine seems conclusive.

[2] I.e. east front $(4 \times 17\frac{1}{2}$ feet$) + (2 \times 24$ feet$) + 28$ feet $= 146$ feet; west front $(4 \times 17\frac{1}{2}$ feet$) + (4 \times 19$ feet$) = 146$ feet; flanks $(18 \times 14\frac{1}{8}$ feet$) + (2 \times 15\frac{1}{2}$ feet$) = 286$ feet, wider spacings (as in the later temple at Samos) being employed toward the east front as a transition to the façade.

suggested in Fig 47.[1] The echinus is carved on the topmost drum of the shaft, with an egg-and-dart clearly showing its origin in the overhanging leaves or petals of the Proto-Ionic pendant girdle; in contrast to the later profile, the upper part of the ovolo recedes even further than the lower part, and the eggs are carved even on the upper surface of the echinus and die into the horizontal bed which carried the volute cushion.[2] The eggs themselves have the typical early rectangular form with rounded corners, the frames or "shells" being formed by rounded astragals, and the darts barely appearing between their bottoms. Below the echinus a smooth astragal, or in some cases a beaded astragal, was carried round the top of the shaft; in the case of the smooth astragal there is an additional feature in that the upper part of the shaft is slightly bell-shaped, increasing in diameter as it rises, and is decorated with a necking of the lotus flower and bud, which may have been the prototype of the well-known anthemion or honeysuckle used on the columns of the Erechtheum. At Naucratis, however, the absence of the palmette emphasises the purely Egyptian

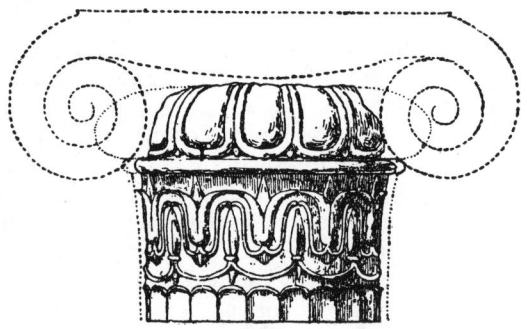

FIG. 47.—CAPITAL FROM THE TEMPLE OF APOLLO AT NAUCRATIS.

influence. The shaft has twenty-five shallow flutes with sharp arrises between, terminating below the necking with slightly projecting fillets such as were later used to surround the tops of the flutes in the north porch of the Erechtheum. The base had, above the usual moulded disc and fluted torus, a high conical member which recurs in no other structure.[3] The columns thus described were of soft limestone as at Samos. Of the superstructure nothing is preserved, except possibly the bed moulding of the cornice, an egg-and-dart like that of the capital, with barrel-shaped beads and reels below; it may be, however, that this moulding belongs to another part of the temple, and that the entablature was wholly of wood. The plan of the temple, also, is not known in detail.

[1] The volutes are now missing, though a portion was found and destroyed by the Arabs before it could be recorded. Lethaby suggests that the volutes were cut in the same block with the echinus, that is, the upper drum of the shaft, making a complicated piece of stone-cutting. But at Samos (Polycrates temple) the volute cushion was separate.

[2] It is sometimes assumed that the ovolo developed from the half-round or Egyptian torus rather than from the Proto-Ionic pendant leaves; but such a derivation is hardly consistent with the greater recession at the top in the earlier examples. Both the profile and the decoration suggest Oriental rather than Egyptian prototypes.

[3] See below with regard to the sculptured drums at Ephesus. The bases at Naucratis have striations caused by a lathe as at Samos.

Toward the middle of the sixth century, when the exploitation of marble as a building material led to a rapid development in Asia Minor and the Aegean islands, many of the Ionic members were still of primitive form. Thus in a temple of Apollo at Myus, near Miletus, the face of the cornice is formed by an ovolo profile, the overhanging bottom deeply undercut to shed rain, and with a torus above; the ovolo is carved, not with the appropriate egg-and-dart, but with the lotus-and-palmette. Similarly in the Letoum at Delos a deeply undercut ovolo forms the face of the cornice, in this case uncarved, with a narrow fillet above.

The most typical of the archaic Ionic temples was the one dedicated to Artemis (Diana) at Ephesus,[1] known as the Croesus temple ('D') because some of the columns were erected at the expense of that Lydian monarch between 560 and 546 B.C., and in fact bear his name on the bases (Fig. 48); it was built over the site of three earlier but much smaller examples ('A'–'C'). The temple was designed by Chersiphron of Cnossus in Crete, who is said to have erected the columns, and by his son Metagenes, who placed upon them the architrave and completed the work; both collaborated also in a book on the subject, now lost but cited by Vitruvius.[2] A third artist, Theodorus of Samos, was said to have been responsible for the bedding of its foundations upon alternate layers of charcoal and fleeces, because of the marshy nature of the ground; Theodorus was apparently regarded as an expert because of his earlier work on the temple in the marshes at Samos. The temple at Ephesus was, like that at Samos (i.e., the later or Polycrates temple hereafter to be described), one of the few temples in the captured cities that was spared by Xerxes at the end of the Ionian Revolt; and the Persians continued to treat it with respect throughout the fifth century. It was, however, burnt in 356 B.C., according to tradition, by an incendiary (Herostratus) on the night of Alexander's birth, and was rebuilt on a platform 8 feet 9½ inches higher, but exactly on the same plan; and it is partly with the assistance of this later plan,[3] combined with the traces of the Croesus structure, and partly as a consequence of the fact that Vitruvius and Pliny did not distinguish between the temple visible in their own day and that described in Chersiphron's book, that the plan of both has to be reconstituted (Fig. 81). The orientation is the reverse of that usually found, the main façade being toward the west because of the tradition inherited from the primitive shrine ('A'), which, refaced and rebuilt, was preserved at the exact centre of the cella, like the special shrine at Samos. As at Samos, furthermore, the platform consisted of only two steps, the stylobate here measuring about 180½ by 377½ feet; and again the peristyle receded considerably from the stylobate edge so that the axial rectangle measured 156 by 353 feet. At Ephesus the platform presents

---

[1] Traces of this temple were found by Wood in 1869–1874 under the fourth-century temple later to be described, the whole being thoroughly re-examined by a British Museum expedition in 1904–1905. The actual remains in place consist only of the lower parts of three column bases, parts of the west cross-wall and south wall, including the southwest anta, considerable patches of the pavement and masses of the foundations.

[2] It is sometimes thought that Chersiphron was the architect, not of the Croesus temple ('D'), but of its non-peripteral predecessor ('C'); but this seems highly improbable in view of the allusions to the great sizes of the column drums and architraves (Vitruvius, X, 2, 11–12) and particularly of the central west architrave (Pliny, XXXVI, 21) as used by Chersiphron and Metagenes.   [3] See p. 224.

THE RISE OF THE IONIC STYLE

a special peculiarity in that it was constructed as a continuous mass of masonry and even with a marble pavement over the whole, regardless of the positions of walls and columns, these being set out upon the pavement as if upon a vast drawing-board and erected without adequate foundations. The west façade was octastyle, with the spacings graded from 20 feet $1\frac{1}{8}$ inches for the two nearest each corner to 23 feet $9\frac{1}{2}$ inches and even 28 feet $1\frac{1}{2}$ inches at the centre, the column diameters being similarly enlarged gradually from 5 feet 2 inches to 5 feet 3 inches, 5 feet 9 inches, and even 6 feet 2 inches at the central span. The rear, on the other hand, was made enneastyle (with nine columns) as at Samos, in order to avoid such extremes of spacing where the absence of an entrance made them unnecessary; the four outer spacings were 20 feet $1\frac{1}{8}$ inches, the four central spacings 18 feet $11\frac{1}{8}$ inches. On each flank were twenty-one columns as at Samos, the spacing being normally 17 feet $1\frac{1}{8}$ inches but increased to 19 feet $4\frac{1}{4}$ inches for the two or three nearest the corners;[1] a curious result of this treatment is a feeling of weakness toward the corners, as contrasted with the strength obtained in the Doric system by the angle contraction (later supplemented by the enlargement of the angle column diameters). Thus there were fifty-five columns in the outer peristyle; the plan being dipteral, the inner peristyle added forty-seven columns; and the main front had also a third row, being tripteral, so that the total number of columns in the peristyle was one hundred and six. The pronaos, deep like that at Samos, contained four pairs of columns, while the shallow opisthodomus had a single row of three, increasing the total to one hundred and seventeen. This, probably, was the total (CXVII) that was reported by Pliny,[2] though the clerical error of some copyist resulted in the insertion of an extra ten (CXXVII) in our surviving manuscripts.[3] It is by no means certain that there were columns within the cella, which may have been largely open to the sky (hypaethral); it seems to have contained a sacred pool, and there was a drain running beneath the west doorway.

The Ionic bases have in this example assumed the characteristic Asiatic form, consisting of a large torus elevated on a horizontally fluted disk; the details of

---

[1] I.e. west front $(4 \times 20 \text{ feet } 1\frac{1}{8} \text{ inches}) + (2 \times 23 \text{ feet } 9\frac{1}{2} \text{ inches}) + 28 \text{ feet } 1\frac{1}{2} \text{ inches} = 156$ feet 1 inch; east front $(4 \times 20 \text{ feet } 1\frac{1}{8} \text{ inches}) + (4 \times 18 \text{ feet } 11\frac{1}{8} \text{ inches}) = 156$ feet 1 inch; flanks $(5 \times 19 \text{ feet } 4\frac{1}{4} \text{ inches}) + (15 \times 17 \text{ feet } 1\frac{1}{8} \text{ inches}) = 353$ feet 2 inches.

[2] The suggestion of nine columns at the rear instead of eight, and of an extra row to be added at the front where the foundations continue far west of the line of the façade restored in the British Museum publication, had been first advanced by Fergusson (who wrongly added an extra row likewise at the rear); and these constructive suggestions were revived by Lethaby. Thus the total number of columns on each flank has been represented as twenty (Wood, Murray, Wilberg, Henderson), twenty-one (Lethaby, Dinsmoor, Krischen), or even twenty-four (Fergusson). Similarly, the total number of columns in the peristyle and porches has been restored as one hundred (Wood, Murray), one hundred and six (Wilberg), one hundred and eight (Henderson), one hundred and seventeen (Lethaby, Dinsmoor), or one hundred and twenty-seven (Fergusson, Krischen). Of the two restorations agreeing with the number in Pliny's text, Fergusson's must be rejected because the temple is unwarrantably lengthened toward the east (rear), while Krischen's attains the total by deepening the opisthodomus to an impossible degree (disregarding the true position of the cross-wall which, though missing, is known because of the impression left in a mass of Byzantine concrete) and filling it with columns. The alternative adopted by Henderson, of counting the assumed interior columns of the cella (where he restores nineteen), seems inadmissible.

[3] Compare the similar clerical errors in the descriptions of the Mausoleum at Halicarnassus.

the profiles are extremely varied. Sometimes the torus moulding is really a cyma reversa, carved with pendant leaves, the heart-and-dart, one of the earliest instances of the employment of the Lesbian cyma with its "triangular rhythm" (Vitruvius, IV, 6, 2; Aeschylus, in Pollux, VII, 122), a variant of the ovolo developed by adding a concave reverse curve at the bottom and adapting to its profile an ornament with double curvature, the heart. The lower discs usually exhibit the developed profile with two wide flutes or scotias (instead of the

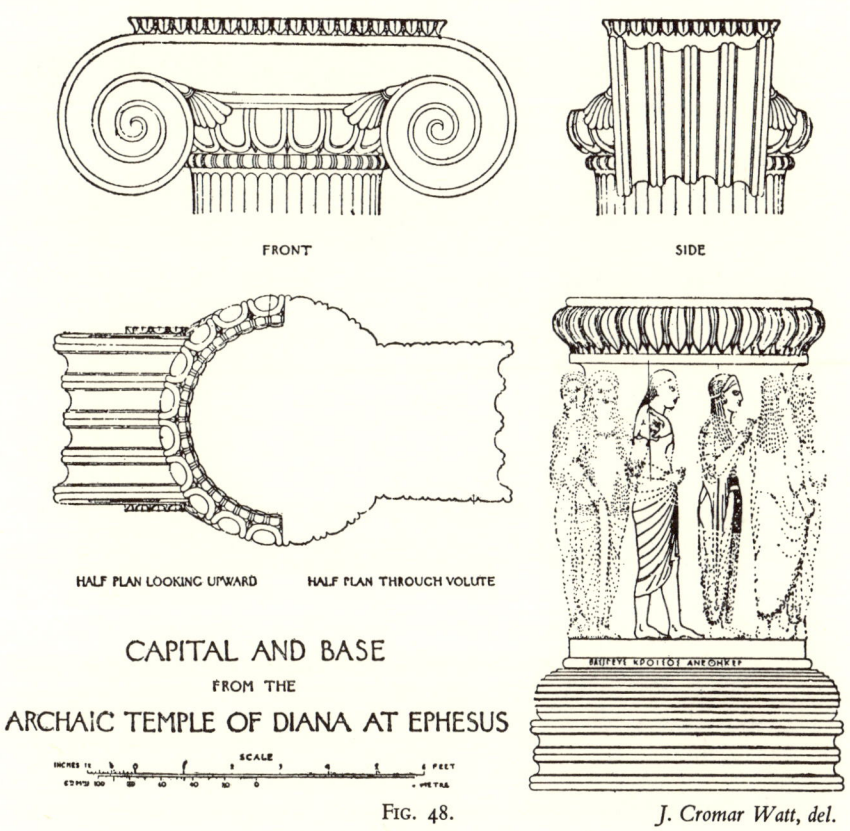

FIG. 48.   J. Cromar Watt, del.

many narrow ones of Samos) separated by astragals. The bases, for the first and only time before the fourth century, rest on square plinths, 7 feet 9 inches wide in the outer row and 6 feet $8\frac{3}{4}$ inches wide in the inner row, probably for the purpose of distributing the weight over more of the platform.[1] Above these bases, in some of the columns, were sculptured lower drums (Fig. 48),[2] the source from which the later Ephesian temple derived the idea of sculptured

---

[1] The plinth is not shown in Fig. 48.

[2] The heart-and-dart moulding utilised by Murray (Fig. 48) as the crowning member of the sculptured drums, to separate them from the fluted shafts, should be transferred to the base, being a variant of the usual torus. In this respect, again, the illustration requires correction.

drums for its columns. Whether the sculptured columns appeared on both façades or merely on the west, and whether the number (thirty-six) mentioned by Pliny should be applied to the archaic temple as well as to its successor, are matters of conjecture.[1] Another problem is that of the sculptured rectangular blocks, which on the analogy of the later temple might reasonably be interpreted as sculptured pedestals employed below columns,[2] thus introducing the additional question of whether they should form part of the total of thirty-six. In view of the almost identical arrangements of the later temple it may reasonably be inferred that Fig. 81 represents the distribution of the archaic sculpture as well. The shafts themselves contain forty, forty-four, or even forty-eight (the last alternately wide and narrow) very shallow flutes, spaced so closely that, as in other early examples of the Ionic column, there were no fillets between the flutes, but merely sharp edges or arrises as in the Doric order. The total height of these early columns at Ephesus, according to Vitruvius and Pliny, was eight diameters; the diameters vary so considerably that it might seem difficult to select the one which should be used as the basis of calculation, though, since this would hardly have been the reduced diameter of the inner peristyle (4 feet 11 inches) nor the exaggerated diameters of the six central columns of the main façade (5 feet 3 inches to 6 feet 2 inches), we may infer that the basic diameter was that on the flanks and rear (5 feet 2 inches), thus giving a height of about 41 feet 4 inches. In any case, it is obvious that the Ionic shaft had from the very beginning a proportion widely different from that of its step-sister the Doric. Its work was less; the whole design of the Ionic temple was lighter and more delicate, particularly the entablature which it had to carry; and it may be accepted as a principle of these early architects that the strength of the columns was determined by what they had to carry. In this way it came about that the Ionic column assumed a proportion of eight or nine diameters in height, while the Doric amounted to four or five only; in proportion to the weight of their respective entablatures there was, however, no great disparity of strength or efficiency.

The normal type of the capitals from Ephesus (Fig. 48; Plate XXX above) shows the undeveloped nature of the spiral band of the volute (convex in profile rather than a concave "canal" as later, with a single separating spiral rib or astragal, and no central eye), of the palmette ornament which fills the triangular gap between the cushion and the echinus, and of the carved egg-and-dart itself. Only the bead below the echinus is carved on the topmost drum of the shaft, the echinus and the volute cushion being carved together in the same block; on the bolster side the echinus is partially sunk in the cushion of the volute, only the lower portion remaining visible. The echinus still shows the traces of its origin in the convex girdle of overhanging leaves, in that the upper portion recedes and is cut off horizontally at the top. But the most remarkable feature is the great length of the very thin abacus moulding at Ephesus, an oblong almost twice its width, instead of the nearly square form to which the later examples have accustomed us, and profiled sometimes as an ovolo carved with the egg-and-dart, sometimes as a cyma reversa carved with the heart-

[1] For the presumable distribution, i.e. that of the fourth century, see p. 225.
[2] The sculptures with straight backgrounds are sometimes assigned to the walls, or to doorways and antae, and sometimes to pedestals as I prefer.

and-dart. The effect is that of a bracket-capital intended to lessen the bearing of the architrave between the columns, and the side elevation of the capital has little of the cushion or bolster shape which it afterwards assumed. Another interesting feature of these capitals is the forward inclination of their volute planes, which are closer together at the bottom than at the top, partly overcoming the distortion due to foreshortening as seen from below. Some of the capitals, presumably those on the main façade, were particularly ornate, with rosettes covering the volutes (Plate XXX below). These were probably the capitals that were provided with neckings carved with lotus-and-palmette bands of varying designs, developing the motive initiated at Naucratis.[1] Some of the capitals had strips of gold inserted between the astragals. As for the angle capitals, which constituted the chief defect of the Ionic order owing to the necessity for making the volutes face in two directions, the exact form is not revealed by the extant fragments. With a single round column at the angle, the later solution was to bend angle-wise in plan the volutes which meet at the external corner; in other words, to unite and turn aside the useless parts of the bracket (cf. Fig. 69). But with the tremendous length and comparative narrowness of the capitals at Ephesus, it would seem that the complete curve of each volute must have been retained at the inner corners,[2] instead of being cut in halves as in most later examples; and this would so completely have overbalanced any outer angle volute as to suggest that the true form was that of two complete intersecting capitals with a cruciform plan, such as we have assumed for the Proto-Ionic type.

Of the entablature at Ephesus only the slightest traces are preserved. There is nothing of the architrave, probably triply divided and stepped, which was so colossal that the mechanical difficulties of its transportation and erection (the central span on the west being 28 feet 1½ inches) caused great distress to its designers, Chersiphron and Metagenes.[3] From these stories, and because of the necessity of supporting the cornice, tympanum, and sima, it is obvious that the architrave must have been of marble. Undoubtedly the frieze was omitted, giving an entablature of the native Asiatic type; the huge egg-and-dart (of which fragments exist) crowning the architrave must at the same time have supported the dentils directly, and these in turn the overhanging cornice.[4] Higher still was one of the most remarkable features of the temple, a monumental exemplification of the primitive terracotta parapet-simas described in

[1] In the British Museum publication the petals of the volute rosettes were restored as pointed; but it so happens that no remains of their terminations survive, and it seems more probable that they had, as now restored, rounded lobes. The lotus-and-palmette necking is omitted in this restoration (Plate XXX), the fragments not having been recognised until recently.
[2] This is shown in Henderson's restoration in the British Museum publication.
[3] The mere fact that the guides were able to relate the fabulous story of the erection of the great central architrave by Artemis herself during the course of a night would seem to be confirmation of the absence of such a central span on the rear, and, consequently, of the use of nine columns rather than eight at the rear end. For the story would have lost its point if the guides had been obliged to account for a second such miracle on the other front. The architraves over the inner rows on the west front, where the great central span was repeated, were undoubtedly of wood.
[4] In the British Museum publication no dentils are shown, an omission contrary to the spirit of archaic work in Asia Minor.

the previous chapter; here the colossal marble sima or gutter in the form of a parapet, 2 feet 10 inches in height, which edged the roof, inclined slightly forward and was carved with figures in low relief, so that it formed a zoophorus, with outlets for rain-water at intervals in the form of lion heads. Grotesque monsters or Gorgons decorated the four corners. The same parapet must have been carried up the sloping pediments.[1] Much of the parapet sculpture is carved in the style of the early fifth century, illustrating the slow progress of the work. Up to this level the entire structure, in contrast to the Doric temples of the west, was constructed in marble. But the great tiles with which the roof was covered, though of marble at the eaves, in the upper parts were of terracotta for the sake of lightness of construction, since they were carried upon wooden beams and rafters.[2]

Several smaller Ionic temples built in the islands during the last third of the sixth century yield additional information and suggest the variety of the Ionic style. The temple of Apollo Phanaeus at Chios, and other temples on this island, displayed a very curious habit of using intricate patterns, superposing relief ornament on the standard patterns, such as eggs carved with pairs of spirals with a scale pattern below, or with pendant palmettes, or with the lotus above a pendant palmette, or even a heart-and-dart wherein the hearts are similarly carved with the lotus above and the pendant palmette below, separated by volutes, while the darts themselves are replaced by spirals. These may have been prototypes of the ornate Persian column bases at Susa. Even the disks of the column bases at Chios sometimes have the astragals carved with rope patterns. At Naxos the only part of the unfinished temple of Dionysus now standing is the great doorway, constructed with marble monolithic jambs and lintel with a threshold of enormous height; the clear opening is 19 feet 6 inches high and 12 feet 2 inches wide. The temple, like the doorway, evidently faced northwest, and had porches distyle in-antis at both ends, with two rows each of four columns inside the cella.[3] At Paros are the remains of another marble temple, probably dedicated to Athena, the foundations indicating that it was likewise in-antis or prostyle rather than peripteral; the doorway was even larger in scale (the jambs 22 feet 4 inches high and the clear span of the lintel 12 feet 5½ inches), the architrave with three fascias surrounded by two contiguous beaded astragals, and above it a frieze of three tiers of egg-and-dart, terminating on either side against volute consoles which supported the cornice. Other portions of this temple include a magnificent egg-and-dart moulding with the joints curved to fit the eggs and thus to become invisible, another with two

---

[1] The theory that the raking sima bent horizontally at the extremities of the pediment in a "Chinese roof" effect, as represented in the British Museum publication, is based on the very improbable evidence from the western colonies, as noted in the previous chapter. As for the theory that the parapet was horizontal all round the temple, edging a hip roof employed to avoid the great weight of pediments above the slender widely spaced columns, it is more probable that the pediments existed but were lightened by windows as in the later temple.

[2] It was at this period, however, that "tiles of stone were first made by Byzes, a Naxian" (Pausanias, V, 10, 3), and such Naxian marble tiles are known.

[3] The total dimensions of the cella as given in the publications are self-contradictory. It has been suggested that a peristyle was planned but abandoned before laying the foundations. Pieces of unfluted columns and bases evidently belong to the porches.

TEMPLES AT DELOS AND DIDYMA

tiers of egg-and-dart, and mouldings with almost Gothic ogee profiles.[1] At Delos the archaic temple of Apollo, later known as the "temple of the Delians," the "temple in which the colossus is," or the "poros temple" to distinguish it from its successors, was presumably hexastyle prostyle, for to it is assigned a marble corner capital, so contracted in length that it was possible to employ a normal canted angle volute, but still with the convex "canal," with an "eye" at the centre, a fillet above the egg-and-dart ovolo, and no abacus. The inner ceiling may have been omitted, exposing the under surface of the roof (as in later buildings at Delos) for the purpose of giving room for the colossal statue by Tectaeus and Angelion. The temple was presumably erected when Peisistratus purified part of the island after 540 B.C.[2] Probably all these temples had (or would have had in the case of Naxos) friezeless entablatures.

Other examples of the archaic Ionic style are far more fragmentary. At Miletus, or rather at Didyma (Branchidae) near by, there was an early temple of Apollo of which only the cella foundations, 65 feet wide, now exist in the court of the great structure later to be described, varying in orientation by $1\frac{1}{2}$ degrees and so pointing directly towards an old circular altar 26 feet in diameter, which is slightly to the left of the axis of the later façade. Probably the old temple was peripteral or dipteral; but only fragments now survive of the marble bases, fluted shafts, and capitals with convex "canals" as at Ephesus; a more striking analogy is the occurrence of sculptured drums, with the fluting carried down between the figures. The marble architrave was sculptured in relief (the prototype of that at Assos) with Gorgons at the corners and great lions and other figures between; for this reason most of the background seems to have been smooth, but on the east front (distinguished by larger corner Gorgons rising up over the crowning mouldings) the usual three fascias appeared between the figures like the fluting on the sculptured columns. The roof tiles were of marble, with semicircular antefixes, lacking the sculptured parapet of Ephesus. This temple was burnt by Darius in 494 B.C. and again destroyed by Xerxes. To a later rebuilding may belong three large anta capitals, 22 inches high, 2 feet $9\frac{1}{2}$ inches wide at the bottom, flaring to 4 feet at the top, the face decorated in typical Asiatic form with superposed tiers of ovolos (Plate XXXI),[3] two carved with the egg-and-dart of more developed form than in the original temple, the third with circumscribed palmettes; the return faces have a characteristic treatment with volutes carved in relief, springing

---

[1] Most of this egg-and-dart is built into the medieval castle on Paros; one slab, apparently once in the collection of the Earl of Arundel, is now in the Ashmolean Museum at Oxford. The double egg-and-dart is built into the "hundred-gated" church at Paros. The "Gothic" profile, of which pieces are built into the pavement of the road leading up to the medieval castle, is unpublished except by Stuart and Revett (*Athens*, IV, ch. VI, p. IV, Fig. 4).

[2] Another theory, that the temple was Doric, seems inappropriate for this island region and is not supported by any actual fragments. The Ionic capital can hardly be assigned to any other building. There is no real evidence for the assumption that the much more archaic running-flying Victory found at Delos was the crowning acroterion of this temple; it is much more probably to be assigned to the base signed by Micciades and Archermus, the inventors of this type. For the later successors of the temple see pp. 183, 184, 221.

[3] Four anta capitals with uncarved ovolos belong to a smaller post-Persian building. It is curious that no archaic anta capitals with single vertical volutes at each edge of the main face, the so-called "Proto-Ionic" or "sofa" form, have yet been discovered in the true Ionic areas, though many occur as Ionic importations in the west (Fig. 32).

one above another and fitting the ovolo profiles of the main face. It may be assumed that, as at Ephesus, the side returns of the antae were typically Ionic in lacking offsets from the walls. Another of the Milesian temples, on the height of Kalabak-tepe, was small and distyle in-antis, $22\frac{1}{2}$ by $28\frac{1}{2}$ feet; it had a simple marble cornice supporting terracotta simas and eaves tiles with antefixes. The latter are moulded with masks or lotus flowers in relief; but the pediment simas have an ovolo profile with large eggs in strong relief, alternately red and black with white shells and darts, the astragal below having the rectangular "Egyptian bead" and the fascia above showing both a maeander and a chevron pattern. Of the later temple at Naucratis only minute fragments are preserved; the smaller mouldings were in marble, with decorative treatments of the corners of egg-and-dart and heart-and-dart motives, while the larger pieces were of limestone, including a cornice soffit decorated with a lotus-and-palmette in relief, all this detail closely resembling that of the Siphnian Treasury at Delphi.[1] On the Greek mainland we find, as yet, no evidence of archaic Ionic temples, apart from the porch columns in the Peisistratid temple on the Athenian Acropolis.[2]

When the great dipteral temple at Samos, built by Rhoecus and Theodorus, was burned at about 530 B.C. during the tyranny of Polycrates, a new and larger temple was planned; the older structure was demolished to its very foundations, the new façade being thrust westward once more by about 130 feet to give still more space before the altar; and at the same time, to avoid conflict with the archaic northwest stoa, the axis was thrust laterally to the south.[3] The plan devised at this time was, as Herodotus correctly remarked, the largest ever executed in the Greek world, a huge rectangle about 179 by 364 feet on the stylobate, which the peristyle closely followed without the broad surrounding promenade occurring in the older temple at Samos and at Ephesus. Another difference from these two predecessors was the fact that the stylobate was high above the surrounding ground, so that a great series of steps must have been planned on all sides, though failure to execute these resulted in the curious effect of a peristyle on a high podium. The columns were arranged in dipteral fashion on the flanks and in three rows (tripteral) across the front and back; the east front had eight columns, the west front nine, and the flanks twenty-four; the deep pronaos had five pairs of columns; there was no opisthodomus. It is probable that the cella was intended to contain two long rows of columns, like its predecessor; but these were never erected, so that the cella always remained an open hypaethral court.[4] The scheme was so vast that it was carried on at

[1] The discoverers were tempted by the rich decoration to date this temple as late as the Erechtheum; but comparison with the Siphnian Treasury shows that its date was a century earlier, and this date is confirmed by pottery suggesting that it was built just after the Persian conquest in 525 B.C.

[2] For the improbable instance of the Olympieum at Athens, see p. 91.

[3] The site was examined by the Dilettanti expedition in 1764, and, after partial excavations by French and Greek archaeologists, the whole was systematically uncovered by German expeditions in 1910-1914 and since 1925. At present only one decapitated and unfinished column, and this of Hellenistic date, stands on the south flank, the fourth from the east front.

[4] It has been suggested that eleven pairs of columns were actually set up in the cella, and that certain poros column bases belong to these; but the evidence from excavation, showing that there never had been any foundations for such columns, would appear to exclude this theory.

THE POLYCRATES TEMPLE AT SAMOS

intervals for centuries and never attained completion. Polycrates himself, perhaps foreseeing the magnitude of the task, limited his work to the essential portions, the cella, pronaos, and portion of the east peristyle corresponding to the pronaos, three rows each of four columns. These three central spans of the façade were equal, 27 feet 7 inches between column centres, not quite as large as the single central span at Ephesus and yet more imposing in that there were three of them; and the maximum diameters seem to have been about 6 feet 8 inches.[1] The columns of the front peristyle and pronaos had marble bases and capitals, though the shafts were of poros limestone; some remained unfluted, while those that are finished reveal a new development: the flutes have become deeper, and so, with the deeper cutting, they could not so well retain the sharp arrises of the earlier examples, with the result that a narrow fillet of the rounded surface of the column was preserved between the flutes, concave and very slightly convex surfaces contrasting over the whole of the shaft. Likewise on account of the deeper cutting and the space required for the fillets, the number of flutes was reduced to what became the normal figure, twenty-four. In the marble capitals the volute cushion and the echinus moulding are carved out of different blocks, the latter being in fact the crowning moulding of the shaft, and carved out of the upper drum of the same, as at Naucratis. The volutes show the same treatment with the convex "canal" and the simple separating astragal that we observed at Ephesus. In a few instances, probably on the façade, a carved necking appeared below the capitals, as at Naucratis and Ephesus. The entablature, though doubtless intended to be of marble, seems to have been temporarily constructed in wood and never replaced, no fragments of marble being preserved.[2] The portions covered by the temporary wooden entablature had a terracotta tile roof. The crucifixion of Polycrates (525 B.C.) was probably responsible for the first interruption. The rectangles of foundations for the peristyle were completed later, though before the time of Herodotus, and in accordance with the original design, with smaller spacings of $21\frac{1}{2}$ feet at the corners of the east front and all across the rear.[3] The disturbed periods of the Ionian Revolt and the Persian Wars,[4] followed by long subjection to Athens, were not conducive to great activity; thus it was not until the Hellenistic period that the missing columns of the east front, the inner row of the peristyle on the three other sides, and part of the outer row on the south flank (including the standing column) were erected with marble for the shafts as well as the bases and capitals. But the outer colonnade was never completed

---

[1] The lower diameter on the south flank has been measured as 6 feet $1\frac{1}{2}$ inches, the disk of the base being 7 feet $1\frac{3}{8}$ inches. On the façade the diameters of the base disks were $2\frac{1}{8}$ and $6\frac{1}{2}$ inches larger, suggesting a corresponding enlargement of the diameters.

[2] Pieces of sculptured friezes in two sizes, of poros limestone, apparently do not belong to the temple so that it is uncertain whether they were at the bottoms or tops of walls.

[3] I.e. east front (2 × 21 feet 6 inches) + (2 × 23 feet $1\frac{1}{2}$ inches) + (3 × 27 feet 7 inches) = 172 feet; west front (8 × 21 feet 6 inches) = 172 feet; flanks (20 × 15 feet $5\frac{1}{8}$ inches) + 15 feet $10\frac{1}{4}$ inches + (2 × 16 feet $2\frac{1}{8}$ inches) = 356 feet 9 inches. The excavators show slight individual variations in the eight equal spacings at the rear and in the three equal spacings at the front, but the evidence for such differences (bringing the smaller at the centre) seems inadequate and illogical.

[4] Pausanias says that the temple was burnt by the Persians; but this seems contrary to the political situation and is probably due to confusion, since Herodotus says nothing of such a fire, implying that the temple was intact (as far as built) in his time.

and never received its entablature or roof; the columns were never fluted, the pavement and stylobate were not dressed off. The disturbed conditions in the first century B.C. ended all hopes of terminating the work; Cicero and Strabo describe it as deserted; and, though a great flight of ten steps was added across the east front in the second century A.D., it was only for the purpose of forming a background for two modest little temples erected as substitutes at that time, close to the altar.

Though our consideration of the archaic Ionic temples should properly terminate with the end of the archaic period in 490 B.C., and so, practically speaking, with the outbreak of the Ionian Revolt in 499 B.C., attention must be called to a few examples of the survival of archaic tradition during the fifth century. Thus at Miletus, when the city was transplanted from the devastated archaic site to the promontory which it occupied after the Persian Wars, a temporary temple was erected in honour of Athena, and was very soon replaced by a more magnificent structure elevated on a high podium, approached by steps only at the south front, apparently imitating this feature from the unfinished temple at Samos. Apart from the unusual orientation, the temple was peculiarly shallow, with only ten columns on the flanks; all these peculiarities seem to have resulted from its constricted location within a city block. The south front was hexastyle, apparently with the three central spacings greater than the others in the usual Ionic manner; and the rear had seven columns. The only remains of the peristyle are one fragment of a marble capital with the convex "canal," with the abacus eliminated, and the egg-and-dart moulding from the corner of an architrave. Again, at Magnesia-on-the-Maeander, the older temple of Artemis Leucophryene was apparently hexastyle peripteral; facing west; the surviving details are sufficient only to indicate that the bases were of the developed Asiatic type with two deep scotias, and that the shafts had thirty-two flutes with wide fillets of developed form between them, the material being limestone rather than marble as in the later temples.[1] And at Neapolis (Kavalla) in Macedonia was erected a peripteral temple in marble, called the Parthenon, of which the capitals, 4 feet 11 inches long and only 2 feet wide (showing the elongated proportions of Ephesus), and omitting the abacus as at Miletus, are most remarkable in that they embody both the old fashion and the new. The inner face of each capital has the convex "canal" with a separating rib or astragal winding to its origin without any "eye"; but the outer face of each capital has the concave canal of later times, with a small rosette serving as the "eye" and with a huge rosette 10 inches in diameter projecting at the middle of the volute cushion.[2]

Another Ionic temple of the fifth century was erected in a spot even more distant from the home of the style, at Locri Epizephyrii in southern Italy, an intruder in the west counterbalancing the Doric temple at Assos in the east. The temple at Locri, on the site called Maraza, was erected on the foundations

[1] The temples at Miletus and Magnesia must be restored on the basis of very slightly preserved foundations, so that the exact spacings of the columns are unknown; but the published restoration with five equal spacings on the south front at Miletus seems unsatisfactory. The carved necking restored at Miletus lacks evidence.

[2] A similar use of the convex "canal" on one side and the concave on the other appears in an Ionic bicolumnar monument at Delphi, probably of the third century B.C.

THE IONIC TEMPLE AT LOCRI

of its primitive predecessor, but with a different orientation; it was heptastyle at the rear, there being six axial spacings of 8 feet 8 inches or 9 Ionic feet across the west end, identical with the sixteen on the flanks;[1] the axial rectangle was laid out with proportions of 3 : 8, or 54 by 144 Ionic feet of $11\frac{9}{16}$ inches. The inner building is of normal distyle in-antis plan, with the central interval unencumbered by a column, so that we may conclude that the missing east front had only six columns, the three central spacings being widened as in the great dipteral temples, averaging 11 feet $6\frac{5}{8}$ inches or 12 Ionic feet. In spite of

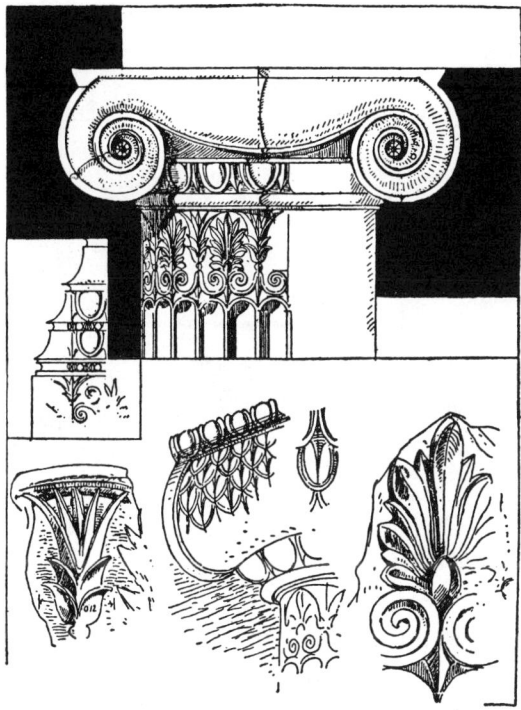

FIG. 49.—DETAILS OF CAPITALS FROM LOCRI. (Durm.)

the use of ordinary limestone, the workmanship of the masonry and the carving of the details are superb. The base is of Asiatic form, though the disk below the torus is more simple than at Samos; the shaft has twenty-four flutes separated by fillets ½ inch wide, and the necking has a lotus-and-palmette border as at Naucratis, Ephesus, and Samos. The capital (Fig. 49) retains the convex "canal" but shows an advance in the specially marked floral "eye" and in the carved imbrication of the baluster side; the absence of an abacus recalls Miletus and Neapolis. The anta capital with three tiers of ovolo mouldings resembles the richly carved but monotonously profiled anta capitals found at Didyma. Of

[1] It is usually assumed that this temple was laid out with spacings of $7\frac{1}{2}$ "Samian feet" (so-called) of $13\frac{7}{8}$ inches; but this unit is very hypothetical and probably was not used in South Italy. For the Ionic foot see p. 222, note 1, p. 229, note 2.

the entablature we have portions of a two-fascia architrave crowned by a heart-and-dart, with a beaded astragal between the fascias; there is no trace of a frieze, which was probably absent, as the cornice had the Asiatic dentils. Marble acroteria crowned the pediments, representing youths riding sea-horses supported by Tritons, derived from the terracotta acroteria of the neighbouring Doric temple. The late style of the architrave and acroteria suggest that the date was no earlier than 450 B.C. Near by, in the Locrian colony of Hipponium, was another Ionic temple, again of peripteral plan; most notable is the sima, carved in relief in fine limestone, crowned by a lotus-and-palmette cut in silhouette.

* * * * *

Among the Ionic treasuries, of which there were several, the most famous were two erected at Delphi, the Cnidian and the Siphnian (Fig. 50), dating

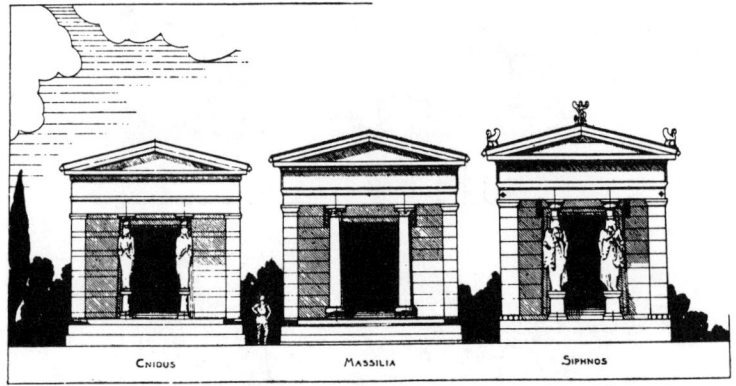

FIG. 50.—CNIDIAN, MASSILIOT AND SIPHNIAN TREASURIES AT DELPHI.
(Restored by Dinsmoor.)

respectively from about 565–555 and 530–525 B.C.[1] Yet both, instead of having Ionic columns in-antis, employed pairs of Caryatid figures on pedestals, prototypes of the much more developed Caryatids of the Erechtheum at Athens.[2] Both treasuries were of marble; but that of the Cnidians was poorly constructed with pseudo-isodomic masonry and was almost devoid of sculpture, except that the idea of Caryatids was probably first exemplified here in monumental form. These figures are of a type resembling the familiar archaic maidens

[1] A recent tendency to assign a later date to the Cnidian treasury, toward 540 B.C., because of the treatment of drapery wrongly assigned to the Caryatids, seems impossible in view of the much earlier ornament (egg-and-dart, bead-and-reel) and technical details (undeveloped lead clamps and dowels, primitive joint tooling, and lack of knowledge of the toothed chisel, cf. p. 72, note 1), as contrasted with the neighbouring Siphnian treasury of 530–525 B.C.

[2] The identities of the Cnidian and Siphnian treasuries were formerly interchanged and even mingled; thus the reconstruction shown in Plate XXXII, and formerly labelled Cnidian, consists chiefly of pieces of the Siphnian treasury, with the wall construction and anta capital of the Massiliot, and the dedicatory inscription of the Cnidian. These three treasuries are shown separately in Fig. 50; the clarification of the problem resulted from a study of their variant techniques and constructive methods.

(*korai*) of the Athenian Acropolis, and carry on their heads a polos (tall cylindrical drum) decorated with reliefs, and above this a wide-spreading capital of Doric profile though with the echinus carved into petals; the figures stood on pedestals, probably circular. Another innovation in the Cnidian treasury was the substitution, for the native Asiatic friezeless entablature, of a full entablature with a frieze between the architrave and cornice (the dentils being omitted). Probably the introduction of the frieze was inspired by the neighbouring Doric treasuries in the same sanctuary; and its purpose was merely to increase the height of the entablature; in the Cnidian treasury the frieze was left plain (or possibly sculptured only on the façade), and because of it the fascias of the architrave were omitted, so that the architrave differs from the Doric only in the richness of its crowning mouldings.[1] The frieze, at first a mere repetition of the architrave, was quickly seized upon as a field for decorative sculpture, as in the richest and most complete of these treasuries, that of the Siphnians. The latter, although of small dimensions, only 20 feet $1\frac{1}{2}$ inch by 28 feet on the stylobate, is one of the most richly decorated of such buildings that ever existed (Plate XXXII). The vestibule consisted of a portico in-antis, with Caryatid figures of heavier proportions, more adapted to their function, raised on square pedestals, and carrying a polos with a peculiar bell capital carved with animals in relief. The doorway behind resembled those at Naxos and Paros, wide in proportion to its height, the monolithic jambs and the lintel having three fascias, the outermost wider than the others and carved with an anthemion, with an enframing astragal; the high threshold, with three similar fascias and with the colossal bead-and-reel of the wall base carried along the bottom, the frieze above the lintel (apparently of three superposed ovolos as at Paros), and the elaborately carved cornice resting on volute consoles (the volutes appearing only at the bottom and not, as in the later S-scroll form, at the top as well), combine to make this the richest of all Ionic doorways. In the outer entablature the frieze, or zoophorus, 2 feet $1\frac{1}{4}$ inches in height, was enriched with sculpture in high relief, painted in red, blue and green, the effect being heightened by bronze spears, wheels of chariots, and bronze harness fastened to the marble. In the pediments were groups of smaller figures, the upper portions of which were carved in the round and detached from the tympanum at the back. On the apex of each gable was a flying victory, on the lower corners seated sphinxes. The whole was built of island marble, and brilliantly coloured; the interior of the cella apparently had even a marble revetment $1\frac{1}{4}$ inches thick. The elaboration and carving of the mouldings, despite their unduly heavy proportions, and the anthemion designs round the architrave of the doorway, on the soffit of the cornice and on the sima (Plate XXXI), are equal to those of the Erechtheum, which it precedes by fully a century.

Two Aeolic treasuries at Delphi, erected by Clazomenae and Massilia during the period between the Cnidian and Siphnian dedications, were likewise of

[1] Owing to the scarcity of fragments the problem of the frieze is difficult. Below the cornice were an ovolo profile and abacus (like an uncarved dentil course) with the top dressed to support an overhanging cornice; but the rectangular eggs are more closely spaced than the barrel-shaped beads on the top of the architrave and so require an intervening course, the frieze. Two plain fragments with barrel-shaped beads spaced to fit the friezecrown must belong to the frieze; but there are also sculptured fragments (with the characteristic bead broken off) which might belong to the façade.

marble; the Clazomenian treasury was destroyed in ancient times and only a few pieces now remain. Apart from the column capitals, these treasuries were distinctly Ionic, the walls surrounded at the base by a fluted torus and beaded astragal, and crowned by a full entablature with architrave, frieze (sculptured in the Massiliot treasury), and cornice; as in the Siphnian treasury the cornices lack dentils, but the soffit of the Massiliot cornice and the face of its sima are carved with rich lotus-and-palmette ornament. The anta capital (preserved in the Massiliot treasury) is merely a cyma reversa (carved with the heart-and-dart) with a beaded astragal below and an abacus above.[1] The columns in-antis are the remarkable features of these two treasuries, having Asiatic Ionic bases (with extra mouldings in the Massiliot bases), fluted shafts with sharp arrises (eighteen in the Clazomenian, twenty-two in the Massiliot), and the peculiar Aeolic basket capitals with drooping petals equal in number to the flutes of the shafts, each supporting a heavy square abacus (Plate XXXIII).[2] Thus the order is merely, like the later Corinthian, an offshoot of the Ionic style, differing only in the form of the capital (which in fact resembles the primitive Ionic echinus with the pendant deeply undercut leaves); but it is of special importance as the probable prototype of the Corinthian.

FIG. 51.—THE ALTAR OF POSEIDON AT CAPE MONODENDRI.
(Restored by Gerkan.)

The great altars of the archaic Ionic sanctuaries set a standard for splendour that was not rivalled until Hellenistic times. Thus the successive seven altars of Hera at Samos were replaced by that designed at about 575 B.C. by Rhoecus, seven times the size of its immediate predecessor, 120 by $54\frac{1}{2}$ feet, with a platform making it exactly 120 feet square. Now for the first time the altar was harmonised with the temple by changing its orientation and placing it on axis. Particularly noteworthy is its rich detail carved in limestone, such as the ovolo carved in relief with the lotus-and-palmette (as at Myus) instead of eggs, above a huge beaded astragal. In imperial Roman times it was carefully replaced by an exact copy in marble, imitating the archaic profiles and decoration. Of nearly the same period is the altar of Poseidon on Cape Monodendri at Miletus (Fig. 51), pseudo-isodomic walls supporting a cap moulding which turned up at the four corners into volutes, with the convex "canal" and without the "eye."

---

[1] It is to be noted that, in this as in the other Ionic treasuries at Delphi, the side returns of the antae were defined only by the capitals, anta offsets being absent as at Ephesus.
[2] Some modern investigators have restored two tiers of petals in each capital; but the actual remains will not permit such a restoration. In the official French publication, moreover, the columns are made disproportionately tall, 13 diameters.

ALTARS WITH IONIC DETAILS

From a later altar of such form may have come the enigmatical pair of "thrones" (the "Ludovisi throne" and the "Boston throne"), of Ionic workmanship and with beautiful relief sculpture above the volutes. Smaller altars, both square and circular, are numerous at Miletus and Samos, and are of particular interest because of their egg-and-dart mouldings. There are also Ionic altars in Greece itself, such as that dedicated to Apollo at Athens by the younger Peisistratus when he was archon about 522 B.C.; below the abacus is a cyma reversa, carved with a heart-and-dart of sixth-century type, undercut beneath and provided with a hawksbeak bed-moulding. Another simple form appears in the altar erected by the Chians for Apollo at Delphi, probably at the time of the Alcmaeonid work on the temple itself,[1] a high pedestal faced by black limestone

FIG. 52.—THE "ALTAR" OF APOLLO AT AMYCLAE.
(Restored by Buschor.)

in pseudo-isodomic masonry (with courses alternately high and low), crowned by a white marble cap, the earliest known instance of such contrasting materials. And perhaps, too, we should number among structures of this kind the great altar or "throne" of Apollo at Amyclae near Sparta (Fig. 52), erected by the Ionian architect Bathycles from Magnesia in Asia Minor as the setting for a primitive xoanon, with hybrid Doric-Ionic forms, Doric capitals from which spring Ionic volute consoles (Plate XXXIII), anta capitals of the "Proto-Ionic" or "sofa" form, and Caryatids, as described by Pausanias. The marble Doric columns are very slender, with sixteen flutes; the capitals vary, some having neckings with a cyma recta profile, separated from the shaft by astragals and fillets, while in others the neckings are hollow with a leaf decoration in relief, and in the hybrid forms the volute "canal" is itself continued round the capital as a necking. Also the cornice face subdivided like an Ionic architrave, the fluted decoration of its crowning moulding, and the cavetto sima carved in relief

[1] The date officially assigned by the French, the second quarter of the fifth century, seems too late.

with the lotus-and-palmette, and other Ionic mouldings used freely throughout the structure, combined to make this one of the most exotic designs of the period; but unfortunately its exact restoration is by no means certain.[1]

Among porticoes or stoas of Ionic design, the foundations of several majestic examples exist at Samos, such as the south stoa destroyed at the time of the Rhoecus temple (575 B.C.) and replaced by the "south building." A little later was the northwest stoa at Samos, of the time of Rhoecus, about 200 feet long, divided into three sections by cross-walls. Another stoa lay southwest of the temple, with about twenty-nine columns between antae on the front and a second row within. The most interesting, however, is the Stoa of the Athenians at Delphi, built against the raised terrace of the temple of Apollo, perhaps to commemorate an Athenian naval victory of 497 B.C.[2] The three steps are of black limestone; the eight Ionic columns are of white marble, so widely spaced that the entablature could only have been of wood. The scale is very small, the lower diameter of the monolithic shafts being only 15 inches, with sixteen flutes separated by fillets. The bases are precursors of the "Attic base," having below the torus and disk (the latter of a peculiar cyma recta or bell profile) of the Asiatic form a lower torus, as yet of diminutive size.

A few unusual buildings, occurring within religious precincts and yet not belonging to the category of temples, require brief mention. One of these is the House of the Naxians at Delos, constructed of Naxian marble in the form of a simple rectangle about 32 by 84 feet, with a single line of eight marble Ionic columns along the main axis.[3] The pronaos, originally closed with a simple doorway, was later opened with two Ionic columns in-antis; and in Hellenistic times was added an opisthodomus with four prostyle Ionic columns. Another curious building at Samos, the so-called "South Building" erected by Rhoecus, has a single line of columns on the axis of the cella and the deep pronaos, and also a peristyle, at least round the rear and both flanks; but the front is cut off at the line of the pronaos, with no evidence that a façade was ever intended.

In the form of smaller monuments, as distinct from temples, the Ionic style freely penetrated into districts which in religious architecture were more strictly devoted to the Doric style. This was particularly true at Athens, where Peisistratus and his sons were closely affiliated with the Ionic tyrants, and at Delphi, where the Ionic states in common with others dedicated offerings. Some of the archaic votive capitals discovered at Athens, and others at Delos, still retain reminiscences of the Proto-Ionic type, with volutes springing vertically or even horizontal volutes as yet not connected; and in technique some are merely masses or blocks with the spirals traced or painted on, in what must have been the primitive manner (Fig. 53). Two of them have the egg-and-dart deeply undercut, with a cavetto which recalls the original form of the

---

[1] The generally accepted date, about the time of the Siphnian treasury, agrees best with the style of the remains; efforts to place it a half-century earlier, on the assumption that certain Laconian vase paintings were inspired by the sculptures of the altar, are nullified by the developed character of the architectural detail.

[2] The Athenian Stoa is sometimes dated as early as 506 B.C.; Amandry now very plausibly suggests 478 B.C.; the date 429 B.C. given by Pausanias is far too late.

[3] Below it are remains of a much earlier building of similar plan, but with two rows each of eight wooden columns dividing the cella into three aisles.

VOTIVE MONUMENTS

pendant leaves; it is in such examples as these that we find the first transition from the overhanging leaves. Among these capitals scarcely a duplicate is to be found; they show infinite variety in design, and any attempt to arrange them chronologically, in accordance with their development from the most primitive type, would be illusory, since they are all of about the same date, their variations being merely the result of playful fantasy.

Among such votive monuments one of the most important for the development of the Ionic order is the column erected by the Naxians at Delphi to support a colossal Sphinx (Plate XXXIII); the whole is carried out in Naxian marble, 47 feet high including the Sphinx. The column itself was 3 feet $1\frac{5}{8}$ inches in diameter, with a height of $12\frac{1}{2}$ diameters, the most slender of all Ionic columns; it has no moulded base, merely a smooth disk 19 inches high supporting a shaft with forty-four shallow flutes with sharp arrises between. The capital has no abacus (recalling the type at Locri), and the volutes, though without "eyes," are unusual for the archaic period in that the "canal" is actually concave; this latter feature seems to be due rather to the individuality of the designer than to the stage of development. For the plan of the capital is as long and narrow as at Ephesus, and the echinus with its receding upper portion and the deep cavetto below is even more reminiscent of the pendant leaves of the Proto-Ionic capital. Two smaller Ionic columns with Sphinxes were erected by the Naxians at Delos. Another column at Aegina, less elaborate, was constructed of poros limestone; the base was a flat disk about 5 feet in diameter, supporting a shaft with thirty-six flutes, about 3 feet in upper diameter. The capital was a simple hemisphere 3 feet $4\frac{1}{2}$ inches in diameter (serving as the echinus) intersected by a horizontal beam $13\frac{1}{2}$ inches wide, of which the ends must have drooped down to form volutes with the details painted on the smooth surfaces.[1]

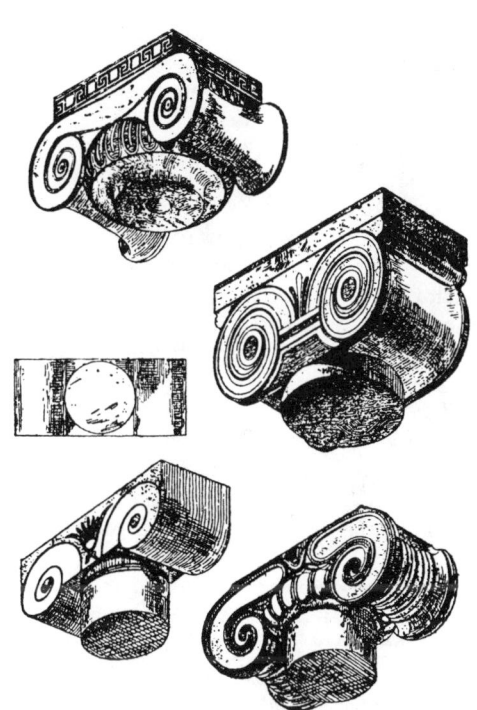

Fig. 53.—Votive Capitals from Athens and Delos. (Chipiez.)

The westward infiltration of Ionic detail, of which we have noted many instances, is marked also by the occurrence of numerous other Ionic capitals, most of them presumably votive, in widely scattered areas. Among them may be cited a little bronze Ionic capital supporting a seated Sphinx from Crete,

[1] The capital no longer exists, except in Cockerell's notebook.

THE RISE OF THE IONIC STYLE

another with a reclining Sphinx from Selinus (Gaggera), as well as small capitals of more architectural character from Selinus, Syracuse, Metapontum, and Capua.

Anta capitals of the so-called "Proto-Ionic" or "sofa" type have been mentioned, apart from those of primitive style in Phoenicia and Cyprus, only in connection with the Ionic infiltration into the west, as in temples on the Silaris (Fig. 32) and Paestum and at Selinus, and in the altar at Amyclae.[1] Indeed, it is curious that most of the early examples of this form are to be found, not in Asia Minor where we might expect them, but in the west. And it is probable that most of these were parts of votive monuments. One comes from Samothrace, the most eastern of the series; several were found in the neighbourhood of Sparta (as at Slavochori and Mistra), others at Tegea in Arcadia, at Monrepos in Corcyra, and, in Sicily, at Acrae, at Syracuse (some of these only $6\frac{1}{2}$ inches high), and at Megara Hyblaea (the last a magnificent example, dating from the fifth century).

Several examples of sculptured Ionic friezes are of uncertain origin; some of them may have belonged to temples or altars, but it seems probable that the majority are from votive monuments or tombs. We have already noted poros examples at Corcyra and Samos;[2] we should mention also several marble friezes, such as the frieze of dancing women from Miletus (Karakeuy) and the Gorgon frieze also from Miletus (Hieronda), as well as the charioteer frieze from Cyzicus, and also the terracotta frieze from Apollonia in Thrace.

The archaic Ionic sepulchral monuments include Asiatic counterparts of the Attic stelae, such as the stele from Dorylaeum with its enframing beaded moulding (of early archaic type) and crowning palmette, the beautiful example from the Troad and the magnificent series from Samos, with their varied combinations of palmettes with S-scrolls paired in lyre patterns (Fig. 54). From these sources the Athenian repertory was enriched; and an imitation even more frankly Ionic is the grave relief of a falling warrior, found at Athens, crowned by an Ionic capital of which the cushion is extremely elongated to cover the entire width. Among the monuments of Asia Minor the most imposing, however, are to be found in Lycia, where the elaborate sepulchral towers at Xanthus, decorated with sculptured friezes and crowned by projecting cornices or by gables (such as the Lion tomb, the Harpy tomb, and many others), foreshadow the development of the Mausoleum type in the fourth century. The Harpy tomb, for instance, rests on a podium 6 feet high, and the shaft is a single marble block 17 feet high, 7 feet 7 inches by 8 feet 2 inches in plan, weighing about 80 tons; on its top rested the marble frieze, 3 feet 4 inches high, enclosing the tomb chamber of which the floor was hollowed out within the shaft to give a clear internal height of $7\frac{1}{2}$ feet; the entrance was through one face of the frieze. Above all was the cap stone in the form of a stepped cornice, weighing more than 15 tons. Other Lycian tombs had gabled tops with ridge roofs, and others again had the ogival curvilinear roofs mentioned in a previous chapter (Fig. 23).[3]

Here, too, should be mentioned the earliest examples of the elaborate Ionic sarcophagi, such as the terracotta series from Clazomenae, the terracotta

[1] See pp. 86, 94, 100, 141.   [2] See p. 73, note 1; p. 135, note 2.
[3] Many portions of these Xanthian tombs of all three types are in the British Museum.

examples found at Gela in Sicily with archaic Ionic columns in the four internal corners, and also the oldest marble sarcophagus with columns on the exterior, found at Samos, with antae at the corners and two archaic Ionic columns standing between them on each end, three on each flank, and a cover in the form of a pedimental roof (an early predecessor of the sarcophagus of the Mourning Women from Sidon). Belonging to the fifth century, but nevertheless to the

FIG. 54.—GRAVE STELAE FROM SAMOS AND THE TROAD.

period under discussion, are the marble sarcophagi from Sidon known as the Satrap and Lycian sarcophagi, the latter distinguished by its ogival vaulted cover.[1]

* * * * *

Such was the artistic expression of that phase of culture known as Archaic Ionic, of which the details from the early temple of Artemis at Ephesus give the best idea. It was at this early period that the structural development of the style was completed; the genius of subsequent architects through centuries was mainly directed to a refining and modifying process, to a close study of every possible elegance and polish consistent with quiet and sound taste, to the obliteration of every crude line, harsh angle, or unseemly form. In such ways they reached the perfection of the temple of Athena Nike and the Erechtheum, which were not so much the works of their particular architects as the matured fruit of a succession of harvests: the result, as we see now, of the dispersion to

[1] Clazomenian sarcophagi are to be found in all the great museums; one from Gela is in the British Museum; the Samian sarcophagus is presumably still at Samos; and the Sidonian sarcophagi are in the Istanbul Museum, having been discovered by Hamdy-Bey in 1887.

Asia, of the atmosphere which the Asiatic colonist breathed, and of the archaic temples of the east. Yet who would affirm that the Greeks were automatons working out unconsciously a line of development, following blindly a predestined course? If ever architects thought or planned or designed with true originality, they were the Greeks. But it was the conservatism, the traditionalism, of the style which, after its constructive form was fixed, gave us the masterpieces of the culmination in Athens.

CHAPTER FIVE

THE CULMINATION IN ATTICA AND THE PELOPONNESUS

AS we have already pointed out in a preceding chapter, during the period described as Archaic the structural development of the styles was completed, few great constructive improvements showing themselves after about 490 B.C. The next two centuries would seem to have been directed chiefly to the beautifying and refining of the constructive features already prescribed: and it was in fact a conservative adherence to the older type, and a traditional respect for previous result, which led ultimately to the production of such masterpieces as the Parthenon, the Propylaea, and the Erechtheum, the perfection of which would have been impossible but for the careful and logical progression of the preceding centuries.

It has been said that behind and beyond any cause that we can specify for a development in art and in civilisation itself there is an economic one; and this theory may be applied to the culmination of Greek art. That a great period in art production should arise, there must be a certain over-production and accumulation of wealth, which may be said to find an outlet in the various channels which architecture and art supply. According to this view of it, we may trace the Egyptian monuments back to the wealth of the Pharaohs, the architecture of Rome to the spoils of the world, and in like manner find an explanation in an economic sense of the central period of Greek art, the age of Pericles. The wars with Persia had enriched Athens, and her naval supremacy, displayed most of all in the battle of Salamis, had raised her to a position of the greatest influence among the Greek cities: so that when the Persians were driven out of Greece, many of the islands and the coast cities of Thrace and Asia Minor, with Athens at their head, in 477 B.C. effected an alliance known as the Delian League, permanently to keep the Persians out of all Greek lands. Athens, gradually assuming greater authority, practically came to treat her allies as subject cities, even exacting tribute and in 454 B.C. transferring the treasury from neutral Delos to the Athenian Acropolis; and thus riches, talent, and power passed into the capital of the hegemony. It was about this time that she, under the leadership of Pericles, took the greatest and proudest place among great cities, built her most beautiful temples, and brought forth her greatest artists; and it is the artistic work of this period, which in its beauty reaches its culminating point of perfection together with all else that was greatest in its history, that we have now to study.

Yet the wonders of the Periclean age would have been impossible but for the long line of Greek artistic tradition, which had been preparing the way not only in Greece but also in Asia Minor. The reflex action of these Ionian cities upon Greece proper can hardly be overestimated, in considering all the causes of the culmination. For, as has been already observed, Athens was an Ionian city from early days, and was influenced largely by, and had much commerce with, her compatriots in Asia Minor. But besides this influence of kinship, there was at work one of almost equal power, namely, the development of Doric principles and manners in the Peloponnesus, by which Athens, if for no other reason than her situation, must have been moulded. Leader of the Ionians in the Grecian motherland, she could not escape the influence of her Dorian neighbours. Hence it came to be, by an irony of fate, that her greatest temple, the Parthenon, and her most popular monument, the Propylaea, were in the Dorian style, though they were in many respects different from the Dorian works elsewhere. In every place except Attica, the cleavage of the styles with the population is quite marked. The Doric so prevails in Sicily, southern Italy, and the Peloponnesus, where the Dorians predominated, that only one or two purely Ionic temples have there been discovered; on the other hand, the temples of Athena at Assos and Pergamum are the only important Greek Doric works in Ionian territory outside of Athens.

Another decisive factor was the appearance of a group of great artists to whom this economic over-production and developed artistic tradition afforded opportunity for the exercise of their skill. We know at least the names of the great architects and sculptors of this period, and we can identify some of their works. Leader among the architects was Ictinus, the designer of the Parthenon, which he made the subject of a book, unfortunately lost but mentioned by Vitruvius; this architect also worked on the Telesterion or Hall of the Mysteries at Eleusis, and designed the temple of Apollo at Bassae, near Phigalia, a work of the greatest interest even though it does not exhibit all the grace of the Parthenon. Ictinus was assisted in his work on the Parthenon by Callicrates, of whom less is known; and the name of Mnesicles has come down to us as that of the creator of the Propylaea, which, as will afterwards appear, he did not leave complete or even as he had originally intended it to be. Many of these works, the Propylaea, the temple at Bassae, and in a lesser degree the Parthenon, embrace both Doric and Ionic principles, as well as their distinctive features; and Callicrates, furthermore, is known as the designer of purely Ionic works, such as the temple of Athena Nike and that on the River Ilissus, while it is quite possible—though our evidence is solely stylistic—that Callicrates likewise designed the "Athenian temple" at Delos, and that Mnesicles was the author of the Erechtheum. The style of another important architect, unfortunately nameless, can be reconstructed on the basis of four temples which may be ascribed to him, the so-called "Theseum" (really the Hephaesteum) at Athens and the temple of Ares in the same city, and the temples at Sunium and Rhamnus on the eastern shore of Attica. Beside these, Phidias, king of sculptors, must have an honoured place. This Athenian, at the time of the erection of the Parthenon, already enjoyed great fame throughout Greece, and consequently he was able to command talent of the highest order in carrying out his work—for it is not to be supposed that he executed with his own hands the pediment, frieze, and metope sculptures of the Parthenon, though they were doubtless all of his conception. Among the greatest works of Phidias were his cult statues and votive monuments; to the latter class belongs the colossal bronze statue of Athena Promachos, made of Persian spoils during 463–454 B.C., which stood on the Acropolis between the Propylaea and the Erechtheum (as shown in the restoration, Plate LI; *cf.* Fig. 74 at S), and whose gilded helmet crest gleamed about 57 feet above the rock, a landmark for sailors far at sea; and in the former class was the world's wonder of the huge Panhellenic Zeus at Olympia. To these, under the patronage of Pericles, he added the colossal gold-and-ivory figure of Athena in the cella of the Parthenon, and the smaller bronze statue of the Lemnian Athena which stood near the Propylaea. In lesser undertakings we meet the names of other sculptors, chiefly the pupils of Phidias, such as Agoracritus who worked at Rhamnus, and Alcamenes who worked in the Hephaesteum and the temple of Ares; and there was also Callimachus, the designer of the Corinthian capital. And there were also the mural painters Polygnotus, Micon, and Panaenus the brother of Phidias. These are merely the names of some of the men in the immediate employ of the Periclean government; but also in other parts of Greece we meet at this time a few prominent names, such as Libon of Elis and Eupolemus of Argos, the architects, and Polycleitus of Argos, Colotes of Elis, and Paeonius of Mende, the sculptors.

Of the rival political centre of that century, Sparta, Thucydides could only say (a true prophecy): "If Lacedaemon were some day to be devastated, and if there remained only the sanctuaries and the foundations of public buildings, posterity in the distant future would have difficulty in believing that its power corresponded to its renown."

Before devoting our attention to the works which owed their inspiration to Pericles and his advisers at Athens, however, it is necessary to recede to the period of the Persian invasions and to note their effects upon architectural development on the Greek mainland. In this respect we are, to a certain extent, retracing our steps; for we have already followed the evolution both in the western colonies and in Asia Minor down to a much later part of the fifth century. But, on the Hellenic mainland, the thirty years immediately preceding the Periclean age are almost inseparably united with the remainder of the century.

* * * * *

At Athens, the single-handed victory over the Persian hosts at Marathon on October 11, 490 B.C., supplied the motive for an architectural renaissance. Another factor was the opening, at about the same time, of the Pentelic marble quarries just outside Athens; hitherto very little material had been extracted from this source, and for architectural and sculptural purposes it had been necessary to import marble at considerable expense from the islands, especially Paros, so that it had been employed very sparingly. The conjunction of these events led to a scheme, presumably sponsored by Aristeides, for the rebuilding of the Acropolis in a material unrivalled in the Greek world. Probably the Athenians were impatient of the poor appearance and tyrannical associations of their chief temples, the poros Hecatompedon and the Peisistratid temple of Athena. The site chosen for the new temple, known as the Older Parthenon, was that on the south side of the Acropolis previously occupied by the old poros Hecatompedon.[1] To make room, the latter was demolished and its remains were either broken up to serve as fill in the great terraces required to

---

[1] Traces of the Older Parthenon were first observed in 1835 and even now can be made out only by close analysis of scattered blocks and of the remains under the present Parthenon.

bring the south slope up to the requisite level, or were squared for second-hand use in the new foundations.[1] A huge platform of solid limestone masonry 252 feet long and 103 feet wide, attaining at one corner a height of 35 feet above bed rock, formed the substructure of the temple; along the south flank it was intended to form a podium rising 7½ feet above the graded earth. Leaving a portion of the platform to form a terrace on all four sides, the three-stepped temple was begun with stylobate dimensions of 77 feet 2½ inches by 219 feet 7½ inches; the lowest step was of pink Kara limestone, the middle step and stylobate of Pentelic marble. The temple was hexastyle, with sixteen columns on the flanks, all uniformly 6 feet 3 inches (5⅝ Doric feet) in lower diameter except those at the corners, which in accordance with a new system of emphasis were thickened by one-fortieth of the diameter. On the other hand, the archaic practice of reducing the flank spacing was retained (13½ and 13⅓ Doric feet on front and flank, respectively). The inner building was tetrastyle prostyle (rather than in-antis) at both ends, the antae being of Ionic form lacking offsets but with base mouldings which were continued along the cella walls. The pronaos gave access to a long cella divided by two rows of interior columns, while through the opisthodomus could be entered what was probably a single large room, the prototype of the west (Parthenon) chamber of the Periclean temple. The chief interest of this temple is that it initiated marble construction in Attica on a large scale, introduced the use of Ionic elements and the application of delicate refinements in upward curvature and column inclinations, and even contributed much of the material and many of the dimensions for the present Parthenon. When the Persians returned in 480 B.C. they completely destroyed it, the unfinished columns at this time having attained a height of only two to four drums (5 to 10 feet) above the stylobate. For more than thirty years it survived merely as a calcined ruin and marble quarry, many of its blocks being built into the north wall of the Acropolis as a memorial of the war in 479 B.C., and the remainder recut or used again in the present Parthenon in 447 B.C., or concealed beneath it and its terrace.

A curious phenomenon was the architectural stagnation resulting in Attica and certain other parts of central and northern Greece which had been exposed to the Persian devastation of 480–479 B.C. The impulse toward monumental building, inspired by Marathon, was smothered by the oath sworn before the battle of Plataea in 479 B.C., namely, that "the sanctuaries which have been burnt and thrown down by the barbarians" are not to be rebuilt, but to be left "as memorials of the impiety of the barbarians." Because of this self-imposed oath, the sanctuaries were encumbered with half-burnt ruins, not only on the Acropolis but also in the lower city of Athens and in other parts of

[1] It is through examination of the broken potsherds in the bottom of the terrace fill, dating in part almost as late as 490 B.C. and thus giving this as the date after which the temple was begun, together with the traces of fire on the new marble structure showing that the erection stopped at the time of the Persian conflagration in 480 B.C., that we may assign the temple to the intervening decade. More specifically, comparison of the orientation of the temple axis with the direction of the actual sunrise on the festival day of Athena, in accordance with the lunar calendar (in other words, obtaining a synchronism between the sun and the moon) for the various intervening years, yields 488 B.C. as the exact year of the beginning. Other theories as to the date, to be sure, are still current, ranging over seventy-five years from 540 to 465 B.C.; but the earlier or later dates will not fit the evidence.

Attica, in Boeotian cities such as Abae, and even as far as Byzantium; they were described not only by Herodotus but even by Strabo and Pausanias, the last more than six centuries later. By exception, an older structure such as the cella of the Peisistratid temple might be reroofed and partly restored for secular use as the state treasury, after the calcined peristyle had been taken down; but the image of Athena brought back from Salamis was placed, not in the east cella of the ruined temple, but in a marble shrine erected just to the north, under the present Erechtheum. Similarly an improvised shrine with rubble walls strengthened by column drums from the injured temple was built at Sunium beside the south flank of the temple. For Athena Nike, hitherto apparently worshipped merely in an open precinct at the west end of the Acropolis, a simple cella was actually erected at this time, very modest in proportions though with excellently cut poros masonry.

It is, therefore, to the Peloponnesus, which had enjoyed immunity from Persian attack, that we must now turn in order to examine one or two temples which form a prelude to the culmination. The most important of these was the main temple in the precinct already described at Olympia, erected from the designs of Libon of Elis and dedicated to Zeus.[1] Pausanias names the architect, and it seems probable that the temple was commenced during the Olympic festival of 468 B.C., and dedicated at the time of the festival of 460 or 456 B.C.[2] Here Zeus—though not Hera—acquired a more spacious home than the old Heraeum which had originally sheltered them both (Fig. 44 at H, Z). The new plan is of the normal hexastyle Doric type (Fig. 55), with thirteen columns on the flanks; in size, however, it was most imposing, one of the largest Doric temples erected in Greece proper. It was built in the coarse shelly limestone of the district, covered with a thin coat of white stucco and painted; but the pediment sculptures, the metopes of the inner porches, and the simas and roof tiles were of Parian marble (partly repaired in later times with Pentelic marble),[3]

---

[1] The temple was totally destroyed by earthquake, probably in the early Byzantine period, so that it was never utilised as a church and was completely built over and forgotten; and the rambling village covering the site was in turn overwhelmed by the thick mass of yellow earth spread over the entire area after a cloudburst perhaps in the seventh century. Some preliminary excavation of the site was attempted by Cockerell and Haller in 1811, and some remains of the temple soon afterward became known as a result of the partial exploration by the French *Expédition de Morée* in 1829. But the complete exposure of the plan by the Germans in 1877 revealed features hitherto unrecorded.

[2] Pausanias wrongly implies that the date was about 570 B.C.; but the monuments buried beneath the temple show that it must have been erected after 480 B.C. and so presumably after the time of the establishment of Elean supremacy during the Olympiad 472–468, and such a date as 468 B.C. agrees with the architectural and sculptural style. The date of completion is fixed approximately by the Spartan dedication of a shield on the apex of the east pediment after the victory at Tanagra in 457 B.C.

[3] Pausanias speaks particularly of the roof of Pentelic marble "wrought into the shape of tiles." It has been suggested that Parian marble was employed for tiles on account of its translucency, which would not only light the space between the roof and the ceilings of the peristyle and cella, but might even partly account for the illumination of the interior of the cella, through openings in the framed ceiling, which otherwise was lighted alone through the open door. But the existence of special tiles with elliptical openings shows that the architect was not disposed to rely solely on the translucency of the material. Tiles with similar pierced openings surrounded with projecting rims have been found at Athens, Calydon (Heroum), Olynthus, Corinth, Tegea, Bassae, Colophon, Priene, and in Italy at Caulonia, Sybaris, and Pompeii ; these were obviously intended merely to light and

THE CULMINATION IN ATTICA AND THE PELOPONNESUS

and the acroteria were of bronze (Plate XXXIV). On the east front a sloping ramp, as at Aegina, formed the approach to the stylobate. In this plan the archaic variation between front and flank survives only in the column diameters, which are 1⅝ inches greater on the fronts, so that the angle columns are not specially enlarged. But the axial spacings are uniform on all sides (except at the contracted corners), being equivalent to 16 Greek (Doric) feet; thus the triglyphs were spaced 8 Greek feet on centres, the mutules and lion heads 4 feet, and the tiles 2 feet. The height of the columns was made 32 Doric feet, exactly twice the axial spacing; and the abacus width of 8 feet (on the flanks) is half of the axial spacing and a quarter of the column height. It seems clear that Libon was attempting to work out some ideal system of proportions. The marble sima reproduces the ovolo profile of the Corinthian terracottas. The pediments contained elaborate sculptured Parian marble groups, representing, on the east, the preparations for the chariot race of Pelops and Oenomaus, and on the west the battle of Lapiths and Centaurs; the design of the group is now skilfully adapted to their triangular frames, and in the subjects, too, we find a subtle distinction, the more dignified scene being placed over the main entrance, while at the rear all is turmoil and confusion.[1] The acroteria consisted of gilded bronze Victories (by Paeonius) at the apex of each pediment, and gilded bronze tripods at the lower extremities.[2] Above the columns of the pronaos and opisthodomus were triglyph friezes, each displaying six marble metopes, the whole representing the twelve labours of Heracles; the returns of the corner triglyphs were narrowed by 10 inches in order to agree with the outer anta returns. The pavement shows traces of the folding gates between the columns and antae of the pronaos, as also of the great door leading into the cella. A range of seven Doric columns on either side, of limestone like those on the exterior, divided the cella into a nave and two side aisles, and carried an upper range of columns, also Doric, to support the ceiling (Plate XXXIV).

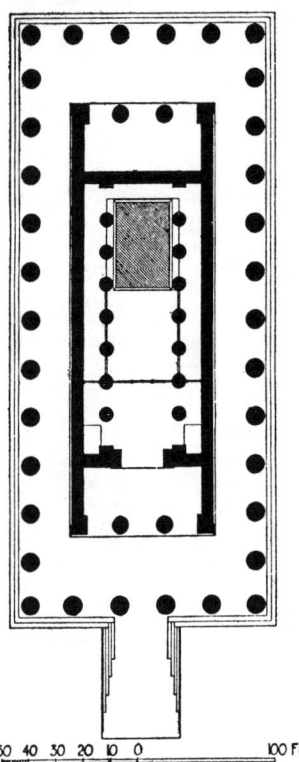

FIG. 55.—TEMPLE OF ZEUS AT OLYMPIA.

ventilate the storage space above the ceiling. We must also reject the idea, so frequently advanced, of a hypaethral opening in the roof, which with its notch in the ridge line would have had a very ugly effect from the exterior.

[1] The tradition given by Pausanias, that these sculptures of the transitional period were designed by Paeonius and Alcamenes, two artists of the latter part of the fifth century, is certainly erroneous and due to some confusion (in the case of Paeonius with the acroteria).

[2] In other words, the bronze Victories (of which we have no traces) may either have been youthful works by Paeonius and thus have borne no resemblance to his famous Messenian Victory, or they may have been added to the temple at a later time.

TEMPLE OF ZEUS AT OLYMPIA

If, as seems probable, the temple was dedicated in 460 B.C., the archaic cult statue of Zeus may have been transferred for the occasion from the Heraeum. A few years later, however, presumably in 454 B.C., Phidias was called from Athens to execute a more appropriate statue; and the result was the colossal chryselephantine seated statue of Zeus Olympius, one of the seven wonders of the ancient world, probably dedicated at the Olympic festival of 448 B.C. The temple had not been planned for so colossal a statue, the cella being much narrower than that afterwards designed in the Parthenon. Thus Phidias was compelled to use the entire width of the nave, the pedestal (about 22 by 32 feet) fitting snugly between the columns (the fifth to seventh on either side). The pedestal was constructed of bluish-black Eleusinian limestone, to which were dowelled gilt bronze figures in relief; and above it, on a throne, sat the gold-and-ivory figure of the god rising $37\frac{1}{2}$ Doric feet (40 feet 2 inches) above the pedestal,[1] of which we have a very detailed description by Pausanias, but no accurate copy. This addition required such drastic alteration of the cella that we must assume the presence of an architect, perhaps Phidias's associate Ictinus, who was not yet busy at Athens. Thus the pedestal was made to rest on a narrow sill of Pentelic marble, flush with the stylobate of the interior columns; and for the sake of uniformity the front portion of the stylobate itself was reconstructed of Pentelic marble, the columns being undercut to receive it. In front of the base of the pedestal was a sunk pavement of bluish-black Eleusinian limestone, enclosed by the raised Pentelic marble sill forming an impluvium, or shallow tank in which the oil, mentioned by Pausanias, was kept, the oil apparently being necessary to prevent the ivory from splitting, and probably the wooden core from swelling, in the damp climate of the Altis.[2] Across the cella are the traces of a stone screen about 5 feet high, with folding gates in the centre; and similar stone screens, from the second to the fifth columns on each side, were fitted within the central flutes of the columns. Beyond the fifth columns, round the spot where the pedestal of the statue stood, are traces of metal enclosures; and metal gates also closed each aisle between the second columns and the walls on either side. Access, therefore, to the inner portions of the cella was given only to privileged persons, so that they could approach nearer to the chryselephantine statue of Zeus. At this time, moreover, the architrave separating the two storeys of interior columns was utilised as the support of a gallery floor, from which the details could be more closely appreciated. Just within the great doorway, on either side, are the bottom steps and the sinkings in which the string-pieces of wooden stairways were fixed, leading, as Pausanias says, to the gallery on either side of the cella, and continued up to the space between the ceiling and the roof (compare the makeshift alteration at Aegina).[3]

[1] The throne was 30 feet high and the god's head 5 cubits higher still (the total probably excluding the pedestal); the Graces and Seasons adorning the throne were 6 feet high (like the Nike at Athens). The dimensions are given by Callimachus in a recently discovered papyrus.
[2] A similar precaution was taken in the Parthenon, except that in the latter only water was required to counteract the intense dryness of the Acropolis.
[3] Among the later vicissitudes of the temple at Olympia during antiquity may be mentioned the repairs after an earthquake of about 175 B.C., involving the dismantling and rebuilding of both façades (in part even nearly to the bottoms of the columns), the replace-

Slightly later in date is the temple of Apollo Epicurius at Bassae in Arcadia, a remarkable example by Ictinus, the architect of the Parthenon, and suggestive of the versatility of its author.[1] The date of the temple and its purpose seem to have been misinterpreted by Pausanias, who transmitted to us the names of the architect and of the god. For Apollo appears actually to have been regarded as the Succourer in time of war rather than of plague, the temple having replaced an earlier one erected in gratitude to Apollo for the aid that he gave to the Phigalians in recapturing their city from the Spartans (soon after 659 B.C.); and, as for the date, it is obvious that Ictinus could never have designed such a temple, and particularly its Doric order, at any time after he had planned the Parthenon. It is possible that Ictinus may have been, like Colotes, a native Elean, an assistant of Libon, enlisted by Phidias for the alterations at Olympia; and after the completion of that work he might well have designed the neighbouring temple at Bassae, which continues the same tradition, toward 450 B.C. Ictinus being called to Athens, through the interest of Phidias, to begin the design of the Parthenon in 447 B.C., the work at Bassae would seem to have languished so that the final touches were not added until about 425 B.C.[2]

The material of the temple is neither the coarse limestone of Olympia nor the marble of Athens, but a fine-grained brittle limestone which was very

ment of some of the capitals, of three of the pediment statues on the west, and of part of the sima and roof tiling; for the new marble work Pentelic was substituted for Parian marble. At the same time the cracked gold-and-ivory statue of Zeus was repaired by Damophon of Messene, and it was probably in connection with this repair that King Antiochus IV in 167 B.C. dedicated behind the statue the embroidered curtain from the despoiled temple at Jerusalem. The shields appearing in the metopes of the east façade (Plate XXXIV) were dedicated by the Roman general Mummius to commemorate his destruction of Corinth in 146 B.C.

[1] The temple at Bassae, because of its isolated position near a mountain top, has remained in a fair state of preservation, with most of the columns and architraves still in place, though smaller blocks had generally been knocked down by earthquakes. It was discovered by a French architect named Bocher in 1765; but he was murdered while attempting to make a more detailed examination, and the temple almost passed into oblivion until it was investigated in 1811 by the international party which had excavated at Aegina (including the architects Cockerell, Foster, and Haller), and was in turn excavated by them (during Cockerell's absence in Sicily) in 1812. The first publication was that of Donaldson, who visited the site in 1820; the *Expédition de Morée* worked here in 1829 and were responsible for a variant publication; but the official publication of the excavators did not appear until 1860, under the editorship of Cockerell, whose collaborators were all by this time deceased, so that, not having been present at the actual excavations, he was forced to rely on discrepant notes and drawings. The Greek authorities reconstructed the walls and interior columns in 1902–1907, placing the scattered blocks approximately in their original positions, but leaving many questions unsolved.

[2] Pausanias dated the temple about 430–429 B.C. on the assumption that Epicurius must refer to aid in time of plague, and so associated the temple with the great plague which afflicted Athens in the lifetime of Ictinus. This date has been widely accepted because it would agree with the style of the sculptured frieze, which seems to be a very few years later. But the architectural details of the exterior, if we accept the ancient attribution to Ictinus, are clearly at variance with such a date. The alternative of disregarding the attribution to Ictinus, on the ground that, as in the case of Sir Christopher Wren, local products might have been associated with a famous name for the sake of prestige, is unsatisfactory not only because it involves the discarding of a very definite statement by Pausanias, but also because the temple is closely related to works at Athens (Parthenon, Hephaesteum), the relation being that of a forerunner rather than that of an imitator. We must also definitely reject other modern suggestions that the temple dates from about 350 or nearer 300 B.C.

TEMPLE OF APOLLO AT BASSAE

difficult to work, quarried in the vicinity. For this reason marble had to be imported for some of the finer details, as noted below. The plan (Fig. 56), moreover, departs from the usual conventional arrangements in detail; the temple runs north and south instead of east and west, and behind the cella is a second chamber with a doorway facing the east. The existence of this inner room or adytum, possibly imitated from that in the archaic temple of Apollo at Delphi, accounts for the unusual length of a temple of this period which, though hexastyle on the façades, has fifteen columns on the flanks.[1] Externally the temple is Doric (Plate XXXV); and the proportions of the columns, the fact that all six columns on the north front are made heavier than the others (as on both fronts at Olympia), the closer spacing of the columns on the flanks, and the triple incisions below the necking of the capitals, all give an archaic flavour which contradicts the theory advanced by Pausanias that the work dates from the time of the great plague at the beginning of the Peloponnesian War. On the other hand there are certain features, such as the sunken panels at the bottoms of the step risers (as at Olympia), to emphasize the regularity of the jointing, and particularly the little vertical cyma reversa at the ends of these panels, which are not paralleled in Attica and so might seem to indicate a later date,[2] were it not that they are probably to be attributed to Peloponnesian taste. In this work, in spite of the harmonious jointing which caught the attention of Pausanias, we do not find the same delicate subtleties of upward curvature in stylobate or entablature, which occur in the Parthenon, probably because the architect recognised that the

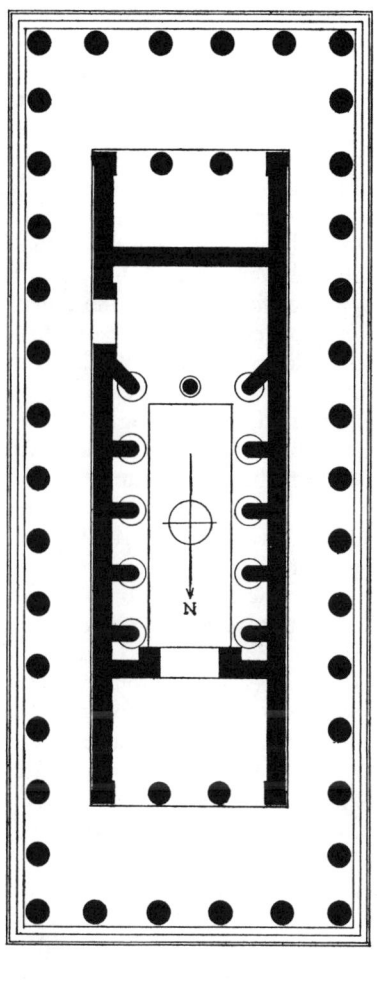

Fig. 56.—Temple of Apollo Epicurius at Bassae.

[1] There has long been current a theory that an older and smaller temple may have run east and west under the adytum, which with its eastern doorway might have been intended to preserve the memory of this structure. The older temple actually existed, to be sure (see p. 43); but it lay under the main cella and probably ran north and south like the present temple.

[2] The little vertical cyma reversa in the step panels had appeared even earlier, it would seem, at Delos, where the two lower steps of the peripteral temple appear to have been erected in preparation for an Ionic temple of Apollo (see p. 184).

extraordinary labour and accuracy required in work at Athens were of too costly a nature to be undertaken in these inaccessible mountains. Another type of curvature, however, the swelling outline of the column shaft known as the entasis, was executed in the columns of the peristyle.[1]

Within, on both sides of the cella are Ionic semi-columns (Plate XXXVI), which are attached to the cella walls by short spur walls as in the Heraeum at Olympia; the southernmost pair of semi-columns, however, had Corinthian capitals, and midway between them stood an isolated Corinthian column, separating the main cella from the adytum; possibly the two intervals between the Corinthian columns were closed off by curtains. The purpose of the employment of Ionic columns was, of course, to dispense with the architrave at midheight, falsely suggesting a gallery, and with the upper tier of columns which would have been required if the Doric order had been employed. The Ionic columns were located, not opposite the outer columns as in the Heraeum, but opposite the centres of the outer intercolumniations, resulting in a peculiarly close juxtaposition of the first pair of spur walls to the massive masonry of the north doorway. Unusual also is the diagonal arrangement of the spur walls at the south end of the cella, like a mitred frame surrounding the bronze statue of the god, 12 feet high, which was transferred in 369 B.C. to Megalopolis (according to Pausanias) and was replaced by one of wood and marble.[2] Between the semi-columns were thus formed niches for votive offerings and statues; and the floor of the central portion of the cella was slightly sunk, not to form an impluvium as at Olympia, but merely to emphasise the Ionic bases by raising them as if on an internal stylobate.

The Ionic bases are of very peculiar profile, with a tremendous flare at the bottom where the diameter is almost twice that of the shaft. The capital of the Ionic order in the cella (Plate XXXVII) is a new and original feature, designed to meet special requirements. Having only a semi-column to deal with, and desiring to detach completely three sides of his capital, the architect designed one with angle volutes at each corner. In a preliminary and rejected model of limestone, which was found buried near the temple, it is evident that Ictinus at first carried across horizontally the astragal connecting the two volutes, and above it executed a simple moulding as an abacus. But this design, as may have been found by actual test, owing partly to the extremely steep angle of vision within the narrow cella and partly to the concave plan of the volutes, would have appeared to dip in the centre. Consequently, in the marble capitals which were actually employed in the temple, Ictinus or more probably his successor raised the upper astragal and with a fine sweep made it a continuation of the curves of the volutes.[3] The curvature of the upper astragal, however,

[1] It has been generally assumed that the entasis, like the horizontal curvature, does not exist at Bassae; but I verified its presence in 1927.

[2] It was suggested by Cockerell that the statue of the god stood in the inner compartment, and was seen in profile, illuminated through the eastern doorway (Plate XXXVI). This theory is not borne out by the facts; the inner room is baldly designed, and its floor pattern contradicts the assumption that a pedestal stood on one side. The statue probably stood in the usual place in the main cella, just in front of the isolated column. Fragments of the marble extremities of the substitute acrolithic statue are in the British Museum.

[3] A later (probably votive) marble capital found in the Heraeum at Olympia imitates this upward curve of the cushion, though without the concavity in plan.

CANTED IONIC AND CORINTHIAN CAPITALS

resulted in another difficulty, that of designing an abacus to fit it; and the eventual decision was to omit the abacus entirely, thus yielding a design which is surprisingly modernistic and functional.[1] The member below the cushion is not the usual egg-and-dart ovolo of Asia Minor, but a cyma reversa such as was employed in early Athenian Ionic capitals of the first half of the fifth century.[2] The capital is not set out on the same axis as that of the shaft, but from a centre 2 inches farther back, so that the side faces are slightly different from that on the front.[3]

As noted above, the capitals of the southernmost semi-columns differed from the others on the flanks in being three-quarter Corinthian capitals,[4] corresponding to the complete Corinthian capital on the isolated central column. This latter, though no longer extant,[5] is the oldest example of the order known (Plate XXXVII); if we accept the story of the invention as related by Vitruvius, assuming that Callimachus was the first to apply the acanthus decoration to the older form of bell capital (as illustrated in the archaic Aeolic treasuries at Delphi), we must regard the example at Bassae as one of the earliest designs produced by him or under his immediate influence.[6] The two girdles of

---

[1] In the first publications of this temple, in the *Antiquities of Athens* (suppl. vol.) and in the *Expédition scientifique de Morée*, no abacus is shown; but Cockerell, and also the Greek authorities who have recently restored the temple, assumed that the abacus had been carved out of a separate block for which a special bed exists at the tops of the spur walls. My examination of the temple in 1927, however, showed that the architrave itself rested in this special bed and that the abacus is quite fictitious; in other words, the earliest publications had been more correct in this respect. [2] See p. 184.

[3] In Cockerell's restoration the lateral faces of the Ionic capitals are shown each with two volutes like the fronts, the inner volute being indicated by dotted lines; but this is merely an erroneous conjecture, contradicted by the form of the spur walls.

[4] The evidence for the Corinthian capitals on the diagonal spur walls, hitherto unknown, consists in the beds existing on the stones from the diagonal spur walls, and also in the fact that additional fragments were reported in 1812 as having been found, besides the complete central capital.

[5] The tradition that the central Corinthian capital was destroyed on the west coast of the Peloponnesus by the Turks who pursued the departing excavators in 1812 is romantic but quite unfounded, since Haller, who was present on that occasion, spoke of the Corinthian capital three years later as still existing at the temple itself.

[6] Vitruvius informs us that the capital was invented by Callimachus at Corinth. Now Callimachus was the craftsman who is said by Pausanias to have made a golden lamp for the goddess Athena Polias in the Erechtheum, and probably also the bronze palm tree reaching to the roof which drew off the smoke. As the earliest Greek Corinthian capitals all suggest a metallic origin, and as Callimachus is known to have worked both in bronze and in marble, it may be conjectured that he worked out the original design in bronze and then reproduced it in marble. Pausanias refers also to Corinthian bronze, which he says "got its colour by being plunged red hot into this water," referring to the fountain of Pirene. Corinthian bronze, for various reasons, was celebrated in ancient times, and Pliny says that the porticus built at Rome by Cneius Octavius was called Corinthian from its brazen Corinthian capitals, just as at Palmyra the acanthus leaves and volutes were of bronze applied to the stone core. The title, therefore, may have been given either because the capital was invented by Callimachus at Corinth, or on account of the material in which he wrought the prototype. In any case, we are undoubtedly to reject the theory of Egyptian influence, which has been advanced for the Corinthian capital as well as for the Doric order; for the application of leaves in relief to the well-known campaniform capitals, transforming them to the type known as "composite" and giving them a superficial resemblance to the Corinthian, began nearly a century later than the earliest Corinthian capital at Bassae and is perhaps to be interpreted rather as an instance of a reversed current of Greek influence on Egypt.

acanthus leaves at the bottom (twenty tiny leaves in each row, corresponding to the flutes of the shaft), the *fleuron* (here a palmette) at the middle of each face, the eight pairs of volutes, and the abacus with its concave sides, are all here present, though in somewhat rudimentary form.[1]

Above the Ionic and Corinthian capitals was a complete Ionic entablature. The architrave is of the archaic type found in the Ionic treasuries at Delphi, as well as in the temple of Athena at Sunium and in that on the Ilissus at Athens, in that it is unbroken by fascias. Above this was a frieze richly carved with figure sculpture, executed in Greek island marble and representing two distinct episodes, the battle of the Greeks and Amazons and that of the Lapiths and Centaurs.[2] The crowning cornice is of very compressed profile. The presence of the frieze might seem to complicate the question of the restoration of the ceiling, in that transverse beams laid across the cella, supporting a horizontal wooden ceiling in the usual manner, must have interfered with adequate lighting of the frieze. Such a ceiling is required, however, by holes on the cornice for tenons fastening horizontal wooden ceiling beams which crossed the cella from side to side; and it seems evident that the sculptured frieze was suffered to remain in semi-obscurity, as poorly shown as the Panathenaic frieze of the Parthenon, an offering to the divinity rather than an exhibit for human visitors. In contrast to the wooden ceilings of the cella and adytum are the coffered limestone slabs above the niches and the stone or marble substituted for wood throughout the rest of the temple. Local limestone was employed for the narrow peristyle ceilings on either flank; but over the great spans at front and rear, and also over the pronaos and opisthodomus, it was necessary to use the more compact marble and various ingenious processes of construction. The variety and richness of these unusual stone ceilings evoked the admiration of Pausanias.

The presence of the unbroken wooden ceiling over the cella is corroborated by the absence of any provision for adequate lighting through the roof.[3] The marble roof tiles, while of ordinary dimensions,[4] were notable because each

---

[1] Because of the loss of these extremely interesting marble Ionic and Corinthian capitals, with the exception of a few fragments, as the result of superstitious demolition by ignorant peasants, most of our knowledge of them comes from the valuable drawings made by Haller and preserved in the British Museum and the Strasbourg Library, utilised in part by Cockerell for his publication.   [2] This sculptured frieze is now in the British Musuem.

[3] It has usually been suggested that one should omit the entire ceiling within the area enclosed by the frieze, and leave a corresponding hypaethral opening in the roof; but this would give the same ugly external effect of a notch in the ridge line to which we have previously found objection. This, nevertheless, was the scheme adopted by Cockerell, though he reduced the area of the hypaethral opening by assuming that at the centre the rafters were self-supporting cantilevers, the ridge being omitted and their weight taken entirely by the Ionic entablature with the wall above; but this large opaion does not seem to be a possible solution of the problem, and, moreover, the moulding represented as enframing it does not exist. The sunken area in the floor below, sometimes regarded as evidence for a hypaethral opening above, in reality had quite another function, as previously noted. We must, therefore, assume that the roof was continuous throughout the length of the temple.

[4] The theory that these tiles were of exceptional size, 3 feet $6\frac{1}{2}$ inches long by 2 feet $5\frac{1}{4}$ inches wide (the largest tiles known), as set forth in Haller's notebooks and accepted by Cockerell and all subsequent writers (including the previous editions of this work), is entirely erroneous, being due to a mistaken combination of various small fragments which Haller had attempted to match together.

cover-tile is worked at one side of the pan-tile in a single slab, as in some Corinthian terracotta examples and also in marble in the Sicyonian treasury at Olympia. And their spacing corresponds exactly to that of the rafters, suggesting that they were supported directly, probably without the transverse cleats and certainly without the interposition of the close boarding and bed of mud which were necessary for the terracotta tiles of other buildings. A few of the tiles were pierced with small rectangular openings with rounded corners and raised rims; but these were so small that they could not have constituted a system of lighting for the interior of the cella and were probably, as at Olympia and elsewhere, intended merely for the lighting and ventilation of the roof space during the rare intervals when this was visited.[1]

Besides the sculptured frieze of the interior, the temple contained also relief sculpture of very beautiful quality in the six metopes above each of the Doric porches, following the example of Olympia. As at Olympia, furthermore, the pediments were prepared for the reception of sculptured groups, the technical details of installation being identical in both instances. No pedimental statues were ever found at Bassae, however, and we must conclude that they were carried off in ancient times, probably for the adornment of Rome.[2] The style of the sculptured internal frieze, and of the anthemion designs carved on the sima of cyma recta profile above the pediments, and of the palmettes on the antefixes spaced at equal intervals along the flanks, is later than that of the general design of the architecture, apparently of about 425 B.C., the date to which we may also attribute the marble Ionic and Corinthian capitals, the metopes of the porches, and the interior cornices and ceilings, both of limestone and of marble. It is tempting to infer that the completion, with its plentiful use of acanthus decoration, was in some way associated with Callimachus.

It is at Athens that we may best study the works of the culminating period. For the prohibition of religious building had been annulled by the act of Pericles in 449 B.C. And so it is on the Acropolis that we find the masterpiece of all these works, the Parthenon. It was officially the temple of Athena Polias, but was distinguished from the other temple of this cult by the name Hecatompedon (or "Hundred-foot Temple") inherited from its predecessors, the name Parthenon being extended a century later from the west room to the whole. The work of Ictinus and Callicrates in partnership, and described in a lost book by Ictinus and a certain Carpion, it was executed in a period of nine years, from 447 to 438 B.C., and after its dedication at the Panathenaic festival in the latter year the labour of the sculptors was continued until the eve of the

---

[1] Cockerell used a piece of one of these pierced tiles for his opaion. But closer study of Haller's notebook showed that there were two corners, and consequently the entire aperture, contained within the individual tiles (far too small, therefore, for an opaion), drawings of which were published by Papworth in 1865. Thus we reject not only Cockerell's opaion with the timber rafters exposed, but also the suggestion of Spiers that the rafters were of marble, and my own proposal (in the previous edition of this work) to restore numerous framed openings in the cella ceiling to correspond to many pierced tiles in the roof.

[2] It so happens that a group of statues found at Rome, the Niobids of which two are now in Copenhagen and a third in the Terme Museum at Rome, would exactly fit the requirements of the temple at Bassae, so that we are probably to restore in its south pediment a scene representing the sons and daughters of Niobe slain by the invisible hands of Apollo and Artemis.

THE CULMINATION IN ATTICA AND THE PELOPONNESUS

Peloponnesian War in 432 B.C.[1] The site was the lofty platform already prepared on the south side of the Acropolis for the Older Parthenon, a site which not only made it the principal crowning feature of the Acropolis as seen from the south and west (Fig. 74 at H; Plates I, L, LII), but on the Acropolis itself rendered it the most imposing structure there (Plates XXXV, XXXVIII, XXXIX) so that it was worthy of the various subtleties both in line and in proportion that it was to receive at the hands of Ictinus and Callicrates, and of its enrichment by Phidias with the most beautiful sculpture that the world has seen.[2]

The plan (Fig. 57) is more sumptuous than that of any other Doric temple erected on the Greek mainland, recalling temple 'GT' at Selinus with its octastyle façades and seventeen columns on the flanks; the size, however, is considerably smaller than in its great Sicilian prototype. The new plan did not agree with that of the older platform (Fig. 74 at OP), which was left unoccupied for a length of 14 feet at the east end, and likewise for $5\frac{1}{2}$ feet at the south; on the other hand, the new building overlapped the old platform by 13 feet at the north, requiring additional foundations of this width along the north flank. The total dimensions of the bottom step are 110 feet $6\frac{3}{4}$ inches by 237 feet $3\frac{3}{8}$ inches, being 24 feet $6\frac{3}{4}$ inches wider than in the Older Parthenon, and 8 feet $8\frac{1}{2}$ inches longer. The purpose of the great increase in width was to allow for a colossal cult statue, as at Olympia, but without crowding it tightly between the internal colonnades; the exact dimensions of the stylobate were determined by the elements composing the peristyle. For the fundamental principle of the new design was that it should incorporate as much as possible of the second-hand material, destined for the Older Parthenon, lying about the Acropolis; even though the lowest drums of many of the columns, having been set in place and exposed to the burning scaffolding, had become unfit for further use, there were still several hundred unfinished drums in fit condition to be incorporated in the peristyle and porches of the present Parthenon, permitting a considerable economy at a time when transportation was one of the most important items in the cost

---

[1] The authorship and date of the temple are given by several passages in ancient literature, combined with the fragments of the marble inscriptions containing expense accounts of the temple and of the gold-and-ivory statue.

[2] The Parthenon remained almost intact for more than 2100 years, apart from the loss of its original roof, the alteration of its interior colonnades, the construction of an apse in the pronaos and the piercing of three doorways in the middle cross-wall, during its transformation into a Byzantine church. Between 1208 and 1458 it served as the cathedral church of the "Frankish" dukes, and a marble campanile was built in the opisthodomus beside the west entrance. After 1458 it became a Turkish mosque, the campanile being continued upward as a minaret. In this condition it remained until a shell from a Venetian battery, on September 26, 1687, exploded a powder magazine temporarily established by the Turks in their mosque, causing the destruction of fourteen of the forty-six columns of the peristyle and of practically all of the inner building with the exception of the opisthodomus. Considerable destruction of the south entablature resulted from Lord Elgin's removal of some of the sculptures in 1801–1803, and slight additional damage was incurred during the sieges of 1822–1823 and 1826–1827. But in 1835–1844 the temple was cleared of modern accretions (with the exception of the minaret) and portions of the columns and walls were unskilfully restored. As the result of an earthquake in 1894 a few scientific repairs were undertaken in 1898–1903, and finally, in 1921–1929, the entire north flank was rebuilt by piecing together the scattered fragments.

THE PLAN OF THE PARTHENON

of stone. Hence the basic element was the normal column diameter of 6 feet 3 inches, equivalent to $5\frac{5}{6}$ Greek (Doric) feet, inherited from the Older Parthenon. The axial spacing of the columns was now related to the old column diameters as 9 : 4 and thus became $13\frac{1}{8}$ Doric feet, except at the corners where, with excessive angle contraction, it became $11\frac{5}{16}$ Doric feet. The reason for this excessive contraction of 24 inches was the octastyle nature of the façade; for the relative spacings and heights of columns, while varying to some degree in individual temples in accordance with scale, nevertheless tended to yield fairly uniform total proportions for normal hexastyle façades, so that the addition of two columns to the width created a violent contrast. It was to mitigate this difference in some degree that the amount of contraction was approximately doubled; and the enlargement of the angle column by one-fortieth of the diameter, for optical reasons, still further reduced the clear interval to 25 inches less than the normal intervals. The resulting width of the stylobate became $94\frac{1}{2}$ Doric feet; and, following the law that the number of columns on the flank should be one more than double the number on the façades, that is, seventeen, the length was made nine axial spacings or $118\frac{1}{8}$ Doric feet more than the width and so became $212\frac{5}{8}$ Doric feet, thus being proportioned to the width exactly as 9 : 4, just as the axial spacing is to the diameter.[1] The total height of the order, that is, of the column and entablature together, was made $3\frac{1}{5}$ times the axial spacing or $7\frac{1}{5}$ lower diameters, that is, exactly 42 Doric feet, and again forms the proportion of 4 : 9 with the width of the stylobate. This consistency in proportions is most unusual and suggests the care with which the entire design was studied.

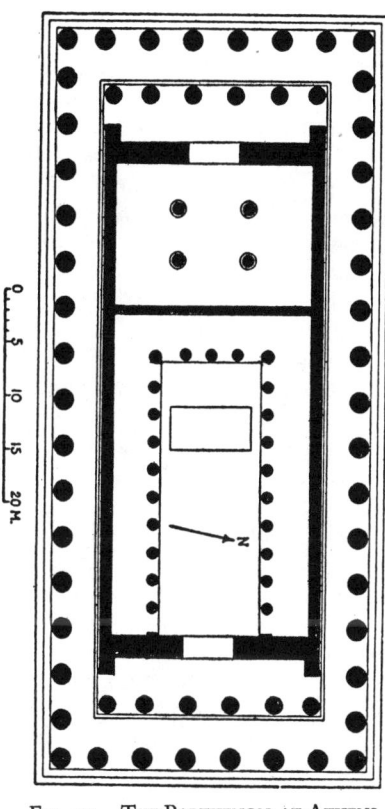

FIG. 57.—THE PARTHENON AT ATHENS.

The jointing of the steps and stylobate was based on the principle that there

---

[1] The stylobate dimensions, while generally recognised as forming the ratio 4 : 9, are often interpreted as 100 by 225 "Greek" feet—but of a foot unit ($12\frac{1}{8}$ inches) which no Greek ever employed. The Doric foot unit actually employed in the Parthenon was 326·85 mm. or 12·868 inches, more than in the Erechtheum but almost identical with that in the Propylaea (see p. 195, note 1; p. 199, note 3). It seems necessary here to insert a word of warning against the validity of the numerous modern attempts to derive the plans of Greek temples, and of the Parthenon in particular, from more or less intricate geometrical diagrams such as interrelated concentric circles and squares, pentagons or pentagrams, hexagons or hexagrams, octagons, decagons, "whirling squares," or the "golden section."

should be three blocks to each axial spacing, every third joint coinciding with a column axis. The columns are barely less than $5\frac{1}{2}$ diameters in height. The profile of the capitals exemplifies the most perfected stage of the Doric style, the echinus very stiff and yet forming a continuous hyperbolic curve. The abacus was originally planned to have a spread of 6 feet $6\frac{7}{8}$ inches, as executed on the west and south sides; but this dimension, apparently regarded as too small, was subsequently enlarged to 6 feet $7\frac{3}{8}$ inches in the west half and to 6 feet $8\frac{1}{2}$ inches in the east half of the north flank, and finally to 6 feet 9 inches on the east façade; the angle capitals in each case showing enlargements proportionate to that of the column diameter, there is a contrast, for instance, between the southeast angle capital and that adjoining it on the south flank amounting to $3\frac{3}{8}$ inches. Apart from these unforeseen irregularities it is interesting to note, in the metopes of the façades, a repetition of the perspective illusion given in the colonnade by the angle contraction; for in the Parthenon, instead of the usual enlarged metopes adjoining the angle triglyphs, we find a careful gradation from excessively wide metopes at the centre to narrow metopes toward the corners, with a maximum difference of $4\frac{1}{8}$ inches in width, and with the result that no triglyph on a façade is exactly centred above the corresponding column. The fascias above the triglyphs and metopes have a crowning beaded astragal as exceptional decoration. The face of the tympanum is recessed 8 inches behind the architrave-triglyph plane, to give a greater depth for pediment sculpture. The sima of the pediment shows, not the cyma recta profile employed at Bassae, nor the type inherited from Corinthian terracottas as at Olympia, but rather a derivative of the latter under Ionic influence, the ovolo dominating with offset fascias below and above, which became peculiarly characteristic of the Periclean designers. On the flanks the sima is replaced by antefixes, located above each mutule so that there are four to each column spacing; but since there were six rows of tiles to each column spacing the antefixes were alternately true and false, the latter corresponding to two lines of cover-tiles. The acroteria were colossal openwork designs in marble, about 9 feet high, consisting of stems and tendrils, springing from nests of acanthus leaves, forming scrolls and finally ending in great palmettes.[1]

The plan of the building within the peristyle included hexastyle porticoes at both ends (rather than tetrastyle as in its predecessor), raised on two steps, of which the lower is accurately located concentrically within the stylobate, while the upper step—and with it the entire inner building—is thrust diagonally toward the northeast so that the width of the tread varies on all four sides. The lateral displacement may have been a result of a clerical error; but the eastward thrust certainly resulted from adjustments required by a peculiar difference in the columns themselves. For the west or opisthodomus columns inherited the diameter of 5 feet $7\frac{1}{2}$ inches, equivalent to $5\frac{1}{4}$ Greek (Doric) feet, employed for the porch columns of the Older Parthenon; but since the new hexastyle opisthodomus utilised the material from six of the original eight columns, it was decided that the remaining drums left for the pronaos were so few as to justify a new design, in which the diameter was reduced to 5 feet $4\frac{7}{8}$ inches.

[1] In the British Museum are representative pieces of the architecture of the Parthenon, a Doric capital and a top drum from the north peristyle, parts of the frieze crowning mouldings, an antefix, and a fragment of an acroterion.

INTERIOR OF THE PARTHENON

The porch column height being uniformly 32 feet $11\frac{7}{8}$ inches, the pronaos columns exhibit the unusually slender proportions of $6\frac{1}{10}$ diameters. On the hexastyle porticoes rested the usual Doric architrave with regulae and guttae, spaced as if they were intended to come below triglyphs;[1] but the regulae appear here merely as the conventional crowning feature of the Doric architrave, carrying up the lines of the columns, while on the flanks of the cella building, where they would have had no such function, they were replaced by a simple band of the height of regula and taenia combined. For above the architrave, instead of the usual triglyphs, was a continuous Ionic frieze such as Ictinus employed inside the cella at Bassae, though above Ionic columns; another precedent was the Peisistratid temple on the Acropolis, where a sculptured frieze was used across the ends of the cella building, likewise above Ionic columns; and while the Parthenon was in course of erection the same treatment was applied to the ends of the cella building in the Hephaesteum, but above Doric columns. The use of a continuous sculptured frieze round the entire inner building of the Parthenon, with a length of 523 feet $7\frac{1}{4}$ inches (top of background), marks a distinct innovation. Above this frieze was a very decorative interior cornice (repeated on the inner face of the main entablature), forming the transition to the marble ceiling.

The plan of the cella building contains two distinct chambers, the cella proper behind the pronaos, and a rear chamber entered from the opisthodomus (Fig. 57). The term Parthenon given to the whole building is a later title, as noted above, and was confined at first to the rear chamber, officially known as the Parthenon (chamber of the Virgin); the cella was known as the Neos Hecatompedos (cella of 100 feet), this being, however, a name inherited from the archaic poros Hecatompedon so that we are not justified in dividing the length by 100 and adopting the quotient as the foot unit.[2] In the cella there were formerly ten Doric columns on either side and five columns across the rear, counting those at the corners twice.[3] They carried an architrave with superposed Doric columns above, as in the temples at Aegina and Paestum already mentioned; the primary object of these columns would seem to have been the support of the beams of the ceiling and roof, as there is no evidence for galleries. The columns returning across the rear constitute a development of the plan employed at Bassae (and again with a central column on axis), in this case forming a true ambulatory with the aisle carried round the interior of the cella, with bronze barriers fixed between the columns, so as to allow privileged travellers like Pausanias to walk round the chryselephantine statue of Athena

[1] It has sometimes been suggested that the regulae imply that a triglyph frieze was once planned here and was replaced by the Ionic frieze; but this is extremely improbable.

[2] Such attempts have frequently been made, but always with erroneous results; the internal length of the cella was actually $91\frac{1}{2}$ Greek (Doric) feet. It would be $100\frac{1}{2}$ Doric feet if the cross-walls at both ends were included; but a literal application of the name does not seem to be indicated.

[3] Most authorities prefer to restore L-shaped piers at the two inner corners; but such would seem too sophisticated for the period, and, furthermore, circular traces were noted by Cockerell and Woods before 1820. The Greek columns were replaced in Roman times, probably after a fire, by second-hand Doric columns of a much later style, of which a few fragments and many of their architraves and triglyph frieze blocks still remain. Recent attempts to prove that these Roman colonnades were Corinthian, and that they supported arches rather than architraves, are quite unfounded.

THE CULMINATION IN ATTICA AND THE PELOPONNESUS

and see it on all sides; a similar arrangement existed in the temple of Zeus at Olympia, except that there were no columns at the west end, a space merely being left at the back of the pedestal to permit one to pass round. The portion of the floor enclosed by the colonnades is sunk $1\frac{1}{2}$ inches, as at Bassae, so that the columns seem to rest on a low stylobate; the sinking of the floor does not, however, indicate that the area was hypaethral. Enough light would have been admitted through the great eastern doorway, $13\frac{3}{4}$ feet wide, between pivots, at the bottom and 32 feet high (an area of 440 square feet). In the middle, located with reference to the columns, was the site of the chryselephantine statue, a large rectangle wherein the marble pavement is economically replaced by poros limestone blocks, surrounded by the engraved outline of the lower step of the pedestal, 26 feet $4\frac{1}{2}$ inches wide and 13 feet $5\frac{1}{4}$ inches deep. The roof over the nave (with a clear span of $33\frac{3}{4}$ feet between the architraves) must have been supported on braced beams (from which the ceiling might in part have been suspended). The ceiling of the Parthenon chamber, on the other hand, was carried by four Ionic columns; the reason for the employment of this order was the desire to avoid the superposed storeys of columns, which in such a shallow room would have seemed rather absurd, and yet at the same time to occupy less floor space than would have been required for Doric columns tall enough to reach the ceiling.[1] It was a principle derived from the temple at Bassae, and soon afterward imitated in the Propylaea.

The temple is so well preserved, in its essential parts, that it is possible even to analyse mathematically those subtle refinements both in design and construction which make it the most remarkable building in the world.[2] Referring to these refinements, it has been said: "The whole building is constructed, so to speak, on a subjective rather than an objective basis; it is intended not to be mathematically accurate, but to be adapted to the eye of the spectator. To the eye a curve is a more pleasing form than a straight line, and the deviations from rigid correctness serve to give a character of purpose, almost of life, to the solid marble construction."[3] Some of the irregularities, however, seem to be due rather to alteration of the design during erection rather than to a desire for spontaneous freedom; and the discrepancies in the spacing of the columns may be traced to a misunderstanding by the workmen who centred them on joints of the stylobate rather than on engraved diameters such as were employed elsewhere. The delicate curves and inclinations of the horizontal and vertical lines include the rising curves given to the stylobate and entablature in order to impart a feeling of life and to prevent the appearance of sagging, the convex curve to which the entasis of the columns was worked in order to correct the optical illusion of concavity which might have resulted if the sides had been straight, and the slight inward inclinations of the axes of the columns so as to

---

[1] While there are several more or less faithful modern replicas of the exterior of the Parthenon, the only reproduction of the interior at full size is that which I designed in 1927 for the Parthenon at Nashville, Tennessee.

[2] These refinements were first noticed by Allason and Cockerell (1814), Donaldson (1820), and Hoffer and Pennethorne (1836-1837), and in 1846 were measured by Penrose, who published his well-known work in 1851 (with a second edition in 1888). Later still, all this evidence was analysed and summarised by Goodyear (1912), whose tendency, however, was to lay too much emphasis on what were really accidental variations or workmen's errors.

[3] Percy Gardner, *Grammar of Greek Art* (1905), p. 39.

OPTICAL REFINEMENTS

give the whole building an appearance of greater strength; all entailed a mathematical precision in the setting out of the work and in its execution which is probably unparalleled in the world. We are justified in regarding these as optical refinements; for, in spite of certain modern experiments made with the purpose of demonstrating that the optical illusions, which these refinements were supposed to correct, might not actually have occurred, we have nevertheless definite evidence that the ancient Greeks believed that such illusions required correctives and, in consequence, must admit that such was the primary purpose of their employment.

Of one group of refinements, consisting of variations from normal dimensions, we have already noted several instances. Such is the contraction of the angle intervals of peristyles, occasioned primarily by the difficulty in the triglyph frieze, but accepted also as an optical refinement because it gave at the end of the colonnade a sense of stability and rest, and at the same time, by emphasising the perspective effect of the narrowing of the more distant intervals, it might seem to increase the length of a colonnade. That this perspective illusion was appreciated is shown, for instance, by the Parthenon, where the contraction was doubled to exaggerate the effect; though here again was a second motive, the improvement of the general proportions. A second refinement of this nature is the repetition of the perspective illusion in the triglyph frieze; this is found, however, only on the façades of the Parthenon, where we noted that the maximum variation is $4\frac{1}{8}$ inches. A third variety is the thickening of the angle columns of a peristyle as mentioned by Vitruvius, "because they are sharply outlined by the unobstructed air round them, and seem to the beholder more slender than they are." Hence this refinement was not applied to the end columns of such prostyle colonnades (as in the porches of the Parthenon and the Propylaea) as were generally seen against solid walls or other obstacles. It was desirable, furthermore, only after the archaic distinction between the sizes of the front and flank columns had been abandoned, and was apparently first used at Aegina and in the Older Parthenon. Vitruvius says that the enlargement should be one-fiftieth of the diameter, which agrees with the Periclean Doric examples (one-fortieth in both Parthenons, one fiftieth in the Hephaesteum).

The second group of refinements consists in the inclination of lines or planes which are supposedly vertical. The most important is the effect of upward tapering, and hence of greater stability, imparted to the whole building by the inward inclination of the column axes, a refinement described by Vitruvius. In the Parthenon the inward inclination of the columns (Fig. 62) is $2\frac{3}{8}$ inches; it may be calculated that the axes of the columns on both flanks, if prolonged, would meet in a line more than $1\frac{1}{2}$ miles above the pavement; the axes on the two façades being inclined at the same rate, it is apparent that the axes of the angle columns, being inclined both ways on a diagonal line, have a greater inclination in the proportion of the diagonal to the sides of a square. In the Propylaea the inclinations are relatively greater, $3\frac{3}{8}$ inches with smaller columns, so that the axes of the flank columns would meet five-eighths of a mile above the stylobate. Such inclinations had appeared earlier than the Periclean period in the Older Parthenon and at Croton in Italy. In some Peloponnesian temples, as Aegina, Olympia, Tegea, and Nemea, only the flank colonnades inclined, confining the effect to the façades (as Vitruvius recommended). Walls likewise sometimes incline inward, either because they taper, as at Bassae (the inner faces being vertical), or in sympathy with the inclinations of the columns, as in the Parthenon and Propylaea; but cross-walls containing doorways are always strictly vertical. In porticoes in-antis the antae sometimes lean backward following the line of diminution of the columns between them, as at Bassae; but in Doric prostyle porticoes the antae lean forward toward the columns, as in the Propylaea and the inner porches of the Parthenon (in the latter to the extent of $4\frac{1}{4}$ inches). Of a similar nature are the inclinations of door and window jambs, resulting in the upward diminution of such openings. The sides of the abacus of a capital in some buildings have slight inclinations, in the Parthenon following the inclined axis of the column, though in other cases, as in the Propylaea, the faces lean outward on all sides, sometimes contrary to the inclination of the axis. Similar inclinations, either backward or forward, occur also in most members of the entablature and pediment; these would seem to be due to the position from which the building was seen, and to its illumination by the sun's rays, or to the desire to correct certain optical illusions or the effect of foreshortening, or even to agree or contrast with other inclinations.

The third group of refinements, the most interesting of all, includes the deviations from apparently straight lines, forming curves, of which we may first consider the horizontal curves.[1] The upward curvature of the stylobate was intended partly to impart a feeling of life to the whole, and even more to prevent any effect of sagging that might otherwise have resulted from the long row of vertical columns bearing down upon the horizontal line of the platform, as mentioned by Vitruvius; but its origin may be traced to the utilitarian function of shedding rain.[2] As a refinement it had already appeared at Corinth, in the Peisistratid temple of Athena, and in the Older Parthenon, but it seems to have been omitted at Bassae, as well as in some of the smaller Periclean temples, and also in the Propylaea platform where the interruption of the stylobate by the central roadway would have neutralised its effect. The upward curvature of the stylobate (cf. Fig. 58) in the Parthenon amounts to $2\frac{3}{8}$ inches on the façades and to $4\frac{5}{16}$ inches on the flanks; the radius of the latter curve, an arc of an enormous circle, is about $3\frac{1}{2}$ miles. In the Hephaesteum the rise amounts to $\frac{3}{4}$ inch on the façades and $1\frac{1}{4}$ inches on the flanks. Even more delicate had been the upward curvature planned for the flanks of the Older Parthenon, with a rise of $2\frac{3}{8}$ inches and a radius of about $7\frac{1}{2}$ miles. But it is not to be supposed that the architect ever troubled to calculate the radius or to establish the form of an arc of such a theoretical circle. His system consisted

---

[1] First noticed by Hoffer and Pennethorne. The fact of their existence was warmly disputed by Bötticher and Durm, with the argument that they resulted from settlement at the corners of temples. But there can be no doubt of their intentional character; apart from the fact that the corners would be the least likely to settle (particularly in the same manner in so many temples), we have such instances as the west end of the temple at Corinth and the northeast quarter of the Parthenon with the solid rock rising almost to the bottom step without any leeway for settlement, also the intensified curve on the south flank of the Parthenon actually countersunk in the top of the older platform, and the measured variations in the Doric column heights of the Propylaea intended to permit their capitals to fit the upward curvature of the architrave even though the bottoms (by exception) rest on a horizontal platform.

[2] Thus in the Croesus temple at Ephesus the pavement slopes up toward the cella, giving somewhat the effect of a deck roof.

rather in deciding first the maximum increment of curvature desired, and then any convenient arbitrary number of equal intervals between the corner and middle of the building (the beginning and apex of the proposed curve); the maximum increment of curvature was next divided by the square of the above-mentioned number of intervals, thus determining the size of the fractional parts of the height, so that the curve could be set out either in diagrammatic form as a parabola with the equally spaced ordinates descending on either side of the apex as successive square numbers of the fractional parts (Fig. 59), or on the actual temple as a colossal arc by replacing the ordinates with corresponding levelling blocks (the *scamilli impares* of Vitruvius.)[1] For at this tremendous scale the resulting parabolic construction would have been indistinguishable from a true circular arc. The general effect of the rising curves upon the platform as a whole (Fig. 58) may be likened to the result obtained by cutting a rectangle from the surface of a melon. The steps of the temple platform being of equal

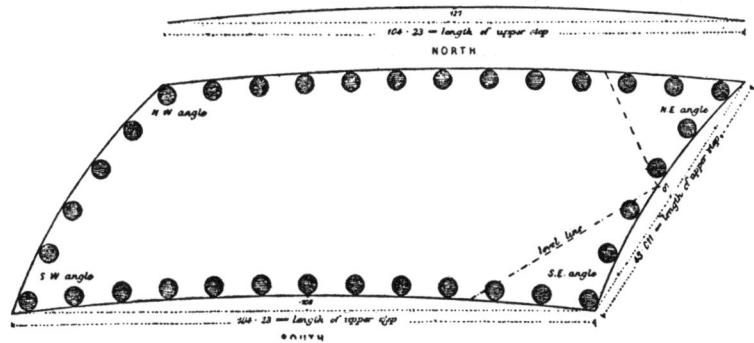

FIG. 58.—UPWARD CURVATURE OF STYLOBATE (HEPHAESTEUM), EXAGGERATED.

height from end to end, it was necessary to start the curvature as low as the foundation. The columns, likewise, were normally of equal height throughout, so that the curvature determined at the bottom was transmitted to the entablature;[2] but in the Propylaea, the stylobate being level, the central columns were made higher than those at the corners in order to obtain an upward curvature

---

[1] For instance, in a length of 228 feet might have been twelve intervals of 19 feet, six on either side of the centre. Then, if the desired curvature were, say, $4\frac{1}{2}$ inches, it would be divided by the square of six, into thirty-six parts of $\frac{1}{8}$ inch each. The first ordinate on either side of the apex would descend $\frac{1}{8}$ inch lower than the apex, the second $\frac{1}{2}$ ($\frac{4}{8}$) inch, the third $1\frac{1}{8}$ ($\frac{9}{8}$) inch, and the fourth 2 ($\frac{16}{8}$) inches, the fifth $3\frac{1}{8}$ ($\frac{25}{8}$) inches, and the corner $4\frac{1}{2}$ ($\frac{36}{8}$) inches. The differences between the successive ordinates were the successive odd numbers, 1, 3, 5, 7, 9, 11 parts (*ad infinitum*); *cf.* Fig. 59. Thus the wooden levelling blocks by means of which these rising curves were executed became *scamilli impares* in two senses: they were not only unequal but they differed by odd (not even) numbers.

[2] Vitruvius seems to have assumed, and probably rightly, that the entablature curve followed and was a consequence of that of the stylobate. Penrose on the other hand argued, with less probability, that the reverse was the case; that Ictinus, in order "to obviate a disagreeable effect produced by the contrast of the horizontal with the inclined lines of a flat pediment," which gave an apparent dip to the former, decided that the horizontal lines must rise towards the middle, requiring a similar rise in the stylobate in order that the columns might be of equal height.

of ¾ inch in the architrave soffit. And through the entablature the curvature was carried up to the top of the cornice or bottom of the tympanum; and since the tympanum triangle retained the ordinates proper to a straight-sided triangle, the sloping tympanum top and the raking cornice were likewise constructed in the form of oblique curves.[1]

The vertical curves, generally confined to columns, are most conveniently expressed by the maximum amount of the entasis, that is, of the deviation of the convex outline of the arris from the straight line or chord connecting the bottom and top of the arris.[2] Thus in the Parthenon the entasis of the tapering column shaft (Fig. 60, II) is probably likewise a circular arc,[3] with a maximum

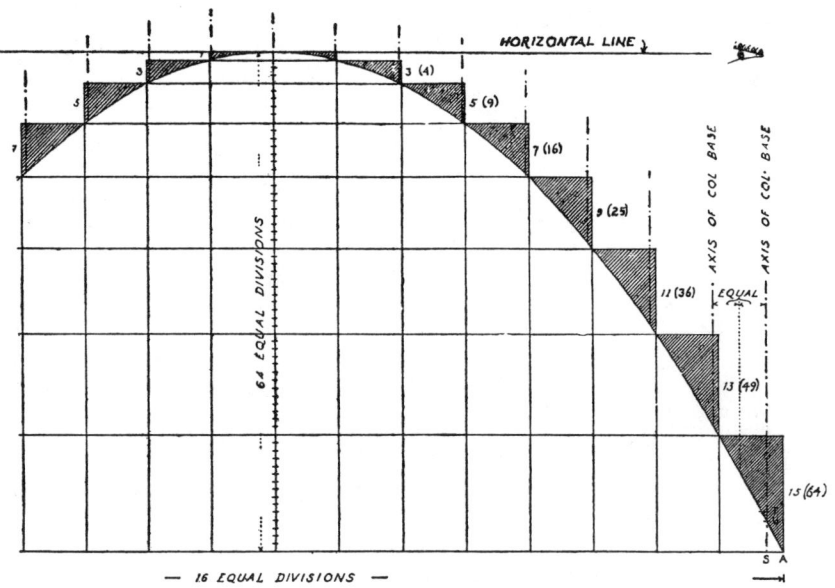

FIG. 59.—DIAGRAM FOR CONSTRUCTION OF STYLOBATE CURVATURE.

increment of about $\frac{11}{16}$ inch, so that the radius would have been nearly half a mile. In the slightly smaller columns of the main porticoes of the Propylaea it is stronger, ¾ inch. The entasis varies in different temples and is not found in some, as, for instance, the temple of Athena Nike and in the east portico of the Erechtheum. The entasis is most delicate in the north porch of the Erech-

[1] Curves in plan, convex or concave to the exterior, have sometimes been mentioned in connection with the Parthenon and the temples at Paestum and Segesta. But these are either imaginary or of doubtful authenticity, those in the upper parts of peristyles being due to accidental deformation of the colonnades. It is to be noted, furthermore, that concave curves in plan at high levels would serve only to neutralise the upward curve transmitted by the columns.

[2] First noticed by Allason and Cockerell, and afterwards measured and verified by Penrose. Delagardette had observed it as early as 1793 at Paestum, but had considered it to be merely Roman recutting.

[3] Penrose argued that it was rather a section of a hyperbola; and others have attempted to prove that it was an even more complicated curve such as the conchoid of Nicomedes.

theum and in the Ionic columns of the Propylaea (the amount of deviation from a straight line in both cases being less than ¼ inch), and is most pronounced in early examples such as the Basilica at Paestum (where the deviation is 2⅛ inches, Fig. 60, I), or in late examples such as the temple of Zeus Olympius at Athens (where it is 1 7/16 inches).[1] No such entasis was applied, during the Periclean period, to walls or antae, except that the slender makeshift pier in the southwest wing of the Propylaea is slightly thicker at the middle of the height than at bottom or top. The entasis had "the purpose of correcting a disagreeable optical illusion, which is found to give an attenuated appearance to columns formed with straight sides, and to cause their outlines to seem concave instead of straight." But it also gave to the column an appearance of elastic strength and vitality; and it was probably this quality that caused its exaggeration even to a cigar shape in later times, when the moderation of the best period had been lost.

With regard to the shorter curves, not properly optical refinements, employed in mouldings and in profiles where perfection of contour was of prime importance, the Periclean architects seem usually to have preferred regular geometrical curves such as true arcs of circles and portions of the hyperbola, parabola, and ellipse, especially for convex mouldings where contour is more important than in concave mouldings. Among the most beautiful examples of such curves are the hyperbolic echinus of the Doric capital, the parabolic soffits of Ionic or raking Doric cornices, and various forms of the hawksbeak and cyma reversa. In the case of the fluting of the columns in the Parthenon an approximate curve struck from three centres, and known as a false ellipse, was adopted; the central portion of the curve had a radius equal to the width of the flute, and the radii of the portions on either side diminished with the decreasing depth of the flutes in the upper portions of the shaft, the principal object throughout being to accentuate the arris. In the Propylaea, as also in most of the earlier Doric examples in south Italy and Sicily, the curves were segments of circles.

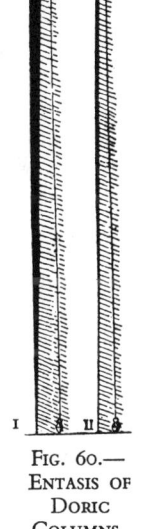

Fig. 60.—Entasis of Doric Columns.

The Parthenon being a completed work, much of the evidence for the method of its construction is derived from other Greek Doric buildings which for various reasons have never been finished, such as the archaic Olympieum at Athens and the older temple at Sunium, the temple 'GT' at Selinus and that at Segesta mentioned in an earlier chapter, also the Older Parthenon, the temples of Nemesis at Rhamnus, Demeter at Eleusis, Apollo Ismenius at Thebes, Zeus at Stratos and Poseidon at Molycrion in Aetolia, of Apollo at Delos, the so-

---

[1] The comparative entasis given approximately by Penrose (*Athenian Architecture*, p. 40) is 12 for the Corinthian temple of Zeus Olympius, 11 for the larger and 9 for the smaller Doric order of the Propylaea, 8 and 6 for the Doric peristyles of the Parthenon and Hephaesteum, and 4 for the Ionic north columns of the Erechtheum; the Ionic columns of the Propylaea (in which Penrose did not perceive the entasis) would fit into the series with the index number 2 (the height of the column being regarded as uniform).

called stoa (telesterion) at Thoricus and the stoa of Philip V at Delos, and, to a lesser degree, the Olympieum at Acragas, the temple at Bassae, and the Propylaea of the Athenian Acropolis, and also from some Ionic temples such as those at Didyma, Samos, and Sardis. From Segesta and Thoricus it may be inferred that the peristyle of a temple was generally the first part erected (Plate XXVII). Similar evidence is derived from the temple at Aegina (where three of the peristyle columns were omitted until the last moment so that material for the cella could be brought in), from the Older Parthenon (where the cella walls never rose higher than the moulded base though the columns were in process of erection to complete height), from the present Parthenon (where the entire cella building was shifted after its lower step had been built in accordance with the peristyle), and from the Hephaesteum (the inner foundation trenches being cut through the fill thrown up inside the outer foundations). As for the point at which the work was begun, it was sometimes the main façade (as in temple 'GT' at Selinus and the temple of Athena at Priene), but frequently the less important rear (as in the archaic temple of Apollo at Delphi and the Parthenon), thus giving the main front the advantage of any last-moment improvements. The foundations of temples of the fifth century were usually of various qualities of poros limestone, carefully coursed and bonded as ashlar masonry, forming concentric hollow rectangles supporting walls and columns but leaving the intervening spaces for mere earth fill, though there was usually a stone grid or a continuous course of underpinning to support the pavement. The Parthenon itself appears to be an exception in this respect, since the foundation erected for the Older Parthenon, doubtless because of its unstable location on the steep declivity of the Acropolis and the extreme depth required on the south flank, was made a solid mass of ashlar masonry. In many of the unfinished buildings the columns are still unfluted, and the treads and risers of the steps retain their rough unworked surfaces; often they retain also the ancones or ears, projecting bosses by which the stones were hoisted and lowered into their positions.[1] The gradual rise of the stylobate was constructed, according to Vitruvius, by means of the *scamilli impares*; his remarks on this subject are not clear, but it is evident that he referred to the formation of the curve, on the top course of the foundations, by means of levelling cubes of various heights, so arranged that when their tops lay in a horizontal plane, their bottoms described the proper curve and indicated to what depth the course below them had to be dressed (Fig. 59). It is clear that, because of the absence of variation in the steps, the exact curvature had to be worked out on the top of the foundation, in the case of the Parthenon the thin marble levelling course on the north and west, the top course of the old basement of poros stone on the south and east. The work was made easier by the fact that the old basement had already been constructed on a curve—though to a lesser degree —through its four topmost courses in order to impart a similar refinement to the Older Parthenon.[2]

[1] It is impossible to assume, as is sometimes done, that the bosses were used also to work the stones backwards and forwards in order to grind the joints (see below, with regard to the centring pins).

[2] To increase the amount of curvature in the present Parthenon, the crown of the curve was retained at its previous level, but the ends were countersunk into the old foundation, thus furnishing one of the proofs of the intentional character of the curvature.

CONSTRUCTION OF COLUMNS

The column drums as delivered from the quarry to the temple site were in the form of roughly dressed disks, coarsely worked with the point and mallet, not only on the cylindrical exterior but also on the top and bottom beds. From four points on the circumference protruded large bosses, as much as 8 to 10 inches wide and 6 to 8 inches in projection, suggesting that they were hewn out of the corners of the square block within which the circular drum was inscribed. Transportation from the Pentelic quarries must have been effected by wheeled carts, drawn by thirty or forty yoke of oxen, mentioned in the Eleusinian inscriptions and responsible for the ruts still remaining in the quarries and on the roads. Only exceptionally huge drums, such as those of Selinus, were transported by the remarkable method of rolling along the ground in the manner described by Vitruvius.[1] The drums were prepared on the ground by dressing the lower bed within an exact circle about 1½ inches outside the proposed final diameter, this circle being marked at the bottom of the face by a drafted margin about 1½ inches high; the rest of the circumference of the drum was then dressed back to the surface indicated by the drafted margin, at first by cutting vertical channels midway between the bosses, then by supplementary channels enframing the bosses, and finally by dressing off the twelve intervening areas with a fine stippled surface from which only the four bosses protruded. On the lowest drum of a Doric column the flutes were finished for 2 or 3 inches in height, the rest being left in its rough cylindrical mantle. Then, with the addition of the special lower bed dressing described below, the drum was ready for hoisting and placing; the corresponding upper bed dressing was not executed until the next drum was ready to be set. Where the stylobate received the lowest drum of the column the surface was sunk to its proper depth (Fig. 61), and on this were traced the diameters marking the axis of the column and in many cases also a circle forming its circumference; the area within the latter was worked lightly over to give some hold to the lower surface of the drum. The bottom surface of the lowest drum of a marble Doric column of the Periclean age was not fastened to the stylobate;[2] but at the upper joints the arrangement was different. There a square sinking was made in the centre of the upper and lower surface of each drum (Fig. 61), about 4 to 6 inches square and 3 to 4 inches deep, in which plugs (empolia) of cypress wood were fixed; at the exact centre of the drum a round hole about 2 inches in diameter was bored in each plug, so that a circular wooden pin, inserted in the hole in the plug at the top of a drum, would fit the corresponding hole at the bottom of the drum above,[3] forming a simple method of centring the drums accurately

---

[1] The frequently mentioned theory that all column drums, including those of the Parthenon, were transported by rolling along the ground, and that the empolion cuttings in their top and bottom beds were used primarily as hub cuttings for the attachment to the oxen, is sufficiently controverted by the presence of the four bosses (effectually preventing rolling) and by the absence of empolion cuttings on unfinished drums which had completed their journey to the Acropolis.

[2] In later work in marble, as well as in soft limestone materials in all periods, the same centring device was often employed also under the bottom drums of Doric columns.

[3] In rare instances all the parts, empolia and pins, were made of bronze, as in the Tholos at Delphi and Philon's porch at Eleusis. In the Tholos the pins are slightly conical with the butt ends fixed in the tops of the lower beds.

one upon another.[1] Between the centre and the circumference several concentric circles appear on the bed of the drum, the outermost ring being smoothly polished to form a joint that was practically invisible, while the next zone was slightly roughened in order to give the drums better hold upon each other; a third zone was slightly depressed, with the object of reducing the amount of surface that was actually in contact; and generally there was an innermost zone, rising again to the level of the joint, immediately round the wooden plug mentioned above. There are from ten to twelve of these drums in each column of the Parthenon. None of the drum joints was truly horizontal, all being per-

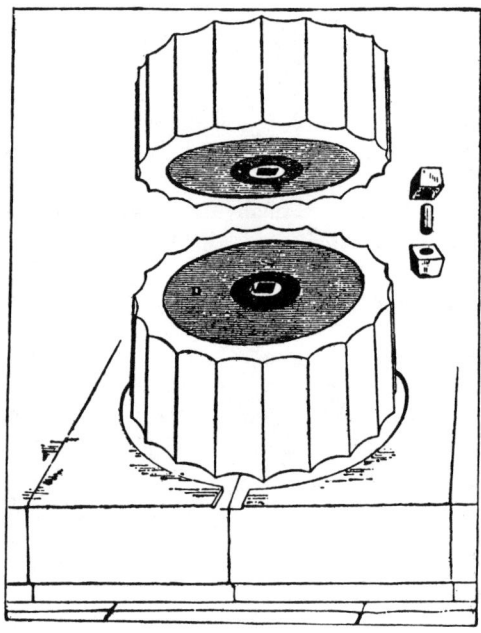

FIG. 61.—CONSTRUCTION OF COLUMNS, SHOWING CENTRING PIN. (Penrose.)

pendicular to the inclined axis of the column (Fig. 62). But on the lowest drum, in consequence of the curve of the stylobate, the side toward the corner of the building had to be carried down a fraction lower than on the side toward the central axis of the building, and likewise, both on account of the curvature and

---

[1] In earlier editions of this work it was assumed that the wooden pins were really pivots on which the drums were worked round so as to grind the blocks closely together, a theory evolved by Penrose, against which there are numerous grave objections. Among these are the occurrences of the same device on semi-columns engaged to wall blocks which obviously could not be rotated, and on column drums of later date into which additional pairs of metal dowels were affixed near the circumference before setting (thus effectually preventing rotation), and even the negative fact that it is absent from the bottoms of Doric columns (which could be centred on the stylobate by comparing the arrises and fluting with the engraved diameters and circles) as contrasted with its presence on the bottoms of Ionic bases which with their undercut torus mouldings could not otherwise have been readily set in their exact positions.

because of the inward inclination of the column axis, the outer face had to be carried down considerably lower than the back (toward the cella wall).[1] Similar difficulties were experienced with the uppermost drums, because of the necessity of presenting for the bed of the capital a plane parallel to the soffit of the architrave. The necking of the capital was also fluted to correspond to the bottom of the shaft, and the echinus was perfectly finished;[2] but on the abacus were sometimes (as at Segesta) left unworked corners to protect them. These processes, in which the painstaking care bestowed upon the erection of the columns was complicated by the rising curves of the stylobate and entablature and by the inward inclinations of the column axes, all entailed a mathematical precision which is almost incredible.

The walls were likewise built up with their faces completely enveloped in the unfinished protective surface, in the case of marble about ⅜ inch outside the proposed final wall planes,[3] or more in other sorts of stone; the lifting bosses still remained on the blocks. The vertical joints were hollowed with the exception of a polished band 2½ or 3 inches wide at the two vertical edges, and across the top (but not across the bottom) the so-called anathyrosis, in order to secure closer contact; and all the joints, both horizontal and vertical, were left with a slight bevel intended to prevent chipping when the blocks were placed together. At internal corners, either vertical or horizontal (as when a wall recedes from a step or a belt course protrudes from a wall), a finished marginal band of about two inches was sunk to the final surface. In all horizontal joints of this character, and likewise in other cases of projecting or receding surfaces where the edges of beds were likely to chip or spall, a relieving margin about $\frac{1}{32}$ inch deep protected the edge from close contact. For hoisting and placing, lifting tongs worked with pulleys and derricks usually gripped bosses left on the exposed faces of the blocks, which could thus be set directly on their final beds and almost in their exact positions, requiring no blocking up or other

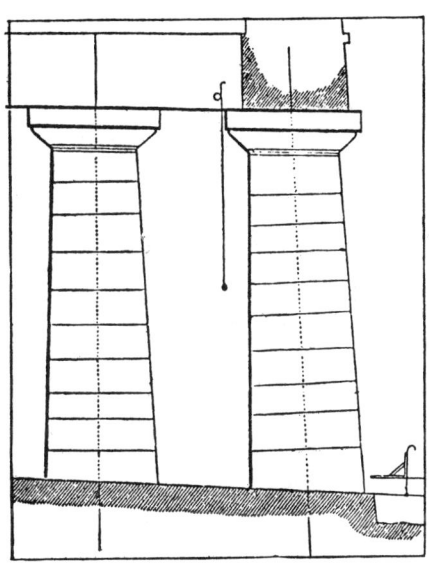

FIG. 62.—INCLINATIONS OF DORIC COLUMNS, EXAGGERATED.

---

[1] Penrose and other authorities have applied to the variations of height on the different sides of the lowest drums, due to their adjustment both to the curved stylobate and to the inclination of the columns, the term *scamilli impares* used by Vitruvius; but the latter was referring only to the stylobate construction.

[2] There is no basis for the statement that it was turned in a lathe.

[3] An exception must be made for the "prefabricated" marble wall blocks of the Hephaesteum, which never had protective surfaces and were therefore provided with relieving margins at the bottom, leaving slightly open joints.

adjustment beyond a lateral shift of a few inches by means of crowbars. For some special work the tongs grasped the joint surfaces of the blocks by means of special tong holes; and the last-laid intermediate block of a course had the tong holes cut in its top so that it could descend accurately into its position between the vertical joints of its neighbours and at the same time leave the tongs free for removal (Fig. 63 c, d). This preoccupation with the removal of

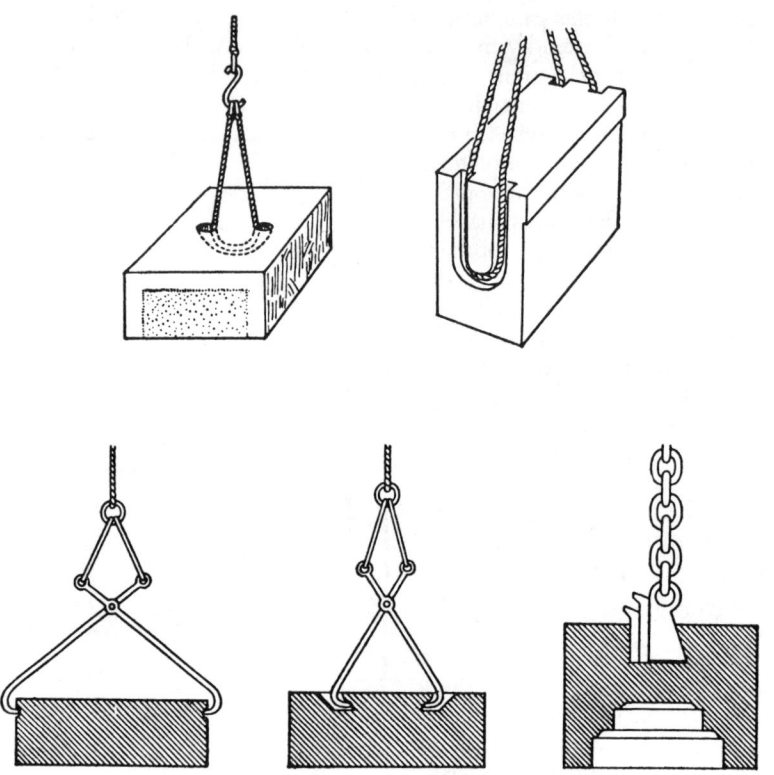

Fig. 63.—Forms of Lifting Devices.
(a, b) Rope loops; (c, d) tongs; (e) lewis.

the lifting appliance underlies all the varied inventions employed both earlier and later: loops of rope passed through tunnels in the tops of blocks (as in the Heraeum at Olympia) or through U-shaped channels in both end joints (as in the Olympieum at Acragas and the temple at Aegina), or lewis irons fitting corresponding wedge-shaped holes in the tops of blocks (tapering on one end only in the best Greek periods, on both ends in late Hellenistic and Roman times). All the blocks were laid dry, without mortar; for a bonding material was used iron, dowels to fasten the blocks to those below them, and clamps of double-T form to connect blocks in the same course, all sealed in molten lead (Fig. 64 d). Special forms of dowels and clamps were employed in unusual positions, even in the work on a single building such as the Parthenon. And

DOWELS AND CLAMPS

in earlier or later buildings we again encounter variant forms of dowels and clamps characteristic of different periods or localities. Thus the archaic dovetail clamp, which in Egypt was of wood, might be either of pure lead (poured molten into the cavity) or of lead reinforced with an iron bar with the ends bent down; the double-T clamp was preceded, and sometimes accompanied, by the double-Γ form, usually with the ends of the bar bent in opposite directions, right and left, rarely in the same direction; and latest of all came the simple bar with both ends bent down to form the Hellenistic and Roman hook clamp.

The members of the entablatures and ceilings appear to have been set in place practically finished.[1] The unworked surfaces with a few exceptions were confined to the platform and columns and walls, these being the portions most liable to injury during the process of erection. On the completion of the

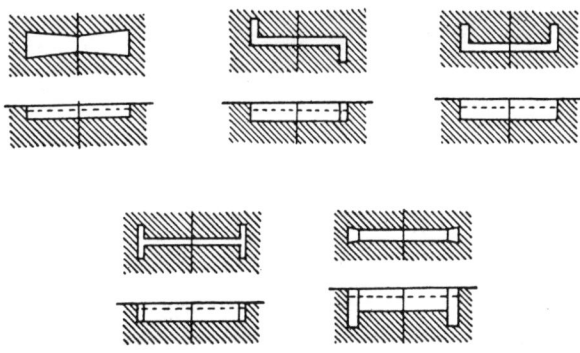

FIG. 64.—FORMS OF CLAMPS.
(a) Dovetail, (b, c) double-Γ, (d) double-T, (e) hook.

temple the faces of the walls were dressed and rubbed so that the bevels at the joints, and almost the joints themselves, disappeared; and the treads and risers of the steps were worked down to their smooth surfaces. Exceptionally careful was the treatment of the columns, of which the cylindrical stippled mantle passed through three additional stages after the columns had been erected and the bosses hewn off (Fig. 65). First, the entire shaft was recut in the form of a polygon of forty sides, twenty of them wider and marking the positions of the flutes, while the twenty narrower facets were to become the sharp arrises. Next, the twenty wider facets were hollowed to form the preliminary fluting, the narrower facets remaining like the fillets of an Ionic column. Finally, all the surfaces were cut back about $\frac{3}{8}$ inch more to the positions of the finished flutes already worked on the bottom drums and the capitals, the fillets then being transformed into the almost razor-edged Doric arrises (actually $\frac{1}{32}$ to $\frac{1}{16}$ inch wide). All these processes may be seen in temple 'GT' at Selinus and are mentioned in the expense accounts of the Erechtheum. And through them

---

[1] In later work narrow protective strips were sometimes left at the vertical joints to prevent chipping or spalling.

all it was necessary to preserve the delicate entasis which gives such beauty to the outline of the shaft.

Among exceptional structural processes required by the use of long spans or heavy masses, such as the hollow marble ceiling beams of Bassae or the balanced cantilevers in the Doric friezes of the Propylaea, none is more interesting than the sparing use of concealed iron beams. In the Parthenon broad flat iron beams were employed as cantilevers to support the heaviest pediment statues; they were imbedded in the tympanum wall and channels were cut beneath them so that their deflection under the weight of the sculpture would not cause them to bear directly on the cornice. In the Propylaea iron beams 6 feet long,

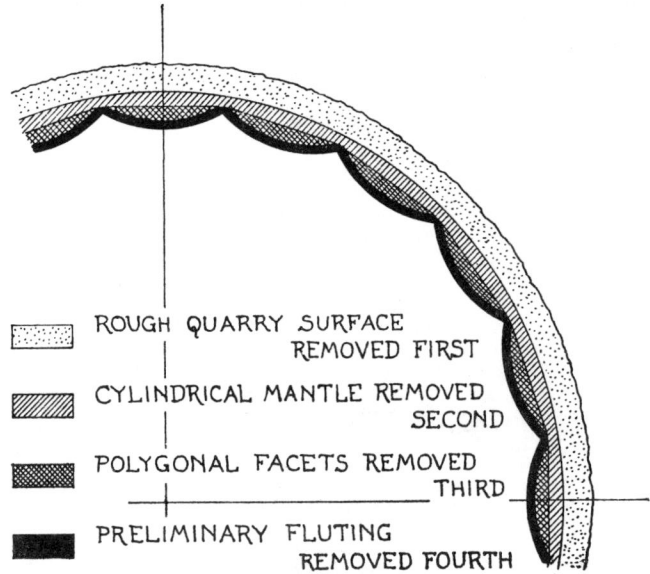

Fig. 65.—Detail of processes of fluting Doric columns.

with similar provision for deflection, transmitted $6\frac{3}{5}$-ton loads from the marble ceiling beams toward the Ionic columns on either side (Fig. 66). At Acragas, as we have noted, the iron beams were 14 feet in length, located in the soffit of the architrave.[1] It is interesting to note that, as contrasted with the traditional Greek suspicion of the strength of stone, there was apparently complete confidence in iron; thus the iron beams in the Propylaea were employed with the low safety factor of 4 (as contrasted with 6 in modern usage), and it must be admitted that this confidence was justified in that they functioned properly for 2,120 years.

The sculptured enrichment of the Parthenon, designed by Phidias, was without doubt the most beautiful that the world has seen. It is apparent that

---

[1] Much less scientific was one iron beam imbedded in a lintel soffit of the Erechtheum, in that the marble lintel itself had to crack (which it did) before the iron beam could begin to function.

SCULPTURE OF THE PARTHENON

the ninety-two metopes (Plate XL), being constructed separately from the triglyphs and afterwards slipped into place between them, were carved on the ground before being raised to their positions; hence they must be earlier than the erection of the cornice, a fact indicated also by the earlier style of the sculptured slabs themselves.[1] Their subjects are, on the east front, the battle of the gods and giants, and on the west the battle of Amazons and Athenians; the long south flank was occupied by the contest of the Centaurs with the Lapiths and on the north flank was the fall of Troy. The sculpture is in such high relief that, in contrast to the metopes of temple 'C' at Selinus, it protrudes far beyond the triglyphs and even overhangs the architrave taenia below. On the other hand, the continuous Panathenaic frieze in low relief on the external walls of the cella formed an integral part of the structure, and was carved *in situ*; a remarkable feature of it is the location of such sculpture in a position where it

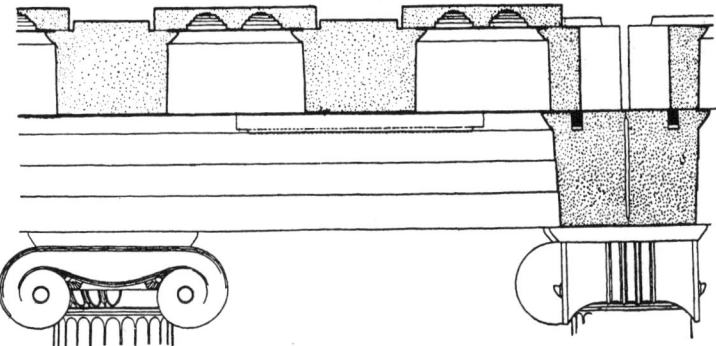

FIG. 66.—STRUCTURAL IRON BEAM IN THE PROPYLAEA.

could hardly be appreciated (Plate XL). Nothing was said by Pausanias about this frieze, 523 feet $7\frac{1}{4}$ inches in length, representing the procession which took place every four years during the Panathenaic festival; it starts from the south-west angle, running east and north, and meeting over the pronaos, where the procession, headed on either side by the maidens selected to work the sacred robe and here represented as bearing religious offerings, arrives before the Athenian officials and the assembled gods who are grouped in the centre, seated, while behind them the old peplos is being folded up to be stored away. The figures decorating the pediments, the latest of the marble sculptures of the temple, are known to have been executed on the ground before being set in place. The only literary notice that we possess of the subject of the pedimental sculptures is from Pausanias, who says, "the whole subject of what is called the pediment over the entrance (i.e., the east pediment) is the circumstances of the birth of Athena; and that at the back is the contest of Poseidon with Athena

---

[1] The earlier style is probably due, not so much to the very slight difference in date, as to the fact that Phidias at this stage had not yet had time to mould the individual styles of the artisans of the old school to his own.

for the land."[1] Attention may be drawn also to the superb lion heads carved as false spouts at the four corners of the temple, not exactly at right angles to the cornice but peering obliquely toward the façades.[2] Finally, a few words should be said about the chryselephantine statue of Athena, Phidias's masterpiece. This was constructed on a wooden core, having ivory for the face, arms, and feet, and gold for the drapery and accessories, the thin gold plates weighing about 2,500 pounds. The engraved outline of the pedestal on the pavement, and the rectangular hole for the central mast, define its exact position.[3] The total height of the statue and its sculptured pedestal was twenty-six cubits (39 Doric feet, and so 41 feet 10 inches); and from the description of it given by Pausanias, and from the numerous smaller marble copies (such as the Varvakeion statuette at Athens) and the representations on marble or gold reliefs or on gems and coins, we obtain a fair idea of its appearance. The column inserted to support the right arm, with a capital that seems to be Corinthian, if not part of the original design, is at least as early as the beginning of the fourth century.

Last of all, a few words must be said with regard to the painting, primarily the architectural polychromy (Plate XL). In general, the most important structural members were free of colour, being left in the natural white of the marble just as, in poros buildings, these portions were covered with white marble stucco.[4] Thus the Doric peristyle contained no colour below the capitals; the deep incision under the necking was painted blue, the annulets at the base of the echinus blue and red. The triglyphs were blue (as Vitruvius also reports) and thus formed the key to the colouring of the entablature: for the regulae and mutules recalling the triglyphs at the top of the architrave and on the soffit of the cornice were likewise blue, and the alternating members, as far as necessary (the taenia of the architrave, the viae between the mutules and the fascia below them and the scotia above), were all in red. In the Parthenon, moreover, the taenia of the architrave had a gold maeander on the red ground and the regulae similarly a gold anthemion on the blue ground. The guttae were apparently dazzling white (at Bassae they were separately inserted bits of marble), often with circles painted on the bottoms. The metopes were always white (except insofar as figure sculpture in relief demanded coloured details); and in poros buildings the metopes were often specially inserted marble slabs for this reason. An uninterrupted frieze such as that of the Panathenaic procession or the Nike temple parapet, however, had in addition to the coloured details of the sculpture a blue painted background, an effect gained in the Erechtheum

[1] Drawings made in 1674 for the French ambassador De Nointel, and sometimes attributed to Jacques Carrey, give the positions of the lost central figures of the west pediment; but in the east pediment the central group was already missing before this time and can be only conjecturally restored.

[2] The best preserved of the sculptures of the Parthenon are in the British Museum, including eighteen of the pediment figures, fifteen of the south metopes, and 247 feet of the Ionic frieze, besides numerous fragments. One metope and one long piece of the frieze are in the Louvre. [3] See p. 164.

[4] The excessive application of polychromy in architectural restorations made during the nineteenth century has led to some misconceptions of its purpose and, consequently, of Greek taste. Some have not hesitated to cover entire columns with yellow or saffron (based apparently on traces of chemical change or oxidation of the iron content in the marble), the echinus with a huge egg-and-dart, the abacus with a maeander, the architrave and cornice faces with elaborate floral patterns, etc.

frieze by an Eleusinian stone background, giving the cameo effect of Wedgwood's jasper ware. Likewise an interior cornice might have elaborately painted maeander or anthemion designs on the main face of the cornice, as well as decorated bed and crowning mouldings. Such mouldings received painted patterns according with their profiles: the hawksbeak had squarish conventional leaves, alternating blue above with red below and *vice versa*, with rims and midribs in gold, green, or white; similar colours were used for the egg-and-dart on the ovolo and the heart-and-dart on the Lesbian cyma (or cyma reversa), red and blue predominating with a sparing use of gold, green, or white where the alternation would otherwise have been confused. The ceiling coffers had successive tiers of egg-and-dart patterns, and the slightly vaulted top panels sometimes contained eight-pointed stars on the blue ground (as in the Hephaesteum, temple of Ares, and east portico of the Propylaea), but in the Parthenon (and also in the west portico of the Propylaea) had elaborate floral patterns. Likewise the square area of cornice soffit at each corner of the temple received a floral pattern (carved in relief in the case of Segesta), and sometimes the viae were similarly painted with palmette compositions. The ovolo sima in the Parthenon received a delicate anthemion, though in the Propylaea it had a huge egg-and-dart. And the alternate red and blue of the petals and scrolls of the antefixes repeated the hieratic finial scheme of the archaic grave stelae. These colours are now preserved only in the most sheltered areas, and elsewhere are distinguishable only by the relative warmth or coolness in the tones of the marble, by discoloration or disintegration of surfaces in accordance with the chemical effects of pigments and their varying degrees of protection, and in some cases by the engraved outlines of the ornament.[1] As for representational painting, mural decoration on a large scale, we know this chiefly from literary sources, such as the decoration of the pronaos walls of the temple of Athena Areia at Plataea by Polygnotus, or those of a temple of Athena at Elis by Panaenus, or also from the preparations for such painting as in the case of the stippled surfaces and waterproofed joints of the porch and cella walls of the Hephaesteum. Sometimes, moreover, additional decoration was applied in later times as, in the Parthenon itself, the series of bronze shields (some dedicated by Alexander the Great) fastened to the architrave, and Nero's great inscription in bronze letters on the architrave of the east façade.

The most complete example of the perfected type of the Doric hexastyle temple exists in the so-called "Theseum,"[2] on a low hill just west of the marketplace at Athens, now known to have been the temple of Athena and Hephaestus mentioned by Pausanias; it contained bronze statues of those divinities designed and executed by Alcamenes, in 421–415 B.C. As at Olympia, however, we must

---

[1] The discoloration, or the effect of relief caused by the disintegration of surfaces in the interstices of the patterns, may be so pronounced as to bring out the patterns clearly by photography, just as paper casts (squeezes) of mouldings may reveal the engraved outlines of patterns.

[2] The temple owes its comparatively perfect preservation to the fact of its having been converted into a church of St. George by the Byzantine Greeks. During this operation the pronaos columns and cross-wall were removed together with the pronaos ceiling, and also the interior columns; the pronaos and cella were covered with a great barrel vault. The pronaos columns were rebuilt by the Greek authorities in 1936–1937, while the neighbourhood and interior were excavated by Americans in 1936–1939.

conclude that the temple was earlier than the cult statues within; a combination of all the evidence suggests 449 B.C. for the beginning of the work, antedating the design of the Parthenon by two years.[1] The Hephaesteum thus becomes the earliest identified design by the nameless "Theseum architect," and its importance is increased by the fact that it reflects the contemporary influence of the Parthenon, not only in the obvious resemblance of the sculpture, but also in the gradual transformations of its architecture. The temple consists of a cella, with a pronaos and opisthodomus, and is surrounded by a peristyle with six columns on the fronts and thirteen on the flanks (Fig. 67; Plates XLI, XLII). Its proportions are less satisfactory than those of the Parthenon, owing to the unfortunate combination of lighter columns with a heavier entablature, and in part also to the different colour and material of the bottom step, which so combines with the surrounding ground as to give the impression that the temple has an inadequate base of only two steps. This idea was borrowed, together with the Ionic moulded base at the foot of the cella wall, from the Older Parthenon, of which the ruins were then visible. Apart from this bottom step, the material is Pentelic marble for most of the architecture, Parian marble for the sculpture. The cella was begun with long and narrow archaic proportions, and with the idea that the inner faces of the walls should be painted with great mural compositions unbroken by internal columns. Under the influence of Ictinus, however, the cella was both widened and shortened, and two storeys of Doric columns as in the Parthenon, returning across the rear with a central column on axis, were placed close against the walls giving almost the effect of the niches at Bassae, apparently causing the abandonment of the scheme for mural decoration. A special feature of this and other plans by the "Theseum architect" is the exact alignment of the pronaos columns and antae with the third column on either flank, thus creating an intimate relation between the outer and inner structures. Notable also is the use of continuous Ionic friezes in pronaos and opisthodomus above Doric columns; even the regulae and guttae of the architrave, retained in the Parthenon, are here replaced by Ionic mouldings. Over the opisthodomus this frieze runs merely from anta to anta; but over the pronaos advantage was taken of the alignment in plan to carry the frieze across also to the north and south peristyles, thus setting off the front pteroma as an enframed compartment. Only eighteen of the external

---

[1] The date and identity of the temple have been subjects of lengthy controversy. The name "Theseum" was formerly applied because of the representation of the exploits of Theseus in the flank metopes; but the real temple or sanctuary dedicated to Theseus is known to have been in quite a different part of the city and was, furthermore, built by Cimon in 475 B.C., far too early for the structure with which we are concerned. Among the numerous other suggested identifications, the only one that fits the topographical description by Pausanias is that of the Hephaesteum, which has recently been confirmed by the numerous surrounding establishments of metal-workers uncovered during the American excavations. Yet the temple cannot be as late, on the other hand, as the statues made by Alcamenes in 421–415 B.C. For the architectural forms and the style of the relief sculpture require a date contemporary with, or barely earlier than, the beginnings of the Parthenon; and the date of the rubbish (chiefly potsherds) excavated among the stonemasons' chips leads to the same conclusion. Taking into account this stylistic evidence, also that of certain inscriptions, and (as in the case of the Older Parthenon) a comparison of the orientation of the axis with the festival day of Hephaestus and Athena and with the lunar calendar, we obtain 449 B.C. as the most suitable date.

metopes are decorated with sculpture; ten on the east front, and the four adjoining the east end on the north and south flanks (Plate XLII), exactly surrounding the special front compartment of the pteroma. The pediments were filled with sculptures which have now disappeared, though some of them have been recovered. Of the cult statues by Alcamenes, in addition to copies on a relief and pieces of the plaster moulds, we have blocks from the pedestal of black Eleusinian limestone, to which were clamped reliefs presumably silhouetted in white marble.

In the Agora just below the Hephaesteum an almost identical but slightly larger temple was seen by Pausanias, dedicated to Ares, with a statue of the god likewise by Alcamenes. This was not, however, its original location; what Pausanias saw was a reconstruction of the temple with the original materials, dating from the time of Augustus, apparently at about 14–10 B.C. It seems to have been transported bodily from the ancient drill-ground farther east, near the Anaceum (sanctuary of the Dioscuri) and the true Theseum, that is, the area subsequently cleared for the Roman market near the Tower of the Winds. Similar temples, likewise of marble, were erected at short distances outside Athens, dedicated to Poseidon at Sunium (Plate XLIII) and to Nemesis at Rhamnus.[1] All three, as well as the Hephaesteum, were by the same unknown "Theseum architect"; and by means of a study of their dimensions, proportions, and ornamental details they may be placed in such a chronological order as to

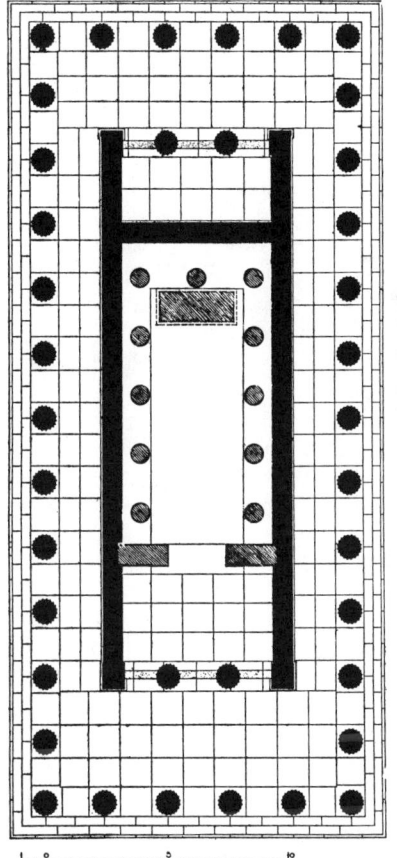

FIG. 67.—THE HEPHAESTEUM. (Restored by Dinsmoor.)

[1] The temple at Sunium was measured by Revett in 1765, and again, as well as that at Rhamnus, by the Dilettanti Society expedition of 1812; the excavations were completed at Rhamnus by the Greeks in 1890, and at Sunium by the Germans in 1884 and by the Greeks in 1899–1915. At Rhamnus nothing now stands above the stylobate except the lowest drums of a few columns; at Sunium twelve of the columns are still erect, nine on the south flank and two on the north, together with portions of the architrave and one column and the two pronaos antae (one reconstructed in 1908). The column diameter at Sunium has always been underestimated, resulting in slender proportions which Herbig regards as an Ionic importation. The foundations of the temple of Ares in the Agora were discovered by American excavators in 1937; but they are of late construction, and the scattered marble blocks and fragments bear masons' letters of Augustan date, for assembling the blocks during a process of rebuilding.

exhibit the development of his style. Thus the temple at Sunium may have been designed about 444 B.C., that of Ares at Athens about 440, and that at Rhamnus in 436 B.C. All three resembled the Hephaesteum in the use of slender column proportions and in the adjustment of the plan, with the pronaos antae aligned with the third column in either flank, to permit the use of continuous friezes extending across the pteroma. In these three later temples, however, the architect returned to his original preference (as exemplified in the first design for the Hephaesteum) for a cella without internal columns. In the latest example, at Rhamnus, the architect experimented with a shorter plan, using only twelve columns on the flanks; but in the others he retained the canonical number of thirteen. At Rhamnus, too, was repeated the experiment of building the lowest step in a darker material, here blue marble; even the foundations are of this same blue marble, so plentiful at Rhamnus that it was used extravagantly. Another peculiarity in the foundations at Rhamnus is the first appearance of a new material, reddish breccia or conglomerate; but with some distrust of its qualities it was limited to underpinning of the pavement. At Sunium the columns are exceptional in having only sixteen flutes, probably an experimental attempt to counteract the slender proportions. The three earlier examples (Hephaesteum, temple at Sunium, temple of Ares) exhibit one of the peculiar tendencies of this period, that of copying dimensions; with different column heights and proportions in all three cases, the entablature heights were identical. The three earlier examples, furthermore, are alike in retaining the old Corinthian ovolo or S-profile of the Doric sima, while the temple at Rhamnus adopts the Periclean Ionic ovolo profile of the Parthenon. In many other respects, too, the Rhamnus temple shows the direct influence of the Parthenon, which was dedicated in 438; and as a result of its late beginning the work at Rhamnus was never finished, steps and walls retaining their rough protective surfaces and the columns remaining unfluted, probably because of the preliminaries of the Peloponnesian War in 432 B.C. Both at Sunium and Rhamnus there was some use of carved ornament, further evidence of the Ionic influence on the Doric buildings of this period. At Sunium the architrave crowning moulding, as in the Hephaesteum, was of Ionic form above the inner porches; but at Rhamnus this inner architrave had the usual regulae and guttae as in the Parthenon. The sculptured Ionic frieze at Sunium lined all four sides of the front pteroma compartment, but the external metopes were blank; we have no remains of the presumable internal frieze in the temple of Ares, but there were apparently eighteen sculptured metopes enframing the front compartment exactly as in the Hephaesteum; and at Rhamnus likewise the façade metopes seem originally to have been sculptured (replaced by plain metopes in Roman times) while the inner frieze was blank only because the temple was unfinished. The pediments contained sculptures at Sunium; the presumable pediment sculptures of the temple of Ares are missing, perhaps having been carried off to Rome when the temple was rebuilt; and at Rhamnus the war apparently caused the omission of such decoration. The acroteria at Sunium were all of the floral type, and on the temple of Ares there were apparently golden Victories; but conventional griffins stood on the outer extremities of the pediments at Rhamnus. The statue of Ares in his temple was by Alcamenes; but that of Nemesis was by Agoracritus, in Parian marble, and the delicate reliefs on her white marble pedestal appear to have been carved at a slightly later date, during the Peace of 421 B.C.[1]

Slightly later in date is a much larger Doric hexastyle temple dedicated to Hera near Argos;[2] it was the work of the local Argive architect Eupolemus, richly decorated with sculpture and carved ornament, and contained the gold-and-ivory statue of Hera wherewith Polycleitus attempted to rival the Zeus of Phidias. The temple replaced the primitive wooden structure which was destroyed by fire in 423 B.C. The new temple, probably erected at about 416 B.C. during the Peace of Nicias, was of the typical hexastyle form, though with only twelve columns on the flanks as at Rhamnus. It would seem that Eupolemus, like Libon at Olympia, attempted to design an ideal temple with column spacings of exactly 10 Doric feet, diameters of 4 Doric feet, triglyphs and metopes of 2 and 3 Doric feet respectively, and other dimensions in proportion. The cella was divided into aisles by two rows each of five columns, probably Doric and therefore arranged in superposed storeys. The material was soft limestone (covered with stucco), with hard grey limestone for the steps, and marble for the architectural sculptures. The triglyph frieze had a crowning ovolo as in the Athenian Propylaea; and the sima, of the Periclean ovolo profile, is unique in its relief decoration, an anthemion interspersed with birds, the sacred cuckoo of Hera. The metopes, for the sake of economy, were carved only at the front and rear, under the pediment sculptures; and the peaks of the gables were crowned by floral acroteria recalling those of the Parthenon.

Less elaborate temples also were erected at this period. On the island of Delos the Athenians commenced a Doric temple to Apollo in 425 B.C., squeezed between the archaic Ionic temple and the unfinished platform which did not receive its peristyle and cella until the Hellenistic age. Because of this cramped location, hexastyle colonnades appeared only on the two fronts, the flanks being solid walls (Plate XLIII).[3] The diameters and spacings of the columns are three-sevenths of those of the Parthenon; and not only this identity of proportion but also other indications of the influence of the Parthenon and of Ionic design suggest that Callicrates was the architect. The pronaos had, instead of columns, four slender piers between the antae (imitated from the piers of the Nike temple), and corresponding slender pilasters protruded from the wall of the rear porch; the front wall was pierced by windows on either side of the door (imitated from the Propylaea at Athens), illuminating an interior lined with a great semicircular pedestal supporting seven statues. The ceiling of the cella was unique in temple design (so far as we know), in being formed by the sloping rafters themselves, the intervals framed and coffered in wood, and the triangles formed by this pitched ceiling at front and back filled

[1] The top of the head of Nemesis is in the British Museum, while portions of her drapery still lie near the temple; the pedestal reliefs are in the Athens Museum. A sculptured metope in the Villa Albani at Rome seems to have been carried off, not in modern times, but in antiquity, since the present blank façade metopes are of Roman construction, dating from the time of the dedication of the temple to Livia, the mother of Augustus.

[2] The Argive Heraeum was excavated by an American expedition in 1892. Only the foundations remain in place; the sculptures are in the Athens Museum.

[3] The foundations were excavated by the French, and their very complete publication of all surviving fragments permits one to form a clear picture of its very unusual design.

by marble internal pediments.¹ The temple was distinguished from its neighbours by the names "Athenian temple" and "temple in which the seven statues are"; it was dedicated in 417 B.C. by the Athenian statesman and general Nicias.² At about the same time Nicias seems to have been responsible for the erection of a prostyle tetrastyle temple of Dionysus at Athens (Fig. 77), likewise apparently Doric.³ The outline of this plan presents an innovation because of its T-shape; the steps, instead of being carried all round the walls where access was impossible, were returned along the flanks only to the extent of the open intercolumniations. In this temple, for the first time, the new material breccia or conglomerate was employed in a responsible position for the actual foundations, whence it was soon to oust poros limestone. On a great pedestal of which the foundations exist within the cella stood, as Pausanias tells us, a gold-and-ivory statue of Dionysus by Alcamenes.

Temples purely Ionic in style likewise arose on Attic soil during this period. One of the most peculiar, and also the earliest, is the lop-sided temple of Athena at Sunium, where an Ionic colonnade was added before 450 B.C. along the east front and south flank of an already existing structure, and so was mentioned by Vitruvius in his series of irregular temples. The additional work is of marble; the capitals show archaic feeling, with a cyma reversa instead of the ovolo between the volutes, and the architrave follows the tradition of the archaic Ionic on the Greek mainland in being unbroken by fascias, and the cornice lacked dentils. Presumably, therefore, a frieze was included in the entablature. The pedimental sima, of terracotta, has an ovolo profile for the first time on the Greek mainland, painted with a large egg-and-dart. At about the same time is probably to be dated the beginning of a great peripteral Ionic temple of Apollo on the island of Delos, hexastyle and with thirteen columns on the flanks. Only the two lower steps were actually erected at this time, and these remained unfinished, though they are of interest because of the sunken panels at the bottoms of the risers to emphasize the regularity of the jointing, and particularly the earliest use of the little vertical cyma reversa at the ends of these panels.⁴ The work seems to have been abandoned as a result of the transfer of the Delian treasury to Athens in 454 B.C.; and when it was resumed at the end of the Athenian domination one hundred and forty years later the style was changed from Ionic to Doric.⁵

¹ See the details of the "Hall of the Bulls at Delos" (p. 290). Extra tympanum slabs found in the peripteral temple of Apollo probably answered a similar purpose.
² The date of the temple is known from the records of the gold crowns dedicated every four years at the Delian festival.
³ The foundations lie near those of the older temple in the theatre precinct, but practically all remains of the architecture have disappeared.
⁴ This treatment appeared, as we have seen, almost immediately afterwards at Bassae.
⁵ The mid-fifth century date of the beginning of the work was first suggested by Courby, but primarily on erroneous grounds, an assumed enlargement of the column spacing on the fronts (later retracted) and finally because of the absence of angle contraction. But the latter would be an archaism only if the peristyle were Doric, and even then would have been inadmissible at any time in the fifth century, or even in the latter part of the sixth, in a Doric temple so close to the centre of development. A Doric temple of such importance in one of the Aegean islands, moreover, would have been a rarity before the tightening of Athenian domination. We may infer from the chequered history of the construction that the early date of the beginning is correct; but we may also assume that the original design followed the Ionic tradition of the islands.

IONIC TEMPLES BY CALLICRATES

At Athens, apparently in 449 B.C. on the occasion of the signing of the peace with Persia, the erection of a temple to Athena Nike (Victory) or Nike Apteros ("without wings") on the Acropolis was authorised by the senate, and the specifications and model were prepared by Callicrates, subsequently an architect of the Parthenon. For some reason—perhaps the new decision to reconstruct the entire Acropolis as a memorial of victory—the scheme was held in abeyance for twenty-two years. It would seem that Callicrates immediately utilised his specifications and model, however, for the erection of another small temple (the Metroum in Agrae?) in Athens, on the bank of the River Ilissus (Plate XLIV).[1] The material was Pentelic marble; the plan was amphiprostyle and tetrastyle—that is to say, it had prostyle porticoes of four Ionic columns each toward east and west, while the pronaos had two columns in-antis[2] and gave access to the cella through a doorway of the usual form. The column bases were of the ultimate form, the "Attic base," which was attained by adding, below the torus and hollow disk (simplified to a single scotia) of the Asiatic type, a lower torus which gradually increased in size until it became somewhat larger than the upper. The echinus of the capitals, which in previous Attic work had generally been the cyma reversa, apart from a few votive capitals in which was employed the Asiatic ovolo, now definitely adopted the latter profile. And the anta capitals, while derived from the triple ovolos of Asia Minor, now assumed the diversified Periclean profile with only one ovolo at the bottom, and a cyma reversa and cavetto above. Although in no sense archaic, the entablature was still of exceptional severity, the architrave being unbroken by fascias; and above a sculptured frieze was a cornice without dentils, showing the same simple bed moulding that we find in the temple of Athena Nike and the Erechtheum. The marble sima was the earliest example of the Ionic ovolo profile in this material, and was undoubtedly the prototype of the profile repeated (with slight simplification) by Callicrates in the Parthenon.[3] At about the same date occurred the employment of the Ionic order inside the temple at Bassae, as mentioned above, and likewise with the simple unbroken architrave (though the actual execution of this upper portion of the order dated about a quarter of a century later).

Some years later the little temple of Athena Nike planned by Callicrates was actually erected, probably between 427 and 424 B.C.[4] Meanwhile the Propylaea

---

[1] The temple was fortunately measured and drawn by Stuart and Revett before its total destruction by the Turks in 1778. Apart from remnants of the foundations, no fragments of the temple have survived with the exception of four slabs of the sculptured frieze carried off as souvenirs by Morosini's army in 1688 (now preserved in the Vienna and Berlin Museums), two small frieze fragments discovered recently, and pieces of the sima.

[2] These two columns in-antis are omitted in all the published plans.

[3] The sima, erroneously restored by Stuart and Revett as a cyma recta, has not hitherto been identified, but is that which I momentarily attributed to, and immediately rejected from, the monument of Nicias (*A.J.A.*, XIV, 1910, pp. 463, 469, 483). The Ionic descent of this profile can be traced from the archaic cornice-sima ovolo (though decorated with a lotus-and-palmette) at Myus, through the terracotta ovolo simas painted with the egg-and-dart at Miletus (Kalabak-tepe) and Sunium.

[4] The date has long been a matter of controversy like that of the Hephaesteum, and the periods assigned have ranged over fifty years. The decisive factors are the overlapping of the construction on that of the neighbouring Propylaea (437-432) showing that the temple is later, the late style of the frieze sculpture, an inscription referring to work on the cult

THE CULMINATION IN ATTICA AND THE PELOPONNESUS

had been constructed, greatly curtailing the site. As finally erected (Fig. 68, 74 at N; Plates XLIV, LI), the temple crowns a bastion on the south side of the west approach to the Acropolis, and was built on the site of the earlier temple and altar; its north side rests in part on the early polygonal wall, and its axis, running south of east, forms a marked angle of nearly 18 degrees with those of the Propylaea and the Parthenon.[1] To fit this site the plan required by the original model was telescoped, so to speak, by diminishing the length of the cella and combining cella and pronaos; the two inner pronaos columns of the temple on the Ilissus were replaced by slender monolithic piers substituted for the front wall of the cella, which would thus have been entirely open but for the bronze screens between piers and antae. The columns are of remarkably stocky proportions, with monolithic shafts and a height of only about $7\frac{5}{6}$ lower diameters, apparently because of a feeling that lighter proportions would be unsuitable on the heavy bastion. While many of the dimensions were slightly reduced from the model (the temple on the Illissus), partly to occupy less space and partly to form a simple relationship (1 : 2) to the Ionic order of the Propylaea, other dimensions and profiles are identical with those in the temple on the Ilissus, suggesting a certain economy of effort on the part of the architect, or more probably an economical use of the old templates.[2] Thus the column bases, while of the typical Attic form, with the scotia between two tori, are identical with those of the temple on the Ilissus so far as the upper torus and scotia are concerned, while the lower torus had

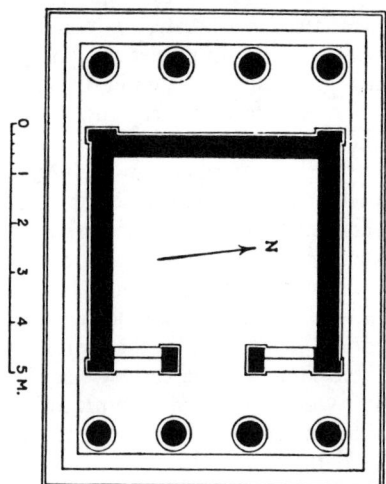

FIG. 68.—TEMPLE OF ATHENA NIKE.

to be very much compressed (resembling that in the Athenian Stoa at Delphi) in order to squeeze the whole base within the permissible height. But certain elements were brought up to date, so to speak; thus the subdivision of the architrave into three fascias, which had been employed internally (where no frieze was required) even in the temple on the Ilissus and then was repeated

statue in 426, allusions to dedications to Athena Nike in 426 and 425 implying unusual activity in her precinct, an inscription now dated 424 B.C. cut on the back of that authorising the erection of the temple in 449 and implying that the work was now finished, and the orientation of the axis which favours 427 rather than 426 B.C.

[1] After having been seen by a few early travellers, this temple disappeared, the Turks having taken it down in 1686 to obtain material for the construction of a central rampart. But on the destruction of this rampart in 1835 the dismembered pieces of the temple were recovered, so that it was rebuilt in the following seven years. Now (1936–1941) it has been rebuilt for the second time from the foundations, but with the columns erroneously rotated to bring fillets on axis under the eggs of the echinus (contrast Fig. 69).

[2] Compare the reproduction of dimensions from the Older Parthenon in the present Parthenon, from the Hephaesteum in the temple of Ares and that at Sunium, from the Nike temple in the Erechtheum, from the Propylaea in the temple at Tegea, etc.

inside the Propylaea, now reappeared on the exterior as had been customary in Asia Minor. The solution adopted for the angle capital in this temple (Fig. 69) was that of leaving the intersecting volutes at the inner corner uncarved, apart from the protruding eyes. The sima reproduces the ovolo form of the temple on the Ilissus. The Nike temple is notable for its sculptured decoration: the frieze contains scenes of combat from the battle of Plataea in 479 B.C.,[1] the probable occasion of the erection of the earlier temple, and even the tiny pediments once contained sculptured figures fastened by pins, while the corners of the pediments supported golden acroteria, apparently winged Nikes. Toward the end of the century was added the series of sculptured slabs which formed a parapet along the north, west, and south edges of the bastion, and these rank among the most beautiful sculptures of all periods, including the famous Victory adjusting her sandal, a fragment from the south side.

The most elaborate of these Ionic temples, however, was that erected opposite the Parthenon, on the north side of the Acropolis, called the Erechtheum (Figs. 70–72, 74 at E; Plates XLV–XLIX, LI); it was to replace the Peisistratid temple of Athena, which it slightly overlapped, just as the Periclean Parthenon was the successor of an earlier temple on the same site. Hence, being likewise a temple of Athena Polias, it was distinguished from the Parthenon by the official name of "the temple in which the archaic image is" or, for convenience, the Archaic (Venerable) Temple (despite its newness). As in the parallel case of the Parthenon, the special name of the west end was eventually applied to the whole. The Erechtheum is a building as complicated in its plan (Fig. 70) as the Parthenon is simple. It was built on two levels, and has four porticoes of different design, and four entrances (not to speak of a subterranean entrance under the north portico); and the interior contained four rooms at different levels, besides a subterranean corridor along the north wall and a niche with a projecting floor elevated high in air at the southwest corner. This irregularity was due primarily to the necessity of preserving intact certain spots sacred to the Athenians,[2] and also in part to changes of plan during the course of erection; but the architect, whose name is unknown, would seem to have accepted the difficulties of the situation and to have designed a building which more than any other shows the elasticity of

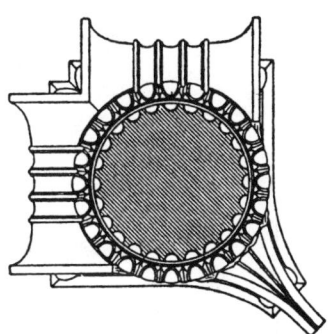

FIG. 69.—PLAN OF ANGLE CAPITAL, TEMPLE OF ATHENA NIKE.

---

[1] Four slabs of the sculptured frieze are in the British Museum, as well as capitals of a column and an anta, all extracted for Lord Elgin from the above-mentioned Turkish rampart.

[2] It was on this site that, according to tradition, Athena and Poseidon are supposed to have contended for the dominion of Athens as represented in the west pediment of the Parthenon; and the mark of the trident in the rock, the well of sea water, and the sacred olive tree are all mentioned by Pausanias.

the Greek style.[1] The manner in which he solved his problems would suggest that he was identical with the architect of the Propylaea, namely, Mnesicles. Perhaps with him was associated the sculptor-architect Callimachus, the inventor of the Corinthian capital; for we know that Callimachus designed the golden lamp within the Erechtheum, and the Caryatids and the anthemion design of the wall and column capitals agree with what we know of his style and choice of subjects. The date of the temple, too, is not definitely fixed; but it is stylistically later than the little temple of Athena Nike (of which, inciden-

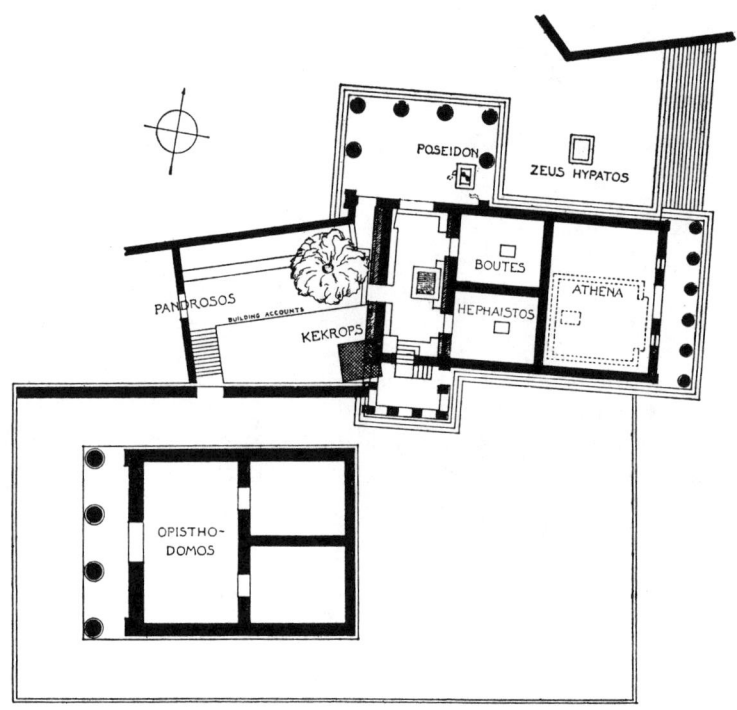

Fig. 70.—The Erechtheum, as begun and as finished.

tally, the axial spacing of the columns was exactly doubled to serve as the corresponding basic element of the new design), so that the time of the Peace of Nicias in 421 B.C. would appear to be most suitable. After being interrupted at the time of the expedition against Syracuse, the work was resumed in the summer of 409 B.C. and completed four years later, under annually appointed

[1] The description of the temple has hitherto involved many uncertainties, not only because of the many alterations in Roman times, but also on account of its subsequent conversion into a Byzantine church and then into a Pasha's residence. After a partial reconstruction in 1837–1846, the entire exterior was rebuilt, so far as the original pieces would permit, in 1903–1909 by the Greek authorities. Most of the problems have now been clarified by the researches of the American School at Athens.

architects of whom we know two by name, Philocles and Archilochus, perhaps supervisors or administrators rather than designers.

The main block, built to be seen from the higher level, covers an area of 38 feet 2 inches by 75 feet on the stylobates, including a prostyle hexastyle portico of six Ionic columns at the east end; the back wall of this east portico had windows on either side of the door (Fig. 72).[1] The west end of the block had four slightly smaller semi-detached Ionic columns between antae, with, in Roman times at least, three windows in the intervening walls.[2] It is uncertain whether the original design had such windows, or whether the three central intercolumniations, and with them the northernmost, had merely low walls capped by sills and carried up by open grilles;[3] it is certain, in any case, that the southernmost intercolumniation both in Greek and Roman times had merely such a low wall, above which it was left completely open, obviously for some cult purpose. These west columns, being at the upper level, were necessarily supported on a lofty basement storey descending to the lower level of the court west of the Erechtheum forming the sanctuary of Pandrosus; and in this basement is a minor entrance to the Erechtheum located exactly under the column to the south of the axis. On the north side of the block was a broad flight of steps leading to the lower level; and at the western end of this north flank, but projecting also westward of the main block, is a prostyle tetrastyle portico of six Ionic columns, four columns in front and one behind each of the corner columns. The back wall of this north portico contains not only the great north doorway but also a minor lateral doorway leading into the sanctuary of Pandrosus at the west, and, toward the east, a subterranean door connecting a crypt under the north portico with a den for snakes below the floor of the interior. On the south side, and likewise close to the west end, is the Caryatid porch, the marble roof of which is carried by six Caryatid figures, four in front and two behind, all facing the south and standing on a podium 5 feet 9¾ inches high,[4] with a seldom used entrance cut through it on the east flank close to the wall, and an L-shaped stairway descending through a minor south doorway to the interior. The plan of this south porch forms an exact pendant, though on a smaller scale, to that of the north portico. At distances of 24 feet and 45 feet 4 inches, respectively, from the east wall of the cella are marks of the attachment of cross-walls, which would divide the area into three compartments. Of these, the eastern chamber, on the higher level, and entered from the hexastyle portico of six columns, is supposed to have been the cella of Athena Polias; and the central and western compartments are at the lower level,

---

[1] The north angle column of this east portico, portions of the entablature above and the anta capital and part of the wall crown behind, as well as one piece of window trim, are in the British Museum. A small fragment of the other (south) anta capital is in the Metropolitan Museum in New York.

[2] These were blown down during a hurricane in October 1852, and the whole front was rebuilt in 1904, after examination of the remains had led archaeologists to the conclusion that both columns and windows were of Roman date, though the column bases are of the original workmanship.

[3] Four wooden grilles, either temporary or permanent, were inserted between these columns in the early summer of 408 B.C., according to the expense accounts.

[4] The Caryatid just to the left of the axis of the porch is in the British Museum, being replaced in the temple by a cast in artificial stone.

the western forming merely a narrow anteroom with entrances from the north portico and south porch and also from the Pandroseum at the west. A marble wall only 12 feet 10½ inches high divided the western from the central compartment, and another subdivided the central compartment longitudinally into two parallel rooms, entered from the anteroom through two doorways each furnished with pairs of marble doors, and having floors differing from each other by 2¼ inches.[1] This threefold group of rooms, the shrine of Erechtheus, opened above toward a single ceiling. The cistern containing the salt sea of Poseidon was evidently under the floor of the western compartment;[2] and the indentations stated by Pausanias to have been produced by the trident of Poseidon were shown on the rock floor of a crypt under the north portico, so that, like marks of the thunderbolt of Zeus, they could be directly exposed to the sky through the floor opening with its altarlike frame and through a corresponding marble-lined shaft in the ceiling and roof above. The olive tree of Athena grew in the sanctuary of Pandrosus west of the Erechtheum.

It seems clear that this irregular scheme was not that which any architect could have desired, and that behind it must have been a much more logical plan.[3] The awkward treatments of the north and south porches overlapping the west wall show a lack of study which would have been incredible in a finished design. We may infer that the original scheme was, while still on paper, a mere translation of the inner building of the Peisistratid temple— which it was intended to replace—into marble, with the same three compartments of which the central one was divided longitudinally, and with prostyle tetrastyle Ionic porticoes at east and west (Fig. 71). The total length measured on the stylobate would have been 100 feet 2 inches; and this would have been located concentrically on the platform of the Peisistratid temple, all at one level. But with the decision to retain the Peisistratid west rooms as a treasury the architect's hope faded, and the new marble temple was transferred to the irregular ground at the north, where only the east end could rest on the high ground, supported by a Mycenaean terrace wall, and the west end was dropped to a level 10 feet 7½ inches lower. In order to avoid too great a discrepancy in the roof levels the high east columns were made smaller, and consequently more numerous, the portico becoming hexastyle and the whole temple slightly widened in order to

---

[1] The evidence for the longitudinal partition, of which even the foundations have disappeared, is the fact of this difference in floor levels (which would have been impossible in a single floor reaching from wall to wall), combined with the mention of the four marble door leaves in the building inventory of 409 B.C.

[2] This was subsequently enlarged to occupy the entire area of the western chamber, but the workmanship is evidently of mediaeval date.

[3] Among those who have attempted to deduce the form of the original plan, Dörpfeld stressed the existence of two axes, the longitudinal axis through the east portico and a transverse axis drawn north and south through the north portico and the Caryatid porch (though the latter is slightly off-axis with respect to the former), and, assuming that the whole was to have been symmetrical about the transverse axis, thus duplicating the present temple, he developed a plan of which the stylobate would have measured 132½ feet from east to west. But not only would the excessive length of this plan have resulted in several unnecessary rooms; there are also other objections such as the lofty podium required to support the proposed west portico, and the inorganic attachment of the box-like Caryatid porch against the middle of the long south flank wall. The Greek architect's scheme must have been something far more logical.

receive the returns of the lower west cornice; and lest the tetrastyle west porch, with its larger columns at a lower level, might seem to be subordinated to the new design on the east, an additional column was placed behind each corner

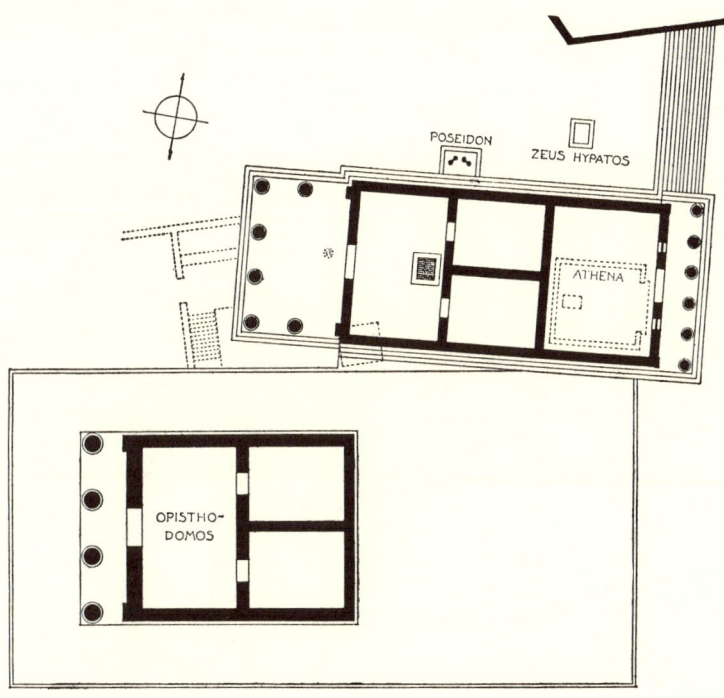

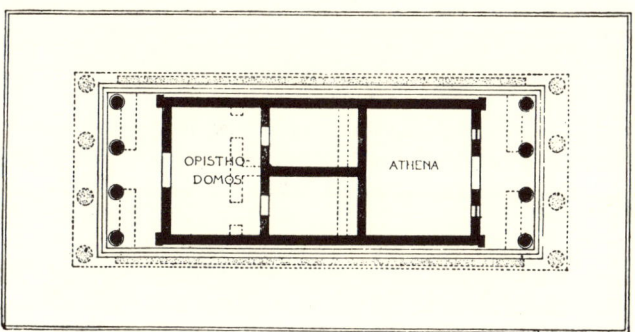

Fig. 71.—The Erechtheum, two earliest stages of design. (Restored by Dinsmoor.)

column on the west. The total length on the stylobates was now increased to 101 feet 10 inches. But this plan had two vital defects: it would have required the decapitation of the very real tomb of the mythical king Cecrops and also the removal of Athena's sacred olive tree, both of them on the site of the proposed west porch. Because of objections from the priesthood it became necessary to rotate the west porch to the north flank and thus, in the words of Vitruvius (IV, 8, 4), to "transfer to the shoulders what ought to have been at the front." The Caryatid porch was next designed to balance the north porch, following the same arrangement of the six columns, though on a smaller scale in order to fit the space left available behind the existing west rooms of the Peisistratid cella (of which the ruined east end had by this time presumably been demolished). The denuded west wall was decorated with the four semi-detached columns between antae to balance the east portico, though their bases were located at a higher level to give room for a doorway below. Even after the foundations had been laid one important alteration was necessary; it was found that the west wall impinged upon the tomb of Cecrops, and it had to be withdrawn eastward by 26 inches, with a corresponding displacement of

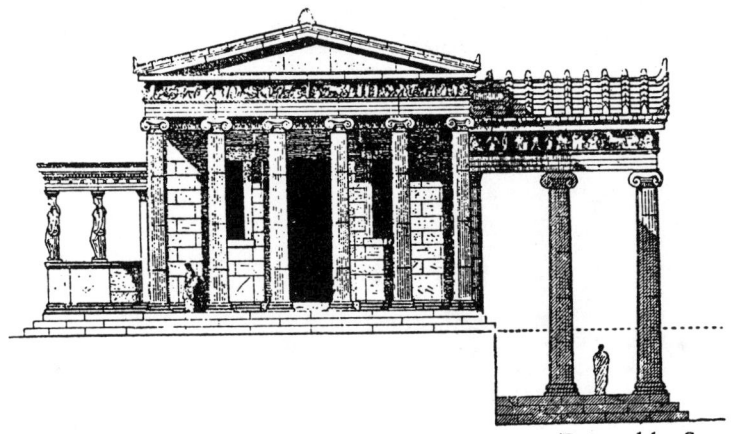

Fig. 72.—East Façade of the Erechtheum, with Windows. (Restored by Stevens.)

the cross-wall just behind by half of this amount, resulting in the narrowing of the south porch and irregular spacing of the Caryatids.

The whole temple was built in Pentelic marble, with black Eleusinian limestone for the frieze, to which figures in white marble were attached by clamps. The intercolumniations and the relative proportions of diameters to heights of columns vary in the different porticoes; in the east portico (Fig. 72; Plate XLV) they are barely more than 2 diameters apart, and the relation of diameter to height is $1 : 9\frac{1}{2}$; but in the north portico (Plate XLVIII) the columns are $2\frac{4}{5}$ diameters apart, and the relation of diameter to height is $1 : 9\frac{3}{8}$. The bases of the columns of the semi-detached columns of the west front (Plate XLVI) are on a level 3 feet $1\frac{3}{4}$ inches higher than those of the east portico; but, while the height of the columns was made exactly equal to 9 diameters, the intercolumniation was made almost the same as in the east portico. While the forms of the orders resemble in general those employed by Callicrates, they are of much greater richness, partly because all the ornament is carved and not merely painted. In the bases, all of the Attic form, the lower torus is always smooth; the upper torus is usually fluted horizontally, but in the north portico is carved with a guilloche of two designs. The capitals are of exceptional richness (Plate XLIX), with compound spiral ribs and intermediate fillets in the volutes, and countersunk between the convolutions in each case was a gilt bronze stem ending in a group of petals filling the triangle left on either side by the sagging curve connecting the volutes; the eyes of the volutes likewise were gilt; above the egg-and-dart, moreover, is a torus moulding richly carved with the guilloche, which, in the case of the north porch, once had the interstices filled with glass beads of four colours. Even the deep cavity below the abacus on the baluster side (where in most examples the receding baluster leaves the abacus quite unsupported) is filled up with a beaded astragal and a cyma reversa moulding. Below the capital proper is a special band or necking carved with the anthemion (as at Naucratis, Ephesus, Samos, and Locri), with a bead-and-reel below it in the east capitals, though in the north portico a simple fillet appears at this point and below it in turn an astragal enframes the head of each flute and descends between them like a series of hanging golden tassels. A similar enriched band, with minor variations in design, decorates the antae (Plate XLVII) and is carried round the entire building, together with the profile of the anta capitals themselves, which reproduce the profile invented for the Ilissus and Nike temples but with carved rather than merely painted decoration. The capitals of the corner columns of both porticoes have, at the internal angles within the porticoes, two fully carved half-volutes intersecting each other at right angles (cf. Fig. 69), a somewhat unsatisfactory solution of the problem.

In the south or Caryatid porch (Plate XLVI), the Caryatid figures perhaps represent the "arrephoroi" alluded to by Pausanias as "the maidens who bear on their heads what the priestess of Athena gives them to carry." What they actually carry on their heads, however, are capitals of a type strikingly like the Roman Doric, the echinus carved with the egg-and-dart. The figures vary in the lines of the folds of their dress and in their pose: the three on the left hand rest on the right leg, and *vice versa*, the vertical folds of the dress (which suggest the fluting of a column) being always on the outer side, that of the supporting limb; and they form the most satisfactory type ever evolved from their archaic predecessors at Delphi.[1]

In the entablature of the main building and of the north portico, following the precedent of the temple of Athena Nike, the architrave retains the three fascias of the Asiatic Ionic style, and above the black limestone frieze the dentils of the cornice which form such prominent features in the Ionic temples of Asia Minor are omitted altogether and replaced by a carved cyma. The entablature of the Caryatid porch, on the other hand, omits the frieze, probably with the idea of diminishing the load carried on the heads of the human figures without excessive reduction in the scale of the members of the entablature; but in compensation the upper fascia of the architrave was slightly widened to receive a frieze-like series of carved rosettes, and the Asiatic dentils reappear in the cornice, though much reduced in projection and becoming merely an intermittent moulding, thus losing all structural significance. The sima of the Caryatid porch, cut in the same block with the cornice, has the ovolo profile

[1] As we have noted above, the Caryatid to the left of the centre (Plate XLVI) is a cast, the original being in the British Museum.

carved with the egg-and-dart, rain water escaping through the interstices as in the Propylaea. The sima above the normal entablatures is now missing, but was replaced by the Romans with what seems to have been a faithful copy, so that we may assume that the original structure likewise had the cyma recta profile already employed at Paestum (temple of Demeter), Bassae, and Delos (Athenian temple), but here surmounted by rampant antefixes, alternating with the lion heads in a manner foreshadowing the fourth century.

Among other details of the temple must be noted the entrance to the shrine of Erechtheus, the magnificent central doorway of the north portico (Plates XLVII, XLVIII), which may be regarded as an example of the finest Greek design.[1] Equally rich are the remains of two windows which flanked on either side the doorway in the wall behind the east portico, leading to the shrine of Athena Polias (Fig. 72); the mouldings of the cornice and architrave of the windows were richly carved with the egg-and-dart, the Lesbian heart-and-dart, and the double guilloche, and there were consoles on either side as in the north doorway.[2] The east doorway itself apparently had a simple enframement, and the small doorway to the Caryatid porch had simple pilasters. Among other notable details, the ceilings of the east, north, and south porticoes were richly coffered in marble, and those over the inner rooms showed, according to inscriptions, a lighter coffered design executed in wood. The deep coffers of the north portico had bronze rosettes suspended from their vaults, while the ceiling inside the west half of the temple had wooden rosettes of two designs. The marble ceiling beams of the north portico are the longest employed by the Periclean builders, $18\frac{3}{4}$ feet in clear span; but across the west half of the cella, with a clear span of $32\frac{1}{4}$ feet, it was necessary to brace the wooden transverse girder (which in turn carried the wooden ceiling beams) by diagonal struts which rested on consoles on the walls. Though the temple was minutely carried out even to the last details of woodwork, carving, and painting, yet certain details, such as the rosettes on the architrave of the Caryatid porch, escaped attention. One of the fascinations of the study of this temple is that such details may be fully explained by means of the building inscriptions of the second period of the work, after the summer of 409 B.C. From these may be ascertained also the numbers and names of the workmen, their social status and distribution among the various crafts—about one hundred and thirty workmen being named, 21 per cent slaves, 54 per cent foreign residents, and 25 per cent full citizens—and the details of the universal daily wage of one drachma (even for the architect, but with various subtle adjustments in accordance with status), and the jobs accomplished by each man on each day. These accounts carved on marble in the last years of the Periclean age go into the most minute details, in great contrast to the summary accounting of the earlier and more prosperous

[1] The lintel, cornice, and left console are repairs of Roman (Augustan) date, exact copies of the original portions which had been injured in a fire; the only differences lie in the character of the carving and the omission of the pierced centres of the rosettes. The inner linings (including the sub-lintel), on the contrary, are accretions of Byzantine times necessitated by another fire which cracked the Roman lintel.

[2] This east wall had been destroyed to make way for the apse of the Byzantine church established in the temple, and apparently the materials were utilised in the foundation of the apse. One piece of window trim is in the British Museum.

years; in the single year 408–407 B.C., for instance, they covered about 2650 lines of writing.¹

A very unusual type of temple was the Telesterion or Hall of the Mysteries at Eleusis,² designed in part by Ictinus, the architect of the Parthenon, though other architects were also involved in the work, Coroebus, Metagenes, and Xenocles. The present plan, nearly four times the size of the archaic temple on the same site, belongs to the work set out by Ictinus and his collaborators, the hall being approximately 170 feet square internally (Fig. 73).³ Earlier than this, however, had been erected an intermediate design, about twice the size of the archaic temple, apparently executed by Themistocles or Cimon to replace the Peisistratid structure destroyed by the Persians in 480–479 B.C. This intermediate plan was unusual in being an oblong, retaining the width but doubling the depth of the archaic square plan, and thus occupying the right-hand half of the present plan. It was apparently felt that, with the narrow plan, the problem of lighting would be no more difficult than in its predecessor, with windows high in the walls; certainly there was no central lantern or opaion, since the columns were arranged in three rows of seven with one coming exactly in the middle.⁴ At about the middle of the century the doubling of this plan was entrusted to Coroebus, who laid out the great square that we see at present, but proposed to fill it merely by extending the three rows of seven columns, thereby obtaining seven rows of seven, forty-nine if we assume that the central one was to have been erected. This scheme was abandoned presumably because of the lighting

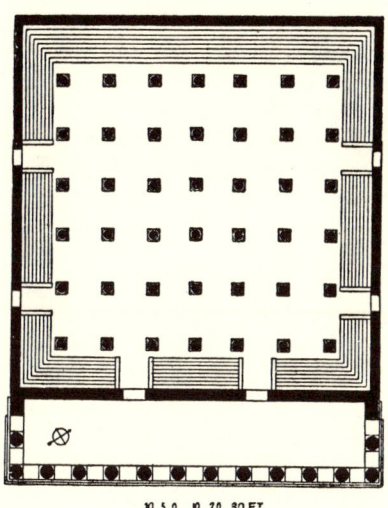

FIG. 73.—HALL OF THE MYSTERIES (TELESTERION), ELEUSIS.

---

¹ The inventory of the summer of 409 B.C. is in the British Museum; the fragments of the accounts of this and the following years are at Athens. It is from these inscriptions, compared with the corresponding portions of the temple, that we learn the true value of the Greek (Doric) foot, exactly 326 mm. or 12·835 inches in this particular example. The usual estimate of 328 mm. does not fit the dimensions of the Erechtheum; and the Athenian foot was never quite so large.

² The Telesterion forms the most conspicuous feature in the conjectural restoration by Gandy-Deering (Plate LXVI); its remains had been studied by Ittar for the Earl of Elgin and by Gandy-Deering for the Society of Dilettanti, but were fully uncovered only during the excavations of the Greek Archaeological Society from 1882 to the present. Some of the recent results are not yet published; the most comprehensive of the available studies, that of Noack in 1927, needs considerable revision.

³ The actual internal dimensions are 169 feet 2 inches in width and 170 feet 6 inches in depth; but the original depth was about 7 feet less.

⁴ Sixteen Ionic column bases and twenty-one wooden architraves stored away among second-hand material in a list of 408–407 B.C. may have come from this building. There are also remains of seven tiers of stone steps lining the walls.

problem.¹ Ictinus thereupon proposed a new solution with an oblong central area covered by a lantern or opaion giving adequate light to the interior; and to adjust the oblong central feature to the square exterior he spaced the columns differently in width and in depth, having five columns in the width but only four in depth, twenty in all. This second solution was likewise abandoned, perhaps because of the tremendous spans involved.² At any rate, the third and present solution, perhaps by Metagenes, is a modification of that of Ictinus, retaining the oblong central opaion but so diminishing the spans as to obtain seven rows of six columns, forty-two in all.³ The lantern itself was built by Xenocles, and probably consisted of a series of piers forming a clerestorey above the main roof, like that of later date at Delos. Because of the oblong patterns formed by the columns and opaion, a hip roof with diagonal rafters at 45 degrees would have been impracticable; and the roofing terracottas show, in fact, that this was not attempted, the main roof having formed a ridge with pediments at front and back. Foundations for a portico were erected on the southeast front, perhaps dodecastyle like the later portico shown on the plan (Fig. 73); but the very fact that the construction of the portico was undertaken on two occasions in the following century suggests that the Periclean design had been left incomplete in this respect, the façade pediment perhaps having been set back in the plane of the front wall. There were two entrance doorways in the front, and also two on the right and on the left sides; and the hall is lined on all sides with eight steps wide enough for use as seats and undercut like those in a theatre, hewn wherever possible in the solid rock.⁴

Eleusis was not the only Attic town to possess a Telesterion of Demeter and Persephone. Another was rebuilt by Themistocles just after the Persian Wars at Phlya, outside Athens. To the same category is probably to be assigned a mysterious "stoa" at Thoricus, dedicated "to the two goddesses" and never finished, presumably because of the Peloponnesian War. Its chief interest lies in the peculiar plan which differentiates it from a normal temple; there are seven columns on the ends and fourteen on the flanks, the central flank intervals being fifty per cent wider than the others (with three metopes above instead of two, as in the Athenian Propylaea) and forming the entrances. No traces of the cella building have been discovered; perhaps it was never begun.

* * * * *

¹ The date of Coroebus, formerly assumed to have been later than Ictinus, is now known approximately from an early building inscription found at Eleusis; he seems to have preceded Ictinus on this site, and to him may be attributed the abortive cuttings in the rock floor discovered by Noack at the back of the left-hand half, showing that it was once intended that there should be forty-nine columns.

² Foundations for these columns exist only in the left-hand half of the plan; it would seem that the Themistoclean structure was permitted to survive in the right-hand half until a definite solution was reached. The restoration of the design of Ictinus as worked out by Noack (conveniently presented by Robertson, *Greek and Roman Architecture*, Figs. 75–76) demands considerable correction, in that the surrounding peristyle is now known to have been, not Periclean, but an abortive fourth-century scheme, while the hip roof and the opaion are unsatisfactory restorations.

³ It was formerly thought that these six rows of seven columns were created during the Roman renovation in the second century A.D.; but it is now evident that, while some of the actual construction dates from this repair, the plan nevertheless must date from the fifth century B.C.

⁴ For the porticoes designed in the fourth century, see the following chapter.

THE ATHENIAN ACROPOLIS

Leaving the subject of temples, we may glance first at the scheme of the Acropolis as a whole (Fig. 74). At the middle of the south and north edges of

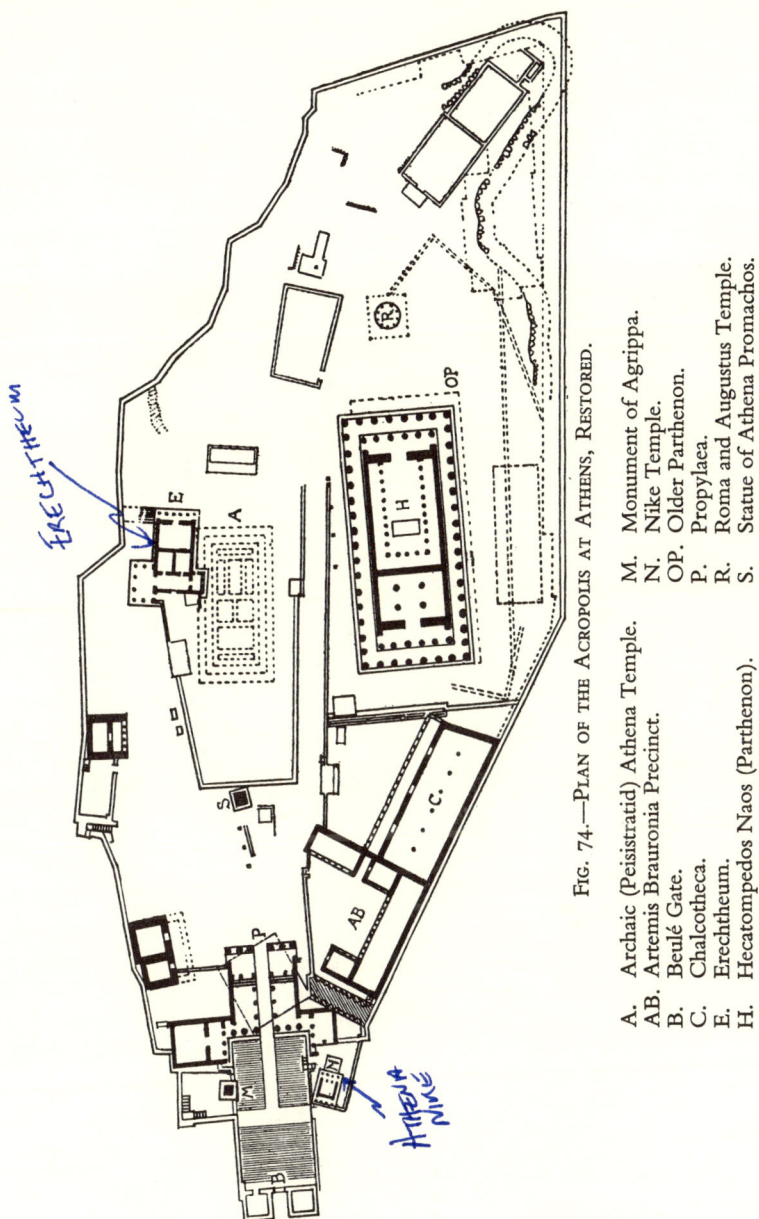

FIG. 74.—PLAN OF THE ACROPOLIS AT ATHENS, RESTORED.

A. Archaic (Peisistratid) Athena Temple.
AB. Artemis Brauronia Precinct.
B. Beulé Gate.
C. Chalcotheca.
E. Erechtheum.
H. Hecatompedos Naos (Parthenon).
M. Monument of Agrippa.
N. Nike Temple.
OP. Older Parthenon.
P. Propylaea.
R. Roma and Augustus Temple.
S. Statue of Athena Promachos.

the long plateau, now terraced up with massive retaining walls in order to form a series of horizontal platforms connected with ramps and steps, stood the Parthenon and the Erechtheum, the former covering the site of the Older

Parthenon, while the latter lay just to the north of its predecessor, the Peisistratid Temple of Athena. Of the latter, the eastern half seems to have been left in ruins as a memorial of the Persian invasion, at least until the time of the erection of the Erechtheum; the western half, known as the Opisthodomus, was repaired to serve as the state treasury, and as such evidently survived until the middle of the fourth century, though fires are reported in 406 and 377 B.C. Farther west, in the centre of the area between the two temples and the Propylaea, stood the colossal bronze statue of Athena Promachos. And at the extreme west end "is the single access to the Acropolis; no other is practicable," says Pausanias, "as the hill rises abruptly on all sides and is fortified with a strong wall." The Propylaea occupied the summit of this approach, originally planned to stretch across the entire width of the Acropolis; the axis of the building is parallel to that of the Parthenon and also points approximately toward the statue of Athena Promachos, thus constituting one of the rare instances of formal relationships between buildings antedating Hellenistic times. Contrasting with this is the marked angle formed by the temple of Athena Nike both with the Propylaea and with the north face of the bastion on which the temple stands. The approach itself seems at this epoch to have been planned as a formal ramp surfaced with clay, and with a broad landing just west of the Propylaea; but only a portion of this was executed, so that it had to be supplemented by an unsymmetrical winding path, probably passing by the foot of the bastion carrying the temple of Athena Nike (Plate LI). Not until Roman times, as will be noted later, did the west approach become strictly formal and symmetrical.[1]

At the head of the ascent had stood some sort of a gateway ever since Mycenaean times; but the earliest traces of a Propylon now remaining are those of the entrance forming part of the reorganisation of the Acropolis after the battle of Marathon, contemporary with the Older Parthenon, and like this destroyed by the Persians. Being a secular building, however, it was repaired after the departure of the Persians, and the traces both of the fire and of the repairs are still evident. It was directed much more sharply toward the north-east than the present building, but so much of it was demolished in 437 B.C. that the plan is now uncertain. It seems to have formed a large square, perhaps with four columns in-antis on each façade, and with a gate wall nearer the inner façade. The steps, antae, columns, and dadoes of the walls were of marble, with plentiful use of poros limestone for the portions covered with stucco; and the upper parts of the flank walls were of half-timbered construction, filled with mud-brick and faced with planks as a ground for mural painting, the "wooden walls" of the Delphic oracle. Before the southwest front lay a hexagonal court, surrounded by steps and a marble revetment, sheltered between the huge Mycenaean walls.[2]

[1] In Plate LI, employed in the absence of a more accurate restoration, some of the most prominent errors are the following: the zigzag path should not be paved and should be combined with a great ramp ascending directly from the west; the roof of the Pinacotheca should be hipped throughout, not gabled towards the south; and the little imaginary temple-like structures shown between the Propylaea and the Parthenon should be replaced by the great porticoed halls of the Brauronion and Chalcotheca, which would, however, have been partly concealed by the lofty Mycenaean west wall, here omitted.

[2] The date of the Old Propylon has sometimes been assumed to have been even as early as Peisistratus; but the workmanship shows that it is contemporary with the Older

PLATE I

Athens: The Acropolis from the West

PLATE II

Delphi: Theatre, Temple of Apollo, and Marmaria

PLATE III

Athens: Corinthian Choragic Columns on the South Slope of the Acropolis

Sunium: Doric Columns of the Temple of Poseidon

PLATE IV

Cnossus: Faience Plaques Showing House-Fronts (Candia Museum)

Melos: Marble Model of Cluster of Round Houses or Granaries (Munich Museum)

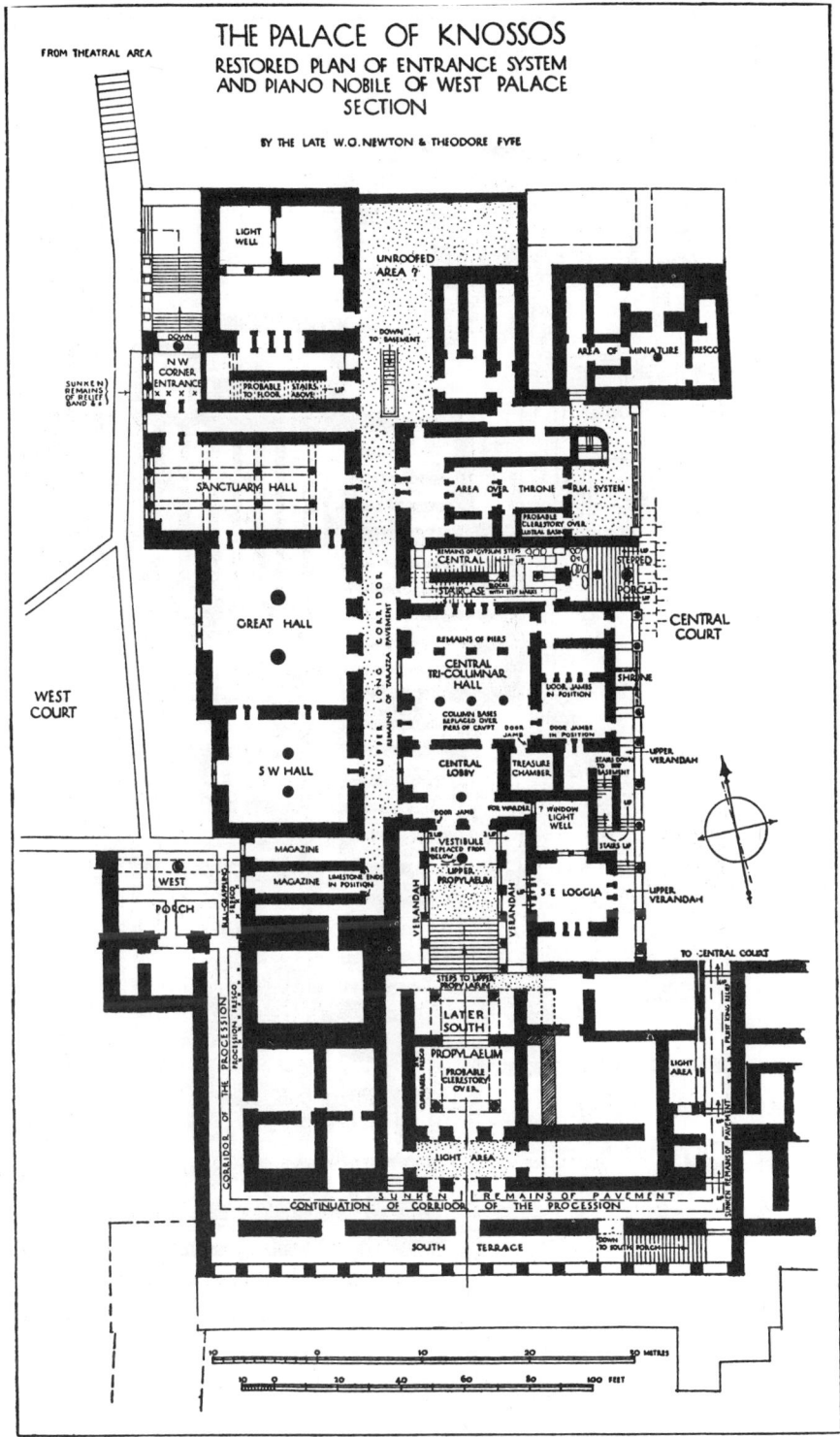

Cnossus: Restored Plan of State Apartments

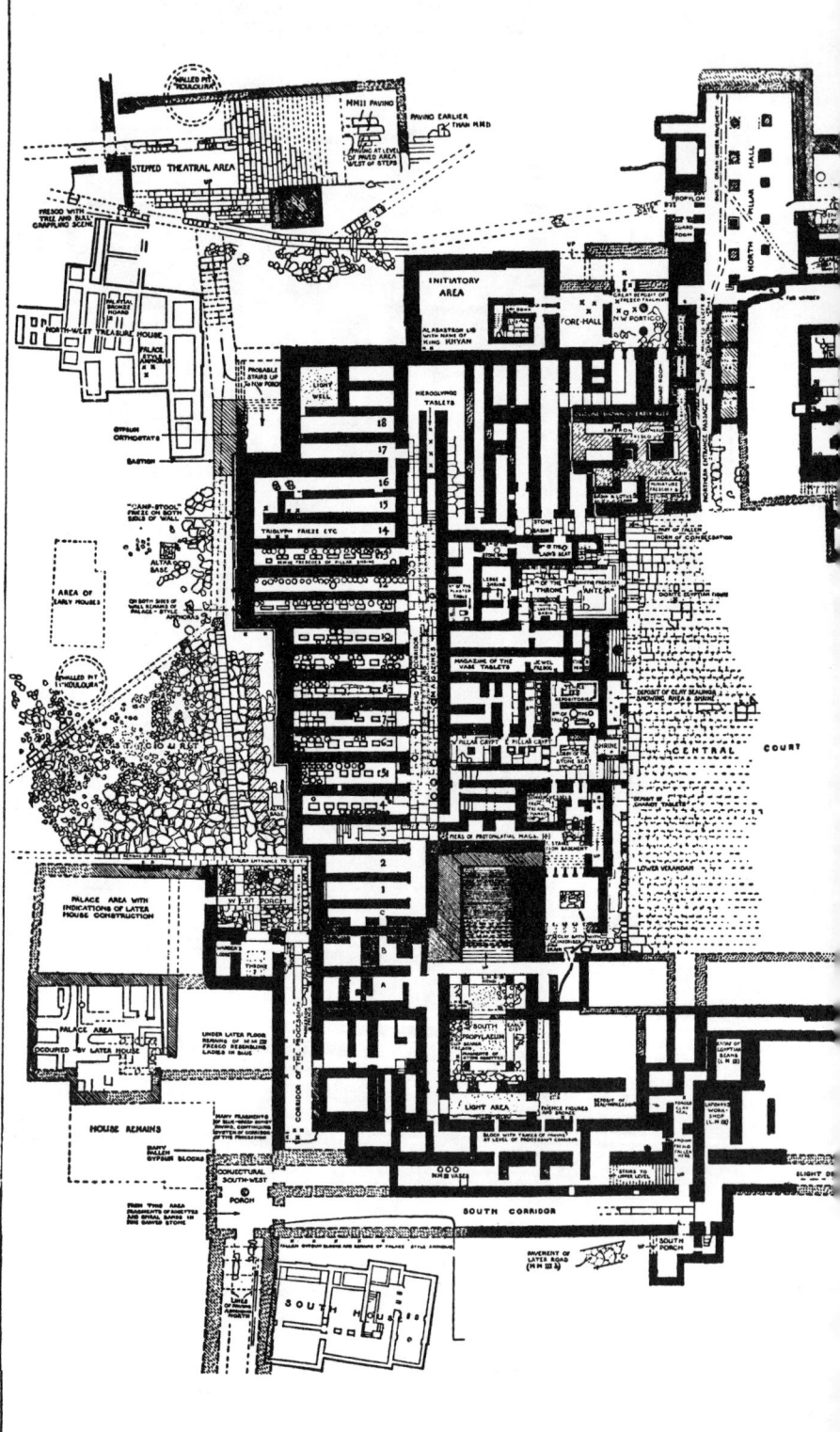

PLATE VI

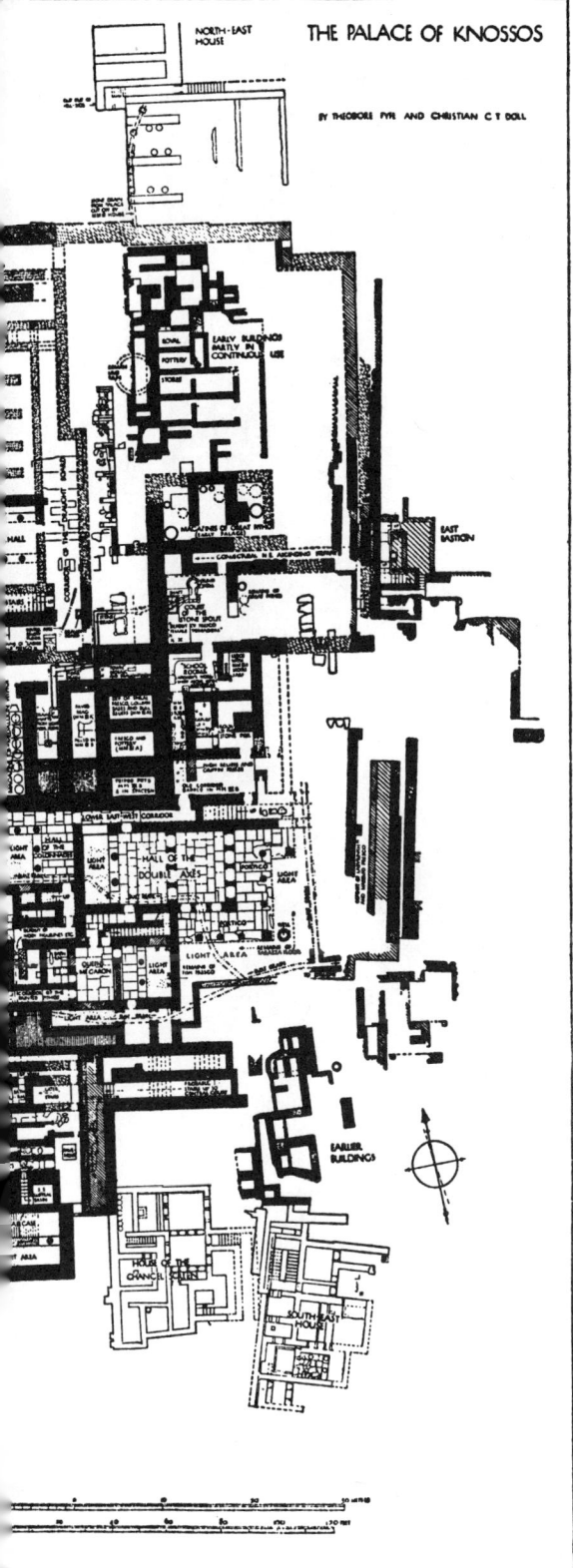

Cnossus: Plan of the Palace

PLATE VII

Cnossus: Throne Room

Cnossus: Alabaster "Triglyph Frieze"

Hagia Triada: Column with Bracket Capital,
Shown in Relief on Stone
Rhyton (Candia Museum)

Cnossus: Staircase and Light Shaft

PLATE IX

Cnossus: So-called Temple Fresco (Candia Museum)

Phaestus: Theatral Area in the Palace

PLATE X

Tiryns: Plan of the Megaron

Tiryns: The Megaron (Restored by Reber)

PLATE XI

Tiryns: Approach to the Inner Gate

Mycenae: The Lion Gate

Mycenae: Sculpture over Lion Gate

PLATE XIII

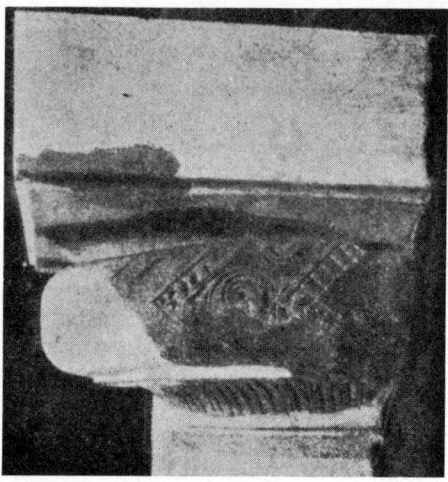

Mycenae: Capital from Tomb of Agamemnon

Mycenae: Column before Tomb of Clytemnestra

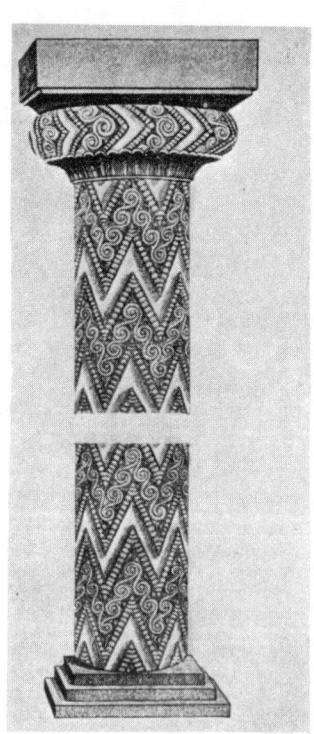

Mycenae: Column from Tomb of Agamemnon

PLATE XIV

Mycenae: Interior of the Tomb of Clytemnestra

Tiryns: Gallery in the Walls

PLATE XV

Mycenae: Entrance to the Tomb of Agamemnon

PLATE XVI

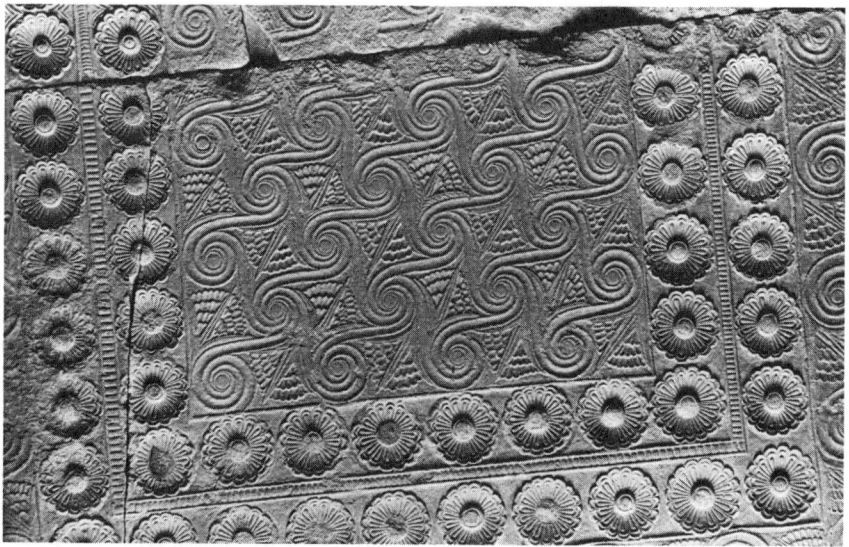

Orchomenus: Detail from Ceiling of Lateral Chamber of Tomb

Mycenae: Fragments of Façade above the Doorway of the Tomb of Agamemnon (British Museum)

PLATE XVII

Thermum: Entablature of the Temple of Apollo (Restored by Kawerau)

Olympia: Corner of the Heraeum, with Rebuilt Columns

PLATE XVIII

Golgoi (Cyprus): Stele (Metropolitan Museum)

Tamassos (Cyprus): Door Jamb of Tomb

Larisa: Proto-Ionic Capital (Istanbul Museum)

PLATE XIX

Myra: Rock-cut Tomb

Telmessus: Rock-cut Tomb

PLATE XX

Athens: Entablature of the Hecatompedon

Athens: Erechtheum Ceiling

PLATE XXI

Selinus: Entablature of Temple 'C' (Palermo Museum)

Selinus: Temple 'C'

PLATE XXII

Corinth: Capitals of the Temple of Apollo

Corinth: Columns of the Temple of Apollo

PLATE XXIII

Metapontum: "Tavole Paladine"

Paestum: So-called Basilica (Hera I), Showing Central Colonnade of Cella

PLATE XXIV

Aegina: Temple of Aphaea, Showing Superposed Columns in Cella

Acragas: Temple of Hera Lacinia

PLATE XXV

Paestum: Temple of Poseidon

Paestum: Temple of Poseidon,
  Showing Superposed
  Columns in Cella

Acragas: Temple of Concord

PLATE XXVII

Segesta: Exterior of Temple

Segesta: Interior of Temple

Delphi: Restoration of Precinct of Apollo (Metropolitan Museum)

PLATE XXIX

Delphi: Athenian Treasury

Delphi: Old Tholos (Restored by Pomtow)

PLATE XXX

Ephesus: Capital from Archaic Temple (British Museum)

Ephesus: Façade Capital from Archaic Temple (British Museum)

PLATE XXXI

Delphi: Cornice and Sima Decoration

Didyma: Anta Capital

Delphi: Reconstruction of Siphnian Treasury (Delphi Museum)

PLATE XXXIII

Delphi: Aeolic Capital from Treasury of Massilia (Restored Cast)

Amyclae: Doric-Ionic Capital from "Altar"

Delphi: Naxian Votive Column

PLATE XXXIV

Olympia: Façade of Temple of Zeus (Restored by J. K. Smith)

Olympia: Section of Temple of Zeus (Restored by J. K. Smith)

PLATE XXXV

Bassae: Temple of Apollo Epicurius

Athens: Parthenon, from the East

PLATE XXXVI

Bassae: Interior of Temple of Apollo, Looking South (Restored by Cockerell)

Bassae: Interior of Temple of Apollo, Looking North

PLATE XXXVII

Bassae: Ionic Order   Bassae: Corinthian Order

PLATE XXXVIII

Athens: Parthenon, from the Northwest

PLATE XXXIX

Athens: Parthenon, Northwest Corner

Athens: Parthenon, South Peristyle, Looking East

PLATE XL

Athens: Parthenon, Detail of Northwest Corner (Restored by Fenger)

Athens: Parthenon, Doric Frieze, Showing Continuous Ionic Frieze Behind, West Front

PLATE XLI

Athens: Hephaesteum

PLATE XLII

Athens: Hephaesteum, from the East

Athens: Hephaesteum, Doric Frieze, South Flank

PLATE XLIII

Sunium: Temple of Poseidon

Delos: Athenian Temple (Restored by Courby)

PLATE XLIV

Athens: Temple of Athena Nike

Athens: Temple on the Ilissus (Restored by Stuart and Revett)

PLATE XLV

Athens: Erechtheum from the Southeast

PLATE XLVI

Athens: Erechtheum from the Southwest

Athens: Erechtheum, Caryatid Portico

PLATE XLVII

Athens: Erechtheum, Anta Capital from East Portico (British Museum)

Athens: Erechtheum, Detail of North Doorway

PLATE XLVIII

Athens: Erechtheum,
North Porch

Athens: Propylaea, East Front

PLATE XLIX

Athens: Propylaea, Doric Capital

Athens: Erechtheum, Angle Capital in North Porch

PLATE L

Athens: Propylaea, North Wing

Athens: Propylaea (Section Restored by Ulmann)

Athens: Acropolis from the West (Restored by Bohn)

PLATE LII

Athens: Acropolis from the South

PLATE LIII

Nemea: Temple of Zeus

Sardis: Temple of Artemis-Cybele

PLATE LIV

Ephesus: West Front of Later Temple of Artemis (Restored by Henderson)

PLATE LV

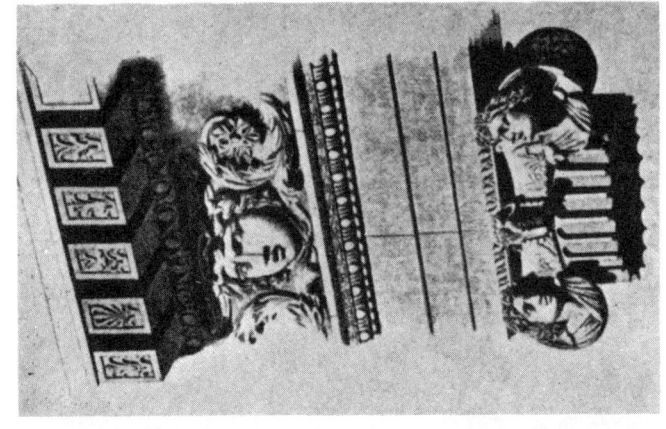

Didyma: Capital and Entablature of Temple of Apollo (Restored by Pontremoli)

Halicarnassus: Capital and Entablature of Mausoleum (British Museum)

Priene: Capital and Entablature of Temple of Athena (Berlin Museum)

PLATE LVI

Ephesus: Temple of Artemis, Sculptured Drum (British Museum)

Didyma: Temple of Apollo, Sculptured Base (Louvre)

PLATE LVII

Didyma: Temple of Apollo, East Front (Restored by Knackfuss)

Delphi: Tholos in the Marmaria

PLATE LVIII

Tegea: Corinthian Capital from Temple of Athena Alea

Didyma: Ionic Pilaster Capital from Temple of Apollo (Louvre)

Epidaurus: Corinthian Capital from Tholos

PLATE LIX

Athens: Choragic Monument of Lysicrates, Detail (Restored by Stuart and Revett)

Delphi: External Order of Tholos (Delphi Museum)

PLATE LX

Athens: Theatre of Dionysus, Throne of Priest

Athens: Choragic Monument of Lysicrates
(Column Drawn by Loviot)

Athens: Choragic Monument of Lysicrates

PLATE LXI

Athens: Theatre of Dionysus, from the Acropolis

PLATE LXII

Epidaurus: Theatre

Athens: Panathenaic Stadium

PLATE LXIII

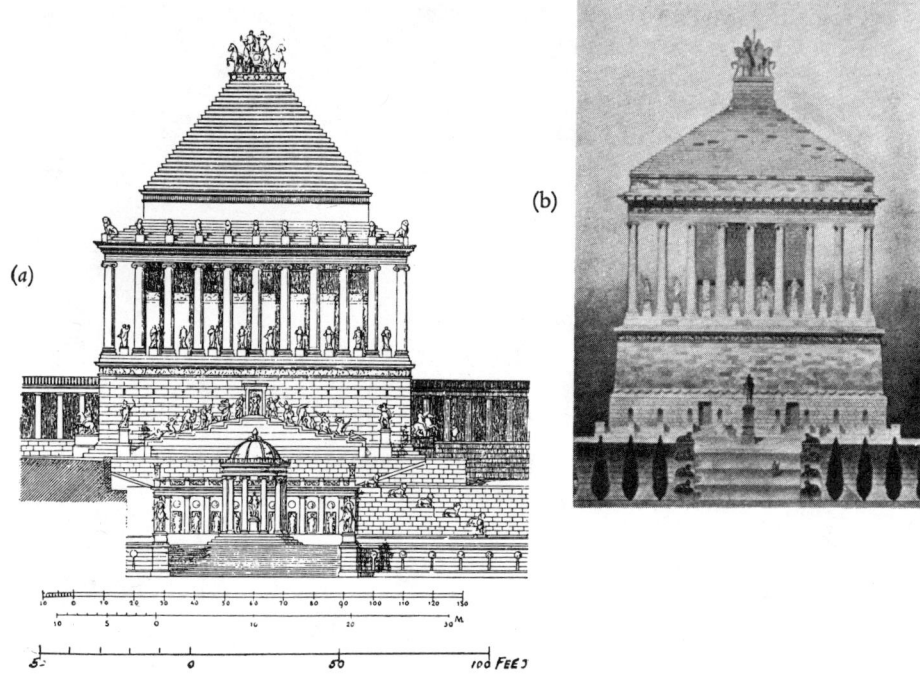

Halicarnassus: Mausoleum, as Restored (a) by Buhlmann and (b) by Dinsmoor

Sidon: Sarcophagus of Mourning Women (Istanbul Museum)

Athens: Temple of Zeus Olympius

PLATE LXV

Magnesia: Capital from Temple of Artemis (Berlin Museum)

Eleusis: Capital from Lesser Propylaea

PLATE LXVI

Eleusis: Precinct of Demeter (Restored by Gandy-Deering)

PLATE LXVII

Eleusis: Doric-Corinthian Entablature from Lesser Propylaea

Pergamum: Detail from Great Altar (Berlin Museum)

PLATE LXVIII

Athens: Tower of the Winds

Alexandria: Lighthouse (Restored by Otero and Asin)

PLATE LXIX

Priene: Theatre

Ephesus: Theatre

PLATE LXX

Delos: House of Cleopatra

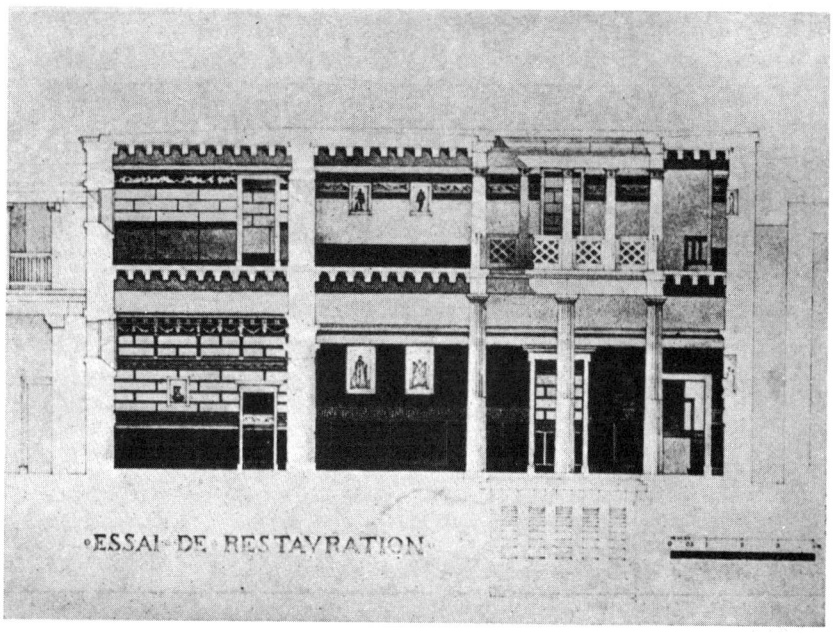

Delos: House on the Hill (Restored by Gabriel)

PLATE LXXI

Mylasa: Tomb (Drawn by William Pars)

Pergamum: Acropolis (Berlin Museum)

THE PROPYLAEA OF THE ACROPOLIS

The new entrance to the Acropolis was known as the Propylaea (Fig. 74 at P; Plates I, LI), the plural name given to the whole pile constructed in 437–432 B.C. from the designs of Mnesicles,[1] including the central building and, as it now stands, two west wings (Fig. 75) forming a lopsided T-shaped plan. It is entirely of Pentelic marble, with a slight use of black Eleusinian stone for polychrome effects, as dadoes or belt courses for walls, copings of terrace walls, thresholds of doorways, and benches. As it now stands, this amputated design occupies a maximum width of 156 feet ½ inch over the extreme north and south walls, though originally, as will be seen, this dimension was intended to be 223 feet 8 inches. The building was left incomplete and unfinished, like so many others in Attica, at the outbreak of the Peloponnesian War, and the work was never resumed.[2]

The central building contained Doric hexastyle porticoes facing west and east, the former resting on a platform of four steps while the latter, owing to the rise in the ground, is not only at a level 5 feet 9 inches higher but also stands merely on a simple stylobate (Plate L). The Doric columns are uniformly $4\frac{3}{4}$ Doric feet (5 feet $1\frac{1}{4}$ inches) in diameter and have normal intervals of exactly $1\frac{1}{3}$ diameters, thus giving a spacing of $11\frac{1}{12}$ Doric feet.[3] In spite of the uniform diameters the height of the western columns, which were always seen from below, is the greater, 28 feet $10\frac{3}{4}$ inches, exactly $5\frac{2}{3}$ diameters or $2\frac{3}{7}$ times the axial spacing; but on the east façade, which was less foreshortened since it was always seen from higher ground, and also with the purpose of avoiding too great a difference in the roof levels (as in the Erechtheum), the columns were reduced nearly 1 foot, approximately by the height of the stylobate, becoming 27 feet $11\frac{3}{4}$ inches, less than $5\frac{1}{2}$ diameters. The central intercolumniation is wider than the others: in the frieze above were three metopes rather than the customary two, increasing the axial spacing to $16\frac{5}{8}$ Doric feet or $3\frac{1}{2}$ diameters, the purpose being to provide easier access for the procession and the beasts of sacrifice (Plates XLVIII, LI). For the same purpose the stylobates and pavements are interrupted by a road more than 12 feet wide, a continuous sloping ramp ascending directly through the building regardless of the individual floor levels (Plate L). It is on this account that the stylobate lacks the usual upward curvature, it apparently having been felt that a curve with the crown cut away would

Parthenon of 488–480 B.C., and the marble revetment of the court (in part against the Mycenaean walls) was composed of second-hand metope slabs from the Hecatompedon demolished in 490–488 B.C. Two other metopes of this series, used not in the court but in the vicinity, contain the great Hecatompedon inscription with the actual date 485–484 B.C.

[1] The date and the name of the architect are known from literary sources, the date being given also on the marble fragments of the expense accounts.

[2] The Propylaea, while remaining intact for the most part, received some additions when it was remodelled to serve as the palace of the "Frankish" dukes of Athens, the southwest wing being sacrificed in the fourteenth century for the erection of a tower 90 feet high. At the middle of the seventeenth century lightning exploded a powder magazine in the east portico, and the Venetian bombardment of 1687 demolished the west façade and the famous ceiling. The Turks erected a rampart over the west portico, but this was cleared away in 1835, and the "Frankish" tower was taken down in 1875. The scientific work of reconstruction was begun in the central building in 1909–1917, and now this process is being extended to the west wings.

[3] This is another instance in which the foot unit can be exactly determined, by means of the engraved construction lines and with reference to the Erechtheum, as 327·2 mm. or 12·880 inches.

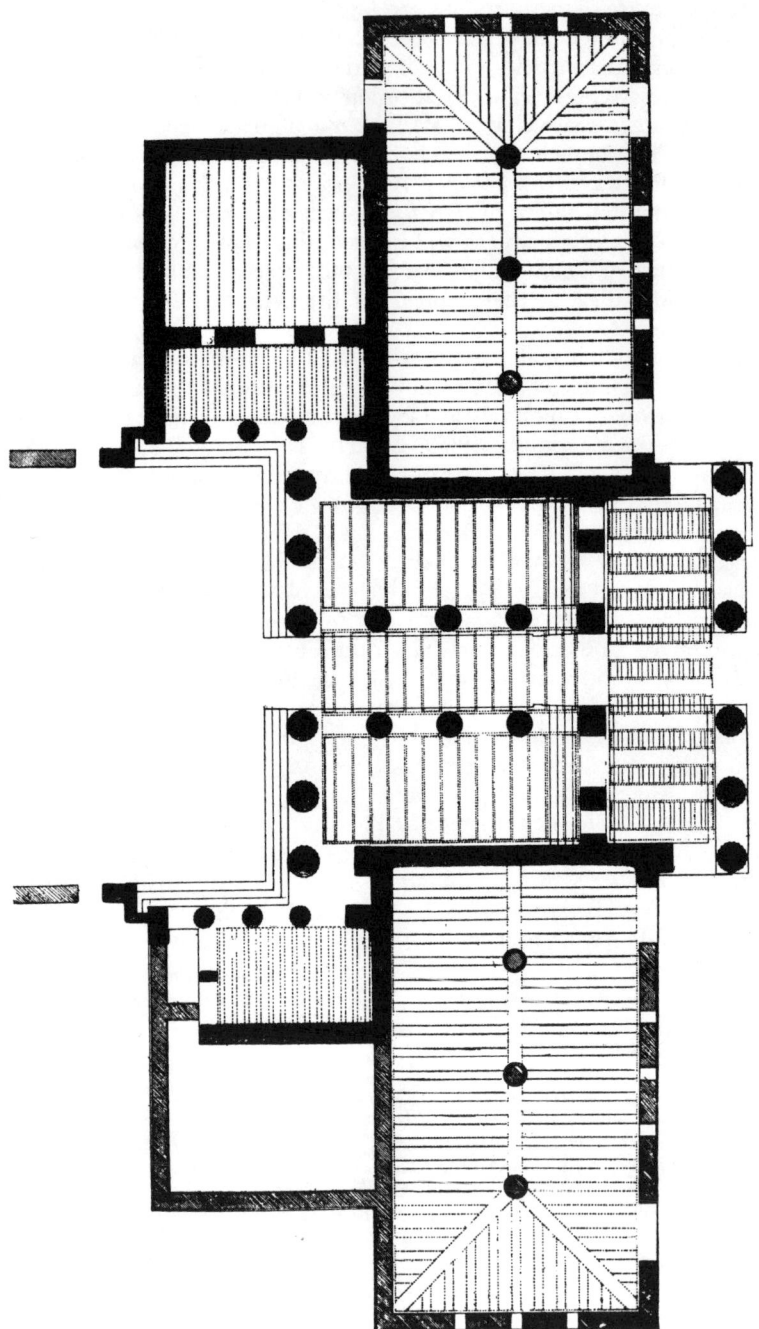

Fig. 75.—Preliminary and Final Plan of the Propylaea. (Restored by Dinsmoor.)

lose its validity; the same reason, however, did not prevail at the architrave level, where the upward curve was properly constructed.[1] The great central span on each façade gave the architect much concern, and the most interesting details of the construction are those by which he succeeded in reducing and distributing the weight of the superstructure. The entablatures were identical in both porticoes; the triglyphs and metopes have a crowning ovolo at the top of the fascia, imitating the Parthenon; and with the same desire for additional decoration, and also to obtain exceptional projection, the horizontal mutular cornice for the first time has a bed moulding, a cyma reversa. The crowning sima imitates the ovolo profile of the Parthenon, but instead of using a palmette or anthemion decoration the architect adhered too closely to the Ionic theory that an ovolo should be decorated with an egg-and-dart, which in this instance is so huge as to be out of scale. An interesting treatment on the flanks is the omission of lion-head spouts, the rain water escaping through triangular interstices between the eggs and the darts, somewhat as in temple 'C' at Selinus (and later imitated, as noted above, in the Caryatid porch of the Erechtheum). The metopes were never intended to contain sculpture; but the absence of pediment statues and of floral and griffin acroteria, for which preparations were made, seems to have been due to the outbreak of the war (Fig. 76).

Parallel to the two porticoes is the most essential part of the Propylaea, the cross-wall pierced with five doorways which correspond approximately in axes and in widths with the varying intercolumniations of the façades, and raised on a flight of five steps which form the transition between the levels of the two porticoes. The doorways themselves are of the simple Doric form, with sunken rebates for the marble revetment of the jambs; the original revetment has disappeared, but portions of that which replaced it in Roman times still remain.[2] The gate wall was placed nearer the inner or east façade, so that the inner vestibule, about a third of the total depth of the building, could be spanned by a marble ceiling without intermediate supports. Hence the depth of the outer vestibule behind the west façade was about two-thirds of the total depth of the building, which was advantageous in that it provided a larger waiting space for pilgrims (for whom benches were erected against the walls) before the gates were opened. For the deep outer vestibule, therefore, interior columns were required to support the marble ceiling; and since two storeys of small Doric columns, with an intervening architrave, could not have been properly terminated against the open west portico, the ceiling in this case was carried by a row of three Ionic columns (33 feet 9 inches or nearly 10 diameters in height) on each side of the central roadway. The slender character of the Ionic order enabled its height to exceed that of the Doric columns, whilst allowing of a far smaller diameter of the base (Plate L), considerations which prevailed, as we have seen, also in the Parthenon; the section through this

[1] This demonstrable variation in the column heights in the Propylaea, increasing towards the centre, constitutes one of the strongest arguments in favour of the intentional character of the curves, which some have argued were due merely to settlement of the foundations.

[2] This Roman revetment is reinforced at the back by horizontal ribs, for which grooves were cut across the reveals of the openings; and the mistaken theory that these grooves were of Greek workmanship gave rise to the current theory that they were intended to contain horizontal planks on which was nailed a wooden sheathing, a supposed survival of primitive architecture such as probably never occurred in the Athenian marble buildings.

vestibule affords a good example of the relation of Doric and Ionic architraves and ceiling, when employed in conjunction without an intervening wall. The

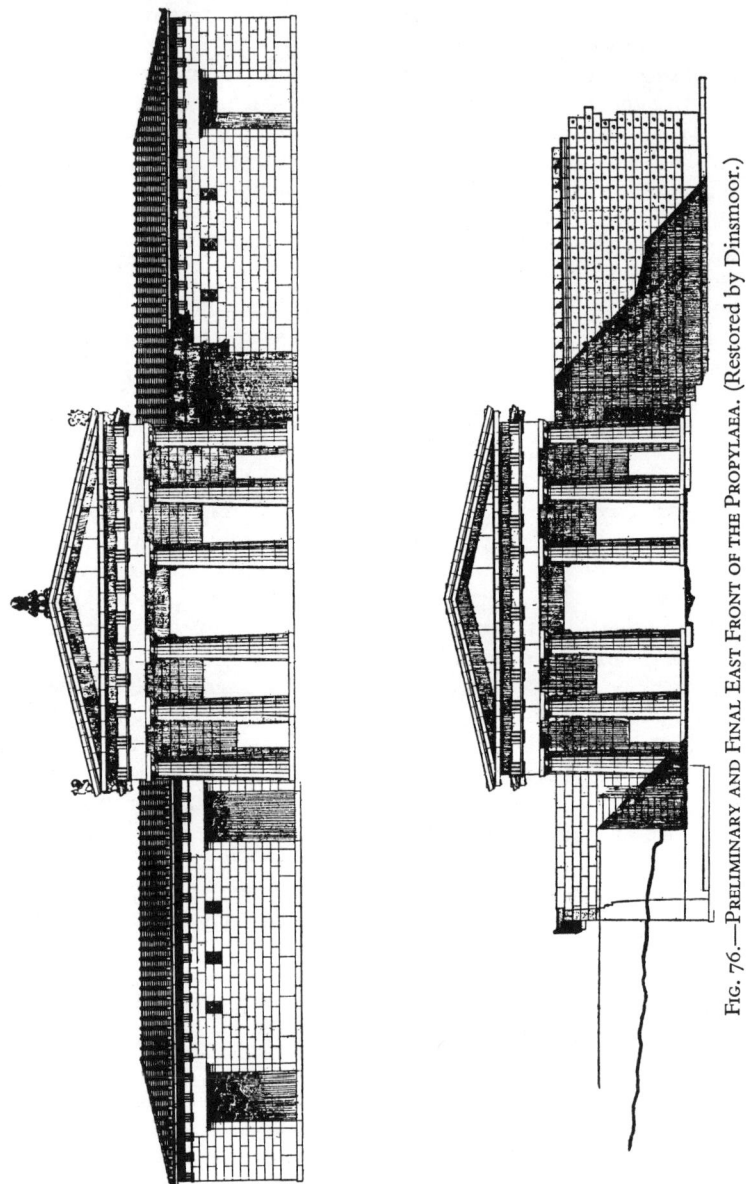

FIG. 76.—Preliminary and Final East Front of the Propylaea. (Restored by Dinsmoor.)

diameter of these Ionic columns, $3\frac{1}{6}$ Doric feet, is exactly two-thirds of the Doric diameter; the developed Attic bases are raised on circular plinths in the absence of a formal stylobate; and the capitals are the most beautiful of the

Periclean age, though they still show the unsupported abacus above the receding baluster side (Plate XLIX) as contrasted with the treatment in the Erechtheum. The three-fascia architrave, though here used internally, probably served as precedent for its appearance externally in the temple of Athena Nike and the Erechtheum. The great ceiling of this outer vestibule represents the supreme effort of the Periclean architects in this direction; even in the days of Antoninus Pius, Pausanias wrote that "the Propylaea has a ceiling of white marble, which in the size and beauty of the stones remains supreme even to my time."[1] The greater spans of the ceiling beams (those above the lateral aisles) were 18 feet in the clear, and each weighed more than 11 tons, thus delivering loads of $6\frac{3}{5}$ tons (including the ceiling coffers) on each face of the Ionic architrave at points midway as well as above the Ionic columns (Fig. 66); these intermediate loads so troubled Mnesicles that he took the perfectly unnecessary, though ingenious, precaution of hollowing the tops of the Ionic architraves and inserting concealed iron beams, undercutting them toward the centre sufficiently to allow for deflection.

The west wings, projecting at right angles, enframed the west or entrance façade of the central building (Fig. 75). That at the left-hand side, the northwest wing, is a small building called the Pinacotheca or picture gallery, from the fact that it was filled with paintings which were described by Pausanias and others. It is entered from the central building through a portico of three Doric columns in-antis, while the chamber behind is lighted by windows on either side of the doorway (Plate L), all unsymmetrically arranged for purely practical reasons of communication. The inner room is provided with a black belt course which suggests that the upper parts of the walls were to have received mural paintings, which, however, were never applied.[2] Above the entablature, instead of a pediment, was a hip roof.[3] On the south side the wing which should have corresponded to the Pinacotheca stops short at the old Mycenaean wall terracing the site which formed part of the sanctuary of Artemis Brauronia; apparently the construction was opposed by the priests of that goddess. For a similar reason the projection of this southern wing westward was curtailed owing to the site being pre-empted by the temple of Athena Nike, which had not yet, to be sure, been actually erected, though the project was under consideration. The peculiar recessed west front of the southwest wing is a most remarkable feature; the portico tristyle in-antis is partly a false front, projecting beyond the curtailed wing merely in order to balance the Pinacotheca, with a great double anta (from which was imitated that built under similar conditions in the north portico of the Erechtheum) standing alone at the northwest corner. With the west wall omitted, the west face of the wing was likewise open, presenting the appearance of a slender monolithic pier (imitated in the Nike temple opposite, and then at Delos) between two antae; the entabla-

[1] Immediately after the visit of Pausanias, however, an exact copy of the Propylaea was erected at Eleusis, with a ceiling of the same magnitude (see p. 285).

[2] This is shown by the fact that the marble wall surfaces were never finished, and by the absence of any stucco which might have concealed the irregularities and filled the open joints.

[3] Hip roofs were restored by Penrose, Dörpfeld, and members of the French Academy at Rome; but Bohn, whose restoration is so frequently reproduced, erroneously showed pediments facing inward towards the main axis of the Propylaea, and even in his revised restoration (Plate LI) compromised with a pediment on the south front of the Pinacotheca.

ture was carried across from the third column to the end of the south wall, supported at mid-span by the slender pier, the triglyphs being omitted from this extemporised frieze while the regulae of the architrave are united to form a continuous member with an uninterrupted row of guttae (Plate LI). The hip roof, following this curtailed plan, had an ell over the key-shaped projection formed by the northwest pier, and a half pediment on the south wall with a sima of cyma recta profile. Another remarkable feature is the bevelled southeast corner, where the southwest wing fitted against the Mycenaean wall; the bevel cuts off this corner from foundation to roof, and the prehistoric wall apparently rose still higher, to a level 44 feet above the Propylaea pavement, surviving in this form throughout antiquity.

It is obvious that this amputated plan is merely the relic of a much more grandiose project. Features now meaningless, such as the antae at the northeast and southeast corners of the central building, and also a stump of wall at the northeast corner of the Pinacotheca, prove that it was the intention of the architect to add further structures, which would have faced the whole west part of the Acropolis (Fig. 75).[1] Preparations for ceilings that were never constructed are sufficient, nevertheless, to reveal the proposed dispositions in exact detail. The main east-and-west axis, parallel to that of the Parthenon, was placed farther north so that the total length of the original design, 223 feet 8 inches, would exactly fit the width of the Acropolis at this point. The central building, apart from a few minor distortions, was erected as planned, with one important change: the distance between the faces of the east and west stylobates, planned as 79 feet 9½ inches, was actually constructed as 78 feet 2½ inches because the main west façade was thrust backward for 19 inches. In consequence, the transverse north-and-south axis, which should have been midway between the east and west stylobates, retained its planned relation to the former but was 19 inches closer to the west stylobate. On the north-and-south axis, and therefore originally but not finally symmetrical with reference to the east and west façades, were laid out two long halls, opening toward the east, the interior of the Acropolis; they are called, therefore, the east halls. These halls were never erected; that toward the south was opposed by the priesthood of Artemis Brauronia, on whose precinct it would have encroached (Fig. 74 at AB), and therefore it was abandoned at an early stage;[2] that toward the north was left until the last, and the work was interrupted by the Peloponnesian War before it could be taken in hand. Neither hall was to have had internal communication with the central building, so that the plan would have been cruciform only on the exterior. Each hall would have been entirely enclosed by walls, with doorways opening toward the east (besides one leading to a precinct at the northwest corner of the Acropolis); and within were to have been in each case a central row of three Ionic columns supporting the ridge beam, from which descended, on all sides except toward the central building, the sloping rafters

[1] Dörpfeld's restoration of these abandoned east halls and of the curtailed southwest wing, which has generally been adopted, has been considerably modified by recent American studies of the building, soon to be published, but here illustrated in Fig. 75.

[2] There is evidence that plans for the southeast hall were resumed later (during the erection of the Propylaea), but in a modified form with the understanding that floor level should be raised to that of the Brauronian precinct; this project in turn was abandoned at the outbreak of the Peloponnesian War.

forming a hip roof, exposed to view from within as in a stoa.[1] It is probable that the northeast hall would have contained the rainwater cistern, with a sunken floor, like the successive cisterns which occupied this low corner of the Acropolis from archaic to Byzantine times, while the southeast hall may have been intended to serve as the arsenal (Chalcotheca).[2] Thus both would have served primarily utilitarian purposes. The two west wings would likewise have been perfectly symmetrical if erected in accordance with the original scheme, both with solid walls toward the west and thus contrasting with the central west portico.[3] The terrace walls supporting the porticoes of the west wings were to have been prolonged much farther westward, enframing the ascent to the hill and pierced by decorative gateways leading to the precinct of Athena Nike at the south and to the corresponding terrace at the north. These, too, were barely begun when the work was stopped, doubtless again on account of the independent plans for the temple of Athena Nike, whose adherents refused to allow it to become a mere appanage of the Propylaea; only one jamb of each gateway was completed, and in the second century B.C. these were utilised as pedestals to support equestrian statues. And in addition to the omission of large sections of the plan, the incompleteness of the building is evidenced by the protective surfaces still covering the walls, pavements, and steps, and even, in the case of outer walls, by the lifting bosses.

Following the inspiration of the Propylaea of the Athenian Acropolis, structures for similar purposes were erected at the entrances to other precincts, as at Sunium, where the cross-wall has only a single doorway, and the façades are distyle in-antis. The influence of the Athenian prototype appears especially in the widened central intercolumniation.

The treasuries at Olympia had all been erected before the fifth century; and those now erected at Delos (a marble structure of the end of the century) and at Delphi (an anonymous Doric marble treasury in the precinct of Athena Pronaea, and those of the Sicyonians and Syracusans in the main precinct) are of limited architectural interest.[4]

The most famous circular building of the fifth century was the Tholos at Athens, erected at about 470 B.C. on the west side of the Agora. This structure, merely a walled circle 60 feet in external diameter, with no columns on the outside, served as the prytaneum or dining club of the presiding section of the Athenian senate, and its roof was sustained by six slender columns arranged in an elliptical plan within the circle; the roof itself was conical, with elaborate rhomboidal terracotta tiles.

[1] It is impossible to reconcile the colonnaded façade towards the east, such as is usually restored (for example, the nine small columns in each wing as proposed by Dörpfeld), with the actual remains. The so-called antae adjoining the east portico would come below metopes rather than below triglyphs, and so must be interpreted as door jambs. The interior, furthermore, requires three columns rather than four as restored by Dörpfeld.

[2] The Chalcotheca was subsequently built farther east, just southwest of the Parthenon (Fig. 74 at C).

[3] Dörpfeld's theory that the west face of the southwest wing was intended to be open from the very beginning, with four Doric columns between great double antae, cannot be reconciled with what was actually built.

[4] The Sicyonian treasury utilised second-hand material from the old tholos (p. 117) and the older Syracusan treasury (p. 116); the demolition of the latter in 413 B.C. to make place for the erection of the later Syracusan treasury, probably indicates the date of the Sicyonian.

Another curved structure—apparently secular though its exact use and even its plan remain unknown—is a wall at Gortyna in Crete, forming part of a circle with a radius of 55 feet, though only a portion of the circumference survives, rebuilt into the Roman odeum. The masonry is pseudo-isodomic, in courses alternately about $12\frac{1}{4}$ and $21\frac{1}{2}$ inches high; at one end of the existing portion is an anta (or door enframement?) with an egg-and-dart carved in the capital, of fifth-century form, more satisfactory evidence for the date than the provincial lettering of the famous law code inscribed on the wall, which gives an erroneous impression of extreme antiquity.[1]

The club-house or Lesche of the Cnidians at Delphi was a simple rectangular structure with eight wooden columns, resting on square limestone plinths, arranged in two rows of four; above the four central columns was probably a clerestorey or lantern by means of which the famous mural paintings of Polygnotus were lighted.

Splendid stoas were constructed during this period, decorated by famous painters, such as the "Painted Stoa" (Poecile, of which we have only a few fragments) and the "Royal Stoa" (Basileios, probably distinct from that of Zeus Eleutherius), erected at the north and northwest edges of the Athenian Agora, while, a little further south, the Stoa of Zeus Eleutherius faced the Agora from the west. The design of the last is known: a Doric portico in a single storey, with widely spaced columns (three metopes above each interval) and with hexastyle pavilions (with more closely spaced columns) projecting forward at either end. An inner row of more lofty Ionic columns, twice as far apart as the Doric, supported the ridge of the roof, the pattern normally followed in the later stoas. The date is toward the end of the fifth century; and already the Doric order begins to show variations, such as the little ovolo added to the top of the architrave taenia. It is possible that the Royal Stoa was a more pretentious structure with even more than two aisles, since it was the forerunner of the Roman basilica or court of justice. Behind the scene building of the theatre at Athens was a long stoa (Fig. 77) to which Vitruvius alludes as intended for sheltering the audience in case of rain; one end of this, being masked by the older temple of Dionysus, was walled up to form an enclosed room.

The old type of Bouleuterion, an elongated temple-like structure with a central line of columns, seems to have been retained in two examples of this period, at Orchomenus in Arcadia and at Delos. The former is a single long hall with a central row of twelve columns; but at Delos one end is cut off to form a square room, while the larger room has a row of seven columns or posts; in both buildings the entrances were in the long walls. The new type already evolved at Athens, with the seats arranged in ⊓-shape in a square building, was repeated also in the New Bouleuterion erected at Athens toward the end of the fifth century just behind its predecessor, which was sacrificed to give space for the Metroum. The original seats were probably of wood; and the columns, instead of following their ⊓-shape, were grouped in pairs toward front and back in order to cause a minimum of obstruction.[2]

The largest administrative structure of the period was the Pnyx at Athens,

[1] It has been variously dated, because of the provincial lettering, even as early as the seventh century B.C.

[2] For the later circular seating arrangement in stone, see p. 297.

SECULAR BUILDINGS

hardly more than a semicircular terrace for the assembly of citizens, as reconstructed in 404 B.C. The orientation of the original Pnyx of Cleisthenes was now reversed, as Plutarch reports, so that the bema faced inland (northeast) rather than toward the sea (southwest), with the result that the earth slope had to be

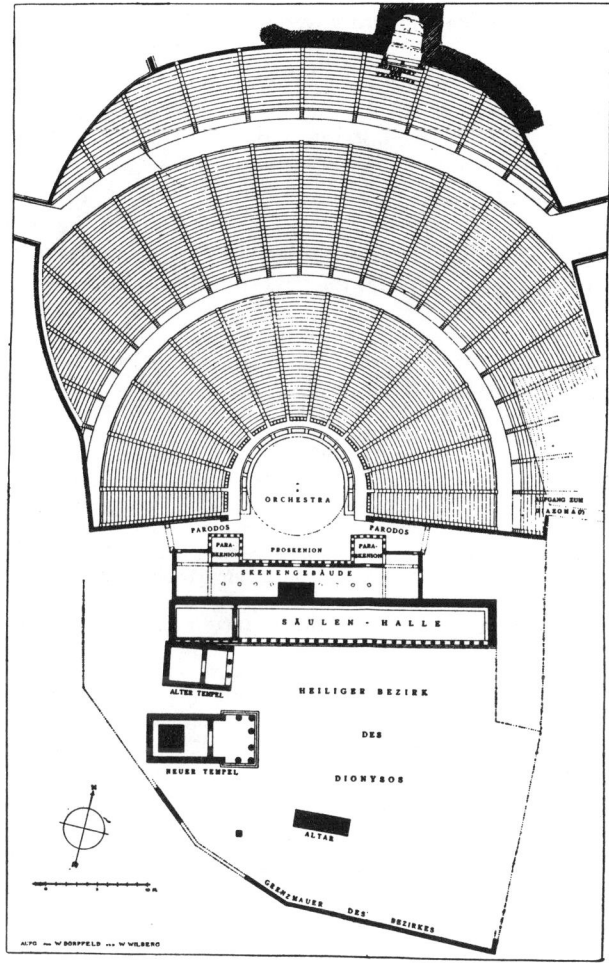

FIG. 77.—THE THEATRE AT ATHENS. (Dörpfeld.)

piled up contrary to the slope of the hill, supported by a semicircular retaining wall about 325 feet in diameter and enclosing an area of about 34,000 square feet. But the anarchical condition of Athens at this time is illustrated by the poor construction in courses only 10 or 12 inches high, each receding 7 inches from that below.

During the fifth century the requirements of the theatre at Athens (Fig. 77) gradually became more complicated. Aeschylus introduced a second actor in

472 B.C., Sophocles a third in 458 B.C. The archaic circular orchestra terrace continued to form the scene of action, the spectators being seated on the hillside or on more or less temporary seats, with scaffolding and bleachers at the sides;[1] but, while the beautiful prospect in itself at first served as the scenery, a special scene building of wood, probably a mere flat wall,[2] was soon introduced at the back of the orchestra. This scene building may first have been required for acoustic reasons, but it was soon employed also for displaying artificial scenery, painted on wood or canvas, which may have been invented by Phormis for use in the theatre at Syracuse, but was created in any case by Agatharchus for Aeschylus (or Sophocles) at Athens in 458 B.C. and served as the basis for early research on perspective by Democritus and Anaxagoras. The theatre was at this unpretentious stage of its development when the great plays were produced in it during the age of Pericles.[3]

Toward the end of the fifth century, apparently during the Peloponnesian War but within the period of renewed Athenian confidence between 425 and 413 B.C., a great change was made: the theatre was transformed from wood to

[1] It has sometimes been assumed (as by Bulle, Fiechter, and now Dörpfeld) that the auditorium was begun almost in its present form as early as 458 or even toward the beginning of the fifth century, the surviving relic of this work being the foundation of the older retaining wall in the west parodos. But the material is breccia, so that it must belong to the end rather than the beginning or middle of the century.

[2] The material and form of this early fifth-century scene building have been disputed, Bulle claiming that it was a stone structure of the parascenium type (with flanking pavilions) lying exactly beneath the existing walls (i.e. of the Lycurgan building), while Fiechter argues that it consisted of the stoa (*skenotheke*) of his preceding period with the addition of the movable wooden timbers (i.e. as in our late fifth-century period). As for those who admit that the early scene building was wholly of wood, there has been speculation as to whether it was a straight wall (as I suggest) or one with projections (parascenia) at either side (Dörpfeld, Noack), or even with a proscenium (Allen) or perhaps a high stage (Puchstein, Petersen) or a low stage (Bethe, Haigh, Bulle, Fensterbusch) between the parascenia. There is also the question of whether the scene building was inscribed within (thus cutting off a small segment) or circumscribed about or tangent to the old orchestra (raising the question of how it was supported). But since the first stone scene building (in the late fifth century) had a straight wall, as did that of the rural theatre at Thoricus, it seems probable that the prototype was a straight wooden wall supported on the orchestra terrace itself. The term "parascenium" is here used throughout in the conventional modern manner, regardless of the doubt as to the exact meaning in antiquity (i.e. at Delos, where the term was used in the third century despite the absence of lateral pavilions); it is first encountered in the oration of Demosthenes against Meidias (XXI, 17), written in 347 B.C.

[3] This absence of monumental construction in the Periclean theatre might seem almost incredible, and indeed has often been disputed. Apart from the erroneous theories previously cited with regard to a stone scene building or auditorium before the middle of the fifth century, the hypothesis of a stone theatre erected during the Periclean age itself (that is, during the third quarter of the century) was eventually supported by Dörpfeld, who after assigning to Pericles the older retaining wall in the west parodos, concluded by placing the lower part of the present auditorium and retaining wall with the present orchestra and gutter, and possibly even parts of the present scene building, within the lifetime of Pericles. So also Fiechter argues that the present scene building foundations were attached to the previously existing stoa (*skenotheke*) in the time of Pericles, and that the auditorium was then built in its present form except that the outermost sectors are assumed to have been prolongations of the circle rather than in U-shape, around a concentric orchestra and gutter. But the fact that the earliest actual remains of monumental building cannot be dated before the last quarter of the fifth century is adverse to all such dates and purely hypothetical restorations; see also p. 247, note 1.

stone.[1] For this purpose, in order to obtain more seating space (the odeum of 446 B.C. having meanwhile encroached upon the eastern part of the area), the axis was moved about 9½ feet toward the west, while at the same time the orchestra circle was moved about 20¼ feet closer to the Acropolis,[2] the earth thereby excavated from the lower part of the hillside being deposited on the upper slope to give the auditorium a steeper gradient. The ends of the auditorium were now supported on earth fill held in by stone retaining walls, those terminating the arc being laid out as radii of the orchestra and enclosing 199 degrees of a circle.[3] It is probable that the total width of the auditorium was then decided as 262 feet, and that it comprised only one storey; for, had more rows of seats been intended, the axis would undoubtedly have been moved sufficiently farther west to accommodate a larger semicircle without conflicting with the odeum. Many of the seats were still of wood,[4] and less important spectators sat on the bare hillside above the auditorium. Another innovation was the erection of a permanent scene wall, serving also as the rear wall of a stoa, to which Vitruvius refers, about 204 feet long and 26 feet deep, with low outer walls at the back and at the east end, where the ground rose to higher levels.[5] This portico faced south toward the precinct of Dionysus,

[1] The date of this transformation was disputable as long as it was regarded as the result of a single operation. For, on the one hand, there is the evidence of the materials and technique which originally induced Dörpfeld to assign it to the Lycurgan period (342–326 B.C.); and, on the contrary, Furtwängler and Bulle inferred that the scene building and the stoa on breccia foundations should be related to the later temple of Dionysus, which apparently belongs in the time of Nicias before 415 B.C. and at least within the lifetime of Alcamenes, whose last known work is dated 403 B.C. The problem was solved by recognition that there were two distinct periods. Dörpfeld had illustrated in 1896, but did not interpret until 1907, the remains of a pre-Lycurgan retaining wall in the west parodos. And only recently did Fiechter show that the scene building itself must be of two periods, and that, since the later portion (the scene building proper with the parascenia) can be no later than Lycurgus, the older portion (the stoa) must be pre-Lycurgan. The pre-Lycurgan period represented by the older retaining wall and the stoa can be no earlier than the last quarter of the fifth century, on account of the breccia material; it is to be regretted that Fiechter, after recognising the anterior construction of the stoa, confused the whole development by dating it more than a century too early (534 B.C.).

[2] The exact location of the centre of this second orchestra circle, while definitely coinciding with the present axis as we know from the position of a projecting platform behind the stoa and now within the scene building (an assumed discrepancy of 4 inches may be dismissed as meaningless and accidental), is not so well defined with respect to the distance from the scene building. Assuming, however, that the second orchestra centre was located at the point where the line of the older west retaining wall foundation of the auditorium intersects the axis, we find that it would have been 20¾ feet south of the third orchestra centre, and so 20¼ feet north of the first orchestra centre (see p. 120, note 3). The finished face of the projecting platform, which presumably would not have cut into the contemporary second orchestra circle, lay 10¾ feet north of the stoa wall, 62½ feet south of the present orchestra centre, and so 41¼ feet south of the second orchestra centre. The fact that the latter is identical with the radius of the first orchestra suggests that the second orchestra exactly reproduced the first but in a different position.

[3] This angle, and the total width of the auditorium, are derived from the breccia foundation of the earlier retaining wall in the west parodos, which some have dated in 458 B.C. or even toward the beginning of the century, as noted above.

[4] Wooden bleachers (*ikria*) were mentioned by Aristophanes as late as 411 B.C.

[5] This portico was formerly assumed to have been merely an appendage to the Lycurgan theatre of about 340 B.C.; but, after Fiechter's discovery that it was older, the date has been variously assigned to the early fifth or even the sixth century, and it has been erroneously

squeezed in so compactly that it impinged upon the steps of the old temple; and at the point where the temple would have masked it the colonnade was continued by a blank wall, with a closed room within separated by a partition from the rest of the portico. The steps and colonnade of the front, as well as the dado of the inner walls, were of marble. Being designed to face the precinct of Dionysus, the portico quite disregarded the axis of the new theatre, extending much farther toward the east than toward the west; but its rear wall formed a scene wall 204 feet in length, of which any desired amount could serve as a background for painted scenery. From its interior, moreover, steps ascended through a wide doorway in the rear wall to the orchestra level 7 feet higher; and outside was constructed a rectangular platform projecting $10\frac{3}{4}$ feet from the stoa wall, on which might be set up, if occasion demanded, a movable porch, temple façade, stairway or altar. To permit the erection of more complicated temporary structures five vertical slots on either side of the platform, in the masonry of the double wall, could be used for a skeleton of upright timbers; and two rows of corresponding sockets may have been set out in front (as was later done for a different reason at Pargamum) for the insertion of vertical posts adapted to various combinations, probably including lateral pavilions (parascenia), as shown on fourth-century South Italian vases.[1]

As for other theatres of the fifth century, it is possible that the rural structure at Thoricus in Attica is of this date, the orchestra being merely a rectangular space with rounded corners, limited at the back by a straight terrace wall on which a temporary wooden scene wall might have been erected as in Periclean Athens. The auditorium fits this rectangular plan, with parallel rows of seats with the ends curved to enclose the orchestra; an extension with additional rows of seats appears to have been built in the fourth century. At Syracuse in Sicily a theatre was erected by the architect Damocopus for Hieron I (478–467 B.C.), apparently with a trapezoidal orchestra,[2] and here Aeschylus produced a play in 476 B.C.; but the present theatre is Hellenistic. Only

interpreted as a *skenotheke* with the floor level, in its original form, as high as the orchestra. But these early dates are impossible for the breccia material employed; and there are no indications that the lower floor level and the colonnaded south front were the results of alteration in the Lycurgan period (as Fiechter suggests). In fact, one floor block built into the structure of the back wall shows that the low floor and colonnade existed from the very beginning; and the late fifth-century date suitable for the technique would agree with the potsherds found beneath the wall, with the mural paintings of the late fifth century described by Pausanias apparently in this very portico, and also with the relationship to the later temple of Dionysus (shortly before 415 B.C.).

[1] In other words, the theatre of about 420 B.C. may be restored in approximately the form assigned by Fiechter to the first half of the century. The number of extra sockets is quite uncertain, Fiechter proposing eighteen (in addition to ten in the back wall), Schleif thirty, while I prefer only sixteen. It will be noted that these earliest actual remains of a stone scene building are quite at variance with most of the restorations of the late fifth-century theatre, that is, with the action taking place on a hypothetical low stage (which did not appear at Athens until A.D. 61), or on or before an assumed high stage or proscenium (which did not appear, even in temporary form, before 315 B.C.), or on the ground between heavy flanking towers or parascenia (of which the foundations were not laid until about 340 B.C.). Furthermore, both Dörpfeld and Fiechter believe that the late fifth-century theatre had an upper storey (episcenium) with great *thyromata* openings (though perhaps only in wood), an anachronism before the Hellenistic theatre.

[2] Anti restores also projecting parascenia on dubious evidence.

at Athens, therefore, do we have remains of a typical theatre of the fifth century.[1]

Adjoining the theatre at Athens was constructed by Pericles a new form of building, the odeum or music hall. This was mentioned by Plutarch, who says that "the odeum, built under the supervision of Pericles, has many seats and pillars within; the roof was made slanting and converging to one point, and they say that it was after the model and as an imitation of the Persian king's tent." Vitruvius also mentions "the odeum as you go out at the left side of the theatre," and says that "it was set out with stone columns and roofed with the yards and masts of ships captured from the Persians." It was restored after the sack of Athens by Sulla, and (as stated by Pausanias) after the original design. Its position, near the theatre, suggests that it was used for rehearsals as well as for musical contests, the latter introduced by Pericles himself in 446 B.C. The building was a perfect square, with the roof supported by a forest of columns in the manner of the Hall of the Mysteries at Eleusis; there were nine rows each of nine columns, though some of the central columns must have been omitted under the presumable octagonal lantern which rose above the hip roof and lighted the interior. There were projecting porches at east and west, and perhaps also at the south; the north wall, as at Eleusis, was backed against the natural rock.[2]

As yet we are hardly in a position to discuss the private houses of this or the preceding periods. The dwellings of Aristeides, Miltiades, Callias, and Alcibiades at Athens were specially mentioned in ancient literature, and that of Alcibiades even had mural paintings. But these have not survived; and the known houses of the poorer quarters in the southwest quarter of Athens, or the rustic houses of Dystus in Euboea, are not sufficient to give us an adequate idea of fifth-century domestic architecture. The best evidence yet available comes from Olynthus in Macedonia, where the houses date from the late fifth century and the first half of the fourth; but in view of this overlapping it will be more convenient to treat of them in the following chapter.

Among votive monuments of this period should be mentioned the low stepped circular platform of black limestone at Delphi, supporting the huge tripod commemorating the victory at Plataea in 479 B.C. The pedestal of Athena Promachos at Athens likewise falls into this class, as it commemorated the battle of Marathon, though erected many years later in 463-454 B.C.; in spite of the colossal size of the bronze statue, the pedestal was probably only about 8 feet high, with a die of black limestone contrasting with the white marble of the base and cap, the latter carved with a huge egg-and-dart moulding, the eggs spaced $12\frac{1}{8}$ inches on centres. Taller pedestals were sometimes employed, the most interesting being the triangular shafts $30\frac{1}{2}$ feet high erected by the Messenians of Naupactus at about 424 B.C. both at Olympia and Delphi,

[1] Excessively early dates have sometimes been suggested, the sixth century for Thoricus, the fifth for the present stone theatre at Syracuse; and the earliest forms of the theatres at Eretria and Oeniadae have sometimes been assigned to the fifth century, but probably follow the fourth-century Lycurgan theatre at Athens.

[2] The odeum has been only partially excavated during intermittent campaigns by the Greek Archaeological Society since 1914. Previously it had been assumed, from the libellous comparison with the "onion-shaped" head of Pericles, that the plan when discovered would prove to be circular.

the former in white marble and the latter in black limestone, with interesting base and cap mouldings, supporting the statue of Victory by Paeonius, respectively in marble and bronze. The Argives set up a characteristic semicircular niche or exedra at Delphi after the battle of Oenoe in 456 B.C., nearly 42 feet in internal diameter and filled with statues. A rectangular niche was employed by the Spartans at Delphi after their victory over the Athenians at Aegospotami in 405 B.C.; it contained thirty-seven statues of Lysander and his captains banked on platforms in the two corners with a single file connecting them. In front was a screen of eight Doric columns arranged with a graded spacing with a maximum difference of 12 inches, diminishing from right to left apparently in order to enhance the effect of perspective by artificially diminishing the more distant intervals with reference to a visitor entering the sacred precinct.[1]

Among sepulchral monuments, the artificial mound or tumulus might persist in open areas, such as that about 160 feet in diameter and 40 feet high, crowned by an inscribed stele, erected over the bodies of the hundred and ninety-two Athenians on the battlefield of Marathon in 490 B.C. A sculptured lion formed the memorial of Leonidas after 479 B.C. on the natural mound at Thermopylae, and there was another lion monument at Thespiae, dating from 424 B.C. Most important, however, was the stele form, which seems to have been temporarily out of favour during the first half of the century but was soon restored to popularity. The Giustiniani stele from one of the Aegean islands, and another from Carystus in Euboea, are of special interest because of the acroteria, with early combinations of the acanthus with the palmette.[2] The Athenian series, in particular, includes the precursors of the typical forms of the fourth century, with a tendency to widen the slab to include more than a single figure. In such instances the widened crowning feature is often in the form of a temple pediment; but the lateral supports in the form of pilasters or even columns, as employed with such architectural features in the fourth century, do not seem to occur in the stelae earlier than the fall of Athens in 404 B.C.

As yet we have had no occasion to discuss the planning of cities as wholes, because Greek designers had not yet so conceived them until the fifth century. A common centre, forming the agora, had always been the natural situation for civic buildings, but these were irregularly placed irrespective of each other and the agora itself was of irregular form, while the streets leading out of it followed traditional routes, without any system, and were generally narrow, crooked, and unsanitary. Nevertheless in a few special instances, such as the wholesale rebuilding of Olbia in South Russia after a fire at the end of the sixth century, order was introduced; here the streets were laid out in chessboard fashion, crossing each other at right angles following the gridiron scheme of the cemeteries and pyramid cities of Egypt; at Olbia there was a main street 33 feet wide. A similar opportunity was afforded after the destruction of Miletus in 494 B.C., the city being rebuilt on a new site out on the peninsula after 479 or

[1] For a similar consideration affecting the design of the adjoining niche of the Argive kings, see p. 253.
[2] Both the Giustiniani stele and the Carystus stele are in the Berlin Museum; the origin of the former is unknown, except that it is of island marble and an island source would agree with Venetian ownership.

more probably after 466 B.C. Here the work was done in two sections. In the older part, at the north tip of the peninsula, the streets are spaced approximately 108 feet on the centres from east to west and, with less regularity, about 90 feet from north to south; the streets being about 12 feet wide, this yielded city

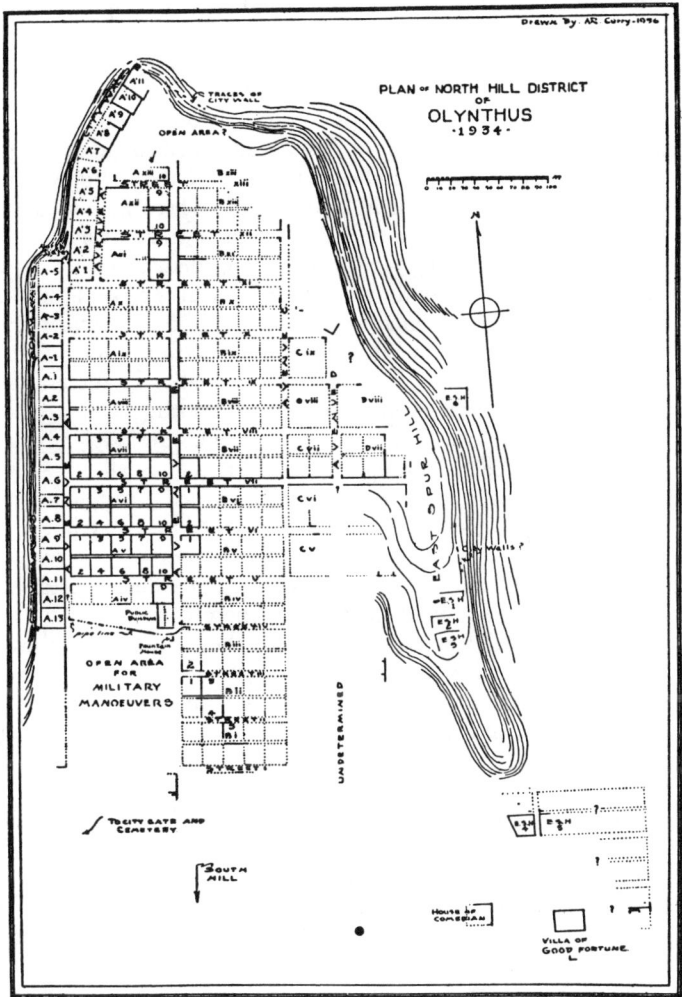

FIG. 78.—CITY PLAN OF OLYNTHUS. (Robinson.)

blocks of about 78 by 96 feet with their greater dimension from east to west. In the south extension of the city, which was more spacious, the orientation was slightly changed and the streets did not carry through, so that it was entirely distinct; there was a main street $25\frac{1}{4}$ feet wide running north and south with twenty-two parallel streets about 14 feet wide, crossed by another main street $24\frac{1}{2}$ feet wide with eleven parallel streets running east and west. The blocks

THE CULMINATION IN ATTICA AND THE PELOPONNESUS

enclosed by these streets measured about 117 feet from east to west and about 138 feet from north to south, their longer dimension being at right angles to the blocks in the older section. The city as a whole covered about four hundred city blocks.

With part of this work at Miletus must have been associated the physician Hippodamus, a native of that city, who gradually developed his studies of meteorology and city-planning into what was known as the Hippodamian system. Pericles called him to Athens and entrusted to him the laying out of the Piraeus. The result was certainly an application of the chessboard scheme, with the agora adjoining the intersection of the two main streets at right angles, though carefully located just off axis so that traffic passed round the edges of the agora rather than through the middle. Later, in 443 B.C., Hippodamus went with Athenian colonists to Thurii in South Italy, where he laid out another chessboard plan, divided into twenty wards by three main avenues crossed by four at right angles; presumably there were intermediate minor streets.[1] At Olynthus in Macedonia, apparently after the Athenian reverses of 429 B.C., the older city on the south hill was enlarged by laying out a new residential suburb on the north hill, with three main avenues (and a fourth subordinate one) running north and south, crossed by thirteen streets at right angles. The cross-streets and the western avenue average $16\frac{1}{4}$ feet in width; the central avenue is $22\frac{3}{4}$ feet wide, the eastern $19\frac{1}{2}$ feet. The main avenues are $283\frac{1}{4}$ feet apart, the cross-streets $116\frac{1}{2}$ feet apart. Through each block ran an alley $4\frac{1}{2}$ feet wide, reducing the blocks to $283\frac{1}{4}$ by 56 feet, each subdivided into five house-lots of about $56\frac{2}{3}$ by 56 feet, or 3,173 square feet. This system of five house-fronts in a row explains why the longer dimension of the blocks did not run, as in the later portion of Miletus, north and south; for the individual houses, as will be noted later, were oriented toward the south.[2] There is no reason for assuming that Hippodamus himself was concerned with the plan at Olynthus. As for another scheme, the radial plan with the harbour as a focus, improvised for Rhodes in 408 B.C., this was attributed to Hippodamus in antiquity, but the date would seem to make it impossible.[3]

* * * * *

In this chapter we have considered together the buildings of the two distinct orders, the Doric temples at Olympia and Bassae, at Rhamnus and Sunium, the Argive Heraeum, and the Parthenon, Propylaea, and Hephaesteum at Athens, as well as the Ionic Erechtheum and temple of Athena Nike and that on the Ilissus. For these two distinct types of Greek work found their culmination and coalesced in the age of Pericles. All of those in Athens, at least, could not by any possibility have been designed elsewhere; for in each of them there are marks of a distinctive Attic style. Familiarity with the Ionic proportions led the Attic artists to refine the ponderous proportions of Doric columns, and to adopt a mean which inclines more closely to the Ionic than any pre-existing examples. Yet the Parthenon and the Hephaesteum, in spite of this and other

---

[1] The plan of Thurii is known to us only from a description by Diodorus; search for the site has been as yet unsuccessful.
[2] For the houses of Olynthus, see p. 252.
[3] For the further development of city-planning, see p. 262.

details which have been noticed, such as their continuous sculptured friezes and many of their ornaments, are substantially Doric. Of the buildings we have examined, the Propylaea and the temple at Bassae combine most freely the Ionic-Doric principles, and most appropriately, each finding its true place. But even in the purely Ionic buildings, such as the Erechtheum, the Doric influence appears in a few details, such as the insertion of a frieze in the entablature, and the projecting antae at the ends of the walls. All of them thus in a measure illustrate the coalescence of types which is characteristic of Athenian work, as it was to some extent typical of the people themselves.

CHAPTER SIX

THE BEGINNING OF THE DECADENCE

THE supremacy of Athens in the Aegean portion of the Greek world was but short lived; for a succession of long wars, the Peloponnesian (431–404 B.C.) and the Corinthian (395–387 B.C.), drained all her energies and deprived her of political leadership. Thus the fall of Athens in 404 B.C. may justly be taken as the beginning of a new epoch; humiliated and impoverished, she was in no condition to maintain the high artistic excellence which she had reached under Pericles. Less cultivated states became dominant powers, such as Sparta (404–371 B.C.) and Thebes (371–362 B.C.); then followed a period of vain struggles against the gradual encroachments by a people hitherto considered foreign, the Macedonians, whose recognised ascendancy in Greek affairs may be dated from the battle of Chaeronea in 338 B.C. It is but natural that these rapid changes of political fortune should have found their echo in the absence of great architectural undertakings. During this century the architecture of the mainland is to be traced only in comparatively minor structures.

In the colonies of the west, conditions were even worse; we find practically no work which can be attributed to the fourth century. The catastrophe of the Carthaginian invasion, the destruction of Selinus and Himera in 409 B.C., of Acragas in 406, and of Gela and Camarina in 405 B.C., seem to have been followed by a period of utter stagnation. In 405 B.C. was drawn up a treaty between Carthage and the new tyrant of Syracuse, Dionysius, according to which Carthage was recognised as dominant in the western part of Sicily, and Syracuse remained the only important Greek state on the island.

Far otherwise was it in Asia Minor, where the Ionic cities had played, as we observed, very little part in the artistic development of the fifth century. They had fallen a prey to the Persians in 494 B.C., and were kept in subjection until the formation of the Delian Confederacy in 477 B.C. Thenceforward until 404 B.C. they were overshadowed by Athens, to whom they were contributory; and the downfall of Athens merely gave them a new master, Sparta. It was not until the Peace of Antalcidas in 387 B.C. that the mainland powers withdrew from Asia Minor, leaving the Ionic cities in a state of comparative quiet under Persian sovereignty. The second naval confederacy founded by Athens in 377 B.C. was less extensive and less oppressive than the first. The luxurious conditions that developed under the Persian satraps find their analogy only in the reigns of the Lydian kings and local tyrants of the archaic period, and they brought about in Asia Minor a revival of architectural grandeur, in which the qualities of the magnificent and ornate are conspicuous; in fact, the outstanding feature of this fourth century is the so-called Ionic Renaissance. The arrival of Alexander the Great in 334 B.C. found many great projects under way; and the new conqueror was quick to seize the opportunity and to make the completion of the great Ionic temples a personal issue. There was no marked break in the

FOURTH-CENTURY POLITICAL CONDITIONS

development until after the partition of Alexander's empire by his generals. For, though it has been customary to adopt, as the terminal event of the political history of this time, the death of Alexander in 323 B.C., yet the employment of this date as a line of demarcation between the periods of artistic evolution is less satisfactory. It would be preferable to select 306 B.C., a moment when the new Hellenistic kingdoms were beginning to take shape, when Demetrius Poliorcetes had seized Athens and been acclaimed as "king," together with his father Antigonus, and when Ptolemy Soter in opposition likewise adopted the regal title in Egypt. Thus the period now to be considered, 404–306 B.C., practically coincides with the fourth century.

Throughout the Greek world the fourth century is characterised by certain general tendencies. In the first place, it marked the beginning of a decline from aesthetic perfection. The religious aspect, the chief inspiration of most styles of art, had reached its culmination in the Periclean temples, and now began to be outweighed by secular elements, a stage of development which indicates that we have passed the crest of the wave of evolution. From the temple, which had previously represented almost the sole aim of architecture, attention was diverted to a great variety of structures, almost as many types of buildings as we erect at the present day, corresponding to the varied activities of a more complex civilisation. And even in religious architecture the same striving for diversity and innovation is manifest in the increase of ornament, at the expense of strength and dignity.

* * * * *

The great temple-building epoch on the Greek mainland had passed with the end of the fifth century; but the recurrence of unforeseen catastrophes, fires, earthquakes, or landslides, demanded unremitting architectural activity. The rebuilding of the temples of Apollo and Athena at Delphi, and of Athena Alea at Tegea, are examples of this process. The Alcmaeonid temple of Apollo at Delphi, for instance, was destroyed by a landslide in 373 B.C., and the expense accounts show that the reconstruction dragged on for more than forty years; the architect is reported to have been a Corinthian, Spintharus, but various others succeeded him such as Xenodorus and Agathon. It was rebuilt almost on the old plan, with very slight readjustment of the dimensions to accord with the contemporary system of proportions. For this reason the plan retains the unusual length of fifteen columns (Plate XXVIII), necessitated by the presence of the adytum. The platform was built òf new material, the hard grey limestone of St. Elias; but for the columns the old fallen drums were employed as far as possible, the injured portions of the fluting being repaired in stucco; and, the old entablature having been utilised for buttressing the foundations, the new entablature was built entirely with fresh material, poros brought from Corinth. The sima is of marble, that on the flanks being of the new form characteristic of the fourth century, a simple vertical fascia carved with *rinceaux* in relief and with antefixes (hitherto used only in the absence of the sima) surmounting the sima in alternation with the lion heads. The pediments were filled with sculpture by Praxias and Androsthenes; and these must have remained intact at least until 175 A.D. when they were described by Pausanias, the absence of any remains suggesting that they were afterwards carried off to Rome or Constantinople.

One of the few Doric temples erected in accordance with the normal fifth-century plan, hexastyle and with thirteen columns on the flanks, and with pronaos and opisthodomus both distyle in-antis, was the later temple of Artemis Laphria at Calydon, erected at about 360 B.C. It was built over the foundations of the earlier temple, the rear portion supported by a high terrace wall of pseudo-isodomic masonry; and it followed the old orientation, facing more nearly south than east. The material was poros limestone up to the roof level; the marble sima had spouts in the form of hunting-dog heads. Since the mutules of the outer cornice were blue, as usual, some triglyphs painted red may have belonged to the inner porches, which had sculptured metopes as at Olympia and Bassae. The cella apparently contained Ionic columns with twenty flutes.

Among the planning innovations appearing in the new temples of the fourth century was the gradual atrophy of the opisthodomus, accompanied by a shortening of the whole peristyle. The first stage appears in the unfinished temple of Apollo Ismenius at Thebes, hexastyle and with twelve columns on the flanks, once decorated with sculpture by Scopas; here the opisthodomus still appears, but in very shallow form with the columns in-antis practically touching the rear wall of the cella. The next step was to terminate the inner building with a simple wall at the back, reducing the width of the pteroma at the rear until it was uniform with that on the flanks. An early and characteristic example was the temple of Asclepius at Epidaurus, hexastyle but with only eleven columns on the flanks because of the fewer elements within. The architect in charge was Theodotus, and the work was begun at about 380 B.C.; an interesting feature is the survival of its expense accounts, containing much information concerning its erection. The pediments contained superb sculpture by Timotheus, who afterwards collaborated with Scopas on the Mausoleum; a battle of the Greeks and Amazons appeared on the east front, and the capture of Troy on the west, while the cella contained a gold-and-ivory statue of the god by Thrasymedes. Likewise in this group belongs the later temple of Apollo at Mt. Ptous, in Boeotia, probably erected at about 316 B.C., hexastyle and with thirteen columns on the flanks on account of the very long cella. In several details this temple reveals the growing tendency to depart from strict Doric details: the abacus of the capital now receives a crowning moulding, the taenia of the architrave is replaced by a cavetto and ovolo, the triglyphs and metopes have a crowning ovolo, and the cornice has complicated bed and crowning mouldings, with a cavetto above the hawksbeak.

As the Doric order in itself was now incapable of being further perfected, architects began to seek variety by introducing additional ornament or combining it with other orders. Typical of the period was the temple of Athena Alea at Tegea (Fig. 79), built from the designs of the sculptor Scopas, and described by Pausanias in the following terms: "The first row of columns is Doric, and the next Corinthian; without the temple,[1] too, stand columns of the Ionic order." This is, incidentally, Pausanias's only reference to the Corinthian order. He regarded the temple as the most beautiful and largest of all those in the Peloponnesus, though two exceeded it, at Corinth and Olympia. The

---

[1] The Greek text says "within the temple," probably by error.

THE TEMPLE AT TEGEA

peristyle was Doric, hexastyle but with the unusual number of fourteen columns on the flanks; the reason for the great length is to be found in the retention of the opisthodomus and in the influence of the neighbouring temple at Bassae, which Scopas appears to have consciously imitated. For the same reason a lateral doorway was opened in the north flank wall. Many of the dimensions of the plan, moreover, were imitated from the Propylaea at Athens; thus the column spacing was exactly reproduced, the axes being set out at intervals of $2\frac{1}{3}$ diameters of $4\frac{3}{4}$ Doric feet. But in elevation the more slender proportions of the fourth century prevailed, the Doric columns being $6\frac{1}{8}$ diameters high, and the entablature only a quarter of the height of the columns. The marble simas are of the new fourth-century type, moulded on the pediments but of the vertical parapet type carved with *rinceaux* on the flanks, surmounted by rampant antefixes; curiously the joints of the raking sima are perfectly vertical rather than normal to the slopes. The pronaos and opisthodomus likewise were Doric; but the cella was lined with semi-detached columns imitating the arrangement at Bassae, though the capitals were Corinthian instead of Ionic. It is possible that the Ionic columns were votive monuments on separate foundations flanking the approach to the temple. The Corinthian capitals (Plate LVIII) have unusually low proportions; Scopas did not, like Theodorus in the Tholos at Delphi, imitate the details at Bassae, but struck out in a new direction, the most important changes being the omission of the central spirals (here replaced by large

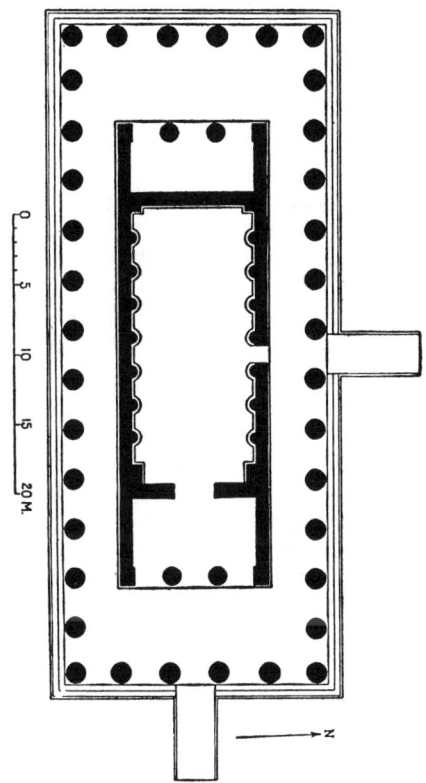

Fig. 79.—The Temple of Athena Alea at Tegea.

acanthus leaves) and the use of the cauliculus or fluted sheath for the corner volutes, appearing here for the first time. The necking joint, as at Bassae, is located slightly below the bottom of the capital; and here again the shafts, if they had been complete, would have had twenty flutes like the Doric. Other indications of the rivalry with Bassae are the stone pteroma ceilings, usually wooden in Peloponnesian temples, and the roof tiles pierced for lighting the attic space and provided with marble lids. The temple was elaborately decorated with sculpture designed by Scopas. The Doric metopes over the inner porches were sculptured like those at Olympia and Bassae, following the Peloponnesian tradition; this sculpture is now lost, though some of the titles are inscribed on

219

the architrave below. But the pediment sculptures were described by Pausanias, representing the Calydonian boar hunt on the east, the battle of Telephus and Achilles on the west; and many of the fragments, particularly heads, have survived to give an idea of the style of Scopas. The present temple replaced an earlier structure destroyed by fire in 394 B.C.; but it does not seem to have been erected until nearly fifty years later, in part by artisans who had worked with Scopas on the Mausoleum at Halicarnassus (355–350 B.C.) and had subsequently followed him to Tegea.[1]

This combination of the orders was characteristic also of other mainland temples of the fourth century, such as those of Zeus at Nemea, of Zeus at Stratos, and of the Mother of the Gods (Metroum) at Olympia (Fig. 44 at M). All three, moreover, follow the fourth-century tendency to omit the opisthodomus and to shorten the peristyle to twelve columns (Nemea) or to eleven (Stratos, Olympia). At Nemea, however, space was left behind the cross colonnade of the cella for a sunken adytum (with a descending stairway) corresponding to the inner room at Bassae. In only one of these examples, at Nemea, do columns exist to their full height; and here the proportions are even more slender than at Tegea, $6\frac{3}{8}$ lower diameters (Plate LIII). Thus, while the height of the columns, 34 feet $\frac{1}{4}$ inch, seems to have been a conscious repetition of the dimension in the Parthenon and the temple of Zeus at Olympia, the diameter is about a foot less than in the Parthenon, about 2 feet less than at Olympia. The temple at Nemea is entirely constructed of poros limestone with the exception of the marble sima, which presents the identical peculiarities and details found at Tegea and suggests that the same artisans were employed on both. The Corinthian colonnade of the interior, however, is free-standing rather than engaged, supporting an upper storey of slender piers, and returns across the rear to enframe the cult statue and segregate the adytum as at Bassae. The temple at Stratos and the Metroum at Olympia had their interior columns, apparently Corinthian in both cases, backed closely against the cella walls; and at Stratos the internal entablature had a denticulated cornice, the top of which is rough, showing as at Bassae that it was never crowned by a sima and suggesting that the cella had a wooden ceiling rather than a hypaethral opening. But the temple at Stratos was never finished, the steps retaining their protective surfaces and the columns remaining unfluted. A similarly unfinished temple in this neighbourhood is that of Poseidon at Molycrion. And a temple similar to the Metroum at Olympia was erected near by at Lepreum.

Among peripteral Doric temples of unusual nature should be mentioned that of Apollo at Cyrene, now rebuilt in more monumental form. The old cella was retained, but the outer orthostates were replaced by others of greater thickness so that the walls could be carried up in masonry. A new peristyle larger than the old was erected at the new and higher ground level outside, leaving the old cella sunk within it; eight steps forming a flight about 17 feet wide descended from the main façade to the cella doorway. This structure was

[1] This relationship to the Mausoleum, and consequently the dating in a later decade than has usually been assumed, is indicated by a votive tablet (now in the British Museum) found near the temple, dedicated by one of the artisans who had worked at Halicarnassus and commemorating the names of Idrieus and Ada, who began to reign in 350 B.C., after the deaths of Mausolus and Artemisia.

destroyed by fire in A.D. 117 and was then rebuilt with unfluted Doric columns and with Roman details. And at Delos, after it became independent of Athens in 314 B.C., work was resumed on the abandoned peripteral temple of Apollo. The stylobate was added, and the design of the peristyle was changed from Ionic to Doric, with a very strange consequence at the corners. For, with the stylobate joints and the columns necessarily spaced in accordance with the existing regular joints of the lower steps, the uniform column spacing of 7 feet $6\frac{1}{4}$ inches was maintained throughout, without the normal angle contraction. The columns were never fluted; but the entablature, imitated from that of the adjacent Athenian temple, was completely finished. This work was continued slowly through a considerable part of the third century.

Of less importance are a few smaller prostyle Doric temples, such as, at Epidaurus again, the hexastyle temple of Artemis (again with the heads of hunting-dogs serving as water-spouts) and two smaller temples which may have been dedicated to Aphrodite and Themis; these had interior Ionic columns lining the cella on three sides. The most interesting, however, is the third temple of Athena Pronaea at Delphi, erected a short distance to the west of the older temple in order to escape the path of landslides; it was beautifully worked in hard grey limestone, and behind the Doric façade were Ionic semi-columns, the two orders appearing in conjunction as in the Athenian Propylaea, with no separating walls.

As for temples of the Ionic order, it is evident that some were erected on the Greek mainland during the fourth century, but their surviving fragments are so few that we lack information on a most vital detail, whether their entablatures included both the mainland frieze and the Asiatic dentils.[1] On the island of Samothrace, to be sure, a marble Ionic temple of the Cabiri was built shortly before the middle of the fourth century, apparently with both members and perhaps the earliest example of this combination, which in such case might have resulted from its intermediate position between the Greek mainland and Asia Minor. The unusual combination of the sima of cyma recta profile, decorated with *rinceaux* in relief, with the rampant antefixes may have been inherited from the Erechtheum.[2]

Turning now to the area across the Aegean Sea, we examine the Ionic temples of this period in Asia Minor. One of the most typical, though not the most imposing, of these is the temple of Athena at Priene, near Miletus, a small but beautiful example begun at about 340 B.C. from the designs of Pythius, who wrote a book about it. It was dedicated by Alexander the Great

[1] A temple of Apollo Patrous, on the west edge of the Athenian Agora, dating from the third quarter of the fourth century, seems to have had Ionic columns on the façade spaced 6 feet $3\frac{3}{8}$ inches on centres, but no fragments have been identified. On a hill just outside Pagasae in Thessaly (included within the city of Demetrias in 293 B.C.) there seems to have been an Ionic temple with elaborately carved mouldings recalling the richness of the Erechtheum (their attribution by Stählin to a precinct wall of the third century seems quite impossible).

[2] The attribution of the sculptured frieze to this temple is not absolutely certain; for the sima and antefixes of the Erechtheum, see p. 194. The discovery of two fragments of a Doric cornice at Samothrace, with the guttae separately inserted in the mutules, has given rise to the suggestion that there was an earlier Doric temple; if this should prove to be the case, it must have been a Doric intrusion in the normally Ionic culture of the islands (that is, if it dates from before the Athenian supremacy), just as Assos was in Asia Minor.

in 334 B.C., and his inscription appeared on one of the pronaos antae. The completion of the west end, and the installation of the cult statue, a copy of the Athena Parthenos in wood and gilded bronze, were delayed until the time of Orophernes (Holofernes) of Cappadocia, 158–156 B.C., probably under the supervision of Hermogenes. The temple is hexastyle, with eleven columns on the flanks, and is of the ordinary plan, with pronaos, cella, and opisthodomus (Fig. 80).[1] As in the temples of Zeus at Olympia and of Hera near Argos, the architect seems in this case to have regarded his design as the embodiment of a canon of proportions. Thus the rectangle formed by the axes of the colonnades is exactly 60 by 120 Ionic feet, the length being twice the width; and the axial spacing is 12 Ionic feet.[2] The column diameter was proportioned to the axial spacing as closely as possible to $1 : 2\frac{3}{4}$, being rounded off to $4\frac{3}{8}$ Ionic feet (actual ratio $1 : 2 \cdot 743$); and the width of each column plinth is exactly half of the axial spacing (like the abaci in the temple of Zeus at Olympia). Since the width of the plinths is 6 Ionic feet, the rectangle enclosing the plinths measures 66 by 126 Ionic feet, with the ratio 11 : 21. The cella building is three by eight axial spacings and so 36 by 96 Ionic feet to the centres of the antae; but, the latter being 4 Ionic feet in width, the enclosing rectangle is exactly 40 by 100 Ionic feet, in the ratio 2 : 5, and the interior length of the cella is 50 Ionic feet or half of the external length. The interpretation of these and other proportions running through the design must have formed the substance of the lost book by Pythius, from which Vitruvius preserved a few paraphrased sentences.

The bases of the columns of the peristyle rested on square plinths, features never found in the earlier Greek temples (except at Ephesus), possibly because they would have interfered with the free passage round. The torus of the base is horizontally fluted only in its lower portion; the upper part retains its smooth parabolic surface, not as a means of shedding rain, but merely as a sign of incompletion or of oversight on the part of the builders.[3] In the capitals the volute cushion still retains the sagging line between the volutes, characteristic of the best periods; the angle capitals have a palmette carved as a decorative motive beneath the canted volute, while at the inner corners the whole plan is

[1] The site was excavated by the first expedition of the Dilettanti Society in 1764, and by the third in 1869, when a capital of the peristyle and one of the anta capitals, as well as numerous other details, were brought to the British Museum. The final excavations were undertaken by a German expedition in 1895–1898, and much of the material was transported to the Berlin Museum, where one complete column is restored with its entablature. Little of the temple remains in place except the stylobate.

[2] Because of the accuracy of these calculations and the careful measurements taken from this temple, it becomes, as checked with the evidence from Didyma (p. 229, note 2), our most trustworthy source of information for the length of the Ionic foot. The stylobate measurements are 19·53 by 37·17 m. or 64·075 by 131·949 feet, from which we subtract 1·89 m. or 6·201 feet for twice the distance to the column centres, obtaining an axial rectangle of 17·64 by 35·28 m. or 57·874 by 125·748 feet, an axial spacing of 3·528 m. or 11·575 feet, and a foot unit of 294 mm. or 11·575 inches. It is to be noted that this is somewhat less than the unit of 295·7 mm. falsely deduced from the Parthenon and usually accepted for Asia Minor.

[3] This peculiar half-fluted torus is generally published as a special treatment, but should not be so considered. The lower part was fluted before setting because it would have been difficult to carve afterwards; and the workmen never happened to give the final touches to the upper part.

slightly distorted in order to give whole volutes (though somewhat contracted) instead of the intersecting volutes usually employed. The anta capitals, as in so many Asiatic examples, differ on front and sides, the front having superposed carved mouldings (a cyma reversa below two ovolos), while the sides are decorated with *rinceaux* and foliage in relief. The walls are curiously constructed with a variety of pseudo-isodomic masonry in which a pair of high courses alternates with one low course, a more complicated form than that in the Cnidian treasury at Delphi. The height of the columns was apparently designed as $8\frac{3}{4}$ lower diameters, this being rounded off to $38\frac{1}{2}$ Ionic feet ($8\frac{4}{5}$ diameters). The entablature at Priene still adheres to the traditional Asiatic type, omitting the frieze, but with very heavy dentils in the cornice (Plate LV).[1] The omission of the frieze yields proportions which seem to our eyes abnormally thin; thus its total height is exactly 7 Ionic feet, or two elevenths of the height of the columns.

A smaller temple at Priene, that of Asclepius, consisting merely of a cella with a prostyle tetrastyle portico, is probably of the period of the temple of Athena or a little later. The entablature undoubtedly lacked a frieze; and the raking sima has the axes of the anthemion set vertically.

At Halicarnassus was a temple of Ares with an acrolithic statue by Leochares (or Timotheus), and so probably of the time of the Mausoleum. Its great Ionic columns, 3 feet 10 inches in diameter, were imitated from those of the Erechtheum, having neckings decorated with a double border of anthemion above and a lyre pattern below, thus constituting a valuable piece of evidence for Athenian influence in Asia Minor at this time. But whether this influence extended to the inclusion of a sculptured frieze is unknown.

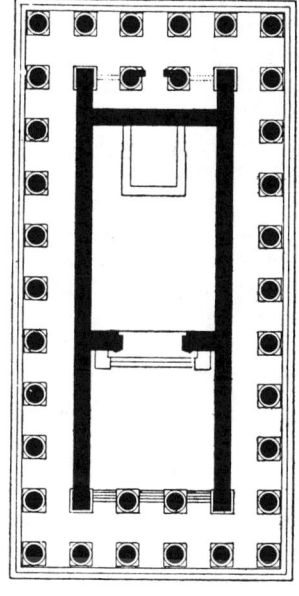

FIG. 80.—THE TEMPLE OF ATHENA POLIAS AT PRIENE.

Though not the largest, the most important temple in Asia Minor was the great temple ('E') of Artemis (Diana) at Ephesus. The archaic temple of the sixth century, known as the Croesus ('D') temple, is stated to have been burnt in 356 B.C., on the night of the birth of Alexander the Great, and was rebuilt immediately afterwards on a platform 8 feet $9\frac{1}{2}$ inches higher, in still greater splendour, though with a plan identical with that of its predecessor, and borrowing from the earlier temple the idea of the sculptured columns, which

---

[1] The two Dilettanti expeditions restored an imaginary frieze, which still appears in many publications of the order at Priene. The evidence that it was omitted, and consequently the entire problem of the native friezeless entablature of Asia Minor, resulted from the investigations of the German expedition: the bed-moulding under the dentils fits directly on the upper fascia of the architrave.

were used only here and in the old temple at Didyma. It was the beauty of these sculptures which caused this temple to be classed among the seven wonders of the ancient world;[1] and Scopas is reputed to have been one of the sculptors of the *columnae caelatae*. The architects of the new temple were Paeonius of Ephesus and Demetrius the slave of Artemis; with this temple is sometimes associated a third name, that of Alexander's architect Deinocrates. The work is reported to have consumed one hundred and twenty years, so that it would not have been completed until 236 B.C.[2]

The plan of the new temple being absolutely identical with that of the archaic temple, column rising above column base and wall above wall, we repeat the same octastyle dipteral plan (tripteral on the west front) that has been previously described, with twenty-one columns on the flanks and nine across the rear, one hundred and seventeen external columns in all. The same plan (apart from the arrangement of the steps) applying to both structures (Fig. 81), the same is true of the statements of Pliny, who obviously did not distinguish between the Croesus and Alexander temples but borrowed his statements indiscriminately from the book of Chersiphron and Metagenes about the old temple and from descriptions of the new temple given by later writers. The chief difference in plan results from the greater elevation of the stylobate, which must have been reached by fourteen steps rather than by two as in the archaic temple. And the extreme dimensions of the bottom step, 239 feet 4 inches by 436 feet 5 inches, must have been due to the presence of a broad passage outside the peristyle, not on the stylobate itself as in the Rhoecus temple at Samos or the Croesus temple at Ephesus, but four or five steps lower.[3] The stylobate dimensions were 168 feet 8 inches by 365 feet 9 inches, and the column plinths lay 2 feet, the column axes 6 feet $3\frac{1}{2}$ inches, inside the stylobate face. The column spacings showed the same variations that occurred in the older temple; but the column diameters seem to have been uniform, 6 feet $\frac{1}{2}$ inch ($6\frac{1}{4}$ Ionic feet). And the column height, according to Pliny, was 60 Ionic feet, considerably greater than in its predecessor, and yielding a more slender proportion of $9\frac{3}{5}$ diameters.

The column bases, as at Priene, are of Asiatic form set on plinths, the latter tending henceforth to become integral members of Asiatic bases.[4] But thirty-six of the columns, according to Pliny, were sculptured, and from these we have

[1] The site of the temple was discovered and excavated by J. T. Wood for the British Museum in 1869–1874, and examples of the architecture and sculpture were brought to the museum. Additional facts were ascertained by a second expedition of the British Museum in 1904–1905, but the new material collected by D. G. Hogarth and A. E. Henderson has not been published. Wood found in place only two of the column bases of the peristyle of the north and south flanks, a length of about 100 feet of the lowest step of the platform on the north side, and the foundations of a great portion of the rest of the structure; these, with Pliny's brief description, form the data for a conjectural restoration.

[2] The period of 120 years mentioned by Pliny is sometimes applied rather to the archaic temple, assuming that its construction was protracted from about 560 to 440 B.C.

[3] Philon of Byzantium speaks of a ten-stepped platform; on the other hand, the dimensions 215 by 425 Ionic feet given by Pliny might easily be applied to the edge of the upper platform if there were nine steps in the lower series and five in the upper (Fig. 81).

[4] There has been some doubt as to whether the course $17\frac{1}{2}$ inches high under the trochilus disk at Ephesus was a plinth or part of the stylobate. It is certainly, however, a plinth, forming part of the base.

THE ALEXANDER TEMPLE AT EPHESUS

both sculptured bottom drums and square sculptured pedestals. The sculptured drums (Plates LIV,[1] LVI) probably belong to the first two rows of columns on the west façade, sixteen in all. The square pedestals may be placed under the twelve columns of the pronaos and the eight of the opisthodomus, their total number twenty being exactly that required to fill out Pliny's thirty-six.[2] These twenty columns on pedestals would have lacked plinths, their circular Asiatic bases resting directly on the pedestals; and their total height, and consequently their diameter, would have been less than in the outer peristyle in accordance with the requirements of the pedestals, exactly like the porch columns of smaller scale on pedestals at Sardis. The great capitals are of excellent design; but not all of them are finished, and one is of particular interest because the eye retains the eight radii and the variously located centre points by which the volute spiral was laid out in octants with compasses. The architrave has three fascias (forming a lintel 3 feet $11\frac{1}{4}$ inches high) and a separate bold egg-and-dart moulding, well suited to support the dentils; the frieze was evidently omitted; and of the cornice we have only the great ovolo (with a cavetto below) which crowned the dentils, and the sima. The total height of this friezeless entablature, apart from the sima, could hardly have been more than a sixth of the height of the columns, and so must have presented a thin and unsatisfactory appearance, in the absence of such a colossal sima parapet as that of its predecessor. In order to relieve the entablature, and particularly the vast central span, of the weight of the pediment, three great openings in the form of windows were left in the tympanum (presumably to be concealed behind sculpture), following a principle already employed in less conspicuous fashion at Acragas (temple of Concord) and Athens (Propylaea).[3]

[1] This restoration is shown as a substitute for that of Murray; but it is to be understood that the sculptured drums and pedestals should not be superposed as here indicated.

[2] This arrangement of the sculptured columns differs considerably from those hitherto proposed. The raising of the *columnae caelatae* to rest on the square pedestals had been proposed many years ago by Fergusson. This arrangement of superposed sculpture was adopted by Murray, whose conjectural restoration, based on long study of the sculptured drums and pedestals which form so important a part of the remains in the British Museum, was formerly generally accepted. But his assumption that there were thirty-six sculptured drums all resting directly on the stylobate, or, in the case of sixteen of which eight were on each façade, on pedestals of which the tops were flush with the stylobate—with nine steps inside each of the façade rows, behind the pedestals, and corresponding to a podium along the flanks—permitted the use of only four steps surrounding the peristyle and so fell far short of attaining the width of the actual remains. And, though the latter difficulty is overcome in Henderson's restoration (Plate LIV), the combination of the sculptured pedestals and drums seems unsatisfactory. Lethaby was undoubtedly correct in separating pedestals and drums; but his arrangements, both with respect to the disposition of the thirty-six sculptured columns and the use of the pedestals on the façades, concealing the sculptured drums behind them, seem unreasonable. The alternative, placing the square pedestals behind the sculptured drums, agrees with the use of the pedestals at Sardis and was suggested by H. C. Butler as the proper restoration for Ephesus. Picard follows this to a certain extent by restoring two rows each of eight sculptured drums at west and east, leaving the remainder of four for pedestals in the pronaos; but this does not fit the probable column distribution. A closer analogy to Sardis would limit the pedestals to the two central rows (ten columns) in the pronaos and to the three central rows (six columns) in the opisthodomus; but the resulting isolation of two sculptured drums before the opisthodomus antae seems less satisfactory than the arrangement in Fig. 81.

[3] These tympanum windows at Ephesus are not actually preserved but appear in coins which represent the façade of the temple.

Another colossal temple dedicated to Artemis in this neighbourhood was that at the Persian seat of government, Sardis, also known as the temple of Cybele (the name of Artemis appears in an inscription on the wall of the temple itself), which replaced an older structure destroyed by the Ionians in 497 B.C. Judging

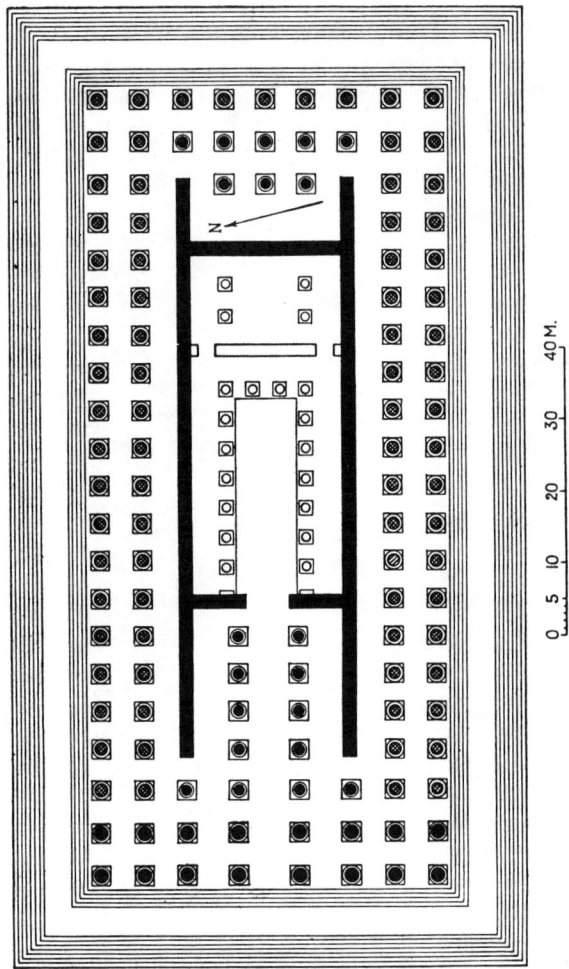

FIG. 81.—THE LATER TEMPLE OF ARTEMIS AT EPHESUS.
(Restored by Fergusson, Lethaby and Dinsmoor.)

from the purity of its original details it was probably contemporary with the temple at Ephesus, which it closely resembles. The temple stands exactly in the path of landslides from the Acropolis; and during an earthquake in A.D. 17 a mass of the hill crushed the east front, thus accounting for the Roman workmanship in that portion of the structure.[1] Again octastyle, with twenty columns

[1] The upper halves of two of the east façade columns had always remained visible, one with the original Greek capital (which Cockerell specially admired) and the other with a

THE TEMPLE AT SARDIS

on the flanks, the façades reproduce the great variety of gradation found at Ephesus, from 17 feet 4¾ inches for the spacing on centres at the corners, through 17 feet 10½ inches and 21 feet 9¼ inches to a maximum of 23 feet 2 inches at the centre. Unlike Ephesus, however, the scheme was not dipteral but pseudo-dipteral, at least in part; for on the flanks the interval between the columns and the cella wall is equal to two intercolumniations, as if the inner row of columns had there been omitted (Fig. 82). On the façades there is an inner row, forming a prostyle arrangement before the pronaos and opisthodomus, directly behind the outer row; it is among these inner columns that we find the square pedestals, two in each porch, left in block form and clearly intended to be sculptured, supporting Ionic columns of a smaller size, which form the best analogies for the treatment at Ephesus (Plate LIII). The stylobate was never laid in place, so that its planned dimensions must be estimated; but in view of the identity of column diameters and widths of plinths with the corresponding dimensions at Didyma, as noted below, it is reasonable to assume that the stylobate would likewise have been about 16 inches outside the column plinths, thus yielding total stylobate dimensions of 148 feet 8 inches by 324 feet. Furthermore, the columns having been erected on separate pier foundations (as was also the case at Didyma) with intermittent gaps which, in the unfinished state of the temple, remained unfilled toward the west end, a more economical mode of access was eventually provided by passing through the foundations and ascending a flight of seven steps within the peristyle, directly to the opisthodomus columns.[1] The pronaos and opisthodomus enclosed great areas about 45 by 60 feet in plan, which must have been almost impossible to roof and may well, therefore, have been hypaethral, giving light to the great doorways nearly 20 feet wide and 39 feet high. The cella, reached by steps from the pronaos, was at a level about 5 feet higher, and was subdivided by interior colonnades and by a screen wall which may have separated an adytum from the cella. From the opisthodomus, on the other hand, was entered a rear chamber or treasury at the lower level, with its ceiling sustained by two interior columns.

The columns of the peristyle are colossal, the largest erected up to that time in Asia Minor; the diameters vary, but were apparently intended to be 6 feet 7½ inches (6⅞ Ionic feet), increasing to 6 feet 9 inches (7 Ionic feet) at the corners. The height followed the proportions of Priene, 8⅘ diameters of the normal size, thus becoming 58 feet 5 inches (60½ Ionic feet) or only ½ Ionic foot more than at Ephesus. The bases are of Asiatic form, with plinths;[2] the torus is in some cases carved with the guilloche and various foliate patterns. Most of the

Roman replacement. The six other columns of the façade had been demolished to the middle of their height, level with the modern ground. The whole area was excavated in 1910–1914 by an American expedition under H. C. Butler; some specimens of the architecture, particularly of the pronaos columns and doorway, are in the Metropolitan Museum in New York.

[1] The excessively complicated restoration of the steps at the west, as represented in the plan, is due in part to the inclusion of the so-called "Lydian building" at a lower level. But it is probable that this would have been completely buried in the fourth century and that the steps would not have broken so meticulously round it. Since the only steps preserved are seven on the north flank of the opisthodomus, the restoration is necessarily largely conjectural.

[2] It has been suggested that the plinths were not intended to count as such but that they were really parts of the pavement; but in view of their construction, their perfect regularity, and the analogy of Ephesus and Didyma, they must be interpreted as plinths.

shafts were never fluted, except those of the smaller order on the pedestals. The latter, since the pedestals are 7 feet 1 inch high, are reduced in height to 51 feet 4 inches, and in diameter to 5 feet 3½ inches (5½ Ionic feet), giving more slender proportions of nearly 9¾ diameters.[1] The capitals are particularly ornate,

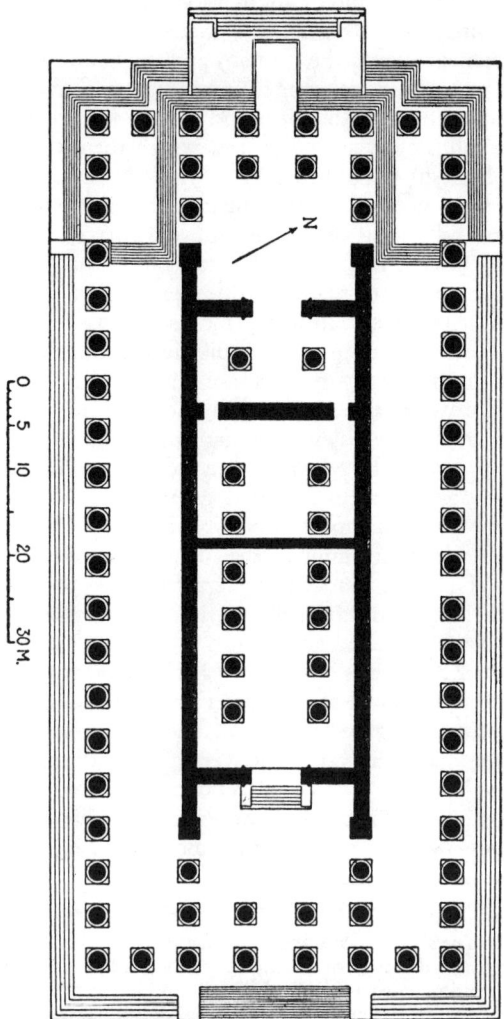

Fig. 82.—The Temple of Artemis-Cybele at Sardis. (Restored by Butler.)

especially those of the smaller order, some with acanthus scrolls or *fleurons* at the middle of the volute cushion, or with inverted palmettes carved on the eggs of the echinus (like the superposed ornament in the archaic temples of

[1] There is no reason for assuming, because of these differences, that the smaller columns were earlier work of the fifth century.

Chios), and perhaps, like the complicated ornament in the Persian palaces at the eastern end of the Sardis-Susa road, a concession to Persian taste. The baluster sides also are variously treated, ribbed, imbricated, or carved with palmettes. Some of the capitals are Roman imitations of the originals, due to the repairs. The entablature seems to betray later influence, suggesting that the work was of long duration; for the crowning moulding of the architrave, a cyma recta with a fillet at the top, would be unsuitable under a dentil course and implies that there was a frieze,[1] such as was eventually added also at Didyma. The anta capitals are also late, of the second century B.C. if not actually Roman; and the enframement of the great east doorway has Roman profiles resulting from the repairs.

Paeonius of Ephesus, one of the architects of the temple of Artemis in that city, was employed together with Daphnis of Miletus to build the temple of Apollo at Didyma (Branchidae) near Miletus; probably the work was undertaken at about 313 B.C., for Strabo's inference that it was rebuilt shortly after the destruction of the archaic temple by Darius in 494 B.C. does not agree with the character of the remains. The work was prolonged for nearly four centuries, as we know from the inscriptions and the treatment of the detail, and finally stopped, leaving the structure still incomplete, at about 41 A.D.[2] It was one of the largest temples in Asia Minor, so large that, according to Strabo,[3] they were unable to roof it; in other words, the cella was hypaethral, one of the few examples about which there is no doubt, though, curiously enough, Vitruvius does not refer to it in this connection. The temple was dipteral, and unique in that the façades were decastyle; on the flanks were twenty-one columns, so that including the twelve columns in the deep pronaos the total number was one hundred and twenty (Fig. 83). The columns have a diameter of 6 feet $7\frac{5}{8}$ inches ($6\frac{7}{8}$ Ionic feet) as at Sardis; the unfinished standing column still retains the figures for the diameters inscribed upon it. Also the plinths are identical in width with those at Sardis, 8 feet 10 inches. The axial spacing is uniformly 17 feet $4\frac{1}{2}$ inches (18 Ionic feet, or 50 per cent greater than at Priene), without the variations found in the other huge Ionic temples. The columns are 64 feet $7\frac{1}{2}$ inches or exactly 67 Ionic feet in height, as close to $9\frac{3}{4}$ lower diameters as the foot unit would permit, and so even more slender than at Ephesus. The

---

[1] The assumption that this was an Asiatic friezeless entablature seems unwarranted.

[2] The temple probably fell during an earthquake in 1493; and the investigation of the ruins by the Dilettanti expeditions of 1764 and 1812, and by a French expedition in 1873, failed to clear up the problem of its history and design. Definite results were obtained through excavations by the French in 1895, and by the Germans in 1906-1913 and 1924-1938. Only three columns, two fluted and carrying part of the architrave on the south flank, and one unfinished and unfluted on the north, still remain standing to their complete height; but the lower portions of the structure were found intact throughout. The unfinished column is of particular interest in that the successive drums are inscribed in Greek notation with the dimensions to which the diameters were to be finished; thus comparison of these figures with the actually finished diameters at bottom and top, and especially with the average axial spacing of 5·2975 m. or 17·380 feet, yields an Ionic foot of 294·3 mm. or 11·587 inches (cf. p. 222, note 2). Gerkan suggests, on less satisfactory grounds, a foot of 294·22 mm. or 11·583 inches. Two of the decorative east façade bases are in the Louvre.

[3] Strabo says, "In after-times the inhabitants of Miletus built a temple which is the largest of all, but which, on account of its vastness, remains without a roof, and there now exist, inside and outside, precious groves of laurel bushes." Its dimensions were in reality exceeded by those of the archaic Polycrates temple at Samos.

peristyle rests on a platform of seven steps; at the middle of the east front is a flight of thirteen more practicable steps enframed by parotids projecting opposite the third column from each corner. The platform has a slight upward curvature, amounting to 2⅜ inches in the façade.

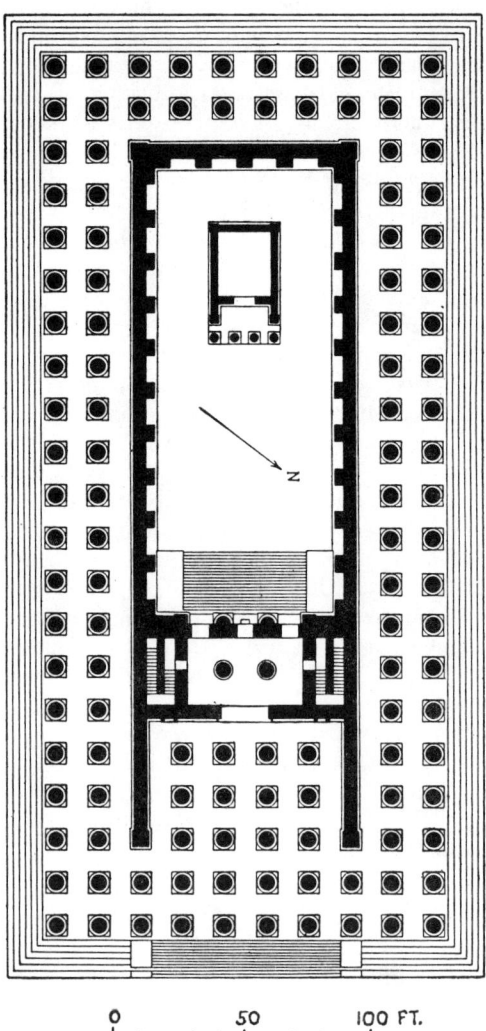

FIG. 83.—THE TEMPLE OF APOLLO AT DIDYMA, MILETUS. (Restored by Wiegand.)

The temple was remarkable not only for its size but also for its design (Plate LVII). Under the columns, above the square plinths, the bases of the principal façade show considerable diversity, the ten bases being arranged in pairs symmetrical with respect to the central axis; only the outermost bases are of the normal Asiatic form with scotias and fluted torus, the first and the third from the centre substituting a circular plinth for the upper torus, while the second and fourth from the centre substitute a plinth for the disk with the two scotias. But the first and third from the centre are further differentiated by having, in the latter case, the Attic profile with a scotia and a lower torus instead of the disk with two scotias below the circular plinth. And the second and fourth from the centre are again differentiated in that the plinth which takes the place of the disk is circular in the fourth and dodecagonal in the second, the latter having each face panelled and decorated within with conventional foliage, or in one case with a Nereid riding a sea-horse (Plate LVI). The circular plinths and the torus mouldings are also richly carved, with maeanders, imbricated patterns of laurel leaves, and anthemion designs. In this exuberant richness of ornament at the bases of the columns the architects would seem to have attempted to rival, though in another direction, the famous *columnae caelatae* of Ephesus. Analogous is the treatment of the corner capitals, with busts of Apollo and other divinities protruding from the normal volutes (Plate LV), with the angle volutes replaced by the foreparts of winged lions or winged horses, and with a bull's head at the centre; and the egg-and-dart of the echinus is replaced by a lotus-and-palmette. The style of these heads bears so strong a resemblance to the sculptures of the Great Altar at Pergamum, built by Eumenes II (197–159 B.C.), as to suggest that the upper portions of the temple were being worked at this late epoch.[1] This is in accord with the design of the ordinary Ionic capitals at Didyma which seem considerably later than the capitals at Ephesus. In the entablature was inserted a frieze, sculptured with heads of Medusa punctuating great *rinceaux* of acanthus; the heads were not, as might have been expected, so arranged as to carry up the lines of the columns, but occurred midway between them.[2] It would be interesting to know whether the frieze was an integral part of the original design, as contrasted with the friezeless entablatures of Priene and Ephesus; probably, however, we may regard it as a Hellenistic revision, for which the architrave was likewise modified as at Sardis, with mouldings unsuitable for the support of dentils. The same florid treatment appears even in the great dentils, of which the faces are carved with palmettes and the like. At the time when the work was abandoned, early in the Roman imperial epoch, only the dentil course of the cornice and the bed moulding above it had been laid, and the temple permanently lacked its cornice and pediments (Plate LVII).

The pronaos, as has been said, was very deep, and this was followed by an antechamber, perhaps the place from which the oracles were delivered; on either side were stone staircases, carried between walls. Though a doorway (18½ feet wide in the clear) opened from the pronaos into the antechamber, this was a mere concession to custom, perhaps due also to the desire for a ceremonial balcony from which oracles might be announced; for there was no direct communication between them, the threshold being 4 feet 9½ inches high. Instead, small doorways on either side give access to descending tunnels with sloping barrel vaults which pass below the winding staircases mentioned above,

---

[1] There seems to be, however, no reason for regarding the façade columns as Imperial Roman. It was formerly assumed that all the façade capitals had heads protruding from the volutes; in this respect Plate LV requires correction.

[2] In this respect also Plate LV must be corrected.

and lead down to the cella, an open court with the pavement 13 feet 2 inches below the stylobate of the peristyle. The mouldings in all this part of the work have Hellenistic profiles. The walls of the cella were decorated with immense pilasters, nearly 6 feet wide and 3 feet in projection, resting upon a podium 17 feet 7 inches high, so that their bases were 4 feet 5 inches higher than those of the peristyle. Thus the height of the pilasters, including capital and base, was so much less than that of the peristyle columns. The pilaster capitals were very varied in design (Plate LVIII), though they are all of the "Proto-Ionic" volute type which is so characteristic of work of this period in Asia Minor, the vertical volutes being connected across the bottom of the capital, and the enclosed panel decorated with foliage and griffins; and between the capitals

FIG. 84.—CAPITAL OF SEMI-COLUMN IN TEMPLE OF APOLLO AT DIDYMA.

ran a band sculptured with griffins and lyres. There were nine pilasters on each side, and three at the west end, besides the responds at each corner, the vast length of the cella being due to the fact that there was no opisthodomus. At the east end of the cella, separating three entrance doorways, were two semi-detached columns ranging with the pilasters, but with Corinthian capitals which are more fully developed than any other examples hitherto noted (Fig. 84); the spirals in the centre of each face, which alone are sheathed in cauliculi carrying the palmette, are, however, too small and leave too much of the surface of the bell uncovered. Access to these three doorways, and through them to the antechamber behind the pronaos, was gained only by means of a great flight of twenty-four steps, 50 feet in width, leading up from the great court. The laurel groves which filled the cella, at least until the time of Strabo, eventually disappeared, and the whole area was covered with a marble pavement. Near the back was a shrine, measuring 28 by 47½ feet, which had the form of a little prostyle tetrastyle Ionic temple; the anta capitals were decorated with a winged figure at the centre and a leaf ornament on either side, and the entablature included both frieze (of cyma profile, decorated with the anthemion) and dentils. In this shrine was placed the archaic bronze figure of Apollo by Canachus, which was brought back by Seleucus from Ecbatana at about 295 B.C., after having been carried off by Xerxes.

With this structure we have passed the limits of the fourth century and have entered the next period, the Hellenistic; the further development in Asia Minor must be deferred until we take up this period in the following chapter. For the present we may turn to the other types of religious and semi-religious buildings that adorned the sanctuaries of the fourth century, and to the structures exemplifying the new advances in secular architecture.

*   *   *   *   *

Much more imposing in scale than most of the normal temples, though designed in the comparative simplicity of the Doric order, were the projects for the addition of the portico, which had apparently been omitted at the time of the fifth-century construction, on the southeast front of that temple of unusual plan already mentioned, the Hall of the Mysteries at Eleusis (Fig. 73; Plate LXVI). There were two successive designs for this work in the fourth century, neither of them finished. The earlier, apparently of 356-352 B.C., was intended to form a partial peristyle, pseudo-dipteral in scheme, across the southeast façade and returning for at least part of the distance along both flanks. The width measured on the stylobate would have been about 245 feet; and from the disposition of the plan it is evident that there would have been sixteen columns on the front, supplementing the twelve of the Ictinus design by two at either corner in order to accommodate the flank peristyles. It seems difficult to assume that a pediment could have been designed for such an enormous width; perhaps the peristyle was conceived as a stoa wrapped round the cella, with its roof leaning against the higher walls. In any case, this project was abandoned after the corners of the peristyle foundations had been erected, together with their diagonal strengthening ribs.[1] The work was resumed between 330 and 310 B.C. by Philon of Eleusis, and assumed the form of a prostyle dodecastyle portico with two intercolumniations on either flank, the stylobate 178¾ feet long and the columns 6 feet 6 inches in diameter, the whole frontispiece being crowned by an enormous pediment. The steps and platform are of black Eleusinian limestone, while the columns and superstructure are of Pentelic marble. This work was never finished, the columns remaining in their unfluted state; and there is considerable reconstruction in the upper parts dating from repairs of the Roman imperial period, after the destruction by Sarmatian Costobocs about A.D. 170.

A few treasuries continued to be erected in the Doric style in the sanctuaries of this period, the most important being those of Cyrene and Thebes at Delphi; the mouldings in the former show a peculiar combination of Doric and Ionic. Here, too, may be mentioned a small marble temple-like structure with an apse

[1] This is the project which has generally been wrongly assigned to the fifth century, and forms the basis of Noack's erroneous restoration of the plan by Ictinus as noted in the preceding chapter. The analysis of the masonry of the foundations, showing that they were built from second-hand stone from walls not demolished until the fourth century, was the result of recent studies by the Greek authorities.

crowned externally with a miniature Doric frieze and internally with a maeander carved in relief, on the island of Paros.[1]

Structures other than temples began in this period to assume more varied forms than had hitherto been the case. Particularly notable, for instance, are the circular buildings, known as tholoi, erected within the precincts at Delphi, Epidaurus, and Olympia. All three consist of circular cellas with concentric rings of outer and inner columns, showing combinations of the orders such as, on the Greek mainland, we find in the temples themselves. The earliest of these is the marble (as contrasted with the archaic limestone) tholos at Delphi (Plate LVII), in the lower precinct of Athena Pronaea (Marmaria), probably designed by a certain Theodorus of Phocaea whose book about the structure was cited by Vitruvius.[2] The Doric external columns are twenty in number (Plate LIX),[3] resulting in exact parallelism between the twenty radii of the plan and the twenty radii of each column, resting on a stylobate 44 feet 9 inches in diameter. The wall sill on the exterior (below the moulding carved with water leaves at the bottom of the white marble orthostates) and the pavement of the interior (all except the white central circle) and a moulded bench lining the cella wall, are of black limestone contrasting with the white marble, recalling Athenian practice in the preceding century. The interior contained, resting on the limestone bench, a girdle of Corinthian columns, half as many as on the exterior (less one omitted because of the doorway), with capitals imitating those at Bassae, placed closely against the face of the cella wall but not actually engaged. The shafts have twenty flutes, and the necking joint lies below the bottom of the capital, as in their prototype. The capitals have two rows of very small leaves at the bottom, sometimes acanthus, in other cases water leaves, and sometimes overlapping in a sort of rotary or wind-blown motion; and the central spirals, instead of springing independently from the leaf girdles as at Bassae, are united with the corner volutes in S-scrolls and thus form lyre patterns. The influence of Bassae, so prevalent in the Doric temples of this period, is apparent also in the diamond-shaped ceiling coffers, and perhaps also in the roof construction with flat and cover-tiles in one piece. The two sizes of entablature recovered (including architraves, triglyph friezes, cornices, and simas), the larger type fitting the circumference of the peristyle and the smaller that of the cella wall, definitely suggest that the roof was broken into two slopes of which the central cone was raised on a vertical drum,[4] following the traditions of the fifth century at Athens (Odeum) and Eleusis (Telesterion). The metopes of both entablatures were filled with delicately carved marble reliefs. The purpose of this and similar tholoi remains debatable; apparently it was not a temple, since Pausanias omits it from his description of the four temples in this precinct;

[1] These structures are as yet insufficiently published. The apsidal structure is immured in the mediaeval castle on Paros, along with the remains of the archaic Ionic temple (p. 132).

[2] The alternative suggestion that Theodorus wrote about the archaic porous tholos is less acceptable, on the one hand because of the rarity of architectural writing at that early period, and again because the marble tholos is so obviously a studied geometrical analysis.

[3] In the modern rebuilding of three columns (Plate LVII), exceptional slenderness is attained by the insertion of an extra drum in each; but the resulting proportions, giving columns of 6·82 diameters and an order of 8·46 diameters, more suitable for the third century than for the early fourth, suggest that the extra drum should be omitted.

[4] The official French restoration is erroneous and omits the vertical drum and ignores the smaller sima.

and we can only regret the loss of the book by Theodorus which might have furnished the requisite information. Also the date is uncertain, some preferring the late fifth century, others the fourth; but details of ornament (the vertical simas with *rinceaux* in both cornices, and the rampant antefixes above them) and construction (the hook clamps) suggest that it is not earlier than the beginning of the fourth century.[1]

The rotunda (tholos) at Epidaurus was the most beautiful of these examples and is stated by Pausanias to have been built by Polycleitus the Younger, who also designed the theatre. The building (Fig. 85) consists of a circular cella, with an external peristyle of twenty-six Doric columns, resting on a stylobate 66 feet 2½ inches in diameter; the entablature which they supported is characterised by the low fourth-century proportions of the architrave and cornice as contrasted with the frieze, and the metopes are filled with great rosettes carved in relief, the earliest instance of this treatment. The interior was lighted by two windows, one on either side of the doorway, displaying to advantage the elaborate pavement of rhomboidal slabs alternating black and white, and the exquisitely carved interior columns and ceiling. The circle of fourteen Corinthian columns, standing free from the wall, has extremely beautiful capitals (Plate LVII), showing a marked advance on that at Bassae, which preceded them by perhaps eighty years; they are, in fact, the most developed of all those dating from the fourth century. Here again, like Scopas at Tegea, the sculptor-architect Polycleitus developed a new approach; and it is to him that we owe the type which ultimately prevailed. One of the Corinthian capitals, differing from the others in that it is unfinished, remains in perfect condition as the result of having been intentionally buried; it was undoubtedly a preliminary model. The entablature supported on these Corinthian columns contains one of the earliest examples of the cyma-profiled frieze.[2] Below the floor are concentric walls with connecting doorways forming an underground labyrinth or maze, which may have had some purpose in the snake cult of Asclepius, being analogous to the snake pits in the stoa of the Asclepieum at Athens and in the Erechtheum.[3] Of the superstructure sufficient remains have been found to permit a conjectural restoration; we may adopt the scheme of the slope broken by a vertical drum as at Delphi, with the apex crowned by a marble floral acroterion of which fragments exist.[4] The details all seem a little later than at Delphi; the vertical

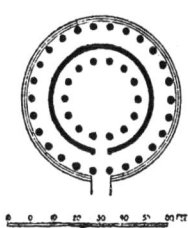

FIG. 85.—THE THOLOS AT EPIDAURUS.

[1] It is to be noted, however, that hook clamps appeared particularly early at Delphi, as in the Aegospotami monument of 405 B.C.

[2] Next in date would come the examples in the propylaea at Epidaurus and in the shrine of the temple at Didyma (about 295 B.C.) as noted above, and in the bicolumnar monument of Aristaeneta at Delphi (about 270 B.C.).

[3] A recent theory that the inner concentric foundations belong to an older tholos is shown to be inacceptable because they contain clamps of the form used throughout the present building.

[4] The published restorations are erroneous in that they represent either a simple conical roof or a drum with a central impluvium; the former seems to be contradicted by the two other tholoi of this century, and the impluvium theory in any case is impossible because of the central acroterion.

sima with the *rinceaux* is similar, but the lower proportions of the architrave and outer cornice, as well as the developed form of the capital, are decisive. Also the surviving accounts of expenditure, inscribed on marble, cover a period of twenty-one years which seem to have formed part of a total of thirty-five or forty, as if the erection had proceeded slowly during about 360-320 B.C.

Last of all comes the circular building at Olympia, called the Philippeum, commenced by Philip in 339 B.C. and completed by Alexander; it consists of a circular cella surrounded by a peristyle of eighteen Ionic columns (Fig. 44 at PH, Fig. 86), resting on a stylobate 45 feet 8 inches in diameter. The Ionic bases are exceptional in having a torus and scotia placed directly on a plinth, the shafts in having twenty-two flutes, and the capitals in lacking the egg-and-dart ovolo. The entablature contained both the mainland frieze and the Asiatic dentils; and, unless we can assume that this combination had appeared slightly earlier at Samothrace, its occurrence in the Philippeum marks the beginning of its long history. The walls, described by Pausanias as of brick, were actually of limestone (above the marble dado courses), faced on the outside with stucco which in Roman times was painted to imitate brickwork (Fig. 86). The interior, again lighted by windows on either side of the doorway, contained a segmental pedestal with gold-and-ivory statues of Amyntas, Philip, Alexander, Olympias and Eurydice, all by Leochares. The inner face of the cella wall was decorated with nine semi-detached columns of the Corinthian order, again half as many as on the exterior. The capitals, as at Tegea, lack the central spirals, having acanthus leaves instead, and for the second time employ the cauliculus for the angle volutes; but the proportions are higher, as at Bassae, which is recalled also in the small leaves round the bare upper part of the bell (though here carved rather than painted). Presumably there was an upper range above them reaching to the roof; the rafters of the roof were, according to Pausanias, held together at the top by a bronze poppy, which formed a central finial.

We have traced the development of the Corinthian capital through six structures (Bassae, Delphi, Epidaurus, Tegea, Olympia, and Didyma—three of them temples and three circular tholoi), all of which employed the capital solely in the interior. Most of these examples were designed, furthermore, by sculptor-architects,[1] possibly Callimachus himself at Bassae, Theodorus at Delphi, Polycleitus at Epidaurus, Scopas at Tegea, and perhaps Leochares at Olympia. It was in a building erected for quite a different purpose that the Corinthian capital for the first time appeared on an exterior.

For convenience, therefore, we may here discuss a group of buildings which, though primarily votive, belong in a separate class from the ordinary votive monuments because of their resemblance to temples and tholoi. These are the choragic monuments, of which simple forms, erected by the patrons of victorious choruses in the contests in the theatre at Athens, had been set up during the fifth century as well as in the fourth, for the purpose of displaying the prize tripods; and most of these monuments were placed in and round the sanctuary of Dionysus, or along the street leading to it, which therefore received the name "Street of Tripods." Originally these monuments had consisted merely of a stepped base or a table-like form, square or circular; but

[1] In this connection may be recalled its use by Phidias or one of his followers in the columnar support of the Athena Parthenos.

THE MONUMENT OF LYSICRATES

with the development of luxury in the fourth century they assumed more extravagant forms, even those of imposing buildings. It is in one of these that we meet the best known example of the Greek Corinthian capital, though a most peculiar type,[1] namely, in another circular building, the choragic monument of Lysicrates (Plates LIX, LX),[2] situated in the Street of Tripods. It was erected to support a tripod won during a choral victory in the theatre in 334 B.C.[3] The monument, with its marble finial, rises to a height of 54 feet, and in addition there was the tripod itself. A high square podium of limestone forms the base, and is surmounted by a cornice supporting the circular steps of blue Hymettian marble, above which everything is of white Pentelic marble; the

FIG. 86.—THE PHILIPPEUM AT OLYMPIA. (Restored by Adler.)

sequence of the three materials is characteristic of the fourth century and of the Hellenistic age. The diameter of the circular lower step is so adjusted that, while it seems to overhang the podium as seen in elevation, it would not so appear as seen in perspective. Six Corinthian columns decorate the exterior; screen walls filling the intervening spaces give them the appearance of being semi-detached, though in reality they are complete, the filling slabs being worked with a hollow to fit them. The capital (Plate LX) is higher than in other examples, being $1\frac{1}{2}$ diameters. The bell subdivides too easily into halves,

[1] Its modern fame is due chiefly to its early publication by Stuart and Revett, at a time when no other pure Greek Corinthian capitals were known.
[2] The monument has always been one of the best known landmarks of Athens, and was known to the first modern travellers as the "Lantern of Demosthenes"; the Jesuit and Capuchin monks incorporated it into their monastery in 1659, and thenceforward the site has belonged to France.
[3] These choragic monuments usually bear dedicatory inscriptions giving their exact dates.

the upper portion with the volutes (which again lack sheaths or cauliculi) not being sufficiently connected with the lower half with its two rows of leaves. The central ornament between the volutes is a palmette, as at Bassae and Didyma, but here raised to the abacus level. The upper row of leaves of the acanthus shows between the leaves eight-petalled flowers or rosettes, which may have been copied from the heads of the pins which in a metallic prototype fastened the leaves to the bell or core of the capital. The lower row of leaves consists of the petals of some water plant, frequently found in Greek decorative sculpture alternating with the acanthus. There is no astragal between the capital and shaft, but merely a sinking which suggests that it was applied in bronze; and below it the fluting of the shaft terminates in leaves, a treatment sometimes found in votive columns. The entablature repeats the mouldings (including the dentils) of the Caryatid portico of the Erechtheum, but has in addition a sculptured frieze. As this was the first example of the Greek Corinthian order to be used externally, it was also the first occasion on which a complete entablature was required; and, while the architect may have derived it from the Ionic entablature of the Philippeum, it is quite as probable that he invented the combination anew for this purpose. Thus was developed a form of entablature, a combination of the Attic and Asiatic Ionic types with the dentils much reduced in projection, which was destined to have great influence on the future history of the Corinthian, and even of the Ionic, style. The frieze, 10 inches high, is carved with a representation of the story of Dionysus and the pirates, who being thrown into the sea became metamorphosed into dolphins. The antefixes, which usually form the terminations of the cover tiles, are here brought out over the front of the corona and carved as a decorative cresting. Set back to the plane of the architrave and frieze is a second superposed cresting with the Greek wave scroll. The roof, which is one block of marble, has its upper surface carved in imitation of bronze scale tiles (Plate LIX). In the centre rises the finial designed to carry the tripod, and from the lower portion of it project three helices or scrolls, which it is thought supported figures or dolphins. In the upper portion of this finial we recognise the further development of a design which we shall see in the Acanthus Column at Delphi; here, in addition to the acanthus leaves, we find the volute used to give variety and greater strength to the support of the tripod.

Other choragic monuments of the period were not so elaborate. A favourite type was that of the temple, which was adopted for instance in the choragic monument of Nicias, of 319 B.C. This consisted of a square cella with a prostyle hexastyle Doric portico, and stood near the theatre of Dionysus; the outline of the plan of the lowest step is of the T-shape characteristic of the prostyle temples of the fourth century.[1] Of particular interest is the economical method of construction, with poros limestone employed for the walls and the triglyphs (to be covered with blue paint), and with marble for columns, antae, architrave, metopes, cornices, and pediments. This monument was carefully taken down, stone by stone, soon after the Herulian invasion of A.D. 267 in order to clear the ground outside the new fortification walls and to furnish

---

[1] The foundations of the monument were not discovered until 1910; portions of the entablature, including the inscription, had been discovered by Beulé in 1852 in the so-called Beulé Gate.

OTHER CHORAGIC MONUMENTS

material for the Roman gate to the Acropolis, later to be described.[1] The other choragic monument of the same year 319 B.C. was erected by Thrasyllus, as a façade enframing a cave just above the theatre (Plate LXI), subsequently crowned by an attic with a statue of Dionysus.[2] The inspiration for this very unusual design clearly came from the makeshift southwest wing of the Propylaea, which as seen from the west presented three piers of varying sizes, carrying an entablature of which the frieze (for the greater part of its extent) is blank while the architrave has a continuous regula and an unbroken row of guttae (Plate LI). So too the Doric monument of Thrasyllus has the three piers,

FIG. 87.—THE CHORAGIC MONUMENT OF THRASYLLUS AT ATHENS. (Restored by Welter.)

the architrave with a chain of guttae, and the frieze without triglyphs, though in this case it is not blank but is adorned with wreaths (Fig. 87).[3] The attic was added to receive dedicatory inscriptions of 279 B.C. erected by the son of Thrasyllus. It seems evident that these two Doric monuments of 319 B.C. were both adaptations of the Propylaea of the Acropolis, one being derived from

[1] The old theory that it was demolished at about A.D. 161 to leave space for a road up to the Acropolis behind the new odeum of Herodes Atticus must now be abandoned.

[2] The monument of Thrasyllus was destroyed by bombardment in 1826, but its appearance had been recorded by Stuart and Revett, and the statue of Dionysus (not shown in Fig. 87, which represents the original form) had been taken by Lord Elgin to London and is now in the British Museum.

[3] This monument in turn inspired many of the features of the Lincoln Memorial in Washington.

the hexastyle central portico and the other from the southwest wing. It is reasonable to suppose, therefore, that another choragic monument of which only fragments have survived, in the Ionic style and copying exactly the forms of the temple of Athena Nike, was erected either just before or just after 319 B.C. It must likewise have stood near the theatre, since it was utilised in 278 B.C. for posting the great list of dramatic victories.[1] In 315 B.C. this expensive rivalry was terminated by the sumptuary laws of Demetrius of Phalerum, restricting choragic monuments to simple memorials erected under public supervision.

Among the more important accessories in the temenos of a great temple were also the stoas or colonnades which afforded protection to the visitors or pilgrims to the shrine. The Echo Colonnade or Stoa Poecile at Olympia (Fig. 44 at EH), so called on account of the paintings which decorated the wall at the back, stood on the east side of the Altis, and consisted of a double corridor 331 feet long, with columns of the Doric order outside, and an inner range of Ionic or Corinthian columns to assist in carrying the roof. At Epidaurus these colonnades, of which there were two forming a continuous line ranging along the north side of the enclosure, were of the Ionic order; and one of them was in two storeys, taking advantage of the lower ground level. The continuous upper storey has Ionic columns both outside and inside; but the basement has simple pilasters on the front and curious heavy square piers with chamfered corners and spreading capitals within. Their use here was of greater importance, in that they served as the temporary refuge (incubation) of the patients who came to the shrine of Asclepius to be healed of their ailments. Similarly in the shrine of Asclepius at Athens there was a Doric stoa in two storeys, with a hip roof, backed against the Acropolis rock; this again was used as a dormitory for patients, and one end, being blocked by the temple, was walled up and contained a stairway leading to a mezzanine storey with a circular pit for the sacred snakes. In the sanctuary of Hera at Perachora was a Doric stoa in an L-shaped plan, with Ionic semi-columns inside, with capitals resembling those at Bassae. Some sanctuaries had as many as four of these stoas, as at Calauria (Poros) and also in the Argive Heraeum. Among those intended for secular use may be mentioned the two begun by Lycurgus above the Pnyx at Athens, forming an open V-shaped plan and intended (like the stoa behind the theatre at Athens) to shelter the citizens in case of rain, but never finished. Usually these stoas, even in Asia Minor, were Doric externally, but if two-aisled the central columns were normally Ionic, spaced either two or three times as far apart as the Doric columns of the front, and reaching to a higher level in order to support the ridge beam directly; or, if the stoa were in two storeys, this use of more lofty columns was applied to the upper storey.

Stoas were frequently employed for commercial purposes as well as for shelter, and then usually required special treatment. The enormous South Stoa at Corinth, facing the open agora, was 525 feet in length and two-aisled, with, as usual, Doric columns (seventy-one on the façade) outside and Ionic within; the unusual feature was the row of thirty-three shops to which doorways in the back wall gave access, and the second row of thirty-three storerooms behind

[1] The Ionic choragic monument has never been published, apart from the discussions of the dramatic records inscribed thereon. It seems improbable that it was built in 278 B.C., the date of the inscription.

these, the front shops having deep wells supplied with water from Pirene, apparently for cold storage. Another example at Corinth is the North Market, which passed through two phases. At first it was solely a market-building, a long hall with a central row of eleven simple columns; and on the back toward the archaic temple of Apollo were ten shops, separated by thin (wooden?) partitions and having in their front walls a central doorway and two flanking windows for each shop, with slender decorative pilasters. A special peculiarity was the hollowing of the window sills to form stone tanks, 11 inches wide and 31 inches long, varying from 10 to 16 inches in depth. This form of the structure may well be earlier than the fourth century; for it was during the fourth century that an open colonnade was built along the east front, returning across the south end, with the Doric columns spaced quite irrespectively of the earlier interior columns behind the wall. Another addition was the placing of little rectangular piers at the centres of all the intervals between the interior columns, apparently for supporting wooden counters of which the ends may have been let into the sides of the columns.

A structure analogous in form, but totally different in purpose, was the Arsenal of the Piraeus near Athens. Although the building no longer exists, having been burnt by Sulla in 86 B.C., the description of it given in the specifications, engraved on a slab of Hymettian marble, is so clear and distinct that we know more about its construction than if its actual remains, rather than the inscription, had been found. It is of particular importance on account of the light that it sheds on the question of the construction of the Greek roofs, about which so little is known, owing to the complete destruction by fire or otherwise of all the timber therein employed. The arsenal was built between 340 and 330 B.C. from the designs of Philon, the architect of the façade of the Hall of the Mysteries at Eleusis; and it was intended for the storing of the rigging, sails, ropes, etc., of the Athenian navy. It was 433 feet 10 inches long by 58 feet 11 inches wide over the walls (405 by 55 Doric feet, or 400 by 50 Doric feet internally, in the ratio of 8 : 1),[1] the walls being of regular ashlar masonry crowned by a triglyph frieze and cornice, below which seventy-eight simple windows (three on each end, thirty-six on each flank) lighted the interior. On each end was a pair of great doorways 9 feet 7½ inches wide and 16 feet 7 inches high, separated by a marble pier 2 feet 1¾ inches wide. The interior was divided into a central passage and two aisles (Fig. 88). The former, 21 feet 6 inches wide, served as a covered promenade; and in the aisles, separated from the nave by stone columns, probably Ionic, 2 feet 11½ inches (2¾ Doric feet) in diameter and 32 feet 1½ inches (30 Doric feet) in height and by screen walls with gates in them, were stored the sails and ropes, with galleries above for the smaller materials. Full specifications are given as to chests, cupboards, and shelving. The columns, thirty-five in number on each side, carried huge beams (32 inches wide by 29 inches high) longitudinally as architraves, serving also as purlins of the roof; and they also carried transverse beams of the same dimensions across the central passage. On the centre of each of these transverse

---

[1] The dimensions recorded in Greek feet, necessarily Doric feet of 12⅞ inches, are here transformed into English feet and inches. Most of the published restorations, based on the Ionic foot of 11⅝ inches erroneously assumed to have been employed at this time in Attica, have deficient dimensions.

THE BEGINNING OF THE DECADENCE

beams rested a block of timber which supported the ridge beam (22½ inches by 17¾ inches). Resting on this ridge beam, on the longitudinal architraves, and on the flank walls were rafters 12 inches wide and 8 inches high, and 16 inches apart. Across the rafters were laid battens, 6½ inches by 1⅝ inches, and 3¼ inches apart, carrying the close boarding ⅞ inch thick on which the Corinthian terracotta tiles were laid, bedded in mud. From this description it follows that the trussing of timber in roofs was yet unknown to the Greeks, and that the rafters were carried by the ridge beam and by other direct vertical supports.[1]

Other stoa-like structures were the ship-sheds for the hulls, the most famous examples being those in the Piraeus harbours called Zea and Mounichia. These consisted of parallel sloping stylobates descending below sea level, with columns

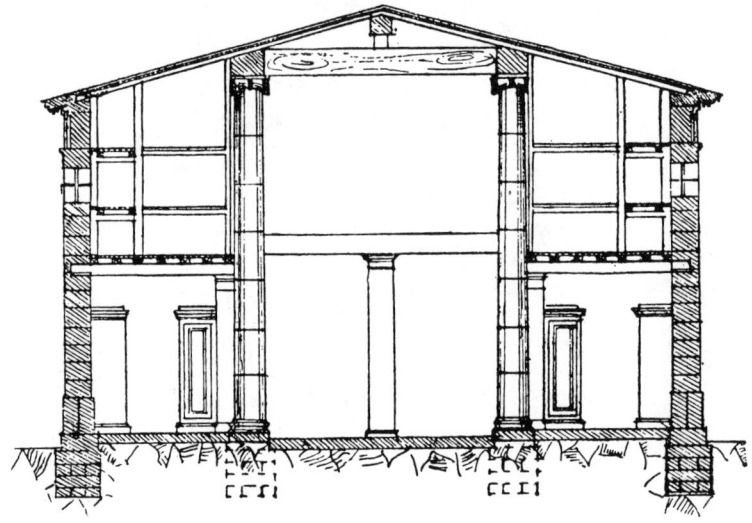

FIG. 88.—TRANSVERSE SECTION OF THE ARSENAL AT THE PIRAEUS.
(Restored by Dörpfeld.)

arranged in rows alternately high and low, the high columns carrying the ridges and the low columns the valleys of an umbrella roof sloping down toward the harbour.

By the fourth century the old type of Bouleuterion with the longitudinal plan and central colonnade had passed out of fashion. The square or the wide rectangle, with the seats arranged in ⊓-shape as developed at Athens, was now universally preferred, appearing in its most elaborate form in the Thersilion or Assembly Hall of the ten thousand Arcadians at Megalopolis (Fig. 89). The plan, measuring 172 by 218½ feet (without the portico), encloses an area of more than 35,000 square feet, and the columns which carried its roof were ranged, as in earlier examples, in lines parallel to three sides of the hall, but in

[1] It is for this reason that we have been obliged to assume that certain large compartments in pre-Hellenistic buildings, such as the pronaos of temple 'GT' at Selinus, and both porches in the temple at Sardis, were designed to be hypaethral. By the Hellenistic period, however, the truss principle had been discovered, and Vitruvius alludes to it.

five concentric series rather than one only. The central series formed an exact square which probably supported a lantern or opaion. In fact, the scheme appears to have been greatly influenced by the Hall of the Mysteries at Eleusis, but it had this important difference, namely, that in order to form the least possible obstruction to the view from any portion of the hall, the columns were arranged on the intersections of lines radiating from the tribune at the middle of the central square. On account of this radiating scheme the axial spacing differs in each row; and it so happens that the third or middle row required either the widest or the narrowest spans; as originally laid out, the more open spans were preferred, but as some weakness developed later additional columns were inserted at the middle of each span. The bases of the columns *in situ* prove by their respective levels that the floor of the assembly hall sloped downwards towards the tribune, probably with wooden seats. Behind the columns

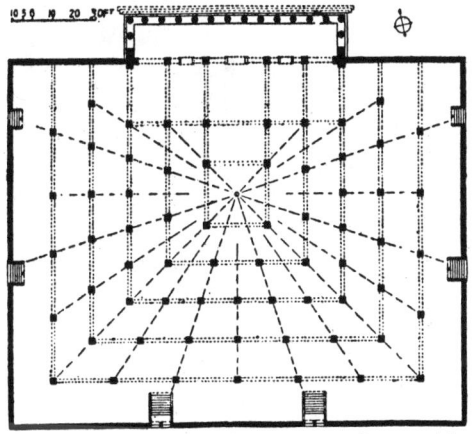

FIG. 89.—THE THERSILION AT MEGALOPOLIS. (Restored by Weir.)

were two entrances on each of the three sides as at Eleusis; but on the fourth side was a great frontispiece, a Doric prostyle portico with fourteen columns on the front, facing towards the theatre, and terminating in line with the third row of interior columns. In terms of the number of columns beneath a single pediment, this outer portico was the most ambitious project known; but its scale was not very large, the columns being spaced barely less than 8 feet on centres. The wall behind the portico was originally open, with four great piers; but at a later date (probably when the intermediate columns were inserted in the third row within) a continuous wall with three smaller doorways was inserted. The building seems not to have been rebuilt after the destruction of the city in 222 B.C., and Pausanias says that only its ruins were to be seen in his time.[1]

A smaller Bouleuterion at Sicyon is a perfect square, and is divided internally by sixteen Ionic columns arranged in four rows of four, again forming an exact square at the centre which probably supported an opaion. Curiously, however, the entire seating arrangement was eccentric, being confined to the rear half of

[1] The building was excavated by the British School at Athens in 1890.

the square, with permanent seats of packed earth and mud-brick covered with stucco. The central square appears to have been occupied by a raised platform surrounded by a grille. On the coast of Asia Minor is a small Bouleuterion at Heraclea near Miletus, with the seats (now perhaps for the first time executed in stone) arranged in ⊓-shape parallel to three walls, and with piers following the same plan but fairly close to the walls in order to leave the auditorium unobstructed.

At Athens the popular assembly-place, the Pnyx, which since the time of Cleisthenes had served for larger assemblies than the Bouleuterion could accommodate, underwent its last transformation at the hands of Lycurgus, but was never quite finished and seems to have been abandoned when the Athenian theatre, as likewise remodelled by Lycurgus, proved to be a more congenial site. The new structure was much larger than that of the end of the fifth century, but approximately concentric, with a diameter of 390 feet, the retaining wall of the auditorium being composed of huge blocks averaging 8 feet in length and $6\frac{1}{4}$ feet in height, forming somewhat irregular ashlar masonry. The largest blocks are 11 feet 10 inches long and 8 feet 3 inches high, weighing about 33 tons. This wall was apparently carried up for a height of only 21 feet, and thence rose about 35 feet higher in the form of an embankment of earth (presumably faced with masonry, forming a sort of crater edge which sloped down gradually toward the bema, enclosing an area of nearly 60,000 square feet and accommodating about 10,000 people. The bema, measuring nearly 22 by 32 feet at the base, has steps ascending to two platforms of which the upper is $9\frac{1}{2}$ by $10\frac{3}{4}$ feet, set in the obtuse angle formed by two rock scarps converging at 148 degrees.[1]

The plan of the theatre, by the fourth century B.C., had become well established and had assumed a monumental form. Most typical, and also one of the best preserved, is the example erected by Polycleitus the Younger (the designer of the tholos) at Epidaurus (Fig. 90; Plate LXII), presumably at about 350 B.C.; and in this structure we are enabled for the first time to study the details. Three parts may be specified—the orchestra circle for the performance, the cavea (*koilon*) or auditorium for the spectators, and the scene building for background and for the storage of properties. The orchestra forms at Epidaurus a complete circle, having in the centre the altar of Dionysus. The basic circle was that of the step on which stand the seats of honour (*proedria*), 80 feet 4 inches (75 Doric feet) in diameter, forming at the same time the outer edge of the gutter.[2] The inner edge of the gutter is formed by the curb delimiting the circle of the orchestra itself, five-sixths of the basic circle or 66 feet 11 inches ($62\frac{1}{2}$ Doric feet) in diameter, the portion facing toward the spectators being decorated with

---

[1] This analysis of the surviving form of the Pnyx, together with the description of its two earlier states (pp. 119, 206), is based on the results of the latest excavations by the American School in Athens, in collaboration with the Greek Archaeological Society, in 1930–1939.

[2] The basic circle, which henceforth plays considerable part in the harmonious adjustment of the plan, was normally that fitting the face of the lowest row of seats; but when the lowest row formed a special bench of honour (*proedria*) there was generally an extra step below it which formed the basic circle. When an ordinary seat formed the basic circle the orchestra gutter was struck out with a lesser radius; but when the extra step under the proedria formed the basic circle, it is obvious that the designer had the choice of making the outer edge of the gutter coincide with this step or of using a smaller radius.

a torus moulding. Between these two stone circles is the stone paved gutter only 7½ inches deep and normally 6 feet 10 inches wide, so that it gave practical service also as an ambulatory. Toward the outer extremities of the auditorium, moreover, this interval was gradually increased to 9 feet 4 inches, not only giving more room for the larger crowds passing the outermost sectors but also opening the horseshoe auditorium so that those seated in the outermost sectors might obtain a better view of the scene. This adjustment was effected by the use of three centres: the auditorium comprised about five-sixths of a semicircle laid out from the orchestra centre, and for the remainder were employed two subordinate centres with the radii lengthened by about 11½ feet. The auditorium thus formed comprises a little more than a semicircle 387 feet in diameter, divided by an ambulatory (diazoma) into two storeys, the lower

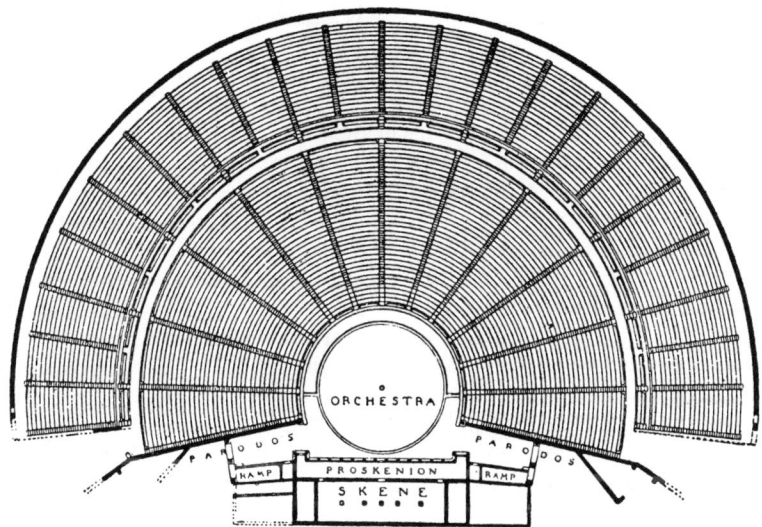

FIG. 90.—THE THEATRE AT EPIDAURUS. (Restored by Dörpfeld.)

containing thirty-four rows of seats and the upper twenty-one. Three of these rows, the lowest and topmost in the first storey and the lowest in the second, form the seats of honour (*proedria*) carved in finer limestone and provided with backs and, at each aisle, with arms. The ordinary rows have the faces hollowed so that one's heels could be drawn back as others passed by, and the rear portions of the seats are slightly depressed to give greater effective height for those above. The height of the ordinary seats is 13 inches in the lower storey (requiring cushions) and 17 inches in the upper, while the width is always 2 feet 5¼ inches (apart from the undercutting), so that the gradient is steeper in the upper storey. The interruption of the slope caused by the diazoma is compensated by a high podium, raising the seats of the upper storey to obtain a clear view of the orchestra. The auditorium is divided by radiating stairways (the use of one on axis being unusual) into wedge-shaped sectors (*cunei, kerkides*), of which there are twelve in the lower storey and theoretically twice as many in the upper, though probably the outermost on either side was omitted (or reduced) in

THE BEGINNING OF THE DECADENCE

order to leave direct approaches to the diazoma. As the stairways pass through the podium they are so steep as to be almost ladders, the risers sharply receding to leave narrow treads.

The scene building at Epidaurus is less satisfactory for study, in that only the foundations date from the time of Polycleitus. The fourth-century form would appear to have consisted of a hall 64 feet long and 20 feet deep (internally), with a narrow room at each end, perhaps protruding forward to form parascenia enframing the scene wall. It is to be noted that, while the length of the scene wall as thus restored is closely related to the orchestra diameter, the face of the scene wall is 45 feet 4 inches from the orchestra centre and so is not tangent to the basic circle (radius 40 feet 2 inches), far less to the orchestra curb (radius 33 feet 4 inches); the latter, however, might be tangent to a line connecting the parascenia (as at Athens), if these projected 12 feet. Such a scene building would probably have been only one storey in height; but its details are quite unknown.[1]

At Athens itself, a little later, beginning with a senatorial decree of 342 B.C., the theatre (Fig. 77) was completely rebuilt and was finished in the time of Lycurgus (338–326 B.C.). In order to utilise more fully the Acropolis slope, and once more to increase the gradient, the centre of the third orchestra was moved $20\frac{3}{4}$ feet north of the second centre, and its level was sunk to a depth of at least 8 inches below the previous surface.[2] From this centre was laid out a basic circle with a diameter of $72\frac{1}{3}$ feet ($67\frac{1}{2}$ Doric feet),[3] nine-tenths of the dimension at Epidaurus and smaller than its predecessors;[4] and this, as at Epidaurus, formed the face of the step below the bench of honour (*proedria*). Within this circle is an open gutter considerably deeper than at Epidaurus, varying from 2 feet 10 inches to 3 feet 7 inches, but much narrower, only 3 feet between the copings; the inner coping forms a circle 64 feet 4 inches (60 Doric feet) in diameter, eight-ninths of the basic circle, though unlike the curb at Epidaurus the portion of the circle toward the scene building was not actually constructed but was left to the imagination. The gutter was crossed by twelve stone bridges opposite the radiating aisles; and during performances the compartments between the bridges were covered in each case by three wooden panels (marked by letters), so that the full area of the orchestra could be employed. But since the wooden floor might sometimes be omitted, and would in any case have been unsuitable for the support of large crowds, the

---

[1] This restoration with wider parascenia in the original plan is Dörpfeld's conjecture, and seems probable, though it must be admitted, in view of the absence of any traces of earlier parascenium foundations, that possibly the scene building was originally a simple rectangle imitating that of fifth-century Athens. The proscenium, ramps, and parodos gateways are Hellenistic and will be described later; but there is no reason to regard the curb of the orchestra circle as another Hellenistic addition.

[2] The earlier orchestra levels are not preserved; but it seems incredible that they were, as has been suggested, as much as 16 inches below the present level. For the second orchestra was presumably high enough to conceal the breccia foundation of the late fifth-century scene building, which still rises 8 inches above the present (third) orchestra level.

[3] The exact dimension is not preserved, the face of the step having been entirely cut away in order to widen the ledge on which was set the Roman marble parapet $4\frac{1}{8}$ inches thick. But the very fact that this trimming was necessary suggests that the amount removed was almost as great as the thickness of the parapet for which it was done.

[4] See pp. 120, 209.

ambulatory was placed outside the basic circle, on the step for the bench of honour. In order to obtain the same logical relation to the amount of traffic that we found at Epidaurus, the centre of the auditorium was moved $3\frac{3}{4}$ feet farther out from the Acropolis (so that the orchestra is eccentric to this extent),[1] and because of the shifting centres the wide step varies from $6\frac{1}{2}$ feet ($6\frac{1}{8}$ Doric feet) on the axis to $10\frac{1}{3}$ feet ($9\frac{5}{8}$ Doric feet) at the sides, the new radius being $46\frac{1}{2}$ feet ($43\frac{3}{8}$ Doric feet). At the back of this wide step was placed the bench of honour, in the position now occupied by the series of later marble thrones.[2] The portions of the auditorium exceeding the semicircle, instead of curving, form straight prolongations and thus give a U-shaped plan, avoidance of the horseshoe improving both visibility and the circulation of spectators. But only in its lowest storey did the auditorium follow the complete plan; the width was limited by the available area to about 285 feet, the maximum radius being about 128 feet at the west and 157 feet at the east. Higher on the slope the maximum width was 364 feet, though the plan is very irregular, and in the upper portions the radius was increased to 280 feet, giving a tremendous depth. The lowest storey contained thirty-three rows of seats, divided by fourteen radiating stairways into thirteen sectors; the second and third storeys contained thirty-one and fourteen rows, respectively, and these upper storeys had, wherever the area permitted, twice as many sectors as were in the lowest storey. The second diazoma was of special width, being, in fact, the street encircling the Acropolis; and at the back of the third storey was the vertical scarp of the Acropolis itself;[3] the top seat was $100\frac{1}{2}$ feet above the orchestra. The seats themselves yield a rise of only $11\frac{3}{4}$ inches and a tread of 30 inches; but the gradient is slightly increased by the downward inclination of all the blocks, giving actually 13 inches in 30. Comfort was slightly increased by hollowing the face of the seat by $3\frac{1}{2}$ inches to permit the feet to be withdrawn as others passed by, and also by depressing the back half of each seat by $1\frac{1}{2}$ inches for the feet of the occupant above; but even so it must have been necessary to bring cushions. The total seating capacity was about 17,000.[4]

The vexed question of the scene building of the Lycurgan theatre at Athens is probably to be solved as follows. The orchestra centre having been removed to a point $73\frac{1}{4}$ feet north of the late fifth-century scene wall, it was necessary to fill the gap by a new structure. Retaining the late fifth-century stoa without

---

[1] A theory that the deep gutter was once preceded by a shallow one as at Epidaurus, and that the orchestra was once concentric with the present stone auditorium, of which the outermost sectors would have curved in horseshoe rather than the present U-shape, and that the scheme thus reconstituted dated from the Periclean age, is quite unfounded (see p. 208, note 3).

[2] It has been suggested that the bench of honour was originally set further forward than the marble thrones, in order to leave a wider space for circulation behind; not only is this unnecessary, however, but it is even contradicted by the careful jointing of the wide step and the use of particularly long stones which were intended to be visible, not to be concealed by the bench and a superposed pavement behind it.

[3] The rear rock wall (*katatome*) was finished before 319 B.C., when the choragic monument of Thrasyllus was erected against it.

[4] Apparently $1\frac{1}{4}$ Doric feet ($16\frac{1}{8}$ inches) were allowed for each person, according to vertical marks on the faces of the seats. But we find also another system of vertical marks 1 Doric foot ($12\frac{7}{8}$ inches) apart, which may have been used for allotting certain lengths of seating space to families, priestly groups, etc.

change,[1] and using its rear wall, the fifth-century scene wall, as a party wall, additional foundations of breccia were constructed to support a scene building 158 feet long and projecting $24\frac{1}{4}$ feet from the older scene wall; from this in turn two lateral pavilions (parascenia), $21\frac{3}{4}$ feet wide and $68\frac{3}{4}$ feet apart, projected $16\frac{3}{4}$ feet more.[2] Thus the new scene wall, 49 feet from the orchestra centre, is tangent neither to the basic circle (radius $36\frac{1}{6}$ feet) nor to the completed circumference of the orchestra coping (radius 32 feet 2 inches); but the latter is exactly tangent to the imaginary line connecting the $16\frac{3}{4}$-foot projections of the parascenia.[3] The wings beyond the parascenia enclosed either narrow stairways or movable scenery to decorate the scene wall, which otherwise appears to have been perfectly blank apart from the traditional three doorways.[4] But the parascenia had marble colonnaded hexastyle fronts of the Doric order, the columns returning for a short distance on either side, so that, while their great projection seemingly obstructed the parodoi, in reality the parascenia were so open that they could be freely traversed.[5] There is no reason to suppose

[1] The assumption that the stoa was first built in the time of Lycurgus was disproved by Fiechter; but his own conclusion that it was reconstructed by Lycurgus lacks foundation (see p. 209, note 4).

[2] This breccia foundation with the projecting parascenia, originally assigned to the Lycurgan theatre, has sometimes been attributed to the Periclean age or to the last quarter of the fifth century (as by Allen, Bethe, Bulle, Fensterbusch, Fiechter, Furtwängler, Haigh, and Puchstein), even at the cost (in Bulle's argument) of the total elimination of the well-attested Lycurgan theatre, with no construction between Pericles and the Hellenistic age. But these early dates are unsatisfactory. The structure is later than the great stoa behind, with which the courses do not coincide or bond, and it nullifies the use of the projecting platform and the upright timber sockets, which must date from the late fifth century.

[3] Of less significance is the fact that the auditorium centre is $45\frac{1}{4}$ feet from the scene wall (almost identical with the corresponding dimension at Epidaurus, 45 feet 4 inches), so that the radius describing the back of the ambulatory (and *proedria*), $46\frac{1}{2}$ feet, would nearly coincide with the middle of the scene wall.

[4] It was assumed by Dörpfeld that the parascenia were connected, even in the Lycurgan period, by a colonnade across the entire wall between them, backed so closely against the wall as to be almost engaged, forming a long portico too shallow to be designated as a proscenium. But no remains of such a colonnade have ever been discovered (as contrasted with the remains of the parascenia) and it is difficult to imagine how the "original proscenium" triglyph spacing of 4 feet $2\frac{1}{8}$ inches (as in the parascenia) could have been increased to 4 feet $4\frac{7}{8}$ inche :in the Hellenistic proscenium while using the same pieces (as Dörpfeld supposed). Furthermore, the foundations will not permit the restoration of both wall and colonnade.

[5] Various interpretations of these parascenia have been published, suggesting that they were open colonnades, or that they were solid lofty towers, or that they were low temple-like structures with solid walls on the fronts and outer returns but with two columns in-antis on the inner returns. Solid walls, however, would seem to obstruct the parodoi; and the fact that they were open is evidenced by the Doric architrave-frieze blocks employed at second hand in the Hellenistic parascenia. Bulle assumes, to be sure, that these come from an older choragic monument of some sort; but since they fit exactly the original parascenium foundations it seems clear that they stood here. The surviving pieces with the architrave soffits well preserved always show the outlines of column capitals on which they rested, with the intervening portion smoothed to be visible; and one of the corner blocks, in particular, according to the letters with which the joints were numbered when the architrave was taken down and reassembled, must have come from the northeast corner of the east parascenium, that is, an outer corner, while a second, which might otherwise fit here, must be assigned to the northeast corner of the west parascenium, showing that there were columns on the corners and fronts. No cornice blocks of the parascenia are preserved; it is therefore unknown whether the roofs were flat or sloping.

OTHER THEATRES

that any portion of this scene building was more than one storey in height; any temporary upper storey must have been of wood.

We have dwelt at some length on the Athenian theatre because of its special literary importance and also because of its complexity. Two other theatres of the late fourth century, apparently directly imitated from the Lycurgan theatre, are the first forms of those at Eretria and Oeniadae. At Eretria the old scene building (later left stranded on a high terrace) consisted merely of a simple structure 98½ feet long, including the terminal parascenia 13 feet wide and projecting 17 feet from the scene wall as at Athens; the construction, above a dado of polygonal masonry, was of mud-brick and timber.[1] The auditorium (later obliterated by deep excavation), being on level ground, seems to have consisted of wooden scaffolding, no remains having survived.[2] But at Oeniadae the auditorium, of the Athenian U-shape, is well preserved; the basic circle, 68 feet 11 inches in diameter, defines the step surrounding the orchestra, and within it, struck out from the same centre, is a gutter 2 feet wide, its inner edge limiting the effective diameter of the orchestra to 55 feet 4 inches; but undoubtedly, as at Athens, it was possible to utilise the entire area by covering the open gutter with movable wooden panels.[3] The auditorium was divided by twelve radiating stairways into eleven sectors; there were at least twenty-seven rows of seats, but no *proedria* and apparently no diazoma. The scene wall is 34 feet 5½ inches from the orchestra centre and so exactly tangent to the basic circle; at either end, 67¾ feet apart (1 foot less than at Athens), were parascenia only 10 feet wide and 10½ feet in projection.

At Megalopolis, considerably after the erection of the Thersilion and so probably toward the end of the fourth century, was built the largest theatre on the Greek mainland, with a diameter of 425 feet. The basic circle has been obliterated by later alterations; the centre of the auditorium is 42 feet 10 inches (40 Doric feet) from the lowest of the three steps added against the façade of the Thersilion; and this may have been the diameter of the original orchestra. Originally, therefore, a wide and shallow gutter may have been planned or even executed. But shortly afterward (though still within the fourth century) the benches of honour (*proedria*) and a new gutter were built by a certain Antiochus at a slightly lower level; this gutter is only 20 inches wide and 12 inches deep, and its inner edge, defining the new orchestra, has a diameter of 99 feet, the largest to be found in all Greek theatres. This enlargement may have been inspired by the use of this particular theatre for armed festivals of Arcadian youths and for the dance-choruses of the entire Arcadian population, men and women, boys and girls. This function, moreover, and the desire to avoid excessive depth, may have reconciled the Arcadians to the resulting amputation of the orchestra circle by the scene building, to the extent of 6 feet

[1] Efforts to date this first form at Eretria too early, in the fifth century, are due to the mistaken assumption that the stone parascenia at Athens are earlier than Lycurgus. It was toward and just after 300 B.C. that the dramatic performances at Eretria assumed special importance and the theatre was probably not much older.

[2] Except, perhaps, the blocks of the outer rim of the orchestra gutter, used later at second hand.

[3] There are at present rough stone slabs laid across the gutter; but these date from a later time after the reduction of the diameter and the raising of the level of the orchestra (see p. 312).

8 inches. It was likewise here for the first time that the scene wall assumed a permanent architectural form, an unvaried colonnade without parascenia; for the portico of the Thersilion originally served also as the back scene of the theatre. The auditorium, unlike the examples hitherto considered, adheres to the circle of the orchestra throughout its extent of about 192 degrees. It is divided by ten aisles into nine sectors, and twice in its total height is subdivided by a horizontal diazoma. There seem to have been about fifty-nine rows of seats, with a capacity of about 21,000 spectators.[1]

The earliest of the extant theatres of Asia Minor, that at Magnesia, appears to have been erected under mainland influence, if we may judge from the plan of the scene building, a series of five rooms of which the endmost project very slightly as parascenia. The auditorium, though rebuilt later in marble, seems originally to have had the same plan, an interesting scheme with three centres, five-sixths of a semicircle being described from the main centre while from secondary centres on the circumference of the basic circle are described the outer sectors of the open horseshoe. The general scheme is obviously derived from Epidaurus, together with the wide shallow gutter; and the fact that the orchestra centre is located so far from the scene wall suggests that it antedates the Hellenistic age.

The stadium or racecourse was an elongated space 600 to 700 feet long, the site for which, like that of the theatre, was selected close to the side of a hill or between two hills, so that, even at the worst, it would be necessary to build up an embankment only on one side. At Athens and at Messene it was placed in a narrow valley, and so could be symmetrical on both sides; but at Delphi, where it was erected on the slope of a hill, the seats on the lower side are only half as numerous as on the upper, while at Priene there are no seats whatever on the lower side. The oldest stadium in Greece, at Olympia (Fig. 44 at ST), originally open towards the precinct with early embankments on three sides, was moved north and east in the fourth century, giving room for an embankment also on the west end, with a length of 631 feet on the running track and of 1090 feet over all.[2] The Panathenaic stadium at Athens (Plate LXII), 850 feet long, was constructed of poros stone by the legislator Lycurgus, who also erected the Athenian theatre in stone at about 340 B.C.; it was only long afterwards, at about A.D. 143, that the stadium was reconstructed in Pentelic marble by Herodes Atticus.[3] The usual stadium plan was the U-shape with one round end, as at Athens and Delphi; but frequently they were square at both ends, as at Olympia, Epidaurus, Miletus, and Priene. In many cases, furthermore, the long sides were slightly bowed outward in order that spectators might have a better view. Of special interest are those examples in which the starting and finish lines are both preserved, yielding the exact length of the course, which, being by definition 600 Greek feet, should have been about $642\frac{3}{4}$ feet if constructed on the Doric system, about $578\frac{3}{4}$ feet if on the Ionic. Actually, however,

[1] Such calculations as that of Durm, that 44,000 spectators could be seated at Megalopolis, are of course fantastic.

[2] The history of the stadium at Olympia is now known in greater detail as a result of the German excavations since 1937; for the vaulted tunnel see p. 319.

[3] Plate LXII shows this stadium of Herodes Atticus as rebuilt for the Olympic Games of 1896.

these stadium lengths are 630 feet 9 inches at Olympia, 627 feet 11 inches at Miletus, 606 feet 10 inches at Athens, 594 feet 10 inches at Epidaurus, and 582 feet 6 inches at Delphi. Even at Olympia the true length of 600 Doric feet is not attained; while at Delphi, strangely, the length approximates 600 Ionic feet. It is hardly reasonable to assume that these stadia were erected with reference to so many local varieties of foot units; the true reason still escapes us.

For horse and chariot racing a longer course was provided, known as the hippodrome; but of such buildings of the Greek periods only the slightest traces exist, as at Delos.

The gymnasium of this period was still informal in plan; the most notable example is that at Delphi (Plate II) well adapted to the natural site, with an upper terrace containing a long Doric portico protecting a covered racecourse 525 feet long (barely shorter than that of the stadium), with a parallel racecourse in the open air beside it. On a lower terrace was the palaestra built round a court 45½ feet square, followed by a pentagonal court measuring 85 feet on a side, containing baths, both shower (a row of eleven bronze spouts in the northeast retaining wall) and plunge (a circular basin 33 feet in diameter and 6 feet deep).

Another secular appurtenance of the great international sanctuary was the hotel or *katagogion*, of which the pattern seems to have been furnished by that described

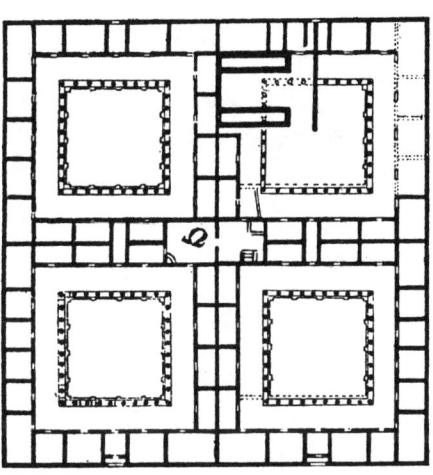

Fig. 91.—The Hotel (Katagogion) at Epidaurus.

by Thucydides as having been erected by the Thebans at Plataea after their destruction of that city in 427 B.C., 200 Greek feet (i.e., 214¼ feet) square with rooms ranged in two storeys round a court. At Epidaurus the hotel (Fig. 91) is slightly larger, 250 feet square, with four square peristyle courts each with ten Doric columns on a side. Each court has twenty rooms of different sizes on each storey, one hundred and sixty rooms in all; and each court has a separate entrance and communicating corridors. The Leonidaeum at Olympia (Fig. 44 at L), built shortly after 338 B.C. by a Naxian named Leonidas, was intended primarily for distinguished visitors and has larger and more varied rooms, especially on the west side which caused it to assume an oblong shape, about 242 by 262 feet, even though the single inner court was exactly square. The exterior was surrounded by Ionic columns, thirty-four on each front and thirty-seven on each side, carrying the friezeless Asiatic entablature with dentils which had been traditional also in the Aegean islands. The inner court had twelve Doric columns on each side. The terraces formed by the roofs of the peristyles formed, in all these instances, the method of communicating with the rooms in the upper storeys.

THE BEGINNING OF THE DECADENCE

In all the earlier classical periods, in contrast to the feeling in prehistoric times, the dwelling houses of the Greeks, even those of the wealthy, seem to have been unpretentious fabrics. Viewed from without, they were of a simple nature, being designed only to shut out "the noise and rattle of the town," the chambers facing inwards towards courtyards, and, in the more important houses, on peristyles. It must be remembered that the Greeks of every period spent their time mostly in the open air and in their places of public assembly, and that their climate failed to develop the home as a place of social intercourse. The writings of the various authors suggest that the ordinary Greek house was simply a residence to which the master of the house returned from his vocation in the city to take his meals and sleep, and that during the daytime it was left in the care of the chief matron of the establishment. It was not until the late fifth and the fourth century that houses began to receive the attention commensurate with that hitherto bestowed on other types of buildings. The house

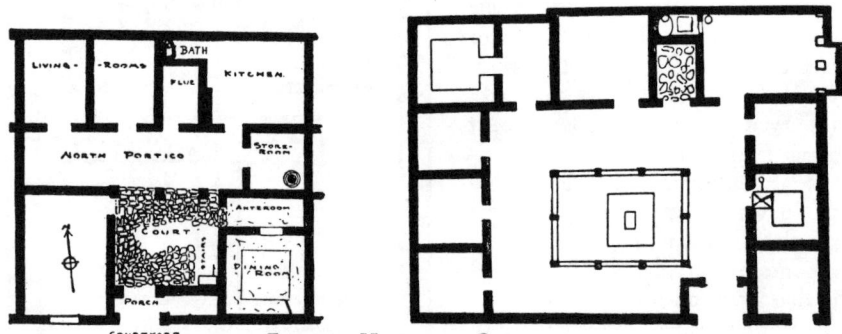

FIG. 92.—HOUSES AT OLYNTHUS.

seems generally to have been of one storey, with walls of mud-brick on a rubble stone foundation; windows were placed very high, if they were in a ground storey, and the door opened on a comparatively narrow street. The examples at Olynthus (Fig. 92), of which more than a hundred are known so that they form the best illustrations of the house type of the late fifth and fourth centuries, are usually almost square, about $56\frac{2}{3}$ by 56 feet as determined by the city plan, though irregularities sometimes resulted through mutual agreement between neighbours. The houses always face south toward the sun, though naturally, when they are built on the south side of the street, the entrances in such cases are at the north or back. Thus there are two types of plans: those with the entrance at the south, with or without a shallow vestibule, giving direct access to a paved court; and those with the entrance at the north, giving indirect access to the court through some room or passage. The court, occupying from a tenth to a fifth of the whole area, is directly against or close to the south wall, and is paved with cobble-stones; sometimes there are simple wooden posts with stone capitals on one, two, or three sides. In any case a sheltered portico of some depth (the pastas) is contrived on the north side of the court, and behind this, facing south, is the main room of the house, the oecus, descended from the old megaron; and, like its ancestor, it very often has a central hearth. Another important room was the andron or dining-room, usually located toward the street in order to obtain better light, so that it was beside the front court in the houses in the south half of each block, but among the back rooms in those in the north half. It usually had a raised border of cement and a sunken central rectangle covered either with cement or with pebble mosaic in elaborate patterns. The same general scheme, though with greater freedom, is displayed in the isolated villas, such as the "House of the Comedian" (Fig. 92, at right) and the "Villa of Good Fortune." In both of these the court has a peristyle of simple piers on all four sides (ten piers in the former, eight in the latter), with deep porticoes all round, so that they are actually forerunners of the late Hellenistic peristyle house.

In the numerous commemorative or votive monuments found both within and outside the sanctuaries we see a parallel development in the employment of architectural forms. In the fifth century a simple base or pedestal sufficed for a statue or tripod; in the fourth century the base often became a complicated design, Long straight or semicircular pedestals might now be placed within exedrae, likewise rectangular or semicircular, such as the enclosure containing the Daochus group at Delphi, or the semicircular niche of the Argive kings in the same sanctuary, with an internal diameter of 45 feet, and with twenty statues of the mythical kings and queens of Argos, the ancestors of Heracles, all located in the left-hand half of the semicircle so that all would be seen immediately by a visitor entering the precinct, and with their genealogical inscriptions lettered in retrograde.[1] Or the façade might even assume the form of an open colonnade, as in Alexander's lion hunt dedicated by Craterus at Delphi (compare the Spartan offering for Aegospotami of the end of the preceding century). In the case of tripods, the contrast may be illustrated by means of the Plataean tripod of 479 B.C. at Delphi, resting merely on a circular pedestal of three steps, and its counterpart of nearly a century later, the Acanthus Column at Delphi (Fig. 93),[2] dating from the very beginning of the fourth century.[3] The lower part of the shaft rises from a calyx of three large ribbed leaves, and at the base of each of the five drums the upward movement of the shaft is interrupted by a girdle of acanthus leaves; from the upper portion of the shaft spring three other acanthus leaves to support the legs of a bronze tripod. The great projection of these leaves, and the vigour shown in their carving, testify that as a decorative feature the foliage of this plant must have been intensively and rapidly developed since its adoption a few years previously.

[1] Compare the perspective effect in the niche of Aegospotami at Delphi, p. 212.

[2] This nameless monument, bearing no inscription and not described by Pausanias, is in consequence ascribed to various dedicating states and occasions but without any unanimity. While exact copies of late date exist at Corinth (*Hesperia*, X, 1941) and in Sta. Prassede at Rome, it is perhaps significant that the idea of the vegetable column with "acanthus" leaves encircling the bottom of the shaft was particularly prevalent in Hellenistic and Roman times in North Africa, as in the column of Protomedes at Cyrene (two tiers of silphium leaves) and the peristyle of the "Hellenistic house" at Tolmeta (for knowledge of these more or less inaccessible examples I am indebted to Major J. B. Ward Perkins), as well as in later examples to be noted hereafter (see p. 276, note 3). In this connection it is of interest to recall the theory of Keramopoullos that the Delphian column was a silphium column dedicated by Cyrene (*Journal Intern. d'Archéol. Numism.*, 1907).

[3] The Acanthus Column was apparently overthrown in the earthquake of 373 B.C.; but its style is hardly earlier than 400 B.C.

Between the tripod legs are poised three marble dancing maidens or Caryatids, apparently as votaries of Artemis at Caryae in Laconia, grouped round the central support for the bronze tripod kettle. The height of the column alone was 29 feet; that of the whole, including the tripod, must have been about 40 feet (apart from the low pedestal).

The favourite type of sepulchral monument in Attica at this time was the vertical slab known as the stele. From the comparatively simple types of the sixth and fifth centuries resulted, in the fourth century, the luxuriant and charming series which was brought to a sudden end by the sumptuary laws of Demetrius of Phalerum in 315 B.C., requiring that henceforth all grave monuments must be mere colonettes or tables. The largest collection of stelae has been preserved in the cemetery of the Outer Cerameicus, lining the roads leading out of the Dipylon Gate and the Sacred Gate, that is, the road to the Academy and the Sacred Way to Eleusis; but other series lined the various roads toward the other suburban towns. Some of these stelae are still of the narrow type used in the archaic period (Fig. 46), but with much more elaborate acroteria in which the acanthus plays a great part; below the floral acroterion, at the upper end of the shaft, generally appear two rosettes in relief and the name of the deceased. Sometimes the face of the shaft contains a small relief panel, or it may be carved in relief with the representation of a sepulchral vase; or the whole monument may take the form of a marble vase, either the one-handled lecythus or the two-handled loutrophorus, carved with ornament and reliefs. Usually, however, the vases were reserved for accessory decoration of family plots. The most characteristic stelae were lower and of a much broader type, giving more scope for relief sculpture. The scenes represented in these sepulchral reliefs are generally of a domestic character, as, for instance, the husband bidding adieu to his wife who is called away to another world. Such a type had already appeared in the Periclean period; but now it was embellished by an enframement consisting of antae or even columns, supporting a simple entablature and generally crowned by a pediment; more rarely was represented the flank of a building, with tiles and antefixes, or perhaps a heraldic composition with rampant goats or mourning Sirens. One of the earliest examples of the fourth century is the beautiful and well-known stele of Hegeso, in very shallow relief. During the course of the fourth century the depth of the relief sculpture tended gradually to increase, until it reached such a point that, instead of carving the whole stele as a single slab, it was made for convenience in five parts, the bottom, the two lateral antae, the crowning feature, and the recessed sculptured panel. More elaborate memorials were sometimes in the form of shallow niches, with the usual architectural enframement but containing a statue in the round; and the ceiling of the niche might even be painted with coffers in perspective. Rarely the monument assumes a symbolic character as in that of Dionysius, a lofty shaft supporting a marble bull.

FIG. 93.—
THE ACANTHUS
COLUMN AT
DELPHI.
(Restored by
Homolle.)

Special interest attaches also to the forms of the burial plots themselves, with their terrace walls of polygonal or ashlar masonry or of sun-dried brick with tile copings, and to the varied grouping of the monuments on these terraces, raised high above the level of the street, and frequently embellished with marble funerary vases or Sirens, and with Molossian hounds or lions as symbolic guardians. Of exceptional interest, because of its adaptation to a corner location, is one of these family burial plots on the Sacred Way, that of Dexileos (Fig. 94), which is unusual also in representing a scene of battle, a known event which gives the date as 394 B.C.

Fig. 94.—Grave Monument of Dexileos at Athens.
(Restored by Kinch.)

An exceptional form, obviously an Asiatic importation, was the temple form of tomb erected by Harpalus, the defaulting treasurer of Alexander the Great, as a memorial for the courtesan Pythionice on the Sacred Way between Athens and Eleusis, adorned with Ionic columns of large size. We may recall in this connection the statement of Pausanias that the Sicyonians erected tomb monuments of unusual form with a stone basement supporting columns and above these "something very like the pediments of temples."

For the evolution of this latter type we may turn to Asia Minor, where the same tendency that induced the erection of colossal temples during the "Ionic renaissance" was responsible for a love of display in sepulchral monuments, contrasting even with the most ostentatious of the Greek mainland. It is necessary, moreover, to recede to a slightly earlier period, since the beginnings of this development were manifested, particularly in Lycia, during the fifth century. Thus at Trysa (Gjölbaschi) a walled enclosure formed a court of about 68 by 78 feet, within which, somewhat diagonally, stands a typical Lycian sarcophagus tomb with a gabled top. The chief interest lies, not in the tomb, but in the surrounding wall, carved with superposed tiers of relief.

This was followed by the so-called Nereid Monument at Xanthus (Fig. 95), apparently erected by a local prince at about 410-400 B.C.[1] The lower portion

FIG. 95.—THE NEREID MONUMENT AT XANTHUS. (Restored by Niemann.)

was a lofty podium or basement, decorated with bands or friezes of sculpture; and the structure carried on the podium was a reproduction of a small Ionic tetrastyle peripteral temple, there being six columns on the flanks, with the figures of Nereids between the columns (apparently symbolising the prince's fleet), and with an Asiatic friezeless entablature with dentils. Though the columns have Asiatic Ionic bases (without plinths), the capitals with their inter-

[1] Dates as early as the middle of the fifth century or as late as the end of the fourth have been suggested for this monument; but the sculptural style and the architectural connections would seem to limit it to the decade 410-400 B.C.

mediate fillets in the volutes are obviously inspired by the Erechtheum (though omitting the anthemion necking on account of the small scale), so that they must be contemporary or slightly later; on the other hand, the peculiar construction of the marble coffered ceiling with overlapping false beams displays an intimate knowledge of the concealed construction in the Propylaea of the Athenian Acropolis such as could have been possessed only by workmen who had been employed on that structure before 432 B.C. We seem to have here a definite instance of craftsmen journeying from Attica to Asia, perhaps native Lycians who had taken advantage of the opportunities available in Periclean Athens until work there was temporarily stopped because of the Syracusan disaster of 413 B.C. Thoroughly Asiatic, however, is the door enframement with a frieze of superposed egg-and-dart above, terminating against consoles with volutes only at the lower ends; Asiatic, too, is the profusion of frieze sculpture, there being two at the bottom and top of the podium, and also a third forming a sculptured architrave like that at Assos,[1] and a fourth at the top of the cella wall. The pediments also were sculptured with reliefs, and there were marble acroteria and guardian lions as well as the Nereids. Even painting was not lacking; while some of the coffer vaults were decorated with radiating palmettes, others were painted with human heads.

During the fourth century a new element was added: above the Greek temple was placed an Egyptian pyramid. This additional step seems to have been taken first in the "Lion Tomb" at Cnidus, which has been associated, though without cogent reasons, with the Athenian naval victory off Cnidus in 394 B.C.; it may well be somewhat later. The architecture, exceptional for the Ionic coast, was Doric, a pseudo-peripteral colonnade attached to the wall supporting the pyramid, which in turn was crowned by a lofty pedestal with a reclining lion,[2] the whole being about 62 feet high. The interior is a tholos $17\frac{1}{4}$ feet in diameter and $39\frac{1}{2}$ feet high (shaped surprisingly like a modern projectile), with corbelled vaulting as at Mycenae, and with twelve radiating cells at the floor level. A slightly smaller example, again with four engaged Doric columns on each side, and a pyramid supporting a seated lion, existed at Amphipolis in Macedonia; and another lion monument stood on the battlefield of Chaeronea.[3]

The most important of these sepulchral monuments was the Mausoleum at Halicarnassus, begun by King Mausolus just before his death in 353 B.C., and continued by Queen Artemisia in memory of her husband and brother, being

---

[1] The remains of the Nereid Monument are for the most part in the British Museum; but the structure has never been satisfactorily restored and there is considerable confusion about the disposition of the friezes. A recent tendency (illustrated by Niemann, Fig. 95) to place the two podium friezes directly above one another, either with the larger below and the smaller above or *vice versa*, is shown to be erroneous by the bonding of the masonry; they must be separated, the larger frieze appearing at the bottom of the podium and the smaller at the top, and the podium itself should be higher than in the restoration. Another error is shown in a recent model in the British Museum, where an ordinary Ionic architrave with three fascias is substituted for the third frieze, of which the tooling clearly shows that it rested directly on the column capitals. Finally, in analysing the design, one should employ the Ionic foot unit of $11\frac{9}{16}$ inches rather than the Doric foot ($12\frac{7}{8}$ inches, Niemann) or the "Samian foot" ($13\frac{3}{4}$ inches, Krischen).

[2] The lion is now in the British Museum.

[3] The lion of Amphipolis, like that of Chaeronea, has now been restored in place but on a much smaller pedestal.

finally completed by their brother and sister Idrieus and Ada, who began to reign in 350 B.C. According to ancient writers, the monument ranked among the seven wonders of the world, and its name became a household word, owing to the novelty of its design and the eminence of the artists who were called in to adorn it with sculpture; their names, as given by Pliny, were Bryaxis, Leochares, Timotheus, and Scopas.[1] These sculptors were apparently brought over from the Greek mainland; we have met Timotheus at Epidaurus, Scopas at Tegea, and Leochares in the Philippeum at Olympia, while an important base signed by Bryaxis was found at Athens. The architects were Pythius, who also sculptured the marble quadriga on the top (and, as we have seen, designed the temple at Priene), and Satyrus; they composed a book about their masterpiece, utilised by Vitruvius, but subsequently lost. Instead, we have a brief description by Vitruvius and a more detailed one by Pliny; but unfortunately Pliny's description is so vague, while the architectural remains are comparatively so few, that the problem is yet far from being solved. Pliny tells us, however, that the perimeter was 440 Ionic (or Roman) feet (424 feet 5 inches),[2] and that the total height of the structure was 140 Ionic feet (135 feet), divided into four parts, the high basement, the pteron or peristyle of thirty-six columns with a height of 25 cubits or 37½ Ionic feet (36 feet 2 inches), the pyramid equal in height to the [element just] below and including twenty-four steps, and finally the crowning quadriga (Plate LXIII).[3]

The lower portion of the structure consisted of the lofty basement or podium, set in the foundation cutting measuring 108 by 127 feet (perimeter 470 feet) and roughly corresponding, if we allow for the spread of the foundations, to the 440 Ionic feet mentioned by Pliny. Above this was the second element, the peristyle of thirty-six columns, as Pliny gives the number, necessarily including the angle supports as is evidenced by the angle capital discovered. With regard to the arrangement of these columns there are two theories:[4] one would place them in a single peristyle large enough to cover the entire area of the foundation cutting, while the other, with less probability, contracts the plan of the peristyle by using dipteral colonnades. The lower diameter of the columns is 3¾ Ionic feet (3 feet 7½ inches), and the axial spacing must have been 10½ Ionic feet

---

[1] The substitution of the name of Praxiteles for that of Scopas, by Vitruvius, is to be rejected on account of the known fact, attested by the Tegean votive slab in the British Museum, that Scopas worked at Halicarnassus at this very time.

[2] This figure is sometimes written as CCCCXL and once as CCCCXI, the latter being an obvious clerical error. We employ the foot of 294 mm. or 11·575 inches as used by the same architect at Priene (p. 222, note 2).

[3] The site was excavated in 1856 by Sir Charles Newton, and the remains discovered were deposited in the British Museum, supplementing thirteen slabs of the sculptured Amazon frieze which had been removed ten years earlier, through the influence of a British ambassador, from the walls of Budrum Castle in which they had been immured four centuries previously by the Knights of St. John. But long previous to their discovery the conjectural restoration of the monument had been a favourite problem with many architects; and some of these restorations, including that of Cockerell, are now exhibited in the British Museum. More evidence might be obtained by a complete examination of Budrum Castle; but the brief studies by Newton in 1856, by the Germans in 1904 and also a few weeks before the armistice in 1918, and by the Italians in 1919, have been inconclusive.

[4] We may disregard the complicated cruciform plan proposed by Oldfield and accepted by Six.

(10 feet $1\frac{1}{2}$ inches) or $2\frac{4}{5}$ lower diameters.[1] With dipteral colonnades the inner row must have had eight columns fewer than the outer, giving fourteen and twenty-two respectively; and an outer row of twenty-two columns must have had five by six intervals, or four by seven, with axial dimensions of $52\frac{1}{2} \times 63$ Ionic feet or $42 \times 73\frac{1}{2}$ Ionic feet, in either case insufficient to explain the deep foundation cutting 108×127 feet, which would hardly have been excavated merely to receive an encircling platform.[2] With a single colonnade of thirty-six columns there must have been nine by nine intervals, or eight by ten, or seven by eleven, requiring axial rectangles of $94\frac{1}{2} \times 94\frac{1}{2}$, 84×105, or $73\frac{1}{2} \times 115\frac{1}{2}$ Ionic feet. But the oblong shape of the foundation cutting and the words of Pliny ("brevius a frontibus") show that it cannot have been a square;[3] and on the other hand the scheme with seven by eleven intervals would bring the columns right up to the edges of the foundation cutting on both fronts but would leave wide margins on either flank. Only the rectangle of eight by ten intervals could fit the cutting,[4] the axial rectangle of 81 feet $\frac{1}{2}$ inch by 101 feet $3\frac{1}{2}$ inches then leaving uniform margins of 13 or $13\frac{1}{2}$ feet on all sides, and agreeing with the proportions of 4 : 5 required by a corner step block of the pyramid above (with treads of $1\frac{1}{2}$ and $1\frac{7}{8}$ Ionic feet on flank and front respectively). Thus we obtain a peristyle of nine by eleven columns, always with a column at the centre.

The height of the order of the peristyle could be made to agree with Pliny's figure of $37\frac{1}{2}$ Ionic feet (10 lower diameters) if we allowed $31\frac{1}{2} + 6 = 37\frac{1}{2}$ Ionic feet for column and entablature (omitting the sculptured frieze 3 Ionic feet in height), or $28\frac{1}{2} + 9 = 37\frac{1}{2}$ Ionic feet including the frieze. But it seems incredible that the column should have been only $28\frac{1}{2}$ Ionic feet ($7\frac{3}{5}$ lower diameters) or even $31\frac{1}{2}$ Ionic feet ($8\frac{2}{5}$ diameters); for, as we have seen, other columns of this period vary from $8\frac{4}{5}$ diameters (Priene and Sardis) to $9\frac{3}{4}$ diameters (Didyma). It seems preferable to adopt $8\frac{4}{5}$ diameters as in the other work by the same architect, giving exactly 33 Ionic feet (31 feet 10 inches). As for the entablature, the restoration depends on the inclusion or omission of the Amazon frieze.[5] But the abundance of sculptured friezes, of which remains of three are preserved (the Amazon, Centaur, and charioteer friezes), suggest that we should dispose of one by inserting it in the entablature. For the alternatives would require the use of one on the podium, the second in the entablature, and the third on the cella wall, or, on the other hand, the combination of two on the podium (as in the Nereid Monument) and the third on the cella wall. As for the use of two friezes on the podium, the fact that the immediate superposition of two friezes is now known to be impossible in the Nereid Monument removes all precedent

1 The sima blocks are $1\frac{3}{4}$ Ionic feet in length, the lion head spouts occurring at every second or third joint ($3\frac{1}{2}$ or $5\frac{1}{4}$ Ionic feet), in either case with six sima blocks requiring $10\frac{1}{2}$ Ionic feet.

2 Of the restorations published since the excavations, Cockerell, Goodchild, Stevenson, and Krüger all wrongly adopt the small dipteral plan.

3 Yet Bernier restored it as square with ten by ten columns as late as 1878.

4 Eight by ten intervals, but with varying dimensions for the axial spacing, were employed by Pullan, Fergusson, Petersen, Arnold, Adler, Dinsmoor, Bühlmann, Lethaby, Krischen, and the recent British Museum model.

5 The Amazon frieze was unanimously inserted in all restorations of the entablature published before 1908, and since that time has been omitted with equal unanimity; both alternatives are shown in reconstructions in the British Museum, that which I prefer being shown in Plate LV.

for such an arrangement in the Mausoleum, while the nearly identical dimensions of the friezes of the Mausoleum would be opposed to the attribution of one to the top and another to the bottom of the podium, as in the Nereid Monument. On the other hand, the attribution of the Amazon frieze to the entablature seems to be vindicated by contrasting the details with those employed by the same architect in the friezeless entablature at Priene.[1] The presence of the frieze in the entablature of the Mausoleum is so un-Asiatic that it must be due to external influence such as the collaboration of the four above-mentioned sculptors brought from the Greek mainland; also the architect Satyrus came from Paros (like Scopas) and had mainland affiliations (as at Delphi).[2] In consequence, the height of the entablature should be 9 Ionic feet (8 feet 8 inches), equivalent to $2\frac{2}{5}$ diameters or $\frac{3}{11}$ of the column height. And the total height of the order may be regarded as $33 + 9 = 42$ Ionic feet (40 feet 6 inches),[3] that is $11\frac{1}{5}$ diameters or exactly 4 axial spacings; with this height of 28 cubits we may interpret Pliny's 25 cubits either as a rough approximation or, as in the case of the number of columns at Ephesus, a clerical error.[4]

The third element of the design is the pyramid of twenty-four steps, crowned by the quadriga; but here again there are two types of solutions, some (especially those with the contracted peristyle) representing a narrow and lofty pyramid, while others use a lower pyramid with a more gradual slope in accordance with the steps found in the excavations, and are therefore obliged to supplement it with an attic above the peristyle and a pedestal below the quadriga; some compromise by using the narrow type of pyramid above the wider peristyle plan, by making it rise from an attic carried by the cella walls rather than by the columns; others again utilise the steps with broad treads (which undoubtedly belong to the roof) for the lower degrees of the pyramid, and raise the upper portion into the form of a meta according to Pliny's description by employing other steep steps which were found on the site—but with a defect in the abrupt change between the two slopes.[5] More recent investigation of the surviving blocks suggests a compromise in the form of the pyramid, starting with the more gradual slopes (2 : 3 on the flanks, 8 : 15 on the fronts), but gradually increasing these slopes by narrowing the treads toward the top so as to form concave curves.[6] The twenty-four steps occupied a height of 24 Ionic feet, and

---

[1] The egg-and-dart crowning the architrave is 28 per cent of the total height of the three fascias below at Priene (30 per cent at Ephesus), and thus adequately supports the dentil course. But in the Mausoleum the crowning egg-and-dart is only 17 per cent of the three fascias below, and seems too weak for this purpose. We obtain satisfactory proportions only by combining the egg-and-dart with the footing moulding of the Amazon frieze, the combined height being exactly 30 per cent of the three fascias below; and the resulting compound profile, with the ovolo surmounted by cyma reversa and fillet, is comparable to the Athenian architrave crowns and anta capitals (as in the Nike temple and Erechtheum), and also to the combination of mouldings employed later at Magnesia where the frieze likewise appeared.

[2] Compare the Athenian influence at Halicarnassus at this time as evidenced in the temple of Ares, p. 223; note also the Athenian embassy in 355 B.C. (Demosthenes, XXIV, 133.)

[3] The height of the order as restored in the British Museum is only 37 feet 3 inches, the column being 3 feet 3 inches lower than the dimension suggested above.

[4] I.e., either Pliny or one of his mediaeval copyists might have omitted the III from XXVIII (cf. note 2, p. 258.)

[5] This is the case, for instance, in Stevenson's restoration in the British Museum.

[6] This scheme was embodied in a small model exhibited in the British Museum since 1927.

so, to be equal to the height of the peristyle below, must have been supplemented by an attic of about $7\frac{1}{2}$ Ionic feet at the bottom of the pyramid and a pedestal of $10\frac{1}{2}$ Ionic feet at the apex. The chariot group on this pedestal was about 14 Ionic feet in height, with four horses and a chariot probably supporting statues of Mausolus and Artemisia.[1] Panthers accompanied the chariot group on a lower plinth at either side. By subtraction, there now remain 42 Ionic feet for the basement; and the division of the total height is seen to fall into four elements of $42 + 42 + 42 + 14 = 140$ Ionic feet (135 feet) in the proportion of 3 : 3 : 3 : 1. We see, furthermore, that the basement was not the excessively lofty and bald mass of masonry shown in most restorations; it was presumably entered only by one or two small doorways at the front,[2] and by a subterranean opening for sepulchral purposes at the rear.[3]

Among the remaining uncertainties is that of supporting adequately the pyramid, which Martial describes as "hanging in open air," while Pliny gives dimensions of 63 feet on the flanks and less on the fronts, apparently intended to apply to a cella within the peristyle, distant either one or two intercolumniations behind the peristyle, the latter fitting Pliny's dimensions.[4] And into the restoration have to be worked, furthermore, not only the two other sculptured friezes, but also the numerous decorative lions, and a host of statues, sculptured groups, and equestrian figures. Possibly one of the sculptured friezes, that of the Centaurs, was imbedded in the podium like the two friezes in the Nereid Monument; that of the Charioteers seems to have been better protected and may have been on the cella wall.[5] The lions are sometimes placed above the peristyle, before the attic; but here they would seem to interfere with the stability of the pyramid, and it seems preferable to locate them on pedestals round the basement. Two colossal sculptured groups, representing a hunt and a sacrifice, may have been applied against the flanks of the podium. And the numerous statues may have stood on pedestals between the columns. The vaults of the ceiling coffers were also decorated with relief sculpture.

Though coming more within the range of sculpture than of architecture, some of the marble sarcophagi found at Sidon are magnificent examples of the decorative sculpture of the fourth century, and in consequence of their good state of preservation show the extent to which polychromy was employed to enrich the elaborately carved mouldings. One of these, of the middle of the

---

[1] Even if the portrait statue of Mausolus and the much mutilated female figure which passes as Artemisia, now exhibited in the British Museum, may seem too well preserved to have been exposed to the weather at the top of this monument, as is argued by some—though they are reported to have been found lying with the fragments of the chariot group—it is apparent that equivalent statues must be restored to fill the otherwise empty chariot (though some prefer to assume that it was empty).

[2] We cannot accept the huge pointed barrel vault piercing the entire structure as shown in a model in the British Museum. It can be proved that the stones assigned to the pointed arch (imitated from Lycian tombs with boat-keel tops) come in reality from different and much later structures, pedestals and exedrae.

[3] The rock-cut stairway descending to the rear entrance, and the great block of stone which sealed it, were found in position by Newton.

[4] I.e. $(10 \times 10\frac{1}{2}) - (4 \times 10\frac{1}{2}) = 63$ Ionic feet, and $(8 \times 10\frac{1}{2}) - (4 \times 10\frac{1}{2}) = 42$ Ionic feet, the axial measurements of the cella.

[5] I see no reason for assuming that the Charioteer frieze was interrupted at frequent intervals by pilaster strips, as has sometimes been suggested.

fourth century, is the so-called "Sarcophagus of the mourning women," of special importance because it reproduces a complete Ionic mausoleum of the type of the "Nereid monument," but with piers rather than columns at the corners (Plate LXIII). Statues of mourning women instead of Nereids fill the intercolumniations; and the entablature omits the frieze in the Asiatic manner. Later still is the so-called "Alexander sarcophagus," in which the architecture is dominated by the sculptured historical reliefs depicting Alexander the Great

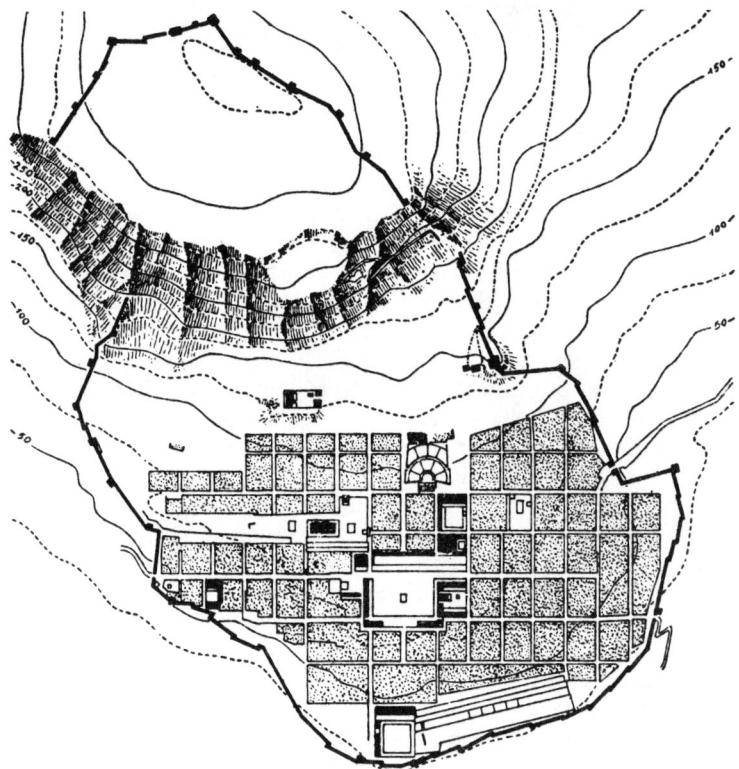

FIG. 96.—CITY PLAN OF PRIENE. (Gerkan.)

in battle with the Persians or engaged in that famous lion hunt during which his life was saved by Craterus. Even here, however, we must stress the beauty of the elaborately carved mouldings, in such a perfect state of preservation as to show the extent to which they were enriched by polychromy.[1]

Turning to the planning of cities, it is apparent that the Hippodamian scheme developed in the fifth century continued to prevail in the fourth, with all the streets crossing each other at right angles. One of the most notable, though smaller, examples of this is Priene (Fig. 96), erected on a steep slope, yet laid out on a regular chessboard plan, with its six main streets running east-and-west, parallel to the slope of the acropolis and so approximately level, but crossed at

[1] See also p. 145, note 1.

right angles by fifteen sloping or stepped streets running north-and-south. The whole is built on terraces on the south slope of the acropolis; the latter is so lofty that it was useless as a site for buildings, and so was left at one side but enclosed within the fortifications. Though the streets form a perfect chessboard, the walls surrounding the whole follow a very irregular plan, taking advantage of the natural defences offered by the ravines which surround the plateau on three sides, the acropolis forming the fourth. At the centre of the city proper is the agora, with the civic buildings in the vicinity; on a higher terrace to the northwest is the dominating precinct of Athena Polias, while still farther to the north, cutting into the slope of the acropolis, is the theatre. The palaestra and stadium are far below to the south, against the city wall. The streets run through from wall to wall on the east and west, and from the wall on the south to the steeper slopes of the acropolis on the north. One of the north-and-south streets, as usual, is wider than the others, $18\frac{1}{4}$ feet as contrasted with $10\frac{1}{4}$ to $12\frac{3}{4}$ feet for the ordinary streets. But, on account of the difficulties of the slope, two of the east-and-west streets were specially emphasised. The second from the south, leading from the "spring gate" at the east, is $18\frac{1}{2}$ to $20\frac{1}{4}$ feet wide, while the third from the south, leading from the city's west gate, is 23 to 24 feet wide; the ordinary east-and-west streets vary from $12\frac{1}{2}$ to $14\frac{1}{2}$ feet in width. These cut the whole area into rectangular blocks each about 116 feet from east to west and 155 feet from north to south (apparently planned as 120 by 160 Ionic feet), and numbering, if there had been no interruptions and irregularities, ninety-five in all. The agora, however, originally covered two blocks; the main east-and-west road, leading from the city's west gate, passed the northern edge of the agora, while the next road to the south would likewise pass the south side of the agora but for the fact that, since it lay in general at a lower level and also because cutting through the agora stoas was undesirable, the direct course of the street was interrupted by steps leading up to the agora level, while all traffic was diverted behind the south stoa; the less important cross streets stopped short against the back walls of the stoas and were not carried through. In the residential districts of the city the blocks were divided into quarters, giving house lots about 58 by $77\frac{1}{2}$ feet (60 by 80 Ionic feet); but nearer the walls the divisions were smaller; it may be calculated, on the basis of eighty habitable blocks with an average of six houses per block, that there were less than five hundred houses in the entire town.

Another example of this application of the chessboard scheme to a city plan in spite of the very steep slopes is Heraclea on the Latmos. Cnidus, too, was laid out on the Hippodamian system. Halicarnassus, on the other hand, is reported by Vitruvius to have formed a semicircle round the harbour, like a theatre, with the agora at the centre dominated by the Mausoleum and the temple of Ares, so that it may have been a radiating plan like that of Rhodes in the preceding century.

Among the important parts of the city were the agoras, where the people assembled for the transaction of public or private business. The agora consisted of a large open area, rectangular or trapezoidal, surrounded by colonnades or stoas, and enriched with temples, fountains and statues; and in the immediate vicinity were the bouleuterion or senate-house, the prytaneum, and other administrative buildings. In the usual type of Greek city, which had grown without any regulating system, these groups of buildings had very little formal relation to each other, apart from a certain amount of alignment along the edges of the agora. In the Hippodamian system, however, the case was different: not only was the position of the agora defined with reference to the main streets, but also, if we can regard the Ionian examples of the fourth century as typical, its shape and general appearance were likewise regulated. The north agora at Miletus was begun in the fourth century by the erection of a portico 445 feet long facing north towards the harbour, with an elbow 104 feet long running north from its west end; the main part of this L-shaped stoa had a row of shops behind it, and behind this in turn a court 88 feet square, surrounded by Doric columns with compound piers at the corners. But the typical Ionian agora, as exemplified at Priene, was an oblong, in this case covering two city blocks; it was surrounded on one long side and both ends by colonnades or stoas, the other long side being open to the main street. This ⊓-shaped plan was apparently typical, though at Priene in order to conserve the area of the agora, 248 feet in length and 152 feet in width, the stoas were built on the actual lines of the streets, which therefore had to be interrupted or diverted behind them. At Priene, furthermore, the agora was greatly extended in the Hellenistic period (158–156 B.C.) by the erection of a stoa, the Hiera Stoa, also on the fourth or open side, though on the opposite side of the main street which thus was permitted to cut through the agora. This north stoa was built for a length of three blocks rather than two; and to match it the ⊓-shaped stoas on the south were also given an eastward extension, the two new stoas then being joined at their eastern extremity by a semicircular arch, 20 feet in span, consisting of no more than a mere archivolt 2 feet wide. On the Greek mainland, however, the agoras continued to be erected in the somewhat haphazard traditional manner, now known as the "older style" by contrast with the Ionian. An example of this was the agora at Elis, where, from Pausanias's description, we gather that the central space, known as the Hippodrome, was used for training horses; on the west (which Pausanias calls the south) side was a stoa with three rows of columns, of which the two inner divided it into three aisles (like the Stoa of Philip at Megalopolis), known as the umpires' hall or Hellanodiceum, separated by a street from the agora; on the south, separated by a street from the first, was a second portico, the double Stoa of the Corcyraeans, with a wall down the centre, against which stood on either side pedestals and statues and colonnades, so that it faced both toward the agora and outward in the opposite direction. The two other sides, the north and east, were lined with smaller buildings of various sorts, forming an irregular quadrilateral.[1]

[1] The agora at Elis, which was previously assumed to have been much more formal, is now revealed by the Austrian excavations.

CHAPTER SEVEN

THE HELLENISTIC AND GRAECO-ROMAN PHASES

THE monuments which testify to the greatness of Greece even in her decline may best be studied, like those of the fourth century, in Asia Minor. For after the supremacy of the mainland cities had been shaken by Philip of Macedonia at the battle of Chaeronea, his successor, Alexander, turned to Asia, and routed the Persian hosts at the Granicus (334) and Issus (333). Now was built up a Greek empire of which Greece proper formed but a small province; the capital lay at Babylon, and the boundaries extended eastward to India and Turkestan, and southward to Nubia. After Alexander's death in 323 B.C. this vast territory was broken up into separate kingdoms ruled by his generals and their successors. For the moment, at any rate, the course of civilisation receded eastward; and it is largely in these Oriental kingdoms, carved out of Alexander's empire, that we must study the last phase but one, an architecture which, imitating the classical styles of the true Hellenic lands, is therefore termed Hellenistic. As we have noted, this phase may be said to have begun at the very end of the fourth century, and may be associated with the new political aspirations of 306 B.C.

Greece proper, during this period, was in great part politically dependent upon Macedonia; but the constant striving for independence resulted in the formation of two great leagues, the Aetolian and the Achaean, though their attempts to free the country were greatly neutralised by their internal strife. As the political importance of the mainland cities declined, and with it their wealth diminished, the incentive which leads to great works of architecture was lost. Athens, however, was kept alive by sentimental and historical associations; even in her decadence her schools were crowded with students from all quarters of the Mediterranean; Asiatic monarchs were proud to be counted honorary citizens of Athens, and vied with each other in showering benefits on the former intellectual centre of the world. Stoas, temples, and votive monuments were built at the cost of the Seleucids of Antioch, of the Attalids of Pergamum; and even later the odeum at Athens was rebuilt by Ariobarzanes of Cappadocia. To a lesser extent the same eastern benefactors showered their favours on other cities of Greece, such as Megalopolis, Tegea, and Lebadea, and the sanctuaries at Delphi, Delos, and Olympia.

This political reconstruction of the Greek world was not long suffered to remain undisturbed. From two quarters arrived external forces to dispute the supremacy of the eastern Mediterranean; and the Greeks successfully repulsed the Gallic invasions of Greece in 279 B.C. and of Asia Minor about 235 B.C., only to fall before others whom they likewise regarded as Barbarians, the Romans. The westward march of empire could no longer be arrested.

THE HELLENISTIC AND GRAECO-ROMAN PHASES

The Romans had come into contact with the Greeks at the very beginning of the Hellenistic period. The rich Greek colonies of southern Italy and Sicily tempted the rapidly expanding state on the Tiber; and as early as 281 B.C. began the annexation of the Greek cities of Italy, and then, with the first Punic war (264-241 B.C.) began the second stage, the penetration of Sicily. The second Punic war (218-202 B.C.), furthermore, brought the Romans into the East; the four Macedonian wars (216-146 B.C.) left Macedonia a Roman province. Though the Greek leagues had at first been the allies of Rome against Macedonia, their continual quarrels invited Roman intervention, and they were crushed by Lucius Mummius (146 B.C.), Corinth being destroyed as an act of terrorism and Greece itself annexed to the province of Macedonia. The war against Antiochus (192-189 B.C.) brought the Romans for the first time into Asia, where the Greek kingdoms one by one fell under Western sway, Pergamum through the bequest of its last king (133 B.C.), and others, as Syria (64 B.C.) and Egypt (30 B.C.), through conquest. Meanwhile, the victories of Sulla over Mithridates (88 B.C.) resulted in the collapse of the great international commercial emporium at Delos, and his capture of Athens itself in 86 B.C. stifled the greatest centre of Greek art and learning.

If we were to adopt a somewhat different interpretation of the term "Hellenistic," the period might be regarded as continuing for several centuries longer. But such an extension of the term to include all architecture in Greek lands down to the fourth century A.D. would result in inextricable confusion with the architecture of imperial Rome, and could be justified only if—as has been done by some—we turned to Rome itself and included the equally "Hellenistic" architecture of the pre-imperial epoch.[1] Not only would the lines of demarcation be difficult to draw; the extension of the investigation would demand a length of treatment far beyond the scope of this book. For convenience, then, we may subdivide the last period of Greek architecture into two parts, restricting the Hellenistic phase to the time of the existence of the Hellenistic kingdoms, from their origin just before 300 B.C. until their final submission to Rome. In general, the capture of Athens on March 1, 86 B.C., may be taken as the end of the Hellenistic phase which had begun so auspiciously two hundred and twenty years earlier.

The last phase of Greek architecture, then, is that of the period when the free states had been subjugated or otherwise annexed to Rome, and which we may therefore call Graeco-Roman. During this epoch, we are not concerned with such outlying regions as Syria and Egypt, to which Greek civilisation was brought only by the Hellenistic kings, and which soon lost their Greek veneer, taking on a new veneer, that of their Roman conquerors. Nor are we concerned with the purely Roman structures with which the later emperors lavishly adorned the main Greek centres, such as Athens, Corinth, and Ephesus. But in Greece proper, in Asia Minor, and in parts of southern Italy and Sicily, the ingrained Hellenism of the native Greek inhabitants lived on, either affecting the architecture of the new rulers or even continuing to produce architecture which might be called Greek. Shiploads of paintings, statues, and decorative architectural pieces were sent to Rome; but, to com-

[1] Such extensions of the term, to cover periods or areas beyond the scope of our study, appear in the works by Delbrück, Butler, Murray, and Fyfe, cited in the Bibliography.

pensate for this, the Roman emperors carried on a vast amount of architectural activity in Greece and Asia Minor, and these late buildings, on which Greek artists would seem to have been invariably employed, are sometimes just as much a part of the development of Greek architecture as are their more purely Hellenic predecessors.

*   *   *   *   *

At this period the erection of Doric temples was virtually abandoned; the the sentiments of the Hellenistic architects of Asia Minor are reflected by Vitruvius: "some 'ancient' architects said that sacred buildings ought not to be constructed of the Doric order, because faults and incongruities were caused by the laws of its symmetry."[1] In consequence, the list of Doric temples of this period includes for the most part imitations of earlier works and completion of earlier undertakings, together with a few sporadic but minor structures in which the style was adopted for conservative reasons. On the island of Delos the erection of the third temple of Apollo, begun at the end of the preceding century, was still in progress. In South Italy was built a peristyle round the temple of Apollo Alius at Crimisa, apparently octastyle and with nineteen columns on the flanks; the primitive cella seems to have been preserved at a low level, enframed by the peristyle at a higher level just as at Cyrene, and presumably again with descending stairs within. The Doric details are very late, particularly the forms of the triglyphs and the profile of the cornice, the latter with heavy bed and crowning mouldings, almost eliminating the face of the cornice itself, while the mutules are horizontal rather than sloping, and of very slight projection; the stone sima is a great cavetto.[2] Conversely, the temple of Apollo at Cyrene which had supplied the precedent for this depressed cella was entirely rebuilt in the second century A.D., with the cella raised to the peristyle level, and the peristyle itself rebuilt with new unfluted Doric columns.

As a strange contradiction of the opinion of the Hellenistic architects of Asia Minor, it was in this very region that the lone example of Assos was now followed by three Doric peripteral temples. Thus at Troy the prehistoric citadel was levelled off in order to establish a precinct of Athena, thereby obliterating the remains of the palace of the Sixth Citadel; and here, on foundations of sand poured into deep trenches, rose a hexastyle temple, with twelve columns on the flanks, apparently erected just before the death of Lysimachus in 281 B.C. The most interesting feature of the exterior is the series of carved metopes, including that of the chariot of Helios; the pronaos had semi-columns combined with the antae, with an architrave crowned by mouldings instead of the usual taenia, and a rosette frieze directly below the marble coffered ceiling.[3] At Pergamum, too, was erected a Doric intruder,

[1] For an actual instance of a temple at Pergamum altered from Doric to Ionic, see p. 273, note 2.

[2] Orsi attributed the temple to the fifth century in an effort to combine the stone Doric peristyle with the archaic terracottas, assuming that only the stone sima was a later replacement of the terracottas.

[3] Carved metopes and sima blocks are in the museums of Berlin and Istanbul; the sima blocks are of two periods, Hellenistic of the third century B.C. and Roman of the first century A.D., indicating a repair.

THE HELLENISTIC AND GRAECO-ROMAN PHASES

a hexastyle temple of Athena Polias, with the short proportions of the Hellenistic period, having only eleven columns on the flanks and no opisthodomus behind the cella. The columns, unfluted and unfinished, are seven diameters in height; and in agreement with these slender proportions the entablature is reduced in height through the expedient of using three metopes, rather than the classical two, for each intercolumniation.[1] The same number of columns and the resulting shortness of the plan, with the omission of the opisthodomus, appear also in the later temple of Asclepius at Cos, of the first half of the second century, with more restrained and conventional details. In Egypt, a hexastyle Doric temple at Hermopolis honoured Ptolemy III and Berenice.

Even shorter was a Doric peripteral temple at Kourno near Cape Matapan in southern Greece, hexastyle but with only seven columns on the flanks; here the angle supports consist of square piers each with a semi-column engaged to its back in such a way as to be visible only from the flank, and among other late features are the bases of the Doric columns and the recurrence of three metopes over each intercolumniation.

Special interest attaches to a more archaeological or anachronistic design, the great temple of Zeus Basileus at Lebadea in Boeotia, begun soon after 175 B.C. as one of the many temples of Zeus undertaken by the mad Asiatic monarch Antiochus IV Epiphanes; and though it remained little more than a beginning, it is of importance because of its elaborate specifications inscribed on marble slabs.[2] The length of the cella building was 151 feet, identical with that at Olympia, and the axial spacing of the columns also was apparently to have been identical, 17 feet $1\frac{3}{8}$ inches,[3] so that we are probably to restore a normal hexastyle plan of six by thirteen columns on a stylobate measuring more than 90 by 210 feet. The interior, however, was redesigned to suit the taste of the period: there was no opisthodomus, but an apse $20\frac{1}{2}$ feet in internal diameter (according to the specifications) was constructed within its rectangular end, presumably intended to enframe a copy of the gold-and-ivory Zeus at Olympia. And at Olympia itself the same king largely rebuilt the temple of Zeus,[4] because of damage caused by an earthquake, and also the gold-and-ivory Zeus by Phidias (the latter superintended by Damophon of Messene), and dedicated there the embroidered curtain taken from the temple of Jehovah

[1] The temple at Pergamum is generally dated too early, in the fourth century or about 300 B.C., but is stylistically much later, though not as late as the surrounding colonnades of Eumenes II (197–159 B.C.).

[2] We have fragments of four sets of specifications, the first being concerned with the erection of a long parapet on which the specifications themselves were to be inscribed, the second dealing with the completion of the stylobate and pteroma pavement, and the third with the construction of the orthostates of the cella walls, and the fourth (now a mere fragment) with the columns, entablature, and pediments.

[3] The cella length may be measured between the ends of the standing orthostate blocks. The column spacing is derived from a single surviving half-buried stylobate block, apparently of half of the axial spacing; but after excavating 8 feet $3\frac{1}{2}$ inches of its width I was obliged to desist, having ascertained that the spacing was more than 16 feet 7 inches. The cornice blocks were to be 4 Doric feet (4 feet $3\frac{3}{8}$ inches), fitting a spacing of 16 Doric feet, and the capitals 7 Doric feet (7 feet $6\frac{1}{4}$ inches) in width, likewise in proportion.

[4] A survey of the fallen blocks shows that both façades were taken down, in part to within one drum of the stylobate, and subsequently rebuilt. To this process we are probably to attribute the three inserted figures of Pentelic marble in the west pediment (the tympanum backgrounds in both pediments apparently being reconstructed in burnt brick, like the

at Jerusalem. Even this last was transformed likewise into a temple of Zeus Olympius, and a replica of the gold-and-ivory statue was erected at the king's own capital of Antioch, in a special temple of which the order is unknown.

A special plan known as the monopteros, because there were no cella walls within the peristyle, was employed for a little temple or chapel usually supposed to have been built in honour of the deified Queen Arsinoe of Ptolemy II (died 270 B.C.), in the guise of Aphrodite Arsinoe, on the promontory of Zephyrium near Alexandria. It had four columns on the fronts and five on the sides, counting the angle supports twice; and the latter were in the form of square piers with half columns engaged on two adjacent sides; the lower third of each shaft had twenty facets, only the upper portions being fluted.[1]

Among Doric prostyle plans, a characteristic example is the later temple of the Cabiri at Samothrace, again with a hexastyle façade, but with a second row of columns two intervals behind as in the archaic peripteral temples of Sicily; the long narrow cella, apparently with two rows of interior columns, had a segmental apse at the rear enclosed within the rectangle, and perhaps lateral doorways. The walls were built of pseudo-isodomic masonry, and the façade pediment was filled with sculpture. Likewise the temple of Despoena (the Mistress) at Lycosura has a hexastyle façade of marble, with the usual proportions of the period, including a low architrave of 1 foot $9\frac{1}{4}$ inches and a higher frieze of 2 feet $5\frac{1}{2}$ inches. The walls were executed in stone only for the height of the dado and belt course, the upper parts being of burnt brick; another detail of interest is the lateral doorway with a high threshold on the south flank. At the back of the cella is the pedestal of the great sculptured marble group by Damophon of Messene.[2] A prostyle hexastyle portico was added at this time to the temple of Apollo at Gortyna in Crete; but here all the columns were engaged to the front wall, with tapering pedestals in the intervals for the posting of inscriptions; as at Pergamum there were three metopes to each intercolumniation, and the cornice had very elaborate and unwieldly mouldings which greatly increased its height. An octastyle prostyle façade, but with the angle columns combined with antae as at Troy, Kourno, and Cape Zephyrium, existed in the sanctuary of Amphiaraus at Oropus in Attica. The order contained normal forms, though the upper edges of the taenias of architrave and frieze were moulded with ovolos. The walls were constructed with a stone dado and projecting belt course, above which was merely rubble covered with stucco; there was also a rear entrance with a small porch formed by two columns; and the cella was divided into aisles by two rows each of five columns.[3] Others of smaller size exist in the Ionic area, including that of Dionysus at Pergamum, about 200 B.C., with numerous

walls of the temple containing Damophon's great group at Lycosura), and also the Pentelic marble roof tiles and some of the simas and lion heads.

[1] This temple was unfortunately destroyed before it had been adequately studied.

[2] The date at Lycosura has been disputed, the arguments ranging from the fourth century B.C. to Roman or even Byzantine times; but the fact that the great pedestal and sculptured group at the back of the cella were the work of Damophon of Messene, whose career can be fixed in the second quarter of the second century B.C. (see p. 268 with regard to the temple of Zeus at Olympia), seems conclusive.

[3] It has been suggested that the temple at Oropus belongs to a much earlier date, about 390 B.C.; but this would seem to be contradicted by its proportions and freedom of detail.

THE HELLENISTIC AND GRAECO-ROMAN PHASES

modifications due to Ionic influence, such as the excessively slender proportions (which in the frieze led to the multiplication of the number of triglyphs), the use of a hybrid Ionic base and Ionic fluting, the substitution of mouldings for the Doric echinus and for the regulae of the architrave, etc. In other words, the supremacy was passing to the Ionic and, as we shall see, also to the Corinthian style, which now for the first time began to be employed on the exteriors of temples. Yet the Ionic victory was by no means complete; even later we meet Doric prostyle temples, such as that of Hera Basileia at Pergamum (built by Attalus II, 159–138 B.C.), with such late features as columns more than $7\frac{1}{2}$ diameters high and with mutules and guttae in the soffit of the raking cornice (a practice which Vitruvius abominated), but with no distinctive Ionic elements. And sometimes, moreover, we meet evidences of a more archaeological tendency, particularly in the reigns of Hadrian and the Antonines, when there were attempts to revive the purity of the classical styles. An instance in point is the little temple of Artemis Propylaea at Eleusis, of which the forms look as if they were designed long before the reign of Marcus Aurelius, its probable date. The plan of this temple is of special interest because it was tetrastyle amphiprostyle like so many of the small Ionic temples; on account of the small scale the shafts were monolithic, raised on a platform of five steps.[1]

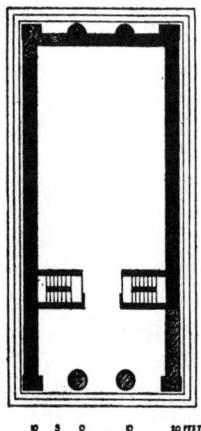

FIG. 97.—THE TEMPLE OF ASCLEPIUS AT ACRAGAS.

The true distyle in-antis Doric plan seems to be represented in the western colonies by the small temple 'B' at Selinus (Fig. 28).[2] Those of Asclepius at Acragas (Fig. 97) and of Serapis at Taormina show also at the rear a false portico of two semi-detached Doric columns between antae; the employment of the semi-detached columns here was undoubtedly inspired by the great temple of Zeus Olympius at Acragas, though it was not warranted by their small dimensions.[3] At Delos, on Mt. Cynthus, is a graceful marble Doric temple of Isis, built during the second period of Athenian domination (166–88 B.C.), with a short cella and a distyle in-antis porch. At Kourno near Cape Matapan, and at Messene, both in southern Greece, are two late distyle in-antis temples with three metopes over each intercolumniation; the latter example is peculiar in that the pronaos is very much wider than the square cella behind, giving a T-shaped plan. Another peculiar plan is that of the temple of Artemis at Lusoi, in Arcadia; both façades form porches tetrastyle in-antis, with two metopes over each intercolumniation; but the flanks seem to have had semi-columns spaced farther apart, with three metopes over each intercolumniation, and corresponding to buttresses projecting into the cella forming

[1] The plan at Eleusis was formerly erroneously restored as distyle in-antis at both ends.
[2] The columns and antae at Selinus were clearly Doric; and the remarkable Ionic capital shown in Hittorff's restoration is probably from a votive column.
[3] The temple of Asclepius at Acragas is usually assigned to the end of the fifth century, a date that is contradicted by its details. The presence of the stairways, in spite of the absence of interior columns, is one more indication that such stairways were not intended to lead up to galleries but only to the roof space.

niches as at Bassae. At a later period narrow aisles were built on either side, each with a flank doorway connecting with the cella.

In a period of so much departure from precedent it is natural that there should have been several examples of mixed orders, as well as temples without any definite orders. Thus a small Doric temple of Apollo Bresaeus on Lesbos, dating from the first century B.C., had its marble architrave sculptured with a continuous band of relief in the manner of the neighbouring archaic temple at Assos. A shrine of Zeus Meilichius at Selinus (Gaggera), measuring only 9 feet 2 inches by 16 feet 8 inches on the stylobate, has Doric columns supporting an Ionic architrave with two fascias crowned by a little cornice and a vertical cavetto sima, all the members above the columns being cut in a single course.[1] Instances of Doric entablatures in Corinthian temples at Paestum and Philae will be cited below. A little temple of Apollo on the island of Sicinos has two unfluted Doric columns in-antis with bases, a cyma-profiled frieze, and dentils in the cornice. More indefinite is the style of the tiny temple of Thea Basileia on the island of Thera (at Marmariani).[2]

From these examples it is evident that in the Hellenistic period, while some Doric temples still obtained their effects in the classical manner, others sought to appeal by new methods. Apses were introduced; lateral and rear entrances ceased to be rare features; wall surfaces were often decoratively modelled, using pseudo-isodomic masonry emphasised by drafted margins, belt courses, or combinations of stone and stucco; the canonical mouldings might be displaced by new and florid profiles. Semi-columns were combined at the corners of peristyles with antae, or as engaged columns formed substitutes for porticoes. The proportions of the order became more slender; the echinus of the capital might be merely a straight line, the abacus might have crowning mouldings, and there might be bases or even Ionic fluting; the time-honoured system with two metopes over each intercolumniation began to give way to that with three; and cornices began to emphasise the bed mouldings and simas, while the mutules might be countersunk in the soffit or even totally omitted. But we never find the characteristic Roman misapprehension of the function of the frieze, with the metopes in the architrave plane and the triglyphs thrust out beyond; nor do we meet any examples of the Vitruvian solution of the angle treatment, with a semi-metope at the end of the frieze.

Among temples of the Ionic style, it should be remembered that most of the work on the great temple of Apollo at Didyma near Miletus was done during the periods with which we are now concerned; and this protraction of the work may well account for the presence of the frieze in the entablature which would have been an anachronism in the fourth century. The same was apparently true at Sardis. It is certain, on the other hand, that the later work of completion at the west end of the temple of Athena at Priene and in the peristyle of the temple of Hera at Samos fairly closely repeated the fourth-century and sixth-century forms, respectively, with only minor variations in detail. At Samos marble was substituted for the poros column shafts; the entablature, which might have embodied the new theory of the frieze, was never erected in stone.

[1] The shrine of Zeus Meilichius is usually regarded as archaic, of the sixth century B.C.
[2] The little temple on Thera is still complete and is used as a church of St. Nicholas.

THE HELLENISTIC AND GRAECO-ROMAN PHASES

One of the earliest, perhaps, of the new Ionic temples of the period is that dedicated to Aphrodite at Messa in the island of Lesbos,[1] both octastyle and pseudo-dipteral, with fourteen columns on the flanks; the purity of the Asiatic bases (reviving the archaic fashion of omitting the plinths) and of the capitals (retaining the depressed curve connecting the volutes) would not be inappropriate for the fourth century, while the pseudo-dipteral plan might at first glance suggest the time of Hermogenes (about 175 B.C.), so that the beginning of the third century is a reasonable date. Late traits are the decoration of the baluster sides of the capitals with carved foliage, the beaded astragals under the fascias of the architrave, and the intrusion of the Attic frieze, never again to be omitted except in a few works at small scale; the use of red stone for the frieze, contrasting with the white of the rest of the structure, may even be a conscious attempt to imitate the Erechtheum at Athens. In spite of the introduction of the frieze, the heavy dentils characteristic of Asia Minor are retained, so that the entablature really consists of four members: architrave, frieze, dentils, and cornice. The sima on the pediments is of the cyma recta profile, but on the flanks it is a simple fascia carved with elaborate *rinceaux*.

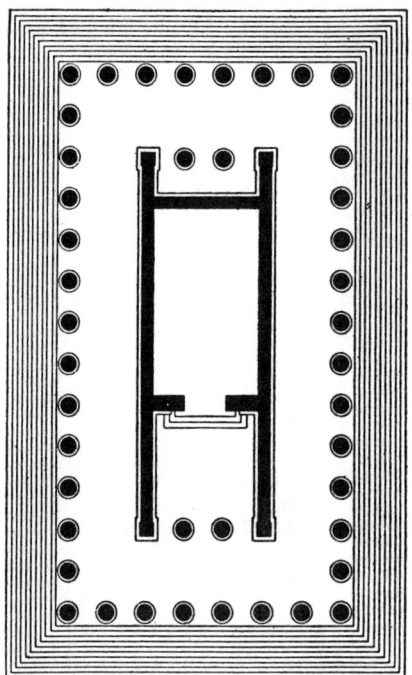

FIG. 98.—TEMPLE OF APOLLO SMINTHEUS (SMINTHEUM) IN THE TROAD.

Another example probably antedating Hermogenes is of almost identical plan, the temple of Apollo Smintheus at Chryse in the Troad, again octastyle pseudo-dipteral, with fourteen columns on the flanks (Fig. 98). The plan anticipates Hermogenes also in the proportions of the cella building, with the length three times the width (i.e. three by nine axial spacings). The peristyle is raised on a high platform of eleven steps.[2]

---

[1] The date assigned to the temple at Messa has varied from the fourth to the second centuries B.C.; I prefer the third, about 280 B.C., as a compromise between the various discrepant details. It has been argued, to be sure, that one of the late elements, the smooth frieze of red breccia $22\frac{1}{2}$ inches high restored by Koldewey between two egg-and-dart mouldings, is to be eliminated, leaving only a single egg-and-dart moulding with the cornice resting directly on the architrave, the normal friezeless entablature of Asia Minor. But the egg-and-dart mouldings are of two differing profiles and cannot be regarded as identical; the traces on their tops are different; and the red breccia frieze is of very peculiar construction for an ordinary wall course.

[2] The temple at Chryse was excavated by the Dilettanti expedition of 1866, and is greatly in need of fresh study. Some have even suggested that the steps occurred only on the façade, the three other sides having a high podium, the whole being of Roman date.

The column bases are of a peculiar transitional form, a combination of the Attic with the Asiatic, a lower torus being substituted for the Asiatic plinth, and thus seems to antedate Hermogenes. The capitals retain the depressed curve between the volutes and also have a branching *rinceau* carved in relief in the canal, very much as at Sardis. In the entablature we find the same beaded astragals on the architrave, and the frieze, that occurs at Messa; the frieze in this instance is sculptured with scenes of combat. In this case the raking cornice also has dentils, placed vertically, the axes of the anthemion ornament of the pediment sima following the same direction. A smaller temple of this period is that of Asclepius at Cos, on a lower terrace and antedating the Doric one described above; it had only a cella and a deep pronaos, with walls of pseudo-isodomic masonry, and with two Ionic columns in-antis, the bases being Asiatic with square plinths, and the entablature including both a frieze (cut in the same stone with the architrave) and a dentil course. And at Magnesia the little temple of Zeus Sosipolis and Tyche, with a tetrastyle prostyle front and a rear porch distyle in-antis, likewise with frieze and dentil course, seems to be earlier than the great work of Hermogenes in the same city, though later than 197 B.C.

The most important architect of the period was Hermogenes of Priene,[1] who codified the rules for the Ionic order in books which influenced Roman architecture and thus, through Vitruvius, our own. He was one of the architects who, according to Vitruvius, wrote that the Doric style ought not to be employed for temples, and even transformed into the Ionic style a temple of Dionysus which had been commenced as Doric.[2] In his studies of the Ionic order he worked out a series of ideal proportions, undoubtedly those which Vitruvius transmitted to us a century later. According to this system, which differed considerably from those of his predecessors, the height of the column varied inversely according to the axial spacing, so that the sum of axial spacing and height was always $12\frac{1}{2}$ diameters, thus: pycnostyle, $2\frac{1}{2}$ and 10; systyle, 3 and $9\frac{1}{2}$; [metriostyle], [$3\frac{1}{2}$] and 9;[3] diastyle, 4 and $8\frac{1}{2}$; araeostyle, $4\frac{1}{2}$ and 8 diameters respectively. But he is said to have preferred an intermediate proportion, eustyle, $3\frac{1}{4}$ and [$9\frac{1}{4}$] diameters.[4] His career would seem to lie between

---

[1] Hermogenes has sometimes been regarded as a citizen of Alabanda, because of a slight ambiguity in Vitruvius (III, 2, 6); but the latter clearly meant only that the temple of Apollo by Menesthes was at Alabanda. The fact that Hermogenes came from Priene is suggested by an inscription of Priene.

[2] We are not told where this temple was located, and it has sometimes been assumed that it was the temple of Dionysus at Teos. But in the neighbouring city of Pergamum is a small unfinished Ionic temple (which may or may not have been dedicated to Dionysus) on the upper gymnasium terrace, dating from the reign of Attalus II (159–138 B.C.), of which the stones originally formed Doric members and have been recut with Ionic profiles; it has been conjectured, not unreasonably, that this was the temple to which Vitruvius referred, particularly as the moulding profiles are more akin to those of Hermogenes at Magnesia than to any others at Pergamum. Another small Ionic temple at Pergamum, on the theatre terrace, largely rebuilt by the emperor Caracalla, is shown by the wall base (of the Attic profile above a plinth) to have some affinity with Hermogenes; it is notable also because of the upward curvature of the platform.

[3] Vitruvius omits the spacing for which I suggest this name; but its omission was probably an oversight, since the height of 9 diameters was cited by Vitruvius as the norm.

[4] Vitruvius cites this height as $9\frac{1}{2}$ diameters like the systyle, probably because he did not understand the principle of Hermogenes.

193 and 156 B.C., beginning with his temple at Teos and ending with his altar at Priene.¹

The earliest of the celebrated works of Hermogenes was the temple of Dionysus at Teos, hexastyle and peripteral, with eleven columns on the flanks, $3\frac{1}{2}$ Ionic feet in lower diameter and spaced exactly 11 Ionic feet on centres, giving the open ratio of $1 : 3\frac{1}{7}$ and so approximating the eustyle arrangement which he seems to have preferred. There is no enlargement of the central spacing, so that the axial rectangle measures 55 by 110 Ionic feet, exactly in the ratio of 1 : 2 as at Priene. The details illustrate the Attic tendencies of Hermogenes; the bases, of the Attic type but set on plinths, and the capitals and entablature (with its sculptured frieze of Dionysiac scenes), all closely resemble those at Magnesia now to be described.²

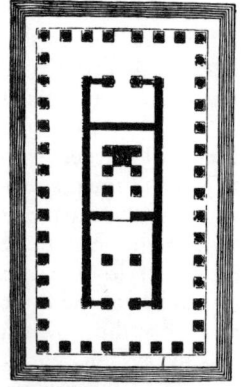

FIG. 99.—TEMPLE OF ARTEMIS LEUCOPHRYENE AT MAGNESIA-AD-MAEANDRUM.

The most remarkable innovation of Hermogenes was, according to Vitruvius, his plan of omitting the inner row of columns in the temple of Artemis Leucophryene at Magnesia-ad-Maeandrum, making it pseudo-dipteral (Fig. 99). The claim that Hermogenes invented this scheme is, however, unfounded, since it can be traced back through four centuries preceding him, to Corcyra, Silaris (Hera), Selinus ('GT'), Acragas (Olympieum, flanks), Sardis (flanks), Messa, and the Smintheum; we can only admit that he transported the lines of the hexastyle peristyle of the fifth-century temple at Magnesia outward by one intercolumniation, and by the discussion of this process in his book acquired an undeserved reputation. The new temple was octastyle, with fifteen columns on the flanks, and, like the temples at Ephesus, Didyma and Chryse, was raised on a lofty platform; seven steps, the lowest measuring 134 feet 8 inches by 221 feet 1 inch, formed a terrace from which the stylobate proper receded as at Ephesus.³ Like Ephesus, too, the temple faced west. The peristyle columns were $4\frac{3}{4}$ Ionic feet in lower diameter; but the angle columns

¹ The date of Hermogenes has generally been assumed to have been at the end of the third century and the beginning of the second, on the assumption that the temple of Artemis at Magnesia was erected at the time of a Delphic oracle regulating the cult of Artemis in 221 B.C., and that the temple of Teos should be associated with an inscription of the peripatetic guild of actors in 193 B.C. There has also been an effort to bring his date down to the latter part of the second century on the assumption that his career began with the altar at Priene. Probably the truth lies between, the sequence of his works being reversed: the temple at Teos would come first, the temple and altar of Artemis at Magnesia later, this altar and that of Athena Polias at Priene (apparently erected for Orophernes in 158–156 B.C.) being directly influenced by the great altar at Pergamum.

² The original capitals at Teos are of the Hermogenes type, but that published by Pullan (*Antiquities of Ionia*, IV) represents a repair of the Roman imperial period with arrow-head darts. The inscription on the architrave belongs to this Roman restoration by Hadrian. The frieze sculptures are mediocre.

³ The site was examined by an expedition of the Society of Dilettanti in 1812 and more thoroughly by a German expedition in 1890; but the lost copperplates of the 1812 expedition, rediscovered in 1912 and published three years later, contain much information elsewhere unrecorded.

were enlarged by 1 dactyl (one-sixtieth), forming the basis of the rule set forth by Vitruvius; and for ease of construction, exactly as in the north porch of the Erechtheum, the base joint was placed below the upper torus (which varied with the column diameter) so that the lower parts of the bases and the plinths could be identical throughout. The columns are spaced $13\frac{1}{3}$ Ionic feet on centres,[1] almost exactly in the ratio $1 : 2\frac{4}{5}$ which had prevailed in the fourth century but not in exact accord with any of the systems that Hermogenes recommended. This uniform spacing is not carried all round the temple: the central spacing on each front is increased by a third (rounded off to $17\frac{2}{3}$ Ionic feet) to give more commodious approach to the cella, another invention which Vitruvius attributed to Hermogenes,[2] though it is found in earlier Ionic temples (Ephesus, Samos, Sardis) and even in Doric buildings (Apollo at Syracuse, Propylaea at Athens). Thus the axial rectangle was $97\frac{2}{3} \times 186\frac{2}{3}$ Ionic feet, differing from the simple ratio $1 : 2$ found at Priene only by the extra third of the central axial spacing of the façade. Like earlier Ionic theorists, Hermogenes was greatly concerned with proportions in plan; to him we probably owe the injunctions quoted by Vitruvius to the effect that the length of the cella building should be three times the width (i.e. $3\frac{1}{3}$ by 10 axial spacings at Magnesia)—though even this had been employed earlier in the Smintheum—and subdivided in simple ratios to give pronaos, cella, and opisthodomus; Vitruvius recommends $2 : 3 : 2$, but at Magnesia it is $2 : 2 : 1$. The interior columns are spaced exactly according to those of the peristyle. The recommendation as to the enlargement of the angle column diameters, as given by Vitruvius for Ionic temples, is also exemplified here. The details show the above-mentioned Attic tendency of Hermogenes: the bases of the columns are of the pure Attic profile but set on plinths, and in the entablature the mainland frieze (employed for special reasons in the Mausoleum, and then reproduced at Messa and Chryse) had now become a regular feature of the Ionic style. The capitals show the tendency of the Hellenistic and Graeco-Roman periods to raise the carved echinus of the capital more and more, so that it ultimately ranged with the top of the second convolution of the volute obliterating the depressed curve connecting the volutes (compare Plates XLIX and LXV), and in this case disappeared entirely under the baluster side of the cushion. The baluster sides of the capitals are variously carved, at least six different patterns having been noted. The architrave mouldings at Magnesia repeat those of the Mausoleum, along with the sculptured frieze, and thus corroborate the restoration of the Amazon frieze in the entablature of the Mausoleum. The frieze at Magnesia is carved with an endlessly monotonous battle of Amazons.[3] The pediments were

[1] Most authorities have assumed that Magnesia was designed according to the "Attic" (Doric) foot of 0·328 m. ($12\frac{7}{8}$ inches), which seems extremely improbable in this Ionic area. According to this system, the axial spacings would be 12 Doric feet (approximately 16 Doric feet at the centre of the façade).

[2] It is of interest to recall that the widened central interval was drawn and measured by the Dilettanti expedition of 1812, but that in their published engravings they were forced by the opinion of William Wilkins to substitute uniform spacing across the façade on the assumption that no Greek temple could exhibit such widening. Another mistake which Wilkins forced upon them was the elimination of the plinths of the column bases, which they likewise had carefully measured and drawn.

[3] A large portion of the Magnesian frieze is in the Louvre, and more is in the museum at Istanbul.

without sculpture, but contained an interesting arrangement of three windows, the central one wider than the others in order to relieve the central intercolumniation of part of the weight of the gable and roof, imitating the arrangement at Ephesus. The delicately carved floral acroteria, perhaps imitated from their mainland prototypes, are marvels of grace.

Another pseudo-dipteral temple of this period was that of Apollo at Alabanda, erected by Menesthes and mentioned by Vitruvius. The plan was octastyle, with thirteen columns on the flanks; the three central openings on both fronts were slightly wider than the others, reflecting the system of Ephesus and Samos; and the frieze was sculptured with an Amazonomachy as at Magnesia, though of better execution.[1] Also at Ancyra (Ankara) was erected the temple of Rome and Augustus—though probably before the time of Augustus, whose inscription is cut directly across the wall blocks without regard for their previously existing drafted margins. The plan was octastyle pseudo-dipteral, with fifteen columns on the flanks; the three central intervals on the façades were enlarged with a gradation as at Ephesus. The peristyle rested on seven steps rising from a broad terrace which in turn had steps only at the front. The porches were tetrastyle prostyle (presumably Corinthian) at the front and distyle in-antis at the rear as in the temple of Zeus Sosipolis at Magnesia. The antae have Attic bases and rich Corinthian capitals with angle volutes springing from acanthus leaves, enframing winged Victories; and the richly decorated walls continue the anta bases (with laurel leaves on the lower torus and a cavetto with the anthemion, upside down, substituted for the scotia and upper torus) and capitals (with a frieze of *rinceaux* and seated Victories with trophies), with the addition of a carved belt course. One of the most interesting details of the temple is the great inscription of the deeds of Augustus carved on the walls, both in the Latin original and the Greek translation.[2]

Another temple of Rome and Augustus—and in this instance undoubtedly erected for that purpose—was that at Mylasa, most unusual not only for its short proportions (with six columns on each front and only seven on each flank, enclosing a perfectly square cella) and the fact that it was set on a podium with steps only at the front, but also because of its detail. The columns had Asiatic bases on plinths; but the six front columns, in addition, were decoratively treated with a single row of great acanthus leaves sprouting above the bases, imitating the Acanthus Column at Delphi.[3] The Ionic capitals, furthermore,

---

[1] Only preliminary reports of the excavation of the temple foundations have been published; nothing remains in place above the foundations except the bases of the pronaos columns.

[2] Only the cella building now stands, adjoining a mosque and the dwellings of the modern city; it was partly excavated by Perrot and Guillaume in 1861, and again by Germans in 1926. Guillaume had restored the plan as hexastyle peripteral with thirteen columns on the flanks; but the Germans ascertained that the foundations were farther out from the cella. Guillaume, moreover, had restored the temple as Corinthian; but the Germans more plausibly regard the peristyle as Ionic, even though no Ionic fragments were found, and even though the porches were probably Corinthian as at Aezani.

[3] This vegetable treatment of the bottom of the shaft with acanthus leaves, in imitation of the Acanthus Columns, occurs not only in the examples previously cited (p. 253, note 2), but also in its more limited form, with a single row of leaves, in many examples of the Roman period, particularly south and east of the Mediterranean. Thus we find it in Syria, as in the monumental arch at Gerasa; in Egypt, as in examples in the Alexandria Museum;

were of the canted variety with volutes on all four sides; but the six front capitals had, in addition, a single row of great acanthus leaves below (cf. Fig. 100), thus forming the forerunner of the composite capital.[1] Below the acanthus leaves the façade shafts had also a necking carved with four festoons, below which the shafts were fluted as usual. The frieze was decorated with bucrania, paterae, and tripods, and there was a window opening on the middle of the pediment.

Similar traditions were observed in the Ionic temples of Aphrodite at Aphrodisias and of Zeus at Aezani in Phrygia; these two are of late date, perhaps in the reign of Hadrian, but were executed by Greek artists still working on ancient tradition, and so retain a much greater purity of style than that found in most Roman work. Both temples are octastyle and pseudo-dipteral, but Aezani has fifteen columns on the flanks, Aphrodisias only thirteen; at Aezani, furthermore, the pronaos was set three intervals behind the façade rather than two.[2] At Aphrodisias only the central interval on the façade is slightly enlarged, while at Aezani three central intervals are increased with a gradation as at Ephesus. The temple at Aezani stood on a high podium on all sides, and in this respect resembled Mylasa, differing both from Ancyra and Aphrodisias. The peristyle bases are of Attic form at Aphrodisias, of the Asiatic form with plinths at Aezani. In the capitals the ovolo is made heavier, its top rising even higher than the second convolution of the volute. The column shafts at Aphrodisias are carved with tablets for dedicatory inscriptions, a practice of which we have noted the forerunner in the Olympian Heraeum, and one which the Romans later "improved" by placing corbels on the shafts of the columns to support statues, as in Syria. At Aezani the tops of the flutes have curious little vases carved in relief within them. The external frieze at Aezani is decorated with vertical fluting,[3] and the cornice has modillions. The porches at Aezani followed the same distribution, prostyle at the front and in-antis at the back, that was employed at Ancyra. The porch columns have Attic bases, contrasting with those of the peristyle, and the capitals of the pronaos also differ; they have canted volutes (Fig. 100) and are decorated with a single row of acanthus leaves under the volutes, forming another precursor of the composite capital as at Mylasa, though in this case the actual date may

in the arch of Marcus Aurelius at Tripoli; in the nymphaeum of Severus and the upper storey of the arcade of the Basilica Severiana at Leptis Magna, as well as in more fantastic examples at Tarentum and in the wall paintings of Pompeii (Curtius, *Die Wandmalerei Pompejis*, p. 129).

[1] The true composite capital first appeared in Rome in the Flavian period, in the Colosseum (A.D. 80) and the Arch of Titus (A.D. 82). But the forerunner at Mylasa is well attested by its dedicatory inscription (in the old *Corpus Inscriptionum Graecarum*, no. 2696) as between 12 B.C. and A.D. 14. It is unfortunate that this temple was seen only by Spon (1675) and Pococke (1740), and had entirely disappeared when the Dilettanti expedition visited the site (1765).

[2] This extra space at Aezani has usually been interpreted as evidence that a second row of columns must be restored behind those of the façade, making it dipteral across the front. But there is no trace of the assumed second row, and there is no possibility of bonding its architrave into that of the flank, either above the second column or the third (if Landron's longitudinal section showing the actual state is correctly drawn).

[3] Texier shows great brackets of acanthus leaves and volutes in the frieze, instead of the vertical fluting; but Landron with more probability assigns the brackets to the propylon of the inner courtyard.

be later than the introduction of this type into Rome. There is a great rectangular niche at the back of the cella, for the cult statue; and under this are contrived small rooms, approached by two doorways from the opisthodomus, one giving access to a stairway down to the crypt. The exterior wall of the cella at Aezani, improving upon the situation at Ancyra, was provided with a blank frieze 24½ inches high, just above the dado, enframed by a maeander pattern below and a projecting cornice above; but, though the space was provided, very little of it was utilized, except for an inscription of Avidius Quietus, proconsul of Asia about A.D. 125, which may be the date of the temple. Both at Aezani and Aphrodisias the temples were set within enormous colonnaded courts, or, in the former case, two concentric courts.

Among less important late Ionic temples in Asia Minor may be cited two hexastyle peripteral examples, one at Termessus, the other a temple of Apollo

FIG. 100.—CAPITAL OF COLUMN IN PRONAOS OF TEMPLE OF ZEUS AT AEZANI.

Clarius at Sagalassus. A distyle in-antis example, the temple of Zeus at Labranda, is of interest because of the numerous windows, one on each side of the doorway in the cross-wall, four in each flank wall (one opening into the pronaos and three into the cella). The temple stood on a podium, and at the back was a rectangular niche, as at Aezani, but in this instance projecting on the exterior.[1]

An unusual design, known to us only from a poetic description, was that of a temple (presumably Ionic) at Cyzicus built by Eumenes and Attalus of Pergamum in honour of their mother Apollonis, at about 160 B.C. It seems to have been tetrastyle peripteral, with seven columns on the flanks, thus giving three by six intervals and a proportion of 1 : 2. The eighteen columns had sculptured pedestals, described in ancient epigrams, and obviously inspired

[1] The temple at Labranda (Yaila) was formerly confused with the Corinthian temple of Zeus at Euromus (Iackly), since early travellers mistook these two sites, both subject towns of Mylasa, and sought Labranda at Euromus (see p. 283 note 1). The two columns in-antis at Labranda are no longer standing, but both Fellows and Lebas noted fallen columns, fluted and Ionic.

by the great temple at Ephesus.[1] Other sculptured pedestals occur in a late prostyle tetrastyle temple at Lagon in Pamphylia, and one exists in the House of the Diadumenos at Delos. Lastly, as an example of the debasement of the Ionic order in its travels toward the East, we may note the temple at Khurka in Mahallat, Persia, with columns attaining a height of 11 diameters and with volutes of so many convolutions that they resemble watch-springs.[2]

We have noted that the Corinthian capital was never raised by the Greeks to the status of an "order," but was generally grafted on to an Ionic shaft and supported an Ionic entablature. In fact Vitruvius, who in this as in other respects seems to be reflecting his Greek authorities, asserts that the Corinthian capital may be equally satisfactorily employed with the Doric entablature (though he condemns the Pergamene combination of Ionic columns with a Doric entablature). This state of mind is reflected in the so-called "Temple of Peace" at Paestum, of which the plan is due to Etruscan influence, dating from the period after the entry of Paestum into the Latin league in 273 B.C. There were originally six columns on the front (later changed to four more widely spaced) and eight on either flank; cella and peristyle together abutted against a continuous rear wall, and the whole was raised on a high podium approached only by two narrow stairways on the front.[3] The simplified bases consist only of a circular plinth with a cavetto, separated from the shaft by an astragal. The capitals have canted volutes, abnormally large for the Corinthian style, separated by human heads; below is a single girdle of acanthus leaves. The entablature is at first glance of normal Hellenistic Doric, with sculptured metopes; but the cornice has dentils below the mutules (a combination against which Vitruvius protested in vain), and the mutules are horizontal, forming mere decorative panels on the soffit rather than the ends of sloping rafters; the face of the cornice is decorated with a rosette above each triglyph. The sima was of terracotta with anthemion and lion heads; the pediment sima apparently had a cresting set into its top. Similar conditions obtained in a temple of Augustus at Philae in Egypt, where four prostyle Corinthian columns, standing on low pedestals, support an architrave with two fascias but crowned with a taenia and double regulae (the lower member recalling the guttae), and a triglyph frieze with four metopes over the central intercolumniation and three over the others. The cornice is a mere mass of monotonous mouldings, with an excessive number of small panels, spaced quite without reference to the triglyphs, recalling the mutules. The raking cornice, instead, has dentils.

The Corinthian style nevertheless attracted the Hellenistic theorists, and

[1] The epigrams (*Palatine Anthology*, III) mention points of the compass in three instances, No. 7 being on the north, No. 10 on the west flank, and No. 16 on the front, suggesting that the description began with No. 1 at the southeast corner, with Nos. 7, 10, and 16 forming the three other corners, the temple facing south.

[2] Similar debased watch-spring Ionic capitals are found in a few late Persian rock-cut tombs, such as two near the villages of Zarzi and Shornakh in Kurdistan, and a third (called "Da-u-Dukhtar") near Persepolis, each with a pair of Ionic columns either free-standing or semi-detached. See Edmonds, *Irak*, I, 1934, pp. 183–192, and Herzfeld, *Archaeological History of Iran* (1935), p. 32, p. V; the latter dates the "Da-u-Dukhtar" about 650–550 B.C.(!)

[3] The arrangement of the two stairways and the separating bema closely resembles that in the prehistoric "megaron" at Eleusis (Fig. 10), with which, of course, it can have no connection.

THE HELLENISTIC AND GRAECO-ROMAN PHASES

Vitruvius even quotes a book on the subject written by Arcesius. With the loss of the book, however, we can only derive our impressions of Hellenistic theory from a few very divergent examples.

One of the earliest of the important examples is the temple of Zeus Olbius at Diocaesarea (Uzundja Burdj) near Olba, in Cilicia, erected by Seleucus I Nicator (306-281 B.C.). It is hexastyle, with twelve columns on the flanks, the columns being about 42 feet high. The lower third of the shaft has facets rather than flutes; and the capitals are of an experimental and not very successful form. There are separate cauliculi for each of the sixteen volutes; the angle volutes are sheathed as high as the abacus level, and the attenuated cauliculi of the very meagre central spirals cross each other almost as if they were knotted.[1]

Another experimental example is the little temple of Artemis Limnatis at Messene in southern Greece; it has merely a cella and pronaos, the latter with two Corinthian columns between double antae giving the effect of six supports on the façade. The capitals are of very low proportions, with only one row of leaves covering the lower half of the bell, while in the upper half only the central spirals have cauliculi, as at Didyma (Fig. 84); and here again they support a palmette, which rises higher than at Didyma and covers the middle of the abacus.

By a curious coincidence, it was a descendant of the above-mentioned Seleucus, namely, Antiochus IV Epiphanes (175-164 B.C.), who was responsible for the erection of the most notable of the Corinthian temples of the Hellenistic age, that dedicated to Zeus Olympius and situated in the plain to the southeast of the Acropolis at Athens.[2] The temple was built on the foundations of the earlier Doric structure begun by the sons of Peisistratus; the new building was commenced by Antiochus in 174 B.C., from the designs of the Roman architect Cossutius, as a gift to the Athenian people and to satisfy his own mania for showing lavish honours to Olympian Zeus. The plan was octastyle, with twenty columns on the flanks (Fig. 102);[3] its dimensions on the stylobate were about 135 by 354 feet, and it was built in the centre of a peribolus measuring 424 by 680 feet. The temple was dipteral, with two rows of columns on each side of the cella, and three rows (tripteral) across the front and rear, a total of one hundred and four columns apart from any that may have been inserted in the pronaos and opisthodomus. The structure as designed by Cossutius was left incomplete; and in 86 B.C. some of the capitals and shafts, probably of monolithic columns prepared for the cella, were transported by Sulla to Rome and used to decorate the temple on the Capitol, thereby exercising a profound influence on the Roman Corinthian style.[4] The work was resumed in the time

[1] All but two of the peristyle columns are still standing; but the temple has never been investigated in detail.

[2] Thirteen columns at the southeast corner, with their architraves, and two isolated columns on the south flank are now standing; a sixteenth column (between the two last) was blown down in 1852, and Stuart and Revett had found the base of another at the west end, which has now disappeared.

[3] The front was formerly regarded as decastyle, but Penrose discovered by excavation in 1884 that it was narrower.

[4] It is possible, of course, that Sulla merely took one or two sample capitals from the peristyle, to serve as models in Rome rather than as actual building material.

of Augustus, but its completion and dedication were reserved for Hadrian in A.D. 132. The temple is one of those described by Vitruvius as hypaethral, but we are left in doubt whether the cella was actually intended to be left uncovered; and it is of course improbable that when completed by Hadrian any portion of the temple was hypaethral, in view of the exposure to which the gold-and-ivory statue of Zeus would then have been subjected. The lower diameter of the columns of the peristyle is 6 feet 3¾ inches, and their height is 55 feet 5 inches, giving a relation of diameter to height as 1 to 8·77, inclusive of the square plinth, an unusually solid proportion for the Corinthian order (Plate LIX). Some of the capitals (Fig. 101) belong to the design by Cossutius, being much too pure in style to have been executed under Augustus, and still less in

FIG. 101.—CAPITAL FROM THE TEMPLE OF ZEUS OLYMPIUS AT ATHENS.

Hadrian's time; the carving of the foliage resembles more that of the tholos of Epidaurus, than that of the arch near the temple and the library both built by Hadrian. The capitals, however, vary in execution, so that part of the work would seem to be that of Hadrian, always copying the original design, with the lesser height of the upper row of acanthus leaves, their sharp lobes, and the sharp corners of the abacus.[1] Now for the first time an angle and a central volute are paired to spring from a single fluted cauliculus. The entablature included both frieze and dentils. Pieces of the sima are quite unfinished, being merely blocked out; but possibly we are to assume that these were merely rejected blocks and that Hadrian's work was actually finished to the roof.[2]

[1] Opinions differ as to the distribution of the work: Gutschow thought that the one drawn by Penrose (Fig. 101) was of the Antiochus type, but Welter and Schober say that it is a Hadrianic copy and that the originals are at the southeast corner.
[2] Only the architrave *in situ* has been published; but the blocks lying about permit a complete restoration apart from the height of the dentils and of the bed moulding of the cornice.

THE HELLENISTIC AND GRAECO-ROMAN PHASES

A later Hellenistic Corinthian temple, dating from the end of the second century B.C., is that of Hecate at Lagina, octastyle and pseudo-dipteral but with only eleven flank columns, giving very short proportions; the three central intervals on the façade were widened as at Alabanda.[1] The peristyle rose from a platform of five steps, and had ordinary Attic bases with plinths and Corinthian capitals, while the pronaos columns were Ionic with Asiatic bases. Both the outer and the inner columns have the upper torus of the base worked on the bottom drum of the shaft, as at Magnesia (and in the North Porch of the Erechtheum), and probably for the same reason, enlargement of the angle column diameter. The anta capitals resemble those at Priene and Magnesia; and the walls are crowned by a frieze of anthemion and egg-and-dart. The frieze of the outer entablature is superior in quality to that at Magnesia.[2]

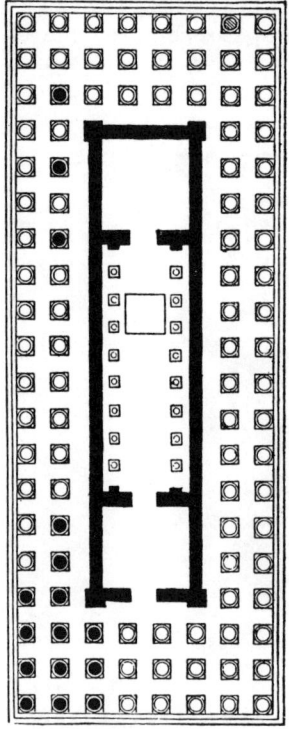

FIG. 102.—TEMPLE OF ZEUS OLYMPIUS AT ATHENS.

In the Graeco-Roman period, naturally, the Corinthian order was that which best suited the increasingly florid taste of the temple-designers, as contrasted with the severe Doric which had prevailed throughout the age of Pericles, or the graceful Ionic of the fourth century and the Hellenistic period. Asia Minor, in particular, was the area in which the new cities gave scope for such construction. Thus a prostyle tetrastyle temple of Men and Augustus, with a copy of the great inscription at Ancyra, stood at Antioch in Pisidia; and another Corinthian temple of Rome and Augustus exists at Apollonia in Pisidia. Later still is the Trajaneum at Pergamum, occupying the site of the palace of the Attalids on the summit of the Acropolis. A Corinthian temple at Euromus (near Ayakli) is hexastyle peripteral, with eleven columns on the flanks; these have tablets worked on them, with inscriptions recording the names of the donors, as is also the case on an isolated votive Corinthian column at Mylasa and on the Ionic columns of the temple at Aphrodisias, and, doubtless because of this method of erection in instalments as in the Heraeum

---

[1] The temple, now a mere heap of ruins, has been variously dated in the first third or last third of the second century B.C. (according to two interpretations of the date of Hermogenes) or in the 80's or in the last quarter of the first century B.C. (on the basis of inscriptions). But an inscription of 81 B.C. on the cella wall implies that the temple was already standing, and another inscription on an anta refers to a restoration of the sanctuary after the Mithridatic War of 88 B.C.

[2] It is difficult to believe that the architrave shown in the restorations, so low in proportion to the frieze (10 inches less in height) as contrasted with the approximate equality found in other temples and with only two fascias, is the true architrave of the peristyle. It seems to be rather the pronaos architrave or the inner face of the peristyle architrave. The sculptured frieze from Lagina is in the museum at Istanbul.

at Olympia, they are in various stages of completion, some being unfluted. The steps of the temple are peculiar in having a projecting moulding at the top of each riser.[1] Another example, of similar plan, was dedicated to Antoninus Pius at Sagalassus.

There are also two colossal temples of Asia Minor that require consideration. One was begun by Hadrian at Cyzicus, though it was not completed and dedicated until A.D. 167 in the reign of Marcus Aurelius; and it was so huge and elaborate that it supplanted the temple of Artemis at Ephesus in the later lists of the seven wonders of the world.[2] The façade was octastyle, the central interval being slightly widened; and, there having been sixty-two columns outside the cella, occupying a rectangle of about 133 by 252 feet, it is evident that there must have been fifteen columns on the flanks (where the scheme was pseudo-dipteral as at Sardis, whereas both fronts were dipteral), besides three pairs of columns in the deep pronaos and one pair in the opisthodomus; the cella had ten additional columns, in two rows of five.[3] The columns had the enormous diameter of 7 feet, greater than any other Ionic or Corinthian columns (exceeding those at Sardis and Didyma by $4\frac{1}{2}$ inches and even those at Baalbek by 2 inches), with a height of 70 feet. The other of these temples was at Tarsus, larger in actual size but smaller in scale; this was the so-called "Tomb of Sardanapalus," a white marble temple occupying a rectangle of about 148 by 329 feet, decastyle and with twenty-one columns on the flanks, the columns being uniformly spaced 16 feet $5\frac{1}{2}$ inches on centres all round.[4] The plan was pseudo-dipteral; and, while there was a second row of columns across the front, this was set two intercolumniations behind the façade, while the pronaos (with four columns in-antis) lay two additional intercolumniations beyond.

Finally, we may examine a few of the late Corinthian temples of Asia Minor containing special peculiarities of detail. Thus a temple at Cnidus, tetrastyle prostyle on the front but distyle in-antis at the rear (like that of Zeus Sosipolis at Magnesia), has engaged columns on the flank walls of the cella, really screen walls filling the intervals since the supports protrude also internally as pilasters, exactly as in the Olympieum at Acragas. The line of the capitals is carried along the walls by a rich frieze, and the true frieze of the entablature is pul-

---

[1] Sixteen of these columns were still standing in 1838–1840, at the site variously called Ayakli, Yiakli, Iackly, or Jakley, which was sometimes mistaken for Labranda, causing confusion with the Ionic temple mentioned on p. 278, note 1. Fellows counted twelve fluted and four unfluted columns.

[2] Nothing survives at Cyzicus except subterranean vaults which supported the platform; but Ciriaco of Ancona in 1431 beheld thirty-three of the columns still intact, 70 feet high, with the entablature and even pediment sculptures. The remains were investigated by Perrot and Guillaume, who found a small fragment of the bottom of a Corinthian capital, giving the spacing of the acanthus leaves and thus enabling them to estimate the upper diameter as 6 feet, and so the lower diameter as 7 feet, one-tenth of the height given by Ciriaco.

[3] The total number of columns is given by Ciriaco, whose dimensions of 110 by 240 cubits, however, do not agree with the remains. We may estimate, approximately, $(6 \times 17\frac{1}{2}) + 21 = 126$ feet (or 133 feet, including the angle column radii); and $(14 \times 17\frac{1}{2}) = 245$ feet (or 252 feet with the angle column radii).

[4] Nothing remains in place at Tarsus except the concrete filling between the missing foundations.

vinated and decorated, while the cornice has both dentils and modillions above them.[1] In two prostyle temples at Termessus, one tetrastyle and the other hexastyle, the columns are unfluted and rest, not on the stylobate, but on low pedestals 14½ inches high in the manner characteristic of late work in Syria. In the larger of these two examples, furthermore, though the central interval is but slightly widened, the entablature over the central span nevertheless is wholly omitted and replaced by an arch resting on the top of the entablature, again in the Roman Syrian manner.[2] With such details, undermining the fundamental principles of the post-and-lintel system, we approach the end of the long series of Greek temples.

In addition to temples of rectangular plan, the circular tholos plan of the fourth century was sometimes imitated, though incompletely, during the periods now being considered. Thus at Samothrace the same Queen Arsinoe who was honoured at Zephyrium donated a circular building known as the Arsinoeum, lacking an external colonnade, though the upper part of the inner face of the wall had a circle of engaged columns as in the Philippeum at Olympia, here only 9 feet 6 inches high, their outer faces formed by simple Doric piers, forty-four in number, carrying a triglyph entablature. The lower parts of the windows thus formed were blocked by parapets, each interval having a central patera flanked by two bucrania on the exterior, while on the interior there were alternating pairs, either bucrania or paterae. The total diameter over the outer wall face was about 67 feet, and the height from the stylobate to the top of the cornice about 34 feet. The conical roof was probably intended to be of marble, but was actually executed in terracotta, with special scale-shaped tiles of diminishing sizes, numbered to fit their tiers; at the top was a marble finial, also imbricated on the exterior, but hollowed like a chimney. Conversely, on the Acropolis of Athens, on the eastward prolongation of the axis of the Parthenon, was erected a temple of Roma and Augustus (Figs. 74 at R, 103), a monopteral plan consisting of a circle of nine Ionic columns imitated from those of the Erechtheum, with a diameter of only 24 feet 6½ inches on the stylobate, and without a cella.[3]

*   *   *   *   *

Among the propylaea erected at this period to serve as the entrances to precincts, the influence of the Athenian Propylaea continued to prevail in those of the Doric style, such as the simple propylon of the precinct of Demeter at Selinus (Gaggera), distyle in-antis on both fronts, with three metopes above all the intercolumniations; six steps ascended to the outer façade, and, while there was no intervening gate-wall as at Athens, two additional steps inside

[1] Leake thought that this was a temple erected (necessarily at some late period) to shelter the Aphrodite by Praxiteles, as described by Lucian. But Newton excavated here without finding any evidence as to its identity.

[2] This is not, of course, the arcuated lintel principle (bending the architrave itself up in arch form), which had also appeared in Syria shortly after 33 B.C.

[3] It was apparently erected by the same architect who was then rebuilding the west front of the Erechtheum after injuries received during a fire, thus accounting for the accuracy in the imitation of the Erechtheum detail. The connection is demonstrated by the discovery of a fragment of the original Greek west cornice of the Erechtheum in the foundations of the temple of Roma and Augustus.

the inner façade caused a change in level in the two porticoes to fit the rising ground. At Epidaurus the propylon of the palaestra (Fig. 116), with the widened central intercolumniation as at Athens, formed an open pavilion which seems to have been added as a frontispiece before the actual gates of the palaestra. After the Athenians resumed possession of Delos in 166 B.C. they erected the southwest propylon in the Doric style, with four columns on the façade. In this connection should be mentioned the gateway to the Roman Agora at Athens, erected in 10 B.C. with four columns on each front, and having as usual the widened central intercolumniation of the great structure on the Acropolis.[1] One of the most imposing examples was that of the precinct of Athena at Lindos in Rhodes, with a long colonnade flanked by terminal towers at the head of a wide flight of steps.

The influence of the Athenian Propylaea is even more apparent in the slavish copy finally erected at Eleusis, known as the outer or Greater Propylaea, exactly copied from the central building of the Propylaea of the Acropolis at Athens (again illustrating the archaeological tendencies of the Antonine period), both in design and in size, except that the hexastyle portico of the main front was raised on a platform of six steps, and the inner portico was at the same level as the outer, while the central passage for processions was omitted (Plate LXVI). In each pediment was a colossal bust of the emperor Marcus Aurelius, who erected the propylaea and restored the sanctuary after its destruction by the Sarmatian Costobocs about A.D. 170. In this structure the complicated wing buildings of the Athenian prototype were omitted.

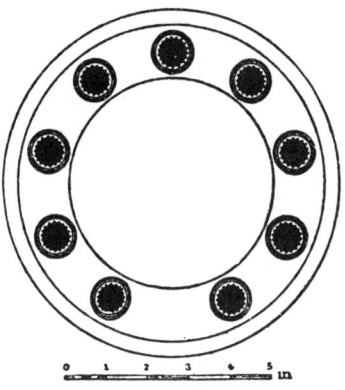

FIG. 103.—THE TEMPLE OF ROMA AND AUGUSTUS AT ATHENS.

It was during this period that the approach to the Athenian Acropolis received its final form. On the north side, approximately balancing the temple of Athena Nike, was built the lofty Pergamene pedestal which eventually supported the chariot of Marcus Agrippa (Fig. 74 at M; Plate L). Later, at the beginning of the reign of Claudius (A.D. 41), was erected the tremendous flight of marble steps, 71 feet in width, which ascended in two flights; the upper of which was subdivided by a central ramp paved with marble, intended for the beasts of sacrifice brought up in the procession which rounded the corner of the bastion of Athena Nike and so attained the landing half-way up the ascent. The marble steps led directly up to the lowest step of the west façade of the Propylaea (cf. Plate L); at the bottom, however, they originally seem to have been left open. Here at the bottom of the flight was eventually built, just after the Herulian invasion of A.D. 267, the so-called Beulé Gate[2] as part

---

[1] The Agora gate is of special interest because it was the first example of the Greek Doric order to be made known in detail to English and American architects, through the first volume by Stuart and Revett in 1762, and thus played a large part in the modern Greek revival.   [2] So named because of its discovery by Ernest Beulé in 1852.

THE HELLENISTIC AND GRAECO-ROMAN PHASES

of the new fortifications of Athens (Fig. 74 at B); the gate and its flanking towers were erected by a certain F. Septimius Marcellinus almost entirely out of material taken from the choragic monument of Nicias.[1]

At Samothrace we find an Ionic version of the Athenian Propylaea, known as the Ptolemaeum, with hexastyle Ionic porticoes on both fronts, erected by Ptolemy II of Egypt (285–246 B.C.). At Priene the propylaeum of the temenos of Athena has tetrastyle porticoes of the Ionic order in the front and rear, with a deep porch inside the gate wall; the outer façade was raised on six steps. One of the column capitals is particularly interesting because the unfinished eye of the volute shows the compass centres used in laying it out.[2] The north entrance to the sanctuary at Epidaurus had hexastyle porticoes on both fronts, Ionic on the outer and Corinthian on the inner, while, this being an unwalled sanctuary, there were no doors whatever. The Ionic or outer front has a frieze sculptured with alternating bucrania and rosettes, while the inner front was obviously imitated from the internal treatment of the tholos at Epidaurus, with its Corinthian capitals and cyma-profiled frieze.[3]

At Eleusis the sacred precinct of the temple was entered in Roman times through two successive gateways known as the Greater and the Lesser Propylaea, of which we have already discussed the former. The latter were built first, by Appius Claudius Pulcher, at about 50 B.C. The plan differs from that of other propylaea (Fig. 104): there is a paved forecourt flanked by two walls at the right and left of the entrance, lined by Ionic columns with crowning entablatures,[4] whilst two columns outside the doorway and two Caryatids inside

---

[1] See p. 238.

[2] The restoration with internal square piers and flat pilaster strips on both faces of the flank walls, as suggested by the Dilettanti expedition in 1812, has no foundation in fact. The rectangular capitals of Proto-Ionic or cradle type formerly utilized for this restoration have now been recognized as statue pedestals (see p. 326). The Ionic capital with the unfinished eyes is in the British Museum.

[3] It has been suggested that the propylaea at Epidaurus date from the latter part of the fourth century, and the fact that friezes of ox-skulls alternating with rosettes or phialae began to appear in red-figured vases of the fourth century is cited as justification. But its position (in the middle of a previously open avenue) and forms suggest that it is later.

[4] Following the conclusions of Libertini (subsequently adopted by Hörmann), who claimed that the lateral walls or parastades were thicker and left no room for a podium supporting columns lining the flanks of the front vestibule, these lateral Ionic columns were omitted in the 1927 edition of this work. But neither of these authorities could find any other position at Eleusis for the Ionic columns, and Hörmann even dismissed them as confused records of the columns of the Greater Propylaea, a manifest absurdity in view of their smaller size (half of that in the Greater Propylaea) and difference of detail. Bedford in 1812 not only meticulously recorded the details, but also noted that the backs of the capitals are uncarved, like that of the architrave; so there can be no doubt of their existence and of their association with the architrave in this particular building. The bottom of the architrave, furthermore, has traces of supports at either end, and the back is much better tooled than if it had been embedded in a wall. Hörmann's recent publication, though detailed, contains other improbabilities. Thus he assumes that the Caryatids of the inner façade occupied two successive positions, first being placed farther apart directly against the wall, and later moved out from the wall and slightly closer together; in the former state the inner parastades are assumed not to have been built and a horizontal entablature is carried merely from Caryatid to Caryatid; in the second stage the parastades are built and a horizontal entablature and ceiling are carried all across, the Caryatids being in-antis. Zschietzschmann showed that even in the first stage the flank parastades of the inner vestibule must have existed, like those of the outer vestibule, but assumed that Hörmann's first

it supported the roofs which merely sheltered the entrance.[1] The capital shown in Plate LXV, of Corinthian type, crowned one of the two outer columns, and is remarkable because of the unique hexagonal plan of the abacus and of the richly carved ornament, with winged horses at three corners. On these rested a mixed Doric-Ionic entablature, carved with emblems of Demeter (Plate LXVII), cists and wheat sheaves on the triglyphs, rosettes and bucrania on the metopes; the combination of Doric and Ionic forms once more illustrates the unsettled character of the Corinthian order in the period antedating the Roman Empire, as described by Vitruvius. Ruts formed by wheels on the pavement imply that before the erection of the outer Propylaea the precinct was accessible for chariots; the central doorway, through which these wheel ruts pass, was closed by massive gates as shown by marks on the pavement, while the lateral doorways (not shown on the plan) are of later origin, cut through the niches.

Among Corinthian gateways, in addition to the inner façade at Epidaurus and the mixed type at Eleusis, one of the most interesting with respect to its detail is that forming the entrance to the courtyard of the Bouleuterion at Miletus, dating from the reign of Antiochus IV (175–164 B.C.), which accounts for the resemblance of its capitals to those of the Olympieum at Athens. Because of their smaller scale, however, they are greatly simplified; there is only a single row of large acanthus leaves covering the lower half of the bell, and above them only a central acanthus leaf as slender as a stalk, leaving the rest of the bell bare; from a single cauliculus spring both the angle volute and the central spiral, the latter strangely attenuated. The Agora Gate on the west side of the Agora at Ephesus, of the early Roman period, is a simple wall with columns before it. Here, too, may be mentioned the stadium gates of Miletus, Athens, and Olympia.

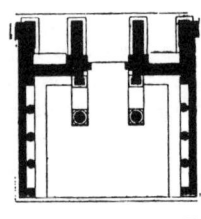

FIG. 104.—LESSER PROPYLAEA, ELEUSIS. (Restored by Bedford.)

Among the structures erected in the sacred enclosures were the altars, which in these later periods were often of considerable size, and sometimes were even the main features of the precincts. One of the largest was the great altar of Zeus the Liberator at Syracuse, built by Hieron II (269–215 B.C.), and intended for an annual sacrifice of 450 oxen. It was famed as being 600 (Doric) feet in length, about 642 feet 8 inches, but very narrow; the total height was about 35 feet. It was in the form of a podium crowned by a small Doric entablature, interrupted at each end of the front by a narrow stairway flanked by Telamones. The Megaron at Lycosura mentioned by Pausanias was another of these monumental altars. The greatest, however, was the Great Altar of Zeus at Pergamum, built by Eumenes II (197–159 B.C.), on the second terrace of the Acropolis overlooking the valley of the river Selinus, and mentioned in the Bible (Revelations) as the "Seat of Satan." It was raised on a podium

---

position for the Caryatids was correct. We may conclude, however, that the first stage never existed, even for the Caryatids; not only would they have made a ridiculous appearance under the long horizontal entablature, but their eventual (and probably original) positions show such careful planning with relation to the outer Corinthian columns as to suggest that they likewise supported a similar entablature and pediment in the form of a distyle porch.

[1] One of these two Caryatids is preserved at Cambridge University.

17 feet 6 inches high, measuring in plan, on the lowest step, 119 feet 6 inches by 112 feet 3 inches. Round the sides, at a height of 8 feet 8 inches above the pavement of the terrace, was a frieze 7 feet 6 inches high, carved in high relief, representing the Gigantomachy, or battle of the Gods and Giants.[1] In the principal front, which was toward the west, was a flight of steps 68 feet 2 inches wide, cutting in to a distance of 30 feet between the wings of the podium and ascending to the court of the altar. The court was surrounded by a wall also carved with reliefs, but in this case of lower relief and on the inner rather than the outer face. The inner face of the wall, furthermore, had a portico of double Ionic columns, or rather of piers with semi-columns attached at front and back, carrying a mere architrave; while on the outside of the wall was an Ionic peristyle, the columns supporting an entablature with dentils but no frieze, returned on each side of the steps above the wings of the podium, and carried as a screen across the top of the stairway itself. In the centre of the court was the actual altar.[2] Smaller imitations of this altar were erected at Priene and Magnesia, before the temples of Athena Polias and Artemis Leucophryene, respectively, and both by the architect Hermogenes. Another, of very similar character and date, stood below the temple of Asclepius at Cos.

The choragic monuments of the Hellenistic and Graeco-Roman periods were generally less pretentious than in the fourth century. Among the latest examples may be noted the isolated columns with triangular Corinthian capitals above the theatre at Athens (Plates III and LXI).

Fountain-houses of the Hellenistic period tended to become more elaborate. On the top of the Acrocorinth, the acropolis of Corinth, the fountain of upper Pirene received a thin shell-like barrel vault after 237 B.C., and at the front of the reservoir was inserted a screen consisting of a column between antae, supporting a low pediment. Similar screens, though with more richly carved Ionic columns and miniature entablatures, were inserted between the older partition walls in the great fountain of Pirene in the lower city, not long before the capture of Corinth in 146 B.C. The early Roman rebuilding of this fountain, with a rectangular court, surrounded by two storeys of engaged Doric and Ionic columns, was likewise Greek in spirit; but the later rebuilding in the time of Herodes Atticus, with great apses and half domes on the three sides of the court not occupied by the fountain proper, belongs in the domain of Roman architecture. The huge apse built by Herodes Atticus at Olympia, and the great nymphaeum at Miletus, likewise fall outside the scope of our study. The double Corinthian portico at Miletus known as the monument of Laodice,

[1] Pieces of the sculptured outer frieze of the podium were discovered by Humann in mediaeval walls, leading to the excavations of Pergamum by the Germans since 1878. Three-quarters of this frieze were until recently in the Pergamum Museum at Berlin, together with a reconstruction of the entire front at full size.

[2] The restoration in Berlin, with the colonnades returned across the top of the steps in front of the altar and thus masking the latter, has been criticised by some on the ground that the sacrifices were probably intended to be seen from the plain below. Moreover, it does not accord with the representation shown on a Pergamene coin struck in the reign of Septimius Severus (A.D. 193–211), on which the altar, of simple design and of less height than the Ionic peristyle, is shown standing clear in the centre. It is probable, however, that the omission of the screen of columns was merely the die-engraver's idea. In the conjectural restoration by Pontremoli, on the other hand, the peristyle is dwarfed by the immense altar shown.

with a friezeless entablature, was apparently a fountain of the Hellenistic period. The so-called temple of Claudius at Ephesus, more probably constructed in the time of Antoninus Pius, resembled a temple with its huge octastyle façade, the Corinthian columns 46 feet 8 inches high (with monolithic shafts) being approached by great flights of steps and giving access to a cella with a niche 24 feet wide at the back. The façade erected by Hadrian before his reservoir at Athens had Ionic columns supporting an entablature which was interrupted by an arch over the wider central span.

Lighthouse towers were generally of simple form, like that at Abusir in Egypt. But an exceptional example was the Pharos at Alexandria, so monumental that it ranked among the seven wonders of the ancient world. It was designed by Sostratus of Cnidus for Ptolemy II (285–246 B.C.), rising from a base about 100 feet square to a height of 440 feet. The lower half was square in plan with slightly tapering sides; then, stepping back, there was an octagonal section, and finally, after another setback, the top portion was circular, with a conical roof and finial. Complicated ramps and staircases filled the interior and permitted a constant supply of fuel for the beacon at the top, where there were apparently also great reflectors.[1]

Among buildings of unusual form was the public clock-tower of Athens, the well-known Tower of the Winds, mentioned by Varro and Vitruvius as having been erected by Andronicus Cyrrhestes,[2] the date probably being the middle of the first century B.C. Presumably it was the first part of the building scheme of Julius Caesar for the Roman Agora at Athens, begun just after the battle of Pharsalus in 48 B.C., the Agora itself being completed by the erection of the above-mentioned west gateway in 10 B.C. The structure designed by Andronicus is an octagonal tower of marble, 25 feet 8 inches in diameter and 47 feet high to the top of the finial (Plate LXVIII) without the Triton, still well preserved and forming one of the most familiar buildings of Greece. On each side was sculptured a relief representing the wind blowing from the quarter facing it; the two figures best seen in the illustration represent, on the left, Sciron the northwest wind, emptying a wide-mouthed jar, and on the right Zephyrus the west wind, with his garment filled with spring flowers. The roof is of twenty-four triangular marble slabs, supporting each other by means of their radiating joints, and carved on their upper surfaces in the form of roof tiles. On the top of the roof was an octagonal Corinthian capital as a finial,[3] supporting a huge bronze Triton working on a pivot, with a rod in his hand which pointed toward the figure representing the quarter in which the wind lay. Also on the faces of the tower were sundials, and inside was a water clock or clepsydra; the turret on the south side contained the cistern which supplied the water. There were two entrances, formed by two small distyle porches on two of the sides of the tower with architraves and pediments. Most notable are their Corinthian capitals, of a special though not infrequent type; the bell is decor-

---

[1] The lower part of the Pharos still exists in the fort of Kaït-Bey at Alexandria; the various modern restorations are based on ancient descriptions and representations on coins, and particularly upon the numerous mediaeval Arabic descriptions.

[2] A sundial and exedra set up by the same Andronicus has been found on the island of Tenos.

[3] The Turkish turban shown in Plate LXVIII has now been removed and replaced by the original octagonal capital.

ated with a single row of acanthus leaves round the base, and with an upper row of water leaves, there being no volutes, while the abacus is perfectly square. Other examples of capitals of the same design exist in the theatre of Dionysus. Another interesting Corinthian detail is the upper of two projecting cornices which form shelves within, at distances of 6 feet 5 inches and 16 feet $5\frac{1}{2}$ inches above the floor. The lower cornice is of no special interest; but the upper has consoles or modillions, one of the earliest instances of this feature; dentils also appear in this cornice, but strangely placed above the corona as a decorative moulding. Higher still is a plain circular belt course with its top 26 feet above the floor; the relation of the circle to the octagon leaves space in each corner for a dwarf Doric column, only 3 feet $8\frac{1}{2}$ inches high, which in turn supports a circular architrave as the transition from the octagonal walls to the roof, which is conical within.

Another tower-like building, in reality a glorified ship-shed, was the "Sanctuary of the Bulls" (Pythium?) at Delos (Fig. 105). It measures 220 feet long by 29 feet wide on the bottom step, with a hexastyle portico at one end, and at the rear end a sanctuary approached through a screen formed by two piers each decorated on one side with two kneeling bulls as bracket capitals, while the other side of each forms a half Doric capital.[1] In the long middle hall the central portion of the floor was depressed about 20 inches to form a basin, 150 feet long and 16 feet wide, in which was dedicated a great war galley;[2] and in the sanctuary was an altar, with the tower rising above it roofed by sloping marble slabs which were coffered beneath and carved as tiles on the exterior.

A series of five long narrow buildings, of like form, erected successively on the extreme northern projection of the citadel of Pergamum (Fig. 121), formed the arsenal of this city. The original structure was about 42 feet wide and 120 feet long; the four others were narrower, only 21 to $26\frac{1}{2}$ feet, and generally longer, $103\frac{1}{2}$ to $156\frac{1}{2}$ feet. All were distinguished by a curious cellular construction of the basement storeys: the earliest had six rows each of six cells running longitudinally, the others single rows varying from fifteen to thirty-five cells running transversely, all connected with doors and with narrow slit windows in the outer walls for the circulation of air and for light. The main storey in every case was constructed entirely of wood; heavy floor beams rested on the transverse walls, carrying a wooden floor; and the walls were of heavy vertical timbers with planks nailed on their outer faces. Long ridge roofs of terracotta tiles, and rows of windows just under the eaves, completed the design of a group of utilitarian structures which externally had a superficial resemblance to the arsenal at the Piraeus.

Of the usual stoa type we find numerous examples dating from the Hellenistic period, usually two-aisled and two-storeyed. Thus the northwest stoa at Corinth had Doric columns both in the lower and in the upper storey on the façade,

[1] A bracket capital formed by two bull heads, from the Agora at Salamis in Cyprus (now in the British Museum), is presumably of this period rather than the fourth century, and is interesting as a connecting link with the Persian capitals of Susa and Persepolis.

[2] It is uncertain whether this was the flagship built by Demetrius Poliorcetes and dedicated by Ptolemy I just after 286 B.C., or that built by Antigonus Gonatas and victorious in the battle of Cos in 256 B.C. The latter would seem to be preferable on account of the analogy with the bull-head triglyphs of the Stoa of Antigonus. The impluvium was not water-tight and must have been dry, though populated by Nereids riding dolphins.

and Ionic columns within, the customary treatment. The Stoa of Philip V at Delos, probably erected between 212 and 205 B.C., was originally of simple form, with only one storey and one aisle, the façade having sixteen columns 19 feet 5 inches in height, with three metopes over each intercolumniation; the unusual feature is that the colonnade is continued in both directions by short pieces of wall, each with a cluster of four windows corresponding exactly to the metopes of the entablature. A complication in the Stoa of Philip was

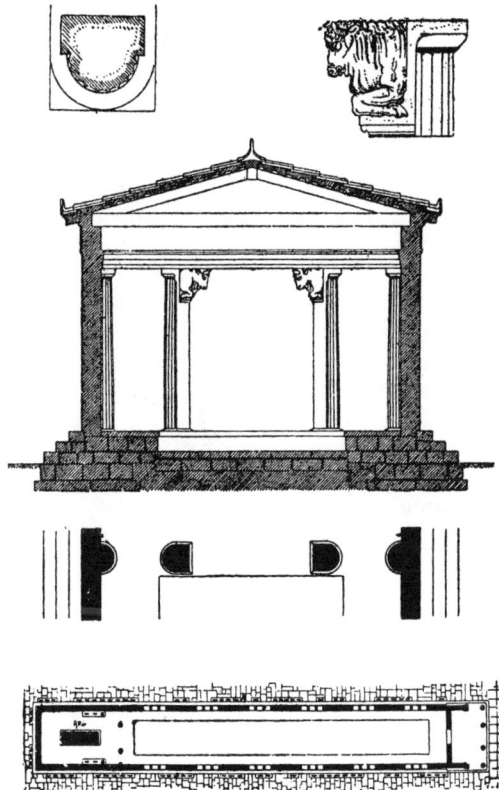

Fig. 105.—"Sanctuary of the Bulls" at Delos.
(Restored by Nenot.)

the addition, a few years later, of a parallel stoa against its back but overlapping it considerably at one end. Thus the Stoa of Philip was not only lengthened but was doubled in depth, with the ridge of the roof now coming above the party wall. The careful planning of the addition, with the same dimensions and column spacing, and particularly the utilisation of the extra space added to the one end of the original stoa, with an Ionic screen of double-columns at the point where the party wall terminates, are worthy of note. The Stoa of Antigonus at Delos (the longest building on the island, measuring 393 feet), erected at about 254 B.C., has terminal pavilions breaking forward and crowned by pediments, enframing the long colonnade; and the details are of special interest because, in spite of the wide spacing of the columns, the architect insisted on maintaining the classic arrangement of two metopes over each intercolumniation, though at the cost of making the metopes horizontal oblongs like those of archaic Syracuse. Alternate triglyphs, furthermore, were carved with bulls' heads which purport to carry the cornice, recalling the capitals in the "Sanctuary of the Bulls." In this and the foregoing examples the internal columns follow the normal scheme in being spaced twice as far apart as those on the façade, and, if the slope of the roof permitted, in being higher as well; for this reason the slender Ionic order was most suitable for interiors of stoas, leaving the heavier Doric for the exteriors. In the Stoa of Antigonus there was a further complication in the valley rafters required by the pavilions; for, while the rafter spans (measured horizontally) were normally 20 feet 9 inches, those at 45 degrees were necessarily 29 feet 4 inches. To improve the situation with regard to the four valley rafters, four extra columns were inserted, one being thrust under each valley rafter until it reached the point where it provided a bearing; the spans were thereby reduced from 29 feet 4 inches to 17 feet 10 inches, but at the cost of having a very curious group of three columns at each end of the stoa. In the Stoa of Philip V at Megalopolis (probably erected in 183 B.C.), the plan is three-aisled and the internal columns (with canted Ionic volutes as at Bassae) were spaced so far apart that they corresponded to every third column on the façade; in this example again, as at Delos, appear the terminal pavilions.

A special style of stoa design was developed in Asia Minor in connection with temple precincts, market-places, and other formal rectangles. These stoas were Doric, even though they might surround Ionic or Corinthian temples. Many of them have capitals of a type which we might be tempted to regard as Roman Doric, but it is clear that it goes back to Hermogenes, as at Teos, Magnesia, and Priene; a moulding usually occurs at the top of the abacus, and the echinus is carved with the egg-and-dart, and sometimes there is even a necking below the echinus.

Another special group of stoas of this period may be designated as the Pergamene type, marked by a curious treatment of details. At Pergamum itself, on the terrace above the Great Altar, the Doric temple of Athena Polias was enclosed within a rectangular court, lined on two sides with a colonnade or stoa in two storeys. A similar colonnade erected at Delphi, outside the enclosure on the east side in order to shelter pilgrims (Plate XXVIII), is known to have been given by Attalus I of Pergamum.[1] His successors, Eumenes II and Attalus II, presented similar stoas to Athens; that of Eumenes is on the south side of the Acropolis, running westward from the theatre, to assist the theatre stoa in accommodating spectators in case of rain (the odeum of Pericles forming a corresponding refuge on the east side). The stoa built by Attalus II at Athens, being located on the Agora, had not only two storeys of columns, arranged in two aisles, but also a row of shops at the back (Fig. 106). In all these Pergamene stoas the lower columns on the façade were Doric, the upper columns Ionic, the latter of elliptical plan in order to provide for the abutment

[1] The stoa of Attalus at Delphi was later transformed by the Romans into a reservoir by walling up the columns.

of stone parapets between them, and supporting a mixed Doric-Ionic entablature, that is, with an Ionic architrave but with Doric triglyphs and metopes, and a cornice with mutules of very simplified form, usually without guttae.[1] The interior capitals were usually of the Aeolic form (*cf.* Plate XXXIII); those of the Stoa of Eumenes are of special interest because of the little petal that fills each corner of the soffit of the abacus where it is left exposed by the bell. Another noteworthy characteristic of the Stoa of Eumenes is the retaining wall behind its back wall, consisting of a series of buttresses connected by arches giving, as now exposed (Plate LII), almost the appearance of a Roman aqueduct. Similar architectural details appear in the stoa on the north side of the agora at Assos, which may be regarded, therefore, as of Pergamene origin.

The above-mentioned stoa at Pergamum, enframing the temple of Athena, served also as the frontispiece of the great library at Pergamum. The arrangement of the chief room of the library, with its central pedestal supporting a free version of the Athena Parthenos at one third-size, and the foundations for the bookcases standing a little free from the walls to avoid dampness, can

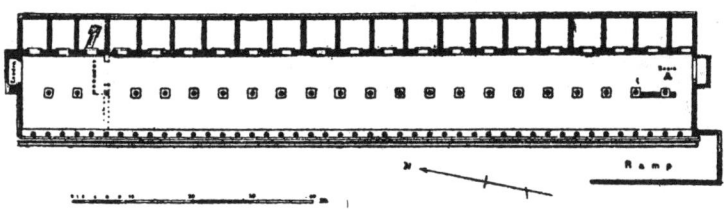

Fig. 106.—The Stoa of Attalus at Athens.

still be traced. Of the great rival library at Alexandria, housed in the Museum, we unfortunately have no remains. The libraries of Celsus at Ephesus and of Pantaenus and Hadrian at Athens are purely Roman designs and can find no place in our discussion.

Another type of structure allied to the stoa is the market-hall. These are most impressive in such cities as Aegae and Alinda and Assos, where the agoras were formed on the slopes of the hills, with artificial terraces to support them. The stoa along the outer side could then be erected in several storeys, the colonnade itself in the top storey facing on the agora, and beneath it one or two storeys which were utilised as markets, though their primary object was the support of the terrace. In these Hellenistic substructures we have some of the few examples of secular Greek architecture which are preserved to any considerable height, and they are of considerable interest as showing extreme simplicity of design with good solid construction. The example at Alinda (Fig. 107) is 332 feet long by 44 feet wide. On the lower storey is a corridor in the rear, 16 feet wide, giving access to a series of rooms in the front, 16 feet deep, some of which were lighted by windows and others through doorways opening on to a terrace. The second or mezzanine storey consists of two long corridors, divided by a series of piers with semi-detached Doric columns facing

---

[1] These simple cornice blocks of the Stoa of Eumenes at Athens are in part built into the theatre stage of Phaedrus, and thus give a clue to the date of the latter.

one another; this storey was lighted only by narrow apertures at the top, in the front wall. The wooden floor dividing these two storeys has disappeared. All this was merely the substructure of the stoa proper: the front wall, 4 feet thick and 28 feet high, is built in coursed masonry, with nineteen courses varying in height apparently as the masons found the blocks to hand, the face of each being worked to a convex curve. The windows or smaller openings have deep architraves, the doorways voussoired arches; and the whole is crowned by an ogee string course. The stoa above this substructure had a row of columns down the centre to support the ridge beam, and on each side piers or pedestals with a solid stone parapet 5 feet high between; all this latter portion is of Roman date. The terrace below the great basement is built on the natural rock, which was left unhewn. The example at Aegae was of similar design, with a front of 270 feet, and a return wing 89 feet long; again it was three-storeyed, with two storeys below the terrace level. The shops at Aegae have in each case one window beside the door. More decorative was the treatment at Assos, each shop having a door flanked by a window on either side (as in the earlier market-hall at Corinth), the doors and windows enframed by decorative pilasters. The windows have slots for the insertion and removal of shutter-boards, and under the lintel of each were three hooks for hanging produce. Heavy piers about $2\frac{1}{2}$ feet square with chamfered corners enframed openings admitting light to the shop storey; and beneath this, in turn, was a basement with cisterns and draw-basins. It is true that these buildings were only substructures of porticoes; but in themselves they make a fine monumental effect, their architectural embellishment, if it may be called so, being confined to the varied heights of the courses of masonry and to their bossed surfaces. The Greeks apparently trusted to this finely-worked masonry alone for the external aspect of many of their buildings.

Fig. 107.—Substructure of Market-Building at Alinda.

At Delos was a great structure, dating from about 210 B.C., officially known as the Stoa of Poseidon, though its plan bears no resemblance to that of a stoa and seems rather to have been derived from the Telesterion at Eleusis. Forming an elongated rectangle rather than a square, however, it seems to be a prototype of the Roman basilica—of the "Oriental" type with the entrance on the long side. For convenience it is preferable to employ its modern designation as the "hypostyle hall." The plan forms a rectangle 185 by $112\frac{1}{2}$ feet, divided internally into six by ten rows of square compartments by means of concentric rectangles of columns. On the long front were fifteen Doric columns between antae, with

Ionic fluting, spaced, as was usual in stoae, twice as closely as the internal columns. The outermost row of internal columns, nine by five, was likewise Doric; but the columns were considerably higher than those on the exterior in order to fit the rising roof slopes. The next row, higher still, consisted of Ionic columns, arranged seven by three; and along the central axis stood an isolated row of columns of the same height, likewise Ionic, which would have been five in number but for the omission of the central one. The employment of columns, rather than interspaces, along the central axes, and the consequent omission of the central one, had its prototypes in the Telesterion at Eleusis (as planned by Coroebus) and the Periclean Odeum at Athens. The purpose of the omission was here the same: to permit the erection of a central lantern which should illuminate the interior. At Delos the remains of this lantern have survived; above the eight Ionic columns forming the central square were eight slender square piers, with parapets between them, rising above the hip roof and admitting light below the more elevated roof of the lantern. Of special interest are the varied forms of the capitals in this building; besides the two Doric types, the Ionic capitals are of three forms, depending on whether they were in normal positions, at the corners of the intermediate rectangle (with one canted volute), or at the ends of the central row (with two canted volutes); all the Ionic capitals are executed in block form, with volutes and ovolo uncarved and the bases have a simple torus profile.

After describing these porticoes used as informal gathering-places, we turn to the great halls intended for popular assemblies. Of these, the senate house or Bouleuterion (sometimes called Ecclesiasterion) at Priene, erected about 200 B.C., is a notable example of such a structure as planned for a small town, seating about 700 citizens. It is not quite square, being about $60\frac{1}{2}$ feet wide and $66\frac{1}{2}$ feet long, besides a rectangular exedra which protrudes into a narrow light court separating the building from the back wall of the great Agora stoa. The various gallery levels within are successfully adapted to the slope of the ground, the highest at the back entered directly from the street above, the lateral galleries eleven steps lower so that the one on the west could be entered from the ascending side street, while the south entrances from the light court are sixteen steps lower still. This surrounding corridor is marked off by a series of sixteen piers (six on each of three sides), leaving a rectangle of about $47\frac{1}{2}$ by 58 feet in clear span, of which the narrower dimension must have been spanned by simple trusses.[1] The seats within this rectangle are arranged in the form of a rectangular theatre, with diagonal aisles at four points, oblique retaining walls as in theatres,[2] an altar at the centre of the rectangular "orchestra," and a bench for officials in a rectangular exedra at the back. Most remarkable is the arch over this exedra, perfectly constructed with radiating voussoirs, $14\frac{1}{2}$ feet in span, and springing from the top of a low dado so that its crown is only 11 feet above the floor; since the arch is in the plane of the main wall, it so happens that the officials on the bench were seated in the

[1] At a later period, when the roof was repaired, these spans were adjudged to be too great and were reduced to $34\frac{1}{2}$ feet by erecting new piers closer together.

[2] In the published plans these retaining walls are wrongly shown in solid black as if they extended to the ceiling, and the two piers which must have rested on their upper ends fail to appear.

THE HELLENISTIC AND GRAECO-ROMAN PHASES

open air, looking in from the outside, though they may perhaps have been protected by an awning.

Similar to that at Priene is the Bouleuterion at Notium, with a central span of about 65 feet, again involving the use of trusses. Simple forms exist in more provincial towns: at Assos the Bouleuterion was a perfect square with four columns arranged concentrically on an inner square, while the front wall was open, with five columns between antae (Fig. 125). At Thasos the Bouleuterion again was square, with a square peristyle within containing five Ionic columns on a side, and with a projecting porch of six Doric columns.

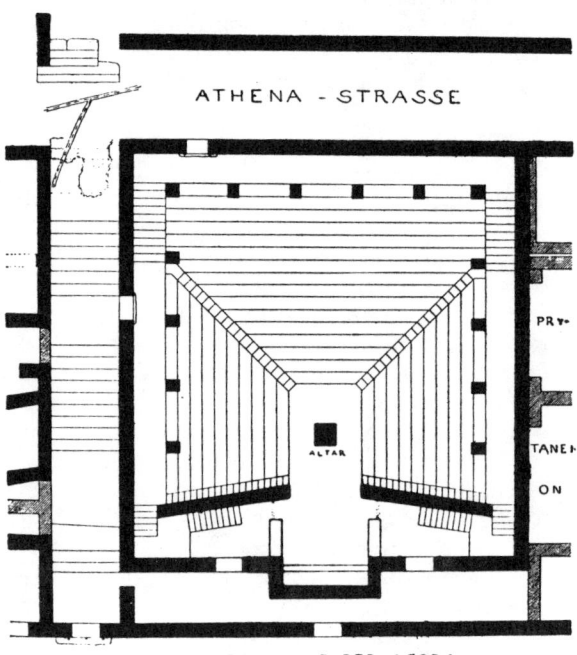

FIG. 108.—THE ECCLESIASTERION AT PRIENE.

More elaborate is the great Bouleuterion at Miletus, erected in the time of Antiochus IV (175–164 B.C.), and providing twice as much seating space as at Priene. The complete design forms a rectangle about $114\frac{1}{2}$ feet by 183 feet, besides the projection of the propylon on the east front. But the main building forms a rectangle of only $79\frac{1}{2}$ by $114\frac{1}{2}$ feet, subdivided into three parts by two pairs of Ionic columns spaced on centres $52\frac{3}{4}$ feet in one direction, $43\frac{1}{4}$ feet in the other. Here again we must assume that simple trusses were employed for the longer spans (this being the direction imposed by the roof) and braced girders for the shorter. In this instance a complete theatre, a little more than a semicircle, is inscribed within the rectangle, the interior thus unsatisfactorily contradicting the external design. The theatre again has four radiating flights of steps, dividing it into three sections, with eighteen rows of seats providing for 1,200 to 1,500 spectators. The triangles left between the semicircle and the rear corners of the hall were utilised for stairways ascending from rear entrances. Even more misleading than the insertion of the theatre is the treatment of the roof with pediments on the shorter ends of the rectangle, disagreeing with the direction of the main axis; a hipped roof would have been more noncommittal. The external treatment recalls the west wall of the Erechtheum, translated into Doric terms: a basement of pseudo-isodomic masonry, rising to the level of the topmost seat, carries a colonnade of twelve semi-detached Doric columns on the fronts, eight on the flanks, besides pilasters at the corners, all with corresponding pilasters on the inner face and in some cases with windows between. The wall panels lacking windows are decorated with shields in relief. Ionic influence appears in the egg-and-dart carved on the echinus of these Doric capitals, and in the dentil course inserted under the cornice instead of mutules. The court to the east of the Bouleuterion is also lined with Doric columns on the three other sides; but the propylon, which breaks through the east colonnade, and the heroum or altar at the centre, are of rich Corinthian forms.[1]

This form of theatral Bouleuterion was by no means isolated; the inscription on that at Miletus records that Antiochus IV simultaneously built another like it at Antioch. Another example with a semicircular theatre inside a square occurs in the Bouleuterion or Synedrion at Messene in the Peloponnesus, where the resemblance to a theatre was heightened by the diazoma in the auditorium, and by the perfect circle of the orchestra. Also at Athens the Bouleuterion was altered in this period to accommodate a theatre-like arrangement of stone seats inserted within the older ⊓-shaped plan; and on one side a portico was added.

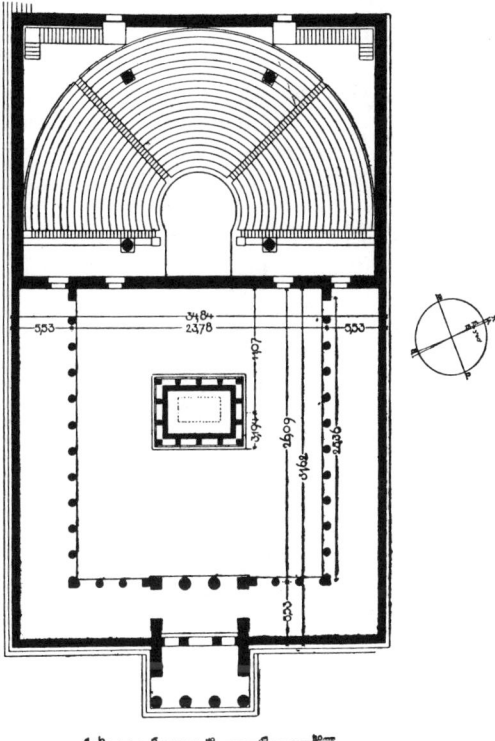

Fig. 109.—The Bouleuterion at Miletus. (Restored by Knackfuss.)

The theatre, during this period, passed through a considerable evolution, from the Greek to the Roman type, involving several distinct processes. The most striking of these are concerned with the scene building, namely, the introduction of the proscenium and the episcenium, and eventually also the appearance of the low Roman stage and of the more elevated Graeco-Roman compromise form. In view of the vast numbers of theatres in all parts of the

[1] For the propylon see also p. 287.

Greek world erected for the first time after 300 B.C., or remodelled after that date to conform to new patterns, it will be impossible to discuss them individually. We may attempt to summarise their outstanding characteristics, taking each part of the theatre separately, and examining the phases through which it passed.

During the early Hellenistic period many older theatres of the characteristic parascenium type of the fourth century survived without change, as at Athens, Epidaurus, Eretria, Oeniadae, and Magnesia.[1] There was also the exceptional form at Megalopolis, where for special reasons there was no scene building apart from the portico of the Thersilion. Among the new theatres built during the early Hellenistic period in Asia Minor, on the other hand, the tendency at first was to omit the parascenia, the straight scene wall formed by the front of the scene building answering all requirements, as at Delos, Assos, and Priene, all of which seem to have been begun at or shortly before 300 B.C.[2] The beginning of this tendency was previously apparent in the very shallow parascenia at Magnesia; and one reason for accepting it may have been the desire to bring the background of the action closer to the audience, instead of having it deeply recessed between parascenia.

Just at this moment, however, a great change in the methods of play-writing was taking place at Athens, requiring considerable modification in the form of the scene building of the theatre. The impulse for the innovation lay in the New Comedy of the Hellenistic period, with its emphasis on dialogue and the clear delineation of a few characters rather than the massive chorus, conditions which were better satisfied by a raised stage for clarity of vision, but shallow to give the effect of relief. On the other hand, conservative adherence to a great classical past was so strong at Athens, involving annual revivals of the classical tragedies and the use of lyrical choruses, that the theatre had to be adaptable to two distinct functions, and the raised stage required for the New Comedy had to be temporary and removable, constructed therefore in wood. The purely temporary character of this structure, known as the "proscenium," is illustrated by Athenian anecdotes of the last decade of the fourth century.[3] This was

[1] Epidaurus is the only doubtful case, no projecting proscenium foundations of the fourth century having been excavated.

[2] The earliest expense accounts for work in the theatre at Delos, dating from 305 B.C., mention the scene building, but as of wood construction, as was also, judging from the low cost, a (parodos) entrance; stone construction was begun only in 297 for the auditorium and in 274 B.C. for the scene building (see p. 299). As for Priene, the oldest document is a reference to seating rights granted to a certain Apellis at about 330 B.C., whence it has sometimes been assumed that the theatre was begun soon after laying out the plan of the town at the middle of the century. Gerkan, on the other hand, because of his theory of the date of the stone proscenium (see note 3, p. 301), hesitates to date the theatre so early and would prefer 300–250 B.C. But the theatre of 330 B.C. may have been provisional; and the stone proscenium is clearly a later addition to the scene building, which may preferably be dated about 300 B.C.

[3] One of these compares the courtesan Nannion, dressed in all her finery, with the proscenium of the theatre (Athenaeus, XIII, 587b; Harpocration and Suidas, *s.v.* Nannion), and the other refers to a painting of Demetrius Poliorcetes set up in the proscenium during the Demetrieia festival (Duris of Samos, quoted by Athenaeus, XII, 536a). The comparison with Nannion suggests that in the minds of her contemporaries the "proscenium" was something that could easily be stripped away, leaving only bald nakedness; it was hardly a permanent architectural colonnade. It may have been some such temporary screen that caused Suidas to define proscenium as a "curtain" before the scene building.

HELLENISTIC THEATRES

exactly the moment at which Menander's influence made the New Comedy the accepted form, presumably shortly after his first victory in 315 B.C., but considerably before his death in 292 B.C. The removable wooden proscenium was probably retained at Athens until about 150 B.C.[1]

Shortly afterward, we may presume, this form of temporary wooden proscenium was inserted in other existing theatres, such as Epidaurus, Oeniadae, Eretria, Delos, Magnesia, Priene, and Assos. The only actual evidence comes from Delos, where the records of expenses tell us of woodwork for the scene building in 305 B.C. and again in 282 (painted wooden *pinakes* for the proscenium), 280 (work on the scene building and proscenium), and 279 (a wooden beam for the "logeion" or proscenium roof). The stone scene wall is first mentioned in 274, but with a wooden upper scene (episcenium) and lower and upper parascenia (parodos entrances?), so that stone for the parascenia in 269 may have been for new flanking auditorium walls; even as late as 250 B.C. there seems to be an allusion to the wooden proscenium.[2] There are records of a temporary wooden proscenium in the stadium at Delphi for the Pythia in the third century.

The next step was the erection of theatres in which a proscenium was planned from the very beginning, as a low colonnade directly in front of the scene building, still employing wood as the material because of the precedent of Athens, though there seems in these later examples to have been no intention of removing it. Among examples are probably to be named Ephesus and Elis.[3] Also the huge rock-cut theatre at Syracuse, as reconstructed by Hieron II between 238 and 216 B.C.,[4] appears to have contained a proscenium from the very beginning, and in front of it provision for a special temporary structure of wood, a removable shallow low Italic stage erected for farces or burlesques (*phylakes*), with a high wooden back wall which when used would conceal the proscenium, and with a subterranean gallery cut in the rock. At New Pleuron in western Greece the theatre was built against the town wall of 234 B.C. and so must be later than that year; it appears to have had some sort of a proscenium from the very beginning.[5] Particularly illuminating is a group of theatres of special type to be found at Oropus, Eretria, Corinth, and Sicyon.[6] In this

---

[1] Dörpfeld believed that he found actual traces of a wooden proscenium at Athens, but did not publish the evidence.

[2] At Delos the inscription on the proscenium for which payment was made in 250 B.C. was undoubtedly on wood; the total cost of 5 drachmas was insufficient for carving in stone, and it is quite impossible that the fragmentary inscription on the architrave of the stone proscenium, *IG.*, XI, 4, 1070, should have been the one mentioned in 250 B.C. as has been suggested.

[3] The situation at Elis and Ephesus is conjectural; in the latter there is no trace of any Hellenistic proscenium, even in stone, all having been uprooted during the Roman alterations.

[4] The supposition that what we see to-day is in part the old fifth-century theatre of Hieron I is undoubtedly fallacious. The work is clearly that of Hieron II (270–216 B.C.), whose name and that of his queen Philistis are carved on the two *kerkides* at the left of the central one (dedicated to Zeus Olympius), followed in the next *kerkis* to the left by that of the princess Nereis who became his daughter-in-law in 238 B.C.

[5] It has been suggested that at New Pleuron the theatre originally had no proscenium; but it is difficult to see how the actors could have circulated with only a single entrance in the tower of the wall exposed to the view of the spectators.

[6] At Oropus Dörpfeld believed that he detected traces of a wooden proscenium earlier than that of stone. At Sicyon what were thought to be actual traces of the stone proscenium

THE HELLENISTIC AND GRAECO-ROMAN PHASES

group the orchestra and scene building were sunk below the natural surface of the ground; the complete area of the scene building was excavated at Oropus, but only two of the three chambers at Sicyon, and only a stairway or a vaulted tunnel in the Hellenistic rebuildings of the theatres at Corinth and Eretria (Fig. 110). The fact that the proscenium must have been planned from the very beginning in these theatres is particularly well illustrated in the two last, where the scene building alone, if used without a proscenium for performances on the sunken orchestra, would not have permitted circulation of the actors out of sight of the audience.[1]

A final step in the evolution was the substitution of stone for the wooden proscenium, a change of which we have definite traces at Eretria, and perhaps also at Athens and Oropus; and at Delos, of course, we have the wooden proscenium attested by the expense accounts and the stone proscenium by the actual remains. At Sicyon the stone proscenium itself passed through two stages, an earlier form in poros limestone, later rebuilt in marble. As for the date of this change from wood to stone, it would seem that Athens conser-

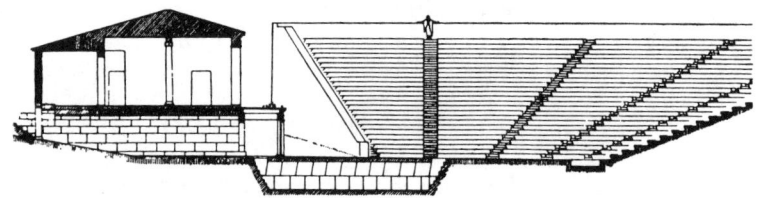

FIG. 110.—SECTION OF THE THEATRE AT ERETRIA.
(Restored by Fiechter.)

vatively adhered to the temporary structure until the latest possible moment, perhaps about 150 B.C.[2] Slightly earlier seem to have been the transformations in the provinces, since the stone successor of the wooden proscenium at Oropus bears a dedicatory inscription of about 200 B.C. The expense accounts would

are now otherwise explained: it is an earlier stylobate of poros, lying behind the later marble stylobate at the same level, but intended for a poros proscenium colonnade. Also at Megalopolis the so-called traces of an old wooden proscenium are now to be rejected; for as a proscenium stylobate the older sill not only extends too far beyond the possible limits of a proscenium but it also encounters the difficulty that the holes assumed to be for the attachment of columns are not arranged symmetrically with reference to the axis of the theatre; its true function in connection with the movable scene building will be explained below (p. 307).

[1] This neglect of the lower storey both at Corinth and Eretria shows that the current dating of these two theatres in the fourth century must be erroneous. Another anomaly occurs at Eretria, where dating of the sunken orchestra in the fourth century would have corresponding implications as to the date of the barrel vault; but the vault and the deepened orchestra probably both date from the middle of the third century. At Eretria, under the later marble proscenium stylobate, is a lower stylobate of poros limestone which clearly supported an earlier Hellenistic wooden proscenium (a fact which is sometimes denied).

[2] Dörpfeld, Bulle, and others regard the present proscenium at Athens as later than 86 B.C. (the Roman conquest), on account of the poor workmanship of the only existing part, the stylobate; nevertheless the very fact that the Piraeus theatre, which with its proscenium is a direct copy of the Athenian, is known to have existed as early as about 150 B.C., would imply that the alteration at Athens had already been made before that date.

INTRODUCTION OF THE STONE PROSCENIUM

suggest that the stone proscenium at Delos was erected in 180 B.C.[1] As for the stone proscenium at Priene (Fig. 111, Plate LXIX), all that can be said is that it must be earlier than statue pedestals of about 135 B.C. erected against it;[2] but whether it dates back as far as 200 B.C. is uncertain.[3]

The foregoing analysis suggests that the proscenium was introduced at Athens and elsewhere in a removable wooden form at some time during the last decade before 300 B.C.; that it was then reproduced in fixed form, though still in wood, in some provincial theatres as early as 250 B.C.; and that it finally appeared in stone, again first in provincial theatres, at about 200 B.C., Athens being one of the last cities to succumb to the idea of the permanent proscenium at about 150 B.C.[4] It is evident that the permanent proscenium could on occasion have been employed as a background for action on the orchestra itself; and it seems clear that, for revivals of the classical drama in the second century and later, it was, in effect, so used. But the very fact that it was so rapidly transformed into a permanent architectural motive, combined with the circumstance that its dimensions agree with those given by Vitruvius (i.e. height 10–12 Roman feet or between 9 feet 8 inches and 11 feet 7 inches, depth 0·2929 of the basic or orchestra circle radius) for the portion of the Greek theatre which, he says, was used as a raised stage, and also the corroborative fact that, at this

[1] The date usually assigned to the marble proscenium at Delos, 274–246 B.C., seems too early; a second period of construction in the theatre is suggested by the account of 179 B.C., mentioning the making of *pinakes* on the logeion (i.e. in the episcenium).

[2] Gerkan, after first dating these statue pedestals 155 and 140 B.C., now dates them 135 and 130 B.C., but employs them only as evidence for the time when the action was transferred from the orchestra (with the proscenium as background) to the top of the proscenium, when blocking two of the intercolumniations would no longer have interfered with the action.

[3] The crucial example for the study of the relation of the proscenium to the scene building is the theatre at Priene, which has been so exhaustively examined by Gerkan that his interpretation has frequently been accepted in recent years. In short, he regards the proscenium as part of the original structure of the theatre; and, since a proscenium implies the existence of an episcenium of some sort, whereas the existing traces of the episcenium at Priene were obviously intended, with the three great *thyromata*, for use at a time when the action took place on the top of the proscenium (and therefore, as Gerkan admits, long after the period to which he assigns the proscenium), he restores an early Hellenistic stone episcenium (without the *thyromata*), of which no evidence survives. Both the stone proscenium and the stone episcenium as early as the original structure of this theatre would be without parallel; and, since it is difficult to imagine that these great advances in theatre design were invented in the small provincial town of Priene, a hypothetical predecessor has been suggested at some important metropolis not yet excavated, such as Alexandria. But it seems unnecessary to indulge in such speculation. As Dörpfeld has pointed out, the late character of the proscenium architecture and its lack of organic connection with the scene building, the fact that all the methods of access to the upper parts (outer and inner stairways and elevator shaft) are later additions, and the late date (admitted by Gerkan) of the only existing traces of the episcenium with its *thyromata*, make it practically certain that before the second century B.C. the scene building at Priene was of a single storey, its front specially finished to be seen from the auditorium without a concealing proscenium.

[4] The date of the introduction of the stone proscenium has been variously given as the fifth century (Puchstein, Allen), or the fourth (Bulle), or the third (Dörpfeld, Bethe Fiechter, Gerkan, Bieber—though Dörpfeld would restore a marble false proscenium or colonnaded screen in the fourth-century Lycurgan theatre, for which the extant foundations give no justification). For none of these early states of the proscenium can actual remains be cited, since even those who adopt a third-century origin regard the present remains as much later (see note 2, p. 300).

THE HELLENISTIC AND GRAECO-ROMAN PHASES

very time, the theatre suddenly received an upper storey which was clearly designed as a background for the action, all make it certain that the true purpose of the proscenium was to serve as the podium or stage on which the action normally took place.[1]

The length of the proscenium was theoretically equal to that of the scene building, which in turn varied from 44¾ feet at Oropus to 137 feet at Ephesus.

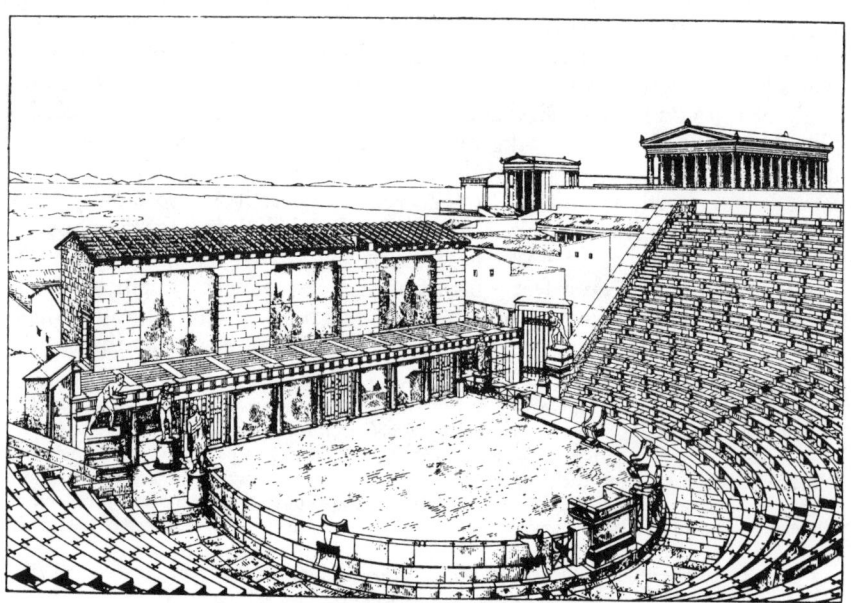

FIG. 111.—THE SCENE BUILDING OF THE THEATRE AT PRIENE.
(Restored by Gerkan.)

In practice, however, while identical in length at Oropus, Sicyon, and Elis, the proscenium might be either longer (as at Priene, Assos, and Delos) or

[1] This is the most warmly disputed point among all the doubtful questions pertaining to the Greek theatre. The situation was obscured, before accurate dates were known, by the obvious incompatibility between the literature (considered chiefly in the light of the great dramas of the fifth century) and the monuments (the remains of the actual theatres showing them in their Hellenistic forms). Scholars were divided, in varying degrees, between two extreme groups: those who attempted to prove that the fifth-century drama was produced on a stage of more or less Hellenistic character, and those who held that it was produced on the orchestra level and that any architectural construction was merely scenic background. The most extreme view is that of Dörpfeld, who held that the action always took place on the orchestra until the Romans generally reconstructed the Greek theatres in the second century A.D.; he insisted that Vitruvius was quite wrong in his interpretation of the Greek proscenium as a high stage. There are three different interpretations now current as to the initial use of the proscenium: (1) That here adopted is that its roof formed a terrace (*logeion*) employed as a raised stage, the action taking place before the upper storey of the scene (Bethe, Bulle, Fiechter, Bieber). (2) The proscenium, like the scene building previously, served merely as the background for action in the orchestra, and its roof was used merely by actors when supposed to appear on roofs of houses (Dörpfeld). (3) A compromise, the proscenium being built first as a background for action in the orchestra, while in the second century B.C. the action was transferred to its roof as a raised stage (Gerkan).

302

shorter (as at Ephesus), these variations being due to the varied manners of getting access to the proscenium roof, as described below. The length of the proscenium might include fifteen intercolumniations (Athens and Megalopolis), thirteen (Assos, Delos, Piraeus, Eretria, Sicyon, and Epidaurus), eleven (Oeniadae, Priene, and Babylon), nine (Oropus and Thera), or only seven (New Pleuron). The central interval is widened at Athens (in this case to double the normal spacing), Piraeus, and Sicyon; otherwise the spacings are uniform.

The proscenium colonnades were usually Doric, the columns being slender and widely spaced, sometimes completely circular (as at Athens, Piraeus, Thera, Thasos, and Magnesia), or circular with slightly projecting flanges on either side just sufficient to counteract the diminution and make the intervals rectangular (as at Megalopolis). Generally, however, they were in the form of semi-columns backed by rectangular piers, rebated for the attachment of panels either in line with the column centres (as at Delos) or farther back (as at Oropus and Priene). Ionic semi-columns were likewise employed, either facing rectangular piers with the rebates set farther back (as at Sicyon) or with peculiar wings projecting from either side to enframe the intervals (as at Epidaurus and Oeniadae). Among smaller details, it may be noted that in the Ionic capitals at Epidaurus, as at Bassae, the volutes are bent anglewise at the corners, and also that the entablature at Epidaurus has both frieze and dentils, whereas at Oeniadae it is of the friezeless Asiatic type. At New Pleuron the columns are nondescript, completely circular, and support merely rude lintels. The heights of the orders, that is, of the proscenium stages, vary from 8 feet 2 inches at Oropus and New Pleuron, to 8 feet $11\frac{1}{4}$ inches at Priene, 10 feet 10 inches at Eretria, 11 feet 7 inches at Epidaurus, and about 12 feet 10 inches at Athens, according very closely with the height of 10–12 Roman feet prescribed by Vitruvius for the Greek (i.e. Hellenistic) stage. The columns themselves vary in height from 6 feet $6\frac{1}{2}$ inches at Oropus, and 6 feet 9 inches at Priene, to 7 feet 1 inch at New Pleuron, 9 feet $\frac{3}{4}$ inch at Epidaurus, and about 10 feet at Athens. The intervals passed through several phases, being at first filled with movable shutter-boards or painted wooden panels (*pinakes*), but later filled or backed by rubble walls which might be painted with formal panels. One or three of the intervals were utilised for actual doorways communicating with the orchestra. The projection of the proscenium colonnade toward the orchestra varied from 6 feet 4 inches at Oropus to the unusually large amount of about 11 feet 4 inches at Babylon and Segesta, 13 feet at Syracuse (as measured to the face of the stylobate);[1] at Athens it projected only 7 feet 4 inches outside the scene wall.

As we have noted, the parascenia of the Lycurgan theatre at Athens were of an unusual type in the form of open colonnades, which survived during the first centuries of the Hellenistic period. At the time of the erection of the proscenium at Athens, the old parascenia were dismantled and rebuilt farther back, projecting only 4 feet from the proscenium and so intruding less upon the

[1] The tremendous projection of 24 feet in the late proscenium at Megalopolis, as measured from the Thersilion stylobate, is difficult to explain. No traces of a scene wall were recorded by the excavators, either on the Thersilion stylobate or closer to the proscenium colonnade which was erected directly above the old poros sill. It is evident that the Megalopolitans had become accustomed, after long use of their rolling stage (see p. 307), to the location of a proscenium in this position; but there must have been a scene wall somewhere behind it, presumably of poor material, that was either destroyed or had become unrecognisable.

parodoi. In the reconstruction at Epidaurus the assumed old parascenia were cut off to reduce the scene building to a simple rectangle; but they were recalled by very narrow colonnaded parascenia, only one interval in width, projecting only $3\frac{1}{4}$ feet from the new proscenium. Likewise the scene building at Oeniadae was reconstructed, with wide parascenia (quite unrelated to their narrow predecessors) consisting of semi-columns attached to piers, projecting only 20 inches from the new proscenium colonnade. Among new theatres of the period, that at Piraeus copied the shallow parascenia of Athens, while the first poros limestone parascenia at Sicyon imitated the almost imperceptible projection at Epidaurus.[1] These colonnaded parascenia in effect increased the length of the proscenium, and might have five intercolumniations (Athens), four (Piraeus), three (Oeniadae), or only one (Epidaurus and Sicyon).

The other type of parascenia with solid walls continued to be erected, when combined with a proscenium, only in a few provincial theatres. Thus at Syracuse there were massive blocks of living rock, $117\frac{1}{2}$ feet apart and projecting 13 feet from the scene wall, enframing the proscenium. The theatres at Tyndaris, Segesta, and Pompeii are later and show more Italic influence, particularly in their upper parts, though each had heavy parascenia enframing the proscenium. At Segesta the fronts of the parascenia are of increased thickness toward their inner corners, in order to support upper parascenia which receded obliquely, while at Pompeii the inner returns of the parascenia themselves were oblique rather than at right angles to the scene wall, both being devices intended to improve the view of the scene. In another type, the little theatre at New Pleuron, where one of the towers flush with the inner face of the city wall served as the central element of the scene building, parascenia were built against the city wall $37\frac{1}{2}$ feet apart and $7\frac{3}{4}$ feet in projection, in this case flush with the proscenium.[2] Similarly at Babylon, where it may have been felt that the use of mud bricks for walls and baked brick for columns required heavy abutments, there are solid parascenia aligning exactly with the proscenium. In this sense, perhaps, the solid terrace walls supporting the lateral ramps at Oropus, Eretria, Sicyon, and Elis might be regarded almost as parascenia flush with the proscenium colonnades, except for the fact that at Epidaurus they lie beyond the true parascenia and so are analogous to the wing walls erected for a similar purpose beyond the parascenia in the Athenian theatre.

With a proscenium masking the scene wall, and the action transferred to the top of the proscenium, the only method of obtaining a background for the action was to carry the scene building up into a second storey (the episcenium), a feature of the Hellenistic theatre.[3] At the beginning, which again we may

[1] On the other hand, some of the second-hand stylobate slabs employed for the later marble proscenium at Sicyon, being second-hand corner slabs, have given rise to a suggestion that there were once wide and deep colonnaded parascenia as in the Lycurgan theatre at Athens. Study of the mason's numerals on the slabs, however, shows that they were derived from a square pavilion which probably bore no relation to the theatre.

[2] It has sometimes been suggested that the theatre at Thera originally had parascenia, in its early Hellenistic form, and that these were later demolished; but re-examination of the evidence at Thera seems to exclude the use of parascenia at any time.

[3] The use of an upper storey (episcenium), even to the extent of including the *thyromata*, was advocated also for the fifth-century theatre by Dörpfeld and Fiechter; but it hardly seems possible that anything more than momentary and exceptional employments of an upper storey could have occurred before the Hellenistic age.

presume to be about 300 B.C., the episcenium seems to have been a removable wooden structure. We have references to the wooden upper scene (and parascenia) in the expense accounts of the theatre at Delos in 274 B.C. Symmetrically arranged sockets for upright timbers occur along the inner face of the scene walls at Elis and Sicyon and Oropus, and at Elis along the rear wall as well. At Oropus (Fig. 112), moreover, the dedicatory inscription shows that the stone episcenium was erected about 150 B.C., fifty years later than the stone proscenium and the wooden episcenium. At Eretria, when the first wooden proscenium on a poros stylobate was erected on the new low level, the upper storey was reconstructed in wood, as a removable framed building set across

FIG. 112.—THE THEATRE AT OROPUS.
(Restored by Fiechter.)

the front of the space between the old parascenia.[1] The timber uprights at Elis are grouped with reference to three great openings in the upper storey.

When the wooden episcenia were reconstructed in stone (as at Delos, Elis, Sicyon, Oropus, Eretria, Priene, and Ephesus),[2] the front wall of the episcenium

---

[1] In connection with this alteration at Eretria the inner faces of the old parascenia were moved about 3 feet so that the parascenia were widened from 13 to 16 feet, and the interval between them was diminished from $72\frac{1}{2}$ to $66\frac{1}{2}$ feet. Traces of the wooden construction at this upper level were noted by Bulle; but Fiechter misinterpreted them and restored an upper proscenium colonnade between the old parascenia, with new parascenia restored at the lower level. It is obvious that the so-called upper proscenium must be contemporary with the deepened orchestra (since it forms a cutting across the top of the barrel vault and so could not be interpreted, for instance, as a proscenium erected while the theatre was still on the upper level); but such a proscenium colonnade on a high terrace is without analogy. The only alternative is to regard the traces as belonging to a wooden episcenium, which, at the time of the building of the marble proscenium, was replaced by a stone episcenium 85 feet long with a row of six interior columns. And the so-called lower parascenia are really the ends of the ramps.

[2] Gerkan, who studied the theatre at Priene in great detail, inferred that there had been an upper storey in stone from the very beginning, but assumed that it originally had only

consisted, not of a bare wall, nor even of a wall with a single doorway,[1] but rather of a series of huge rectangular openings, three at Priene, five at Oropus and Oeniadae, seven at Ephesus and Miletus, separated by rectangular piers.[2] These openings (*thyromata*)[3] could be temporarily closed by movable painted scenery; or one or more could be left open to increase the depth of the stage or to accommodate settings of interiors of any desired size. The widths of the openings were usually graded, with the greatest in the centre; at Oropus the central one was also higher, the architrave here terminating with consoles so that only the triglyph frieze was carried across in the form of a lintel.

For ascending to the proscenium or stage floor, and especially to permit lateral entrances, various expedients were adopted. In an Eastern type, with the proscenium extending slightly beyond the scene building at either end, ladders placed against these protrusions at first presumably gave access from the rear; but for convenience second-storey passages or galleries were soon added against each flank of the scene building, as at Priene, Assos, Magnesia, Miletus (the third stage), and Delos, so that lateral entrances, as well as those through the scene wall, could be made directly from the second storey. Likewise at Ephesus and Miletus (the fourth stage), where the endmost of the seven *thyromata* lay beyond the ends of the proscenuim, the latter had triangular extensions and thus permitted lateral entrances from the outermost *thyromata*.[4] But in a mainland type, following classical precedent, lateral entrances were made along the parodoi, by means of ramps aligned with the proscenium and ascending if the orchestra were on level ground (as at Epidaurus, Sicyon, and the earlier form at Elis), but horizontal if the orchestra itself were sunk to the height of the proscenium (Eretria, Oropus, and the second form at Elis). When there were projecting parascenia, they were normally of a single storey with their tops level with that of the proscenium, so that, as at Epidaurus and Sicyon, the ramp approaches gave access to the top of the parascenia and thence to the

a single narrow central doorway and that it was later rebuilt to form the three *thyromata*. This, if accepted, would profoundly modify our conception of the initial use of the proscenium, since a single narrow opening would have been insufficient for the action of a play. But, as Dörpfeld has shown, there is no evidence whatever for an earlier stone episcenium at Priene. The episcenium of which traces actually remain is, as both Gerkan and Dörpfeld agree, a later alteration; but Dörpfeld also shows that other features which would have been required to give access to the hypothetical earlier episcenium are likewise additions, namely, the interior cross-walls with the stairway and elevator shaft, as well as the outer west stairway and the doorway at the top. The corresponding doorway in the upper east wall probably never existed, and the later extension on the east elbow of the proscenium, which would be required to give access to this hypothetical east doorway and thus was regarded by Gerkan as evidence for transferring the action from orchestra to proscenium at about 150 B.C., was more probably an addition of Roman times to fit the deeper stage. Also at Ephesus the episcenium appears to be an addition to the lower storey.

[1] Gerkan restored a single doorway in his assumed original stone episcenium at Priene, just as Dörpfeld had in his old (but subsequently abandoned) theory of the Greek episcenium.

[2] The first *thyroma* opening to be discovered was the central one at Oropus, and it was then thought that there was only one. Multiple openings were first observed at Ephesus. There is slight uncertainty as to the number at Oropus, three or five.

[3] Dörpfeld insists that the term *thyromata* refers to the swinging wooden doors analogous to the wooden *pinakes* in the proscenium below; but in fact the term means the door opening itself with its enframement, and was officially applied to the great north door of the Frechtheum, there referring to the marble enframement.

[4] Gerkan calls these outermost *thyromata* at Ephesus and Miletus the upper parodoi.

RAMPS AND MOVABLE SCENE BUILDINGS

proscenium. The same was true of the larger parascenia at Athens and the Piraeus, where stairways were undoubtedly inserted in the narrow wings beyond the parascenia. But in some of the late Hellenistic theatres of the western colonies, and so presumably under Italic influence, as at Tyndaris, Segesta, and Pompeii, the parascenia had upper storeys forming decorative pavilions (oblique at Segesta) enframing the stage, while the scene wall itself was much more elaborately decorated with pilasters and columns instead of the simple rectangular openings. These monumental methods of ascending to the proscenium (particularly as contrasted with the inadequacy of some of the lower storeys as at Eretria and Corinth) form additional corroboration of the use of the proscenium roof by the actors in general, rather than by an occasional visitor to the housetops. And as the latter, in turn, had to go higher, special provision might be made; at Priene there was a stone elevator shaft through which an actor might be hoisted to the roof of the episcenium.[1]

Three theatres of the period had exceptional wooden removable scene buildings, due to special circumstances. At Pergamum, the theatre erected by Eumenes II (197–159 B.C.) was so close to the edge of a terrace that, in order to leave room for a street, the scene building was erected with a skeleton of vertical timbers which could be dismantled and assembled at will. A series of sixty-four sockets, consisting of holes about 14 inches square cut through blocks of special hard stone (rebated for movable covers) imbedded in the terrace pavement, are arranged in three rows with symmetrical groups and angle treatments, permitting varied architectural schemes; the slightly smaller distance between the first and second rows indicates that this was the site of the proscenium;[2] and it is clear that the timber uprights were grouped with reference to three great openings (*thyromata*) in the episcenium. At Megalopolis, where the portico of the Thersilion had to be respected and the area of the orchestra had to be left open for popular festivals, a third-century modification was the great wooden scene building which, instead of being dismantled at the end of a performance, was rolled away on wheels and stored in a great shed (the *skenotheke*) erected for the purpose in the left-hand parodos, with internal dimensions of 27 by 116 feet and a clear height of perhaps 24 feet. Inside the shed is a stone "guard-rail" close to one wall and a foundation for a windlass at the entrance; and across the orchestra, $23\frac{3}{4}$ feet outside the Thersilion stylobate, runs a sill course with holes and slots for fastening a wooden screen to conceal the wheels and the gap under the movable scene building when it was in place. At a later time, when Megalopolis was partially restored after the devastation of the city in 222 B.C., the unwieldy movable scene building was discarded and an ordinary stone proscenium was erected, with its stylobate directly on top of the older sill; the Thersilion must at this time have been in ruins (as Pausanias saw it later), and there was no longer any reason for respecting its portico. At Sparta, where physical contests likewise predominated, the area behind the orchestra was open to the fields beyond; but for dramatic performances a rolling stage was erected in the Augustan period and stored in a great brick shed (called the *skenotheke*) in the right-hand parodos. Three rows

[1] Bethe and Dörpfeld prefer to interpret this shaft, only $2\frac{1}{4}$ by $2\frac{1}{2}$ feet in area, as a well for the upright mast of a crane.
[2] Also the holes of the first row are only $2\frac{1}{4}$ feet deep, the others $3\frac{1}{4}$ feet deep.

of stone sills indicate that the scene building, about 16 feet deep, was moved on rollers, and that the proscenium, about 6½ feet deep, was dragged on wheels for which tracks were provided in the first and second sills.

It is possible that the great Hellenistic theatre at Mytilene was the one imitated by the architects of Pompey for the great theatre built for him at Rome, though with greater richness of the *scaenae frons*; through this process the Hellenistic theatre, with its high but shallow stage, and its large orchestra, may have become the model which Vitruvius describes as the Greek theatre. Actually, however, the Vitruvian description of the Greek theatre strictly applies to the Hellenistic theatre only through the fact that the theatre of Pompey may have been imitated, with modifications, from that at Mytilene.

Before turning to the other type described by Vitruvius, the Roman theatre, it is desirable to examine a type which he did not describe at all, for the reason that it was not invented until just after his time, at the beginning of the Empire, so that most of the surviving examples are of the first and second centuries A.D. This was a Hellenistic invention of Asia Minor, or, more strictly, a Hellenistic compromise with Roman requirements, spreading to the Greek mainland.[1] In this type the high Hellenistic proscenium and the deep Roman stage might be reconciled, in already existing theatres, in one of two ways. The more conservative method was to retain the older Hellenistic proscenium as a high podium, obtaining the deeper stage simply by demolishing the old scene wall, with its *thyromata*, and building a new scene wall (*scaenae frons*) farther back. Such a method was adopted at Oropus, Sicyon, and Priene. In the last, for example, the Roman *scaenae frons* was set back 16½ feet from the proscenium (7½ feet from the old scene wall) and decorated with two great niches and three doorways. Sometimes, as at Sicyon, a solid wall was erected just behind the existing proscenium columns so that they became engaged; or, as at Priene, the proscenium intercolumniations were walled up and decorated with painted panels, except three in which door openings were left; or, as at Babylon, the proscenium colonnade might be entirely removed and a solid wall substituted. The alternative method of deepening the stage was to retain the scene wall where it stood, but to build out in the orchestra a new podium, generally a simple panelled wall, though retaining the former height of the proscenium. Such a method was followed at Miletus, Magnesia, and Ephesus. At Ephesus, for example, the new stage front was built about 30 feet in front of the old scene wall; but in this case a new *scaenae frons* of massive construction 14 feet thick was erected on the site of the old scene wall, extending both before and behind it so that the actual depth of the stage became 20 feet. The new stage front, 8½ feet high, consisted of a Roman imitation of a Doric proscenium with twenty-one intervals, the central one widened; but the columns are only 5 feet 4 inches high, less than the height of a man, set on a high double socle (just as at Babylon), so that one cannot assume that this was the Hellenistic proscenium transferred outward;[2] and under the stage was a forest of supporting

[1] Dörpfeld, who denied that Vitruvius described the true Hellenistic theatre, claimed that what he had in mind was this "Asia Minor theatre"; but this seems impossible, first because all the examples are later than Vitruvius, and second because the depth of the stage is too great to fit his prescription, being as great as that in the Roman theatre.

[2] Wilberg, in publishing the theatre at Ephesus, argued that this was the original Hellenistic proscenium transferred to a new position.

piers arranged in three rows. Later a double stairway ascending from the orchesra was added against the middle of the stage front. Similarly at Magnesia, where the stage was only 7½ feet high, the front was formed by a new wall of rubble and behind it were thirty piers of various forms to support the stage, with a double stairway at the middle. Both the three rows of supporting piers and the central double stairway recur in the theatre at Tralles.

Among new theatres of this period, the compromise scheme of the high stage is best represented at Termessus, with a stage 7 feet 9 inches high and 17¾ feet deep, and at Sagalassus, with a stage 9 feet 2 inches high and 24¾ feet deep. As in the remodelled theatres, the heights approximate those of the Hellenistic proscenia while the depths are vastly greater. The stage front was merely panelled and might have several small doorways, only 3 feet 2½ inches high at Termessus and 2 feet 10¼ inches high at Sagalassus, probably used for animals or gladiatorial paraphernalia.

A few comparatively shallow stages, even in theatres which must be regarded as belonging to this compromise type, are to be found in Asia Minor. Thus at Pergamum a permanent stone stage was eventually erected, decorated with semi-columns; but on account of the restricted site, the depth of the stage was only 9 feet 2 inches.

The other type of theatre discussed by Vitruvius is the Roman, characterised by its low but deep stage; he specifies that its height should be no more than 5 Roman feet (4 feet 10 inches) while its depth should be the distance from the stage front (at the centre of the orchestra) to the parallel line formed by the base of an inscribed equilateral triangle (the location of the *scaenae frons*), and thus mathematically half the orchestra radius. This low Roman stage appeared for the first time in Greek lands in the reconstructed theatre of Dionysus at Athens, as dedicated by Nero in A.D. 61; the stage was 5 feet 2¼ inches high and extended forward 32 feet from the Lycurgan scene wall, of which the site became the Roman *scaenae frons*; the front of the stage seems to have been decorated with sculptured reliefs,[1] and behind the stage front was a trench containing the apparatus for lowering the curtain.[2] Very much later, at about A.D. 270, the stage itself was rebuilt by the archon Phaedrus,[3] employing the same marble reliefs but now cutting them down to obtain a height of only 4 feet 8¼ inches, with interrupting niches occupied by crouching Sileni apparently taken from Nero's *scaenae frons*, and with a central stairway descending to the orchestra. Strangely enough, the colonnaded Doric parascenia of

[1] The exact height of Nero's stage depends on the assumption that the marble reliefs originally belonged to it and that their backgrounds were cut down about 6 inches, as was Dörpfeld's former assumption. Later he suggested that Nero's theatre had no stage at all (which seems improbable), while others consider that the reliefs came from an independent structure, perhaps an altar of the time of Hadrian, thus would give no evidence for the Neronian stage. It seems most probable, however, that the reliefs actually belong to the stage of Nero.

[2] Other remains of the curtain apparatus appear in the Roman alterations at Corinth, Sparta, Syracuse, Taormina, Herculaneum, and Pompeii.

[3] The date of Phaedrus, after vacillating from the end of the third to the end of the fourth centuries, appears to be settled by the fact that his inscription on the stage is cut on a second-hand cornice block of the Stoa of Eumenes, dismantled just after the Herulian invasion of A.D. 267 along with the monument of Nicias, the temple of Ares, and other structures to clear the area just outside the new fortifications.

THE HELLENISTIC AND GRAECO-ROMAN PHASES

Lycurgus, as rebuilt in the Hellenistic period, were retained even in the Roman theatre, flanking the deep stage.[1] Another instance of adaptation of a Roman stage to an existing Greek theatre is that at Corinth, where, after the erection of a special amphitheatre outside the city in late imperial times, the theatre was restored to its proper use, with the rows of seats carried down to the orchestra level, and the scene wall rebuilt as a Roman colonnaded frontispiece. Similar reconstructions took place in the later theatres at Syracuse, Taormina, Herculaneum, and Pompeii. But at Sparta, when the movable scene building was destroyed by fire, the emperor Vespasian in A.D. 78 built a permanent architectural frontispiece or screen exactly on the site of the wooden scene wall (the middle sill), decorated with columns enframing eleven narrow passages of which the thresholds are at the orchestra level. Because of the requirements of athletic events there could be no fixed proscenium or stage; but the column bases rest on a podium about 5 feet high so that a temporary stage could be erected at this level for dramatic performances without interfering with the architecture. A permanent low stage of this height was erected much later at Sparta, about A.D. 200, when eight of the passages were blocked up and the three others were widened, with their thresholds raised to the stage level, enframed by pairs of free-standing columns and giving access to three rooms behind;[2] a new stage front was now built 27 feet from the scene wall,[3] Among the new theatres erected in accordance with the Roman type the most perfect is that at Aspendus, designed by the architect Zenon in the reign of Marcus Aurelius (A.D. 161–180); here the stage was 4 feet 6¾ inches high and about 25 feet deep, with a removable floor of wood. The only Roman theatre known to have been erected in Greek lands without any preparation whatever for a stage is that at Stobi in Macedonia, dating from the Hadrianic period; the *scaenae frons* contains five doorways through each of which descends a flight of six steps to the floor of the arena.

At the back of the stage of the Graeco-Roman or of the Roman type was erected, not the simple scene wall with the *thyromata* of the Hellenistic period, but the colonnaded *scaenae frons* of Roman invention (as used first in Pompey's adaptation of the theatre at Mytilene), rising in two or sometimes even in three storeys above the stage level and thus forming permanent architectural scenery, gradually becoming more and more enriched (Fig. 113).[4] Thus in Nero's theatre at Athens there were two storeys of decorative Corinthian colonnades,

---

[1] This accounts for the preservation of so many pieces of the parascenia, as contrasted with the absence of fragments of the Hellenistic proscenium, of which all except the stylobate was removed during the Roman alterations.

[2] Bulle infers that when these three pairs of columns were erected the permanent low stage did not yet exist; he concludes that not until the third century or later was the stage added, together with the raising and widening of three doorways. But the pairs of columns of about A.D. 200 are so obviously designed to enframe the widened lateral doorways that these and the raised stage must all have been contemporary.

[3] Behind it are "rubbish pits," interpreted by Bulle as post-holes for a wooden stage, but more probably for the curtain poles.

[4] Dörpfeld's derivation of the *scaenae frons* as the functional descendant of the proscenium, merely raised to a higher level so that it could continue to form the background for the acting, is contrary both to the actual fact that the proscenium was often undisturbed or merely rebuilt at the orchestra level, and to the interpretation of the proscenium as a stage for the acting.

THE SCAENAE FRONS

breaking forward and backward to form alternate niches and pavilions. The Corinthian capitals are of a peculiar type without volutes, merely two tiers of great acanthus leaves, the upper ones occurring only at the four corners and enframing horned chimaera heads between winged rosettes.[1] Also incorporated in this fantastic design were both standing and crouching marble statues of Satyrs and Sileni, and arched heads of openings enclosed within rectangular frames, cut in single blocks of Hymettian marble.[2] The *scaenae frons* at Ephesus dates from A.D. 66, though the top storey is of the third century A.D.; when this was added there were, including the peculiar stage front, four superposed storeys of colonnaded architecture. In many of these great frontispieces there were niches between the columns, filled with statues; sometimes there were large apses. There was a tendency to use alternating triangular and segmental pediments, staggered in superposed storeys. At Aezani the back wall was decorated with a series of columns standing 6 feet from the wall and carrying a second tier of columns, the lower storey being of the composite order, and

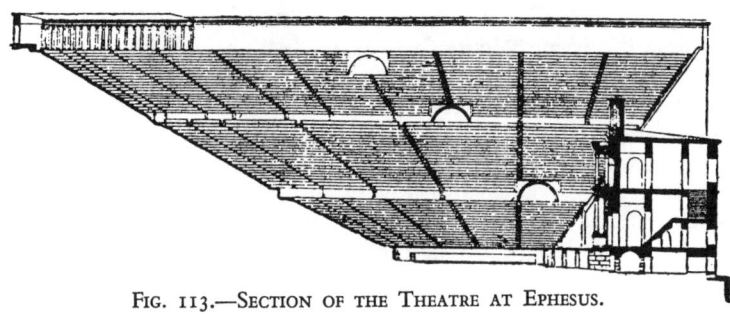

FIG. 113.—SECTION OF THE THEATRE AT EPHESUS.
(Restored by Wilberg.)

the upper Corinthian; these columns were arranged in pairs, with doorways between them, the central doorway being flanked by columns of greater size. Also at Ephesus, Termessus, and Myra the composite order was employed, with capitals like those in the arches of Titus at Rome and of Trajan at Beneventum. At Aspendus the back wall of the scene had the usual three doorways and the tiers of columns, entablatures, and pediments; the stage was roofed, above the two colonnaded storeys, by means of cantilever trusses rising from back to front.[3] The exterior of the rear wall at Aspendus, 80 feet in height and 360 feet in length, has no other architectural embellishment than that of its drafted and rusticated masonry in courses of varying heights, showing the simplicity of treatment which lasted in Asia Minor even down to Roman times, the only Roman elements to creep in being the moulded archivolts of the range of arches in the upper portion of the wall.

We now return to the early Hellenistic theatre, for the purpose of examining the orchestra. In the earliest theatres of the period, before the erection of the

[1] Similar capitals are known from Eleusis, Corinth, Delphi, Patras, Corcyra, Tarentum, the sunken ship off Mahdia (Tunis), Pompeii, and Rome, all of the imperial period.
[2] This is the type of arched opening made famous, through the Roman Porta de' Borsari at Verona, in the Cancelleria Palace at Rome.
[3] Similar traces of the stage roof exist in the Roman theatre at Orange in France.

311

permanent proscenium, the orchestra was imagined as a full circle; and at Priene, in fact, the basic circle (that of the $1\frac{1}{2}$ inch projection of the nosing of the lowest seat) was actually marked out as an engraved circumference with a diameter of 62 feet $2\frac{1}{2}$ inches, exactly tangent to the scene building (without the proscenium). At Assos and Delos the basic circles are slightly larger, 64 feet $2\frac{1}{2}$ inches (the face of the lowest seat) and 66 feet $1\frac{1}{2}$ inches (the step below the *proedria*), respectively;[1] and at Assos the scene building lies $13\frac{3}{4}$ inches outside this basic circle, while at Delos the scene building intersects the basic circle to the extent of 19 inches, though it intersects the effective orchestra circle (the inner edge of the gutter) by only $7\frac{1}{2}$ inches.

When the permanent form of proscenium came into existence, with the transference of the acting to its top, the orchestra became less important and tended to suffer gradual encroachment. But in many cases, as at Athens with its conservative adherence to a great classical past, and also in other centres where lyrical choruses and revivals of the classical tragedies required the use of an orchestra, its subordination was at first hardly perceptible. In some of the remodelled theatres, as at Athens and Epidaurus and Magnesia, where the scene building had been so designed as to recede far behind the orchestra circle, even the insertion of the proscenium left the circle intact. Similarly at Oeniadae the desire for a complete orchestra circle caused a shift of 2 feet in the centre, from which was struck out a smaller circle 51 feet 8 inches in diameter, having toward the auditorium a new curb with a moulded face $14\frac{1}{2}$ inches high, the orchestra surface being raised to this new level. The surviving portion of the old orchestra surface at Oeniadae now became a sunken ambulatory (as at Epidaurus), the width logically diminishing from 8 feet 8 inches on either side to 6 feet 8 inches at the middle, and with the original narrow gutter sunk in its floor.[2] Among new theatres erected at this period, the full orchestra circle was respected also at Piraeus, Corinth, Eretria, Thera,[3] and Syracuse. In two of these, moreover, the greater spaciousness was obtained by the use of shifted centres for the auditorium (as at Athens and Oeniadae), the differences being 2 feet 5 inches at Piraeus and 5 feet 4 inches at Corinth, the auditorium centres in all cases being closer to the scene buildings. Just outside the orchestra circle was a narrow gutter with covers at Syracuse; at Piraeus and Corinth the deep Athenian gutter with bridges and movable covers was reproduced; and at Eretria was used the broad shallow gutter of Epidaurus, 6 feet 4 inches wide and 16 inches deep, with a roll moulding on the inner edge facing the auditorium.

In most of the new theatres, however, the proscenium overlaps the orchestra circle, though by varying amounts. We have noted that the scene building was exactly tangent to the basic circle at Priene, and almost so at Assos and Delos. So also in two of the new theatres planned for proscenia from the very first, Sicyon and New Pleuron, with basic circles 79 feet 8 inches and 35 feet 2 inches

[1] The dimensions at Assos must be restored, the lowest seat having been removed in Roman times. The basic circles were planned as $62\frac{1}{2}$ (Priene), $66\frac{1}{2}$ (Assos), and $68\frac{1}{2}$ Ionic feet (Delos, using this unit while independent from Athens); the effective orchestra circle inside the gutter at Delos, $64\frac{1}{4}$ feet or $66\frac{1}{2}$ Ionic feet (like the basic circle at Assos), is identical with the orchestra circle at Athens (60 Doric feet).

[2] The proscenium architrave at Oeniadae has a dedicatory inscription showing that the orchestra was remodelled at the same time.

[3] At Thera the orchestra and auditorium are later than scene building and proscenium.

in diameter, the circumferences are exactly tangent to the scene buildings; and this rule was repeated by Vitruvius in his description of the Greek (i.e. Hellenistic) theatre (Fig. 114). In theory, therefore, the proscenium should intersect the basic circle by the full amount of its projection; and this, too, was recognised by Vitruvius, who says that the proscenium should intrude upon the circle to the extent of the segment cut off by an inscribed square, this segment fixing the depth of the proscenium as about three-tenths (or 0·2929) of the radius of the basic circle. In actuality, the proscenium overlapped the basic circle by $11\frac{3}{4}$ feet (or 36 per cent) at Delos, by $10\frac{3}{4}$ feet (or 27 per cent) at Sicyon, by 9 feet (or 29·28 per cent) at Priene, by $7\frac{3}{4}$ feet (or 44 per cent) at New Pleuron, and by $6\frac{3}{4}$ feet (or 21 per cent) at Assos. Only at Priene, therefore,

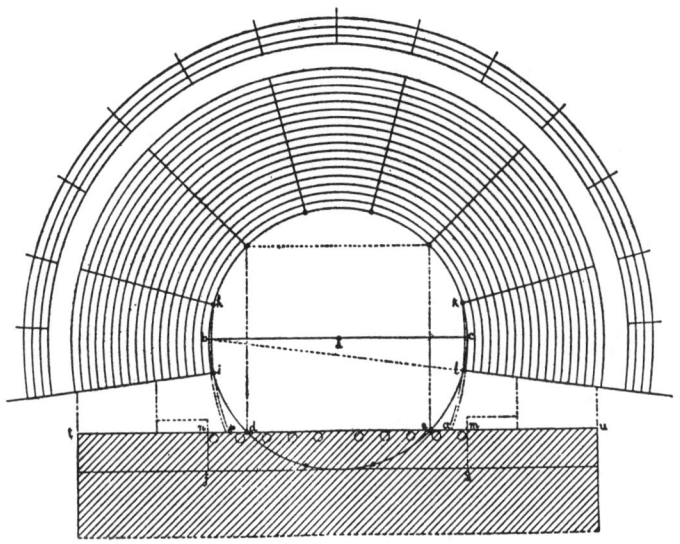

Fig. 114.—Scheme of the Greek (Hellenistic) Theatre, after Vitruvius.

does the face of the proscenium stylobate exactly coincide with the side of a theoretical square inscribed in the basic circle; for at Sicyon and Assos the proscenium fails to attain the square by 9 and 28 inches, respectively, while at Delos and New Pleuron it overlaps the square by 29 and 32 inches, respectively. But on account of the variant forms of the gutters, omitted in the little theatre at New Pleuron, narrow at Delos and Assos, deep and wider with bridges at Sicyon, and shallow but 6 feet wide at Priene, the proscenium overlaps the effective orchestra circle by 1 foot 10 inches at Priene, 4 feet 8 inches at Assos, 6 feet at Sicyon, $7\frac{3}{4}$ feet at New Pleuron, and $10\frac{3}{4}$ feet at Delos.

In a group of small or simple theatres constructed without gutters so that (as at New Pleuron) the orchestra coincides with the basic circle, the latter was set out at some distance from the scene wall in order to avoid excessive overlapping. This was the case, for instance, at Oropus, where the proscenium overlaps the orchestra by 2 feet 1 inch, and at Segesta and Babylon, where the overlapping is 4 and 5 feet, respectively.

Conversely, in a group of more monumental theatres, there was a tendency to thrust the basic circle even closer to the scene building than in the formula given by Vitruvius, so that, instead of being tangent, the basic circle was intersected by the scene wall to the extent of 1 foot at Tyndaris, 1¾ feet at Sparta (the rolling wooden scene), 3¼ feet at Ephesus, and about 5½ feet at Miletus. In all these instances, however, the amount of the basic circle thus cut off is exactly or nearly identical with the reduction of the radius by the orchestra drain, so that the orchestra circle itself is tangent to the scene wall, and the area of the orchestra is cut off by the full depth of the proscenium.[1] The extremes in the curtailment of the orchestra are represented at Pergamum, where the movable wooden proscenium overlapped the orchestra circle by about 23½ feet, and at Megalopolis, where both the wooden rolling proscenium and its stone successor overlapped by 26½ feet.

At Corinth occurs the unique peculiarity of a quadrangle inscribed within the circle of the orchestra, so to speak, even though the circle was so laid out as to be respected by the proscenium. For this quadrangle, varying in width from 73 feet at the back to 69 feet at the front, projects 48½ feet from the scene wall, while the orchestra circle is apparent only in a bubble-like segment projecting 16¼ feet from the quadrangle; the "wings" protruding beyond the circle on either side nearly fill the ambulatory, the gutter here being completely covered over. The curious outline of this area, defined by a curb with a cyma reversa moulding facing outward at the bottom, is strangely reminiscent of the presumable trapezoidal orchestra in the daughter-city of Syracuse.[2]

Among other peculiarities of the orchestra were the tunnels reached by steps from within the scene building or proscenium, and giving access to the middle of the orchestra by means of another flight of steps, so that actors in revivals of classical dramas might make sudden appearances from the lower world, as at Eretria, Sicyon, Magnesia, Tralles, Syracuse, and Segesta. At the centre of the orchestra, too, was usually an altar of Dionysus; but at Priene an altar was erected on the circumference, toward the middle of the auditorium, at about 200 B.C. At a later moment, and therefore unsymmetrically, five marble thrones were set out on the circumference at Priene, three on one side and two on the other; and at about the same time five thrones were likewise distributed about the circumference at Oropus and others again at Eretria; for these were three of the theatres in which no provision had been made for seats of honour in the lowest tier of the auditorium.[3] Later still at Priene the five thrones were pushed farther back toward the gutter, with *proedria* benches inserted between them.

[1] The unknown dimensions in this group are the radius of the original orchestra at Tyndaris and the projection of the proscenium at Ephesus, no traces of either having been recorded. At Tyndaris, to be sure, even the basic circle has been obliterated by the removal of the lowest seats; but the diameter of 79½ feet restored by Bulle seems incredible in such a small theatre, and it seems more reasonable to assume that the Romans, instead of lowering the level about 3 feet 2 inches as he assumes, in reality raised it (as at Corinth) by 2 feet, thereby eliminating eight rather than four rows of seats. The diameter of the circle of the lowest seat would thus have been 59½ feet.

[2] This arrangement belongs to the original Hellenistic theatre, and was completely buried under the arena and orchestra levels of the successive Roman theatres.

[3] The seats at Oropus have inscriptions of about the time of Sulla (86 B.C.), and thus are later than the proscenium and episcenium.

GRAECO-ROMAN MODIFICATIONS OF THE ORCHESTRA

The orchestra of the Graeco-Roman theatre of the compromise type, with the high but deep stage, was naturally unaffected if the remodelled theatre retained the proscenium in its original location. But when the stage front, on the other hand, was thrust out into the orchestra, the distance from the orchestra centre was reduced to 17½ feet (Magnesia), 13 feet (Miletus), or even 10 feet (Ephesus). In new theatres, however, space was allowed for the deep stage by locating the scene wall or *scaenae frons* far outside the circumference of the orchestra circle, by 8 feet 10 inches at Termessus and by 17 feet 1 inch at Sagalassus. Thus the orchestra circle is overlapped by the stage only to the extent of 8 feet 10 inches (28 per cent of the radius) at Termessus and by 7 feet 8 inches (18 per cent of the radius) at Sagalassus. It is evident that, in spite of the depth of the stage, its front adheres very closely to the rule given by Vitruvius for the Greek (Hellenistic) theatre, that it should overlap the orchestra to the extent of the segment cut off by an inscribed square (i.e. three tenths or 0·2929 of the radius). It appears, moreover, that at Termessus the circumference of the orchestra circle intersects the exact middle of the stage, between the front line and the *scaenae frons*.

In many of these remodelled or new theatres of the imperial period the orchestra was made unusually large because of the desire for gladiatorial shows or wild beast combats. In the case of remodelled theatres this result was attained by cutting away the lowest tiers of seats, thereby increasing the diameter of the orchestra from 64 feet 2½ inches to 67 feet 4½ inches at Assos, from about 60 feet to 70 feet 10½ inches at Magnesia, from 50 feet 6 inches to 76 feet 6 inches at Pergamum. In some cases the enlargement was much more considerable; at Corinth, and likewise at Tyndaris in Sicily, about eight or ten rows of seats were eliminated, increasing the diameters of the arenas from 56¼ feet to 121 feet at Corinth and from 59½ feet to 82 feet at Tyndaris.[1] In both cases the former proscenium was demolished and the face of the scene building itself constituted the flattened further side of the arena (the transition from the semicircle being formed by flattened curves), so that the depth of the arena, from front to back, was 28½ feet less than the width at Corinth and 14 feet less at Tyndaris. The above-mentioned stageless theatre at Stobi belongs to this period of evolution. The orchestra now served as an arena (*konistra*) rather than for theatrical performances; the effect of this treatment upon the auditorium will be mentioned below. It is noteworthy that at Corinth, when in much later times a regular Roman amphitheatre was erected just outside the city, the theatre was restored to its proper use, with the lower tiers of seats replaced and with a new shallow gutter and ambulatory of hard Acrocorinth limestone framing the orchestra.

Among the theatres remodelled to receive stages of the low and deep Roman type, the stage front at Athens was pushed forward 32 feet from the Lycurgan scene wall and so to within 17 feet of the centre of the orchestra, while at Sparta the stage front was built 27 feet from the scene wall and so only 14¾ feet from the orchestra centre. Even in new theatres of the Roman type, as at Aspendus, the stage front was at some distance from the orchestra centre, in this instance 21 feet. In Greek lands, at least, the Vitruvian method of placing the

---

[1] For Bulle's supposition that only four rows were eliminated at Tyndaris, as contrasted with my calculation of eight rows, see p. 314, note 1.

centre of the orchestra exactly at the front of the stage (Fig. 115) was not followed. Instead, the orchestra formed a stilted semicircle, which at Athens was paved with marble, with marble slabs perforated in rosette patterns laid across the Lycurgan gutter. In the exceptional little theatre at Acrae in Sicily, where the Hellenistic proscenium already coincided with the diameter of the orchestra, a low Roman stage was built out into the orchestra for 8 feet, thus reducing it to less than a semicircle.

In all the Hellenistic theatres (with the exception of those designed or remodelled in imitation of Athens, namely, Piraeus, Corinth, and Oeniadae), the auditorium and orchestra centres coincided. The auditorium (koilon or cavea) lacked stone seats—that is, utilised the bare hillside or wooden benches

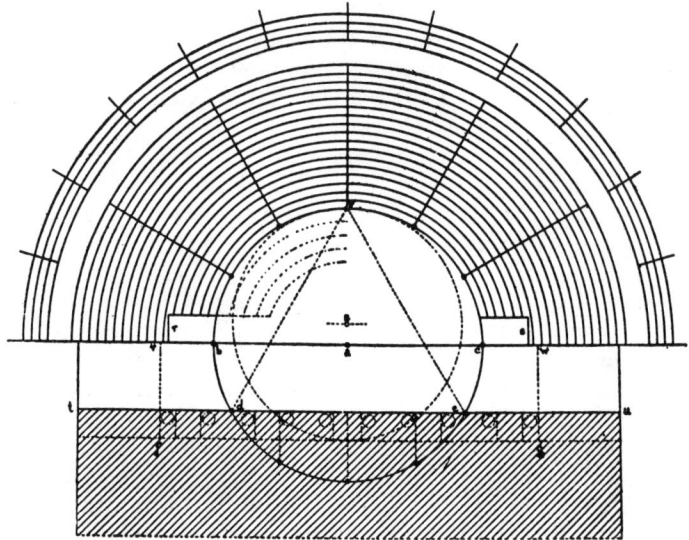

Fig. 115.—Scheme of the Roman Theatre, after Vitruvius.

—at Oropus, Thespiae, Mycenae, and Elis throughout their history, and at Sparta until Roman times. Even at Corinth the auditorium was very economically constructed, only the fronts of the seats being of stone, resting on small blocks under each joint, and packed between with earth; likewise the stairways had stone fronts with earth packing behind; and the slope was very moderate, only $1 : 3\frac{1}{8}$.[1] Conversely, in many cases the auditorium was carved more or less completely out of the living rock, as at Syracuse, Argos, and Chaeronea.

Only rarely was the plan of the auditorium an exact semicircle, as at Acrae and in the restricted site at New Pleuron, or less than a semicircle, as in the even more restricted site at Pergamum. Usually the circular arc was continued for a little more than a semicircle (as previously at Megalopolis), giving a horseshoe plan as at Sicyon, Delos, Miletus, Ephesus, Aezani, Termessus, Sagalassus, Side, Perge, Myra, Iassus, and Patara. The scheme of opening the

[1] The Romans, in rebuilding the theatre at Corinth, raised the auditorium on radiating rib walls of rubble to increase the gradient.

horseshoe by constructing only about five-sixths of the semicircle and then shifting to two additional centres with longer radii (as at Epidaurus and Magnesia) was reproduced at Priene, Syracuse, and possibly also at Corinth,[1] as well as in the Roman auditorium at Sparta; and this was recommended by Vitruvius. Another variant was the Athenian U-shape or stilted semicircle, with straight prolongations, repeated at Piraeus, Eretria, Assos, Aspendus, and Segesta. The number of sectors (kerkides or cunei) varied considerably, but was generally odd (in the lower storey) for the purpose of placing spectators on axis; there were five sectors at New Pleuron, Thera, Priene, Magnesia, Miletus, Termessus, and Iassus (the central one abnormally wide in the last); six at Assos and Soli; seven at Delos and Pergamum; eight at Babylon, Sagalassus, and Patara; nine at Syracuse, Sparta, and Aezani; eleven at Eretria, Ephesus, Side, and Aspendus; twelve at Perge; thirteen at Piraeus; fourteen at Corinth; and fifteen at Sicyon. Two diazomata, resulting in three storeys, were used at Corinth, Sparta, Ephesus, and Miletus.

The seating capacity of these theatres varied considerably. At Priene, where the auditorium receded 143 feet from the centre, there were twenty-two tiers of seats in the lower storey, twenty-five in the upper, sufficient for 6,000 spectators with the same seating allowance ($16\frac{1}{8}$ inches) that was permitted at Athens. At Syracuse, with an outer diameter of 454 feet, there were twenty-eight tiers of seats in the lower storey and thirty-nine in the upper, accommodating about 22,000 spectators; in spite of the vast size of the auditorium the gradient was unusually low, on account of the expense of cutting in rock, rising only 66 feet from orchestra to top seat.[2] The largest auditorium of all was that employed for the theatre at Ephesus (493 feet in diameter), with twenty-two tiers of seats in each of the three storeys, sixty-six in all. Among later theatres, at Aezani the external diameter was 380 feet; and at Aspendus, where the diameter is 318 feet, the auditorium had two ranges of seats, twenty-one in the lower and nineteen in the upper, and an arcaded gallery running round the theatre at top, like the colonnade erected in late imperial times in a corresponding position at Ephesus (Fig. 113).

The lowest row of seats in the auditorium generally had backs and served as the benches of honour (proedria). At Mycenae this single row of *proedria* benches was the only part of the auditorium constructed in stone (apart from the radiating stairways). At New Pleuron the only distinction was an extra course of slabs laid on the lowest tier of seats, to give them greater height. Particularly impressive is the series inserted during the late Hellenistic period

[1] The surviving remains at Corinth are inconclusive on this point; but the published restoration with a single centre combines very awkwardly with the quadrangular "wings" of the orchestra, and also, since they form a trapezoid, the Athenian U-shape with parallel sides would seem unsuitable.

[2] The only detailed publication of the theatre, by Rizzo, is so inadequately dimensioned that our calculations are in many cases approximate. There are also disturbing discrepancies, not only as to interpretation and date, but also as to actual facts; he states that the lower and upper storeys contained respectively twenty-three and thirty-six rows, making fifty-nine, while his plan and section show twenty-five and thirty-nine, making sixty-four. Not only are the twelve lowest rows of seats Roman alterations (excavated more deeply in the rock), but the same is true of the ambulatory 8 feet wide, just below them, its edge forming the face of the original lowest seat (preserving even the traces of the radiating aisles), so that we must add three more rows of seats at the bottom, making sixty-seven in all.

in the theatre of Dionysus at Athens (Plate LX), where there were sixty-seven marble thrones inscribed with the names of the priests or other dignitaries who occupied them (Plate LXI), that of the priest of Dionysus being at the exact centre.[1]

In front of the lowest tier of seats there was sometimes, even in the Hellenistic period, a fence of wooden posts let into mortise holes to keep the audience off the orchestra, as at Priene, Assos, and Eretria. Analogous in position, though very different in purpose, were the marble parapets such as that erected just in front of the thrones at Athens, waterproofed so that the orchestra could be used for naval combats as well as those of gladiators on foot. There was a similar parapet in the final period of the theatre at Corinth.

More frequent in imperial times, in connection with gladiatorial and wild beast combats, was the abrupt termination of the tiers of seats at the top of a podium, leaving the orchestra in the form of a sunken pit or arena (*konistra*). In the remodelled theatres this arrangement was obtained merely by cutting away the lowest tiers of seats, a process which also had the advantage of enlarging the diameter of the arena, as noted above, and of giving the lowest seats a better view of the rear portion of the high and deep stage. The height of the podium varies from 1 foot 11 inches at Aspendus to 8 feet 1 inch at Myra. As an additional safeguard, the edge of the podium was sometimes faced or crowned by a marble parapet. At Assos, where the podium was low (formed by the top of the second seat), the parapet was set on the orchestra level and only its upper portion rose above the feet of the spectators. At Stobi the podium was 5 feet 3 inches high, and the parapet on its top about 3 feet more. Later, at Stobi, this system was replaced by a high pit wall, rising 10 feet 8 inches above the arena and carried not only round the auditorium but also across the *scaenae frons*. Similarly at Corinth and Tyndaris the pit walls attained exceptional height, about $9\frac{1}{2}$ feet and $8\frac{1}{4}$ feet respectively, without the parapets, or 12 feet and 11 feet with them. The parapet at Corinth was part of the face of the podium, its top curving forward to overhang the arena, and the entire surface of stuccoed poros, about 12 feet in height, was painted with gladiatorial scenes and combats with wild animals. Three refuges were entered through openings in the high podium, those at Corinth being cut in the rock like caves (the central one having a stairway ascending to the auditorium) while those at Tyndaris were vaulted (those at either side connected with the parodos by a tunnel). Also at Stobi there were similar refuges under the seats.

The connection, or lack of connection, between the auditorium and the scene building had always been one of the least satisfactory features of the Greek theatre. In some of the Hellenistic theatres the parodoi assumed greater regularity, enframed between the oblique retaining walls of the auditorium and the approximately parallel terraces of the ramps to the proscenium. An organic connection was established in some cases by the insertion of parodos gateways, likewise oblique and at no logical angle to anything else, as at Priene,

---

[1] These thrones at Athens have been variously dated between the fourth and first centuries B.C.; the latest analysis of the inscriptions suggests an Augustan date, and earlier dates could be assumed for the thrones only if we could regard the inscriptions as later additions, as some, indeed, are (as late as the second century A.D.). But the style of the sculpture on the throne of the priest of Dionysus seems to be Neo-Attic and so not much before Augustus.

Delos, and Epidaurus; in the last they are double, the smaller opening giving access to the ramp.[1] And in a few instances such gateways are placed in more orderly fashion at right angles to the scene building, as at Assos, Babylon, and Segesta; likewise at Pergamum were removable wooden parodos gateways at right angles. This lack of unity persisted even in imperial times, not only in many of the remodelled theatres, but even in some of the new structures of that period, as at Aezani. In other instances, however, the auditorium was built out over the parodoi, or the parodoi were turned under the auditorium in L-shaped plan, in either case forming vaulted tunnels in the Roman manner; at Ephesus, Termessus, and Side, for instance, the vaulted parodoi are oblique, while at Babylon, Corinth, and Syracuse the ends of the auditorium were cut off and, with the vaulted parodoi, made parallel to the scene building. Only in this Roman version was it finally possible to unite auditorium and scene building into a continuous and harmonious structure as at Aspendus.

Purely Roman theatre forms were employed also for the small roofed theatre or odeum, of which the earliest surviving example is the small theatre at Pompeii, dating from about 75 B.C., with its semicircular auditorium enclosed within rectangular outer walls in order to simplify the roofing problem. Similar arrangements of a semicircular auditorium within a rectangular enclosure were adopted for the odeum built by Agrippa (about 14 B.C.) in the middle of the Agora at Athens, and that at Epidaurus inserted in the rectangular court of the gymnasium. Even closer to the theatre form, in that the exterior of the auditorium is semicircular, is the odeum of Herodes Atticus at Athens, erected on the south slope of the Acropolis at about A.D. 161. Like the neighbouring theatre of Dionysus, it is partly hewn out of the rock. The plan is merely that of the ordinary Graeco-Roman theatre, but is slightly smaller in size; the auditorium had a diameter of 250 feet. It is said to have been roofed with cedar wood; and, though this statement might perhaps be regarded as an allusion to the roof over the stage alone, it does not seem probable that such a feature of ordinary occurrence would have been stressed by an ancient writer; nor does it seem physically possible to have covered the entire area without internal supports, of which there is no evidence. Possibly the roof covered merely the seats, even so having tremendous spans effected with cantilevered trusses and chains, leaving the central portion to be temporarily covered with an awning. The same theatre plan was employed, apparently likewise by Herodes Atticus, for the odeum at Corinth and another at Patras. Similar structures were erected at Butrinto in Albania, at Taormina, and at Naples.

Amphitheatres of Roman form were in a few cases erected in Greek lands during the imperial period; but they are not properly examples of Greek architecture. One, partly excavated in the rock, exists at Corinth; there were others at Pergamum and Cyzicus in Asia Minor, and at Syracuse in the west.

The stadium retained in later times the form which it had assumed in the fourth century, though with more magnificent treatments. At Olympia a west embankment was added, with a barrel-vaulted tunnel 12 feet wide and 105 feet long giving access from the precinct. At Athens the whole structure was

[1] The parodos gates at Epidaurus have been variously dated from the fourth century to the first; probably the actual date is the third century, antedating, according to the style of the mouldings, the proscenium of the second century.

rebuilt in marble by Herodes Atticus, and a vaulted passage was constructed, providing an entrance for the contestants under the seats on the east flank, while at the opposite or open end of the U-plan was built a screen of marble Corinthian columns. At Delphi was built a corresponding screen, formed by piers and arches.[1] The most important stadia erected in the periods now under discussion are those in Asia Minor. The stadium at Ephesus was cut into the hill only on the south flank and supported by masonry on the north; additional tiers of seats were built on the hillside (Fig. 122), which had incidentally the result of giving a more monumental appearance to those who entered the town through the northeast gate, though its real purpose, as shown in other examples, was to take advantage of the natural slope on one side and to economise in the amount of artificial embankment required on the other. Similarly at Priene there were seats on one side only, with a portico behind; the other side, open toward the bay, was supported by a great retaining wall, upon which the erection of seats would have been a needless extravagance. At Aezani, Magnesia, and Perge the stadia were built on level ground, more in the Roman manner; in the first of these the great frontispiece forming the entrance at the open end of the U-plan was at the same time the *scaenae frons* of the theatre, which was on axis with the stadium; that at Perge, 809 feet in length, had arcaded walls with fifty-nine sloping barrel vaults supporting the seats. The largest stadium, but built in Roman times, was that at Laodicea-ad-Lycum, 1,000 feet in length, with semicircular terminations at each end; also at Aphrodisias the stadium had semicircular colonnades at each end.

A circus or hippodrome of the Roman type was erected at Pessinus in Asia Minor, combined with the theatre in a single composition; but in this case, instead of being on a single axis (like the stadium and theatre at Aezani) the theatre is at right angles, its scene building forming a gallery at the middle of one flank of the hippodrome, with a corresponding gallery opposite.

The gymnasium now assumed a more formal plan than that of the fourth century. The gymnasium proper was the open athletic ground for running, jumping, and throwing, while the name palaestra was given to the enclosed structures wherein wrestling and the like were practised. The palaestra at Olympia (Fig. 44 at PA) consisted of a large open court 135 feet square with a Doric peristyle round it, and, on all four sides, a series of rooms for exercise under cover, dressing-rooms, baths, lectures, etc.; on the south side was an inner colonnade for the entire width of the court, while on the north, though not for the entire width, there was a deeper room screened by a row of columns, the ephebic exedra or ephebeum mentioned by Vitruvius. Of similar form was the palaestra at Delos, where the court was smaller, 104 feet square, but again with the prominent ephebeum on the north side. A new principle appears in the palaestra (lower gymnasium) at Priene, where the north colonnade is doubled to give greater depth and protection from the sun, and the ephebic exedra is pushed farther back. So also in the palaestra at Epidaurus (Fig. 116), where great colonnaded dining halls lie at the south and east, the north side has the double colonnade and behind it a long ephebeum (with a shrine in an exedra). On the north side, too, is the propylon mentioned above.

[1] Pausanias says that Herodes Atticus finished the stadium at Delphi in Pentelic marble; but this is certainly an error, no marble having been used.

THE GYMNASIUM AND PALAESTRA

As for the gymnasium proper, the great gymnasium, at Olympia (Fig. 44 at G), which must have been an establishment of considerable importance, the great double-aisled porticus (690 feet long) on the east side, together with a single portico on the south side backed against the palaestra, and the monumental propylon at the point of junction of the two porticoes, form the most distinctive features. At Pergamum was the great triple gymnasium, built in successive terraces at levels varying by 40 feet and connected by vaulted stairways; the lowest was devoted to the boys; the middle terrace, for the ephebes of eighteen to twenty, measured about 118 by 500 feet, with a double colonnade along the north side and a small Corinthian temple at the east end; the upper terrace, called

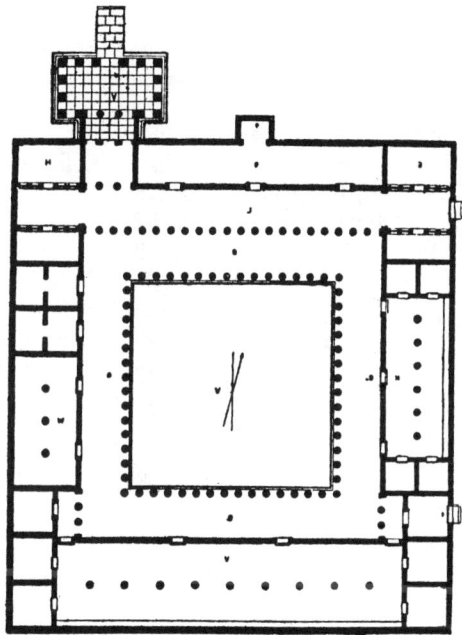

FIG. 116.—THE PALAESTRA AT EPIDAURUS.

the Panegyric gymnasium, was the largest, with an open court 118 by 243 feet surrounded by a Doric colonnade (changed by Hadrian to Corinthian) and by many rooms, including a great hall and a theatre, and with a covered racecourse built out over the middle terrace. The later gymnasia would appear to have been the prototypes of the Roman thermae, except that they were built for gymnastic exercises of various kinds, the baths being subordinated. Thus the so-called "gymnasium" at Alexandria Troas is in reality a bath, which in actual date is Roman (about A.D. 150), showing the axial composition in a rectangular block and the great vaulted halls which are characteristic of the Roman thermae; but in details it is far more closely related to the Greek gymnasium than to the Roman thermae, the principal hall containing a series of shower baths corresponding to those in the far earlier gymnasium at Delphi. But other baths, as at Ephesus, Corinth, etc., are of a more developed type rivalling in magnificence the Roman thermae and showing a very great departure from the gymnasium plan.[1]

Of buildings erected before the Graeco-Roman period primarily for use as baths, reference may be made to a rectangular structure at Colophon in Asia Minor, and to a circular room outside the Dipylon Gate at Athens. But the baths at Oeniadae in Acarnania, of the second century B.C., are the most interesting examples of the hot baths that preceded the Roman thermae. Here the arrangements are still very primitive, though the three main elements are already present: the frigidarium, a small rectangular room with a square tank; the tepidarium, a large circular room with eight basins in the floor and probably with a bronze caldron in the centre; and the caldarium, a smaller circular room with a ring of seventeen circular basins in the floor.

A type of building which came into existence in the late Hellenistic period, combining some of the characteristics of the palaestra with many features of domestic architecture, was the guildhall or place of reunion for the various national groups of bankers, traders, and warehousemen. After the destruction of Corinth in 146 B.C., when Delos became for a brief period the commercial centre of the Greek world, business groups from opposite ends of the Mediterranean had their guildhalls there, such as the so-called "Agora" of the Italians (apparently from Campanian cities such as Naples and Pozzuoli) and the "Agora" of the Poseidoniastae of Berytus (Beirut).[2] The latter, for example, erected in 110 B.C., contained an approximately rectangular peristyle court, with Doric columns $16\frac{1}{4}$ feet high and with a great rain-water cistern beneath. From the peristyle access was obtained to storerooms for merchandise, a great reunion hall, and particularly, through a columned screen at one corner, a smaller court on which faced a religious structure with four Doric columns in-antis, containing four chapels of varying sizes, dedicated (from left to right) to Heracles-Melcarth, to Aphrodite Astarte, to the Semitic Poseidon of Berytus, and to the goddess Roma.

In the private houses of the Hellenistic and Graeco-Roman periods the tendency toward increasing luxury, of which the beginnings were observable in the fourth century, becomes more evident. The examples discovered at Priene and Delos (Figs. 117, 118) customarily have the narrow entrance (D), a single courtyard (A), with an exedra (B) sheltered from the sun and the winds,[3] and one large room (C) forming the oecus as at Olynthus, and with smaller rooms and offices round the court and lighted from it. The earlier examples, as those of the third century at Priene (Fig. 117), still show in the arrangement of the oecus, with its prodomus usually with two columns in-antis, facing the north side of the court (so that the prodomus corresponds to the pastas at Olynthus), the survival of the megaron type which underlies the temple plan, a type which had been developed by the Achaean and Dorian invaders of Greece. The house proper, at Priene, usually consists of a block of four rooms, the prodomus and the megaron forming the main axis, and

---

[1] The four monumental gymnasia at Ephesus, identified by Falkener and Wood as those of the theatre and stadium (that of Vedius) and those adjoining the Thermae and the Magnesian Gate (see pp. 331–333), are of Roman design and do not fall within our scope.

[2] The term "Agora" commonly applied to these structures is a modern misnomer.

[3] Figs. 117 and 118 are oriented with north at the top.

two lateral rooms opening respectively from the prodomus and megaron; sometimes the wall separating the main rooms from the lateral rooms is straight, as if the main rooms were carried up higher than the rest with a ridge and gable in temple form (the lateral rooms merely leaning against it), while in other cases the wall jogs and could not well have been carried up as an external wall, so that the whole group of four rooms must have been under one hip roof. The long entrance passage, coming either from the south or the north according to the position of the house in the block, emerges to form one side of the courtyard, and sometimes has an informal colonnade along this side of the court, at right angles to that of the prodomus. The low buildings on the other side of the court are for servants and storerooms, and are often separated from the main block by a passage to a lateral entrance. The entire house lot at Priene, as we have noted,[1] was regularly 58 by 77½ feet (60 by 80 Ionic

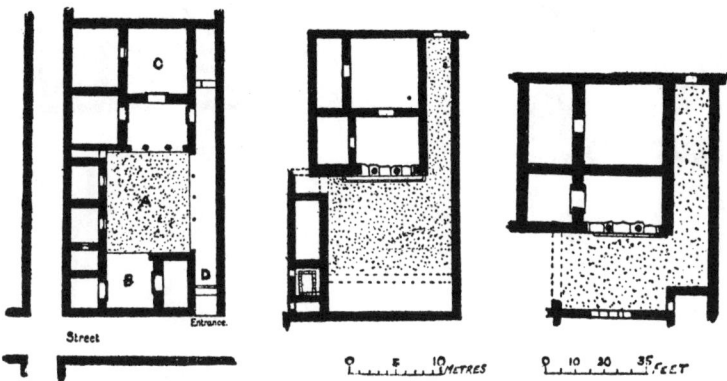

FIG. 117.—HOUSES AT PRIENE.

feet), the larger dimension running north and south, and so barely wider but considerably deeper than those at Olynthus.

By the second century B.C. a change had been brought about in the general appearance of the house, as we see in some of the altered houses of this period at Priene. The suggestion of a peristyle court in house No. XXXIII (Fig. 117 at left), as given by the larger columns of the prostas at the north and the small columns of the passage at the east, was now developed into a complete peristyle court, as when this very house was remodelled with the prodomus widened into a pastas with three large columns between piers or antae, while nine smaller columns surrounded the three other sides. This system with larger columns on one side is that which Vitruvius designates as the Rhodian type: and it was at this period, of course, that the commercial influence of Rhodes was paramount. Another feature of the altered house No. XXXIII at Priene is the annexation of the adjoining house, the two being thrown into one so that it became one of the few known Greek houses with two courts, corresponding to the andronitis and gynaeconitis of Vitruvius.

It is at Delos that we meet in full perfection this peristyle type (which of

[1] See p. 263.

course had already been foreshadowed at Olynthus). Here at Delos, in the second century B.C. (Fig. 118), the predominating type was the peristyle, often very graceful with its slender marble columns (Plate LXX), and giving almost the effect of the Roman atrium. The Delian houses are of irregular shapes, due to the absence of an organised city plan; but they follow the same principles of orientation, with one or two exceptions such as the "House of the Trident" (Fig. 118, upper right corner), which faces west. The large courtyard usually has a perfectly square peristyle of Doric columns, rarely Ionic; enclosed by

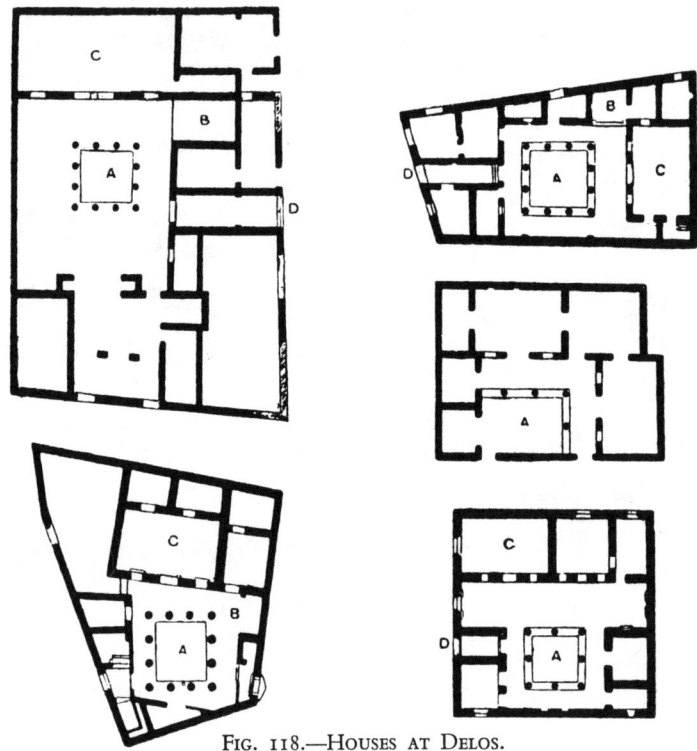

FIG. 118.—HOUSES AT DELOS.

them is a sunken impluvium, one step lower, often with an elaborate mosaic pavement. Beneath is a great rain-water cistern, covered over by arches and heavy wooden beams; the supply system consisted of lead conductors leading from the roof and down one of the columns, to which they were fastened; and water was drawn through a circular well-curb at one side of the impluvium. The columns were often of marble, sometimes only of stone with stucco; the lower parts, in the case of Doric columns, were often cylindrical or faceted rather than fluted. There might be only four columns, one at each corner; but eight or twelve were typical numbers. Sometimes, as in the "House of the Masks," the four columns forming the deeper portico facing south were larger and higher than the others, with brackets to receive the ends of the entablature coming from the adjoining lower sides; this was the Rhodian type, which we have met at Priene. Facing south toward the court was always an elaborately decorated room of great width, usually with a wide doorway between two windows, the oecus which replaced the megaron of Priene; like the impluvium, the oecus often had a pictorial mosaic floor, while the walls were of coloured stucco, sometimes imitating masonry in an incrustation style as at Pompeii. Thresholds were of marble, likewise the moulded jambs and lintels, but in more modest houses the jambs and lintels were of unmoulded gneiss. Staircases gave access to upper rooms, which often faced upon a gallery or upper storey of columns and piers carried upon the peristyle.

Even as far afield as Nippur, in Mesopotamia, such a peristyle house of Hellenistic date was constructed, interesting in that it is transitional in plan, retaining the megaron while it introduces the peristyle. The columns are Doric, of debased type, constructed of specially moulded baked brick; those of the

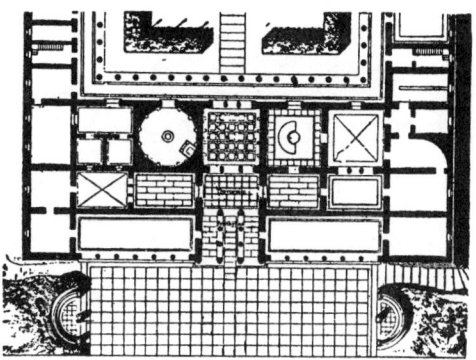

FIG. 119.—PORTION OF THE PALACE AT PALATITZA.
(Restored by Daumet.)

prodomus are elliptical in plan, while at the angles of the court are compound piers.[1]

The first portion of the description of the Greek house given by Vitruvius is in accordance with the remains of these later houses, with the peristyle and the narrow passage leading from the street, flanked by the doorkeeper's rooms on one side and the stables on the other. Beyond is the peristyle, of which the portico facing south is called the prostas (as at Priene) or pastas (as at Olynthus); from this in turn open the thalamus and other rooms of the gynaeconitis or women's quarter, including a dining-room (in ordinary houses called the andron). For Vitruvius's description applies to late houses with more luxurious additions, a second and larger peristyle court with suites of rooms intended solely for the entertainment of men (adronitis), with larger dining-rooms, picture gallery, library, and guest chambers.

An example of a residence on a more magnificent scale is the summer palace near Palatitza, in Macedonia (Fig. 119). The principal front of the palace, which faced east, measured about 250 feet; at the centre was a spacious entrance, and

[1] This is the house to which fantastically early dates, in the Aegean age, were assigned in the excavation reports.

on either side were deep open porticoes of the Doric order. The entrance was subdivided into three aisles by two rows of Ionic columns similar to those found in the Propylaea at Athens, and beyond was an open anteroom. Passing through this, one entered an immense court, about 200 feet wide, surrounded by a peristyle giving access on the north and south to various chambers, and also, on the east, to two great halls on either side of the anteroom. The southern hall was circular, with a diameter of 36 feet, decorated with marble, and in it were the foundations of a throne; this may have been the hall where foreign envoys or statesmen or generals were received and entertained, as in the throne room at Cnossus. To the south of the circular hall were the private apartments of the king. On the north was a corresponding hall, but square, apparently forming a state dining-room; it opened on to a court farther north, and beyond this, in the north wing of the building, lay the offices, kitchen, etc.

The palaces on the east edge of the citadel at Pergamum (Fig. 121), on the other hand, were in fact two rather luxurious peristyle houses, the courts surrounded by rooms elaborately decorated with mosaic floors and stuccoed walls in the incrustation style, imitating courses of variously coloured marbles.[1] Three adjoining buildings of similar type appear to have housed the courtiers.

Among the votive monuments which crowded the precincts and cities, we have already noted the simple rectangular pedestal which the Pergamene kings erected on the Athenian Acropolis in 178 B.C. (later known as the Agrippa pedestal),[2] the shaft of blue Hymettian marble in alternating courses of pseudo-isodomic masonry, with white marble base and crowning mouldings, thus raising the victorious quadriga to a much higher level than had been customary in previous centuries. Similar pedestals rose in great profusion at Delphi, among them four erected by Attalus I and Eumenes II (very similar to that at Athens), another for an equestrian statue of Prusias king of Bithynia, the great pedestal of Aemilius Paullus with its sculptured frieze commemorating the defeat of King Perseus of Macedonia at Pydna in 168 B.C., and that supporting the Rhodian chariot. There were similar pedestals at Delos, such as those of Philetaerus of Pergamum and of Antiochus the Great of Syria. A special type of pedestal or pier capital is found at Priene, characterised by the vertical Proto-Ionic volutes of the cradle type, and used both as statue pedestals and as terminal motives of exedras; those used as statue pedestals have an additional member above the abacus to serve as the plinth of the statue (Fig. 120), with sinkings in which were leaded the tenons below the feet of bronze statues.[3]

The old custom of erecting statues on the tops of tall columns was repeated in two Ionic columns at Olympia supporting statues of Ptolemy II and Arsinoe of Egypt. A more interesting type is the bicolumnar monument, with two columns set on a single podium and connected at the top by an entablature in the form of a conventional representation of an architectural order. Ten

[1] The use of incrustation imitating marble revetment suggests that coloured marbles were likewise used for this purpose; but of such we have no actual examples before Roman times. Even our literary evidence is limited to statements by Vitruvius and Pliny that Mausolus was the first to cover the brick walls of his palace at Halicarnassus with marble revetment; but this does not seem to have been coloured marble.

[2] See p. 285.

[3] These capitals at Priene were formerly assumed to have been employed in such buildings as the propylaeum at Priene; three are now in the British Museum.

of these monuments, all of the Ionic style, about 31 feet high apart from the crowning statues, were erected at Delphi alone; the capitals in one case imitated the elaborate Erechtheum examples, and in another showed the usual concave canal on one side and the convex "canal" on the other-in the manner of the archaic capitals at Kavalla. The entablatures sometimes had neither frieze nor dentils, and in other cases had both; and the frieze itself might have a cyma profile.[1] Such monuments were surmounted by family groups, or by an equestrian statue; and they are of particular importance as having been, apparently, the source of inspiration for the Roman triumphal arch.[2]

Among structures of the exedra type with colonnaded façades, of which several were erected at Delphi in the late fifth and fourth centuries, the most important Hellenistic example is the monument of Mithridates at Delos, built

FIG. 120.—CAPITAL OF PIER CARRYING A STATUE IN THE TEMENOS AT PRIENE.

in 102–101 B.C. The monument is small in comparison with its prototypes, being only $16\frac{1}{4}$ feet wide and 11 feet deep, with two slender Ionic columns between antae supporting a pediment. The interior is of interest because of the frieze of portrait medallions, containing busts in high relief, six on the rear wall and three on each end wall.

Among carved pedestals and commemorative monuments of exceptional form may be cited the galley prow on which the Nike of Samothrace was supported, also the heaped mass of shields carved in marble in the Aetolian trophy at Delphi, and two huge tripods about $13\frac{3}{4}$ feet high in the Bouleuterion at Miletus.

Among the tomb monuments of this period, we need refer only to a few.

[1] Later examples of bicolumnar monuments occur in Syria, such as a Corinthian example dated A.D. 132 near Sermeda, a Doric example dated A.D. 195 at Katura, and others at Benabil and Kefr Ruma.
[2] The actual Roman triumphal or commemorative arches erected in Greece, as at Athens (by Hadrian) and Eleusis, at Corinth (the Agora gate or "propylaea") and Salonica (by Galerius), lie outside the scope of this survey.

The sumptuary laws of Demetrius of Phalerum, which had interrupted the development of choragic monuments at Athens, had an equally disastrous effect upon the tomb stele. Henceforth the prevalent memorial was a simple colonette two or three feet high, generally tapering downward and embellished only by a collar near the top. Outside Athens, however, grave stelae continued to be used in many localities; particularly noteworthy are the carefully painted stelae of Demetrias (near Volo), and the carelessly executed examples from Alexandria in Egypt. In Roman times the stele returned to Athens, with sculpture poorly designed and executed, though sometimes with a significant enframing motive, an arch inside a rectangular frame, with rosettes in the spandrels.[1]

Another frequent form of tomb at this period was the tumulus, of which the architectural importance generally consists solely in the vaulted chamber itself, rectangular and covered by a simple barrel vault regularly constructed with stone voussoirs. Such examples are numerous in Macedonia (as at Pydna, Pella, Palatitza, Niausta, and Langaza) as well as in other areas of Macedonian influence, as in Asia Minor (tomb of Alcestas at Termessus), Egypt (Alexandria), and the island of Euboea (at Eretria and the neighbouring Vathia). The tumulus itself might vary from 130 feet in diameter and 28 feet in height (Eretria) to 250 feet in diameter and 64 feet in height (Langaza). The tomb chamber itself was frequently off-centre. The vaults vary in width from $9\frac{1}{4}$ feet (Vathia) to $17\frac{3}{4}$ feet (the vestibule at Langaza), and in height from 10 feet (Eretria) to 20 feet 10 inches (the vestibule at Langaza). These chambers were usually provided with elaborately carved and painted marble furniture, funerary beds and thrones; but special interest lies in their swinging marble doors (as much as $10\frac{1}{4}$ feet high) with elaborate bronze ornament, door handles, medallions, etc. The façade, likewise, might be extremely decorative, even though it was to be covered by earth, as at Langaza; here are Ionic semi-columns, antae, and a pediment, elaborately painted and provided with wooden doors (the marble doors in this case being at the back of the vestibule) with bronze ornaments, even though the actual door opening had to be filled with carefully cut and removable blocks of stone, for protection when it was buried. An example at Pergamum is of special interest because the chamber is covered by two intersecting barrel vaults regularly constructed with stone voussoirs, a notable prototype of Roman construction; and the perfection of the execution in this tomb at Pergamum suggests that this was by no means the first attempt.

Still another class of underground tomb began to come into favour in this period, the catacomb, such as those at Alexandria in Egypt, where the catacombs of Mustapha Pasha show purely Greek detail while those of Kom-el-Shugafa and of Anfushy show Greek and Egyptian elements intermingled. Square courts with engaged Doric columns, coupled at the corners, cut in the rock with full entablatures, and finished with fine stucco and colour, give access through numerous doorways to tomb chambers and stairways. Similar details occur on tomb façades at Hermopolis in middle Egypt.

Hellenistic tombs of temple form are numerous, though not always of

[1] The same motive appears in Roman arcades at Athens (e.g. behind the Tower of the Winds, and the stage building of Nero), and also in Roman works in Italy (e.g. the Porta de' Borsari at Verona).

individual importance. The so-called "oratory of Phalaris" at Acragas, really the heroum dedicated to a Roman matron at about 85 B.C., had a prostyle tetrastyle Ionic portico raised on a podium, supporting a Doric entablature A tomb-temple at Djambazli in Cilicia has two Corinthian columns in-antis supporting a pediment, with a high double-podium carried forward with parotids to flank the steps of the façade. Numerous examples of such structures were found at Assos. An example at Delphi, a heroum, has a vaulted chamber beneath.

An unusually complicated heroum was erected at Calydon, in the cemetery southwest of the city, in honour of a certain Leon "the new Heracles," at about 100 B.C., adding to the usual elements some of the characteristics of the palaestra; for it is probable that athletic contests formed part of the memorial services. The entire structure measures 113 by 142 feet; its centre is a peristyle court 55 feet square, surrounded by twenty-eight Doric columns. On two sides, the east and north, are series of rooms, one in each case having pairs of Ionic double-columns between antae. Of these, the T-shaped chapel at the north is the focal point of the whole scheme. The head of the T is a compartment $41\frac{1}{2}$ feet wide and $18\frac{1}{2}$ feet deep, both ends being fitted as exedrae with ⊓-shaped benches, and on the walls were medallion busts of the gods as in the contemporary monument of Mithridates at Delos. A third exedra opens from the back of the chapel compartment and, because of the thickness of the walls (6 feet), may be assumed to have been vaulted (the span being $15\frac{1}{2}$ feet); it contained a parapet or chancel, a black limestone altar-table, and a great pedestal of black limestone supporting the family portrait statues. Below this in turn was the usual vaulted crypt, but of very small dimensions, the barrel vault being only $6\frac{1}{4}$ feet wide and $8\frac{1}{2}$ feet high, provided with limestone rather than marble doors, the nailheads merely being carved in relief. In this tomb the ostentation was all for the living rather than the dead.

The heroum of the family of Charmylus (the Charmyleum) at Cos had a podium 31 feet wide and 25 feet deep, with a central flight of steps descending into a crypt beneath, while on either side of this flight are stairs ascending to the top of the podium, which supported a two-storeyed building. The lower storey, with doorways opposite each of the two ascending stairways, contained two chambers or chapels, while the upper was a partly open Ionic portico. The crypt beneath is a barrel vault 8 feet 4 inches in span, with six cells on either side at the floor level (like those radiating from the inner tholos of the Lion Tomb at Cnidus).

In Asia Minor as a general rule, however, the mausoleum type, inspired by the example at Halicarnassus, was employed for the most monumental designs. Thus at Belevi near Smyrna a great tomb was erected in the third century, either for Antiochus II of Syria who died here in 246 B.C., or for some slightly earlier Hellenistic monarch. The plan was perfectly square, the podium measuring $97\frac{1}{4}$ feet on each side of the bottom step, forming a facing for a core of natural rock, in which was hollowed out a tomb chamber, lined with stone and covered with a barrel vault 11 feet 2 inches wide, its crown 12 feet above the floor. Within is a marble sarcophagus, its cover supporting the reclining figure of the deceased king. The podium was crowned by a full Doric entablature, and above this were twenty-eight Corinthian columns arranged eight on a side. The Corinthian capitals are of normal form, with two rows of acanthus leaves and with a single cauliculus sheathing an angle and a central volute together. Statues greater than life size stood between the columns; the twenty-four large ceiling coffers were decorated with reliefs (as in the Mausoleum), depicting the funeral games of the deceased in the seven compartments on the north front, the Centauromachy in the seventeen others; and on the edge of the cornice stood figures of various kinds, three pairs of heraldically opposed griffins on each front with stone vases between them, and life-size horses and attendants serving as corner acroteria. The form of the top is still conjectural; there may have been a receding attic above the cella wall, supporting either a row of decorative figures or perhaps a pyramid.

A tomb at Mylasa, likewise of the Corinthian order, was also based on the design of the great Mausoleum, and possesses the three divisions of podium, pteron, and pyramid. While it is of much smaller dimensions, the pyramid still exists and in a sense recalls Martial's description of its prototype, as it is entirely supported by the square piers at the four corners, and by the intermediate supports consisting of columns of elliptical plan with narrow pilaster strips on each side (Plate LXXI), the angles being tied inside by diagonal beams of stone across the four corners.[1] The tomb of Hamrath at Suweida in the Hauran (Syria), of about 75 B.C., is a structure about 30 feet square, to which are engaged Hellenistic Doric columns, six on each side, supporting a pyramidal roof. Of about the same date is the so-called tomb of Theron at Acragas, with a lofty podium; the engaged Ionic columns at each corner have canted volutes and support a Doric entablature.

The great number of new cities founded or rebuilt by the successors of Alexander, the various Alexandrias and Antiochs and Seleucias, afforded unprecedented opportunities for the development of city planning. Practically all, however, continued to follow the Hippodamian scheme with minor variations in orientation, widths of streets, and sizes of blocks. Thus Dura-Europus, founded by Seleucus I Nicator or more probably by Nicanor before 313 B.C., had its main street, 30 feet wide, running from northeast to southwest, with nine other parallel streets about 15 feet wide, crossed by twelve narrow streets at right angles. The blocks average about 123 by 235 feet, their longer dimensions being from northwest to southeast, at right angles to the main street as at Olynthus and Priene; but the size of the blocks is much greater than in either of those cities. It may have been at this time that a gridiron scheme, with a main street running north and south, crossed by another at right angles, was inserted between the archaic temples on the Acropolis of Selinus.[2] At Nicaea in Bithynia, founded in 316 but enlarged after 285 B.C., we are told by Strabo that the plan was perfectly square and that from a stone at the central gymnasium, looking down the main avenues, could be seen the gates at the four sides of the city. The physician Oribasius insisted that the gridiron plan was most desirable, and that the streets should be oriented by

[1] On account of this resemblance to Martial's description the tomb at Mylasa has sometimes served as an inspiration for restorations of the Mausoleum at Halicarnassus.
[2] The plan at Selinus is sometimes attributed to the period of fortification against the Carthaginians in 409 B.C.; but such a crisis was not a propitious moment, and, in fact, most of the houses are Hellenistic. See note 2 on p. 122.

the cardinal points of the compass in order that they might be the more easily swept clear by the four winds!

A very different system was applied to Pergamum, or at least to its citadel (Fig. 121), as laid out by Attalus I (241–197) and Eumenes II (197–159 B.C.). Here was recognised the value of utilising the steep slopes for the building of successive terraces with winding approaches. Thus the gymnasium alone, as noted above, was erected on three terraces; higher up were the theatre, the Great Altar of Zeus, and higher still the royal library and the temple of the chief divinity of the city, Athena Polias; while the very top was dominated by the royal palaces.

The rich new city of Ephesus, founded on a new site on the west slope of Mount Pion by Lysimachus at about 290 B.C., in order to regain access to the receding harbour, may here be described as an instance of the splendour of the last Graeco-Roman phase. Although most of the actual remains are Roman or even early Byzantine, they are in many cases built on Greek foundations or follow the general lines of the Hellenistic city, and thus will serve equally well to illustrate the plan, and the general employment of axes at right angles (Fig. 122).[1] The main axis, running east and west from Mount Pion to the harbour, is parallel to the higher Mount Coressus at the south;[2] and upon this axis, beginning at the port, lie the great baths or Thermae, next one of the four gymnasia with exedras at north and south, the two structures having in common an entrance from the south through a circular colonnaded court and a three aisled "atrium"; east of these lie the three-aisled porticoes of Verulanus surrounding a rectangular court of about 650 by 800 feet, and east of this in turn the theatre gymnasium.[3] Along the south side of this complex runs the straight street known as the Arcadiane, a third of a mile in length, paved with marble for a

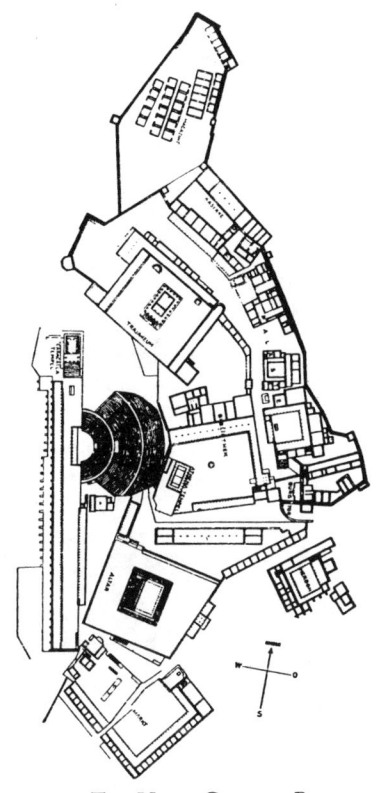

FIG. 121.—THE UPPER CITADEL, PERGAMUM.

---

[1] This plan by Falkener is here reproduced in spite of its many inaccuracies and imaginative additions, because, in the absence of any other detailed plan of the site, it will serve to give us a general idea of the monumental qualities of the scheme. Some of the necessary corrections will be made in the text and notes.

[2] These two mountains, rightly identified by Falkener, were interchanged by Wood.

[3] These four structures are not accurately shown in detail by Falkener, and the court of Verulanus is called the "agora civilis" or grand forum.

THE HELLENISTIC AND GRAECO-ROMAN PHASES

width of 36 feet, with colonnades 17 feet deep on either side, with mosaic floors, and shops in turn behind these; at the west end is a monumental gate opening on the port, at the east end a similar gate opening on the place before the theatre; on the north side are the entrances to two gymnasia and the court of Verulanus, and in the middle of the road is a notable columnar monument marking the cross-roads.[1] South of this street is another, parallel to it, leading

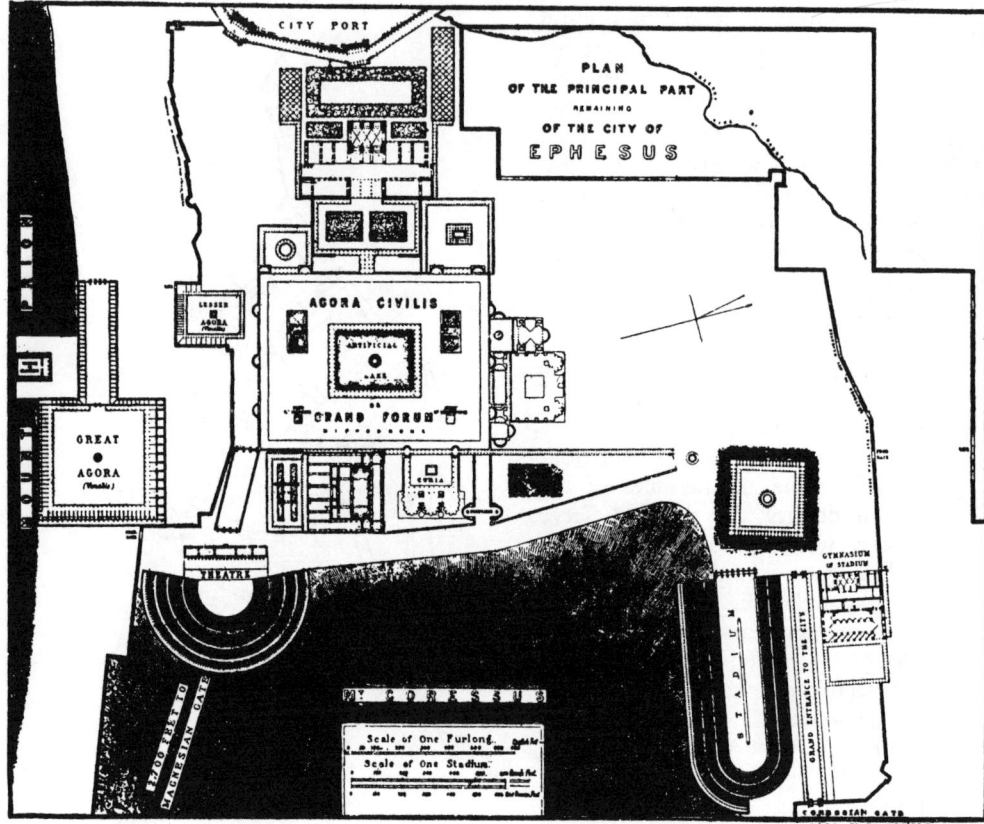

FIG. 122.—PLAN OF THE CITY OF EPHESUS (after Falkener).

east to the great agora; and the area between this and the Arcadiane street was dominated by the back of the great theatre which cuts into the slope of the hill. The great agora is an open area about 525 feet square, surrounded with porticoes, and with a clock at the centre; adjoining it are smaller courts, one at the west with a colossal nymphaeum or fountain-house,[2] and one at the south with the beautiful library of Celsus. The road to the Magnesian gate passes south along the east side of the agora, then eastward, passing the odeum on the

[1] Falkener's plan does not include the Arcadiane street, which lies between his "agora civilis" and the winding Byzantine fortification wall.
[2] The so-called "temple of Claudius," of the Corinthian order.

THE FORMAL "IONIAN" AGORA

south slope of Mount Pion, and finally reaches the Magnesian Gate, inside which is another great gymnasium. On the north slope of Mount Pion lies the stadium, with a square court surrounding a circular building opposite its west end, and the stadium gymnasium, that of Vedius, at the north; between the latter and the stadium runs a colonnaded road, with shops on either side, leading to the northeast gate.[1] From the latter, as from the Magnesian Gate, roads lead east and northeast to the temple of Artemis, distant respectively three-quarters and one and one-quarter miles.

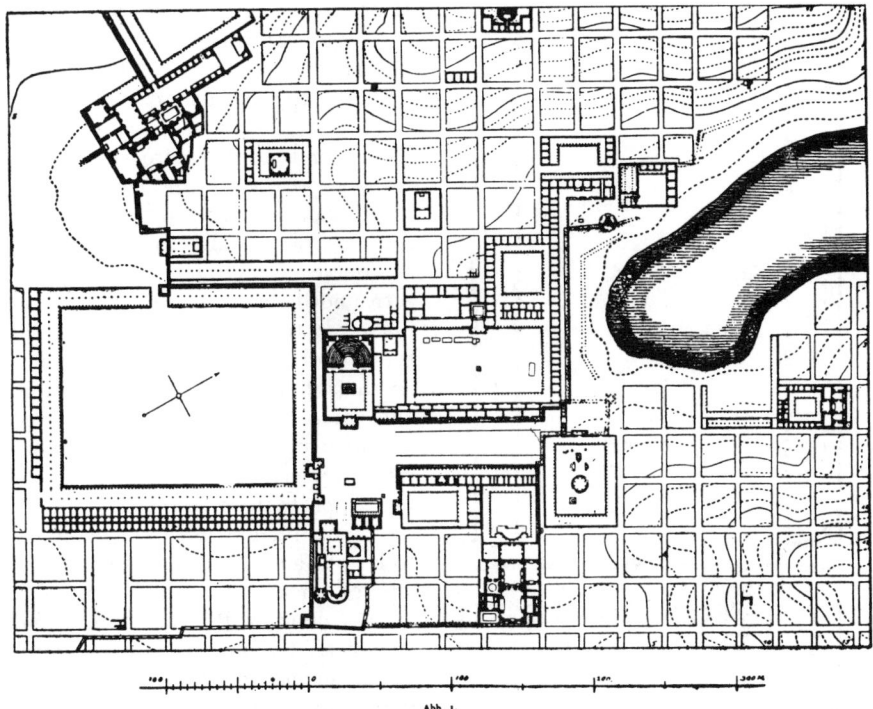

FIG. 123.—THE AGORAS AT MILETUS. (Restored by Gerkan.)

The formal plan of the agora, of which we have discussed the earlier development,[2] now tended to become even more regular in the Ionian examples, or, if the area had been laid out previously, to receive great additions and annexes. Thus the north agora at Miletus (Fig. 123) in the Hellenistic period received two ⊓-shaped annexes, both with their open sides towards the east, one being located behind the older west elbow which had the effect of closing its fourth side (though a street lay between), and a larger annex south of the main stoa and backed against the small square court, this new area enclosed between the arms of the ⊓-shaped stoas being 287 by 164 feet. Later in the Hellenistic period the fourth side was closed by a propylon, and in the imperial period this was replaced by a stoa so that all four sides were colonnaded,

[1] Wood called this the Coressian Gate.   [2] See p. 263.

enclosing an area of 287 by 141 feet.[1] The greatest of these was the south agora at Miletus, originally covering sixteen city blocks, its ⊓-shaped stoas facing east and enclosing an area of 530 by 380 feet. Here again a stoa was built later in the Hellenistic period to close the east side, the area within now becoming 530 by 419 feet, the whole with its colonnades covering twenty city blocks. The most typical example of the new form is Magnesia (Fig. 124), with a perfectly rectangular plan enclosing an area of 318 by 617 feet, interrupted only by the Propylaea forming its entrances; but even here one of the narrow ends was separated from the rest by a street passing through. These agoras all had Doric columns, often with the egg-and-dart carved on the echinus, at Magnesia supporting an Ionic friezeless entablature with dentils. At Aphrodisias was the largest of all the agoras, measuring 360 by 672 feet, the enclosing wall being lined by a double stoa facing inward, and surrounded by a single stoa facing outward: the interior stoas included four hundred and sixty Ionic columns. As the agora tended to become more and more monumental, it remained a market-place only in name, serving rather for civic purposes and for the higher professions and trades. Under such circumstances, it became necessary to lay out a subordinate agora for the sale of meat, fish, and vegetables, as was done at Priene, Tralles, and elsewhere. On the other hand, many of the smaller Hellenistic towns continued to exist with a single agora for all purposes, as at Assos (Fig. 125), where the trapezoidal shape and the long stoas on the flanks, two-storeyed on the upper side and one-storeyed on the lower (but with two storeys of markets below), with the bouleuterion at one end and a temple at the other, and all the appurtenances of a busy commercial life within, gave an effect of great dignity and charm even though it was not entirely planned in advance.

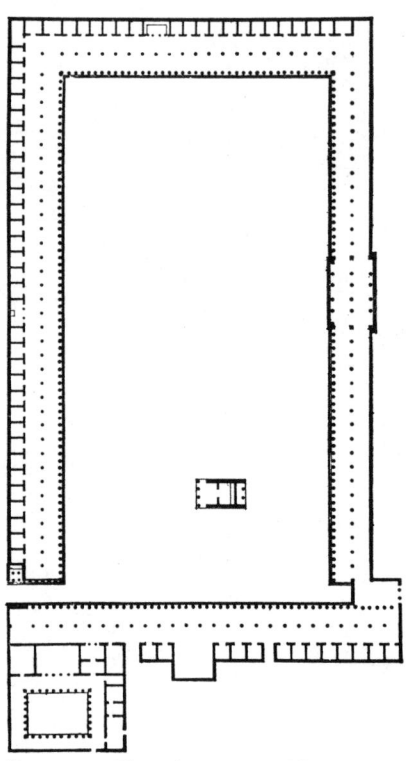

FIG. 124.—THE AGORA AT MAGNESIA. (Restored by Dinsmoor, for Marquand.)

A completely new element of the Hellenistic city was the colonnaded street, a feature occurring not only in Greece and Asia Minor but also throughout Syria; the remains now existing belong, however, to the Roman period. But under the Seleucidae the town of Antioch in Syria was laid out with wide colonnaded streets, crossing one another at right angles, the principal street,

---

[1] We have noted the addition of a stoa likewise on the fourth side at Priene.

from east to west, being about two miles in length. The central avenue for carriage traffic was open to the sky; the side avenues, bordered with shops and houses, had flat roofs over them. This arrangement formed the prototype for

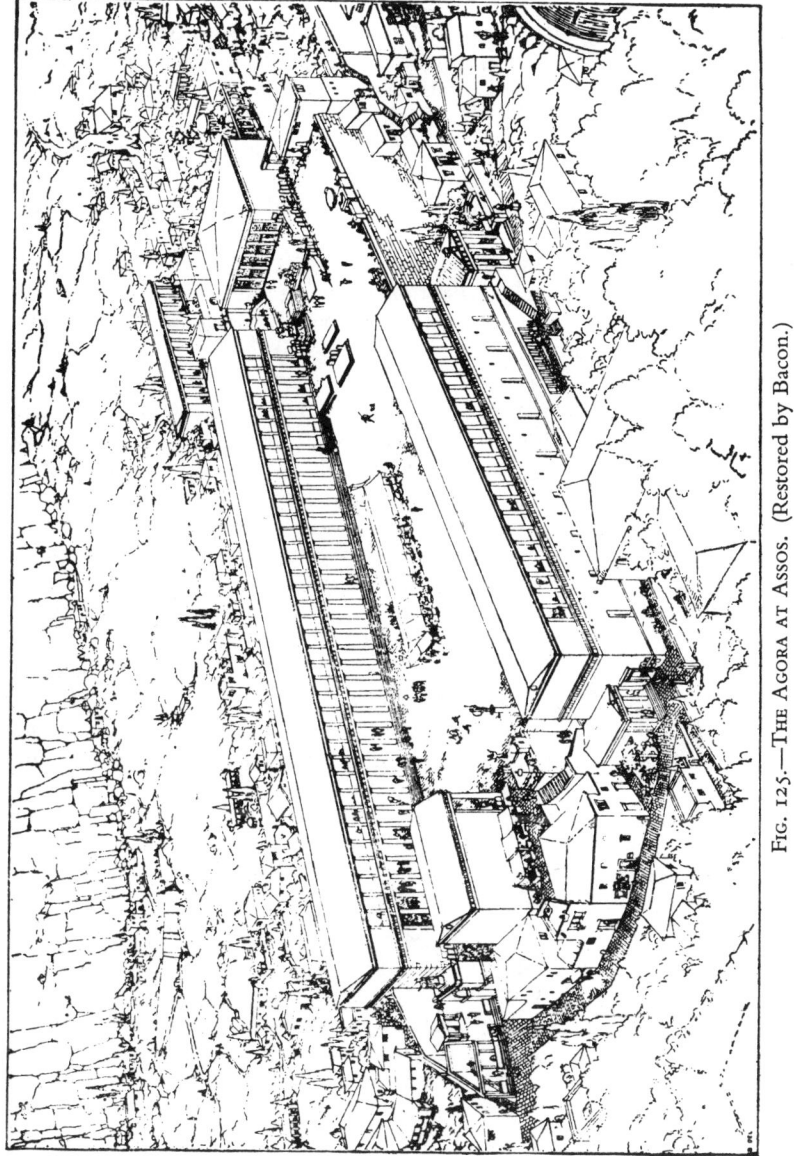

Fig. 125.—The Agora at Assos. (Restored by Bacon.)

the numerous existing colonnaded streets of Corinth in Greece (the "straight road to Lechaeum"), of Ephesus (Arcadiane street), of Olba and Pompeiopolis in the south of Asia Minor, and of Amman, Apamea, Bosra, Damascus, Gadara,

Gerasa, Kanawat, Palmyra, Pella and Samaria in Syria, all of which, however, are of Roman times.

* * * * *

We have now passed in review the evolution of the Greek orders of architecture and the various forms of the buildings that they adorned, the temples, altars, treasuries, stoas, tholoi, propylaea, and votive monuments enclosed within the sacred precincts, and also the agora with its colonnades, clock-towers, fountain-houses, market-halls, the guildhall, the bouleuterion and the theatre, the odeum and the stadium, the palaestra and the gymnasium, the baths, arsenals and lighthouses, the houses and the city plans and the tombs outside the cities. For the further developments of classical architecture it is necessary to turn to that of imperial Rome.

The story of Greek architecture, however, does not end at this point. New impetus was given to Greek civilisation by the transfer of the Roman capital in A.D. 324 to Byzantium which, under its new name of Constantinople, became the centre of an empire which was essentially Greek, and Roman only in name. Simultaneously occurred a change of even greater importance, the official adoption of Christianity; the old religion was gradually extinguished, and by the fifth and sixth centuries A.D. such noted temples as the Parthenon, the Erechtheum, the Hephaesteum, the temple on the Ilissus, and the temple of Concord at Acragas, among many others, had been devoted to the new service. Such makeshifts, however, could not long suffice; and the innate versatility of the Greeks caused them to take the lead in the great problem of mediaevalism, that of vaulting the church. Their sense of fitness, however, resulted in the abandonment of the classical orders; and the new style which they created, Byzantine architecture, was as homogeneous and as logical in its use of the arch and vault as classical Greek architecture had been with respect to the post and lintel. Nor was this due to chance; for, though working with different elements, Isidorus of Miletus was of the same race, and gifted with the same genius, as his ancestor Daphnis of Miletus. Hagia Sophia at Constantinople piles up in exactly the same fashion, dome buttressed by semi-domes and these in turn by other semi-domes, as do the Propylaea of the Acropolis with their pyramidal grouping of pediments, hip roofs, and leaning walls. For the second time Greece created a lasting style, which not only became official with the Orthodox Church but also spread east and south through Islam, and west through Ravenna, Venice, Milan, Aix-la-Chapelle, and Perigueux, playing its part in the formation of the Romanesque and Gothic.

And yet once more Greece directly influenced the world's architecture. The Renaissance, to be sure, was Greek only at second hand, Rome and Vitruvius being the direct sources. But later, as the result of the studies and contacts which we discussed in the introduction to this survey, classical Greece became the direct inspiration for the creations of men like Stuart and Revett, Cockerell, Hittorff and Labrouste, von Klenze and Schinkel and Hansen, and more recently Henry Bacon, a Greek revival which has been one of the most vital phases of modern architecture.

APPENDIX

METRIC MEASUREMENTS OF TEMPLES

SINCE archaeologists, even in English-speaking countries, generally prefer to record and publish their measurements in metres rather than in feet, and since, in fact, measurements in the metric system formed the actual basis of the foregoing table (converted into feet and inches with the equations 1 foot = 0·304800 m. and 1 inch = 0·025400 m.), the original figures are here reproduced for the convenience of those who may prefer them in this form.[1]

For our present purpose a tabular arrangement would be less suitable, inasmuch as the record of unintentional variations on fronts and flanks of peripteral temples (too small to be given accurately in inches), and of deviations from normal dimensions toward the corners (which deserve mention), would greatly encumber a table. Accordingly, for each temple the main dimensions are presented in the following sequence: (a) width and length of stylobate, (b) axial spacings of external columns, (c) lower diameters of external columns, (d) height of external columns, and (e) height of entablatures, so far as known.

DORIC

Olympia, Heraeum: (a) 18·75 × 50·01 m.; (b) 3·56 m. normal average fronts (3·325 m. at corners) and 3·26 m. normal average flanks (3·12 m. at corners); (c) 1·20–1·28 m. fronts and 1·00–1·24 m. flanks; (d) 5·22 m.

Syracuse, Apollo: (a) 21·57 × 55·33 m.; (b) 3·772 m. fronts (4·45 m. central) and 3·331 m. flanks; (c) 2·01 m. fronts and 1·84 m. flanks; (d) 7·98 m.

Syracuse, Olympieum: (a) c. 22·40 × c. 62·05 m.; (b) 4·08 m. fronts and 3·753 m. flanks; (c) 1·84 m. flanks; (d) c. 8·00 m. (estimated).

Selinus, 'C': (a) 23·937 × 63·720 m.; (b) 4·399 m. fronts and 3·860 m. flanks; (c) c. 1·91 m. fronts and 1·81 m. flanks; (d) 8·653 m.; (e) 4·48 m.

Assos, Athena: (a) 14·03 × 30·31 m.; (b) 2·61 m. fronts and 2·45 m. flanks; (c) 0·915 m.; (d) 4·78 m.; (e) 2·02 m.

Corinth, Apollo: (a) c. 21·484 × c. 53·824 m.; (b) 4·028 m. fronts (3·758 m. at corners) and 3·744 m. flanks (3·506 m. at corners); (c) 1·744 m. fronts and 1·645 m. flanks; (d) 7·24 m.

Selinus, 'D': (a) 23·626 × 55·679 m.; (b) 4·368 m. fronts and 4·491 m. flanks; (c) 1·701 m.; (d) 8·31 m.; (e) 3·953 m.

Paestum, Basilica: (a) 24·51 × 54·27 m.; (b) 2·871 m. fronts and 3·102 m. flanks; (c) 1·442 m.; (d) 6·445 m.

Selinus, 'FS': (a) 24·370 × c. 61·88 m.; (b) 4·468 m. fronts and 4·604 m. flanks; (c) 1·79 m.; (d) c. 9·11 m.; (e) 3·955 m.

Athens, Peisistratid Temple: (a) 21·30 × 43·15 m.; (b) 4·042 m. fronts (3·732 m. at corners) and 3·834 m. flanks (3.467 m. at corners); (c) c. 1·63 m. fronts and c. 1·55 m. flanks; (d) c. 7·40 m. (estimated); (e) 3·999 m.

[1] A considerable number of the examples, having been measured by myself, may be considered as completely revised with respect to the dimensions hitherto published. This statement applies to all the examples cited on the Greek mainland (with the partial exceptions of Aegina, Eleusis, Epidaurus, Olympia, and Tegea), those in Sicily (with the exception of Syracuse), and those in South Italy (with the exception of Metapontum). As for examples to which I have not had personal access, such as the temples of Asia Minor, in such cases I have employed the latest and most authoritative publications. Even among the latter, however, discrimination is necessary in correcting errors of measurement or typography. For instance, the American publication of Sardis gives the width over the column plinths as 45·51 m., which would yield 42·81 m. between the corner column centres, whereas the addition of the axial spacings is 41·81 m.; the plan is unfortunately unfigured, so that only by means of the scale can we be sure that 41·81 m. is to be preferred. Such instances, of which many occur not only in this publication but also in others, will illustrate the care with which all published measurements must be checked if one cannot obtain access to the buildings themselves.

METRIC MEASUREMENTS OF TEMPLES

Selinus, 'GT': (*a*) 50·07 × *c*. 110·12 m.; (*b*) 6·53 m. east front, 6·61 m. west front (6·29 m. at corners) and 6·61 m. flanks (6·57 m. at west corners only); (*c*) *c*. 2·97 m. east front and flanks, and *c*. 3·26 m. west front; (*d*) *c*. 14·69 m.; (*e*) *c*. 6·56 m.

Acragas, Olympieum: (*a*) *c*. 52·74 × *c*. 110·095 m. (finish); (*b*) 8·042 m. fronts and 8·185 m. flanks (7·985 m. for two at each corner on flanks); (*c*) 4·05 m.; (*d*) *c*. 17·265 m.; (*e*) *c*. 7·555 m.

Paestum, Demeter: (*a*) 14·541 × 32·880 m.; (*b*) 2·629 m. fronts and 2·625 m. flanks; (*c*) 1·267 m.; (*d*) 6·127 m.; (*e*) *c*. 2·653 m.

Delphi, Athenian Treasury: (*a*) 6·621 × 9·687 m. (no stylobate projection at rear); (*b*) 2·175 m.; (*c*) 0·759 m.; (*d*) 4·128 m.; (*e*) 1·617 m. fronts and 1·671 m. flanks.

Metapontum, Tavole Paladine: (*a*) 16·06 × 33·46 m.; (*b*) 2·956 m. fronts and 2·9255 m. flanks; (*c*) *c*. 1·06 m.; (*d*) 5·135 m.

Acragas, Heracles: (*a*) 25·284 × 67·040 m.; (*b*) 4·614 m. fronts (4·501 m. at corners) and 4·614 m. flanks; (*c*) *c*. 2·085 m.; (*d*) 10·07 m.; (*e*) 3·71 m.

Delphi, Athena Pronaea: (*a*) 13·25 × 27·464 m.; (*b*) 2·485 m. fronts (2·345 m. at corners) and 2·421 m. flanks (2·285 m. at corners); (*c*) 1·005 m. fronts and 0·975 m. flanks; (*d*) 4·60 m.

Sunium, Poseidon (old): (*a*) *c*. 13·06 × *c*. 30·20 m. (finish); (*b*) 2·449 m. (*c*. 2·306 m. at corners); (*c*) 0·98 m. (*c*. 1·00 m. at corners).

Aegina, Aphaea: (*a*) 13·770 × 28·815 m.; (*b*) 2·618 m. fronts (2·40 m. at corners) and 2·5605 m. flanks (2·327 m. at corners); (*c*) 0·989 m. (1·01 m. at corners); (*d*) 5·272 m.; (*e*) 1·966 m. fronts and 2·041 m. flanks.

Athens, Older Parthenon: (*a*) 23·533 × 66·940 m. (finish); (*b*) 4·413 m. fronts (4·075 m. at corners) and 4·359 m. flanks (4·0645 m. at corners); (*c*) 1·903 m. (1·95 m. at corners).

Syracuse, Athena: (*a*) *c*. 22·00 × *c*. 55·02 m.; (*b*) 4·15 m. fronts (4·08 m. and 3·87 m. for two at each corner) and 4·165 m. flanks (3·995 m. and 3·80 m. for two at each corner); (*c*) 1·92 m.; (*d*) 8·71 m.; (*e*) *c*. 3·90 m.

Himera, Nike: (*a*) 22·455 × 55·955 m.; (*b*) 4·175 m. fronts (*c*. 4·11 m. and *c*. 3·997 m. for two at each corner) and 4·198 m. flanks (*c*. 4·084 m. and 3·970 m. for two at each corner); (*c*) *c*. 1·875 m.

Selinus, 'ER': (*a*) 25·324 × *c*. 67·735 m.; (*b*) 4·712 m. (4·405 m. at corners); (*c*) 2·268 m.; (*d*) *c*. 10·15 m.; (*e*) 4·47 m.

Olympia, Zeus: (*a*) 27·68 × 64·12 m.; (*b*) 5·2265 m. fronts (4·793 m. at corners) and 5·221 m. flanks (4·748 m. at corners); (*c*) 2·25 m. fronts and 2·21 m. flanks; (*d*) 10·43 m.; (*e*) 4·08 m. fronts and 4·155 m. flanks.

Paestum, Poseidon: (*a*) 24·264 × 59·975 m. (finish); (*b*) 4.471 m. fronts (4·295 m. at corners) and 4·503 m. flanks (4·362 m. and 4·223 m. for two at each corner); (*c*) *c*. 2·112 m. fronts and 2·036 m. flanks; (*d*) 8·88 m.; (*e*) 3·788 m.

Acragas, Hera Lacinia: (*a*) 16·910 × 38·100 m.; (*b*) 3·118 m. fronts (3·033 m. at corners) and 3·064 m. flanks (2·985 m. at corners); (*c*) *c*. 1·387 m. fronts and 1·332 m. flanks; (*d*) 6·36 m.; (*e*) *c*. 2·90 m.

Selinus, 'A': (*a*) 16·129 × 40·303 m. (finish); (*b*) 2·997 m. fronts (2·929 m. and 2·875 m. for two at each corner) and 2·9975 m. flanks (2·903 m. at corners); (*c*) *c*. 1·32 m.; (*d*) 6·235 m.; (*e*) 2·78 m.

Bassae, Apollo: (*a*) 14·478 × 38·244 m. (finish); (*b*) 2·714 m. fronts (2·506 m. at corners north, 2·526 m. at corners south) and 2·673 m. flanks (2·432 m. at corners); (*c*) 1·161 m. north front and 1·121 m. south front and flanks; (*d*) 5·957 m.; (*e*) 1·948 m.

Athens, Hephaesteum: (*a*) 13·708 × 31·769 m.; (*b*) 2·583 m. fronts (2·413 m. at corners) and 2·581 m. flanks (2·413 m. at corners); (*c*) 1·018 m. (1·038 m. at corners); (*d*) 5·713 m.; (*e*) 2·020 m. fronts and 1·980 m. flanks.

Athens, Parthenon: (*a*) 30·880 × 69·503 m.; (*b*) 4·2965 m. fronts (3·6815 m. at corners) and 4·2915 m. flanks (3·689 m. at corners); (*c*) 1·905 m. (1·948 m. at corners); (*d*) 10·433 m.; (*e*) 3·295 m.

Sunium, Poseidon (new): (*a*) 13·470 × *c*. 31·124 m.; (*b*) 2·522 m. (*c*. 2·374 m. at corners); (*c*) 1·043 m. (*c*. 1·063 m. at corners); (*d*) 6·024 m.; (*e*) 2·010 m. fronts and 1·990 m. flanks.

Athens, Ares: (*a*) *c*. 14·344 × *c*. 33·174 m.; (*b*) 2·690 m. (*c*. 2·53 m. at corners); (*c*) *c*. 1·10 m. (*c*. 1·12 m. at corners); (*d*) *c*. 6·275 m.; (*e*) *c*. 2·027 m. fronts and *c*. 1·967 m. flanks.

Athens, Propylaea, Central Building: (a) 21·125 (east) × 23·836 m. (finish); (b) 3·628 m. (5·436 m. central, 3·382 m. at corners); (c) 1·558 m.; (d) 8·8075 m. west (8·824 m. central) and 8·528 m. east (8·5445 m. central); (e) 2·725 m. fronts and 2·710 m. flanks. West Wings: (b) 2·506 m.; (c) 1·074 m.; (d) 5·8515 m.; (e) 1·913 m.

Rhamnus, Nemesis: (a) c. 9·996 × 21·420 m. (finish); (b) 1·904 m. (c. 1·730 m. at corners); (c) 0·714 m. (c. 0·728 m. at corners); (d) c. 4·10 m.; (e) 1·394 m. fronts and 1·356 m. flanks.

Acragas, Concord: (a) 16·925 × 39·420 m.; (b) 3·195 m. fronts (3·100 m. and 3·005 m. for two at each corner) and 3·206 m. flanks (3·111 m. and 3·015 m. for two at each corner); (c) 1·452 m.; (d) 6·70 m.; (e) c. 2·96 m.

Delos, Apollo (Athenian): (a) c. 9·686 × c. 17·014 m.; (b) 1·832 m. (c. 1·647 m. at corners); (c) 0·814 m.; (d) c. 4·65 m.; (e) 1·476 m.

Segesta: (a) 23·120 × 58·035 m. (finish); (b) 4·334 m. fronts (4·230 m. and 4·113 m. for two at each corner) and 4·3595 m. flanks (4·225 m. and 4·100 m. for two at each corner); (c) 1·955 m.; (d) 9·366 m.; (e) 3·585 m.

Argos, Heraeum: (a) c. 17·305 × c. 36·90 m.; (b) 3·266 m. (c. 3·041 m. at corners); (c) 1·32 m. (c. 1·345 m. at corners); (d) c. 7·40 m. (estimated); (e) c. 2·48 m.

Epidaurus, Asclepius: (a) c. 11·76 × c. 23·06 m.; (b) c. 2·27 m. (c. 1·99 m. at corners); (c) c. 0·93 m.; (d) c. 5·20 m.; (e) 1·520 m.

Delphi, Apollo: (a) c. 21·68 × c. 58·18 m.; (b) 4·138 m. fronts (3·708 m. at corners) and 4·083 m. flanks (3·667 m. at corners); (c) 1·806 m.; (d) c. 10·59 m.

Tegea, Athena Alea: (a) 19·19 × 47·55 m.; (b) 3·613 m. fronts (3·342 m. at corners) and 3·585 m. flanks (3.224 m. at corners); (c) 1.55 m. (c. 1·575 m. at corners); (d) 9·474 m.; (e) 2·421 m. fronts and 2·352 m. flanks.

Nemea, Zeus: (a) 20·09 × 42·555 m.; (b) 3·750 m. fronts (3·453 m. at corners) and 3·746 m. flanks (3·452 m. at corners); (c) 1·63 m. (c. 1·655 m. at corners); (d) 10·368 m.; (e) 2·567 m. fronts and 2·484 m. flanks.

Stratos, Zeus: (a) 16·57 × 32·42 m. (finish); (b) 3·17 m. (2·835 m. at corners); (c) c. 1·31 m.; (d) c. 7·095 m.; (e) 2·071 m.

Olympia, Metroum: (a) 10·62 × 20·67 m.; (b) 2·01 m. (1·82 m. at corners); (c) 0·85 m.; (d) unknown; (e) 1·488 m.

Athens, Nicias Monument: (a) 11·095 × c. 15·22 m.; (b) 2·094 m. (c. 1·944 m. at corners); (c) 0·844 m.; (d) c. 5·102 m.; (e) 1·467 m.

Delos, Apollo (peripteral): (a) 12·47 × c. 28·53 m.; (b) 2·2905 m. (same at corners); (c) 0·945 m. (0·965 m. at corners); (d) c. 5·20 m.; (e) 2·060 m.

Pergamum, Athena Polias: (a) 12·27 × 21·77 m.; (b) 2·367 m. fronts (2·175 m. at corners) and 2·371 m. flanks (2·175 m. at corners); (c) 0·754 m.; (d) 5·260 m.; (e) 1·225 m.

Pergamum, Dionysus (market temple): (a) c. 6·765 × c. 10·135 m.; (b) 2·022 m. (1·891 m. at corners); (d) c. 0·620 m.; (d) 4·49 m.; (e) 0·85 m.

Eleusis, Artemis Propylaea: (a) c. 6·44 × c. 12·33 m.; (b) 1·976 m. (1·783 m. at corners); (c) 0·782 m.; (d) 4·53 m.; (e) 1·419 m.

IONIC

Ephesus, Artemis (old): (a) 55·10 × 115·14 m.; (b) c. 8·62 m. central west front, c. 7·25 m. adjoining centre, 6·12 m. two at each corner on both fronts, 5·78 m. four central east front, and 5·216 m. normal flanks (5·88 m. three at west corners and two at east corners); (c) 1·51 m. normal flanks, increasing gradually to c. 1·725 m. at centre of west front; (d) c. 12·08 m. (8 diameters, Vitruvius, Pliny).

Samos, Heraeum: (a) c. 59·70 × c. 115·80 m. (estimated, stylobate never built); (b) 8·406 m. three central east front, 7·046 m. two adjoining, 6·552 m. at corners east front and average west front, and 4·701 m. normal flanks (4·835 m. third and 4·935 m. second and first spacings at east corners); (c) 1·868 m. normal flanks, increasing gradually to 2·014 m. at centre of east front.

Locri Epizephyrii, Maraza: (a) 17·320 × 43·728 m.; (b) 2·641 m. (3·521 m. three central on east front); (c) 1·134 m.

Athens, Ilissus temple: (a) c. 5·849 × 12·686 m.; (b) 1·679 m. (spread to 1·730 m. at corners probably later distortion); (c) 0·543 m.; (d) 4·478 m.; (e) 1·0995 m.

METRIC MEASUREMENTS OF TEMPLES

Athens, Athena Nike: (*a*) 5·397 × 8·166 m. (5·383 × 8·152 m. on finished bottom margin); (*b*) 1·5485 m.; (*c*) 0·518 m.; (*d*) 4·049 m.; (*e*) 1·077 m.

Athens Erechtheum, North Porch: (*a*) 10·717 m.; (*b*) 3·097 m. (3·149 m. at corners, 3·067 m. on flanks); (*c*) 0·817 m. (0·824 m. at corners); (*d*) 7·635 m.; (*e*) 1·678 m. East Portico: (*a*) 11·633 m.; (*b*) 2·113 m.; (*c*) 0·692 m.; (*d*) 6·586 m.; (*e*) 1·535 m. front and 1·509 m. flanks. West Front: (*b*) 1·970 m.; (*c*) 0·62 m.; (*d*) 5·613 m.; (*e*) 1·535 m.

Halicarnassus, Mausoleum: (*a*) *c.* 26·39 × *c.* 32·57 m.; (*b*) 3·090 m.; (*c*) 1·105 m.; (*d*) *c.* 9·71 m.; (*e*) *c.* 2·40 m. (*c.* 2·65 m. with sima).

Priene, Athena Polias: (*a*) 19·53 × 37·17 m.; (*b*) 3·528 m.; (*c*) 1·289 m.; (*c*) *c.* 11·40 m.; (*e*) 1·696 m. (2·071 m. with sima).

Ephesus, Artemis (new): *c.* 51·44 × *c.* 111·48 m.; (*b*) exactly like archaic spacings; (*c*) 1·840 m.; (*d*) *c.* 17·65 m. (60 Ionic feet, Pliny).

Sardis, Artemis-Cybele: (*a*) *c.* 45·73 × *c.* 99·16 m. (estimated, stylobate never built); (*b*) 7·05 m. central fronts, 6·635 m. adjoining centre, 5·445 m. second and 5·30 m. first spacings at each corner, and 5·002 m. normal flanks (5·103 m. one at each corner); (*c*) 1·99 m. (2·022 m. at corners, 1·61 m. pronaos columns on pedestals); (*d*) 17·81 m. (15·65 m. pronaos columns on pedestals).

Didyma, Apollo: (*a*) 51·13 × 109·34 m.; (*b*) 5·301 m. fronts and 5·296 m. flanks; (*c*) 2·022 m.; (*d*) 19·70 m.; (*e*) unfinished.

Messa, Aphrodite: (*a*) *c.* 22·098 × *c.* 39·756 m.; (*b*) 2·943 m.; (*c*) 1·04 m.; (*d*) unknown; (*e*) 2·36 m. (2·61 m. with sima).

Chryse, Apollo: (*a*) 22·578 × 40·436 m.; (*b*) 2·976 m.; (*c*) 1·180 m.; (*d*) unknown; (*e*) 2·258 m. (2·592 m. with sima).

Teos, Dionysus: (*a*) 18·63 × 34·98 m.; (*b*) 3·265 m. fronts and 3·2675 m. flanks; (*c*) 1·03 m.; (*d*) unknown; (*e*) 1·870 m. (2·200 m. with sima).

Magnesia, Artemis Leucophryene: (*a*) *c.* 31·60 × *c.* 57·89 m.; (*b*) *c.* 5·23 m. central fronts and 3·94 m. normal throughout; (*c*) 1·387 m. (1·407 m. at corners); (*d*) unknown; (*e*) 2·50 m. (2·952 m. with sima).

Aphrodisias, Aphrodite: (*a*) 19·945 × 32·57 m.; (*b*) 2·863 m. central fronts and 2·582 m. normal throughout; (*c*) 1·129 m.; (*d*) 9·288 m.; (*e*) 2·176 m. (2·426 m. with sima).

Aezani, Zeus: (*a*) 21·350 × 36·590 m.; (*b*) 3·740 m. central fronts, 3·110 m. adjoining centre, 2·520 m. normal fronts and flanks; (*c*) 0·0964 m.; (*d*) 9·55 m.; (*e*) 1·92 m. (2·19 m. with sima).

CORINTHIAN

Athens, Olympieum: (*a*) 41·11 × 107·89 m.; (*b*) 5·494 m. fronts and 5·540 m. flanks (5·525 m. at corners of flanks); (*c*) 1·918 m. (1·940 m. at corners); (*d*) 16·890 m.

Sagalassus, Antoninus Pius: (*a*) 13·875 × 26·635 m.; (*b*) 2·53 m.; (*c*) 0·79 m.; (*d*) unknown; (*e*) 1·54 m. (1·78 m. with sima).

Euromus, Zeus: (*a*) 14·375 × 27·455 m.; (*b*) 2·616 m.; (*c*) 0·872 m.; (*d*) 8.30 m.; (*e*) 1·692 m. (*c.* 1·905 m. with sima).

Cnidus: (*a*) 8·030 × 14·635 m.; (*b*) 2·360 m. fronts and 1·955 m. flanks; (*c*) 0·632 m.; (*d*) unknown; (*e*) 1·213 m. (1·406 m. with sima).

CHRONOLOGICAL LIST
OF GREEK TEMPLES

CHRONOLOGICAL LIST OF GREEK TEMPLES[1]

GIVING THEIR APPROXIMATE DATES AND PRINCIPAL DIMENSIONS AND PROPORTIONS[2]

Date[3]	Name of Temple	No. of Columns	Top of Stylobate[4] Front	Top of Stylobate[4] Flank	Ratio Width to Length 1:	Axial Spacing[5]	Lower Column Diameter[5]	Height of Column
			ft. in.	ft. in.		ft. in.	ft. in.	ft. in.
	DORIC							
c. 590	Olympia, Heraeum	6 by 16	61 6	164 1	2·667	11 8, 10 8½	{4 2½, 3 3½ / 3 11½, 4 1}	17 1½
c. 565	Syracuse, Apollo	6 ,, 17	70 9	181 6½	2·565	{12 4½, 10 11 / 14 7}	6 7, 6 0½	26 2
c. 555	Syracuse, Olympieum	6 ,, 17	73 6	203 7	2·770	13 4½, 12 4	6 1	c. 26 3
c. 550–530	Selinus, 'C'	6 ,, 17	78 6½	209 0½	2·662	14 5, 12 8	6 3, 5 11½	28 4½
c. 540	Assos, Athena	6 ,, 13	46 0½	99 5½	2·160	8 7, 8 0½	3 0	15 8
c. 535	Corinth, Apollo	6 ,, 15	70 6	176 11	2·505	13 2½, 12 3½	5 8½, 5 5	23 9
c. 535	Selinus, 'D'	6 ,, 13	77 6	182 8	2·367	14 4, 14 9	5 7	27 3
c. 530	Paestum, Basilica	9 ,, 18	80 5	178 0½	2·214	9 5, 10 2	4 9	21 1½
c. 525	Selinus, 'FS'	6 ,, 14	79 11½	203 0	2·544	14 8, 15 1½	5 10½	29 10½
529–515	Athens, Athena (Peisistratid)	6 ,, 12	69 10½	141 7	2·026	13 3, 12 7	c. 5 4, 6 5 1	c. 24 3

[1] Including for comparison a few other accurately dated buildings, the Athenian Treasury at Delphi, the Propylaea and the Monument of Nicias at Athens, and the Mausoleum at Halicarnassus.
[2] Dimensions are normally given to the nearest half-inch in limestone buildings, to the nearest quarter or eighth in marble buildings (for measurements in metres see Appendix).
[3] All dates are B.C. unless otherwise stated.
[4] In the case of unfinished stylobates, the finished dimensions are given (subtracting protective surfaces).
[5] When two dimensions or proportions appear side by side in the same column, the first always refers to the fronts and the second to the flanks; but when variations (other than the contracted corner spacings in Doric buildings) occur within either front or flank, the normal is shown above and the extreme variation below, respectively.

Name of Temple	Height of Entablature[6]	Proportions in Lower Diameters[5]			in Axial Spacings[5]		in Column Heights[5]
		Axial Spacing	Height of Column	Height of Entablature	Height of Column	Height of Order	Order
	ft. in.						
DORIC							
Olympia, Heracum	?	2·76, 3·26 2·97, 2·69	4·08, 5·22 4·35, 4·21	?	1·46, 1·60	?	?
Syracuse, Apollo	?	1·88, 1·81 2·21	3·97, 4·34	?	2·12, 2·40 1·79	?	?
Syracuse, Olympieum	?	2·21, 2·03	c. 4·32	?	c. 1·96, c. 2·13	?	?
Selinus, 'C'	14 8½	2·30, 2·13	4·53, 4·78	2·35, 2·48	1·97, 2·24	2·99, 3·40	1·52
Assos, Athena	6 7½	2·85, 2·68	5·22	2·21	1·83, 1·95	2·61, 2·78	1·42
Corinth, Apollo	?	2·31, 2·28	4·15, 4·40	?	1·80, 1·93	?	?
Selinus, 'D'	12 11½	2·57, 2·64	4·89	2·32	1·90, 1·85	2·81, 2·72	1·48
Paestum, Basilica	?	2·00, 2·15	4·47	?	2·24, 2·08	?	?
Selinus 'FS'	12 11½	2·50, 2·57	5·09	2·21	2·04, 1·98	2·92, 2·84	1·43
Athens, Athena (Peisistratid)	11 2	c. 2·48	c. 4·54, c. 4·77	c. 2·46, c. 2·58	c. 1·83, c. 1·93	c. 2·82, c. 2·97	c. 1·54

[5] When two dimensions or proportions appear side by side in the same column, the first always refers to the fronts and the second to the flanks; but when variations (other than the contracted corner spacings in Doric buildings) occur within either front or flank, the normal is shown above and the extreme variation below, respectively.

[6] The height of the entablature is always measured to the top of the corona, omitting the sima which forms in reality part of the roof; but for Asiatic Ionic and Corinthian the total, including the sima, is given in parentheses.

Date	Name of Temple	No. of Columns	Top of Stylobate		Ratio Width to Length	Axial Spacing	Lower Column Diameter	Height of Column
			Front	Flank				
c. 520–450	Selinus, Apollo ('GT')	8 ,, 17	164 3	361 3	2·199	{ 21 5, 21 8 / 21 8	{ 9 9 / 10 8½, 9 9	48 2½
c. 510–409	Acragas, Zeus Olympius	7 ,, 14	173 0½	361 2½	2·088	26 4, 26 10	13 3½	56 8
c. 510	Paestum, Demeter	6 ,, 13	47 8½	107 10½	2·261	8 7½	4 2	20 1
507	Delphi, Athenian Treasury	2 in-antis	21 8¾	31 9½	1·463	7 1¾	2 6	13 6½
c. 500	Metapontum, Tavole Paladine	6 by 12	52 8½	109 9½	2·021	9 8½, 9 7	3 5½	16 10
	Acragas, Heracles	6 ,, 15	82 11½	219 11½	2·651	15 1½	6 10	33 0½
	Delphi, Athena Pronaea	6 ,, 12	43 5½	90 1½	2·073	8 2, 7 11½	3 3½, 3 2½	15 1
498	Sunium, Poseidon (old)	6 ,, 13	42 10½	99 1	2·312	9 0½	3 2½	?
c. 495–485	Aegina, Aphaea	6 ,, 12	45 2	94 6½	2·093	8 7, 8 5	3 3	17 3½
488–480	Athens, Older Parthenon	6 ,, 16	77 2½	219 7½	2·845	14 5¾, 14 3½	6 3	?
480	Syracuse, Athena	6 ,, 14	72 2	180 6	2·501	13 7½, 13 8	6 3½	28 7
	Himera, Nike	6 ,, 14	73 8	183 7	2·492	13 8½, 13 9½	6 2	?
c. 480–460	Selinus, Hera ('ER')	6 ,, 15	83 1	222 2½	2·675	15 5½	7 5½	33 3½
468–460	Olympia, Zeus	6 ,, 13	90 10	210 4½	2·316	17 1¾, 17 1½	7 4½, 7 3	34 2½
c. 460	Paestum, Poseidon	6 ,, 14	79 7½	196 9	2·472	14 8, 14 9½	6 11, 6 8	29 1½
	Acragas, Hera Lacinia	6 ,, 13	55 6	125 0	2·253	10 3, 10 0½	4 6½, 4 4½	20 10½
	Selinus, 'A'	6 ,, 14	52 11	132 2½	2·499	9 10	4 4	20 5½
c. 450–425	Bassae, Apollo	6 ,, 15	47 6	125 5¾	2·642	8 10¾, 8 9¼	3 9¾, 3 8¼	19 6½
449–444	Athens, Hephaesteum	6 ,, 13	44 11¾	104 2¾	2·318	8 5⅝	3 4⅛	18 9
447–432	Athens, Parthenon	8 ,, 17	101 3¾	228 0⅜	2·251	14 1⅛, 14 1	6 3	34 2¾
444–440	Sunium, Poseidon (new)	6 ,, 13	44 2¼	102 1¼	2·311	8 3¼	3 5	19 9⅛
440–436	Athens, Ares	6 ,, 13	47 0¾	108 10	2·313	8 9⅞	c. 3 7¼	c. 20 7
437–432	Athens, Propylaea—							
	Central Building	6 amphi-prostyle	69 3¾	78 2½	1·128	{ 11 10¾ / 17 10	5 1⅜	{ 28 10¾ / 27 11¾
	West Wings	3 in-antis	—	—	—	8 2⅝	3 6¼	19 2⅜
436–432	Rhamnus, Nemesis	6 by 12	32 9½	70 3¼	2·143	6 3	2 4⅛	13 5½
c. 430	Acragas, Concord	6 ,, 13	55 6½	129 4	2·329	10 6, 10 6¼	4 9	22 0
425–417	Delos, Apollo (Athenian)	6 amphi-prostyle	31 9¼	55 9¾	1·757	6 0⅛	2 8	15 3

Name of Temple	Height of Entablature	Proportions in Lower Diameters			in Axial Spacings		in Column Heights
		Axial Spacing	Height of Column	Height of Entablature	Height of Column	Height of Order	Order
Selinus, Apollo ('GT')	21 6½	2·20, 2·23 2·03, 2·23	4·95 4·51, 4·95	2·21 2·01, 2·21	2·25, 2·22 2·22	3·25, 3·22	1·45
Acragas, Zeus Olympius	24 9½	1·98, 2·02	4·26	1·86	2·15, 2·11	3·09, 3·03	1·44
Paestum, Demeter	8 8½	2·07	4·84	2·09	2·33	3·34	1·43
Delphi, Athenian Treasury	5 3¾, 5 5¾	2·87	5·44	2·13, 2·20	1·90	2·64, 2·67	1·39, 1·40
Metapontum, Tavole Paladine	?	2·79, 2·76	4·84	?	1·74, 1·76	?	?
Acragas, Heracles	12 2	2·21	4·84	1·78	2·18	2·99	1·37
Delphi, Athena Pronaea	?	2·47, 2·48	4·58, 4·72	?	1·85, 1·90	?	?
Sunium, Poseidon (old)	?	2·50	?	?	?	?	?
Aegina, Aphaea	6 5½, 6 8½	2·65, 2·59	5·32	1·99, 2·06	2·01, 2·05	2·76, 2·86	1·37, 1·39
Athens, Older Parthenon	?	2·32, 2·29	?	?	?	?	?
Syracuse, Athena	12 9½	2·11, 2·12	4·54	2·03	2·10, 2·09	3·04, 3·03	1·45
Himera, Nike	?	2·23, 2·24	?	?	?	?	?
Selinus, Hera ('ER')	14 8	2·08	4·48	1·97	2·15	3·10	1·44
Olympia, Zeus	13 4¾, 13 7½	2·32, 2·37	4·64, 4·72	1·81, 1·88	2·00, 1·99	2·78, 2·79	1·39, 1·40
Paestum, Poseidon	12 5	2·12, 2·21	4·20, 4·36	1·79, 1·86	1·99, 1·97	2·83, 2·81	1·43
Acragas, Hera Lacinia	9 6	2·25, 2·30	4·59, 4·77	2·09, 2·18	2·04, 2·08	2·97, 3·02	1·45
Selinus, 'A'	9 1½	2·27	4·72	2·11	2·08	3·01	1·45
Bassae, Apollo	6 4½	2·34, 2·38	5·13, 5·31	1·67, 1·74	2·19, 2·23	2·91, 2·96	1·33
Athens, Hephaesteum	6 7½, 6 6	2·54	5·61	1·98, 1·95	2·21	2·99, 2·98	1·35
Athens, Parthenon	10 9¾	2·25	5·48	1·73	2·43	3·19, 3·20	1·32
Sunium, Poseidon (new)	6 7⅛, 6 6⅜	2·42	5·78	1·93, 1·91	2·39	3·19, 3·18	1·33
Athens, Ares	6 7¾, 6 5½	2·45	5·70	1·84, 1·79	2·33	3·09, 3·06	1·32, 1·31
Athens, Propylaea—							
Central Building	8 11¼, 8 10¾	2·33 3·49	5·65 5·47	1·75, 1·74	2·43, 2·35 1·62, 1·57	3·18, 3·10 2·12, 2·07	1·32, 1·31
West Wings	6 3⅜	2·33	5·45	1·78	2·33	3·10	1·33
Rhamnus, Nemesis	4 6⅞, 4 5⅜	2·67	5·74	1·95, 1·90	2·15	2·89, 2·87	1·34, 1·33
Acragas, Concord	9 8½	2·20, 2·21	4·61	2·04	2·10, 2·09	3·02, 3·01	1·44
Delos, Apollo (Athenian)	4 10	2·25	5·71	1·81	2·54	3·34	1·32

Date	Name of Temple	No. of Columns	Top of Stylobate		Ratio Width to Length	Axial Spacing	Lower Column Diameter	Height of Column
			Front	Flank				
424–416	Segesta	6 by 14	75 10	190 5	2·510	14 2½, 14 3½	6 5	30 9
423–416	Argos, Hera	6 ,, 12	56 9½	121 1	2·132	10 8½	4 4	c. 24 3½
c. 380	Epidaurus, Asclepius	6 ,, 11	38 7	75 8	1·961	7 5½	c. 3 1	c. 17 1
366–326	Delphi, Apollo	6 ,, 15	71 1½	190 10½	2·684	13 7, 13 4¾	5 11	c. 34 9
c. 350	Tegea, Athena Alea	6 ,, 14	62 11½	156 0	2·478	11 10, 11 9⅛	5 1	31 1
c. 340	Nemea, Zeus	6 ,, 12	65 11	139 7½	2·118	12 3⅝, 12 3½	5 4¼	34 0
c. 321	Stratos, Zeus	6 ,, 11	54 4½	106 4½	1·957	10 4¾	4 3½	c. 23 3½
c. 320	Olympia, Metroum	6 ,, 11	34 10	67 10	1·946	6 7	2 9½	?
319	Athens, Nicias Monument	6 prostyle	36 4¾	49 11	1·372	6 10½	2 9¼	16 9
c. 460–454 c. 314–280	Delos, Apollo (peripteral)	6 by 13	40 11	c. 93 7¼	2·288	7 6¼	3 1¼	c. 17 1
c. 250	Pergamum, Athena Polias	6 ,, 10	40 · 3	71 5	1·774	7 9¼	2 5¾	17 3
c. 170	Pergamum, Dionysus	4 prostyle	22 2½	33 3	1·498	6 7½	2 0½	14 8¾
c. A.D. 125	Eleusis, Artemis Propylaea	4 amphi-prostyle	c. 21 1½	c. 40 5½	1·915	6 5¾	2 7	14 10½
	IONIC							
c. 560–460	Ephesus, Artemis (old)	8 (9) by 21	180 9	377 9	2·090	18 11½, 17 1⅜ 28 3¼, 19 3½	4 11½ c. 5 8, 4 11½	c. 39 7½
c. 530–100	Samos, Hera	8 (9) ,, 24	c. 195 10½	c. 379 11	c. 1·940	21 6, 15 5 27 7, 16 2¼	?, 6 1½ 6 7¼, ?	?
c. 450–425	Locri Epizephyrii, Maraza	6 (7) ,, 17	56 10	143 5½	2·525	8 8 11 6½, 8 8	3 8½	?
449	Athens, Ilissus	4 amphi-prostyle	19 2¼	41 7½	2·169	5 6	1 9½	14 8¼
427–424	Athens, Athena Nike	4 amphi-prostyle	17 8½	26 9½	1·513	5 1	1 8½	13 3½
421–405	Athens, Erechtheum— North Portico	4 prostyle	35 2	—	—	10 2, 10 0¾ 10 4	2 8¼	25 0½
	East Portico	6 prostyle	38 2	—	—	6 11¼	2 3¼	21 7¼
	West Front	4 in-antis	—	—	—	6 1½	2 0½	18 5

Name of Temple	Height of Entablature	Proportions in Lower Diameters			in Axial Spacings		in Column Heights
		Axial Spacing	Height of Column	Height of Entablature	Height of Column	Height of Order	Order
Segesta	11 9	2·23	4·79	1·83	2·16, 2·15	2·99, 2·97	1·38
Argos, Hera	c. 8 1½	2·47	c. 5·61	c. 1·88	c. 2·27	c. 3·02	c. 1·33
Epidaurus, Asclepius	5 0	c. 2·44	c. 5·59	c. 1·63	c. 2·29	c. 2·96	c. 1·29
Delphi, Apollo	?	2·29, 2·26	c. 5·86	?	c. 2·56, 2·59	?	?
Tegea, Athena Alea	7 11½, 7 8½	2·33, 2·31	6·11	1·56, 1·52	2·62, 2·64	3·29, 3·30	1·26, 1·25
Nemea, Zeus	8 5, 8 1¾	2·29	6·35	1·57, 1·52	2·76, 2·77	3·45, 3·43	1·25, 1·24
Stratos, Zeus	6 9½	2·42	c. 5·42	1·58	c. 2·24	c. 2·89	c. 1·29
Olympia, Metroum	4 10½	2·36	?	1·75	?	?	?
Athens, Nicias Monument	4 9¾	2·48	6·05	1·74	2·44	3·14	1·29
Delos, Apollo (peripteral)	4 0¼	2·42	c. 5·50	1·30	c. 2·27	c. 2·80	c. 1·24
Pergamum, Athena Polias	4 0	3·14	6·98	1·62	2·22	2·74	1·23
Pergamum, Dionysus	2 9½	3·26	7·24	1·37	2·22	2·64	1·19
Eleusis, Artemis Propylaea	4 7⅞	2·53	5·76	1·81	2·29	3·01	1·31
IONIC							
Ephesus, Artemis (old)	?	3·82, 3·46 4·99, 3·89	c. 8·00 c. 7·00, c. 8·00	?	c. 2·09, c. 2·31 c. 1·40, c. 2·05	?	?
Samos, Hera	?	? , 2·52 4·17, 2·68	?	?	?	?	?
Locri Epizephyrii, Maraza	?	2·33 3·19, 2·33	?	?	?	?	?
Athens, Ilissus	3 7¼	3·09	8·25	2·02	2·67	3·32	1·25
Athens, Athena Nike	3 6½	2·99	7·82	2·08	2·61	3·31	1·26
Athens, Erechtheum—							
North Portico	5 6	3·79, 3·76 3·85, 3·76	9·35	2·05	2·42, 2·49 2·46, 2·49	2·96, 3·03 3·01, 3·03	1·22
East Portico	5 0½, 4 11½	3·05	9·52	2·22, 2·18	3·12	3·84	1·23
West Front	5 0½	3·18	9·05	2·48	2·85	3·63	1·27

Date	Name of Temple	No. of Columns	Top of Stylobate		Ratio Width to Length	Axial Spacing	Lower Column Diameter	Height of Column
			Front	Flank				
355–350	Halicarnassus, Mausoleum ..	9 by 11	c. 86 7	c. 106 10¼	c. 1·234	10 1⅝	3 7½	c. 31 10
c. 340–156	Priene, Athena Polias	6 ,, 11	64 1	121 11½	1·903	11 7	4 2¾	c. 37 5
c. 356–236	Ephesus, Artemis (new)	8 (9) ,, 21	168 9	365 9	2·167	{ 18 11½, 17 1⅜ 28 3¼, 19 3½	6 0½	c. 57 11
c. 350–300	Sardis, Artemis-Cybele	8 ,, 20	c. 150 0	c. 325 4	c. 2·168	{ 17 4¾, 16 5 23 1½, 16 8⅞	6 2⅞	58 2¼
313–A.D. 41	Didyma, Apollo	10 ,, 21	167 9	358 8½	2·138	17 4¾, 17 4½	6 7½	64 8
c. 280	Messa, Aphrodite	8 ,, 14	72 6	130 5	1·791	9 7⅞	3 5	?
c. 250	Chryse, Apollo	8 ,, 14	74 1	132 8	1·791	9 9⅛	3 10½	?
193	Teos, Dionysus	6 ,, 11	61 1½	114 10½	1·878	10 8¾	3 4½	?
c. 175	Magnesia, Artemis Leucophryene	8 ,, 15	c. 103 8	c. 189 11	c. 1·832	{ 12 11⅛ 17 2, 12 11⅛	4 6⅝	?
c. A.D. 125	Aphrodisias, Aphrodite	8 ,, 13	65 5	106 10	1·633	{ 8 5⅝ 9 4¾, 8 5⅝	3 8½	30 5¾
	Aezani, Zeus	8 ,, 15	70 0½	120 0½	1·714	{ 8 3¼ 12 3¼, 8 3¼	3 2	31 4
	CORINTHIAN							
515–510 174–A.D. 132 }	Athens, Zeus Olympius	8 ,, 20	134 10½	354 0	2·624	18 0¼, 18 2⅛	6 3½	55 5
c. A.D. 140	Sagalassus, Antoninus Pius ..	6 ,, 11	45 6¼	87 4½	1·920	8 3½	2 7	?
	Euromus, Zeus	6 ,, 11	47 2	90 1	1·909	8 7	2 10¼	27 3
	Cnidus	4 ,, 8	26 4	48 0	1·823	7 9, 6 5	2 1	?

Name of Temple	Height of Entablature	Proportions in Lower Diameters			in Axial Spacings		in Column Heights
		Axial Spacing	Height of Column	Height of Entablature	Height of Column	Height of Order	Order
Halicarnassus, Mausoleum ..	c. 7 10½ (8 8⅜)	2·80	8·79	2·17 (2·40)	3·14	3·92 (4·00)	1·25 (1·27)
Priene, Athena Polias	5 6¾ (6 9½)	2·74	8·84	1·32 (1·61)	3·23	3·71 (3·82)	1·15 (1·18)
Ephesus, Artemis (new)	?	3·14, 2·84 4·68, 3·20	c. 9·60	?	c. 3·06, c. 3·34 c. 2·05, c. 3·00	?	?
Sardis, Artemis-Cybele	?	2·66, 2·52 3·54, 2·55	8·95	?	3·36, 3·56 2·52, 3·49	?	?
Didyma, Apollo	?	2·62	9·74	?	3·72	?	?
Messa, Aphrodite	7 9 (8 6¾)	2·83	?	2·27 (2·51)	?	?	?
Chryse, Apollo	7 5 (8 6)	2·52	?	1·81 (2·08)	?	?	?
Teos, Dionysus	6 1½ (7 2½)	3·17	?	1·82 (2·14)	?	?	?
Magnesia, Artemis Leucophryene	8 2⅜ (9 8¼)	2·84 3·84, 2·84	?	1·80 (2·13)	?	?	?
Aphrodisias, Aphrodite	7 1½ (7 11½)	2·29 2·54, 2·29	8·23	1·93 (2·15)	3·60 3·24, 3·60	4·44 (4·54) 4·00, 4·44 (4·54)	1·23 (1·26)
Aezani, Zeus	6 3½ (7 2¼)	2·61 3·88, 2·61	9·91	1·99 (2·27)	3·79 2·55, 3·79	4·55 (4·66) 3·07, 4·55 (4·66)	1·20 (1·23)
CORINTHIAN .							
Athens, Zeus Olympius	?	2·86, 2·89	8·81	?	3·07, 3·05	?	?
Sagalassus, Antoninus Pius ..	5 0½ (5 10)	3·20	?	1·95 (2·25)	?	?	?
Euromus, Zeus	5 6½ (6 3)	3·00	9·52	1·94 (2·18)	3·17	3·82 (3·90)	1·20 (1·23)
Cnidus	7 0 (4 7¼)	3·73, 3·09	?	1·92 (2·22)	?	?	?

SELECTED BIBLIOGRAPHY

(A) ANCIENT SOURCES

(1) *VITRUVIUS:*

CHOISY (A.)—*Vitruve*. 4 vols. Paris, 1909.
GRANGER (F.)—*Vitruvius on Architecture* (Loeb Classical Library). 2 vols. London and New York, 1931–34.
MORGAN (M. H.)—*Vitruvius, the Ten Books on Architecture*. Cambridge (Mass.), 1914.
See also E6 (Birnbaum, Schlikker), F3 (Carpenter), F5 (Picard).

(2) *PLINY THE ELDER:*

JEX-BLAKE (K.) and SELLERS (E.)—*The Elder Pliny's Chapters on the History of Art*. London, 1896.
RACKHAM (H.)—*Pliny, Natural History* (Loeb Classical Library). 10 vols. London and New York, 1938- (in progress).

(3) *PAUSANIAS:*

FRAZER (Sir J. G.)—*Pausanias's Description of Greece*. 6 vols. London, 1898. (Reprinted 1913.)
HITZIG (H.) and BLÜMNER (H.)—*Des Pausanias Beschreibung von Griechenland*. 3 vols. Berlin, 1896–1910.
JONES (W. H. S.)—*Pausanias, Description of Greece* (Loeb Classical Library). 4 vols. London and New York, 1918–35.
VAN BUREN (A. W.)—*Graecia Antiqua, Maps and Plans to illustrate Pausanias's Description of Greece*. London, 1930.
See also G1 (Harrison–Verrall), G2 (Jahn–Michaelis), I6 (Daux).

(4) *OTHER WRITERS AND COLLECTIONS:*

JONES (H. S.)—*Select Passages from Ancient Writers, illustrative of the History of Greek Sculpture*. London and New York, 1895.
MILLER (W.)—*Daedalus and Thespis, the Contributions of the Ancient Dramatic Poets to our Knowledge of the Arts and Crafts of Greece*. 3 vols. New York and Columbia (Mo.), 1929–32 (especially vol. I, Architecture and Topography).
OVERBECK (J.)—*Die antiken Schriftquellen zur Geschichte der bildenden Künste*. Leipzig, 1868.
REINACH (A.)—*Recueil Milliet; I, Textes grecs et latins relatifs à l'histoire de la peinture ancienne*. Paris, 1921 (no more published).
See also K13 (Meyer).

(5) *INSCRIPTIONS AND TERMINOLOGY:*

CHOISY (A.)—*Études épigraphiques sur l'architecture grecque*. Paris, 1883–84.
EBERT (F.)—*Fachausdrücke des griechischen Bauhandwerks, I, Der Tempel*. Würzburg, 1910 (Diss.).
FABRICIUS (E.)—*De architectura graeca commentationes epigraphicae*. Berlin, 1881.
Inscriptiones Graecae, especially I–III, *Inscriptiones Atticae*. Berlin, 1873–97 (better in the Editio Minor, Berlin, 1913–40). Also XI, *Inscriptiones Deli*. Berlin, 1912–27, and Paris, 1926–37.
LATTERMANN (H.)—*Griechischen Bauinschriften*. Strasbourg, 1908.
See also G2 (Dinsmoor, Smith), G7 (Paton-Stevens), G22 (Dörpfeld, Marstrand), G24 (Caskey, Davis, Noack), H11 (Baunack), I6 (École Française iii), I11 (Bundgaard, Ridder), J8 (Davis), K20 (Haussoullier), K33 (Kalinka).

BIBLIOGRAPHY

(B) GENERAL REFERENCE WORKS

(1) *ANCIENT HISTORY:*
BOTSFORD (G. W.) and ROBINSON (C. A.)—*Hellenic History.* 3rd ed., New York, 1948.
BURY (J. B.), BARBER (E. A.), BEVAN (E.) and TARN (W. W.)—*The Hellenistic Age, Aspects of Hellenistic Civilisation.* 2nd ed., Cambridge, 1925.
Cambridge Ancient History. 12 vols. and 5 vols. plates. Cambridge, 1923–39.
FERGUSON (W. S.)—*Hellenistic Athens.* London, 1911.
MEYER (E.)—*Geschichte des Altertums,* especially vol. III, 2nd ed., Stuttgart, 1937; vol. IV, 3rd ed., Stuttgart, 1939.
ROSTOVTZEFF (M. I.)—*The Social and Economic History of the Hellenistic World.* 3 vols. Oxford, 1941.
TARN (W. W.)—*Hellenistic Civilisation.* 2nd ed., London, 1930.

(2) *PROGRESS OF DISCOVERY:*
GARDNER (P.)—"Fifty Years of Progress in Classical Archaeology." (In his *New Chapters in Greek Art,* Oxford, 1926.)
KOEPP (F.) and WIEGAND (T.)—"Geschichte der Archäologie" and "Die Denkmäler, ihr Untergang, Wiedererstehen." (In Otto, *Handbuch der Archäologie,* vol. I, Munich, 1939.)
MARSHALL (F. H.)—*Discovery in Greek Lands: A Sketch of the Principal Excavations and Discoveries of the Last Fifty Years.* Cambridge, 1920.
MICHAELIS (A.)—*Ein Jahrhundert kunstarchäologischer Entdeckungen.* 2nd ed., Leipzig, 1908.
——— *A Century of Archaeological Discoveries.* New York and London, 1908.
STARK (C. B.)—"Geschichte der archäologischen Studien." (In his *Handbuch der Archäologie der Kunst,* vol. I, Leipzig, 1880.)
See also annual reports in *A.J.A., Arch. Anz., B.C.H., J.H.S.,* and *Rev. Et. Gr.*; also in the *Year's Work in Classical Studies,* I, 1906, ff.

(3) *GUIDE-BOOKS:*
BAEDEKER (K.)—*Greece: Handbook for Travellers.* 4th ed., Leipzig, 1909.
——— *Konstantinopel und Kleinasien.* 2nd ed., Leipzig, 1914.
——— *Southern Italy and Sicily.* 17th ed., Leipzig, 1930.
BÉQUIGNON (Y.)—*Grèce (Guides Bleus).* Paris, 1935.
TOURING CLUB ITALIANO—*Guida d'Italia;* 15, *Campania;* 17, *Puglie;* 18, *Lucania e Calabria;* 19, *Sicilia e Isole minori;* 22, *Isole Egee;* 23, *Libia.* Milan, 1937–40.

(4) *TOPOGRAPHICAL PHOTOGRAPHS:*
BAUD-BOVY (D.) and BOISSONNAS (F.)—*En Grèce par monts et par vaux.* Geneva, 1910. (Also English trans.)
——— *Des Cyclades en Crète au gré du vent.* Geneva, 1919.
BON (A.) and CHAPOUTHIER (F.)—*En Grèce.* Athens, 1932.
——— *Retour en Grèce.* Athens, 1934.
CHISHOLM (H.) and HOYNINGEN-HUENE (G.)—*Hellas, a Tribute to Classical Greece.* New York, 1943.
HOLDT (H.) and HOFMANNSTHAL (H. v.)—*Picturesque Greece.* London, 1929.

(5) *MUSEUM COLLECTIONS:*
BLÜMEL (C.)—*Staatliche Museen zu Berlin: Katalog der Sammlung antiker Skulpturen.* Vols. III–IV. Berlin, 1931–38.
CASKEY (L. D.)—*Catalogue of Greek and Roman Sculpture of the Boston Museum of Fine Arts.* Boston, 1925.
DICKINS (G.) and CASSON (S.)—*Catalogue of the Acropolis Museum.* 2 vols. Cambridge, 1912–21.
LETHABY (W. R.)—*Greek Buildings Represented by Fragments in the British Museum.* London, 1908.
——— "Greek Afternoons at the British Museum." (In *Builder,* CXVIII–CXIX, 1920.)
——— "More Greek Studies." (In *Builder,* CXXXVI–CXXXVII, 1929.)

BIBLIOGRAPHY

MENDEL (G.)—*Musées impériaux ottomans, Catalogue des sculptures grecques, romaines, et byzantines*. 3 vols. Constantinople, 1912.
PAPASPYRIDI (S.)—*Guide du Musée national*. Athens, 1927.
PRYCE (F. N.)—*British Museum, Catalogue of Sculpture in the Department of Greek and Roman Antiquities*. London, 1928– (in progress).
RICHTER (G. M. A.)—*Metropolitan Museum of Art: Handbook of the Greek Collection*. New ed., New York, 1930.
SMITH (A. H.)—*A Catalogue of Sculpture in the Department of Greek and Roman Antiquities, British Museum*. 3 vols. London, 1892–1904.
STAIS (V.)—*Marbres et bronzes du Musée national*. 2nd ed., Athens, 1910.
SVORONOS (J. N.)—*Das athener Nationalmuseum*. 3 vols. Athens, 1908–13.
WOLTERS (P.)—*Führer durch die Glyptothek König Ludwigs I*. Munich, 1935.
See also E3 (Wolters), G3 (Heberdey, Langlotz, Payne, Schrader), J7 (Cesnola, Dikaios, Myres), K26 (Massow).

(6) DICTIONARIES AND ENCYCLOPAEDIAS:

BAUMEISTER (A.)—*Denkmäler des klassischen Altertums*. 3 vols. Munich and Leipzig, 1885–88.
DAREMBERG (C.) and SAGLIO (E.)—*Dictionnaire des antiquités grecques et romaines*. 6 vols. Paris, 1873–1919.
EBERT (M.)—*Reallexikon der Vorgeschichte*. 15 vols. Berlin, 1924–32.
LONGFELLOW (W. P. P.)—*Cyclopaedia of Architecture in Italy, Greece, and the Levant*. New York, 1895.
PAULY (A.) and WISSOWA (G.)—*Real-Encyclopädie der classischen Altertumswissenschaft*. New ed., Stuttgart, 1894– (in progress).
SMITH (Sir W.)—*Dictionary of Greek and Roman Antiquities*. 2 vols. London, 1895.
STURGIS (R.)—*Dictionary of Architecture and Building*. 3 vols. New York, 1901.
THIEME (U.) and BECKER (F.)—*Allgemeines Lexikon der bildenden Künstler von der Antike. bis zur Gegenwart*. 36 vols. Leipzig, 1907–47.

(7) BIBLIOGRAPHIES:

MAU (A.), MERKLIN (E. v.), and MATZ (F.)—*Katalog der Bibliothek des deutschen archäologischen Instituts in Rom*. 2 vols. in 5. 2nd ed., Berlin, 1913–32.
SMITH (A. H.)—*A Classified Catalogue of the Books, Pamphlets and Maps in the Library of the Societies for the Promotion of Hellenic and Roman Studies*. London, 1924. (MS. revised ed., 1936, in the library.)
See also annual bibliographies in *A.J.A., J.H.S.* ("Supplement to the Subject Catalogue of the Joint Library"), *Jahrb. Arch. Inst.* ("Bibliographie"), and *Bibliotheca Philologica Classica* (part of Bursian's *Jahresberichte über die Fortschritte der classischen Altertumswissenschaft*). See also N1 (Bérard).

(C) GENERAL HANDBOOKS (AEGEAN AND GREEK TOGETHER)

1) ART IN GENERAL:

CURTIUS (L.)—*Die antike Kunst: die klassische Kunst Griechenlands*. Potsdam, 1938.
DUCATI (P.)—*L'Arte classica*. Turin, 1920.
FOWLER (H. N.) and WHEELER (J. R.)—*Handbook of Greek Archaeology*. New York and Cincinnati, 1909.
RIZZO (G. E.)—*Storia dell' arte greca*. Turin, 1913–27 (unfinished).
RODENWALDT (G.)—*Die Kunst der Antike, Hellas und Rom*. Berlin, 1927.
SCHUCHHARDT (W. H.)—*Geschichte der Kunst: I, Altertum, 1, Die Kunst der Griechen*. Berlin, 1940.
SPRINGER (A.) and WOLTERS (P.)—*Handbuch der Kunstgeschichte: I, Die Kunst des Altertums*. 12th ed., Leipzig, 1923.
TARBELL (F. B.)—*History of Greek Art*. Meadville and New York, 1896.
WALTERS (H. B.)—*The Art of the Greeks*. New York and London, 1906.
WHIBLEY (L.)—*Companion to Greek Studies*. 4th ed., Cambridge, 1931.

BIBLIOGRAPHY

(2) *ARCHITECTURE:*
BENOIT (F.)—*L'Architecture: I, antiquité.* Paris, 1911.
BORRMANN (R.) and NEUWIRTH (J.)—*Geschichte der Baukunst: I, Die Baukunst des Altertums.* Leipzig, 1904.
CHOISY (A.)—*Histoire de l'architecture.* Vol. I. Paris, 1899.
DURM (J.)—*Handbuch der Architektur: Die Baukunst der Griechen.* 3rd ed., Leipzig, 1910.
FIECHTER (E.)—"Haus." (In Pauly-Wissowa, *R.E.*, VII, 1912.)
NOACK (F.)—*Die Baukunst des Altertums.* Berlin, 1910.
PFUHL (E.)—"Vorgriechische und griechische Haustypen." (In *Festgabe H. Blümner*, Zurich, 1914.)
RIDER (B. C.)—*The Greek House: its History and Development from the Neolithic Period to the Hellenistic Age.* Cambridge, 1916.
ROBERTSON (D. S.)—*Handbook of Greek and Roman Architecture.* 2nd ed., Cambridge, 1943.
ROBINSON (D. M.)—"Prähistorische und griechische Häuser." (In Pauly-Wissowa, *R.E.*, Suppl. VII, 1939, *s.v.* "Haus.")
WARREN (H. L.)—*The Foundations of Classic Architecture.* New York, 1919.

(3) *ALLIED FIELDS:*
SWINDLER (M. H.)—*Ancient Painting from the Earliest Times to the Period of Christian Art.* New Haven and London, 1929.

(D) THE AEGEAN AGE

(1) *GENERAL:*
BELL (E.)—*Prehellenic Architecture in the Aegean.* London, 1926.
BOSSERT (H. T.)—*Alt-Kreta.* 2nd ed., Berlin, 1923.
——— *The Art of Ancient Crete.* London, 1937.
CHARBONNEAUX (J.)—*L'Art égéen.* Paris and Brussels, 1929.
CHILDE (V. G.)—*The Dawn of European Civilization.* New ed., London and New York, 1939.
——— *The Bronze Age.* Cambridge and New York, 1930.
DUSSAUD (R.)—*Les Civilisations préhelléniques dans le bassin de la mer Égée.* 2nd ed., Paris, 1914.
FIMMEN (D.)—*Die kretisch-mykenische Kultur.* 2nd ed., Leipzig, 1924.
GLASGOW (G.)—*The Minoans.* London, 1923.
GLOTZ (G.)—*La Civilisation égéenne.* Paris, 1923.
——— *The Aegean Civilization.* New York, 1925.
HALL (H. R.)—*Aegean Archaeology.* London, 1915.
——— *The Civilization of Greece in the Bronze Age.* London, 1928.
KARO (G.)—"Mykenische Kultur." (In Pauly-Wissowa, *R.E.*, Suppl. VI, 1935.)
KAVVADIAS (P.)—Προιστορικὴ Ἀρχαιολογία. Athens, 1909.
LICHTENBERG (R. v.)—*Die ägäische Kultur.* Leipzig, 1918.
MYLONAS (G. E.)—Ἡ νεολιθικὴ Ἐποχὴ ἐν Ἑλλάδι. Athens, 1928.
NILSSON (M. L.)—*The Minoan-Mycenaean Religion.* Lund, 1927.
PARIBENI (R.)—*Architettura dell' oriente antico.* Bergamo, 1937.
PERROT (G.) and CHIPIEZ (C.)—*Histoire de l'art dans l'antiquité: VI. La Grèce primitive, l'art mycénien.* Paris, 1894.
——— *Art in Primitive Greece.* 2 vols. London, 1894.
SCHUCHHARDT (C.)—*Schliemann's Excavations.* London and New York, 1891.
THOMPSON (G. D.)—*The Prehistoric Aegean.* London, 1948.
TSOUNTAS (C.) and MANATT (J. I.)—*The Myceanaean Age.* London, 1897.
   See also C1, C2 (Benoit, Borrmann-Neuwirth, Choisy, Durm, Noack, Robertson, Warren).

(2) *ARCHITECTURAL FORMS:*
DOMBART (T.)—"Die nach unten verjüngten Säulen des Altertums." (In *Wilhelm Dörpfeld Festschrift*, Berlin, 1933.)
DURM (J.)—"Über vormykenische und mykenische Architekturformen." (In *Jahresh. Oest. Arch. Inst.*, X, 1907.)

BIBLIOGRAPHY

MEURER (M.)—"Form und Herkunft der mykenischen Säule." (In *Jahrb. Arch. Inst.*, XXIX, 1914.)
REBER (F. v.)—"Beiträge zur Kenntnis des Baustiles der heroischen Epoche." (In *Sitzb. Mün. Akad.*, 1888.)
——— "Über das Verhältnis des mykenischen zum dorischen Baustil." (In *Abh. Mün. Akad.*, XXI, 1898.)
WURZ (E.)—*Der Ursprung der kretisch-mykenischen Säulen.* Munich, 1913.

(3) *HOUSES AND PALACES:*
AKERSTRÖM (A.—"Zur Frage der mykenischen Dacheindeckung." (In *Skrift. Sven. Inst.*, V, 1941.)
BASSETT (S. E.)—"The Palace of Odysseus." (In *A.J.A.*, XXIII, 1919.)
BLEGEN (C. W.)—"The Roof of the Mycenaean Megaron." (In *A.J.A.*, XLIX, 1945.)
BOETHIUS (C. A.)—"Mycenaean Megara and Nordic Houses." (In *B.S.A.*, XXIV, 1919-21.)
DINSMOOR (W. B.)—"Notes on Megaron Roofs." (In *A.J.A.*, XLVI, 1942.)
DÖRPFELD (W.)—"Kretische, mykenische, und homerische Paläste." (In *Ath. Mitt.*, XXX and XXXII, 1905 and 1907.)
HOLLAND (L. B.)—"Primitive Aegean Roofs." (In *A.J.A.*, XXIV, 1920.)
ISHAM (N. M.)—*The Homeric Palace.* Providence, 1898.
MACKENZIE (D.)—"Cretan Palaces and the Aegean Civilisation." (In *B.S.A.*, XI–XIV, 1904-5 to 1907-8.)
MARINATOS (S.)—"Greniers de l'Helladique ancien." (In *B.C.H.*, LXX, 1946.)
MÜLLER (V.)—"Development of the Megaron in Prehistoric Greece." (In *A.J.A.*, XLVIII, 1944.)
NOACK (F.)—*Homerische Paläste.* Leipzig, 1903.
——— *Ovalhaus und Palast in Kreta.* Leipzig, 1908.
OELMANN (F.)—*Haus und Hof im Altertum.* Vol. I. Berlin and Leipzig, 1927.
REUTHER (O.)—"Urformen des Sparren- under Pfettendaches." (In *Ath. Mitt.*, L, 1925.)
SMITH (E. B.)—"The Megaron and its Roof." (In *A.J.A.*, XLVI, 1942.)
    See also C2 (Fiechter, Pfuhl, Rider, Robinson), D6 (Evans *Palace*, Pendlebury), D7 (Pernier), D8 (Chapouthier, Charbonneaux, Hatzidakis), D10 (Blegen, Dörpfeld), D11 (Bulle, Goldman, Noack, Ridder, Tsountas, Wace-Thompson), D13 (Schliemann, Wace), D14 (entire), D15 (Blegen, Frödin-Persson, Holmberg, Valmin, G7 (Holland).

(4) *TOMBS:*
BELGER (C.)—*Beiträge zur Kenntniss der griechischen Kuppelgräber.* Berlin, 1887.
VALMIN (N.)—"Tholos Tombs and Tumuli." (In *Skrift. Sven. Inst.*, II, 1932.)
    See also D6 (Evans *Tombs*), D8 (Seager, Xanthoudidis), D9 Gjerstad, Westholm), D11 (Schliemann), D12 (Gropengiesser, Lolling-Bohn), D13 (Evans, Karo, Simpson, Thiersch, Wace), D15 (Blegen *Prosymna*, Persson), D16 (entire).

(5) *CRETE IN GENERAL:*
BAIKIE (J.)—*The Sea-Kings of Crete.* 4th ed., London, 1926.
BURROWS (R. M.)—*The Discoveries in Crete.* 2nd ed., London, 1908.
DEMARGNE (P.)—*La Crète dédalique.* Paris, 1947.
HAWES (C. H. and H. B.)—*Crete the Forerunner of Greece.* 3rd ed., London and New York, 1916.
KARO (G.)—"Kreta." (In Pauly-Wissowa, *R.E.*, XI, 1922.)
MARAGHIANNIS (G.) and others—*Antiquités crétoises.* 3 vols. Candia and Athens, 1906-15.
MOSSO (A.)—*The Palaces of Crete and their Builders.* 2nd ed., London, 1910.
PENDLEBURY (J. D. S.)—*The Archaeology of Crete.* London, 1939.

(6) *CNOSSUS:*
EVANS (Sir A. J.)—"Bird's-eye View of the Minoan Palace of Knossos, Crete." (In *Journal R.I.B.A.*, X, 1902-3.)
——— "The Palace of Knossos." (In *B.S.A.*, VI–XI, 1899-1900 to 1904-5.)
——— *The Palace of Minos at Knossos.* 4 vols. and index in 7. London, 1921-36.

EVANS (Sir A. J.)—"The Prehistoric Tombs of Knossos." (In *Archaeologia,* LIX, 1905.)
―――― "The Tomb of the Double Axes." (In same, LXV, 1914.)
PENDLEBURY (J. D. S.)—*A Handbook to the Palace of Minos at Knossos*. London, 1933.

(7) *PHAESTUS AND HAGIA TRIADA:*
HALBHERR (F.)—"Scavi della Missione italiana ad Hagia Triada nel 1902." (In *Mem. Ist. Lomb.*, XXI, 1899-1907.)
PERNIER (L.)—"Scavi della Missione italiana a Phaestos." (In *Mon. Ant.*, XII and XIV, 1902 and 1904.)
―――― *Il Palazzo minoico di Festos*. Rome, 1935- (in progress).
STEFANI (E.) and BANTI (L.)—"La Grande tomba a tholos di Haghia Triada." (In *Ann. Scuol. Ital.*, XIII-XIV, 1930-31.)

(8) *SMALLER CRETAN SITES:*
BOSANQUET (R. C.) and DAWKINS (R. M.)—"Excavations at Palaikastro." (In *B.S.A.*, VIII-XII, 1901-2 to 1905-6, Suppl. 1923.)
CHAPOUTHIER (F.), CHARBONNEAUX (J.) and JOLY (R.)—*Fouilles executées à Mallia*. 3 vols. Paris, 1928-42.
CHARBONNEAUX (J.)—"L'Architecture et la céramique du palais de Mallia." (In *B.C.H.*, LII, 1928.)
HATZIDAKIS (J.)—*Tylissos à l'époque minoenne*. Paris, 1921.
HAWES (H. B.) and others—*Gournia, Vasiliki, and other Prehistoric Sites on the Isthmus of Hierapetra, Crete*. Philadelphia, 1908.
SEAGER (R. B.)—*Excavations in the Island of Pseira*. Philadelphia, 1910.
―――― *Explorations in the Island of Mochlos*. Boston and New York, 1912.
XANTHOUDIDIS (S. A.)—*The Vaulted Tombs of Mesará*. London, 1924.

(9) *AEGEAN AND ASIATIC ISLANDS:*
ATKINSON (T. D.) and others—*Excavations at Phylakopi in Melos* (Suppl. Papers Soc. Prom. Hellenic Studies, IV). London, 1904.
CASSON (S.)—*Ancient Cyprus, its Art and Archaeology*. London, 1937.
GJERSTAD (E.) and others—*The Swedish Cyprus Expedition*. 4 vols. Stockholm, 1934-9. (in progress).
HILL (Sir G. F.)—*A History of Cyprus*. Vol. I. Cambridge, 1940.
LAMB (W.)—*Excavations at Thermi in Lesbos*. Cambridge, 1936.
WESTHOLM (A.)—"Built Tombs in Cyprus." (In *Skrift. Sven. Inst.*, V, 1941.)

(10) *TROY:*
BLEGEN (C. W.)—"Excavations at Troy." (In *A.J.A.*, XXXVI-XLIII, 1932-39.)
BLEGEN (C. W.), CASKEY (J. L.), and RAWSON (M.)—*Troy, Excavations conducted by the University of Cincinnati, 1932-38*. 4 vols. (In preparation.)
DÖRPFELD (W.) and others—*Troja und Ilion*. 2 vols. Athens, 1902.
LEAF (W.)—*Troy, a Study in Homeric Geography*. London, 1912.
SCHLIEMANN (H.)—*Troy and its Remains*. London, 1875.
―――― *Ilios: the City and Country of the Trojans*. London, 1880; New York, 1881.
―――― *Troja: Results of the Latest Researches and Discoveries on the Site of Homer's Troy*. London, 1884.

(11) *NORTHERN GREECE:*
BULLE (H.)—"Orchomenos." (In *Abh. Mün. Akad.*, XXIV, 1907.)
CASSON (S.)—*Macedonia, Thrace, and Illyria*. Oxford, 1926.
DÖRPFELD (W.)—*Alt-Ithaka, ein Beitrag zur Homer-Frage, Studien und Ausgrabungen auf der Insel Leukas-Ithaka*. 2 vols. Munich, 1927.
GOLDMAN (H.)—*Excavations at Eutresis in Boeotia*. Cambridge (Mass.), 1931.
HANSEN (H. D.)—*Early Civilization in Thessaly*. Baltimore, 1933.
HEURTLEY (W. A.)—*Prehistoric Macedonia*. Cambridge, 1939.
KERAMOPOULLOS (A. D.)—"Θηβαϊκά." (In 'Αρχ. Δελτ., III, 1917.)

BIBLIOGRAPHY

NOACK (F.)—"Arne." (In *Ath. Mitt.*, XIX, 1894.)
RHOMAIOS (K. A.)—"Ἐκ τοῦ προιστορικοῦ Θέρμου." (In *Ἀρχ. Δελτ.*, I, 1915.)
RIDDER (A.)—"Fouilles de Gha." (In *B.C.H.*, XVIII, 1894.)
SCHLIEMANN (H.)—*Orchomenos*. Leipzig, 1881.
TSOUNTAS (C.)—*Αἱ προιστορικαὶ Ἀκροπόλεις Διμηνίου καὶ Σέσκλου*. Athens, 1908.
WACE (A. J. B.) and THOMPSON (M. S.)—*Prehistoric Thessaly*. Cambridge, 1912.

(12) *ATHENS AND ATTICA:*
BRONEER (O.)—"A Mycenaean Fountain on the Athenian Acropolis." (In *Hesperia*, VIII, 1939.)
GROPENGIESSER (H.)—*Die Gräber von Attika der vormykenischen und mykenischen Zeit*. Athens, 1907 (Diss.).
KÖSTER (A.)—*Das Pelargikon*. Strasbourg, 1909.
KOUROUNIOTIS (K.) and MYLONAS (G. E.)—*Ἐλευσινιακά*. Athens, 1932.
LOLLING (H.) and BOHN (R.)—*Das Kuppelgrab bei Menidi*. Athens, 1880.
MYLONAS (G. E.)—"The Temple of Demeter at Eleusis." (In *A.J.A.*, XLVI, 1942.)
―――― *The Hymn to Demeter and her Sanctuary at Eleusis*. St. Louis, 1942.
See also G7 (Holland).

(13) *MYCENAE:*
EVANS (Sir A. J.)—*The Shaft Graves and Bee-hive Tombs of Mycenae and Their Interrelation*. London, 1929.
KARO (G.)—"Die Schachtgräber von Mykenai." (In *Ath. Mitt.*, XL, 1915.)
―――― *Die Schachtgräber von Mykenai*. 2 vols. Munich, 1930–33.
ROBERTSON (D. S.)—"New Light on the Façade of the Treasury of Atreus." (In *J.H.S.*, LXI, 1941.)
RODENWALDT (G.)—*Der Fries des Megarons von Mykenai*. Halle, 1921.
SCHLIEMANN (H.)—*Mycenae: a Narrative of Researches and Discoveries at Mycenae and Tiryns*. New York, 1880.
SIMPSON (W.)—"Notes upon the Smaller 'Treasuries' at Mycenae." (In *Journal R.I.B.A.*, II, 1894–95.)
THIERSCH (F.)—"Die Tholos des Atreus zu Mykenae." (In *Ath.Mitt.*, IV, 1879.)
WACE (A. J. B.) and others—"Excavations at Mycenae." (In *B.S.A.*, XXIV–XXV. 1919–21 to 1921–23; and *Archaeologia*, LXXXII, 1932.)
―――― "The Date of the Treasury of Atreus." (In *J.H.S.*, LXVI, 1926.)
―――― "The Treasury of Atreus." (In *Antiquity*, XIV, 1940.)
――――*Mycenae*. Princeton, 1949.
See also B5 (Pryce i l), H1 (Blouet ii).

(14) *TIRYNS:*
DEUTSCHES ARCHÄOLOGISCHES INSTITUT—*Tiryns: Die Ergebnisse der Ausgrabungen*. Athens, 1912– (in progress).
KARO (G.)—*Führer durch Tiryns*. 2nd ed., Athens, 1934.
SCHLIEMANN (H.)—*Tiryns: the Prehistoric Palace of the Kings of Tiryns*. New York, 1885; London, 1886.

(15) *SMALLER PELOPONNESIAN SITES:*
BLEGEN (C. W.)—*Korakou, a Prehistoric Settlement near Corinth*. Boston and New York, 1921.
―――― *Zygouries, a Prehistoric Settlement in the Valley of Cleonae*. Cambridge (Mass.), 1928.
―――― *Prosymna, the Helladic Settlement Preceding the Argive Heraeum*. 2 vols. Cambridge (Mass.), 1937.
―――― "Excavations at Pylos, 1939." (In *A.J.A.*, XLIII, 1939.)
FRÖDIN (O.) and PERSSON (A. W.)—*Asine, Results of the Swedish Excavations, 1922–1930*. Stockholm, 1938.
HARLAND (J. P.)—*Prehistoric Aigina*. Paris, 1925.
HOLMBERG (E. J.)—*The Swedish Excavations at Asea in Arcadia*. (In *Skrift. Sven. Inst.*, XI.) Lund, 1944.

Persson (A. W.)—*Royal Tombs at Dendra near Midea.* Lund, 1931.
—— *New Tombs at Dendra near Midea.* Lund, 1943.
Valmin (M. N.)—*The Swedish Messenia Expedition.* Lund, 1938.

(16) *UGARIT (RAS SHAMRA):*

Dussaud (R.)—*Les Decouvertes de Ras Shamra (Ugarit) et l'Ancien Testament.* 2nd ed., Paris, 1941.
Friedrich (J.)—*Ras Schamra. (Alte Orient,* XXXIII), Leipzig, 1933.
Schaeffer (C. F. A.)—"La [première] onzième campagne de fouilles à Ras Shamra." (In *Syria,* XIV–XVII, XIX–XX, 1933–36, 1938–39.)
—— "Die Stellung Ras Shamra-Ugarits zur kretischen und mykenischen Kultur." (In *Jahrb. Arch. Inst.,* LII, 1937.)
—— *Ugaritika I (Mission de Ras Shamra,* III). Paris, 1939.

(E) THE HELLENIC AGE: GENERAL SURVEYS

(1) *ART IN GENERAL:*

Carpenter (R.)—*The Esthetic Basis of Greek Art.* Bryn Mawr and New York, 1921.
Gardner (P.)—*The Principles of Greek Art.* London, 1914 (reprinted 1926).
Gardner (P.) and Blomfield (Sir R.)—*Greek Art and Architecture.* (Reprinted from Livingstone, *The Legacy of Greece.*) London, 1922.
Ridder (A. de) and Deonna (W.)—*L'Art en Grèce.* Paris, 1924.
—— *Art in Greece.* London, 1927.
Zervos (C.)—*L'Art en Grèce.* 2nd ed., Paris, 1946.
See also C1 (entire).

(2) *ARCHITECTURE:*

Bell (E.)—*Hellenic Architecture, its Genesis and Growth.* London, 1920.
Blomfield (Sir R.)—"Architecture." (In Livingstone, *The Legacy of Greece,* Oxford, 1922.)
Boutmy (E.)—*Philosophie de l'architecture en Grèce.* Paris, 1870.
—— *Le Parthénon et le génie grec* (new ed. of preceding). Paris, 1897.
Brooks (A. M.)—*Architecture* (Our Debt to Greece and Rome). Boston, 1924.
Kohte (J.)—*Die Baukunst des klassischen Altertums.* Brunswick, 1915.
Laloux (V.)—*L'Architecture grecque.* Paris, 1888.
Marquand (A.)—*Greek Architecture.* New York and London, 1909.
Riehl (H.)—*Griechische Baukunst.* Munich, 1932.
Stevens (G. P.)—"Architecture." (In Fowler-Wheeler, *Greek Archaeology,* New York and Cincinnati, 1909.)
Valery (P.)—*Eupalinos, or the Architect.* London, 1932.
See also C2 (Benoit, Borrmann-Neuwirth, Choisy, Durm, Noack, Robertson, Warren).

(3) *ALLIED FIELDS:*

Beazley (J. D.) and Ashmole (B.)—*Greek Sculpture and Painting to the End of the Hellenistic Period.* Cambridge, 1932.
Blümel (C.)—*Griechische Bildhauerarbeit.* Berlin and Leipzig, 1927.
Brunn (H.) and Bruckmann (F.), and Arndt (P.)—*Denkmäler griechischer und römischer Skulptur.* Munich, 1888– (in progress).
Buschor (E.)—*Greek Vase Painting.* London, 1921.
—— *Griechischer Vasen.* Munich, 1940.
Casson (S.)—*The Technique of Early Greek Sculpture.* Oxford, 1933.
Charbonneaux (J.)—*La Sculpture grecque archaïque.* Paris, 1938.
—— *La Sculpture grecque classique.* Paris, 1945.
Furtwängler (A.)—*Masterpieces of Greek Sculpture.* London, 1895.
Langlotz (E.)—*Zur Zeitbestimmung der strengrotfigurigen Vasenmalerei und der gleichzeitigen Plastik.* Leipzig, 1920.
Lawrence (A. W.)—*Classical Sculpture.* 2nd ed., London, 1944.
—— *Later Greek Sculpture.* New York, 1927.

BIBLIOGRAPHY

MACH (A. W. v.)—*A Handbook of Greek and Roman Sculpture.* Boston, 1905.
MARKMAN (S. D.)—*The Horse in Greek Art.* Baltimore, 1943.
PFUHL (E.)—*Masterpieces of Greek Drawing and Painting.* New York, 1926.
PICARD (C.)—*La Sculpture antique des origines à Phidias.* Paris, 1923.
―――― *La Sculpture antique de Phidias à l'ère byzantine.* Paris, 1926.
―――― *Manuel d'archéologie grecque, la sculpture.* Paris, 1935- (in progress).
REINACH (S.)—*Répertoire de la statuaire grecque et romaine.* 6 vols. Paris, 1897-1930.
―――― *Répertoire des reliefs grecs et romains.* 3 vols. Paris, 1909-12.
RICHTER (G. M. A.)—*The Sculpture and Sculptors of the Greeks.* 3rd ed., New Haven, 1950.
―――― *Kouroi, a Study of the Development of the Greek Kouros from the Late Seventh to the Early Fifth Century B.C.* New York, 1942.
―――― *Greek Painting: the Development of Pictorial Representation from Archaic to Graeco-Roman Times.* New York, 1944.
―――― *Attic Red-figured Vases.* New Haven, 1946.
―――― *Archaic Greek Art against its Historical Background.* London and New York, 1949.
RODENWALDT (G.)—*Das Relief bei den Griechen.* Berlin, 1923.
SALIS (A. v.)—*Die Kunst der Griechen.* Leipzig, 1919.
SCHRADER (H.)—*Phidias.* Frankfurt-am-Main, 1924.
SELTMAN (C. T.)—*Attic Vase-Painting.* Cambridge (Mass.), 1933.
SÜSSEROTT (H. K.)—*Griechische Plastik des 4. Jahrhunderts vor Christus.* Frankfurt, 1938.
WOLTERS (P.)—*Die Gipsabgüsse antiker Bildwerke in historischer Folge erklärt.* Berlin, 1885.
See also C3 (Swindler).

(4) PRIMITIVE AND ARCHAIC PERIODS:

DÖRPFELD (W.)—"Der antike Ziegelbau und sein Einfluss auf den dorischen Stil." (In *Hist. u. Philol. Aufsätze Ernst Curtius gewidmet.* Berlin, 1884.)
MARSH (A. R.)—"Ancient Crude-brick Construction and its Influence on the Doric Style." (Summary of preceding, in *A.J.A.*, I, 1885.)
PERROT (G.) and CHIPIEZ (C.)—*Histoire de l'art dans l'antiquité: VII-VIII, La Grèce de l'epopée, La Grèce archaique.* Paris, 1898-1903.
POULSEN (F.)—*Der Orient und die frühgriechische Kunst.* Leipzig, 1912.
RODENWALDT (G.)—"Zur Entstehung der monumentalen Architektur in Griechenland." (In *Ath. Mitt.*, XLIV, 1919.)
WEICKERT (C.)—*Typen der archaischen Architektur in Griechenland und Kleinasien.* Augsburg, 1929.

(5) CULMINATING PERIOD:

DINSMOOR (W. B.)—"The Correlation of Greek Archaeology with History." (In *Studies in the History of Culture, Leland Volume*, Menasha, 1942.)
―――― "The Dawn of Periclean Architecture." (In *A.J.A.*, LIII, 1949.)
―――― *Athenian Architecture in the Age of Pericles.* (In preparation.)

(6) LATER PERIODS:

BIRNBAUM (A.)—"Vitruvius und die griechische Architektur." (In *Denk. Akad. Wien*, LVII, 1914.)
DELBRÜCK (R.)—*Hellenistische Bauten in Latium.* 2 vols. Strasbourg, 1907-12.
FYFE (T.)—*Hellenistic Architecture, an Introductory Study.* Cambridge, 1936.
SCHLIKKER (F. W.)—*Hellenistische Vorstellungen von der Schönheit des Bauwerks nach Vitruv.* Berlin, 1940.

(F) GREEK ARCHITECTURE: ANALYTICAL STUDIES

(1) ORDERS:

BÖTTICHER (K. G. W.)—*Die Tektonik der Hellenen.* 2 vols. 2nd ed., Berlin, 1869-81.
BÜHLMANN (J.)—*The Architecture of Classical Antiquity and of the Renaissance.* Berlin, 1892.
CHIPIEZ (C.)—*Histoire critique des origines et de la formation des ordres grecs.* Paris, 1876.

ESPOUY (H. d')—*Fragments d'architecture antique*. 2 vols. Paris, 1896, 1905.
—— *Monuments antiques relevés et restaurés par les architectes pensionnaires de l'Académie de France à Rome*. Vols. I, IV. Paris, 1906, 1923.
MAUCH (J. M. v.)—*Die architektonischen Ordnungen der Griechen und Römer*. 7th ed., Berlin, 1875.
SEMPER (G.)—*Der Stil in den technischen und tektonischen Künsten*. 2 vols. 2nd ed., Frankfurt-am-Main, 1878-79.
SPIERS (R. P.)—*The Orders of Architecture, Greek, Roman and Italian*. 3rd ed., London, 1897.
WURZ (E. and R.)—"Die Entstehung der Saülenbasen des Altertums unter Berücksichtigung verwandter Kapitelle." (In *Zeitschr. Gesch. Architektur*, Beiheft 15, 1925.)

(2) DORIC:

BÜHLMANN (M.)—"Die altdorische Säule." (In *Zeitschr. Gesch. Architektur*, VI, 1913.)
DEMANGEL (R.)—"Sur l'origine des mutules doriques." (In *Rev. Arch.*, XXXIV, 1931.)
—— "Fenestratum imagines." (In *B.C.H.*, LV and LXX, 1931 and 1945.)
—— "Triglyphes bas." (In same, LXI, 1937.)
—— "Regula." (In same, LXVI-LXVII, 1942-43.)
—— "Anecdota dorica." (In same, LXXI-LXXII, 1947-48.)
HOLLAND (L. B.)—"The Origin of the Doric Entablature." (In *A.J.A.*, XXI, 1917.)
KAWERAU (G.)—"Holzsäulen im dorischen Bau." (In *Zeitschr. Gesch. Architektur*, II, 1908-9.)
KRELL (P. F.)—*Geschichte des dorischen Styls*. Text and atlas. Stuttgart, 1870.
MONTUORO (P. Z.)—"La Struttura del fregio dorico." (In *Palladio*, IV, 1940.)
WASHBURN (O. M.)—"The Origin of the Triglyph Frieze." (In *A.J.A.*, XXIII, 1919; cf. XXII, 1918.)
WILBERG (W.)—"Die Entwicklung des dorischen Kapitells." (In *Jahresh. Oest. Arch. Inst.*, XIX-XX, 1919.)
See also E4 (Dörpfeld, Marsh), H24 (Sulze), I6 (Amandry-Bousquet, Coste-Messelière *Chapiteaux*), N15 (Griffo), N16 (Patroni).

(3) IONIC:

ANDRAE (W.)—*Die ionische Säule, Bauform oder Symbol*. Berlin, 1933.
BAKALAKIS (G.)—"Zum ionischen Eckkapitell." (In *Jahresh Oest, Arch. Inst.*, XXXVI, 1946.)
BRAUN-VOGELSTEIN (J.)—"Die ionische Säule." (In *Jahrb. Oest. Arch. Inst.*, XXXV, 1920.)
See also G7 (Paton-Stevens), G9 (Martin), G23 (Möbius), H6 Dinsmoor *Temple*, Rhomaios ἐσωτερικά), I6 (Replat *Rémarques*), I13 (Bakalakis), K21 (Koldewey), K27 (Stevens).
BÜHLMANN (J.)—"Die Entstehung der Volutenkapitelle." (In *Zeitschr. Gesch. Architektur*, VII, 1914-19.)
CARPENTER (R.)—"Vitruvius and the Ionic Order." (In *A.J.A.*, XXX, 1926.)
DANTHINE (H.)—*La Palmette-dattier et les arbres sacrés dans l'iconographie d'Asie occidentale ancienne*. 2 vols. Paris, 1937.
DEMANGEL (R.)—*La Frise ionique*. Paris, 1933.
DRERUP (H.)—"Konstruktionsprinzipien des griechisch-ionischen Kapitells." (In *Arch. Anz.*, LII, 1937.)
KAWERAU (G.)—"Eine ionische Säule von der Akropolis zu Athen." (In *Jahrb. Arch. Inst.*, XXII, 1907.)
LEHMANN-HAUPT (C. F.)—"Zur Herkunft der ionischen Säule." (In *Klio*, XIII, 1913.)
LICHTENBERG (R. von)—*Die ionische Säule als klassisches Bauglied rein hellenischen Geistes entwachsen*. Leipzig, 1907.
LUSCHAN (F. v.)—*Entstehung und Herkunft der ionischen Säule*. (*Alte Orient*, XIII.) Leipzig, 1912.
PRZYLUSKI (J.)—"La Colonne ionique et le symbolisme oriental." (In *Rev. Arch.*, VII, 1936.)
PUCHSTEIN (O.)—*Das ionische Capitell*. Berlin, 1887.
—— *Die ionische Säule als klassisches Bauglied orientalischer Herkunft*. Leipzig, 1907.
REBER (F. v.)—"Über die Anfänge des ionischen Baustiles." (In *Abh. Mün. Akad.*, XXII, 1900.)
SCHEFOLD (K.)—"Das äolische Kapitell." (In *Jahresh. Oest. Arch. Inst.*, XXXI, 1939.)
WEICKERT (C.)—"West-östliches." (In *Röm. Mitt.*, LIX, 1944.)

BIBLIOGRAPHY

(4) *CORINTHIAN:*
GÜTSCHOW (M.)—"Untersuchungen zum korinthischen Kapitell." (In *Jahrb. Arch. Inst.*, XXXVI, 1921.)
HOMOLLE (T.)—"L'Origine du chapiteau Corinthien." (In *Rev. Arch.*, IV, 1916.)
RONCZEWSKI (K.)—"Description des chapiteaux corinthiens et variés du musée d'Alexandrie." (In *Acta Universitatis Latviensis*, XVI, 1927.)
SCHLUMBERGER (D.)—"Les Formes anciennes du chapiteau corinthien en Syrie, en Palestine et en Arabie." (In *Syria*, XIV, 1933.)
WEIGAND (E.)—*Vorgeschichte des korinthischen Kapitells*. Würzburg, 1920.
See also G11 (Welter), G23 (Möbius), H6 Dinsmoor (Temple, Wotschitzky), K17 (Schober); cf. I6 (Dinsmoor *Aeolic*), K18 (Kjellberg).

(5) *CARYATIDS:*
HOMOLLE (T.)—"L'Origine des Caryatides." (In *Rev. Arch.*, V, 1917.)
PICARD (C.)—"Vitruve, le portique des Perses à Sparte, et les origines de l'ordre Persan." (In *Comptes Rendus Acad. Inscr.*, 1935.)

(6) *ARCHITECTURAL FORMS IN VASE PAINTINGS:*
KRISCHEN (F.)—"Architektur auf Vasenbildern." (In *Ber. VI. Kong. Arch.*)
ORLANDOS (A. K.)—"Παραστάσεις κρηνῶν ἐπὶ ἀγγείων." (In *'Αρχ. Δελτ.*, II, 1916.)
TARBELL (F. B.)—"Architecture on Attic Vases." (In *A.J.A.*, XIV, 1910.)
VALLOIS (R.)—"Étude sur les formes architecturales dans les peintures de vases grecs." (In *Rev. Arch.*, XI, 1908.)
See also F25 (Dunkley).

(7) *DOORS AND WINDOWS:*
DONALDSON (T. L.)—*A Collection of the Most Approved Examples of Doorways, from Ancient Buildings in Greece and Italy*. London, 1833.
HERBIG (R.)—"Fenster an Tempeln und monumentalen Profanbauten." (In *Jahrb. Arch. Inst.*, XLIV, 1929.)
See also G7 (Paton-Stevens, Schultz-Gardner-Barnsley), I12 (Heuzey-Daumet, Macridy-Bey).

(8) *BASEMENTS AND UPPER STOREYS:*
GERSBACH (A.)—*Geschichte des Treppenbaus der Babylonier, Assyrier, Aegypter, Perser und Griechen*. Strasbourg, 1917.
MÜFID (A.)—*Stockwerkbau der Griechen und Römer*. Berlin and Leipzig, 1932.
VETTER (M.)—*Der Sockel, seine Form und Entwicklung in der griechischen und hellenistisch-römischen Architektur und Dekoration*. Strasbourg, 1910.
See also G9 (Allen-Caskey), G12 (Dinsmoor, Hill), G13 (Adler, Bohn), K2 (Bohn-Schuchhardt), K9 (Bacon-Clarke-Koldewey), K16 (entire), K26 (Staatliche Museen vi), K33 (entire), N15 (Labrouste).

(9) *MOULDINGS:*
SHOE (L. T.)—*Profiles of Greek Mouldings*. 2 vols. Cambridge (Mass.), 1936.
——— "Greek Mouldings of Kos and Rhodes." (In *Hesperia*, XVIII, 1949.)
——— *Profiles of Western Greek Mouldings*. (In preparation.)
WEICKERT (C.)—*Das lesbische Kymation*. Leipzig, 1913 (Diss.).

(10) *DECORATION AND ARCHITECTURAL SCULPTURE:*
BENNDORF (O.)—"Ueber den Ursprung der Giebelakroterien." (In *Jahresh. Oest. Arch. Inst.*, II, 1899.)
HOMANN-WEDEKING (E.)—*Archaische Vasenornamentik in Attika, Lakonien, und Ostgriechenland*. Athens, 1938.
JACOBSTHAL (R.)—*Ornamente griechischer Vasen*. 2 vols. Berlin, 1927.

KÄHLER (H.)—*Das griechische Metopenbild*. Munich, 1949.
KATTERFELD (E.)—*Die griechischen Metopenbilder*. Strassburg, 1911.
KEMPTER (F.)—*Akanthus; die Entstehung eines Ornamentmotivs*. Leipzig, 1934.
LAPALUS (E.)—*Le Fronton sculpté en Grèce, des origines à la fin du IV siècle*. Paris, 1947.
MEURER (M.)—*Vergleichende Formenlehre des Ornamentes und der Pflanze*. Dresden, 1909.
MÖBIUS (H.)—*Die Ornamente der griechischen Grabstelen*. Berlin, 1929.
MONTUORO (P. Z.)—"L'Origine della decorazione frontale." (In *Mem. Accad. Lincei*, I, 1925.)
NAPP (A. E.)—*Bukranion und Guirlande, Beitrag zür Entwicklungsgeschichte der hellenistischen und römischen Dekorationskunst*. Wertheim, 1933 (Diss.).
PALLOTTINO (M.)—"Tipologia dei frontoni arcaici." (In *Rendiconti pontif. Accad. romana*, VIII, 1931–32.)
PAYNE (H.)—*Necrocorinthia: A Study of Corinthian Art in the Archaic Period*. Oxford, 1931.
PRASCHNIKER (C.)—*Zur Geschichte des Akroters*. Brünn, 1929.
SCHEDE (M.)—*Antikes Traufleisten-Ornament*. Strassburg, 1909 (Diss.).
SCHUCHHARDT (W. H.)—*Archaische Giebelkompositionen*. Freiburg, 1940.
TATHAM (C. H.)—*Etchings of Ancient Ornamental Architecture*. 3rd ed., London, 1810.
——— *Etchings of Grecian and Roman Architectural Ornament*. New ed., London, 1893.
VOLKERT (K.)—*Das Akroter: I, Archaische Zeit*. Düren, 1932 (Diss.).
VULLIAMY (L.)—*Examples of Ornamental Sculpture in Architecture*. London, 1824.
WATT (J. C.)—*Examples of Greek and Pompeian Decorative Work*. London, 1897.
See also G23 (Möbius).

(11) POLYCHROMY:

DURM (J.)—*Constructive und polychrome Details der griechischen Baukunst*. Berlin, 1880.
FENGER (L.)—*Die dorische Polychromie*. Text and atlas. Berlin, 1886.
HITTORFF (J. I.)—*Restitution du temple d'Empédocle à Sélinonte: ou, l'architecture polychrôme chez les Grecs*. Text and atlas. Paris, 1851.
SHOE (L. T.)—"Dark Stone in Greek Architecture." (In *Hesperia*, Suppl. VIII, 1949.)
SOLON (L. V.)—*Polychromy, Architectural and Structural*. New York, 1924.
See also G3 (Wiegand), H2 (Cockerell, Furtwängler, Garnier), H20 (Curtius-Adler ii).

(12) ROOF TERRACOTTAS:

ANDREN (A.)—*Architectural Terracottas from Etrusco-Italic Temples*. (In *Skrift. Sven. Inst.*, VI, especially pp. lxxi–cxv.) 2 vols., Lund, 1939–40.
BORRMANN (R.)—*Die Keramik in der Baukunst*. (In *Handbuch der Architektur*, IV, 1.) Stuttgart, 1897.
DARSOW (W.)—*Sizilische Dachterrakotten*. Berlin, 1938 (Diss.).
DÖRPFELD (W.) and others—*Über die Verwendung von Terrakotten am Geison und Dache griechischer Bauwerke*. Berlin, 1881.
KOCH (H.)—*Dachterrakotten aus Campanien*. Berlin, 1912.
——— "Studien zu den Campanischen Dachterrakotten." (In *Röm.Mitt.*, XXX, 1915.)
VAN BUREN (E. D.)—*Archaic Fictile Revetments in Sicily and Magna Graecia*. London, 1923.
——— *Greek Fictile Revetments in the Archaic Period*. London, 1926.
See also F10 (Payne, Schede), F11 (Hittorff, Solon), G3 (Buschor *Tondächer*, Wiegand), G13 (Thompson *Tholos*), H6 (Kourouniotis, Rhomaios ἀρχαιοτέρου), H8 (Fowler iv l), H20 (Curtius-Adler ii), H23 (Dawkins), I4 (Dyggve, Poulsen-Rhomaios, Rhomaios), I5 (Rodenwaldt *Korkyra* i), I10 (Goldman), I22 (entire), J6 (Bosanquet, Demargne, Forster, Kjellberg, Pfuhl, Savignoni, Sieveking), K4 (Macridy-Bey), K15 (Körte), K18 (Kjellberg-Böhlau ii), K20 (Wiegand *Milet* i 8), K21 (Koldeway), K25 (Kosay), K28 (Butler *Sardis* x, Haufmann), N1 (Säflund), N4 (Orsi), N5 (Orsi), N6 (Orsi), N12 (Orsi), N14 (Galli, Luynes, Petra), N17 (Putorti), N19 (Gabrici *Storis*), N20 (Orsi).

(13) CONSTRUCTION:

ATKINSON (R.) and BAGENAL (H.)—*Theory and Elements of Architecture*. Vol. I, London and New York, 1926.
DINSMOOR (W. B.)—"Structural Iron in Greek Architecture." (In *A.J.A.*, XXVI, 1922.)

ORLANDOS (A. K.)—"Preliminary Dowels." (In *A.J.A.*, XIX, 1915.)
TSCHIRA (A.)—"Keildübel." (In *Ath. Mitt.*, LXVI, 1941.)
See also A5 (Choisy), C2 (Durm), E2 (Stevens), E3 (Blümel, Casson), F11 (Durm), C4 (Balanos, Carpenter), G5 (Dinsmoor), G6 (Orlandos), G7 (Paton-Stevens), G12 (Dinsmoor), I11 (Bundgaard), N1 (Koldewey-Puchstein).

(14) *MODELS:*
BENNDORF (O.)—"Antike Baumodelle." (In *Jahresh. Oest. Arch. Inst.*, V, 1902.)
See also H4 (Müller, Oikonomos), H8 (Payne).

(15) *PERSPECTIVE:*
BUNIM (M. S.)—*Space in Medieval Painting and the Forerunners of Perspective.* New York, 1940.
LEVY (G. R.)—"The Greek Discovery of Perspective, its Influence on Renaissance and Modern Art." (In *Journal R.I.B.A.*, L, 1942–43.)
RICHTER (G. M. A.)—"Perspective, Ancient, Mediaeval and Modern." (In *Scritti in Onore di Bartolomeo Nogara*, Vatican City, 1937.)

(16) *OPTICAL REFINEMENTS:*
BASILE (G. B. F.)—*Curvatura delle linee dell' architettura antica.* 2nd ed., Palermo, 1896.
DOMBART (T.)—"Entasis." (In Pauly-Wissowa, *R.E.*, Suppl. IV, 1924.)
GOODYEAR (W. H.)—*Greek Refinements: Studies in Temperamental Architecture.* New Haven, 1912.
HAUCK (G.)—*Die subjektive Perspektive und die horizontalen Curvaturen des dorischen Styls.* Stuttgart, 1879.
PENNETHORNE (J.)—*The Geometry and Optics of Ancient Architecture.* London and Edinburgh, 1878.
PENROSE (F. C.)—*An Investigation of the Principles of Athenian Architecture.* 2nd ed., London, 1888.
STEVENS (G. P.)—"Entasis in Roman Architecture." (In *Mem. Amer. Acad. Rome*, IV, 1924.)
THIERSCH (A.)—"Optische Täuschungen auf dem Gebiete der Architektur." (In *Zeitschr. Bauwesen*, XXIII, 1873.)
See also G4 (Balanos, Hoffer, Stevens, Ziller).

(17) *PROPORTIONS:*
CASKEY (L. D.)—*Geometry of Greek Vases.* Boston, 1922.
CHIPIEZ (C.)—*Le Système modulaire et les proportions dans l' architecture grecque.* Paris, 1891.
DINSMOOR (W. B.)—"How the Parthenon was Planned: Modern Theory and Ancient Practice." (In *Architecture*, XLVII–XLVIII, 1923.)
HAMBIDGE (J.)—*The Parthenon and Other Greek Temples, Their Dynamic Symmetry.* New Haven, 1924.
LUND (F. M.)—*Ad Quadratum, a Study of the Geometrical Bases of Classic and Medieval Religious Architecture, with Special Reference to Their Application in the Restoration of the Cathedral of Nidaros-Throndjem, Norway.* 2 vols. London, 1921.
RAPHAEL (M.)—*Der dorische Tempel.* Augsburg, 1930.
RICHTER (I. A.)—*Rhythmic Form in Art.* London, 1932.
THEUER (M.)—*Der griechisch-dorische Peripteraltempel.* Berlin, 1918.
WOLFER-SULZER (L.)—*Das geometrische Prinzip der griechisch-dorischen Tempel.* Winterthur, 1939.
See also H10 (Dumon, Fossum), K16 (Breen, Krischen, Krüger), K33 (Krischen), N2 (Krischen).

(18) *METROLOGY:*
DÖRPFELD (W.)—"Beiträge zur antiken Metrologie." (In *Ath. Mitt.*, VII and XV, 1882 and 1890.)
LEHMANN-HAUPT (C. F.)—"Stadion." (In Pauly-Wissowa, *R.E.*, IIIA, 1929.)
RIEMANN (H.)—*Zum griechischen Peripteraltempel.* Düren, 1935 (Diss.).
See also H10 (Fossum), I5 (Riemann), K16 (Dinsmoor), K20 (Gerkan *Tempel*), M2 (Aurès), N15 (Aurès).

BIBLIOGRAPHY

(19) *ORIENTATION:*

DINSMOOR (W. B.)—"Archaeology and Astronomy." (In *Proc. Amer. Phil. Soc.*, LXXX, 1939.)
NISSEN (H.)—*Orientation, Studien zur Geschichte der Religion.* Berlin, 1906–10.
PENROSE (F. C.)—"On the Orientation of Certain Greek Temples and the Dates of their Foundation." (In *Proc. Roy. Soc.*, LIII, LXI, LXV, LXVIII, 1893–1901; and *Trans. Roy. Soc.*, CLXXXIV, CXC, CXCVI, 1893–1901.)
See also F27 (Doxiadis), N1 (Koldeway-Puchstein).

(20) *LIGHTING:*

DÖRPFELD (W.)—"Die Beleuchtung der griechischen Tempel." (In *Zeitschr. Gesch. Architektur*, VI, 1913.)
LAUNAY (R. de)—"Le Temple hypèthre." (In *Rev. Arch.*, XIX–XX, 1912.)
See also F7 (entire).

(21) *TEMPLES:*

GRINNELL (I. H.)—*Greek Temples.* New York, 1943.
HANELL (K.)—"Zur Entwickelungsgeschichte des griechischen Tempelhofes." (In *Skrift. Sven. Inst.* II, 1932.)
HUSSEY (G. B.)—"The Distribution of Hellenic Temples." (In *A.J.A.*, VI, 1890.)
LAPPO-DANILEWSKI (O.)—*Untersuchungen über den Innenraum der archaischen griechischen Tempel.* Würzburg, 1942 (Diss.)
LECHAT (H.)—*Le Temple grec.* Paris, 1902.
LEHMANN-HARTLEBEN (K.)—"Wesen und Gestalt griechischer Heiligtümer." (In *Antike*, VII, 1931.)
RAVE (P. O.)—*Griechische Tempel.* Marburg, 1924.
RODENWALDT (G.) and HEGE (W.)—*Griechische Tempel.* Berlin, 1941.
SCHLIKKER (F. W.)—"Der Schaubildentwurf im griechischen Tempelbau." (In *Arch. Anz.*, LVI, 1941.)
SCRANTON (R. L.)—"Interior Design of Greek Temples." (In *A.J.A.*, L, 1946.)
Since most of the sites contain temples, individual references are not listed; see especially G1–4, 6–8, 10–12, 24–27; H2, 4, 6, 8, 11–13, 19–20, 24; I4–6, 18–19, 22; J5–6, 8, 11–13, 15–16; K3, 6–9, 14, 17, 19–21, 26–28, 30–31; M2, 4, 6, 8; N2–6, 8–9, 12, 14–16, 18–21.

(22) *MONUMENTS:*

LOEWY (E.)—"Die Anfänge der Triumphbogen." (In *Jahrb. kunsthist. Samml. Wien*, XI, 1928.)
NILSSON (M. P.)—"Les Bases votives à doubles colonnes et l'arc de triomphe." (In *B.C.H.*, XLIX, 1925.)
REISCH (E.)—*Griechische Weihgeschenke.* Vienna, 1890.
ROUSE (W. H. D.)—*Greek Votive Offerings.* Cambridge, 1902.
See aslo G19 (entire), G20 (entire), I3 (entire), I6 (École française ii–iii, Pomtow *Tanzerinnen* and *Paionios*, Replat (*Rémarques*), I18 (Guillon).

(23) *TOMBS:*

COLLIGNON (M.)—*Les Statues funéraires dans l'art grec.* Paris, 1911.
GARDNER (P.)—*Sculptured Tombs of Hellas.* New York and London, 1896.
MATZ (F.)—"Hellenistische und römische Grabbauten." (In *Antike*, IV, 1928.)
MÖBIUS (H.)—"Stele." (In Pauly-Wissowa, *R.E.*, IIIA, 1929.)
VOLLMÖLLER (K. G.)—*Griechische Kammergräber mit Totenbetten.* Bonn, 1901.
See also D9 (Westholm), F10 (Möbius), G1 (Lebas-Landron), G21 (entire), I4 (Dyggve-Poulsen-Rhomaios), I12 (entire), I15 (Robinson xi), I24 (entire), J1 (Choiseul-Gouffier i), J5 (Schazmann), J9 (Vollmöller), J14 (*Clara Rhodos*, Kinch), J15 (*Buschor Altsamische*), K1 (Beundorf-Niemann, Dilettanti ii and v, Laborde, Petersen-Luschan, Texier i–iii), K9 (Bacon-Clarke-Koldewey), K10 (entire), K11 (Newton), K16 (entire), K32 (entire), K33 (entire), L7 (entire), L8 (Edmonds), M1 (Noshy),

BIBLIOGRAPHY

M2 (Adriani, Breccia, Pagenstecher, Schreiber), M4 (Maioletti, Pacho, Smith-Porcher), M5 (Gabra), N21 (Klumbach).

(24) *THEATRES:*
ALLEN (J. T.)—"The Greek Theater of the Fifth Century Before Christ." (In *Univ. Cal. Publ. Class. Phil.*, VII 1, 1919.)
——— *Stage Antiquities of the Greeks and Romans and Their Influence* (Our Debt to Greece and Rome). New York, 1927.
ANTI (C.)—*Teatri greci arcaici da Minosse e Pericle*. Padua, 1947.
ARIAS (P. E.)—*Il Teatro greco fuori di Atene*. Florence, 1934.
BETHE (E.)—*Prolegomena zur Geschichte des Theaters im Alterthum*. Leipzig, 1896.
——— "Das griechische Theater Vitruvs." (In *Hermes*, XXXIII, 1898.)
——— "Die hellenistische Bühne und ihre Decorationen." (In *Jahrb. Arch. Inst.*, XV, 1900.)
BIEBER (M.)—*Die Denkmäler zum Theaterwesen im Altertum*. Berlin and Leipzig, 1920.
——— *The History of the Greek and Roman Theater*. Princeton, 1939.
BRONEER (O.)—"The 'Οχετός in the Greek Theatre." (In *Classical Studies presented to Edward Capps*, Princeton, 1936.)
BULLE (H.)—"Untersuchungen an griechischen Theatern." (In *Abh.Mün. Akad.*, XXXIII, 1928.)
DILKE (O. A. W.)—"The Greek Theatre Cavea." (In *B.S.A.*, XLIII, 1948.)
DÖRPFELD (W.)—"Das griechische Theater Vitruvs." (In *Ath. Mitt.*, XXII, 1897; cf. XXIII, 1898.)
——— "Thymele und Skene." (In *Hermes*, XXVII, 1902.)
——— "Die griechische Bühne." (In *Ath. Mitt.*, XXVIII, 1903.)
——— "Zur baugeschichtlichen Entwicklung des antiken Theatergebäudes." (In *Arch. Anz.*, XXX, 1915.)
DÖRPFELD (W.) and REISCH (E.).—*Das griechische Theater*. Athens, 1896.
FENSTERBUSCH (C.)—*Das griechishe Theater in klassischer Zeit*. Leipzig, 1927.
——— "Theatron." (In Pauly-Wissowa, *R.E.*, VA, 1934.)
FIECHTER (E.)—*Die baugeschichtliche Entwicklung des antiken Theaters*. Munich, 1914.
——— *Antike griechische Theaterbauten*. Stuttgart, 1930– (in progress).
See also reviews by O. Broneer (*A.J.A.*, XLII, 1938), A. v. Gerkan (*Gnomon*, IX, XIV, XVII, 1933, 1938, 1941).
——— "Einige Beobachtungen über die Chronologie der Rand-Formen der griechischen Orchestra." (In *Mélanges Octave Navarre*, Toulouse, 1935.)
FLICKINGER (R. C.)—*The Greek Theater and its Drama*. 4th ed., Chicago, 1936.
FRICKENHAUS (A.)—*Die altgriechische Bühne*. Strassburg, 1917.
——— "Skene." (In Pauly-Wissowa, *R.E.*, IIIA, 1927.)
HAIGH (A. E.) and PICKARD-CAMBRIDGE (A. W.)—*The Attic Theatre*. 3rd ed., Oxford, 1907.
LIBERTINI (G.)—*Il Teatro greco e la sua evoluzione*. Catania, 1933.
MÜLLER (A.)—*Lehrbuch der griechischen Bühnenalterthümer*. Freiburg, 1886.
——— *Das attische Bühnenwesen*. 2nd ed., Gütersloh, 1916.
NOAK (F.)—"Das Proskenion in der Theaterfrage." (In *Philologus*, LVIII, 1899.)
PUCHSTEIN (O.)—*Die griechische Bühne: eine architektonische Untersuchung*. Berlin, 1901.
STRACK (J. H.)—*Das altgriechische Theatergebäude*. Potsdam, 1843.
VALLOIS (R.)—"Les Théatres greca; skené et skenai." (In *Rev. Et. Anc.*, XXVIII, 1926.)
WIESELER (F.)—*Theatergebäude und Denkmäler des Bühnenwesens bei Griechen und Römern*. Göttingen, 1851.
See also G1 (Lebas-Landron), G15 (entire), G16 (entire), G28 (Arias, Cushing-Miller), H8 (Fowler x, Stillwell), H11 (Defrasse-Lechat, Dumon, Fossum, Kavvadias, *Fouilles* and ἱερόν), H15 (Gardner-Schultz), H22 (Brownson-Earle-McMurtry-Young), H23 (Bulle, Dawkins-Woodward), H24 (Vallois), I14 (Powell-Sears), I17 (Collart), J6 (Pernier *Odeum*), J8 (Bequignon-Replat, Chamonard, Dörpfeld, Vallois *Architecture*), J9 (Richardson), J19 (Fiechter), K1 (Benndorf-Niemann, Dilettanti ii, iii and v, Laborde, Lanckoronski-Niemann-Petersen i–ii, Petersen-Luschan, Texier i and iii), K9 (Bacon-Clarke-Koldewey), K14 (Dörpfeld, Hörmann, Oesterreichisches Institut ii), K19 (Humann), K20 (Krauss), K26 (Pontremoli-Collignon, Staatliche Museen iv), K27 (Dörpfeld, Gerkan *Theater*), L3 (Schmidt), N18 (Marconi), N20 (Anti, Rizzo).

(25) *SECULAR BUILDINGS:*
CALLMER (C.)—"Antike Bibliotheken." (In *Skrift. Sven. Inst.*, X, 1944.)
CHARBONNEAUX (J.)—"Tholos et prytanée." (In same, XLIX, 1925.)
DUNKLEY (B.)—"Greek Fountain-Buildings before 300 B.C." (In *B.S.A.*, XXXVI, 1935-36.)
FRICKENHAUS (A.)—"Griechische Banketthäuser." (In *Jahrb. Arch. Inst.*, XXXII, 1917.)
GÖTZE (B.)—"Antike Bibliotheken." (In same, LII, 1937.)
KRISCHEN (F.), WULZINGER (K.) and GERKAN (A. v.)—*Antike Rathäuser*. Berlin, 1941.
LEROUX (G.)—*Les Origines de l'édifice hypostyle en Grèce, en Orient et chez les Romains*. Paris, 1913.
MCDONALD (W. A.)—*The Political Meeting Places of the Greeks*. Baltimore, 1943.
ROBERT (F.)—*Thymélè: Recherches sur la signification et la destination des monuments circulaires dans l'architecture religieuse de la Grèce*. Paris, 1939.
THIERSCH (H.)—"Antike Bauten für Musik." (In *Zeitschr. Gesch. Architektur*, II, 1908-9.)
See also F27 (Krischen), G13 (Adler, Bohn, Shear, Thompson), G14 (entire), G22 Dörpfeld, Marstrand), H8 (Fowler i-ii), H11 (Delorme), H15 (entire), H20 (Curtius-Adler ii, Gardiner, Wrede), H22 (Orlandos, Philadelpheus), H26 (Welter), J8 (Audiat, École française vi and xix), K2 (Bohn-Schuchhardt), K9 (Bacon-Clarke-Koldewey), K12 (Holland), K14 (Heberdey-Keil, Oesterreichisches Institut i and iii), K19 (Humann), K20 (Wiegand *Milet* i 2, i 5 and i 9), K26 (Staatliche Museen ii, vi and x), K27 (Krischen, Wiegand-Schrader), L3 (Kirk), M2 (Adler, Asín Palacios, Monnert de Villard, Reincke, Thiersch).

(26) *HOUSES:*
BIE (O.)—"Zur Geschichte des Haus-Peristyls." (In *Jahrb. Arch. Inst.*, VI, 1891.)
FALKENER (E.)—"The Grecian House as Described by Vitruvius." (In *Journal R.I.B.A.*, I, 1893-94.)
GARDNER (E. A.)—"The Greek House." (In *J.H.S.*, XXI, 1901.)
PUCHSTEIN (O.)—"Die Gestalt des altgriechisches Hauses." (In *Arch. Anz.*, VI, 1891.)
RUMPF (A.)—"Zum hellenistischen Haus." (In *Jahrb. Arch. Inst.*, L, 1935.)
WISTRAND (E.)—"Om grekernas och romarnas Hus." (In *Eranos*, XXXVII, 1939.)
See also C2 (Fiechter, Pfuhl, Rider, Robinson), I15 (Robinson ii, viii and xii), J7 (Gjerstad), J8 (École française viii), J9 (Johnson, Wiegand), J19 (Hiller von Gaertringen), K12 Holland), K26 (Staatlich Museen v 1), K27 (Wiegand-Schrader), L5 (Fisher, Marquand), M1 (Lewis, Luckhard, Rubensohn, Schütz), M3 (entire), M7 (Vanderborght).

(27) *CITY PLANS:*
CULTRERA (G.)—"Architettura ippodamea, contributo alla storia dell' edilizia nell' antichità." (In *Mem. Accad. Lincei*, XVII, 1923-24.)
DOXIADIS (K. A.)—*Raumordnung im griechischen Städtebau*. Heidelberg, 1937.
ERDMANN (M.)—"Hippodamos von Milet und die symmetrische Städtebaukunst der Griechen." (In *Philologus*, XLII, 1883.)
FABRICIUS (E.) and LEHMANN-HARTLEBEN (K.)—"Städtebau." (In Pauly-Wissowa, *R.E.*, IIIA, 1929.)
GERKAN (A. v.)—*Griechische Städteanlagen*. Berlin and Leipzig, 1924.
HAVERFIELD (F.)—*Ancient Town Planning*. Oxford, 1913.
KRISCHEN (F.)—*Die griechische Stadt, Wiederherstellungen*. Berlin, 1938.
LEHMANN-HARTLEBEN (K.)—*Die antiken Hafenanlagen des Mittelmeeres* (*Klio*, Beiheft XIII). Leipzig, 1923.
TRITSCH (F.)—"Die Stadtbildungen des Altertums und die griechische Polis." (In *Klio*, XXII, 1928.)
TSCHERIKOWER (V.)—"Die hellenistischen Städtegründungen von Alexander dem Grossen bis auf die Römerzeit." (In *Philologus*, Suppl. XIX, 1927.)
WYCHERLEY (R. E.)—"The Ionian Agora." (In *J.H.S.*, LXII, 1942.)
—— *How the Greeks Built Cities*. London and New York, 1949.
WYMER (J. E.)—*Marktplatz-Anlagen der Griechen und Römer*. Munich, 1920.
See also G13 (entire), G14 (entire), H8 (Fowler i-ii), H10 (Tritsch, Walter), I15 (Robinson ii, viii and xii), K9 (Bacon-Clarke-Koldewey), K11 (Newton), K14 (Falkener, Keil, Oesterreichisches Institut i and iii), K19 (Humann), K20 (Wiegand *Milet* i 6

and i 7), K27 (Schede, Wiegand-Schrader), L4 (entire), M2 (Breccia *Alexandrea*), M7 (Viereck), N19 (Gabrici *Acropoli*, Hulot-Fougères).

(28) *CITY AND TERRACE WALLS:*
DODWELL (E.)—*Views and Descriptions of Cyclopean or Pelasgian Remains in Greece and Italy.* London, 1834.
GELL (Sir W.)—*Probestücke von Städtemauern des alten Griechenlands.* Berlin, 1831.
PETIT-RADEL (L. C. F.)—*Récherches sur les monuments cyclopéens et description de la collection des modèles en relief composant la galérie pélasgique de la bibliothèque Mazarine.* Paris, 1841.
SÄFLUND (G.)—"The Dating of Ancient Fortifications in Southern Italy and Greece." (In *Skrift. Sven. Inst.*, IV, 1935.)
SCRANTON (R. L.)—*Greek Walls.* Cambridge (Mass.), 1941.
See also G1 (Lebas–Landron), G22 (Noack), G23 (Wrede *Mauern*), G24 (Noack), H1 (Blouet i–ii), H8 (Fowler i and iii 2), H14 (Fougères), I1 (entire), I2 (Woodhouse), I7 (Stählin), I10 (Goldman), I14 (Powell-Sears), K1 (Benndorf-Niemann, Lanckoronski-Niemann-Petersen i–ii, Petersen-Luschan, Texier ii–iii), K9 (Bacon-Clarke-Koldewey), K20 (Wiegand *Milet* i 8, ii 3 and iii 2), K26 (Staatliche Museen i 2), K27 (Wiegand-Schrader), N1 (Krischen), N7 (Gabrici), N10 (Crispo), N20 (Mauceri).

(G) LOCAL WORKS: ATHENS AND ATTICA

(1) *ATHENS IN GENERAL:*
BAUDOT-LAMOTTE (E.)—*Athènes et l'Attique.* Paris, 1941.
CURTIUS (E.)—*Die Stadtgeschichte von Athen.* Berlin, 1891.
DÖRPFELD (W.)—"Zu den Bauwerken Athens." (In *Ath. Mitt.*, XXXVI, 1911.)
FERGUSON (W. S.)—*Hellenistic Athens.* London, 1911.
FOUGÈRES (G.)—*Athènes.* Paris, 1912.
GARDNER (E. A.)—*Ancient Athens.* New York and London, 1902. (Reprinted 1923.)
HARRISON (J. E.) and VERRALL (M. G.)—*The Mythology and Monuments of Ancient Athens.* London and New York, 1890.
HARRISON (J. E.)—*Primitive Athens as Described by Thucydides.* Cambridge, 1906.
JUDEICH (W.)—*Topographie von Athen.* 2nd ed., Munich, 1931.
KARO (G.)—*Athen und Umgebung* (Grieben Reiseführer). Berlin, 1937.
LABORDE (L. de)—*Athènes au XVe, XVIe et XVIIe siècles.* 2 vols. Paris, 1854.
LEBAS (P.) and LANDRON (E.)—*Voyage archéologique en Grèce et en Asie Mineure fait par ordre du gouvernement français 1843–44.* Paris, 1847–77. (Reprinted by S. Reinach.) Paris, 1888.
MAURRAS (C.)—*Athènes antique.* Paris, 1919.
MIDDLETON (J. H.)—*Plans and Drawings of Athenian Buildings* (Suppl. Papers Soc. Prom. Hellenic Studies, III). London, 1900.
OMONT (H. A.)—*Athènes au XVIIe siècle.* Paris, 1898.
STUART (J.) and REVETT (N.)—*The Antiquities of Athens.* 4 vols. London, 1762–1816. Suppl. vol., London, 1830. 2nd ed. (edited by W. Kinnard), 4 vols. London, 1825–30.
WELLER (C. H.)—*Athens and its Monuments.* New York, 1913.

(2) *ACROPOLIS IN GENERAL:*
BEULÉ (C. E.)—*L'Acropole d'Athènes.* 2 vols. Paris, 1853–54.
BÖTTICHER (A. G.)—*Die Akropolis von Athen.* Berlin, 1888.
BURNOUF (E. L.)—*La Ville et l'acropole d'Athènes.* Paris, 1877.
DINSMOOR (W. B.)—"Attic Building Accounts." (In *A.J.A.*, XVII and XXV, 1913 and 1921.)
D'OOGE (M. L.)—*The Acropolis of Athens.* New York and London, 1908.
ELDERKIN (G. W.)—*Problems in Periclean Buildings.* Princeton, 1912.
JAHN (O.) and MICHAELIS (A.)—*Arx Athenarum a Pausania Descripta.* 3rd ed., Bonn, 1901.
KAVVADIAS (P.) and KAWERAU (G.)—*Die Ausgrabung der Akropolis.* Athens, 1906.
PICARD (C.) and BOISSONNAS (F.)—*L'Acropole d'Athènes, l'enceinte, l'entrée, le bastion d'Athéna Niké, les Propylées.* Paris, 1930.
——— *L'Acropole d'Athènes, le plateau supérieur, l'Erechtheion, les annexes sud.* Paris, 1930.

RODENWALDT (G.) and HEGE (W.)—*Die Akropolis*. Berlin, 1930.
—— *The Acropolis*. London, 1930.
SCHEDE (M.)—*Die Burg von Athen*. Berlin, 1922.
—— *The Acropolis of Athens*. Berlin, 1924.
SMITH (A. H.)—"The Building Inscriptions of the Acropolis of Athens." (In *Journal R.I.B.A.*, XXXIV, 1926-27.)
STEVENS (G. P.)—*The Periclean Entrance Court of the Acropolis of Athens*. Cambridge (Mass.), 1936 (also in *Hesperia*, V, 1936).
—— *The Setting of the Periclean Parthenon* (*Hesperia*, Suppl. III). Cambridge (Mass.), 1940.
WALTER (O.)—*Athen, Akropolis*. Vienna, 1929.
See also G1 (entire).

(3) ARCHAIC ACROPOLIS BUILDINGS:

BUSCHOR (E.)—"Burglöwen" and "Die Wendung des Blaubarts." (In *Ath. Mitt.*, XLVII, 1922.)
—— *Die Tondächer der Akropolis*. 2 fasc. Berlin and Leipzig, 1929-33.
DINSMOOR (W. B.)—"The Burning of the Opisthodomos at Athens." (In *A.J.A.*, XXXVI, 1932.)
—— "The Hekatompedon on the Athenian Acropolis." (In *A.J.A.*, LI, 1947.)
DÖRPFELD (W.)—"Der alte Athena-Tempel auf der Akropolis." (In *Ath. Mitt.*, XI, XII, XV, and XXII, 1886-87, 1890, and 1897; also *Ant. Denk.*, I, 1891.)
—— "Das Hekatompedon in Athen." (In *Jahrb. Arch. Inst.*, XXXIV, 1919.)
HEBERDEY (R.)—*Altattische Poros-Skulptur*. Text and atlas. Vienna, 1919.
LANGLOTZ (E.) and SCHUCHHARDT (W. H.)—*Archaische Plastik auf der Akropolis*. 2nd ed., Frankfurt, 1943.
PAYNE (H.) and YOUNG (G.)—*Archaic Marble Sculpture from the Acropolis*. London, 1936.
SCHRADER (H.)—"Die Gorgonakrotere." (In *Jahrb. Arch. Inst.*, XLIII, 1928.)
SCHRADER (H.) and others—*Die archaischen Marmorbildwerke der Akropolis*. 2 vols. Frankfurt-am-Main, 1939.
SCHUCHHARDT (W.)—"Die Sima des alten Athenatempels der Akropolis." (In *Ath. Mitt.*, LX-LXI, 1935-36.)
WIEGAND (T.)—*Die archaische Poros-Architektur der Akropolis zu Athen*. Text and atlas. Cassel and Leipzig, 1904.
See also B5 (Dickins-Casson i), D12 (Köster), G1 (Harrison), G2 (Kavvadias-Kawerau, Picard, Rodenwaldt, Schede, Walter), G4 (Dinsmoor *Date* and *Peisistratos*, Dörpfeld *Aeltere* and *Zeit*, Hill, Kolbe, Tschira), G5 (Stevens, Weller), G6 (Welter).

(4) PARTHENON:

BALANOS (N. M.)—*Les Monuments de l'Acropole*. 2 vols. Paris, 1938.
CARPENTER (R.)—"New Material for the West Pediment of the Parthenon." (In *Hesperia*, I, 1932.)
—— "The Lost Statues of the East Pediment of the Parthenon." (In same, II, 1933.)
COLLIGNON (M.) and BOISSONNAS (F.)—*Le Parthénon, l'histoire, l'architecture et la sculpture*. Paris, 1910-12 (smaller edition, 1914). 2nd ed. (revised by G. Fougères), Paris, 1926.
DINSMOOR (W. B.)—"The Repair of the Athena Parthenos." (In *A.J.A.*, XXXVIII, 1934.)
—— "The Date of the Older Parthenon." (In same, XXXVIII, 1934.)
—— "Peisistratos, Kleisthenes, Themistokles, Aristeides, oder Kimon: Wer hat den älteren Parthenon begonnen?" (In *Jahrb. Arch. Inst.*, LII, 1937.)
—— "The Construction and Arrangement of the Panathenaic Frieze of the Parthenon." (In *J.H.S.*, LXVIII, 1948.)
—— *The Parthenon and its Predecessors*. (In preparation.)
DÖRPFELD (W.)—"Untersuchungen am Parthenon." (In *Ath. Mitt.*, VI, 1881.)
—— "Der ältere Parthenon." (In same, XVII, 1892.)
—— "Die Zeit des älteren Parthenon." (In same, XXVII, 1902.)
HILL (B. H.)—"The Older Parthenon." (In *A.J.A.*, XVI, 1912.)
HOFFER (J.)—"Der Parthenon in Athen, in seinen Haupttheilen neu gemessen." (In *Wiener Allgemeine Bauzeitung*, III, 1838.)

BIBLIOGRAPHY

Kolbe (W.)—"Die Neugestaltung der Akropolis nach den Perserkriegen." (In *Jahrb. Arch. Inst.*, LI, 1936.)
Laborde (L. de)—*Le Parthénon, documents pour servir à une restauration.* Paris, 1848 (unfinished).
Lücken (G. v.)—*Die Entwicklung der Parthenonskulpturen.* Augsburg, 1930.
Magne (L.)—*Le Parthénon.* Paris, 1895.
Michaelis (A.)—*Der Parthenon.* Text and atlas. Leipzig, 1870–71.
Murray (A. S.)—*The Sculptures of the Parthenon.* London, 1903.
Niemann (G.)—"Aufbau der nordostecke des Parthenon." (In *Vorlegeblätter für archäologische Uebungen*, series 7, pl. XII, Vienna, 1875.)
Orlandos (A. K.)—"Notes on the Roof Tiles of the Parthenon." (In *Hesperia*, Suppl. VIII, 1949.)
Praschniker (C.)—"Die Akroterien des Parthenon." (In *Jahresh. Oest. Arch. Inst.*, XIII, 1910.)
——— *Parthenonstudien.* Augsburg and Vienna, 1928.
Smith (A. H.)—*British Museum; Sculptures of the Parthenon.* London, 1910.
Stevens (G. P.)—"Concerning the Curvature of the Steps of the Parthenon." (In *A.J.A.*, XXXVIII, 1934.)
——— "The Sills of the Grilles of the Pronaos and Opisthodomus of the Parthenon." (In *Hesperia*, XI, 1942.)
——— "The Curves of the North Stylobate of the Parthenon." (In same, XII, 1943.)
Tschira (A.)—"Die unfertigen Säulentrommeln auf der Akropolis zu Athen." (In *Jahrb. Arch. Inst.*, LV, 1940.)
Ziller (E.)—"Ueber die ursprüngliche Existenz der Curvaturen des Parthenon." (In *Zeitschr. Bauwesen*, XV, 1865.)
See also F16 (Hauck, Pennethorne, Penrose), F17 (Dinsmoor, Hambidge), G1 (Stuart-Revett ii and iv), G2 (entire).

(5) PROPYLAEA:

Bohn (R.)—*Die Propyläen der Akropolis zu Athen.* Berlin and Stuttgart, 1882.
Dinsmoor (W. B.)—"The Gables of the Propylaea." (In *A.J.A.*, XIV, 1910.)
——— *The Propylaea and the Entrance to the Acropolis.* (In preparation.)
Dörpfeld (W.)—"Die Propyläen der Akropolis von Athen." (In *Ath. Mitt.*, X, 1885.)
Stevens (G. P.)—"Architectural Studies concerning the Acropolis of Athens." (In *Hesperia*, XV, 1946.)
Weller (C. H.)—"The Pre-Periclean Propylon of the Acropolis at Athens." (In *A.J.A.*, VIII, 1904.)
See also F16 (Penrose), G1 (Dörpfeld, Harrison-Verrall, Stuart-Revett ii), G2 (entire).

(6) ATHENA NIKE TEMPLE:

Blümel (C.)—*Der Fries des Tempels der Athena Nike.* Berlin, 1923.
Carpenter (R.)—*The Sculpture of the Nike Temple Parapet.* Cambridge (Mass.), 1929.
Dinsmoor (W. B.)—"The Sculptured Parapet of Athena Nike." (In *A.J.A.*, XXX, 1926.)
——— "The Nike Parapet Once More." (In same, XXXIV, 1930.)
Heberdey (R.)—"Die Komposition der Reliefs an der Balustrade der Athena Nike." (In *Jahresh. Oest. Arch. Inst.*, XXI–XXII, 1922–24.)
Kekule von Stradonitz (R.)—*Die Reliefs an der Balustrade der Athena Nike.* Stuttgart, 1881.
Orlandos (A. K.)—"Zum Tempel der Athena Nike." (In *Ath. Mitt.*, XL, 1915.)
——— "Nouvelles observations sur la construction du temple d'Athéna Niké." (In *B.C.H.*, LXXI–LXXII, 1947–48.)
Ross (L.), Schaubert (E.) and Hansen (C.)—*Der Tempel der Nike Apteros.* Berlin, 1839.
Stevens (G. P.)—"The Cornice of the Temple of Athena Nike." (In *A.J.A.*, XII, 1908.)
Welter (G.)—"Vom Nikepyrgos." (In *Ath. Mitt.*, XLVIII, 1923.)
——— "Vom Nikepyrgos." (In *Arch. Anz.*, LIV, 1939.)
See also G1 (Lebas-Landron), G2 (entire), G10 (Möbius).

BIBLIOGRAPHY

(7) *ERECHTHEUM:*

DELL (J.)—*Das Erechtheion in Athen, bauanalytisch untersucht, erklärt und ergänzt*. Brunn, 1934.
DÖRPFELD (W.)—"Der ursprünglichen Plan des Erechtheion." (In *Ath. Mitt.*, XXIX, 1904.)
——— "Zur ursprüngliche Plan des Erechtheion, eine Entgegnung." (In *Neue Jahrb. für das klassische Altertum*, XLVII, 1921.)
DÖRPFELD (W.) and SCHLEIF (H.)—*Erechtheion*. Berlin, 1942.
ELDERKIN (G. W.)—"The Cults of the Erechtheum." (In *Hesperia*, X, 1941.)
HOLLAND (L. B.)—"Erechtheum Papers." (In *A.J.A.*, XXVIII, 1924.)
INWOOD (H. W.)—*The Erechtheion at Athens*. London, 1831.
PATON (J. M.) and STEVENS (G. P.)—*The Erechtheum*. Text and atlas. Cambridge (Mass.), 1927.
RODENWALDT (G.)—"Die Form des Erechtheions." (In *Neue Jahrb. für das klassische Altertumsgeschichte*, XLVII, 1921.)
SCHULTZ (R. W.), GARDNER (E. A.) and BARNSLEY (S. H.)—"The North Doorway of the Erechtheum." (In *J.H.S.*, XII, 1891.)
WELLER (C. H.)—"The Original Plan of the Erechtheum." (In *A.J.A.*, XXV, 1921.)
See also F16 (Penrose), G1 (Sturt-Revett ii), G2 (entire), G3 (Dinsmoor *Burning*, Dörpfeld).

(8) *ROMA AND AUGUSTUS TEMPLE:*

KAWERAU (G.)—"Der Tempel der Roma und des Augustus auf der Akropolis von Athen." (In *Ant. Denk.*, I. 1888.)
SNIJDER (G. A. S.)—"De Tempel van Roma en Augustus en het Erechtheum op de Acropolis te Athene." (In *Mededeelingen van het Nederlandsch Historisch Instituut te Rome*, III, 1923.)
——— "Sur le temple de Rome et Auguste et l'Erechtheion sur l'Acropole d'Athènes." (In *Rev. Arch.*, XIX, 1924.)

(9) *ASCLEPIEUM:*

ALLEN (G.) and CASKEY (L. D.)—"The East Stoa of the Asclepieum at Athens." (In *A.J.A.*, XV, 1911.)
GIRARD (P.)—*L'Asclépieion d'Athènes d'après de récentes découvertes*. Paris, 1881.
MARTIN (R.)—"Chapiteaux ioniques de l'Asclépieion d'Athènes." (In *B.C.H.*, LXVIII–LXIX, 1944–45.)
TRAVLOS (J.)—"Τὸ 'Ασκληπιεῖον." (In 'Εφ. 'Αρχ., 1939–41.)

(10) *ILISSUS TEMPLE:*

MÖBIUS (H.)—"Zu Ilissosfries und Nikebalustrade." (In *Ath. Mitt.*, LIII, 1928.)
——— "Das Metroon in Agrai und sein Fries." (In same, LX–LXI, 1935–36.)
STUDNICZKA (F.)—"Zu den Friesplatten vom ionischen Tempel am Ilissos." (In *Jahrb. Arch. Inst.*, XXXI, 1916, and *Ant. Denk.*, III, 1916.)
See also G1 (Stuart-Revett i).

(11) *OLYMPIEUM:*

BEVIER (L.)—"The Olympieion at Athens." (In *Papers of the American School of Classical Studies at Athens*, I, 1882–83.)
WELTER (G.)—"Das Olympieion in Athen." (In *Ath. Mitt.*, XLVII–XLVIII, 1922–23.)
See also F4 (Gütschow), F16 (Penrose), K17 (Schober).

(12) *HEPHAESTEUM:*

BATES (W. N.)—"Notes on the 'Theseum' at Athens." (In *A.J.A.*, V, 1901.)
DINSMOOR (W. B.)—*Observations on the Hephaisteion* (*Hesperia*, Suppl. V). Cambridge (Mass.), 1941.
GULLINI (G.)—"L'Hephaisteion de Atene." (In *Archeologia Classica*, I, 1949.)
GURLITT (W.)—*Das Alter des Bildwerkes und die Bauzeit des sogenannter Theseion in Athen*. Vienna, 1875.
HILL (B. H.)—"The Interior Colonnade of the Hephaisteion." (In *Hesperia*, Suppl. VIII, 1949.)

KOCH (H.)—"Untersuchungen am sogenannten Theseion in Athen." (In *Arch. Anz.*, XLIII, 1928.)
SAUER (B.)—*Das sogenannte Theseion und sein plastischer Schmuck.* Leipzig, 1899.
STEVENS (G. P.)—"The Ceiling of the Opisthodomus of the Theseum." (In *A.J.A.*, XV, 1911.)
THOMPSON (D. B.)—"The Garden of Hephaistos." (In *Hesperia*, VI, 1937.)
See also G1 (Stuart-Revett iii, suppl. vol.).

(13) *GREEK AGORA:*
ADLER (F.)—"Die Stoa des Königs Attalos II zu Athen." (In *Zeitschr. Bauwesen*, XXV, 1875.)
BOHN (R.)—"Die Stoa König Attalos des Zweiten zu Athen." (In same, XXXII, 1882.)
DINSMOOR (W. B.)—"The Temple of Ares at Athens." (In *Hesperia*, IX, 1940.)
DÖRPFELD (W.)—*Alt-Athen und seine Agora.* 2 parts. Berlin, 1937–39.
SHEAR (T. L.) and others—"The American Excavations in the Athenian Agora." (In *Hesperia*, II–XVIII, 1933–49.)
THOMPSON (H. A.)—"The Buildings on the West Side of the Agora." (In same, VI, 1937.)
——— *The Tholos of Athens and its Predecessors.* (*Hesperia*, Suppl. IV). Cambridge (Mass.), 1940.
TRAVLOS (J.)—"The West Side of the Athenian Agora Restored." (In *Hesperia*, Suppl. VIII, 1949.)

(14) *ROMAN AGORA AND TOWER OF THE WINDS:*
DINSMOOR (W. B.)—"The Athenian Theater of the Fifth Century."
GRAINDOR (P.)—"Le Plus ancien exemple de rachat du plan octogonal." (In *Byzantion*, III, 1926.)
ROBINSON (H.)—"The Tower of the Winds and the Roman Market-place." (In *A.J.A.*, XLVII, 1943.)
See also G1 (Stuart-Revett i).

(15) *THEATRE OF DIONYSUS:*
ALLEN (J. T.)—"The Key to the Reconstruction of the Fifth-century Theater at Athens." (In *Univ. Cal. Publ. Class. Phil.*, V 2, 1918.)
——— "The Orchestra Terrace of the Aeschylean Theater." (In same, VII 2, 1922.)
——— "On the Athenian Theater before 441 B.C." (In *Univ. Cal. Publ. Class. Arch.*, I 6, 1937.)
——— "On the Odeum and the Periclean Reconstruction of the Theater." (In same, I 7, 1941.)
BRONEER (O.)—"The Tent of Xerxes and the Greek Theater." (In same, I 12, 1944.)
DINSMOOR (W. B.)—"The Orchestra and Scene Buildings of the Athenian Theater." (In *Studies presented to D. M. Robinson*, 1950.)
DÖRPFELD (W.)—"Zum Dionysos-Theater in Athen." (In *Jahrb. Arch. Inst.*, XXIII, 1908.)
——— "Das Proskenion des Kaisers Nero im Dionysos-Theater von Athen." (In *Mélanges Octave Navarre*, Toulouse, 1935.)
FENSTERBUSCH (C.)—"Die baugeschichtliche Entwicklung des athenischen Dionysostheaters im V. Jahrhundert." (In *Philologus*, LXXXV, 1930.)
FURTWÄNGLER (A.)—"Zum Dionysostheater in Athen." (In *Sitzb. Mün. Akad.*, 1901.)
GERKAN (A. v.)—"Die Neronsiche Scaenae Frons des Dionysostheaters in Athen." (In *Jahrb. Arch. Inst.*, LVI, 1941.)
NOACK (F.)—Σκηνὴ τραγική, *eine Studie uber die scenischen Anlagen auf der Orchestra des Aischylos.* Tübingen, 1915.
PETERSEN (E.)—"Nachlese in Athen: Das Theater des Dionysos." (In *Jahrb. Arch. Inst.*, XXIII, 1908.)
PICKARD-CAMBRIDGE (A. W.)—*The Theatre of Dionysus in Athens.* Oxford, 1946.
SCHLEIF (H.)—"Die Baugeschichte des Dionysostheaters in Athen." (In *Arch. Anz.*, LII, 1937.)
VALLOIS (R.)—"Promenade au théâtre de Dionysos." (In *Rev. Et. Anc.*, LVI, 1941.)
VERSAKIS (F.)—"Das Skenengebäude des Dionysos-Theaters." (In *Jahrb. Arch. Inst.*, XXIV, 1909.)
See also F24 (entire, except Arias).

(16) *ODEUMS OF PERICLES AND HERODES ATTICUS:*
KASTRIOTIS (P.)—"Περίκλειον ᾠδεῖον." (In 'Εφ. 'Αρχ., 1922.)
TUCKERMANN (W. P.)—*Das Odeum des Herodes Atticus und der Regilla in Athen.* Bonn, 1868.
VERSAKIS (F.)—"Μνημεῖα τῶν νοτίων προπόδων τῆς 'Ακροπόλεως." (In 'Εφ. 'Αρχ., 1912.)
See also G1 (Stuart-Revett ii and iv).

(17) *PNYX:*
KOUROUNIOTIS (K.) and THOMPSON (H. A.)—"The Pnyx in Athens." (In *Hesperia*, I, 1932.)
THOMPSON (H. A.)—"Pnyx and Thesmophorion." (In same, V, 1936.)
THOMPSON (H. A.) and SCRANTON (R. L.)—"Stoas and Later Walls on the Pnyx." (In same, XII, 1943.)

(18) *STADIUM:*
KÖSTER (A.)—*Das Stadion von Athen.* Berlin, 1906.
ZILLER (E.)—"Ausgrabungen am panathenäischen Stadium." (In *Zeitschr. Bauwesen*, XX, 1870.)

(19) *CHORAGIC MONUMENTS:*
DINSMOOR (W. B.)—"The Choragic Monument of Nicias." (In *A.J.A.*, XIV, 1910.)
DÖRPFELD (W.)—"Das choragische Monument des Nikias." (In *Ath. Mitt.*, X and XIV, 1885 and 1889.)
LÜTZOW (C. v.)—*Das choragische Denkmal des Lysikrates.* Leipzig, 1868 (also in *Zeitschrift für bildende Kunst*, III, 1868).
PHILADELPHEUS (A.)—" 'Ανασκαφὴ παρὰ τὸ Λυσικράτειον μνημεῖον." (In 'Εφ. 'Αρχ., 1921.)
WELTER (G.)—"Das choregische Denkmal des Thrasyllos." (In *Arch. Anz.*, LIII, 1938.)

(20) *VOTIVE AND RECORD MONUMENTS:*
BINNEBÖSSEL (R.)—*Studien zu den attischen Urkundenreliefs des 5. und 4. Jh.* Kaldenkirchen, 1932 (Diss.).
BORRMANN (R.)—"Stelen für Weihgeschenke auf der Akropolis zu Athen." (In *Jahrb. Arch. Inst.*, III, 1888.)
KJELLBERG (E.)—*Studien zu den attischen Reliefs des V Jahrhunderts v. Chr.* Upsala, 1926.
RAUBITSCHEK (A. E.)—"Zur Technik und Form der altattischen Statuenbasen." (In *Bulletin de l'Institut archéologique bulgare*, XII, 1938.)
—— "Early Attic Votive Monuments." (In *B.S.A.*, XL, 1939–40.)
—— *Dedications from the Athenian Akropolis.* Cambridge (Mass.), 1949.
See also F3 (Kawerau), F22 (entire).

(21) *CERAMEICUS CEMETERY AND TOMB MONUMENTS:*
BRÜCKNER (A.)—*Ornament und Form der attischen Grabstelen.* Strasbourg, 1886.
—— *Der Friedhof am Eridanos bei der Hagia Triada zu Athen.* Berlin, 1909.
BRÜCKNER (A.) and PERNICE (E.)—"Ein attischer Friedhof." (In *Ath. Mitt.*, XVIII, 1893.)
BULAS (K.)—*Chronologja attyckich Stel nagrobnych Epoki archaicznej.* Cracow, 1935.
CONZE (A.)—*Die attischen Grabreliefs.* 4 vols. Berlin, 1893–1922.
DIEPOLDER (H.)—*Die attischen Grabreliefs des 5. und 4. Jahrhunderts.* Berlin, 1931.
HOLWERDA (J. H.)—*Die attischen Gräber der Blüthezeit, Studien über die attischen Grabreliefs.* Leiden, 1899.
KARO (G.)—*An Attic Cemetery, Excavations in the Kerameikos at Athens.* Philadelphia, 1943.
KRAIKER (W.) and KÜBLER (K.)—*Kerameikos: Die Ergebnisse der Ausgrabungen.* Berlin, 1939– (in progress).
KÜBLER (K.)—"Die Graber des zwölften bis achten Jahrhunderts im Kerameikos." (In *Ber. VI. Kong. Arch.*)
MÜHSAM (A. F.)—*Die attischen Grabreliefs in römischer Zeit.* Berlin, 1936 (Diss.).
NOACK (F.)—"Die Mauern Athens." (In *Ath. Mitt.*, XXXII, 1907.)
RICHLER (G. M. A.)—*Archaic Attic Gravestones.* Cambridge (Mass.), 1944.
See also F10 (Möbius), F23 (Collignon, Gardner, Möbius).

BIBLIOGRAPHY

(22) *PIRAEUS:*

DÖRPFELD (W.)—"Die Skeuothek des Philon." (In *Ath. Mitt.*, VIII, 1883.)
MARSTRAND (V.)—*Arsenalet i Piraeus, og Oldtidens Byggeregler*. Copenhagen, 1922.
NOACK (F.)—"Bemerkungen zu den Piraeusmauern." (In *Ath. Mitt.*, XXXIII, 1908.)

(23) *ATTICA OUTSIDE ATHENS AND PIRAEUS:*

DILETTANTI SOCIETY—*The Unedited Antiquities of Attica*. London, 1817.
MÖBIUS (H.)—"Attische Architekturstudien." (In *Ath. Mitt.*, LII, 1927.)
WREDE (W.)—*Attische Mauern*. Athens, 1933.
——— *Attika*. Athens, 1934.

(24) *ELEUSIS:*

CASKEY (L. D.)—"Notes on Inscriptions at Eleusis Dealing with the Building of the Porch of Philon." (In *A.J.A.*, IX, 1905.)
DAVIS (P. H.)—"The Foundations of the Philonian Portico at Eleusis." (In same, XXXIV, 1930.)
——— *Some Eleusinian Building Inscriptions of the 4th Century B.C.* Geneva (N.Y.), 1931.
DEUBNER (O.)—"Zu den grossen Propyläen von Eleusis." (In *Ath. Mitt.*, LXII, 1937.)
HÖRMANN (H.)—*Die inneren Propyläen von Eleusis*. Berlin, 1932.
KOUROUNIOTIS (K.)—*Eleusis, a Guide to the Excavations and the Museum*. Athens, 1936.
KOUROUNIOTIS (K.) and TRAVLOS (J.)—"Τελεστήριον καὶ ναὸς Δήμητρος." (In ᾿Αρχ. Δελτ., XV, 1933-35.)
LIBERTINI (G.)—"I Propilei di A. Claudio Pulcro ad Eleusi." (In *Ann. Scuol. Ital.*, II, 1916.)
NOACK (F.)—*Eleusis, die baugeschichtliche Entwicklung des Heiligtums*. 2 vols. Berlin and Leipzig, 1927.
ORLANDOS (A. K.)—῾Ο ἐν Ἐλευσῖνι ναὸς τῆς Προπυλαίας ᾿Αρτέμιδος. Athens, 1920. (Reprinted in Kourouniotis, ᾿Ελευσινιακά, I, 1932.)
TRAVLOS (J.)—"The Topography of Eleusis." (In *Hesperia*, XVIII, 1949.)
ZSCHIETZSCHMANN (W.)—"Die inneren Propyläen von Eleusis." (In *Arch. Anz.*, XLVIII, 1933.)
See also D12 (Kourouniotis-Mylonas), G23 (Dilettanti).

(25) *OROPUS:*

VERSAKIS (F.)—"Der Tempel und die Stoa im Amphiaraeion bei Oropos." (In *Ath. Mitt.*, XXXIII, 1908.)
See also F24 (Fiechter *Antike*.).

(26) *RHAMNUS:*

LANGLOTZ (E.)—"Eine Metope des Nemesistempels in Rhamnus." (In *Scritti in Onore di Bartolomeo Nogara*, Vatican City, 1937.)
ORLANDOS (A. K.)—"Note sur le Sanctuaire de Némésis à Rhamnonte." (In *B.C.H.*, XLVIII, 1924.)
ZSCHIETZSCHMANN (W.)—"Die Tempel von Rhamnus." (In *Arch. Anz.*, XLIV, 1929.)
See also G23 (Dilettanti).

(27) *SUNIUM:*

DÖRPFELD (W.)—"Der Tempel von Sunion." (In *Ath. Mitt.*, IX, 1884.)
FABRICIUS (E.)—"Die Skulpturen vom Tempel in Sounion." (In same.)
HERBIG (R.)—"Untersuchungen am dorischen Peripteraltempel auf Kap Sunion." (In same, LXVI, 1941.)
ORLANDOS (A. K.)—"Τὸ ἀέτωμα τοῦ ἐν Σουνίῳ ναοῦ τοῦ Ποσειδῶνος." (In ᾿Αρχ. Δελτ., I, 1915.)
——— "Τοῦ ἐν Σουνίῳ ναοῦ τοῦ Ποσειδῶνος τοῖχοι καὶ ὀροφή." (In same, 1917.)
STAIS (V.)—" ᾿Ανασκαφαὶ ἐν Σουνίῳ." (In same, 1900.)
——— "Σουνίου ἀνασκαφαί." (In same, 1917.)
——— Τὸ Σούνιον καὶ οἱ ναοὶ Ποσειδῶνος καὶ ᾿Αθηνᾶς. Athens, 1920.

ZSCHIETZSCHMANN (W.)—"Zum Innen-Architrave von Sunion." (In *Arch. Anz.*, XLIV, 1929.)
See also G23 (Dilettanti), H1 (Blouet), K1 (Dilettanti ii).

(28) *THORICUS:*

ARIAS (P. E.)—"Il Teatro di Torico in Attica." (In *Historia*, VII, 1933.)
CUSHING (W. L.) and MILLER (W.)—"The Theatre of Thoricus." (In *Papers Amer. School of Class. Studies in Athens*, IV, 1885–86.)
STAIS (V.)—" 'Ανασκαφαὶ 'εν Θορικῷ." (In Πρακ., 1893.)
See also G23 (Dilettanti).

(H) LOCAL WORKS: PELOPONNESUS

(1) *PELOPONNESUS IN GENERAL:*

BLOUET (A.)—*Expédition scientifique de Morée, architecture . . . du Péloponnèse, des Cyclades, et de l'Attique.* 3 vols. Paris, 1831–38.
See also G1 (Lebas-Landron).

(2) *AEGINA:*

COCKERELL (C. R.)—*The Temples of Jupiter Panhellenius at Aegina and of Apollo Epicurius at Bassae near Phigalia in Arcadia.* London, 1860.
FURTWÄNGLER (A.) and others—*Aegina: Das Heiligtum der Aphaia.* 2 vols. Munich, 1906.
GARNIER (C.)—*Ile d'Egine, temple de Jupiter panhellénien.* Paris, 1884.
SCHMIDT (E.)—"Zu den Giebeln von Aigina." (In *Ber. VI. Kong. Arch.*)
THIERSCH (H.)—"Aeginetische Studien." (In *Nachrichten der Gesellschaft der Wissenschaften zu Göttingen*, 1928; see also *Arch. Anz.*, XLIII, 1928.)
WELTER (G.)—"Aeginetica." (In *Arch. Anz.*, LIII, 1938.)
——— *Aigina.* Berlin, 1938.
See also H1 (Blouet iii), K1 (Dilettanti ii).

(3) *AMYCLAE:*

BUSCHOR (E.) and MASSOW (W. v.)—"Vom Amyklaion." (In *Ath. Mitt.*, LII, 1927.)
FIECHTER (E.)—"Der Thron des Apollon." (In *Jahrb. Arch. Inst.*, XXXIII, 1918.)
KLEIN (W.)—"Zum Thron des Apollon von Amyklae." (In *Ath. Mitt.*, XXXVIII, 1922.)

(4) *ARGIVE HERAEUM:*

EICHLER (F.)—"Die Skulpturen des Heraions bei Argos." (In *Jahresh. Oest. Arch. Inst.*, XIX–XX, 1916–19.)
FRICKENHAUS (A.) and MÜLLER (W.)—"Aus der Argolis." (In *Ath. Mitt.*, XXXVI, 1911.)
MÜLLER (K.)—"Gebäudemodelle spatgeometrischer Zeit." (In same, XLVIII, 1923.)
OIKONOMOS (G. P.)—"'Ο ἐκ τοῦ 'Αργείου 'Ηραίου πήλινος οἰκίσκος κατὰ νέαν συμπλήρωσιν. (In 'Εφ. 'Αρχ., 1931.)
WALDSTEIN (Sir C.) and others—*The Argive Heraeum.* 2 vols. Boston and New York, 1902–5.

(5) *ARGOS:*

BOETHIUS (A.)—"Zur Topographie des dorischen Argos." (In *Strena philologica Upsaliensis: Festskrift tillägnad Per Persson*, Upsala, 1922.)
VOLLGRAFF (W.)—"Fouilles d'Argos." (In *B.C.H.*, XXXI and XLIV, 1907 and 1920.)
See also H1 (Blouet ii).

(6) *BASSAE:*

DINSMOOR (W. B.)—"The Temple of Apollo at Bassae." (In *Met. Mus. Studies*, IV, 1933.)
——— "Lost Pedimental Sculptures of Bassae." (In *A.J.A.*, XLIII, 1939.)
——— "A Further Note on Bassai." (In same, XLVII, 1943.)
——— *The Temple of Apollo at Bassae.* (In preparation.)

JOHNSON (F. P.)—"Three Notes on Bassai." (In *A.J.A.*, XLVII, 1943.)
KENNER (H.)—*Der Fries des Tempels von Bassae-Phigaleia*. Vienna, 1946.
KOUROUNIOTIS (K.)—"'Ανασκαφὴ ἐν Κωτίλῳ." (In 'Εφ. 'Αρχ., 1903.)
—— "Τὸ ἐν Βάσσαις ἀρχαιότερον 'ιερὸν τοῦ 'Απόλλωνος." (In same, 1910.)
PICARD (C.)—"Acrotères latéraux au temple d'Apollon de Phigalie-Bassae." (In *Monuments et Mémoires Fondation Piot*. XXXIX, 1943.)
RHOMAIOS (K. A.)—"Τὰ ἐσωτερικὰ κιονόκρανα τοῦ ναοῦ τῶν Βασσῶν." (In same, 1914.)
—— "Ἐκ τοῦ 'αρχαιοτέρου ναοῦ τῆς Φιγαλείας." (In same, 1933.)
STACKELBERG (O. M. v.)—*Der Apollotempel zu Bassae in Arcadien*. Rome, 1826.
WOTSCHITZKY (A.)—"Zum korinthischen Kapitell im Apollontempel zu Bassae." (In *Jahresh. Oest. Arch. Inst.*, XXXVII, 1948.)
See also F4 (Gütschow), G1 (Stuart-Revett suppl. vol. or 2nd ed. iv), H1 (Bouet ii), H2 (Cockerell).

(7) *CALAURIA (POROS)*:
WIDE (S.) and KJELLBERG (L.)—"Ausgrabungen auf Kalaureia." (In *Ath. Mitt.*, XX, 1895.)
See also H26 (Welter).

(8) *CORINTH AND PERACHORA*:
CARPENTER (R.)—*Ancient Corinth, a guide to the Excavations and Museum*. 4th ed., Athens, 1947.
DINSMOOR (W. B.)—"The Largest Temple in the Peloponnesos." (In *Hesperia*, Suppl. VIII, 1949.)
DÖRPFELD (W.)—*Der Tempel in Korinth*. (In *Ath. Mitt.*, XI, 1886.)
FOWLER (H. N.) and others—*Corinth: Results of Excavations Conducted by the American School of Classical Studies at Athens*. Cambridge (Mass.), 1929- (in progress).
PAYNE (H.)—*Perachora, the Sanctuaries of Hera Akraia and Limenia*. Oxford, 1940- (in progress).
POWELL (B.)—"The Temple of Apollo at Corinth." (In *A.J.A.*, IX, 1905.)
STILLWELL (R.)—"The Theater at Corinth." (In same, XXXIII, 1929.)
WEINBERG (S.)—"On the Date of the Temple of Apollo at Corinth." (In *Hesperia*, VIII, 1939.)
See also G1 (Stuart-Revett iii), H1 (Blouet iii)

(9) *CORONE (LONGA)*:
VERSAKIS (F.)—"Τὸ ἱερὸν τοῦ Κορύνθου 'Απόλλωνος." (In 'Αρχ. Δελτ., II, 1916.)

(10) *ELIS*:
TRITSCH (F.)—"Die Agora von Elis und die altgriechische Agora." (In *Jahresh. Oest. Arch. Inst.*, XXVII, 1932.)
WALTER (O.)—"Vorläufiger Bericht über die Ausgrabungen in Elis." (In same, Beibl., XVI and XVIII, 1913 and 1915.)

(11) *EPIDAURUS*:
BAUNACK (J.)—*Aus Epidauros, eine epigraphische Studie*. Leipzig, 1890.
CATON (R.)—*The Temples and Ritual of Asklepios at Epidaurus and Athens*. 2nd ed., London, 1900.
DEFRASSE (A.) and LECHAT (H.)—*Épidaure, restauration et description des principaux monuments du sanctuaire d'Asclépios*. Paris, 1895.
DELORME (J.)—"Recherches au gymnase d'Épidaure." (In *B.C.H.*, LXX, 1946.)
DUMON (K.)—*Le Théâtre de Polyclète reconstitué d'après un module*. Paris, 1889.
FOSSUM (A.)—"Harmony in the Theatre at Epidaurus." (In *A.J.A.*, XXX, 1926.)
HEROLD (R.) and DÖRPFELD (W.)—"Der Rundbau in Epidauros." (In *Ant. Denk.*, II, 1891–92.)
KAVVADIAS (P.)—*Fouilles d'Épidaure*. Athens, 1893.
—— Τὸ ἱερὸν τοῦ 'Ασκληπίου ἐν 'Επιδαύρῳ. Athens, 1900.
—— "Περὶ τῶν ἐν 'Επιδαύρῳ ἀνασκαφῶν καὶ 'εργασιων." (In Πρακ., 1905, 1906.)
—— "Die Tholos von Epidauros." (In *Sitzb. Berl. Akad.*, 1909.)

BIBLIOGRAPHY

NOACK (F.)—"Der Kernbau der Tholos von Epidauros." (In *Jahrb. Arch. Inst.*, XLII, 1927.)
ROBERT (F.)—"La Date du labyrinthe d'Épidaure." (In *Rev. Arch.*, X, 1937.)
See also H1 (Blouet ii).

(12) *LUSOI*:

REICHEL (W.) and WILHELM (A.)—"Die Heiligtum der Artemis zu Lusoi." (In *Jahresh. Oest. Arch. Inst.*, IV, 1901.)

(13) *LYCOSURA*:

DICKINS (G.)—"Damophon of Messene." (In *B.S.A.*, XII, 1905-6.)
KAVVADIAS (P.)—*Fouilles de Lycosoura*. Athens, 1893.
LEONARDOS (V.)—"'Ανασκαφαὶ τοῦ ἐν Λυκοσούρᾳ ἱεροῦ τῆς Δεσποίνης." (In Πρακ., 1896.)
THALLON (I. C.)—"The Date of Damophon of Messene." (In *A.J.A.*, X, 1906.)

(14) *MANTINEA*:

FOUGÈRES (G.)—*Mantinée et l'Arcadie orientale*. Paris, 1898.
See also H1 (Blouet ii).

(15) *MEGALOPOLIS*:

BENSON (E. F.) and BATHER (A. G.)—"The Thersilion at Megalopolis." (In *J.H.S.*, XIII, 1892-93.)
GARDNER (E. A.), SCHULTZ (R. W.) and others—*Excavations at Megalopolis, 1890-1891* (Suppl. Papers Soc. Prom. Hellenic Studies, I). London, 1892.
See also F24 (Fiechter *Antike*), H1 (Blouet ii).

(16) *MESSENE*:

OIKONOMOS (G. P.)—"Ἀνασκαφαὶ ἐν Μεσσήνῃ." (In Πρακ., 1909, 1925.)
See also G1 (Lebas-Landron), H1 (Blouet i).

(17) *MESSENIA*:

VALMIN (M. N.)—*Études topographiques sur la Messénie ancienne*. Lund, 1930.

(18) *MYCENAE*:

KOUROUNIOTIS (K.)—"Porossculpturen aus Mykene." (In *Jahrb. Arch. Inst.*, XVI, 1901.)
RODENWALDT (G.)—"Metope aus Mykenai." (In *Corolla Ludwig Curtius*, Stuttgart, 1937.)

(19) *NEMEA*:

BLEGEN (C. W.)—"Excavations at Nemea 1926." (In *A.J.A.*, XXXI, 1927.)
BLEGEN (C. W.) and HILL (B. H.)—*Nemea, Excavations conducted by the University of Cincinnati*. (In preparation.)
DINSMOOR (W. B.)—"Dimensions of the Temples at Tegea and Nemea." (In *Hesperia*, XIX, 1950.)
VALLOIS (R.) and CLEMMENSEN (M.)—"Temple de Zeus à Némée." (In *B.C.H.*, XLIX, 1925.)
See also H1 (Blouet iii), K1 (Dilettanti ii).

(20) *OLYMPIA*:

BUSCHOR (E.) and HAMANN (R.)—*Die Skulpturen des Zeustempels zu Olympia*. Marburg, 1924.
CURTIUS (E.) and others—*Die Ausgrabungen zu Olympia*. 5 vols. Berlin, 1876-81.
CURTIUS (E.), ADLER (F.) and others—*Olympia: Die Ergebnisse der vom Deutschen Reich veranstalteten Ausgrabungen*. 5 vols. text and 5 vols. atlas. Berlin, 1890-97.
DINSMOOR (W. B.)—"An Archaeological Earthquake at Olympia." (In *A.J.A.*, XLV, 1941.)

DINSMOOR (W. B.) and SEARLS (H.)—"The Date of the Olympia Heraeum." (In same, XLIX, 1945.)
DÖRPFELD (W.)—*Alt-Olympia, Untersuchungen und Ausgrabungen zur Geschichte des ältesten Heiligtums von Olympia.* 2 vols. Berlin, 1935.
GARDINER (E. N.)—*Olympia, its History and Remains.* Oxford, 1925.
HAMPE (R.)—"Ein bronzenes Beschlagblech aus Olympia." (In *Arch. Anz.*, LIII, 1938.)
KUNZE (E.) and SCHLEIF (H.)—*IV. Bericht über die Ausgrabungen in Olympia.* Berlin, 1944.
—— *Olypische Forschungen*, I. Berlin, 1945.
KUNZE (E.) and WEBER (H.)—"The Olympic Stadium, the Echo Colonnade, and an 'Archaeological Earthquake' at Olyppia." (In *A.J.A.*, LII, 1948.)
LALOUX (V.) and MONCEAUX (P.)—*Restauration d'Olympie.* Paris, 1889.
RODENWALDT (G.) and HEGE (W.)—*Olympia.* London, 1936.
SCHLEIF (H.)—*Die neuen Ausgrabungen in Olympia und ihre bisherigen Ergebnisse für die antike Bauforschung.* Berlin, 1943.
SMITH (J. K.)—"A Restoration of the Temple of Zeus at Olympia." (In *Mem. Amer. Acad. Rome*, IV, 1924.)
VACANO (O. W. v.)—*Das Problem des alten Zeustempels in Olympia.* Naumburg, 1937 (Diss.).
WIESNER (J.) and ZIEHEN (L.)—"Olympia." (In Pauly-Wissowa, *R.E.*, XVII–XVIII 1937–39.)
WREDE (W.) and others—"Olympiabericht I–III." (In *Jahrb. Arch. Inst.*, LII, LIII, and LVI, 1937, 1938, and 1941.)
WUNDERER (W.)—*Olympia* (Berühmte Kunststätten). Leipzig, 1935.
See also H1 (Blouet i).

(21) *ORCHOMENUS (ARCADIAN)*:
BLUM (G.) and PLASSART (A.)—"Orchomene d'Arcadie." (In *B.C.H.*, XXXVIII, 1914.)

PERACHORA (See CORINTH)
PHIGALIA (See BASSAE)

(22) *SICYON*:
BROWNSON (C. L.), EARLE (M. L.), MCMURTHY (W. J.) and YOUNG (C. H.)—"Excavations at the Theatre of Sicyon." (In *A.J.A.*, V, VII–VIII, 1889, 1891–92.)
FOSSUM (A.)—"The Theatre at Sicyon." (In *A.J.A.*, IV, IX, 1900, 1905.)
ORLANDOS (A. K.)—"Ἀνασκαφαὶ Σικυῶνος." (In *Πρακ.*, 1932–41.)
—— "La Fontaine de Sicyone." (In *A.J.A.*, XXXVIII, 1934.)
PHILADELPHEUS (A.)—"Note sur le Bouleuterion (?) de Sicyon." (In *B.C.H.*, L, 1926.)
See also F24 (Fiechter *Antike*).

(23) *SPARTA*:
BULLE (H.)—"Das Theater zu Sparta." (In *Sitzb. Mün. Akad.*, 1937.)
DAWKINS (R. M.) and others—*The Sanctuary of Artemis Orthia at Sparta* (Suppl. Papers Soc. Prom. Hellenic Studies, V). London, 1929.
DAWKINS (R. M.), WOODWARD (A. M.) and others—"Excavations at Sparta." (In *B.S.A.*, XII–XXX, 1905–6 to 1928–30.)
See also H1 (Blouet ii).

(24) *TEGEA*:
DUGAS (C.), BERCHMANS (J.) and CLEMMENSEN (M.)—*Le Sanctuaire d'Aléa Athéna à Tégée au IVe siècle.* Paris, 1924.
VALLOIS (R.)—"Le Théâtre de Tégée." (In *B.C.H.*, L, 1926.)
See also H19 (Dinsmoor).

(25) *TIRYNS*:
SULZE (H.)—"Das dorische Kapitell der Burg von Tiryns." (In *Arch. Anz.*, LI, 1936.)
See also D14 (entire), D15 (Blegen *Korakou*).

(26) *TROEZEN:*
WELTER (G.)—*Troizen und Kalaureia.* Berlin, 1940.
See also F25 (Frickenhaus).

(I) LOCAL WORKS: NORTHERN GREECE, MACEDONIA, RUSSIA

(1) *ACARNANIA:*
HEUZEY (L.)—*Le Mont Olympe et l'Acarnanie.* Paris, 1860.
KIRSTEN (E.)—"Aitolien und Akarnanien in der älteren griechischen Geschichte." (In *Neue Jahrb. für antike und deutsche Bildung,* III, 1940.)
NOACK (F.)—"Untersuchungen in Aetolien und Akarnanien." (In *Arch. Anz.,* XXXI, 1916.)

(2) *AETOLIA:*
WOODHOUSE (W. J.)—*Aetolia, its Geography, Topography, and Antiquities.* Oxford, 1897.
See also I1 (Noack).

(3) *AMPHIPOLIS:*
BRONEER (O.)—*The Lion Monument at Amphipolis.* Cambridge (Mass.), 1941.
ROGER (J.)—"Le Monument au lion d'Amphipolis." (In *B.C.H.,* LXIII, 1939.)

(4) *CALYDON:*
DYGGVE (E.—*Das Laphrion, der Tempelbezirk von Kalydon.* Copenhagen, 1948.
DYGGVE (E.), POULSEN (F.) and RHOMAIOS (K. A.)—"Das Heroon von Kalydon." (In *Kgl. Danske Vidensk. Selsk. Skrifter, Historisk og Filosofisk Afd.,* 7 Raekke IV, 4, 1934.)
POULSEN (F.) and RHOMAIOS (K. A.)—"Erster vorläufiger Bericht über die dänisch-griechischen Ausgrabungen von Kalydon." (In *Kgl. Danske Vidensk. Selsk., Historisk-filologiske Meddelelser,* XIV, 3.) Copenhagen, 1927.
RHOMAIOS (K. A.)—"'Ο κέραμος τοῦ Λαφριαίου τῆς Καλυδῶνος." (In 'Εφ. 'Αρχ., 1937.)

(5) *CORCYRA (CORFU):*
DINSMOOR (W. B.)—"Additional Note on the Temple at Kardaki." (In *A.J.A.,* XL, 1936.)
DÖRPFELD (W.)—"Grabungen auf Korfu." (In *Arch. Anz.,* XXVII, 1912.)
———— "Die auf der Insel Korfu unternommenen Grabungen." (In same, XXIX, 1914.)
———— "Die Ausgrabungen auf Korfu im Frühjahre 1914." (In *Ath. Mitt.,* XXXIX, 1914.)
JOHNSON (F. P.)—"The Kardaki Temple." (In *A.J.A.,* XL, 1936.)
RIEMANN (H.)—"Zum Artemistempel von Korkyra." (In *Jahrb. Arch. Inst.,* LVIII, 1943.)
RODENWALDT (G.)—*Altdorische Bildwerke in Korfu.* Berlin, 1940.
RODENWALDT (G.) and others—*Korkyra, Archaische Bauten und Bildwerke.* Vols. I–II, Berlin, 1939–40.
VERSAKIS (F.)—"'Ανασκαφαὶ Κερκύρας." (In Πρακ., 1911.)
See also G1 (Stuart-Revett suppl. vol. or 2nd ed. vol. IV).

(6) *DELPHI:*
AGARD (W.)—"The Date of the Metopes of the Athenian Treasury." (In *A.J.A.,* XXVII, 1923.)
AMANDRY (P.)—"Le Portique des Athéniens à Delphes." (In *B.C.H.,* LXX, 1946.)
AMANDRY (P.) and BOUSQUET (J.)—"La colonne dorique de la tholos de Marmaria." (In same, LXIV–LXV, 1940–41.)
BOURGUET (E.)—*Les Ruines de Delphes.* Paris, 1914.
———— *Delphes.* Paris, 1925.
BOUSQUET (J.)—"Le Trésor de Syracuse à Delphes." (In *B.C.H.,* LXIV–LXV, 1940–41.)
COSTE-MESSELIÈRE (P. de la)—*Au Musée de Delphes.* Paris, 1936.
———— "Chapiteaux doriques de Delphes." (In *B.C.H.,* LXVI–LXVII, 1942–43.)
———— *Delphes.* Paris, 1943.
———— "Les Alcméonides à Delphes." (In *B.C.H.,* LXX, 1946.)

BIBLIOGRAPHY

COURBY (F.)—"Sur la frise du trésor de 'Cnide' à Delphes." (In *Rev. Arch.*, XVII, 1911.)
——— "La Tholos du trésor de Sicyone à Delphes." (In *B.C.H.*, XXXV, 1911.)
DAUX (G.)—*Pausanias à Delphes*. Paris, 1936.
DAUX (G.) and COSTE-MESSELIÈRE (P. de la)—"La Frise du trésor de Siphnos." (In *B.C.H.*, LI, 1927.)
DINSMOOR (W. B.)—*Studies of the Delphian Treasuries*. (In same, XXXVI and XXXVII, 1912 and 1913.)
——— "The Aeolic Capitals of Delphi." (In *A.J.A.*, XXVII, 1923.)
——— "The Athenian Treasury as Dated by its Ornament." (In same, L, 1946.)
——— "The Naxian Column at Delphi." (In *B.C.H.*, LXXIII, 1949.)
ÉCOLE FRANÇAISE D'ATHÈNES—*Fouilles de Delphes*. Paris, 1902- (in progress).
GRAINDOR (P.)—*Delphes et son oracle*. Cairo, 1930.
KENNEDY (C.)—*The Treasury of the Siphnians at Delphi*. Northampton (Mass.), 1935.
KOLDEWEY (R.)—"Die Halle der Athener zu Delphi." (In *Ath. Mitt.*, IX and XIV, 1884 and 1889.)
PICARD (C.) and COSTE-MESSELIÈRE (P. de la)—*La Sculpture grecque à Delphes*. Paris, 1929.
POMTOW (H.)—*Beiträge zur Topographie von Delphi*. Berlin, 1889.
——— "Die Tänzerinnen-Säule in Delphi." (In *Jahrb. Arch. Inst.*, XXXV, 1920.)
——— "Die Paionios-Nike in Delphi." (In same, XXXVII, 1922.)
POMTOW (H.) and SCHOBER (F.)—"Delphi." (In Pauly-Wissowa, *R.E.*, Suppl. IV-V, 1924-31.)
POULSEN (F.)—*Delphi*. London, 1920.
——— *Delphische Studien*. (In *Kgl. Danske Vidensk. Selsk., Historisk-filologiske Meddelelser*, VIII, 5.) Copenhagen, 1924.
REPLAT (J.)—"Note sur la restauration partielle de l'autel de Chios à Delphes." (In *B.C.H.*, XLIV, 1920.)
——— "Rémarques sur un chapiteau ionique attribué à l'ordre intérieur du temple d'Apollon à Delphes." (In same, XLVI, 1922.)
See also F22 (Loewy, Nilsson).

(7) *DEMETRIAS AND PAGASAE:*
STÄHLIN (F.) and others—*Pagasai und Demetrias*. Berlin and Leipzig, 1934.

(8) *DODONA:*
CARAPANOS (C.)—*Dodone et ses ruines*. 2 vols. Paris, 1878.
DYGGVE (E.)—"Dodonaeiske Problemer." (In *Festskrift til F. Poulsen*, Copenhagen, 1941.)
EVANGELIDIS (D.)—Ἡ ἀνασκαφὴ τῆς Δωδώνης. (In Ἠπειρώτικα Χρόνικα, X, 1935.)

(9) *GONNOS AND HOMOLIUM:*
ARVANITOPOULLOS (A. S.)—"Ἀνασκαφαὶ καὶ ἔρευναι ἐν Θεσσαλίᾳ." (In Πρακ., 1910, 1911.)

(10) *HALAE:*
GOLDMAN (H.)—"The Acropolis of Halae." (In *Hesperia*, IX, 1940.)

KAVALLA (See NEAPOLIS)

(11) *LEBADEA:*
BUNDGAARD (J.)—"The Building Contract from Lebadeia." (In *Classica et Mediaevalia*, VIII, 1946.)
RIDDER (A. de)—"Devis de Livadie." (In *B.C.H.*, XX, 1896.)
See also A5 (Choisy, Fabricius).

(12) *MACEDONIA:*
HEUZEY (L.) and DAUMET (H.)—*Mission archéologique de Macédoine*. 2 vols. Paris, 1867-76.
KINCH (K. F.)—"Le Tombeau de Niausta." (In *Kgl. Danske Vidensk. Selsk. Skrifter, Historisk og Filosofisk, Afd.*, 7 Raekke, IV 3, 1920.)

MACRIDY-BEY (T.)—"Un Tumulus macédonien à Langaza." (In *Jahrb. Arch. Inst.*, XXVI, 1911.)
See also D11 (Casson).

(13) *NEAPOLIS (KAVALLA)*:
BAKALAKIS (G.)—"Νεάπολις-Χριστούπολις-Καβάλα." (In 'Εφ. 'Αρχ., 1936.)

(14) *OENIADAE*:
POWELL (B.) and SEARS (J. M.)—"Oeniadae." (In *A.J.A.*, VIII, 1904.)
See also F24 (Fiechter *Antike*).

(15) *OLYNTHUS*:
GUDE (M.)—*A History of Olynthus*. Baltimore, 1933.
ROBINSON (D. M.) and others—*Excavations at Olynthus*. 12 vols., Baltimore, 1929–46.

(16) *PHERAE*:
BEQUIGNON (Y.)—*Récherches archéologiques à Phères de Thessalie*. Strasbourg, 1937 (Diss.).

(17) *PHILIPPI*:
COLLART (P.)—"Le Théâtre de Philippes." (In *B.C.H.*, LII, 1928.)
——— *Philippes, ville de Macedoine*. Paris, 1937.

(18) *PTOUS, MOUNT*:
GUILLON (P.)—*Les Trépieds de Ptoion*. 2 vols., Paris, 1943.
ORLANDOS (A. K.)—" Ὁ ναὸς τοῦ 'Απόλλωνος Πτῴου." (In 'Αρχ. Δελτ., I, 1915.)

(19) *STRATOS*:
ORLANDOS (A. K.)—" Ὁ ἐν Στράτῳ τῆς 'Ακαρνανίας ναὸς τοῦ Διός." (In 'Αρχ. Δελτ., VIII, 1923.)
PICARD (C.) and COURBY (F.)—*Récherches archéologiques à Stratos d'Acarnanie*. Paris, 1924.

(20) *TAXIARCHI (AETOLIA)*:
RHOMAIOS (K. A.)—" 'Αρχαῖον ἱερὸν παρὰ τὸν Ταξιάρχην τῆς Αἰτωλίας." (In 'Αρχ. Δελτ., X, 1926.)

(21) *THEBES*:
WOLTERS (P.) and BRUNS (G.)—*Das Kabirenheiligtum bei Theben*. Vol. I, Berlin, 1940.
See also D11 (Keramopoullos).

(22) *THERMUM*:
KAWERAU (G.) and SOTERIADIS (G.)—"Der Apollotempel zu Thermos." (In *Ant. Denk.*, II, 1902–8.)
KOCH (H.)—"Zu den Metopen von Thermos." (In *Ath. Mitt.*, XXXIX, 1914.)
PAYNE (H.)—"On the Thermon Metopes." (In *B.S.A.*, XXVII, 1925–26.)
POULSEN (F.)—"Thermos." (In *Det Filologisk-historiske Samfund, Studier fra Sprog- og Oldtidsforskning*, no. 133, Copenhagen, 1924.)
RHOMAIOS (K. A.)—" 'Ανασκαφὴ ἐν Θερμῳ." (In Πρακ., 1931.)
SOTERIADIS (G.)—" 'Ανασκαφαὶ ἐν Θέρμῳ." (In 'Εφ 'Αρχ., 1900, 1903.)
See also D11 (Rhomaios).

(23) *THESSALY*:
STÄHLIN (F.)—*Das hellenische Thessalien*. Stuttgart, 1924.
WESTLAKE (H. D.)—*Thessaly*. London, 1935.

(24) *RUSSIA:*
DURM (J.)—"Die Kuppelgräber von Pantikapaion." (In *Jahresh. Oest. Arch. Inst.*, X, 1907.)
KIESERITZKY (G. v.) and WATZINGER (C.)—*Griechische Grabreliefs aus Sudrussland.* Berlin, 1909.
MINNS (E. H.)—*Scythians and Greeks, a Survey of Ancient History and Archaeology on the North Coast of the Euxine, from the Danube to the Caucasus.* Cambridge, 1913.
——— "Thirty Years of Work at Olbia." (In *J.H.S.*, LXV, 1945.)
ROSTOVTZEFF (M. I.)—*Iranians and Greeks in South Russia.* Oxford, 1922.

(J) LOCAL WORKS: AEGEAN AND ASIATIC ISLANDS

(1) *GENERAL:*
CHOISEUL-GOUFFIER (Duc de)—*Voyage pittoresque de la Grèce.* 2 vols. in 3, Paris, 1782–1824.
See G1 (Lebas-Landron), H1 (Blouet).

(2) *ANDROS:*
SAUCIUC (T.)—*Andros, Untersuchung zur Geschichte und Topographie der Insel.* Vienna, 1914.

(3) *CARTHAEA (CEOS):*
BRÖNDSTED (P. O.)—*Reisen und Untersuchungen in Griechenland.* Part 1. Paris, 1826.
GRAINDOR (P.)—"Fouilles de Karthaia (Ile de Kéos)." (In *B.C.H.*, XXIX–XXX, 1905–6.)

(4) *CHIOS:*
KOUROUNIOTIS (K.)—" Ἀνασκαφαὶ καὶ ἔρευναι ἐν Χίῳ." (In *Ἀρχ. Δελτ.*, I–II, 1915–16.)

(5) *COS:*
HERZOG (R.) and others—*Kos, Ergebnisse der deutschen Ausgrabungen und Forschungen.* Berlin, 1932– (in progress).
SCHAZMANN (P.)—"Das Charmyleion." (In *Jahrb. Arch. Inst.*, XLIX, 1934.)

(6) *CRETE:*
BOSANQUET (R. C.)—"Excavations at Palaikastro; the Temple of Dictaean Zeus." (In *B.S.A.*, XI, 1904–5.)
——— "Dicte and the Temples of Dictaean Zeus." (In same, XL, 1939–40.)
DEMARGNE (P.)—"Terres cuites archaiques de Lato." (In *B.C.H.*, LIII, 1929.)
FORSTER (E. S.)—"Praesos, the Terracottas." (In *B.S.A.*, VIII, 1901–2.)
KIRSTEN (E.)—*Das dorische Kreta; I, Die Insel Kreta in fünften und vierten Jahrhundert.* Würzburg, 1942.
KJELLBERG (L.)—"Panionismus oder Pankretismus." (In *Symbolae Philologicae O. A. Danielsson*, Upsala, 1932.)
LEVI (D.)—"Arkades, una città cretese all' alba della civiltà ellenica." (In *Ann. Scuol. Ital.*, X–XII, 1931.)
MARINATOS (S.)—"Le Temple géometrique de Dréros." (In *B.C.H.*, LX, 1936.)
PERNIER (L.)—"Tempii arcaici sulla Patela di Prinias." (In *Ann. Scuol. Ital.*, I, 1914.)
——— "L'Odeum nell' agora di Gortina presso il Leteo." (In same, VIII–IX, 1925–26.)
——— "New Elements for the Study of the Archaic Temple of Prinias." (In *A.J.A.*, XXXVIII, 1934.)
PFUHL (E.)—"Die Terrakottareliefs aus dem Heiligtum des diktäischen Zeus in Palaikastro." (In *Ath. Mitt.*, XLVIII, 1923.)
SAVIGNONI (L.)—"Sima ionica con bassorilievi." (In *Röm. Mitt.*, XXI, 1906.)
——— "Il Pythion di Gortyna." (In *Mon. Ant.*, XVIII, 1907.)
SIEVEKING (J.)—"Zur Sima von Palaikastro." (In *Arch. Anz.*, XXXVI, 1921.)
See also D5 (Demargne, Pendlebury), D8 (Bosanquet-Dawkins).

(7) *CYPRUS:*
CESNOLA (L. P. di)—*Descriptive Atlas of the Cesnola Collection of Cypriote Antiquities in the Metropolitan Museum of Art, New York.* 3 vols. in 6. Boston, 1885–1903.

BIBLIOGRAPHY

Dikaios (P.)—*A Guide to the Cyprus Museum*. Nicosia, 1947.
Gjerstad (E.)—"The Palace at Vouni." (In *Skrift. Sven. Inst.*, II, 1932.)
Myres (Sir J. L.)—*Metropolitan Museum, Handbook of the Cesnola Collection of Antiquities from Cyprus*. New York, 1914.
Myres (Sir J. L.) and Ohnefalsch-Richter (M. H.)—*Catalogue of the Cyprus Museum*. Oxford, 1899.
Ohnefalsch-Richter (M. H.)—*Kypros, the Bible, and Homer*. London, 1893.
Westholm (A.)—*The Temples of Soli*. Stockholm, 1936.
See also D9 (Casson, Gjerstad, Hill, Westholm).

(8) *DELOS*:

Audiat (J.)—"Le Gymnase de Délos et l'inventaire de Kallistratos." (In *B.C.H.*, LIV, 1930.)
Béquignon (Y.) and Replat (J.)—"Le Trace du théâtre de Délos." (In same, LI, 1927.)
Chamonard (J.)—"Théâtre de Délos." (In same, XX, 1896.)
Courby (F.)—"Notes topographiques et chronologiques sur le sanctuaire d'Apollon délien." (In same, XLV, 1921.)
Davis (P. H.)—"The Delian Building Contracts." (In same, LXI, 1937.)
Davis (P. H.) and Holland (L. B.)—"The Porch-ceiling of the Temple of Apollo on Delos." (In *A.J.A.*, XXXVIII, 1934.)
Dörpfeld (W.)—"Le Théâtre de Délos et la scène du théâtre grec." (In *B.C.H.*, XX, 1896.)
École Française d'Athènes—*Exploration archéologique de Délos*. Paris, 1909– (in progress).
Homolle (T.)—"L'Autel des cornes à Délos." (In *B.C.H.*, VIII, 1884.)
Laidlaw (W. A.)—*A History of Delos*. Oxford, 1933.
Lebègue (J. A.)—*Récherches sur Délos*. Paris, 1876.
Picard (C.) and Replat (J.)—"Récherches sur la topographie du Hieron délien." (In *B.C.H.*, XLVIII, 1924.)
Poulsen (G.)—"Note sur la couverture du sanctuaire dit 'des taureaux' à Délos." (In *Mélanges Holleaux*, Paris, 1913.)
Roussel (P.)—*Les Cultes égyptiens à Délos du IIIe au Ier siècle av. J.C.* Nancy, 1916.
——— *Délos colonie athénienne*. Paris, 1916.
——— *Délos*. Paris, 1925.
Vallois (R.)—"Topographie délienne." (In *B.C.H.*, XLVIII–XLIX, 1924–25.)
——— *Architecture hellénique et hellénistique à Délos jusqu'à l'eviction des Déliens, 166 av. J. C.; I, Les Monuments*. Paris, 1944.
See also G1 (Stuart–Revett iii–iv and suppl. vol.), H1 (Blouet iii).

(9) *EUBOEA*:

Johnson (F. P.)—"The Dragon-houses of Southern Euboea." (In *A.J.A.*, XXIX, 1925.)
Richardson (R. B.) and others—"Excavations at Eretria." (In same, VII and X–XI, 1891 and 1895–96.)
Wiegand (T.)—"Dystos." (In *Ath. Mitt.*, XXIV, 1899.)
Vollmöller (K. G.)—"Ueber zwei euböische Kammergräber mit Totenbetten." (In same, XXVI, 1901.)
See also F24 (Fiechter *Antike*).

(10) *LEMNOS*:

Fredrich (C.)—"Lemnos." (In *Ath. Mitt.*, XXXI, 1906.)

(11) *LESBOS*:

Rouse (W. H. D.)—"Lesbos." (In *B.S.A.*, II, 1895–96.)
Koldewey (R.)—*Die antiken Baureste der Insel Lesbos*. Berlin, 1890.

(12) *NAXOS*:

Welter (G.)—"Altionische Tempel." (In *Ath. Mitt.*, XLIX, 1924.)
See also H1 (Blouet iii), J1 (Choiseul-Gouffier i).

BIBLIOGRAPHY

(13) *PAROS:*
RUBENSOHN (O.)—"Paros." (In *Ath. Mitt.*, XXV–XXVII, 1900–2.)
——— "Der ionische Burgtempel auf Paros." (In *Arch. Anz.*, XXVIII–IX, 1923–24.)
——— "Paros." (In Pauly-Wissowa, *R.E.*, XVIII, 1947.)
See also G1 (Stuart-Revett iv), J12 (Welter).

(14) *RHODES:*
BLINKENBERG (C.)—"De danske Udgravninger i Lindos." (In *Festskrift til F. Poulsen*, Copenhagen, 1941.)
BLINKENBERG (C.) and KINCH (K. F.)—*Lindos, fouilles et récherches*, 1902–1914. Berlin, 1931– (in progress).
Clara Rhodos, Studi e materiali publicati a cura dell' Instituto Storico Archeologico di Rodi. I (1927) ff.
KINCH (K. F. and H.)—*Fouilles de Vroulia.* Berlin, 1914.
TORR (C.)—*Rhodes in Ancient Times.* Cambridge, 1885.
ZERVOS (S.)—*Rhodes, capitale du Dodecanèse.* Paris, 1920.

(15) *SAMOS:*
BUSCHOR (E.)—"Heraion von Samos, frühe Bauten." (In *Ath. Mitt.*, LV, 1930.)
——— "Altsamische Grabstelen." (In same, LVIII, 1933.)
BUSCHOR (E.) and SCHLEIF (H.)—"Heraion von Samos, der Altarplatz der Frühzeit." (In same, LVIII, 1933.)
JOHANNES (H.)—"Die Säulenbasen vom Heratempel des Rhoikos." (In same, LXII, 1937.)
SCHEDE (M.)—"Zweiter vorläufiger Bericht über die Ausgrabungen in Samos." (In *Abh. Berl. Akad.*, 1929.)
SCHLEIF (H.)—"Der grosse Altar der Hera von Samos." (In *Ath. Mitt.*, LVIII, 1933.)
——— "Heraion von Samos, das Vorgelände des Tempels." (In same.)
WIEGAND (T.)—"Erster vorläufiger Bericht über die Ausgrabungen in Samos." (In *Abh. Berl. Akad.*, 1911.)
See also J1 (Choiseul-Gouffier i), K1 (Dilettanti i).

(16) *SAMOTHRACE:*
CONZE (A.) and others—*Archäologische Untersuchungen auf Samothrake.* Vienna, 1875.
——— *Neue archäologische Untersuchungen auf Samothrake.* Vienna, 1880.
LEHMANN-HARTLEBEN (K.)—"Excavations in Samothrace." (In *A.J.A.*, XLIII–XLIV, 1939–40.)
SCHOBER (A.)—"Der neue Tempel von Samothrake." (In *Jahresh. Oest. Arch. Inst.*, XXIX, 1934–35.)

(17) *SICINOS:*
DAWKINS (R. M.)—"The Apollo Temple on Sikinos." (In *B.S.A.*, XVIII, 1911–12.)

(18) *THASOS:*
BAKER-PENOYRE (J. ff.)—"Thasos." (In *J.H.S.*, XXIX, 1909.)
FREDRICH (C.)—"Thasos." (In *Ath. Mitt.*, XXXIII, 1908.)
LAUNEY (M.)—*Etudes thasiennes:* 1, *Le Sanctuarire et la culte d'Heracles à Thasos.* Paris, 1944.
PICARD (C.)—"Le Porte de Zeus à Thasos." (In *Rev. Arch.*, XX, 1912.)
PICARD (C.) and others—"Fouilles de Thasos." (In *B.C.H.*, XLV, XLVII, and LVI, 1921, 1923, and 1932.)
SEYRIG (H.) and BON (A.)—"Le Sanctuaire de Poseidon à Thasos." (In same, LIII, 1929.)

(19) *THERA (SANTORIN):*
DURAZZO-MOROSINI (Z.)—*Santorin, die fantastische Insel.* Berlin, 1936.
FIECHTER (E.)—"Das Theater in Thera." (In *Wilhelm Dörpfeld Festschrift*, Berlin, 1933.)
HILLER VON GAERTRINGEN (F.) and others—*Thera, Untersuchungen, Vermessungen, und Ausgrabungen in den Jahren 1895–1902.* 4 vols. Berlin, 1899–1909.

BIBLIOGRAPHY

(K) LOCAL WORKS: ASIA MINOR

(1) *GENERAL:*

AMERICAN SOCIETY FOR ARCHAEOLOGICAL RESEARCH IN ASIA MINOR—*Monumenta Asiae Minoris Antiqua.* 6 vols., Manchester, 1928–39.
BENNDORF (O.) and NIEMANN (G.)—*Reisen in Lykien und Karien.* Vienna, 1884.
DILETTANTI SOCIETY—*The Antiquities of Ionia.* 5 vols. London, 1797–1915.
FELLOWS (Sir C.)—*Journal Written during an Excursion in Asia Minor.* London, 1839.
——— *Travels and Researches in Asia Minor, More Particularly in Lycia.* London, 1852.
——— *An Account of Discoveries in Lycia.* London, 1841.
FELLOWS (Sir C.) and SCHARF (G.)—*Lycia, Caria, and Lydia.* London, 1847.
HEBERDEY (R.) and WILHELM (A.)—"Reisen in Kilikien." (In *Denk. Akad. Wien*, XLIV, 1896.)
HIRSCHFELD (G.)—"Paphlagonische Felsengräber." (In *Abh. Berl. Akad.*, 1885.)
LABORDE (A. de)—*Voyage en Orient: Asie Mineure et Syrie.* 2 vols. Paris, 1838.
LANCKORONSKI (K.), NIEMANN (G.) and PETERSEN (E.)—*Städte Pamphyliens und Pisidiens.* 2 vols. Vienna, 1890–92.
LEONHARD (R.)—*Paphlagonia.* Berlin, 1915.
NEWTON (Sir C. T.)—*Travels and Discoveries in the Levant.* 2 vols. London, 1865.
PERROT (G.) and GUILLAUME (E.)—*Exploration archéologique de la Galatie et de la Bithynie, d'une partie de la Mysie, de la Phrygie, de la Cappadoce et du Pont.* 2 vols. Paris, 1872.
PETERSEN (E.) and LUSCHAN (F. v.)—*Reisen in Lykien, Milyas, und Kibyratis.* Vienna, 1889.
REBER (F. v.)—"Die phrygischen Felsdenkmäler." (In *Abh. Mün. Akad.*, XXI, 1897.)
TEXIER (C.)—*Description de l'Asie Mineure.* 3 vols. Paris, 1839–49.
TEXIER (C.) and PULLAN (R. P.)—*The Principal Ruins of Asia Minor.* London, 1865.
TREMAUX (P.)—*Exploration archéologique en Asie Mineure.* Paris, 1852.
See also G1 (Lebas-Landron.)

(2) *AEGAE:*

BOHN (R.) and SCHUCHHARDT (C.)—*Die Altertümer von Aegae.* Berlin, 1889.

(3) *AEZANI:*

KÖRTE (A.)—"Das Alter des Zeustempels von Aizanoi." (In *Festschrift Otto Benndorf*, Vienna, 1898.)
See also G1 (Lebas-Landron), K1 (Laborde, Texier i).

(4) *AK-ALAN:*

MACRIDY-BEY (T.)—"Une Citadelle archaïque du Pont." (In *Mitt. vorderasiat. Gesell.*, XII, 1907.)

(5) *ALABANDA:*

EDHEM-BEY—"Fouilles d'Alabanda en Carie." (In *Comptes rendus Acad. Inscr.*, 1905–6.)

(6) *ANCYRA (ANKARA):*

KRENCKER (D.) and SCHEDE (M.)—*Der Tempel in Ankara.* Berlin and Leipzig, 1936.
See also K1 (Perrot-Guillaume, Texier i).

(7) *ANTIOCH (PISIDIAN):*

ROBINSON (D. M.)—"A Preliminary Report on the Excavations at Pisidian Antioch and at Sizma." (In *A.J.A.*, XXVIII, 1924.)
——— "Roman Sculptures from Colonia Caesarea (Pisidian Antioch)." (In *Art Bulletin*, IX, 1926–27.)

(8) *APHRODISIAS:*

BOULANGER (A.)—"Note sur les fouilles executées à Aphrodisias en 1913." (In *Comptes rendus Acad. Inscr.*, 1914.)

COLLIGNON (M.)—"Les Fouilles d'Aphrodisias." (In *Revue de l'art ancien et moderne*, XIX, 1906.)
GAUDIN (P.)—"Note sur les fouilles executées à Aphrodisias." (In *Comptes rendus Acad. Inscr.*, 1904, 1906.)
VAGTS (R.)—*Aphrodisias in Karien*. Borna-Leipzig, 1920.
See also K1 (Dilettanti iii, Laborde, Texier iii).

(9) *ASSOS:*
BACON (F. H.), CLARKE (J. T.), and KOLDEWEY (R.)—*Investigations at Assos*. Cambridge (Mass.), 1902–21.
CLARKE (J. T.)—*Report on the Excavations at Assos, 1881–1883*. 2 vols. Boston, 1882, 1898.
SARTIAUX (F.)—*Les Sculptures et la reconstruction du temple d'Assos en Troade*. Paris, 1915 (also in *Rev. Arch.*, XXII–XXIII, 1913–14).
See also B5 (Mendel ii), K1 (Texier ii).

(10) *BELEVI:*
KEIL (J.)—"Vorläufiger Bericht." (In *Jahresh. Oest. Arch. Inst.*, Beibl., XXVIII–XXX, 1933–37.)
PRASCHNIKER (C.)—"Die Skulpturen des Mausoleum von Belevi." (In *Ber. VI. Kong. Arch.*)

(11) *CNIDUS:*
NEWTON (Sir C. T.)—*History of Discoveries at Halicarnassus, Cnidus, and Branchidae*. Text and Atlas. London, 1861–63.
KRISCHEN (F.)—Löwenmonument und Maussolleion." (In *Röm. Mitt.*, LIX, 1944.)
See also K1 (Dilettanti iii, Laborde, Texier iii).

(12) *COLOPHON:*
HOLLAND (L.B.—"Colophon." (In *Hesperia*, XIII, 1944.)

(13) *CYZICUS:*
HASLUCK (F. W.)—*Cyzicus, Being some Account of the History and Antiquities of that City*. Cambridge, 1910.
MEYER (H.)—*De Anthologiae Palatinae epigrammatis Cyzicensis*. Königsberg, 1911 (Diss.).

DIDYMA (See MILETUS)

(14) *EPHESUS:*
DÖRPFELD (W.)—"Ueber das Theater in Ephesos." (In *Arch. Anz.*, XXVIII, 1913.)
FALKENER (E.)—*Ephesus and the Temple of Diana*. London, 1862.
FERGUSSON (J.)—"The Temple of Diana at Ephesus, with special reference to Mr. Wood's Discoveries of its Remains." (In *Trans. R.I.B.A.*, 1883.)
FYFE (T.)—"Some Aspects of Greek Architecture." (In *Journal R.I.B.A.*, XXI, 1914–15.)
GJERSTAD (E.)—"Studies in Archaic Greek Chronology, II, Ephesus." (In *Liverpool Annals of Archaeology and Anthropology*, XXIV, 1937.)
HEBERDEY (R.) and KEIL (J.)—"Vorläufiger Bericht über die Ausgrabungen in Ephesos." (In *Jahresh. Oest. Arch. Inst.*, Beibl. I–XXX, 1898–1937.)
HENDERSON (A. E.)—"The Hellenistic Temple of Artemis at Ephesus." (In *Journal R.I.B.A.*, XXII, 1915–16.)
——— "The Temple of Diana at Ephesus." (In same, XL, 1932–33.)
HOGARTH (D. G.)—*British Museum: Excavations at Ephesus, the Archaic Artemisia*. Text and atlas. London, 1908.
HÖRMANN (H.)—"Die römische Bühnenfront zu Ephesos." (In *Jahrb. Arch. Inst.*, XXXVIII–IX, 1923–24.)
KEIL (J.)—*Ephesos, ein Führer durch die Ruinenstätte und ihre Geschichte*. 2nd ed., Vienna, 1930.
KRISCHEN (F.)—"Das Artemision in Ephesos." (In *Wilhelm Dörpfeld Festschrift*, Berlin, 1933.)

BIBLIOGRAPHY

LETHABY (W. R.)—"The Sculptures of the Later Temple of Artemis at Ephesus." (In *J.H.S.*, XXXIII, 1913.)

—— "Another Note on the Sculptures of the Later Temple of Artemis at Ephesus." (In same, XXXVI, 1916.)

—— "The Earlier Temple of Artemis at Ephesus." (In same, XXXVII, 1917.)

LOEWY (E.)—"Zur Chronologie der frühgriechischen Kunst, Die Artemistempel von Ephesos." (In *Sitzb. Wien. Akad.*, CCXIII, 1932.)

MURRAY (A. S.)—"The Sculptured Columns of the Temple of Diana at Ephesus." (In *Journal R.I.B.A.*, III, 1895–96.)

OESTERREICHISCHES ARCHÄOLOGISCHES INSTITUT—*Forschungen in Ephesos*. Vienna, 1906– (in progress).

PICARD (C.)—*Ephèse et Claros*. Paris, 1922.

—— "Sur les reconstructions de l'Artemision d'Ephèse." (In Λαογραφία, VII, *Mélanges Politis*, 1922.)

—— "Βομόσπειρα d'Ionie et *columnae caelatae*." (In *Rev. Et. Anc.*, XXIX, 1927.)

TRELL (B.L.)—*The Temple of Artemis at Ephesos (Numismatic Notes and Monographs*, 107). New York, 1945.

WEBER (G.)—*Guide du voyageur à Ephèse*. Smyrna, 1891.

WOOD (J. T.)—*Discoveries at Ephesus*. London, 1877.

VALLOIS (R.)—"L'Artemision d'Ephèse, le temple A, les architectes du temple D." (In *Mélanges Glotz*, Paris, 1932.)

See also B5 (Pryce i 1, Lethaby), J1 (Choiseul-Gouffier i), K1 (Dilettanti ii), K27 (Butler, *Elevated Columns*).

(15) GORDIUM:

KÖRTE (G. and A.)—*Gordion, Ergebnisse der Ausgrabungen im Jahre 1900*. Berlin, 1904.

(16) HALICARNASSUS:

ADLER (F.)—"Das Mausoleum zu Halikarnass." (In *Zeitschr. Bauwesen*, 1900.)

BREEN (J. van)—*Het Reconstructieplan voor het Mausoleum te Halikarnassos, ontworpen volgens een meetkundig systeem in gebruick van de oudete tijden tot in de XVIe eeuw*. Amsterdam, 1942.

BÜHLMANN (J.)—"Das Mausoleum in Halikarnass." (In *Zeitschr. Gesch. Architektur*, II, 1908–9.)

DINSMOOR (W. B.)—"The Mausoleum at Halicarnassus." (In *A.J.A.*, XII, 1908.)

FERGUSSON (J.)—*The Mausoleum at Halicarnassus Restored in Conformity with the Recently Discovered Remains*. London, 1862.

KRISCHEN (F.)—"Ionische Bauten Kleinasiens und der Aufbau des Mausoleums von Halikarnass." (In *Bonn. Jahrb.*, CXXVIII, 1923.)

—— "Die Statue des Maussollos." (In *Jahrb. Arch. Inst.*, XL, 1925.)

—— "Der Entwurf des Maussoleions von Halikarnass." (In *Arch. Anz.*, XLII, 1927.)

KRÜGER (E.)—"Der Aufbau des Mausoleums von Halikarnass." (In *Bonn. Jahrb.*, CXXVII, 1922.)

LAW (H. W.)—"The Mausoleum." (In *J.H.S.*, LIX, 1939.)

LORENTZ (F. v.)—*Maussollos und die Quadriga auf dem Maussollion zu Halikarnassos*. Neuruppin, 1931 (Diss.).

NEUGEBAUER (K. A.)—"Das Maussolleion von Halikarnass und sein bildnerischer Schmuck." (In *Neue Jahrb. für antike und deutsche Bildung*, V, 1942.)

—— "Pytheos oder Bryaxis?" (In *Jahrb. Arch. Inst.*, LVIII, 1943.)

PRYCE (F. N.)—"The Order of the Mausoleum." (In *British Museum Quarterly*, II, 1927–28.)

STEVENSON (J. J.)—*A Restoration of the Mausoleum at Halicarnassus*. London, 1909.

WALTERS (H. B.)—"A New Reconstruction of the Mausoleum." (In *British Museum Quarterly*, I, 1926–27.)

See also B5 (Lethaby), J1 (Choiseul-Gouffier i), K1 (Dilettanti ii), K11 (Newton, Krischen.)

(17) LAGINA:

CHAMONARD (J.)—"Les Sculptures de la frise du temple d'Hécate à Lagina." (In *B.C.H.* XIX, 1895.)

BIBLIOGRAPHY

SCHOBER (A.)—*Der Fries des Hekateions von Lagina*. Baden-Vienna, 1933.
See also B5 (Mendel i).

(18) *LARISA:*
KJELLBERG (L.)—"Das äolische Kapitell von Larisa." (In *Skrift. Sven. Inst.*, II, 1932.)
KJELLBERG (L.) and BOEHLAU (J.)—*Larisa am Hermos, die Ergebnisse der Ausgrabungen, 1902–1934*. Stockholm and Berlin, 1940– (in progress).
See also B5 (Mendel ii).

(19) *MAGNESIA:*
GERKAN (A. v.)—"Der Altar des Artemistempels in Magnesia a.M." (In *Arch. Anz.*, XXXVIII–IX, 1923–24.)
────── *Der Altar des Artemistempels in Magnesia am Mäander*. Berlin, 1929.
HAHLAND (W.)—"Datierung der Hermogenesbauten." (In *Ber. VI. Kong. Arch.*)
HERKENRATH (E.)—*Der Fries des Artemisions von Magnesia am Maeander*. Berlin, 1902 (Diss.).
HUMANN (C.) and others—*Magnesia am Maeander: Bericht über die Ergebnisse der Ausgrabungen der Jahre 1891–1893*. Berlin, 1904.
See also B5 (Mendel i), K1 (Dilettanti v).

(20) *MILETUS AND DIDYMA:*
GERKAN (A. v.)—"Der Tempel von Didyma und sein antikes Baumass." (In *Jahresh. Oest. Arch. Inst.*, XXXII, 1940.)
────── "Der Naiskos im Tempel vpn Didyma." (In *Jahrb. Arch. Inst.*, LVII, 1942.)
HAUSSOULLIER (B.)—"Le Temple d'Apollon didyméen." (In *Rev. Philol.*, XXII, 1898.)
────── *Études sur l'histoire de Milet et du Didymeion*. Paris, 1902.
KNACKFUSS (H.)—*Didyma, I, Die Baubeschreibung*. 3 vols. Berlin, 1941.
KRAUSS (F.)—"Das Theater von Milet in seiner griechischen und römischen Gestalt." (In *VI Kong. Arch. Berlin*, 1939.)
PONTREMOLI (E.) and HAUSSOULLIER (B.)—*Didymes, fouilles de 1895 et 1896*. Paris, 1904.
RAYET (O.) and THOMAS (A.)—*Milet et la golfe latmique, Tralles, Magnésie du Méandre, Priène, Milet, Didymes, Héraclée du Latmos*. Text and atlas. Paris, 1877–85 (unfinished).
VAN ESSEN (C. C.)—"Notes sur le deuxième Didymeion." (In *B.C.H.*, LXX, 1946.)
WIEGAND (T.)—"Siebenter vorläufiger Bericht über die in Milet und Didyma unternommenen Ausgrabungen." (In *Abh. Berl. Akad.*, 1911.)
────── "Achter vorläufiger Bericht über die Ausgrabungen in Milet und Didyma." (In same, 1924.)
WIEGAND (T.) and others—*Milet: Ergebnisse der Ausgrabungen und Untersuchungen seit dem Jahre 1899*. Berlin, 1906– (in progress).
See also B5 (Mendel i), J1 (Choiseul-Gouffier i), K1 (Dilettanti i, Laborde, Rayet-Thomas, Texier ii).

(21) *NEANDRIA:*
KOLDEWEY (R.)—*Neandria*. Berlin, 1891.
See also B5 (Mendel ii).

(22) *NOTIUM:*
DEMANGEL (R.) and LAUMONIER (A.)—"Fouilles de Notion." (In *B.C.H.*, XLVII, 1923.)

(23) *NYSA:*
DIEST (W.)—*Nysa ad Maeandrum*. Berlin, 1913.
KOUROUNIOTIS (K.)—"'Ανασκαφαὶ ἐν Νύσῃ τῇ ἐπὶ Μαιάνδρῳ." (In 'Αρχ. Δελτ., X, 1926.)

(24) *OLBA:*
HERZFELD (E.)—"Olba." (In *Arch. Anz.*, XXIV, 1909.)
KEIL (J.) and WILHELM (A.)—*Denkmäler aus dem rauhen Kilikien* (Vol. III of *Monumenta Asiae Minoris Antiqua*, Manchester, 1931).

BIBLIOGRAPHY

(25) *PAZARLI:*
KOŞAY (H. Z.)—*Pazarli Hafriyati Raporu: Les Fouilles de Pazarli.* Ankara. 1941.

(26) *PERGAMUM:*
CONZE (A.) and others—*Die Ergebnisse der Ausgrabungen zu Pergamon, vorläufiger Bericht,* 1880–1886. 3 vols. Berlin, 1880–88.
—— "Vorläufiger Bericht über die Arbeiten zu Pergamon 1886–1898." (In *Ath. Mitt.,* XXIV, 1899.)
DEUBNER (O.)—*Das Asklepieion von Pergamon, kürze vorläufige Beschreibung.* Berlin, 1938.
HANSEN (E. V.)—*The Attalids of Pergamon.* Ithaca (N.Y.), 1947.
MASSOW (W. v.)—*Führer durch das Pergamon-Museum.* Berlin, 1932.
NAPP (A. E.)—*Der Altar von Pergamon.* Munich, 1936.
OHLEMUTZ (E.)—*Die Kulte und Heiligtümer der Götter in Pergamon.* Würzburg, 1940.
PONTREMOLI (E.) and COLLIGNON (M.)—*Pergame, restauration et description des monuments de l'acropole.* Paris, 1900.
SALIS (A. v.)—*Der Altar von Pergamon.* Berlin, 1912.
SCHOBER (A.)—"Zur Datierung Eumenischer Bauten." (In *Jahresh. Oest. Arch. Inst.,* XXXII, 1940.)
SCHUCHHARDT (W. H.)—*Die Meister des grossen Frieses von Pergamon.* Berlin, 1925.
STAATLICHE MUSEEN ZU BERLIN—*Altertümer von Pergamon.* Berlin, 1885- (in progress).
ZSCHIETZSCHMANN (W.)—"Pergamon." (In Pauly-Wissowa, *R.E.,* XIX, 1937.)
See also K1 (Texier ii).

(27) *PRIENE:*
DÖRPFELD (W.)—"Das Theater von Priene und die griechische Bühne." (In *Ath. Mitt.,* XLIX, 1924.)
GERKAN (A. v.)—"Zum Gebälk des Athenatempels in Priene." (In same, XLIII, 1918.)
—— *Das Theater von Priene.* Munich, 1921.
—— "Der Altar des Athenatempels in Priene." (In *Bonn. Jahrb.,* CXXIX, 1924.)
KRISCHEN (F.)—"Das hellenische Gymnasion von Priene." (In *Jahrb. Arch. Inst.,* XXXVIII–IX, 1923–24.)
SCHEDE (M.)—*Die Ruinen von Priene, kurze Beschreibung.* Berlin, 1934.
—— "Heiligtümer in Priene." (In *Jahrb. Arch. Inst.,* XLIX, 1934.)
STEVENS (G. P.)—"The Volute of the Capital of the Temple of Athena at Priene." (In *Mem. Amer. Acad. Rome,* IX, 1931.)
WIEGAND (T.) and SCHRADER (H.)—*Priene: Ergebnisse der Ausgrabungen und Untersuchungen in den Jahren 1895–1898.* Berlin, 1904.
WILBERG (W.)—"Zum Athena-Tempel in Priene." (In *Ath. Mitt.,* XXXIX, 1914.)
See also B5 (Lethaby), K1 (Dilettanti i and iv, Rayet-Thomas).

(28) *SARDIS:*
BUTLER (H. C.)—"First (Fifth) Preliminary Report on the American Excavations at Sardes in Asia Minor." (In *A.J.A.,* XIV–XVIII, 1910–14.)
—— "The Elevated Columns at Sardis and the Sculptured Pedestals from Ephesus." (In *Anatolian Studies W. M. Ramsay,* Manchester, 1923.)
BUTLER (H. C.) and others—*Sardis.* Leyden and Princeton, 1922- (in progress).
HANFMANN (G. M. A.)—"Horsemen from Sardis." (In *A.J.A.,* XLIX, 1945.)

(29) *TARSUS:*
GOLDMAN (H.)—"Excavations at Gözlü Kule, Tarsus." (In *A.J.A.,* XXXIX, XLI–XLII, and XLIV, 1935, 1937–38, and 1940.)
KOLDEWEY (R.)—"Das sogenannte Grab des Sardanapal zu Tarsus." (In *Aus der Anomia Carl Robert dargebracht,* Berlin, 1890.)

(30) *TEOS:*
BÉQUIGNON (Y.) and LAUMONIER (A.)—"Fouilles de Téos." (In *B.C.H.,* XLIX, 1925.)
See also J1 (Choiseul-Gouffier i), K1 (Dilettanta i and iv).

BIBLIOGRAPHY

(31) *TROY:*
ZSCHIETZSCHMANN (W.)—"Der Athenatempel von Ilion und seine Entstehungszeit." (In *Ber. VI. Kong. Arch.*)
See also D10 (Dörpfeld, Schliemann).

(32) *TRYSA (GJÖLBASCHI):*
BENNDORF (O.) and NIEMANN (G.)—*Das Heroon von Gjolbaschi-Trysa*. Vienna, 1889–91. (Also in *Jahrb. Kunstsamml. Wien*, IX and XI, 1889 and 1891.)
See also K1 (Petersen-Luschan).

(33) *XANTHUS:*
AKURGAL (E.)—*Griechische Reliefs des VI. Jhr. aus Lykien*. Berlin, 1941.
FELLOWS (Sir C.)—*The Xanthian Marbles, their acquisition and transmission to England*. London, 1843.
―― *Account of the Ionic Trophy Monument Excavated at Xanthus*. London, 1848.
KALINKA (E.)—*Tituli Asiae Minoris*. Vols. I–II, Vienna, 1901–44.
KRISCHEN (F.)—"Der Aufbau des Nereidenmonumentes in Xanthos." (In *Ath. Mitt.*, XLVIII, 1923.)
LETHABY (W. R.)—"The Nereid Monument Re-examined." (In *J.H.S.*, XXXV, 1915.)
LLOYD (W. W.)—*Xanthian Marbles, the Nereid Monument*. London, 1845.
NIEMANN (G.)—*Das Nereiden-Monument in Xanthos*. Vienna, 1921.
PRYCE (F. N.)—"The Nereid Monument." (In *British Museum Quarterly*, III, 1928–29.)
SCHUCHHARDT (W. H.)—"Die Friese des Nereiden-Monumentes." (In *Ath. Mitt.*, LII, 1927).
TRITSCH (F. J.)—"False Doors on Tombs." (In *J.H.S.*, LXIII, 1943.)
See also B5 (Lethaby, Pryce i 1), K1 (Benndorf-Niemann).

(L) LOCAL WORKS: SYRIA AND MESOPOTAMIA

(1) *GENERAL:*
BUTLER (H. C.)—*Architecture and Other Arts (in Syria)*. New York, 1903.
MURRAY (S. B.)—*Hellenistic Architecture in Syria*. Princeton, 1921.
See also K1 (Humann-Puchstein, Laborde).

(2) *ANTIOCH:*
FÖRSTER (R.)—"Antiochia am Orontes." (In *Jahrb. Arch. Inst.*, XII, 1897.)
MÜLLER (K. O.)—*Antiquitates Antiochenae*. Göttingen, 1839.
PRINCETON UNIVERSITY—*Antioch-on-the-Orontes*. Princeton and London, 1934– (in progress).

(3) *BABYLON:*
KIRK (G. E.)—"Gymnasium or Khan, a Hellenistic Building at Babylon." (In *Iraq*, II, 1935.)
SCHMIDT (E.)—"Die Griechen in Babylon und das Weiterleben ihrer Kultur." (In *Arch. Anz.*, LVI, 1941.)

(4) *DURA-EUROPOS:*
CUMONT (F. V. M.)—*Fouilles de Doura-Europos, 1922–1923*. 2 vols. Paris, 1926.
ROSTOVTZEFF (M. I.)—*Dura-Europos and its Art*. Oxford, 1938.
YALE UNIVERSITY—*The Excavations at Dura-Europos, Preliminary Report*. New Haven, 1929– (in progress).

(5) *NIPPUR:*
FISHER (C. S.)—"The Mycenaean Palace at Nippur." (In *A.J.A.*, VIII, 1904.)
MARQUAND (A.)—"The Palace at Nippur not Mycenaean but Hellenistic." (In same.)

(6) *SAMARIA:*
CROWFOOT (J. W.), KENYON (K. M.), and SUKENIK (E. L.)—*The Buildings at Samaria (Samaria-Sebaste I)*. London, 1942.

(7) SIDON:

HAMDY-BEY (O.) and REINACH (T.)—*Une Nécropole royale à Sidon*. 2 vols. Paris, 1892-96.
WINTER (F.)—*Der Alexandersarcophag aus Sidon*. Strasbourg, 1912.
See also B5 (Mendel i).

(8) THE EAST:

EDMONDS (C. J.)—"A Tomb in Kurdistan." (In *Iraq*, I, 1934.)
MARSHALL (Sir J.)—*A Guide to Taxila*. 3rd ed., Delhi, 1936.
ROWLAND (B.)—"Notes on Ionic Architecture in the East." (In *A.J.A.*, XXXIX, 1935.)

(M) LOCAL WORKS: EGYPT AND NORTH AFRICA

(1) GENERAL:

LEWIS (N.)—"New Light on the Greek House from the Zenon Papyri." (In *A.J.A.*, XXXVI, 1933.)
LUCKHARD (F.)—*Das Privathaus im ptolemäischen und römischen Aegypten*. Bonn, 1914 (Diss.).
NOSHY (I.)—*The Arts in Ptolemaic Egypt*. London, 1937.
RUBENSOHN (O.)—"Aus griechisch-römischen Häusern des Fayum." (In *Jahrb. Arch. Inst.*, XX, 1905.)
SCHÜTZ (A. R.)—*Der Typus des hellenistisch-ägyptischen Hauses in Anschluss an Baubeschreibungen griechischer Papyrusurkunden*. Würzburg, 1936 (Diss.).

(2) ALEXANDRIA:

ADLER (F.)—*Der Pharos von Alexandria*. Berlin, 1901.
ADRIANI (A.)—*La Nécropole de Moustafa Pacha*. Alexandria, 1936.
ASÍN PALACIOS (M.)—"Una Descripción nueva del Faro de Alejandría." (In *Al-Andalus*, I, 1933.)
ASÍN PALACIOS (M.) and OTERO (M. L.)—"The Pharos of Alexandria." (In *Proc. Brit. Acad.*, XIX, 1933.)
AURÈS (A.)—"Étude des dimensions du temple que Ptolémée Philadelphe a fait construire sur le cap Zéphyrium près Alexandrie d'Égypte en l'honneur de Vénus Arsinoé." (In *Rev. Arch.*, XX, 1869.)
BRECCIA (E.)—*La Necropoli di Sciatbi*. Cairo, 1912.
—— *Alexandrea ad Aegyptum*. Bergamo, 1922.
CECCALDI (G. C.)—"Le Temple de Vénus Arsinoé au Cap Zéphyrium." (In *Rev. Arch.*, XIX, 1869.)
LOHDE (L.)—"Römischer Tempel zu Alexandrien." (In *Arch. Zeit.*, XXIV, 1866.)
MONNERT DE VILLARD (U.)—"Il Faro di Alessandria, secondo un testo a disegni arabi inediti da Codici Milanesi Ambrosiani." (In *Bull. Soc. Archéologique d'Alexandrie*, no 18, 1921.)
PAGENSTECHER (R.)—*Nekropolis: Untersuchungen über Gestalt und Entwicklung der Alexandrinischen Grabanlagen und ihrer Malereien*. Leipzig, 1919.
REINCKE (G.)—"Pharos." (In Pauly-Wissowa, *R.E.*, XIX, 1937.)
ROWE (A.) and DRIOTON (E.)—"Discovery of the Famous Temple and Enclosure of Serapis at Alexandria." (In *Annales du Service des Antiquités*, Suppl. 2, Cairo, 1946.)
SCHREIBER (T.)—*Die Nekropole von Kom Esch-Schukafa* (*Expedition Ernst von Sieglin*, I). 2 vols., Leipzig, 1908.
SIEGLIN (E. v.)—*Expedition Ernst von Sieglin, Ausgrabungen in Alexandria*. Leipzig, 1908- (in progress).
THIERSCH (H.)—*Pharos, Antike Islam und Occident*. Leipzig and Berlin, 1909.

(3) CARANIS:

BOAK (A. E. R.)—*Karanis, the Temples, Coin Hoards, Botanical and Zoological Reports*. Ann Arbor, 1933.
BOAK (A. E. R.) and PETERSON (E. E.)—*Karanis, Topographical and Architectural Report of Excavations during the Seasons 1924-28*. Baltimore, 1933.

BIBLIOGRAPHY

(4) CYRENE:
MAIOLETTI (B.)—"L'Architettura delle necropoli di Cirene." (In *Riv. Colon.*, V, 1931.)
NORTON (R.)—"The Excavations at Cyrene." (In *Bull. Arch. Inst. Amer.*, II, 1910.)
——— "The Ruins of Messa." (In same.)
PACHO (J. R.)—*Relation d'un voyage dans la Marmarique, la Cyrénaïque.* Paris, 1827–29.
PERNIER (L.)—"L'Artemision di Cirene." (In *Africa Italiana*, IV, 1931.)
——— *Il Tempio e l'altare di Apollo a Cirene.* Bergamo, 1935.
PESCE (G.)—"Il 'Gran Tempio' in Cirene." (In *B.C.H.*, LXXI–LXXII, 1947–48.)
SMITH (R. M.) and PORCHER (E. A.)—*History of the Recent Discoveries at Cyrene made during an Expedition to the Cyrenaica in 1860–61.* London, 1864.

(5) HERMOPOLIS:
GARBA (S.)—Preliminary reports in *Illustrated London News*, CLXXXIV, 1934 (April 21), CLXXXVI, 1935 (June 8).
WACE (A. J. B.)—Preliminary reports in *Bulletin of the Faculty of Arts, Farouk I University*, Alexandria.

(6) NAUCRATIS:
GJERSTAD (E.)—"Studies in Archaic Greek Chronology, I, Naucratis." (In *Liverpool Annals of Archaeology and Anthropology*, XXI, 1934.)
PETRIE (W. M. F.) and GARDNER (E. A.)—*Naukratis.* 2 vols. London, 1886–88.

(7) PHILADELPHIA:
VANDERBORGHT (E.)—"La Maison de Diotimos à Philadelphie." (In *Chroniques d'Égypte*, XVII. 1942.)
VIERECK (P.)—*Philadelpheia, die Gründung einer hellenistischer Militärkolonie in Aegypten.* (Morgenland, XVI), Leipzig, 1928.

(8) PHILAE:
BORCHARDT (L.)—"Der Augustustempel auf Philae." (In *Jahrb. Arch. Inst.*, XVIII, 1903.)

(N) LOCAL WORKS: SICILY AND MAGNA GRAECIA

(1) GENERAL:
BÉRARD (J.)—*Bibliographie topographique des principales cités grecques de l'Italie meridionale et de la Sicile dans l'antiquité.* Paris, 1941.
DUNBABIN (T. J.)—*The Western Greeks.* Oxford, 1948.
DÜRR (K.)—*Aus dem classischen Süden.* Lübeck, 1896.
GIANNELLI (G.)—*Culti e miti della Magna Grecia.* Florence, 1924.
HITTORFF (J. I.) and ZANTH (L.)—*Architecture antique de la Sicile: Recueil des monuments de Ségeste et de Sélinonte.* Text and atlas. 2nd ed., Paris, 1870.
KOLDEWEY (R.) and PUCHSTEIN (O.)—*Die griechischen Tempel in Unteritalien und Sicilien.* Berlin, 1899.
KRISCHEN (F.)—*Die Stadtmauern von Pompeji und griechische Festungsbaukunst in Unteritalien und Sizilien.* Berlin, 1941.
LARIZZA (P.)—*La Magna Grecia, ricerche storiche, archeologiche e numismatiche.* Rome, 1929.
LENORMANT (F.)—*La Grande-Grèce, paysages et histoire.* 3 vols. Paris, 1881–84.
PACE (B.)—"Arti ed artisti della Sicilia antica." (In *Mem. Accad. Lincei*, XV, 1917.)
——— *Arte e civiltà della Sicilia antica.* 3 vols. Milan, 1935–46.
RANDALL-MACIVER (D.)—*Greek Cities in Italy and Sicily.* Oxford, 1931.
SÄFLUND (G.)—"Ionisches und Dorisches in Magna Graecia." (In *Skrift. Sven. Inst.*, V, 1941.)
SERRADIFALCO (Duca di)—*Le Antichità della Sicilia.* 5 vols. Palermo, 1834–42.
WILKINS (W.)—*Antiquities of Magna Graecia.* Cambridge and London, 1807.
See also F12 (Darsow, Van Buren Sicily).

(2) ACRAGAS (AGRIGENTO, GIRGENTI):
DINSMOOR (W. B.)—"The Olympieum at Acragas." (In *Mem Amer. Acad. Rome*, XX, 1950.)

BIBLIOGRAPHY

DRERUP (H.)—"Der Tempel des Zeus Olympios in Akragas." (In *Ber. VI. Kong. Arch.*)
GRIFFO (P.)—*Ultimi scavi e ultime scoperte in Agrigento*. Agrigento, 1946.
KLENZE (L. v.)—*Der Tempel des olympischen Jupiter zu Agrigent*. Stuttgart and Tübingen, 1821.
KRISCHEN (F.)—"Das Olympieion von Akragas." (In *Arch. Anz.*, LVII, 1942.)
MARCONI (P.)—"Girgenti, ricerche ed esplorazioni." (In *Notiz. Scav.*, LI, 1926.)
—— "La Grondaia a protomi leonine del tempio di Demetra a Girgenti." (In *Boll. Arte*, VI, 1926-27.)
—— "I Telamoni dell' Olimpieion agrigentino." (In same.)
—— *Agrigento, topografia ed arte*. Florence, 1929.
—— "Studi agrigentini." (In *Rivista del R. Istituto d'archeologia e storia dell' arte*, I, 1929.)
—— "Agrigento; Studi sulla organizzazione urbana." (In same, II, 1930.)
—— "Agrigento arcaica." (In *Atti e Mem. Soc. Magna Grecia*, 1931.)
—— "Novità nell 'Olympieion di Agrigento." (In *Dedalo*, XII, 1932.)
—— *Agrigento*. Rome, 1933.
PACE (B.)—"Il Tempio di Giove Olimpico in Agrigento." (In *Mon. Ant.*, XXVIII, 1922.)
PATRICOLO (G.)—"Tempio della Concordia in Girgenti." (In R. Commissario degli scavi e musei per la Sicilia, *Studi e documenti relativi alle antichità agrigentine*, Palermo, 1887.)
See also G1 (Stuart-Revett suppl. vol. or 2nd ed. iv), N1 (Koldewey-Puchstein, Serradifalco iii), N15 (Labrouste).

(3) CAMARINA:

ORSI (P.)—"Camarina." (In *Mon. Ant.*, IX, 1899.)
—— "Camarina, scavi del 1899 e 1903." (In same, XIV, 1903.)
PACE (B.)—*Camarina, topografia, storia, archeologia*. Catania, 1927.

(4) CAULONIA:

ORSI (P.)—"Caulonia, campagne archeologiche del 1912, 1913 e 1915." (In *Mon. Ant.*, XXIII, 1916.)
—— "Caulonia, II Memoria." (In same, XXIX, 1923.)
See also N1 (Säflund).

(5) CRIMISA:

ORSI (P.)—"Templum Apollinis Alaei ad Crimisa-Promontorium." (In *Atti e Mem. Soc. Magna Grecia*, 1932.)

(6) CROTON:

ABATINO (G.)—*La Colonna del tempio di Hera Lacinia*. Naples, 1901.
—— "Note sur la colonne du temple de Hera Lacinia à Capocolonna (Crotone)." (In *Mélanges d'archéologie et d'histoire, École française de Rome*, XXIII, 1903.)
EMERSON (A.)—"The Temple of Hera Lakinia." (In *Annual Report, Archaeological Institute of America*, VIII, 1886-87.)
ORSI (P.)—"Croton." (In *Notiz. Scav.*, XXXVI, 1911, Suppl.)
See also N1 (Koldewey-Puchstein).

(7) CUMAE:

GABRICI (E.)—"Cuma." (In *Mon. Ant.*, XXII, 1913.)

(8) GELA:

ORSI (P.)—"Gela, scavi di 1900-1905." (In *Mon. Ant.*, XVII, 1907.)
—— "Nuovo tempio greco arcaico in contrada Molino a vento, Gela." (In *Notiz. Scav.*, XXXII, 1907.)
See also N1 (Koldewey-Puchstein).

(9) HIMERA:

MARCONI (P.)—*Himera, lo scavo del tempio della Vittoria e del temenos*. Rome, 1931. (Also in *Atti e Mem. Soc. Magna Grecia*, 1930.)

MAUCERI (L.)—"Cenni sulla topografia di Imera e sugli avanzi del tempio di Bonfornello." (In *Mon. Ant.*, XVIII, 1907.)
See also N1 (Koldewey-Puchstein).

(10) *HIPPONIUM*:
CRISPO (C. F.)—"Di Hipponio e della Brettia nel V sec. a. C." (In *Atti e Mem. Soc. Magna Grecia*, 1928.)
See also F28 (Säflund).

(11) *LEONTINI*:
ORSI (P.)—"Scava di Leontini-Lentini." (In *Atti e Mem. Soc. Magna Grecia*, 1930.)

(12) *LOCRI EPIZEPHYRII*:
OLDFATHER (W. A.)—"Lokroi." (In Pauly-Wissowa, *R.E.*, XIII, 1927.)
ORSI (P)—"Locri Epizephyrii." (In *Notiz. Scav.*, XXXVI, 1911, Suppl. and XXXVII, 1912, Suppl.)
PETERSEN (E.)—"Tempel in Locri." (In *Röm. Mitt.*, V, 1890, and *Ant. Denk.*, I, 1891.)
See also N1 (Koldewey-Puchstein).

(13) *MEGARA HYBLAEA*:
CAVALLARI (F. S.) and ORSI (P.)—"Megara Hyblaea." (In *Mon. Ant.*, I, 1890.)
ORSI (P.)—"Megara Hyblaea 1917-1921, villaggio neolitico e tempio greco arcaico." (In *Mon. Ant.*, XXVII, 1921.)

(14) *METAPONTUM*:
GALLI (E.)—"Metaponto, esplorazioni archeologiche e sistemazione dell' area del tempio delle Tavole Palatine." (In *Atti e Mem. Soc. Magna Grecia*, 1926-27.)
LACAVA (M.)—*Topografia e storia di Metaponto*. Naples, 1891.
LUYNES (Duc de) and DEBACQ (F. J.)—*Métaponte*. Paris, 1833. (Italian trans. by G. Gallo, Castrovillari, 1882.)
NORMAND (C.)—"Metaponte, essai de restitution." (In *Ami des Monuments*, V, 1891.)
PETRA (G. de)—"Il Geison nel tempio di Apollo Lycio a Metaponto." (In *Atti Accad. Napoli*, XVII, 1896.)
SANTE SIMONE—*Studii sugli avanzi di Metaponto*. Bari, 1875.
SESTIERI (P. C.)—"Metaponto, Saggi eseguiti presso il tempio di Apollo Liceo." (In *Notiz. Scav.*, LXV, 1940.)
See also N1 (Koldewey-Puchstein).

(15) *PAESTUM (POSEIDONIA AND SILARIS)*:
AURÈS (A.)—*Études des dimensions du grand temple de Paestum*. Text and atlas. Nîmes and Paris, 1868.
DINSMOOR (W. B.)—"The Greek Temples at Paestum." (In *Mem. Amer. Acad. Rome*, XX, 1950.)
FRENKEL (W.)—*Paestum, nuova guida*. Torre del Greco, 1935.
GRIFFO (P.)—*I Capitelli della 'Basilica' e del tempio di Demetra a Paestum*. Palermo, 1937.
KRAUSS (F.)—"Die Giebelfront des sog. Cerestempels in Paestum." (In *Röm. Mitt.*, XLVI, 1931.)
——— *Paestum, die griechischen Tempel*. 2nd ed., Berlin, 1943.
KRAUSS (F.) and HERBIG (R.)—*Der korinthisch-dorische Tempel am Forum von Paestum*. Berlin, 1939.
LABROUSTE (H.)—*Les Temples de Paestum*. Paris, 1877.
LAGARDETTE (C. M. de)—*Les Ruines de Paestum ou Posidonia*. Paris, VII (1799).
LAMB (C.)—*Die Tempel von Paestum*. Leipzig, 1944.
MAJOR (T.)—*The Ruins of Paestum otherwise Posidonia in Magna Graecia; Les Ruines de Paestum ou de Posidonie dans la Grande-Grèce*. London, 1768.
MARZULLO (A.)—*Paestum*. Salerno, 1933.

MONTUORO (P. Z.) and ZANOTTI-BIANCO (U.)—"Heraion alla foce del Sele." (In *Notiz. Scav.*, LXII, 1937.)
PAOLI (P. A.)—*Paesti quod Posidoniam etiam dixere rudera.* Rome, 1784.
See also N1 (Koldewey-Puchstein).

(16) *POMPEII:*

DUHN (F. v.) and JACOBI (L.)—*Der griechische Tempel in Pompeii.* Heidelberg, 1890.
PATRONI (G.)—"La Forma originaria dell'antica colonna etrusca e delle colonne del tempio sul foro triangolare in Pompeii." (In *Atti Accad. Napol.*, XXV, 1908.)
PATRONI (G.) and COZZI (S.)—"I Nascimenti delle colonne dallo stilobato nel cosi detto tempio greco di Pompeii." (In *Mem. Accad. Napol.*, I, 1911.)
See also N1 (Koldewey-Puchstein).

(17) *RHEGIUM:*

PUTORTI (N.)—"Terrecotte architettonische di Reggio-Calabria." (In *Italia Antichissima*, I, 1929.)

(18) *SEGESTA:*

MARCONI (P.)—"Segesta, esplorazioni della scena del teatro." (In *Notiz. scav.*, LIV, 1929.)
See also N1 (Hittorff-Zanth, Koldewey-Puchstein, Serradifalco i).

(19) *SELINUS:*

ANGELL (S.) and EVANS (T.)—*Sculptured Metopes Discovered amongst the Ruins of the Temples of the Ancient City of Selinus in Sicily.* London, 1826.
BENNDORF (O.)—*Die Metopen von Selinunt.* Berlin, 1873.
GABRICI (E.)—"Il Santuario della Malophoros a Selinunte." (In *Mon. Ant.*, XXXII, 1927-28.)
——— "Acropoli di Selinunte." (In same, XXXIII, 1929.)
——— "Per la storia dell' architettura dorica in Sicilia." (In same, XXXV, 1933-35.)
HULOT (J.) and FOUGÈRES (G.)—*Sélinonte, colonie dorienne en Sicile.* Paris, 1910.
See also F11 (Hittorff), N1 (Hittorff-Zanth, Koldewey-Puchstein, Serradifalco ii).

(20) *SYRACUSE:*

ANTI (C.)—*Teatro antico di Siracusa.* Syacuse, 1948.
CULTRERA (G.)—"Consolidamento e restauro di due colonne dell' Artemision di Ortygia in Siracusa." (In *Rivista del R. Istituto d'archeologia e storia dell' arte*, IX, 1942.)
GUARDUCCI (M.)—"L'Iscrizione dell' Appollonion di Siracusa." (In *Archeologia Classica*, I, 1949.)
HOLM (A.) and CAVALLARI (F. S.)—*Topografia archeologica di Siracusa.* Palermo, 1883-91. (Transl. by B. Lupus, *Die Stadt Syrakus im Altertum.* Strasbourg, 1887.)
MAUCERI (L.)—*Il Castello Eurialo nella storia e nell' arte.* Rome, 1928.
ORSI (P.)—"L'Olympieion di Siracusa." (In *Mon. Ant.*, XIII, 1903.)
——— "Scavi intorno a l'Athenaion di Siracusa." (In same, XXV, 1918.)
RIZZO (G. E.)—*Il Teatro greco di Siracusa.* Milan and Rome, 1923.
See also N1 (Koldewey-Puchstein, Serradifalco iv).

(21) *TARENTUM:*

KLUMBACH (H.)—*Tarentiner Grabkunst.* Reutlingen, 1937.
LENORMANT (F.)—"Notes archéologiques sur Tarente." (In *Gazette Archéologique*, VII, 1881.)
VIOLA (L.)—"Taranto." (In *Notiz. Scav.*, VI, 1881.)
WUILLEUMIER (P.)—*Tarente des origines à la conquête romaine.* 2 vols. Paris, 1939.
See also N1 (Koldewey-Puchstein.)

(22) *VELIA (ELEA):*

MAIURI (A.)—"Velia, prima ricognizione ed esplorazione." (In *Atti e Mem. Soc. Magna Grecia*, 1926-27.)

BIBLIOGRAPHY
(O) LOCAL WORKS: FRANCE AND SPAIN

(1) *GENERAL:*

BOSCH GIMPERA (P.)—*La Arqueologia preromana hispánica.* Barcelona, 1920.
CARPENTER (R.)—*The Greeks in Spain.* Bryn Mawr, 1925.
PARIS (P.)—*Promenades archéologiques en Espagne.* Paris, 1910–21.
SCHULTEN (A.)—"Hispania." (In Pauly-Wissowa, *R.E.*, VIII, 1913.)

(2) *EMPORIUM:*

PARIS (P.)—"Emporion." (In *Rev. Arch.*, IV–V, 1916–17.)

(3) *MASSILIA:*

CLERC (M.)—*Massalia, histoire de Marseille dans l'antiquité des origines à la fin de l'Empire romain d'occident.* 476 ap. J.C. 2 vols. Marseilles, 1927–29.

(4) *TARTESSUS:*

BONSOR (G. E.)—*Tartesse.* New York, 1922.
SCHULTEN (A.)—*Tartessus, ein Beitrag zur ältesten Geschichte des Westens.* Hamburg, 1922.

BIBLIOGRAPHY

LIST OF PERIODICALS ABBREVIATED

A(merican) J(ournal of) A(rchaeology).
Abh(andlungen der) Berl(iner) Akad(emie).
Abh(andlungen der) Mün(chner) Akad(emie).
Ann(uario della) Scuol(a) Ital(iana di Atene).
Ant(ike) Denk(mäler).
Arch(äologische) Anz(eiger: in Jahrb. Arch. Inst.).
"Αρχ(αιολογικὸν) Δελτ(ίον).
Ath(enische) Mitt(eilungen, Deutsches Archäologisches Institut).
Atti (della R.) Accad(emia di archeologia . . . in) Napoli.
Atti e Mem(orie della) Soc(ietà) Magna Grecia.
Ber(icht über den) VI. (internationalen) Kong(ress für) Arch(äologie, Berlin 21–26 August, 1939. Berlin, 1940).
Boll(ettino d') Arte.
Bonn(er) Jahrb(ücher).
B(ulletin de) C(orrespondance) H(ellénique).
B(ritish) S(chool at) A(thens, Annual).
Comptes rendus (de l') Acad(emie des) Inscr(iptions et Belles-Lettres).
Denk(schriften der) Akad(emie zu) Wien.
'Εφ(ημερὶς) 'Αρχ(αιολογική).
J(ournal of) H(ellenic) S(tudies).
Jahrb(uch des Deutschen) Arch(äologischen) Inst(ituts).
Jahrb(uch der) Kunstsamml(ungen des allerhöchsten Kaiserhauses in) Wien.
Jahresh(efte des) Oest(erreichischen) Arch(äologischen) Inst(ituts).
Journal (of the) R(oyal) I(nstitute of) B(ritish) A(rchitects).
Klio (; Beiträge zur Alten Geschichte).
Mem(orie della R.) Accad(emia Nazionale dei) Lincei.
Mem(oirs of the) Amer(ican) Acad(emy at) Rome.
Mem(orie del R.) Ist(ituto) Lomb(ardo).
Met(ropolitan) Mus(eum) Studies.
Mitt(eilungen der) vorderasiat(ischen) Gesell(schaft).
Mon(umenti) Ant(ichi della R. Accademia Nazionale dei Lincei).
Notiz(ie degli) Scav(i della R. Accademia Nazionale dei Lincei).
Πρακ(τικὰ τῆς ἐν Αθήναις 'Αρχαιολογικῆς 'Εταιρείας).
Proc(eedings of the) Amer(ican) Phil(osophical) Soc(iety).
Proc(eedings of the) Roy(al) Soc(iety).
R(eal-) E(ncyclopädie).
Rend(iconti della) pontif(icia) Accad(emia) romana (di archeologia).
Rev(ue) Arch(éologique).
Rev(ue des) Ét(udes) Anc(iennes).
Rev(ue des) Ét(udes) Gr(ecques).
Röm(ische) Mitt(eilungen, Deutsches Archäologisches Institut).
Sitz(ungsberichte der) Mün(chner) Akad(emie).
Skrift(er utgivna av) Sven(ska) Inst(itutet i Rom: Acta Instituti Romani Regni Sueciae).
Trans(actions of the) R(oyal) I(nstitute of) B(ritish) A(rchitects).
Trans(actions of the) Roy(al) Soc(iety).
Univ(ersity of) Cal(ifornia) Publ(ications in) Class(ical) Phil(ology).
Zeitschr(ift für) Bauwesen.
Zeitschr(ift für) Gesch(ichte der) Architektur.

GLOSSARY

ABACUS.—The uppermost member of a capital. Plain in the Doric order, moulded in the Ionic and Corinthian orders. The sides are concave in the Corinthian capital, and curve out over the canted volute of the special Ionic capital used at the corner of a building.

ABUTMENT.—The masonry, brickwork, or earth which counteracts the thrust of an arch or vault.

ACANTHUS.—A prickly plant of which the spiny leaves were copied in later Greek decoration, particularly in the Corinthian capital; the Romans preferred acanthus leaves with more rounded lobes.

ACROLITHIC.—With stone (or marble) extremities; applied to statues (generally wooden) with only the head, arms, and feet of stone.

ACROTERION (*pl.* ACROTERIA).—The figures or ornaments at the lower angles or apex of a pediment, generally supported on plinths.

ADYTUM.—The inner or most holy room of a temple, generally separated from the cella by a wall with a doorway.

AEOLIC.—The palmiform capital evolved by the Aeolic Greeks of northwest Asia Minor; sometimes confusingly used of the Proto-Ionic capital.

AGORA.—A public square or market-place in Greek cities corresponding to the Forum in Roman cities.

AISLE (Lat., *ala*, a wing).—Term given to the side passages in a hall or cella, separated from one another and from the central nave by columns or piers.

AMPHIDISTYLE IN-ANTIS.—A temple with two columns between antae at both front and rear. *See* TEMPLES.

AMPHIPROSTYLE.—Temple with porticoes of columns in front and rear only. *See* TEMPLES.

ANACTORON.—A palace; but applied also to the Telesterion or Hall of the Mysteries at Eleusis.

ANATHYROSIS.—The smooth marginal dressing or contact band of a joint surface (usually vertical, but sometimes applied also to horizontal joints as in column drums), of which the central portion is roughened and sunk to avoid contact. Being applied only to the top and two vertical edges of a vertical joint, it assumes the appearance of the trim of a door ($\theta \acute{v} \rho a$), hence the name.

ANCONES.—Projecting bosses left on masonry blocks.

ANDRON.—The room reserved for men in a Greek house, particularly a dining-room.

ANNULET.—A projecting ring, generally one of several at the bottom of a Doric echinus.

ANTA (*pl.* ANTAE).—Pilaster (or corner post) of slight projection terminating the end of the lateral walls of a cella, and usually serving as respond to a column. In the latter case the columns are said to be in-antis.

ANTEFIX (*pl.* ANTEFIXES, *not* ANTEFIXAE).—The decorative termination of the covering tiles over the joints between the flat tiles of a roof, placed either directly on the eaves tiles or on the top of the sima, sometimes also on the crest of the ridge.

ANTHEMION (Gr. $\mathring{a}\nu\theta o\varsigma$, a flower).—A continuous pattern of alternating palmette and lotus (the latter generally much conventionalised and so sometimes, but erroneously, called honeysuckle), often rising from nests of acanthus leaves and connected by scrolls.

ANTITHEMA.—A backing block, generally used of the inner unmoulded face of an architrave or frieze if constructed separately from the outer face.

APOPHYGE ($\mathring{a}\pi \acute{o}$, from, and $\phi\varepsilon\acute{v}\gamma\omega$, I flee).—(*a*) The cavetto or concave sweep taken by the end of the shaft in the Ionic and Corinthian Orders in its junction with the upper or lower fillet. (*b*) The similar curve of the necking beneath the Doric echinus, forming the junction between the capital and the shaft.

APSE.—A semicircular termination of a building or recess in a wall, often vaulted.

APTEROS.—Without wings; as applied to the statue and temple of Wingless Victory (Nike Apteros), at Athens.

GLOSSARY

ARAEOSTYLE.—Wide-spaced. The term given by Vitruvius to wide intercolumniations, carrying an architrave in timber. See INTERCOLUMNIATION.

ARCH.—The form devised for spanning an opening with small units of brick or stone, generally arranged radially and forming a semicircular head over the opening, but sometimes pointed, elliptical, or even flat (horizontal). For a false arch, see CORBEL.

ARCHITRAVE.—A lintel in stone or beam of timber carried from the top of one column or pier to another; the lowest member of the entablature (q.v.). Applied also to the lintel and side posts or jambs of a door or window.

ARCHIVOLT.—A moulded architrave carried round an arch.

ARRIS.—A sharp edge formed by two surfaces meeting at an external angle as in the flutings of the Doric column.

ASHLAR MASONRY.—Regular masonry of squared stone, with horizontal courses and approximately or perfectly vertical joints.

ASIATIC BASE.—The type of Ionic base developed in Asia Minor, composed of a lower disk generally decorated with horizontal fluting or scotias (normally two large scotias with separating astragals), and of an upper torus decorated with horizontal fluting or relief ornament. A plinth might be added below the disk.

ASTRAGAL.—A small moulding of rounded, convex section.

ATLANTES.—The Greek term for the male figures employed in architecture in place of columns. See TELAMONES.

ATRIUM.—The entrance court of a Roman house, roofed over at the sides, but open to the sky in the centre. In an atrium of large size four or more columns would be introduced to carry the roof.

ATTIC.—A storey above the main cornice, sometimes decorated with bas-reliefs or utilised for an inscription; or space under the roof. Also the adjective derived from Attica.

ATTIC BASE.—The favourite type of Ionic base, consisting of an upper and lower torus and a scotia between, with fillets; the upper torus was often decorated with horizontal fluting or sometimes with guilloche or scale patterns, and below the lower torus a plinth was added in later examples.

BALTEUS.—The decorative girdle or restraining band which encircles and compresses the middle of the baluster side of an Ionic capital.

BALUSTER SIDE.—The return face of a normal Ionic capital, reaching from volute to volute in the form of a concave roll. See PULVINUS.

BARREL VAULT.—The covering of a room or compartment on the principle of the arch, and therefore generally semicircular in cross-section.

BASE.—The lowest member of a column, anta, or wall, and therefore usually appearing only in the Ionic and Corinthian styles, rarely also in the Doric. See ASIATIC, ATTIC.

BASILICA.—The Roman exchange and court of law. An oblong rectangular building usually with aisles around and provided at the middle of one side or at one or both ends with a recess used as the Tribune; the name is derived from the Stoa Basileios at Athens.

BEAD-AND-REEL.—The pattern employed when an astragal was decorated, usually carved but sometimes only painted. The beads were at first squat barrel shapes, later globular and finally more and more elongated and pointed. The reels were at first rounded, later pointed in section.

BED-MOULDING.—The lower or supporting moulding under a projecting member such as a cornice.

BIBLIOTHECA (Library).—A chamber provided with cases to hold manuscript rolls.

BOULEUTERION.—The Greek Senate House.

BRACE.—A diagonal wooden or iron strut sometimes applied inside the joints of masonry, in addition to dowels, to prevent the joints from opening from the effects of earthquakes; used also of a diagonal strut for a braced beam.

BRECCIA.—Conglomerate or pudding-stone, with large pebbles embedded in hardened red clay, unsuitable for any use except in foundations.

BRICK.—Normally sun-dried, square in plan and fairly large; baked or burnt brick, though early developed in Mesopotamia, did not appear in Greek lands before the middle of the fourth century and was used only rarely even in the Hellenistic period, apart from its special forms in roof tiling.

GLOSSARY

BUCRANIUM.—The bull's head or ox-skull carved in frontal view, sometimes in a panel, sometimes combined with swags or festoons.

CABLING.—The convex filling sometimes employed within the fluting of the lower parts of Hellenistic and Roman columns.

CANALIS (Canal or Channel.—The space between the fillets or astragals of an Ionic volute: in early work, convex; in the fully developed types, concave.

CANTILEVER.—A beam fixed at one end with other end free, or fixed in the middle with both ends free.

CAPITAL.—The topmost member of a column, anta, or wall, being in the case of columns the most distinctive member of the order.

CARCERES.—A row of stalls or horse-boxes at one end of a hippodrome or circus, enclosed by double doors, within which the chariots waited till the signal was given for starting, when the doors were simultaneously thrown open.

CARYATID.—Figure of a maiden (*kore*, *pl. korai*) taking the place of a column in supporting an entablature, as in the South Porch of the Erechtheum, Athens.

CAULICULUS.—The stalk or stem from which spring the acanthus leaves supporting the volutes or *fleurons* in the Corinthian capital.

CAVEA.—The auditorium of a theatre, so called because originally it was excavated in the rocky side of a hill.

CAVETTO.—A concave moulding, generally a quarter round, derived from the typical Egyptian concave cornice.

CELLA.—The enclosed chamber or sanctuary of a temple, also known by the Greek term naos or neos.

CENTRING.—The wooden frame or pattern temporarily supporting an arch or vault before it is sufficiently complete to become self-supporting.

CHANNEL.—Used not only of the Ionic capital (*see* CANALIS) but sometimes also for the flutes of column shafts and bases.

CHRYSELEPHANTINE.—A statue in which a wooden core is overlaid with gold and ivory, the drapery and ornaments being of the former and the flesh of the latter material.

CLAMP (sometimes but less properly known as a Cramp).—The wooden, lead, iron, or bronze link (for the forms, see Fig. 64) employed for bonding blocks of stone, instead of mortar.

CLEPSYDRA.—A vessel employed in ancient days to measure time by the running out of a certain quantity of water. There was one in the Tower of the Winds at Athens.

COFFER.—A sunk panel in a vault or ceiling, sometimes even in a cornice.

COLONNADE.—A range of columns. See PORTICO.

COLUMNAE CAELATAE.—The term given by Pliny to the sculptured columns of the Temple of Artemis at Ephesus.

COMPOSITE.—A late type of capital formed by superimposing Ionic volutes on a Corinthian bell.

CONCRETE.—A composition of lime, cement and stone aggregate employed for mass construction in Roman times.

CONSOLE.—A carved corbel or bracket, generally used for the "ears" flanking doors and windows and supporting their cornices, or for modillions.

CORBEL, CORBELLING.—A projecting bracket (generally uncarved), or an overhanging course of masonry successively repeated on opposite sides of an opening until it is completely covered with a false arch or vault, which may be trimmed into semicircular form even though the courses are all horizontal rather than radial.

CORINTHIAN.—The bell type of capital decorated with volutes and acanthus leaves, invented as a substitute for the Ionic, supposedly at Corinth (*see* p. 157).

CORNICE.—The upper member of the entablature (*q.v.*) subdivided into bed-moulding, corona, and sima, though the last properly belongs to the roof; a term also employed for any projection on a wall, provided to throw the rain-water from the face of the building.

CORONA.—The projecting member of the cornice having a vertical face.

COVER-TILE.—The roof tile (*imbrex*) of terracotta or marble, normally semicircular (Laconian) or triangular (Corinthian) in section, bridging the open joint between two rows of flat or pan-tiles (*tegulae*).

GLOSSARY

CREPIDOMA.—The stepped platform of a Greek temple.

CUNEI.—The wedge-shaped groups into which the seats of a theatre are divided by radiating passages.

CYCLOPEAN MASONRY.—The rude but massive masonry employed by the Aegean peoples and by the early Greeks in the walls of their cities and citadels.

CYMA or CYMATIUM.—A wave moulding of double curvature. When the concave portion protrudes (normally at the top) it is called a cyma recta; when the convex part protrudes it is called cyma reversa; the Doric hawksbeak is another example of such a moulding, related to the cyma recta.

DADO.—The lower portion of a wall when treated as a continuous pedestal or wainscot; sometimes only the plain surface between the base and top mouldings of such a pedestal.

DECASTYLE.—Temple front with ten columns. See TEMPLES.

DECATETRASTYLE.—Front with fourteen columns.

DENTIL.—Rectangular blocks in the bed-mould of a cornice, or occupying the place of a frieze, originally representing the ends of joists which carried a flat roof.

DIASTYLE.—Fairly widely spaced columns. See INTERCOLUMNIATION.

DIAULOS.—The peristyle round the great court of the Palaestra described by Vitruvius.

DIAZOMA.—The Greek term for a horizontal passage which separated the several ranges of seats in a theatre or stadium.

DIE.—The vertical face of a pedestal or podium.

DIMINUTION.—The amount of tapering or reduction in the diameter of a column shaft from bottom to top, generally two-ninths to one-fifth of the lower diameter in Doric and one-sixth to one-seventh of the lower diameter in Ionic and Corinthian columns.

DIPTERAL.—A temple surrounded by two rows of columns, a double peristyle. See TEMPLES.

DISTYLE IN-ANTIS.—Temple or porch front with two columns between antae. See TEMPLES.

DODECASTYLE.—Temple front with twelve columns. See TEMPLES.

DOME.—The hemispherical form of vault employed above a circular or, with adjustments, above a square plan, and constructed either as a true radial vault or as a false corbelled vault.

DORIC.—The order evolved in the Dorian and western regions of Greece.

DOWEL.—The wooden, lead, iron, or bronze attachment for securing blocks to the course below them.

DROMOS.—A long narrow passage or runway, used of the entrances to Aegean chamber or tholos tombs, and even of one of the main streets of Athens.

DRUM.—One of the cylindrical sections or courses of a column shaft; also used of a cylindrical wall interrupting a conical roof and raising its central portion.

EAVES.—The overlapping edge of a sloping roof, on the flanks of temples.

EAVES-TILE.—The flat tile or pan-tile with a decorative nosing employed on the eaves (with antefixes) as a substitute for the sima.

ECCLESIASTERION.—A special name sometimes applied to the Bouleuterion, as at Priene.

ECHINUS.—The convex moulding of circular plan which supports the abacus of a Doric capital. Also the similar moulding carved with egg-and-dart placed under the cushion of the Ionic capital and appearing between the volutes.

EGG-AND-DART or EGG-AND-TONGUE.—The pattern applied to the Ionic ovolo profile, in early times with squarish eggs touching each other and concealing all but the tips of the darts, later with more pointed or oval eggs separated to reveal the darts, which in Roman times are sometimes even arrow-shaped.

EMPOLION.—A wooden block at the centre of a column drum joint holding the wooden centring pin; the same device was sometimes made of bronze (as at Eleusis).

ENGAGED COLUMN.—A semi-detached column exactly or slightly more than semi-circular in plan.

ENNEASTYLE.—Temple front with nine columns. See TEMPLES.

ENTABLATURE.—The superstructure carried by columns; it is occasionally used to complete, architecturally, the upper portion of a wall, even when there are no columns, and in the case of pilasters or detached or engaged columns is sometimes profiled round them.

GLOSSARY

It is usually divided into three parts: viz. the architrave (the supporting member, carried from column to column); the frieze (the decorative portion); and the cornice (the crowning and projecting member). The frieze is often omitted in the Asiatic Ionic order.

ENTASIS.—The slight convex curve given to the arris of a Doric column, or to the fillets between the flutes of other columns, in order to correct an optical illusion; if the shaft tapered upward in absolutely straight lines, the silhouette of the column would appear concave.

EPICRANITIS.—The Greek term for a wall capital or an interior cornice.

EPISCENIUM.—The upper storey of the scene building of a theatre, generally receding behind the proscenium colonnade.

EPISTYLE.—The Greek term for the architrave (*q.v.*).

EUSTYLE.—Well-spaced columns. See INTERCOLUMNIATION.

EUTHYNTERIA.—The Greek term for the special top course of a foundation used as a levelling course.

EXEDRA.—A semicircular stone or marble seat, or a rectangular or semicircular recess.

EYE.—The decorative centre point of an Ionic volute.

FASCIA.—The term given to the planes into which the architrave of the Ionic and Corinthian Orders is subdivided, or to a flat projecting band (cf. TAENIA).

FILLET.—A narrow flat moulding, used also of the flattened arris between the deeper flutes of Ionic columns.

FINIAL.—The crowning decoration, usually floral, on a stele or at the peak of a conical roof, corresponding to the acroteria on pediments.

FLAT TILE.—The roof tile (*tegula*) or pan-tile of terracotta or marble, normally slightly concave (Laconian) or flat (Corinthian), with upturned lateral rims which meet at open joints protected by the cover-tiles.

FLEURON.—The floral form adorning the middle of each face of the abacus of the Corinthian capital, or each face of the bell between the volutes.

FLUTES.—The vertical channels (segmental, elliptical, or semicircular in horizontal section) employed in the shafts of columns in the classic styles. The flutes are separated one from the other by an arris in the Greek Doric and early Ionic Orders, and by a fillet in the developed Ionic and Corinthian Orders. In early and late Doric columns the flute was usually segmental, but at the best period, in order to emphasise the arris, it was formed of three arcs constituting what is known as a false ellipse; a deeper curve was given to the flutes in Greek Ionic and Corinthian columns; in later work the flute was semicircular. In rare examples the flutes were carried spirally round the columns.

FRIEZE.—The middle member of the entablature. Applied also to any horizontal band enriched with sculpture. See ZOPHOROS.

GEISON.—The Greek term for the cornice or corona (*q.v.*).

GROIN.—The arris formed by the intersection of two barrel vaults.

GUILLOCHE.—A continuous plaited pattern of interwoven fillets, leaving circular centres, sometimes filled with rosettes.

GUTTAE (drops).—Small pendant tapering cylinders like pegs under the triglyphs and mutules of a Doric entablature. See TRUNNEL.

GYMNASIUM.—A school for physical education and training, particularly for exercises requiring considerable space, such as running.

GYNAECONITIS.—The women's quarter of the Greek house.

HAWKSBEAK.—The Doric moulding of multiple curvature, related to the cyma recta and similarly derived from the Egyptian cavetto, decorated with upright conventionalised squarish leaves painted alternately red and blue.

HEART-AND-DART or LEAF-AND-DART.—The Lesbian pattern with pendant conventionalised pointed leaves reproducing the profile of, and normally applied to, the cyma reversa or Lesbian cyma.

HELIX.—The Greek term for a volute spiral, as used in the Ionic or Corinthian capitals.

HEMICYCLE.—Term given to semicircular recesses of great size, sometimes vaulted.

HENOSTYLE IN-ANTIS.—Temple or porch front with a single column between antae. See TEMPLES.

GLOSSARY

HEPTASTYLE.—Temple front with seven columns. See TEMPLES.

HEROUM.—A small shrine or chapel of a demigod or mortal, in the latter case for the worship of the dead.

HEXASTYLE.—Temple or porch front with six columns. See TEMPLES.

HIERON.—The name given to a temple, or more particularly to the sacred enclosure or Temenos of some Greek temples, as at Epidaurus.

HIP ROOF.—Sloping roof applied to a rectangular plan and descending in all directions, the planes meeting in hips which bisect the rectangular corners at 45 degrees, or even (in more complicated plans such as the Propylaea of the Athenian Acropolis) in valleys.

HIPPODROME.—The course provided by the Greeks for horse and chariot racing.

HYPAETHRAL.—A temple the naos of which was wholly or partly open to the sky, with a hypaethron.

HYPOTRACHELIUM (Gr., under the neck).—One or more grooves under the necking or gorge of the Greek Doric capital which mask the junction of capital and shaft.

IMBREX.—The Latin term for cover-tile (q.v.).

IMPLUVIUM.—A shallow tank in the floor of the atrium of a house, provided to receive the rain falling through the roof; used also of any shallow tank sunk in a floor.

INTERAXIAL.—The measurement of column spacing from centre to centre, and thus greater than the intercolumniation (as set forth by Vitruvius) by the diameter itself.

INTERCOLUMNIATION.—The distance between the columns of a colonnade, defined in terms of the lower diameter of the columns. They are thus set forth by Vitruvius (III. 3).—Pycnostyle (where the columns are $1\frac{1}{2}$ diameters apart), Systyle (2 diameters), Eustyle ($2\frac{1}{4}$ diameters), Diastyle (3 diameters), and Araeostyle ($3\frac{1}{2}$ diameters or more), the latter carrying architraves in wood only; he accidentally omitted Metriostyle ($2\frac{1}{2}$ diameters). Very different spacings, however, were used in the better periods of Greek architecture.

INTRADOS.—The soffit or under surface of an arch or vault.

IONIC.—The order evolved in the Ionian and eastern regions of Greek lands.

JAMB.—One of the vertical lateral members of a door or window enframement, supporting the lintel.

LACUNAR.—A coffer of the ceiling (q.v.).

LEAF-AND-DART.—Another name for heart-and-dart (q.v.).

LESBIAN CYMA.—Another name for the cyma reversa (q.v.).

LEWIS.—A wedge-shaped lifting iron inserted into a hole in the top of a block, spreading at both ends in late Hellenistic and Roman (as in modern) times, but at one end only (vertical at the other) in the best Greek times.

LINTEL.—The horizontal beam covering a door or window opening or spanning the interval between two columns or piers.

LOGEION.—Literally "speaking-place," the roof of the proscenium colonnade in the Hellenistic theatre.

LOTUS.—The Egyptian floral conventional form at first imitated faithfully, though in an upright rather than pendant position, and later transformed into the so-called honeysuckle.

LOTUS-AND-PALMETTE.—See ANTHEMION.

MAEANDER.—A continuous fret or key pattern, like a rectangular spiral.

MARBLE.—Always white unless otherwise specified, and usually in one of two main varieties, the close-grained Pentelic from Athens, and the coarse-grained translucent Parian, Naxian, and other types from the Aegean islands. Less frequent were the pure white soft marble found near Sunium, and the blue-clouded marbles of Hymettus near Athens and of Doliana near Tegea.

MEGARON.—The principal, or men's, hall in the Mycenaean palace or house, and so used infrequently of temples (as of Athena at Athens, of Demeter at Eleusis and Megara).

METOPE (Gr., between the holes).—Originally the panels of brick wall between the holes left for the ends of the beams of the Doric ceiling, and applied afterwards to the sunk panels between the triglyphs (q.v.).

METRIOSTYLE.—Medium spaced columns. See INTERCOLUMNIATION.

MODILLION.—The horizontal corbels carrying the corona of a Corinthian cornice.

GLOSSARY

MODULE.—The unit of a design; defined by Vitruvius as the half diameter of the lower part of the shaft of a Doric column, or the full lower diameter of an Ionic column.

MONOLITHIC.—Composed of a single block of stone, in the case of a column extending from the top of base or stylobate to the bottom of the capital.

MONOPTERAL.—Temple with columns only, lacking a cella, usually circular. See TEMPLE.

MOULDING.—A narrow profiled decorative member employed to divide or define the edges of surfaces, to support or crown more important members, or to separate other mouldings. See ANNULET, ASTRAGAL, BED-MOULDING, CAVETTO, CYMA or CYMATIUM, FASCIA, FILLET, HAWKSBEAK, LESBIAN CYMA, OGEE, OVOLO, SCOTIA, TAENIA, TORUS, TROCHILUS.

MUTULE.—A projecting slab on the soffit of the Doric cornice, between the viae.

NAOS.—The cella of the Greek temple.

NECKING.—A narrow transitional member through which the lines of the shaft are sometimes carried up into the capital, as in the Doric (see TRACHELIUM) and rarely also in Ionic (as at Naucratis, Ephesus, Samos, Locri, in the Erechtheum, etc.).

NYMPHAEUM.—A chamber (sometimes subterranean) in which were plants and flowers and a fountain or running water.

OCTASTYLE or OCTOSTYLE.—Temple front with eight columns. See TEMPLES.

ODEUM.—A roofed building in which rehearsals and musical contests took place.

OECUS.—Literally "house," the main room of a Greek house (successor of the old megaron); used as the dining-room in more elaborate Roman houses and presumably also in Greek prototypes, since according to Vitruvius the four kinds were the Tetrastyle, the Corinthian, the Egyptian, and the Cyzicene.

OGEE.—An abnormal moulding composed of two cyma reversa meeting in a sharp edge, an ogival or "Gothic" profile occurring once in archaic Greece (at Paros).

OPAION.—The Greek word for the clerestorey formed by a lantern projecting above a roof. Applied also to an hypaethral opening in a roof, or even in a single roof tile.

OPISTHODOMUS.—The recessed porch in the rear of a Greek temple, sometimes enclosed with bronze grilles and serving as a treasury; hence used also as the name of the sacred treasury on the Athenian Acropolis.

ORCHESTRA.—The "dancing-place" and hence the place of action for the chorus and at first even for the actors in the Greek theatre; generally circular in plan.

ORDER.—The architectural system composed of column and entablature taken together.

ORTHOSTATES.—The bottom course of the walls of the naos of a Greek temple, generally twice or three times the height of the upper courses.

OVOLO.—A convex moulding which, though sometimes closely related to a torus, generally shifts the point of maximum projection toward the top and finally degenerates into a quarter-round.

PALAESTRA.—A training school for physical exercises, smaller than the gymnasium and used for such events as wrestling, boxing, etc.

PALMETTE.—A floral decoration of Mesopotamian origin, related to the "sacred tree," at first imitated faithfully by the Greeks and later varied with pointed or even flame-shaped petals.

PAN-TILE.—Another term of flat tile or *tegula*.

PARAPET.—A low protective wall or "balustrade" at the edge of a platform.

PARASCENIUM.—One of the symmetrical wings of the scene building which project into the orchestra, according to modern usage; but the Greeks seem to have used the term for other lateral features of the scene building, such as the side porticoes at Delos.

PARASTADE.—A flanking wall generally terminating in an anta, such as the side walls of porches in Greek temples.

PARODOS.—One of the lateral or main entrances to the orchestra of the theatre, often an irregular passage left between the auditorium wall and the scene building.

PASTAS.—A monumental alcove in the Greek house with one side open on a court.

PATERA.—The representation of a flat, round dish or disk, usually decorated; used to ornament a panel, frieze, etc.

GLOSSARY

PEDIMENT.—The triangular termination of a ridge roof, including the tympanum and the raking cornice above.

PENTASTYLE.—Temple front with five columns. See TEMPLES.

PERIAKTOI (Gr., "revolving").—Triangular machines with differing scenery painted on each of the three faces, sometimes placed in the parascenia or the endmost intercolumniations of the proscenium, later at the ends of the episcenium above the proscenium.

PERIBOLUS.—Another word for Hieron or Temenos (*q.v.*).

PERIPTERAL.—A temple, the cella of which is surrounded by a peristyle. See TEMPLES.

PERISTASIS.—Another term for Peristyle.

PERISTYLE.—(1) A covered colonnade which surrounds a building. (2) An inner court lined with a colonnade.

PIER.—A free-standing rectangular support having the function of a column, but generally of heavier mass, in carrying an entablature or arch.

PILASTER.—An engaged or semi-detached pier, analogous to the anta.

PILLAR.—A somewhat ambiguous or poetic term applied to a column or pier.

PINACOTHECA.—A picture gallery.

PINAX (*pl.* Pinakes).—The Greek term for a plate, plaque, tablet, plank, or panel, such as the decorated panels filling the proscenium intercolumniations.

PLINTH.—Literally, a brick, and hence used also of rectangular blocks in ashlar masonry, and of the brick-shaped member sometimes forming the bottom of a column base, used even of the abacus of a Doric capital.

PODIUM.—The Greek term for a low wall or continuous pedestal on which columns, or even entire temples, are carried. It consisted of a plinth, a dado and a cornice.

POLOS.—The cylindrical axis or centring pin of wood or metal employed in column drums (*see* EMPOLION); used also of the tall cylindrical headdress of Caryatids.

POLYGONAL MASONRY.—The term applied to carefully fitted masonry in which the stones are not squared, but are hewn into polygons or wavy shapes which approximate the original shapes of the rough stones, but permit accurate adjustment to their neighbours, the exposed faces afterwards dressed perfectly smooth, so that the finished wall presents the appearance of a picture puzzle.

POLYTRIGLYPHAL.—Having more than the usual single triglyph above the interval between Doric columns.

PORCH.—A more limited term for portico, implying that it forms an entrance and hence used also of a vestibule without columns.

POROS.—A buff or brown limestone, soft and coarse as contrasted with marble, often filled with fossil shells; this is the most frequent building stone employed by the Greeks.

PORTICO.—A colonnade or a colonnaded porch or entrance to a building. The term, when applied to a Greek temple, is classed as Henostyle or Distyle or Tristyle or Tetrastyle in-antis (one, two, three or four columns between antae). Tetrastyle (four columns in front without antae), Pentastyle (five columns), Hexastyle (six columns), Heptastyle (seven columns), Octastyle (eight columns), Enneastyle (nine columns), Decastyle (ten columns), Dodecastyle (twelve columns), and Decatetrastyle (fourteen columns). See TEMPLES.

POSTICUM.—The Latin term for the opisthodomus in the rear of a temple.

POUR-CHANNEL.—A groove cut on the top of a block, but sometimes bored through from a convenient surface, as a method of getting molten lead into the dowel hole.

PRODOMUS.—Corresponding to the pronaos in the case of ordinary houses.

PRONAOS.—The porch in front of the naos or cella.

PROPYLAEUM.—The entrance gate-building of the Temenos or sacred enclosure of a temple, when there is one doorway only; when there is more than one doorway, as at Athens and Eleusis, the plural form *propylaea* is used.

PROPYLON.—A very simple building of the propylaeum type.

PROSCENIUM.—A colonnade six to eleven feet deep and eight to thirteen feet high between the orchestra and the scene building, often terminated at either end with a parascenium.

PROSTAS.—Another term for Prodomus or Pronaos.

PROSTYLE.—A temple with a portico of columns in the front. See TEMPLES.

PROTECTIVE SURFACE.—The preliminary dressed surface left on ancient masonry, projecting ⅜ inch in marble, 1 inch or more in coarse stone (German *werkzoll*), before the entire surface was cut back to the finished plane.

GLOSSARY

PROTHYRON.—Another term for Prodomus or Porch.

PRY-CUTTING.—A small irregular cavity hacked in the upper bed of a block to give purchase for the point of a crowbar.

PRYTANEUM.—The state dining-room and senate committee building in a Greek city.

PSEUDO-DIPTERAL.—A dipteral temple with the inner row of columns omitted. See TEMPLES.

PSEUDO-ISODOMIC.—Irregular masonry of squared stone (ashlar), usually with low and high courses alternating, but sometimes with more high than low (bonding) courses, permitting an economical construction with slabs or mere facing.

PSEUDO-PERIPTERAL.—A peripteral temple where some or all of the columns are engaged in the wall of the cella. See TEMPLES.

PTEROMA.—The passage between the walls of the cella and the peristyle colonnade.

PTERON (Gr., Wing).—The wing or flank colonnade of a temple, and so used by Pliny of the colonnade carrying the superstructure of the tomb of Mausolus.

PULVINUS.—In an Ionic capital, the return or baluster side ($q.v.$).

PURLIN.—A horizontal roof beam parallel to the ridge beam, supporting the rafters at a lower part of the sloping roof.

PYCNOSTYLE.—Very closely spaced columns. See INTERCOLUMNIATION.

QUADRIGA.—The ancient four-horsed chariot.

RAFTER.—A roof beam resting on (normally at right angles to) the ridge beam, purlins, and eaves; but special hip rafters and valley rafters occur in hip roofs, at 45 degrees to the other beams.

RAKING CORNICE.—The sloping cornice of a pediment, above the tympanum.

RAMP.—A sloping causeway, or a sloping approach to a temple engulfing the steps.

REEDING.—Applied to columns when decorated with convex reeds, the opposite of fluting, though sometimes filling the flutes and giving the effect of cabling.

REGULA.—A narrow strip under the taenia of a Doric architrave, beneath which the guttae are carved.

RELIEVING MARGIN.—A very slight depression of the edge, only $\frac{1}{32}$ to $\frac{1}{16}$ inch in marble, so that flaking or spalling will not result from pressure on projecting parts below (as of a fluted Doric column on a stylobate) or from the pressure exerted by projecting members above (as of a lintel resting on the edge of a capital).

RELIEVING TRIANGLE.—A false arch of triangular form used as a relieving arch in Mycenaean construction.

RESPOND.—(1) The wall pilaster behind a column. (2) The wall pier carrying either the end of an architrave or beam or the springing of an arch.

REVETMENT, REVETTED.—Applied decorative or more expensive facing.

RHYTON.—A conical funnel vase with a hole in the bottom.

RINCEAU.—A foliated branching pattern with curves and S-scrolls.

ROSETTE.—A circular floral ornament with petals, derived from the Assyrian rather than the Egyptian form.

SCENE (Gr., Tent).—A term used first of the player's booth, and afterwards of the building which replaced it, the back scene of the theatre; hence the words proscenium, episcenium and parascenium.

SCOTIA.—A "shaded" or concave moulding generally more or less semicircular (as in Ionic bases), but sometimes merely a quarter-circle (as under the nose of the Doric cornice).

SHAFT.—The main body of a column or pier, between the base and the capital.

SHIFT-CUTTING.—Rough cutting for a lever or crowbar, made at the bottom or top of a vertical joint.

SIMA.—The terracotta or marble gutter of a building, on the gables and sometimes on the flanks; it may or may not be moulded; if it occurs on the flanks it is provided with outlets for rain-water at intervals, often in the form of lions' heads.

SOCLE.—A slightly projecting footing of a wall or pedestal, sometimes used even of the projecting dado of a wall.

SOFFIT.—The exposed lower surface of a lintel or architrave, of an arch (see INTRADOS), or of a cornice.

GLOSSARY

SPINA.—The podium wall down the centre of the hippodrome.

STADIUM.—A racecourse of fixed dimension, viz. six hundred Greek feet; a term applied also to that measure of length.

STELE.—(1) An upright Greek tombstone. (2) Any upright stone slab used for sculptured reliefs or for inscriptions.

STEREOBATE.—The substructure of a temple.

STOA.—In Greek architecture a term corresponding to the Latin porticus, a building with its roof supported by one or more rows of columns parallel to the rear wall.

STUCCO.—The thin lime facing applied to mud-brick walls for protection, or to poros to conceal coarse inequalities; good Greek stucco on poros is of paper-like thinness and does not obscure the profiles, whereas the thick later stucco is full of sandy particles and alters the profiles.

STYLOBATE.—The upper step of a temple, which formed a platform for the columns. The term is sometimes misapplied to the three steps, properly known as the crepidoma.

SWAG.—A festoon of leaves, flowers, and fruit, carved as a frieze decoration.

SYSTYLE.—Fairly closely spaced columns. See INTERCOLUMNIATION.

TAENIA.—The projecting broad fillet or band which crowns the architrave of the Doric entablature.

TEGULA.—The Latin term for flat tile or pan-tile (*q.v.*).

TELAMONES.—The Roman term for male figures forming supports. See ATLANTES.

TELESTERION.—A hall of ceremonies, employed for a "hall of the mysteries" connected with the worship of Demeter, and primarily for that at Eleusis. See ANACTORON.

TEMENOS.—The sacred enclosure in which one or more Greek temples stand.

TEMPLES.—*Types of Plan (see also* PORTICO).

Henostyle in-antis—Temple 'A' at Prinias (primitive).

Distyle in-antis—Older Temple of Nemesis at Rhamnus, Temple 'B' at Selinus (Doric).

Amphidistyle in-antis—No examples known, except those with engaged columns at the rear, viz. Temples of Asclepius at Acragas and of Serapis at Taormina (Doric).

Tristyle in-antis—Hecatompedon at Athens (Doric).

Tetrastyle in-antis—Temple of Artemis at Lusoi (Doric).

Tetrastyle prostyle—Temple of Dionysus at Pergamum (Doric).

Tetrastyle amphiprostyle—Temple of Artemis Propylaea at Eleusis (Doric); Temples on the Ilissus and of Nike Apteros at Athens (Ionic).

Tetrastyle peripteral—Temple of Apollonis at Cyzicus, Nereid Monument at Xanthus (Ionic).

Tetrastyle pseudo-peripteral—Temple at Cnidus (Corinthian).

Pentastyle peripteral—Temple of Apollo, Thermum (Doric).

Hexastyle prostyle—Temple of the Cabiri at Samothrace (Doric), Erechtheum east front at Athens (Ionic).

Hexastyle amphiprostyle.—Athenian temple of Apollo, Delos (Doric).

Hexastyle peripteral—Heraeum at Olympia, Temples at Syracuse (Apollo, Zeus, Athena), Selinus ('A,' 'C,' 'D,' 'ER,' 'FS'), Acragas (Heracles, Hera, Concord), Paestum (Demeter, Poseidon), and Segesta, Tavole Paladine at Metapontum, Older Parthenon and Hephaesteum at Athens, Temples of Athena at Assos, Athens (Peisistratid or Old Temple), Pergamum, and Tegea, of Apollo at Corinth, Bassae, and Delphi, of Zeus at Olympia, Nemea, and Stratos, of Hera at Argos, of Poseidon at Sunium, of Asclepius at Epidaurus, of Nemesis at Rhamnus, Metroum at Olympia (Doric); Temples of Athena Polias at Priene, of Dionysus ay Teos, and the Temples at Sagalassus and Euromus (Ionic).

Heptastyle pseudo-peripteral—Temple of Zeus at Acragas (Doric).

Octastyle peripteral—The Parthenon, Athens (Doric).

Octastyle dipteral—Temples of Artemis at Ephesus, of Hera at Samos (Ionic), and of Zeus Olympius at Athens (Corinthian).

Octastyle pseudo-dipteral—Temple 'GT' at Selinus (Doric); Temples of Artemis at Magnesia and Sardis, of Apollo at Chryse, of Aphrodite at Aphrodisias, and at Messa in Lesbos, of Zeus at Aezani (Ionic).

Enneastyle prostyle—Older Telesterion at Eleusis (Doric).

Enneastyle peripteral—The so-called Basilica at Paestum.

GLOSSARY

Decastyle dipteral—Temple of Apollo at Didyma (Ionic).
Dodecastyle prostyle—Telesterion at Eleusis (Doric).
Decatetrastyle prostyle—No temples known, but see the Thersilion at Megalopolis (Doric).
Circular temples:
Monopteral—Temple of Roma and Augustus at Athens (Ionic).
Peripteral—Tholos at Epidaurus and at Delphi (Doric); Philippeum at Olympia (Ionic).

TETRASTYLE.—Temple front with four columns. *See* TEMPLES.

THALAMUS.—The bedroom of a Greek house.

THEATRON (Gr., "seeing-place").—The seating-place or auditorium of the Greek theatre, and consequently the theatre as a whole.

THOLOS.—A Greek circular building with or without a peristyle.

THYMELE.—An altar, particularly that at the centre of a theatre orchestra; consequently sometimes used as the name of other circular sacred structures, as the Tholos at Epidaurus.

THYROMA (*pl.*, THYROMATA).—Literally, a great doorway, used of the monumental north doorway of the Erechtheum and also of the huge openings in the episcenium of the theatre.

TILE.—Roofing material either of terracotta or of marble, moulded or cut in special forms. *See* ANTEFIX, COVER-TILE, EAVES TILE, FLAT TILE, IMBREX, PAN-TILE, SIMA, TEGULA.

TORUS.—A convex moulding of semicircular profile, larger than an astragal.

TRACHELIUM (Gr.).—The necking or gorge of the Greek Doric capital between the annulets on the echinus and the grooves which mask the junction of capital and shaft.

TRIGLYPH.—A projecting member separating the metopes, emphasised with two vertical channels and two chamfers (total three), a survival of the primitive beam end.

TRIPTERAL.—Temple or porch front with three rows of columns.

TRISTYLE IN-ANTIS.—Temple front with three columns between antae. *See* TEMPLES.

TROCHILUS.—Greek term for scotia (*q.v.*).

TRUNNEL.—A pin or peg, carved in stone beneath the regula of the architrave and the mutule of the cornice. *See* GUTTAE.

TYMPANUM.—The triangular wall enclosed by the raking cornice of the pediment and the horizontal cornice of the entablature beneath.

VAULT.—The application of the arch principle to the covering of a compartment rather than a mere opening. *See* BARREL VAULT, CORBEL, DOME, GROIN.

VIA.—The Latin term for street, road, or way, applied to the sloping path left between the mutules in the soffit of the Doric cornice.

VOLUTE.—The spiral scroll of the Ionic capital.

VOUSSOIR.—A wedge-shaped stone which forms one of the units of an arch.

XOANON.—A rude and primitive image of a deity, carved in wood, sometimes used of a primitive stone image.

XYSTUS.—A Roman garden planted with groves of plane trees, and laid out with flower-beds. In Greece the xystus was a covered promenade or covered running track.

ZOPHOROS or ZOOPHOROS.—A continuous frieze sculptured in relief with the forms of human beings and animals.

INDEX TO TEXT AND ILLUSTRATIONS

A. PLACES

In this and the following sections italicised references are bibliographical; references to notes are followed by the letter n; main references are designated if necessary by asterisks (*).

Abae, burnt temple, 151
Abusir, Lighthouse, 289
Acarnania, xxi, *368*
Achaeans, xi, 2, 3, 8n, 29, 35n, 36, 37, 39, 58, 65, 96, 123, 322; League, 265
Acrae, colonised, 37; Theatre, 316; votive capital, 144
Acragas, 69, *382*; Altar of Zeus, 117; circular altar, 118; colonised, xi, 37; destroyed, 105, 112, 216; excavated, xix, xxiii; Olympieum, 91, *101–106, 109, 170, 174, 176, 270, 274, 283, 338, figs. 40, 41; Oratory of Phalaris, 329; situation, 100–101; Temple of Asclepius, 104n, 111n, *270, fig. 97; Temple of Athena (S. Maria dei Greci), 100, *109; Temple of Castor and Pollux, 101, *111–112; Temple of Concord, 55n, 101, *111, 225, 336, 339, Pl. XXVI; Temple of Demeter, 109; Temple of Hephaestus, 77n, 101, *111–112; Temple of Hera Lacinia, 101, *110, 111, 338, Pl. XXIV; Temple of Heracles, xxiii, 101, *105, 111n, 338; Tomb of Theron, 330
Actium, Battle of, xii
Aegae, *374*; Market-hall, 293–294; Proto-Ionic (?) capital, 62n
Aegina, *347, 364*; Aegean settlement, 3; Altar of Aphaea, 39; Propylon, 115; Temple of Aphaea (first), 41; (second), 71; (third), xxiii, *105–107, 152, 153, 163, 165, 170, 174, 338, fig. 42, Pl. XXIV; Temple of Aphrodite, 107n; Temple of Apollo, 107; votive column, 143
Aegospotami, Battle of, 212
Aeolis, Aeolians, 36, 44, 58, *368*
Aetolian League, 265; monument, *see* Delphi
Aezani, *374*; Stadium, 320; Temple of Zeus xxiii, 276n, 277–278, 340, fig. 100; Theatre, 311, 316, 317, 320
Ak-Alan, *374*; simas, 64
Alabanda, *374*; Temple of Apollo, 273n, 276, 282
Alalia, colonised, 37
Alberobello, trulli, 5n
Alexandria, *380*; catacombs, 328; founded, xii; Lighthouse (Pharos, 289, Pl. LXVIII; Museum (ancient), 293; (modern), 276n; painted stelae, 328; Temple of Aphrodite Arsinoe, 269, 284; vaulted tombs, 328
Alexandria Troas, Baths, 321
Alinda, Market-hall, 293–294, fig. 107
Amathus, sarcophagus, 60
Amman, colonnaded streets, 335
Amorgos, house model, 6

Amphipolis, *368*; Lion monument, 257
Amyclae, *364*; tholos tomb (Vaphio), 31, 34; Throne of Apollo, 141–142, 144, fig. 52, Pl. XXXIII
Anatolia, 60
Ancyra, *374*; Temple of Roma and Augustus, xxii, 276–278
Andros, *371*
Antioch (Pisidian), *374*; Sanctuary of Men Ascaenus, 10n; Temple of Men and Augustus, 282
Antioch (Syrian), *379*; Bouleuterion, 297; colonnaded streets, 334–345; founded, xii; Statue and Temple of Olympian Zeus, 269
Antiphellus, rock-cut tombs, 67
Apamea, colonnaded streets, 335
Aphrodisias, *375*; Agora, 334; Stadium, 320; Temple of Aphrodite, 277–278, 282, 340
Apollonia (Pisidian), Temple of Roma and Augustus, 282
Apollonia (Thracian), frieze, 144; simas, 64
Arcades, *371*; Aeolic capital, 59
Argive Heraeum, *347, 364*; Aegean settlement, xxiii, 3; chamber tombs, 27; excavated, xxii, xxiv; house model, 42–43, 65, fig. 15; houses, 5; statue of Hera, 183; stoas, 240; Temple of Hera (first), xi, 53, 55–56, 183; (second), xxii, 53, *183, 222, 339; tholos tomb, 29, 31
Argos, 38, *364*; Aegean settlement, 3; chamber tombs, 26; Theatre, 316
Arkhanes, water-basin, 28n
Arslan Tash, ivories, 60
Artemisium, Temple of Artemis Prosoea, 49
Arycanda, rock-cut tombs, 67
Asea, *347*
Asia Minor, 59, *374–379*; exploration, xix–xxiii
Asine, *347*; Aegean settlement, 3; houses, 7, 65, Temple of Apollo, 43
Aspendus, Theatre, 310, 311, 315, 317–319
Assos, *375*; Agora, 293, 334, fig. 125; Bouleuterion, 296, 334; excavated, xxii; heroa, 329; Market-hall, 293, 334; Stoa, 293; Temple of Athena, 46, *88, 117, 133, 221n, 257, 271, 337, fig. 33; Theatre, 298, 299, 302, 303, 306, 312, 313, 315, 317–319
Assur, capitals, 60, 61n
Assyria, 58
Atheniu, Proto-Ionic capital, 60
Athens, 69, *357–362*; Acropolis (in general), 113, 197–198, *346, 357–358*, fig. 74, Pls. I, LI, LII; Acropolis ascent, 198, 285, fig. 74, Pl. LI; Acropolis excavated, xxi, xxii; Acropolis walls, 22, 65, 91, 113, 150, 198, 203, 204, fig.

398

INDEX OF PLACES

74, Pls. LI, LXI; Aegean settlement, 3, *346*; Agora (Greek), vii, xxii, 206, *361*; (Roman), 181, 289, *361*; Agora gate, 285, 289; Altar of Apollo Pythius, 141; Altar of Athena Nike, 186; Altars of Butes, Hephaestus, Poseidon, and Zeus Hypatos, 90, 190, figs. 70, 71; Anaceum, 181; Arch of Hadrian, 281, 327n; Base of Bryaxis, 258; Bastion of Athena Nike, 187, 188, 198, 285; Beulé Gate, 238n, 285–286, fig. 74, Pl. I; Bouleuterion (first), 65; (second), 119; (third), 206, 297; bronze palm tree, 157n; Cerameicus, vii, xxii, 254, *362*; Chalcotheca, 198n, 205, fig. 74; chamber tombs, 27; choragic columns, 288, pls. III, LXI; choragic monuments, 236–240 (*see also* Monuments); destruction of Athens (480), xi, 150; Dipylon Gate, 254, 322, *362*; Dipylon graves, 65, *362*; Dromos, 390; Enneacrunus, 118; Erechtheum, vii, xxiii, 55n, 81n, 90n, 104n, 124n, 138, 139, 148, 151, 161n, 168, 169n, 175, 178–179, 186n, *187–195, 197–199, 201, 203, 215, 221, 235, 238, 257, 260n, 272, 275, 282, 284, 297, 326, 336, 340, *360*, 389, figs, 70–72, 74, Pls. I, XLV, XLVI, XLVII, XLVIII, XLIX, LI, LII; Fall of Athens (404), xii, 212, 216; Fountain-house in Agora, 118n; golden lamp, 157n, 188; grave colonettes, 328; grave monuments, *see* Stelae; Hecatompedon, *71–73, 80, 89, 91, 149, 163, 199n, *358*, Pl. XX; Hecatompedos Neos, 159, 163, fig. 74; Hephaesteum, vii, 148, 149, 163, 165, 166, 169n, 170, 173n, *179–182, 186n, 336, 338, *360–361*, figs. 58, 67, Pls. XLI, XLII; houses, 7n, 41, 65, 211; Hydra pediment, 71; Lenaeum theatre, 120n; Library of Hadrian, 281, 293; Library of Pantaenus, 293; Metroum, 206; Monument of Lysicrates, 237–238, *362*, Pls. LIX, LX; Monument of Nicias, 185n, *238–239, 286, 309n, 339, *362*; Monument of Thrasyllus, *239, 247n, *362*, figs. 77, 87, Pl. LXI; Museum (Acropolis), *342*; (National) xxiv, 6n, 13n, 183n, *343*, fig. 46; Odeum of Agrippa, 119n, 319; Odeum of Herodes Atticus, 239n, 319, *362*, Pl. LII; Odeum of Pericles, 206, 209, *211, 234, 265, 292, 295, *362*; Old Propylon, 198, *359*, fig. 74; Older Parthenon, 72, 89n, *149–150, 160, 165, 166, 169, 170, 172, 180, 186n, 198, 338, *358–359*, fig. 74; olive tree of Athena, 71n, 187n, 190, 191, fig. 70; Olympieum (earlier), *91, 134n, 169, 280, *360*; (later), xii, 106, 169, *280–281, 340, *360*, figs, 101, 102, Pl. LXIV; opaion tile, 151n; Opisthodomus (The), 91, 198, figs. 70, 71; Orchestra (Agora), 119–120; Palace of Erechtheus, 21–22, 58; Parapet of Athena Nike, 178, 187; Parthenon (first), *see* Hecatompedon; (second), *see* Older Parthenon; (third), vii, xi, xxi, xxiii, 72, 90, 108n, 110n, 116n, 148, 150, 153, *159–180, 183, 185–187, 201, 220, 336, 338, *358–359*, figs, 57, 59, 60, 74, Pls. I, XXXV, XXXVIII, XXXIX, XL, LI, LII; Pedestal of Agrippa, 285, 326, fig. 74, Pl. L; Peisistratid temple of Athena, 22, 71n, 72n, *90–91, 94n, 134, 149, 163, 166, 187, 190, 192, 198, 337, *358*, figs, 70, 71, 74; Pinacotheca, 198n, 203, 204, fig. 75, Pls. L, LI; Pnyx, *362*; (first), 119; (second), 206–207; (third), Precinct of Artemis Brauronia, 198n, 203–205, fig. 74; Precinct of Asclepius, 235, 240, *360*; Precinct of Dionysus Eleuthereus, 119–120, 184n, 209, 236, fig, 77; Precinct of Pandrosus, 189, 190, fig, 70; Precinct of Theseus, 180n, 181; "Pre-Erechtheum," 71n; Propylaea, 57, 81n, 161n, 165–167, 169, 170, 176, 179, 183, 185n, 186, 187, 194, *198–205, 219, 221, 225, 257, 275, 284–285, 326, 336, 339, *359*, figs, 61, 66, 74, 75, 76, Pls. I, XLVIII, XLIX, L, LI, LII; Proto-Ionic capital, 62n; Sacking of Athens (86), xii, 211, 266; (A.D. 267), xii, 309n; Sacred Way, 254, 255; sepulchral offering tables, 122; spiral column, 121; Stadium, 250, 251, 319–320, *362*, Pl. LXII; Stadium gate, 287; Statue of Ares, 181, 182; Statue of Athena Hephaestia, 179, 180n, 181; Statue of Athena Lemnia, 149; Statue of Athena Nike, 185–186n; Statue of Athena Parthenos, xi, 149, 160, 163, 164, 178, 222, 236n; Statue of Athena Promachos, 148–149, 198, 211, fig. 74, Pl. LI; Statue of Dionysus (marble), 239; Statue of Dionysus Eleuthereus, 184; Statue of Hephaestus, 179, 180n, 181; Statue of Zeus Olympius, 281; Stelae, *362*; (primitive), 65; (archaic), 121–122, 144, fig. 46; (classical), 212, 254–255, fig. 94; (Roman), 328; Stoa Basileios (Royal), 206, 388; Stoa Poecile (Painted), 206; Stoa of Asclepieum, 235, 240; Stoa of Attalus, 292–293, *361*, fig. 106; Stoa of Eumenes, 292–293, 309n, Pl. LII; Stoa of Theatre, 206, 208n, 209–210, 292, fig. 77; Stoas on the Pnyx, 240; Street of Tripods, 239; Temple 'A,' 71; Temple 'Aa,' 50, 71; Temple 'B', 41n, 71n, 89, 91; Temple 'C,' 71n, 89, 91; Temple 'D,' 71n; Temple 'E,' 71n, 91; Temple of Apollo Patrous, 221n; Temple of Ares, 148, 149, 179, *181–182, 186n, 309n, 338, *361*; Temple of Athena (Homeric), 40, 58; Temple of Athena Nike (first), 151, 186, 187, *359*; (second), xxi, xxiii, 148, 168, 183, *185–188, 193, 198, 203, 205, 240, 260n, 340, *359*, 387, figs, 68, 69, 74, Pls. XLIV, LI, LII; Temple of Dionysus Eleuthereus (first), 89, 120, 206, 210, fig. 77; (second), 184, 209n, 210n, fig. 77; Temple of Dionysus-in-the-Marshes, 43; Temple of Roma and Augustus, 284, *360*, figs, 74, 103; Temple of Zeus Olympius, *see* Olympieum; Temple on the Ilissus (Metroum in Agrae?), 148, 158, *185, 186, 336, 339, *360*; Pl. XLIV; temporary shrine of Athena, 151; Theatre of Dionysus, 119–120, 207–210, 211n, 246–249, 290, 298–301, 303, 304, 307, 309–312, 315–318, 328n, *361*, fig. 77, Pls. LX, LXI; Tholos, 205, *361*; Tomb of Cecrops, 191, 192, figs. 70, 71, 74; Tomb of Dexileos, 255, fig. 94; Tomb of Dionysius, 254; Tomb of Pythionice, 255; Tower of the Winds, 181, *289–290, 328n, *361*, 389, Pl. LXVIII; trident marks and sea of Poseidon, 187n, 190, figs. 70, 71; tumuli (miniature), 121; votive capitals, 59, 142–143, fig. 53; votive pedestals,

INDEX OF PLACES

121, *362*; walls of Athens, 362; xoanon of Athena, 151, 187
Attica, *363*; Invasion of, xii

Baalbek, Temple of Bel, 283
Babylon, xii, 265, *379*; Palace of Nebuchadnezzar, 61; Theatre, 303, 304, 308, 313, 317, 319
Baeza (Spain), columns, 13n
Bassae, *364-365*; Statues of Apollo, 156; Temple of Aphrodite, 43; Temple of Apollo (first), 43, 155n; Temple of Apollo Epicurius (second) vii, xxi, xxiii, 47, 96, 116, 148, 151n, *154-159, 162-164, 166, 170, 176, 178, 180, 184n, 185, 194, 219, 220, 234-236, 240, 292, 303, 338, fig. 56, Pls. XXXV, XXXVI, XXXVII; Temple of Artemis, 43
Belevi, *375*; Mausoleum, 329-330
Benabil (Syria), bicolumnar monument, 327n
Beneventum, Arch of Trajan, 311
Beni-Hasan (Egypt), columns, 56
Berlin Museums, 23n, 32n, 212n, 222n, 267n, 288n, *342*, Pls. LV, LXV, LXVII
Berytus (Beirut), merchants from, 322
Bithynia, xxi
Boeotia, funerary vases, 65
Boghazkeuy, lily capital, 60
Bosra, colonnaded streets, 335
Boston Museum, 88n, 122n, 141, *342*
Butrinto (Albania), Odeum, 319
Byblus, sarcophagus, 60
Byzantium, xii, 336; colonised, 37; burn temple, 151

Calauria (Poros); *365*, stoas, 240
Calydon, *368*; excavated, vii, xxii; Heroum, 151n, 329; Temple of Apollo Laphrius, 52, 82n; Temple of Artemis Laphria (earlier), 52; (later) 218; Temple of Dionysus, 52n
Camarina, *382*; colonised, 37; destroyed, 112, 216; Temple, 112n
Cambridge, Fitzwilliam Museum, 287n
Canaan, Canaanites, 60
Candia Museum, xxiv. Pls. IV, VII, IX
Capua, votive capital, 144
Caranis, *381*
Caria, Carians, 58
Carlsruhe Museum, 32n
Carthaea (Ceos), *371*
Carthage, Carthaginians, xii, 69, 100, 101n, 104, 105, 112, 122n, 216, 330n
Caryae, Sanctuary of Artemis, 254
Carystus, Stele, 212
Catana, colonised, 37
Caulonia, *382*; opaion tile, 151n; sima, 81n; Temple, 112n
Cephallenia, Aegean settlement, 3
Chaeronea, Battle of, xii, 216, 265; Lion monument, 257; Theatre, 316
Chalcedon, colonised, 37
Chalcis, coloniser, xi, 37
Chalia, Aegean settlement, 3
Chios, *371*; neolithic settlement, 4; Temple of Apollo Phanaeus, 132, 229

Chryse, Temple of Apollo Smintheus, 272-275, 340, fig. 98
Cimmerians, 40
Clazomenae, sarcophagi, 144-145
Cnidus, *375*; city plan, 263; Lion tomb, 104n, 257, 329; Statue of Aphrodite, 284n; Temple, 283-284, 340
Cnossus, 59, *346*; Aegean settlement, 3; beehive hypogeum, 15; destroyed, 22; excavated, vii, xxiv; house model, 46; Little palace, 16; Neolithic stratum, 4; Palace of Minos (earlier), 15; (later), 9-13, 326, fig. 5, Pls. V, VI, VII, VIII, IX; Royal villa, 16; Skoteino cave, 24; "Temple fresco," 13, 24, Pl. IX; Temple tomb, 28; Tholos tombs, 28n; "Town mosaic," 4-5, 22, Pl. IV
Colophon, *375*; Baths, 322; opaion tile, 151n; tholos tomb, 28
Constantinople, Hagia Sophia, 326; renamed, xii.
Copenhagen, Glyptotek, 159n
Corcyra, *368*; Altar of Artemis, 117-118; colonised, xi, 37; excavated, vii, xxiii; Temple at Kardaki, 92; Temple of Artemis ("Gorgon temple"), 55, *73-75, 92, 274, fig. 25; Tomb of Menecrates, 122; votive capitals, 122, 144
Corinth, 69, *365*; Acanthus columns, 253n; Acrocorinth, 288; Aegean settlements, 3; Agora, 240; Amphitheatre, 310, 315, 319; Baths, 321; coloniser, xi, 37; destroyed, xii, 266, 288, 322; excavated, vii, xxii; Fountain in Agora, 118; Fountain of Glauce, 118; Fountain of Pirene, 118, 157n, 288; Fountain of Upper Pirene, 288; invention of pediments, 43; Lechaeum Road, 335; North market, 241, 294; North-west stoa, 290; Odeum, 319; opaion tile, 151n; Porpylaea of Agora, 327n; refounded by Romans, xii; shaft graves, 25; South Stoa, 240-241; Temple (colossal), 90n, 218; Temple 'B' (oracle), 41n, 89; Temple of Apollo, *89-92, 166, 337, fig. 35, Pl. XXII; Theatre, 299, 300, 307, 309, 310, 312, 314-319
Corone (Longa), *365*; Temple of Apollo Corynthius, votive capital, 121
Cos, *371*; Altar of Asclepius, 288; Battle of, 290n; Charmyleum, 329; colonised, 37; excavated, vii, xxii; Temple of Asclepius (Doric), 268; (Ionic), 273
Crete, Cretans, xi, 1, 2, 59, 345-346, *371*; neolithic settlement, 4. *See also* list of Cretan sites above (p. 399)
Crimisa, *382*; Temple of Apollo Alius, 84, 86, 267, fig. 31
Croton, *382*; colonised, 37; Temple of Hera Lacinia, 81n, *110, 165
Cumae, *382*; colonised, xi, 37
Cyaneae, rock-cut tombs, 67
Cyprus, 60, *346, 372*; Aegean raids, 2; colonised, 36; excavated, vii, xxi, xxii; orientalising motifs, 59, 60, 63; source of copper, 1, 3
Cyrene, *381*; colonised, xvii, 37; column of Protomedes, 253n; excavated, xxi, xxii, 86n; Statue of Zeus, 88; Temple of Apollo (earlier), 86; (later), 220-221, 267; Temple of Zeus, 86-88

INDEX OF PLACES

Cyzicus, *375*; Amphitheatre, 319; charioteer frieze, 144; Temple of Apollonis, 278–279; Temple of Hadrian, 283

Da-u-Dukhtar (Persia), rock-cut tomb, 279n
Damascus, 60; colonnaded streets, 335
Daulus, Phocicon, 119
Delian Confederacy (first), xi, 123, 147, 216; (second), xii, 216; Festival, xi, 184n
Delos, *372*; Aegean ivories, 23n; "Agoras" of the Italians and of the Poseidoniastae, 322; annexed by Athens, xii, 285; Bouleuterion, 206; Cave temple, 24n; decline, 266; excavated, vii, xviii, xxii; Exedra of Methridates, 327, 329; Hippodrome, 251; houses, 279, 322–325, fig. 118, Pl. LXX; Hypostyle hall, 294–295; Letoum, 127; magazine hall, 104n; Naxian columns, 143; Naxian house, 142; Palaestra, 320; Pedestals of Antiochus and Philetaerus, 326; "Sanctuary of the Bulls" (Pythium?), 184n, 290, 292, fig. 105; Southwest propylon, 285; Statue (colossus) of Apollo, 133; Statues (Seven), 183–184; Stoa of Antigonus, 290n, 291–292; Stoa of Philip, 170, 291; Temple of Apollo (arachaic), 38, 133; (Athenian), 96, 148, *183–184, 194, 203, 221, 339, Pl. XLIII; (peripteral), 155n, *184, *221, 267, 339; Temple of Isis, 270; Theatre, 208n, 298–300, 302, 303, 305, 306, 312, 313, 316, 317, 319; treasuries, 205; votive capitals, 142–143, fig. 53
Delphi, *368–369*; Acanthus column, 238, 253–254, 276, fig. 93; Aetolian monument, 327; Altar of Apollo, 141; apsidal shrine, 41n; Argive Niche (earlier), 212; (later), 212n, 253; Athenian Stoa, 142, 186; Athenian Treasury, xxiii, *117, 338, Pl. XXIX; bicolumnar monuments, 136n, 235n, 326–327, Pl. XXVIII; Bouleuterion, 119; Clazomenian Treasury, *139–140, 157; Cnidian Lesche, 206; Cnidian Treasury, *138–139, 223, fig. 50; Corinthian Treasury, 116; Cyrenaic Treasury, 253; Daochus monument, 253; Doric Treasury in Precinct of Athena, 205; excavated, vii, xxii; Gymnasium, 251, 321, Pl. II; Heroum, 329; Marathon base, 117; Massiliot Treasury, 138n, *139–140, 157, fig. 50, Pl. XXXIII; Messenian Victory monument, 211–212; Museum, Pls. XXXII, LIX; Naxian column, 143, Pl. XXXIII; Niche of Craterus, 253; Palaestra, 251, Pl. II; Pedestals of Aemilius Paullus, Attalus, Eumenes, and Prusias, 326; Plataean tripod, 211, 253; Precinct of Apollo, Pl. XXVIII; Precinct of Athena Pronaea, 205, 234; raided by Gauls, xii; Sicyonian Treasury, 116n, 117, 205; Siphnian Treasury, 94, 134, *138–139, 142n, fig. 50, Pls. XXXI, XXXII; situation, 113, Pls. II, XXVIII; Spartan niche, 212, 235n, 253; spiral column, 121; Stadium, 250, 251, 299, 320; Stoa of Attalus, 292, Pl. XXVIII; Syracusan Treasury (earlier), 78, *116–117, 205n; (later), 205; Temple of Apollo (Homeric), 38, 40; (primitive), 41; (fourth), xi, 71, 86; (fifth), xii, *91–92, 155, 170, 217; (sixth), 91, *217–218, 339, Pl. XXVIII; Temple of Athena Pronaea (first), 56n, 72–73, fig. 24; (second), 92, 338; (third), 217, 221; Theatre, Pl. XXVIII; Theban Treasury, 233; Tholos (earlier), 117, 205n, 234, Pl. XXIX; (later), 171n, 219, 234–236, Pls. LVII, LIX.
Demetrias (Pagasae), *369*; painted stelae, 328
Dendra, *347*; Aegean settlement, 3; chamber tombs, 7n, 27n
Der-el-Bahari (Egypt), columns, 56
Didyma, *377*; altar, 133; destroyed, 229; excavated, vii, xxii; smaller anta capitals, 133n; Statue of Apollo, 233; Temple of Apollo (earlier), 88, *133–134, 137, 224, Pl. XXXI; (later), 103n, 106, 170, 222n, 227, *229–233, 235n, 236, 259, 271, 274, 280, 283, 340, figs, 83, 84, Pls. LV, LVI, LVII, LVIII
Dimini, *346*; Aegean settlement, 3; houses, 8
Diocaesarea, Temple of Zeus Olbius, 280
Djambazli (Cilicia), Heroum, 329
Dodona, 38, *369*
Dorians, xi, 2, 8n, 36, 37, 39, 40, 50, 58, 65, 322
Dorylaeum, Stele, 144
Dreros, *371*; Temple of Apollo Delphinius, 45, 46
Dura-Europus, *379*; city plan, 330
Dystus, *372*; houses, 211

Ecbatana (Persia), 233
Egypt, 2, *380–381*; annexed by Rome, 266; architectural motifs, 58, 59, 124–216, 328
Eleusis, *347, 363*; Aegean settlement, 3; Aegean temple, 24, 113n, 279n, fig. 10; destroyed, xii; excavated, vii, xxii; Porch of Philon, 169, 171n, *233, 241, fig. 73, Pl. LXVI; Precinct of Demeter, Pl. LXVI; Propylaea (Greater), 203n, *285, 326, Pl. LXVI; (Lesser), ix, 286–287, fig. 104, Pls. LXV, LXVII; Telesterion or Hall of the Mysteries (primitive), 38, 113n; (Peisistratid), 113; (transitional), 195; (Periclean), 148, *195–196, 211, 234, 243, 294, 295, fig. 73; Temple of Artemis Propylaea, 270, 339, Pl. LXVI: triumphal arches, 327n
Elis, *365*; Agora, 264; Corcyraean stoa, 264; Hellanodiceum, 264; Temple of Athena, 179; terracotta triglyphs, 53; Theatre, 299, 302, 304–306, Pl. LIX; Tomb of Oxylus, 53
Emporium, *385*
Ephesus, *375–376*; Agora, 332, fig. 122; Altar of Artemis, 40; Arcadiane street, 331, 332, 335; Baths, 321, 331; city plan, 331-333, fig. 122; colonised, 36, 123; Court of Verulanus, 331–332; excavated, xxi, xxiii; Gymnasia, 322n, 331–333; Library of Celsus, 293, 332; Nymphaeum ("Temple of Claudius"), 289, 332; Odeum, 332; Stadium, 320, 333; streets, 331–333; Temple of Artemis ('A'), 38, 40, 127; ('B'), 40, 41n, 127; ('C'), 47, 127; ('D,' Croesus), xii, 81, 82n, 91, 126n, *127–135, 137, 140, 166n, 193, 222–224, 339, figs. 48, 81, Pl. XXX; ('E,' Alexander), vii, xxi, 55n, 129, 130, *223–225, 227, 229, 231, 260n, 274–277, 279, 283, 333, 340, 389, fig. 81, Pls. LIV, LVI; Theatre, 299, 302, 303, 305, 306,

401

INDEX OF PLACES

308–309, 311, 304–317, 319, 332, fig. 113, Pl. LXIX
Epidaurus, *365–366*; excavated, xxii; Hotel (Katagogion), 251, fig, 91; Odeum, 319; Palaestra, 320, fig. 116; Propylaea (North), 235n, 286; Propylaea of Palaestra, 285, 320, fig. 116; Stadium, 250, 251; Statue of Asclepius, 218; Stoa, 240; Temple of Asclepius, 218, 258, 339; Temples of Aphrodite, Artemis, and Themis, 221; Theatre, 120n, 244–246, 248n, 298, 299, 303, 304, 306, 312, 317, 319, fig. 90, Pl. LXII; Tholos, 235–236, 286, fig. 85, Pl. LVIII
Eretria, *372*; coloniser, 37; Temple of Apollo Daphnephorus (earlier), 41; (later), 82n, 91; Theatre, 211n, 249, 298–300, 303–307, 312, 314, 317, 318, tumulus, 328
Erythrae, colonised, 36
Euboea, *372*
Euromus (Ayakli, Jackly), Temple of Zeus, 278n, 282, 340
Eutresis, *346*; houses, 5, 13n

Florence, François vase, 73

Gadara, colonnaded streets, 335
Gasi, Temple, 41
Galatia, xxi
Gauls, xii
Gela, 108, *383*; colonised, 37; destroyed, 112, 216; sarcophagi, 145; Temple, 112n
Gerasa, colonnaded streets, 336; monumental arch, 276n
Gla, *346*; Aegean settlement, 3; Palace, 21; Walls, 23n
Golgoi, Proto-Ionic capital, 60, Pl. XVIII
Gonnos, *369*; Temple of Athena Polias, 41
Gordium, *376*; simas, 64
Gortyna, *371*; curved building, 206; Odeum, 206; Temple of Apollo Pythius, 46, 269
Goths, xii
Gournia, *346*; Aegean settlement, 3; bricks, 12n; house tombs, 34; Megaron, 22; Palace 15
Granicus, Battle of the, 265

Hagia Marina, Aegean settlement, 3
Hagia Triada, *345*; grave circle, 29n; Megaron, 22; Palace, 13, 21n; stone rhyton, 13, Pl. VII
Hagios Onouphrios, grave circle, 29n
Halae, *369*
Halicarnassus, *376*; Agora, 263; Budrum castle, 258n; city plan, 263; colonised, 37; Mausoleum, xii, 128n, 220, 223, *257–261, 275, 330, 340, Pls. LV, LXIII; statue of Ares, 223 Temple of Ares, 223, 260n
Hemeroscopion, colonised, xvii, 37
Heraclea-on-the-Latmos, *377*; Bouleuterion, 244; city plan, 263
Heraclea Minoa, Temple of Aphrodite and Tomb of Minos, 28
Herakleion. *See* Candia
Herculaneum, Theatre, 309n, 310
Hermopolis, *381*; temple, 268; tombs, 328

Herulians, xii, 238, 285, 309n
Himera, *383*; Battle of, xi, 69, 101n, 104, 108; colonised, 37; destroyed, 112, 216; excavated, xxiii; Temple of Victory, 83n, *108–111, 338
Hipponium, *383*; Doric temple, 112n; Ionic temple, 138
Hissarlik. *See* Troy
Hittites, 36, 60, 121
Homolium, *369*; Temple, 53

Iassus, Theatre, 316, 317
Icaria, Precinct of Dionysus, 119
Ida (Mt.), Kamares cave, 24
Idalium, Proto-Ionic capital, 60
Ilium, 3
Ionia, Ionians, 36, 44, 50, 58; Revolt, xi, 123, 127, 135, 136
Isopata, Royal tomb, 28, 35n, 66
Issus, Battle of, 265
Istanbul Museum, 62n, 88n, 145n, 267n, 275n, 282n, *343*, fig, 21, Pls. XVIII, LXIII
Italy, *381–385*; colonisation, 37–38: explored xix–xxiii
Ithaca, Palace of Odysseus, 22

Jerusalem, Temple of Jehovah, 60, 61, 154n, 268–269
Juktas (Mt.), sanctuary, 24

Kanawat, colonnaded streets, 336
Karnak (Egypt), columns, 13n, 56
Karphi, Aegean settlement, 3; altar, 39
Katura (Syria), bicolumnar monument, 327n
Kavousi, tholos tombs, 65
Kefr Ruma (Syria), bicolumnar monument, 327n
Khorsabad, Palace of Sargon, 61
Khurka (Persia), Temple, 279
Korakou (Corinth), *347*; Aegean settlement, 3; houses, 6, 7, figs, 3, 4
Kourno, Temple (in-antis), 270; (peripteral), 268
Koumasa, grave circle, 29n

Labranda, Temple of Zeus, 278, 283n
Lagina, *377*; Temple of Hecate, 282
Lagon, Temple, 279
Lamptrae, Stele, 122
Langaza, tumulus, 328
Laodicea-ad-Lycum, Stadium, 320
Larisa-on-the-Hermos, *377*; excavated, vii, xxii; Palace, 121; simas, 64, 116n; Temple, 40, 43, 61–64, Pl. XVIII; temple model, 63
Lato, *371*
Lebadea, *369*; Temple of Zeus Basileus, xii, 41n 268
Lemnos, *372*; false site of Labyrinth, 124n; fountain-house models, 65; neolithic settlement, 4
Leontini, *383*; colonised, 37
Lepreum, Temple, 220
Leptis Magna, Basilica Severiana, 277n; Nymphaeum of Severus, 277n

INDEX OF PLACES

Lesbos, *372*; neolithic settlement, 4; Temple of Apollo Bresaeus, 88n, 271
Leucas, *346*: Aegean settlement, 3; cist graves, 26n
Lianokladi, Aegean settlement, 3; houses, 7
Limyra, rock-cut tombs, 67
Lindian Chronicle cited, 76n
Lindos, *373*; excavated, xxii; Propylon, 285; Temple of Athena, 76
Locri Epizephyrii, *383*; colonised, 37; Doric Temple (Casa Marafioti), 81n, *98, 138, fig. 39; Ionic Temple (Maraza, earlier), 45, 49; (later), 94, *136–138, 193, 339, fig. 49
London, British Museum, xx, xxi, 32n, 127n, 128n, 131n, 132n, 144n, 145n, 156n, 158n, 162n, 178n, 183n, 187n, 189n, 193n, 194n, 220n, 222n, 224n, 225n, 239n, 257n, 258n, 259n, 260n, 261n, 286n, 290n, 326n, *342–343*, figs. 23, Pls. XVI, XXX, XLVII, LV, LVI
Lusoi, *366*; Temple of Artemis, 270–271
Lycia, Lycians, 58, 123, *374*; Sarcophagus (see Sidon); tombs, 66–68, 144
Lycosura, *366*; Megaron, 287; Temple of Despoena, 268n, 269
Lydia, Lydians, xi, 36, 66, 123; tombs, 66

Macedonia, Macedonians, xii, xxi, 216, *346*, *370*
Maenace, colonised, 37
Magasa, house, fig. 1; Neolithic remains, 4n
Magnesia-ad-Maeandrum, 141, *377*; Agora, 334, fig. 124; Altar of Artemis Leucophryene, 274n, 288; excavated, xxii; Stadium, 320; Stoa, 292; Temple of Artemis Leucophryene (earlier), 40, 136, 274; (later), 260n, *274–276, 282, 340, fig. 99, Pl. LXV; Temple of Zeus Sosipolis and Tyche, *273, 276, 283, fig. 124; Theatre, 250, 298, 299, 303, 306, 308, 309, 312, 314, 315, 317
Mallia, *346*; Aegean settlement, 3; Palace, 15
Mallorca, Talayots, 13n
Mantinea, *366*; Doric capital, 121
Marathon, Battle of, xi, 69, 117, 123, 149, 150, 198, 211, 212; Tumulus, 212
Massilia, *385*; colonised, xvii, 37, 123; house, 7n
Medeibiyeh (Transjordan), Proto-Ionic capital, 60
Megalopolis, *366*; excavated, xxii; Statue of Apollo Epicurius, 156; Stoa of Philip, 264, 292; Theatre, 249–250, 298, 300n, 303, 307, 314, 316; Thersilion, 242–243, 250, 298, 303n, 307, fig. 89
Megara, coloniser, 37; Fountain-house of Theagenes, 118
Megara Hyblaea, *383*; colonised, 37; Temple, 112n, Votive capital, 144
Megiddo (Syria), incense stand, 61; Proto-Ionic capitals, 60
Melos (Phylakopi), *346*; Aegean settlement, 2, 3; house model, 6, 7n, Pl. IV; houses, 5, 7, 22; Palace, 22; Walls, 23n
Menidi, *347*; Aegean settlement, 3; ivories, 23; Tholos tomb, 33–34
Mesara, *346*; grave circles, 4, 29
Mesopotamia, 59
Messa, *372*; Temple of Aphrodite, 272, 274, 275, 340

Messene, *366*; Bouleuterion (Synedrion), 297; Stadium, 250; Temple (in-antis), 270; Temple of Artemis Limnatis, 280
Messenia, *347*, *366*
Metapontum, *383*; colonised, 37; excavated, xx; Tavole Paladine, 97, 338, Pl. XXIII; Temple of Apollo, 97, 98; Temple of Hera, 53; votive capital, 144
Midea, Aegean settlement, 3; walls, 23n
Miletus, *377*; Aegean settlement, 3; Altar of Poseidon (Monodendri), 140, fig. 51; altars (small), 141; Bouleuterion, 104n, 296–297, fig. 109; city plan, 212–214, 333–334, fig. 123; colonised, 36; coloniser, 37; destroyed, xi, 212; excavated, xxi, xxii; friezes from Hieronda and Karakeuy, 144; Heroum, 297, fig. 109; houses, 65, Monument (fountain-house?) of Laodice, 288–289; North Agora, 264, 333–334, fig. 123; Nymphaeum, 288; Propylon of Bouleuterion, 287, 297, fig. 109; South Agora, 334, fig. 123; Stadium, 250, 251; Stadium gate. 287; Stoas, 264; Temple at Kalabek-tepe, 134, 185n; Temple of Athena, 136, 137; Theatre, 306, 308, 314–317; tripods in Bouleuterion, 327
Minorca, Talayots, 13n
Minyans, xi, 2, 8n
Mochlos, *346*; Aegean settlement, 3; house tombs, 34
Molycrion, Temple of Poseidon, 169, 220
Mosul-Diarbekr, Kurdish houses, 5n
Munich Museum, 6n, 107n, *343*, Pl. IV
Mycenae, *347*, *366*; Aegean settlement, 2, 3; altar, 51n?; chamber tombs, 7n, 26–27, fig. 12; excavated, xxiv, 17n; gold temple plaque, 24; Grave circle, 26, fig. 11; intaglio, 7n; ivory tusk, 13n, 59; Lion Gate, 23, 56, 66, 67, fig. 11, Pls. XI, XII; Lion Tomb, 29; Palace 17–18, fig. 8; shaft graves, 25–26; silver rhyton, 22; Temple, 18, 50–51, 58; Theatre, 34n, 316, 317; Tholos tombs, 29–33; Tomb of Aegisthus, 29; Tomb of Agamemnon, 20n, 25n, 30–33, 56, fig. 13, Pls. XIII, XV, XVI; Tomb of Clytemnestra, 30–33, 34n, Pls. XIII, XIV; Tomb of the Genii, 30; walls of citadel, 23, 25, Pls. XI, XIV, walls of town, 23n
Mylasa, Temple of Roma and Augustus, 276–277; Tomb, 330, Pl. LXXI; votive column, 282
Myra, rock-cut tombs, 67, Pl. XIX; Theatre, 311, 316, 318
Mysia, 123
Mytilene, Proto-Ionic capital, 61–62; Theatre, 308
Myus, Temple of Apollo, *127, 140, 185n

Nape, Temple, 61–64
Naples, colonised, 37; merchants from, 322; Odeum, 319
Nashville (Tennessee), copy of Parthenon, 164n
Naucratis, *381*; colonised, 123; excavated, xxii; Temple of Apollo (earlier), *125–126, 131, 135, 137, 193, fig. 47; (later), 134
Nauplia, Aegean settlement, 3; chamber tombs, 7n; Museum, 32n

INDEX OF PLACES

Naxos, *373*; Aegean settlement, 3; Temple of Dionysus, 132, 139
Naxos (Sicily), colonised, 37
Neandria, *377*; Temple, 40, 45, *61-64, figs. 21, 22
Neapolis (Kavalla), *370*; Parthenon, 136, 137, 326
Nemea, *366*; excavated, xxii; Temple of Zeus, 165, 220, 339, Pl. LIII
New Pleuron, Theatre, 299, 303, 304, 312, 313, 316, 317
New York, Metropolitan Museum, 122n, 189n, 227n, *343*, Pl. XVIII
Niausta, tumulus, 328, *370*
Nicaea, city plan, 330
Nimrud, ivories, 60
Nippur, Hellenistic house, 325, *379*
Notium, *377*; Bouleuterion, 296
Nysa, *377*

Oeniadae, *370*; Baths, 322; Theatre, 211n, 249, 298, 299, 303, 304, 306, 312, 316
Oenoe, Battle of, 212
Olba, *378*; colonnaded streets, 335
Olbia, *371*; colonised, xvii; city plan, 212
Olympia, 366-367; Aegean settlement, 3; Altar of Zeus, 38, 39, 117; apsidal houses, 6, fig. 44; Bouleuterion, 41n, 65, 89n, 118-119, fig. 44; circular altar, 118; excavated, vii, xix, xxi, xxii; Exedra of Herodes Atticus, 288, fig. 44; Geloan Treasury, 115-116, figs. 44, 45; Gymnasium, 321, fig. 44; Heraeum (first), 47; (second), 47, *53-58, 77n, 86, 89, 151, 153, 156, 174, 277, 282, 337, figs. 19, 44, Pl. XVII; House of Oenomaus, 53; houses (Aegean), 6; Leonidaeum, 251, fig. 44; Megarian Treasury, 116; Messenian Victory Monument, 152n, 211-212; Metapontine Treasury, 116; Metroum, 220, 339, fig. 44; Palaestra, 320, fig. 44; Philippeum, 236, 238, 258, 284, figs. 44, 86; Precinct of Zeus, 113, fig. 44; Propylon of Gymnasium, 321; Selinuntine Treasury, 116; Shrines of Myron, 41n; Sicyonian Treasury, 116, 159; sima, 81n; Stadium, 250-251, 319, fig. 44; Stadium Gate, 287; Statue of Hermes, 55n; Statue of Zeus Olympius, 88, 149, 153, 154n, 183, 268; Stoa Poecile (Echo Colonnade), 240, fig. 44; Syracusan Treasury, 116; Temple of Zeus, 53, *151-153, 155, 156, 159, 162, 164, 165, 218, 220, 222, 268-269, 338, figs. 44, 55, Pl. XXXIV; Treasuries, 115, fig. 44; votive capital, 156n
Olynthus, *370*; city plan, 214, 330, fig. 78; excavated, vii, xxii; houses, 211, 252-253, 322-325, fig. 92; opaion tile, 151n
Orange, Theatre, 311n
Orchomenus (Arcadian), *367*; Bouleuterion, 206
Orchomenus (Boeotian), *346*; Aegean settlement, 3; houses, 5, 6, fig. 2; Palace, 21; Tholos tomb ("Treasury of Minyas"), 30-32, 34, Pl. XVI
Oropus, *363*; Temple of Amphiaraus, 269; Theatre, 299, 300, 302-306, 308, 313, 314, 316, fig. 112
Oxford, Ashmolean Museum, 133n

Paestum, *383-384*; Altars of Poseidon, 92, 117; Basilica, 56, *92-97, 100, 110, 144, 169, 337, figs. 36, 37, 60, Pl. XXIII; colonised, 37; excavated and studied, vii, xix-xx; Temple of Demeter, 82n, *92-98, 100, 194, 338, figs. 36, 38; Temple of Peace, 271, 279; Temple of Poseidon, 73n, *110-111, 163, 338, fig. 36, Pl. XXV
Pagasae, *369*; Temple, 221n. *See also* Demetrias
Palaikastro, *346-371*; Aegean settlement, 3; bricks, 12n; house tombs, 34; Temple of Dictaean Zeus, 46n, 64
Palatitza, Palace, 325-326, fig. 119; tumulus, 328
Palermo Museum, 81n, Pl. XXI
Palestine, 60
Pallantium, Temple, 53
Palmyra, colonnaded streets, 336; Corinthian capitals, 157n
Panticapaeum, *371*
Paphos, Temple of Aphrodite, 38
Paris, Louvre, 88n, 178n, 229n, 275n, Pls. LVI, LVIII
Paros, *373*; Aegean settlement, 3; apsidal shrine, 41n, 233-234; explored, xviii; houses, 6; Temple of Athena, 132-133, 139, 234n
Patara, Theatre, 316, 317
Patras, Odeum, 311n. 319
Pazarli, *378*; terracotta revetment, 64
Pella (Macedonian), tumulus, 328
Pella (Syrian), colonnaded streets, 336
Peloponnesian War, xi, xii, 155, 160, 190, 196, 204, 208, 216
Perachora, *365*; excavated, xxii; house models, 27n, 41-42, 65, Stoa, 240; Temple of Hera Acraea (first), 41; (second), 92; Temple of Hera Limenia, 43
Pergamum, *378*; Acropolis, 287, 331, fig. 121, Pl. LXXI; Altar of Zeus, 231, 274n, *287-288, 292, 331, Pls. LXVII, LXXI; Amphitheatre, 319; annexed by Rome, 266; Arsenal, 290; excavated, xxii; Corinthian temple, 321; Ionic temple on gymnasium terrace, 267n, 273n; Ionic temple on theatre terrace, 273n, 321; Library, 293, 331; Panegyric gymnasium, 321; Royal palaces, 282, 326, 331; Statue of Athena Parthenos, 293; Stoa of Athena Polias, 268n, 292, 293; Temple of Athena Polias, *267-268, 292, 331, 339; Temple of Dionysus, 269-270, 339; Temple of Hera Basileia, 270; Theatre, 210, 307, 309, 314-317, 319, 331, Pl. LXXI; Trajaneum, 282; Triple gymnasium, 321, 331
Perge, Stadium, 320; Theatre, 316, 317
Persepolis, Palace and Tomb of Darius, 62n, 64; Palace of Xerxes, 62n
Persia, Persians, xi, xxiv, 59, 69, 91, 123, 125, 127, 134n, 135n, 150, 195, 198, 216, 226, 262, 265; Persian Wars, 135, 147, 149, 198
Pessinus, Circus and Theatre, 320
Petsofa, sanctuary, 24
Phaestus, *345-346*; Aegean settlement, 3; Disk, 68n; Palace (earlier), 15; (later), 10n, 14-15, fig. 6, Pl. IX; Temple of Rhea, 46
Pharsalus, Battle of, 289
Phellus, rock-cut tombs, 67
Pherae, *370*
Philadelphia (Egypt), *381*

INDEX OF PLACES

Philae, Temple of Augustus, 271, 279, *381*
Philippi, *370*
Phlya, Telesterion, 196
Phocaea, colonised, 36; coloniser, 37
Phoenicia, Phoenicians, 37, 58–60
Phrygia, Phrygians, 36, 38, 66, 123; rock-cut tombs, 66
Pinara, rock-cut tombs, 67
Piraeus, *363*; Arsenal, *241–242, 290, fig. 88; city plan, 214; Ship-sheds, 242; Theatre, 300n, 302–304, 307, 312, 316, 317
Plataea, Battle of, xi, 69, 150, 187; Hotel (Katagogion), 251; Oath of, 150, 159; Temple of Athena Areia, 179; Tripod (*see* Delphi)
Platanos, grave circle, 29n
Pompeii, *384*; colonised, 37; Doric temple, 84–85; houses, 324, 325; incrustation style, 325; mural painting, 277n; Odeum (Teatro coperto), 319; opaion tile, 151n; Theatre (Teatro scoperto), 304, 307, 309n, 310
Pompeiopolis, colonnaded streets, 335
Poseidonia. *See* Paestum
Pozzuoli, merchants from, 322
Praesus, *371*; houses, 65; simas, 64; tholos tombs, 65
Priene, 273, *378*; Acropolis, 263; Agora, 263, 264, 334n; Agora for produce, 334; Altar of Athena Polias, 274, 288; city plan, 262–263, 330, fig. 96; Ecclesiasterion, 295–296, fig. 108; excavated xxi, xxii; houses, 322–323,325, fig. 117; opaion tile, 151n; Palaestra, 263, 320; Pedestals, 326, fig. 120; Propylaeum of Athena, 286, fig. 111; Stadium, 250, 263, 320; Statue of Athena Polias, 222; Stoas, 264, 292; Temple of Asclepius, 223; Temple of Athena Polias, 170, *221–223, 227, 229, 231, 258–260, 263, 271, 340, fig. 80, 111, Pl. LV; Theatre, 263, 298, 299, 301, 303, 305–308, 312–314, 317, 318, fig. 111, Pl. LXIX
Prinias, *371*; Temple 'A,' 45–47, 59, 64
Pseira, *346*; Aegean settlement, 3
Psychro, Dictaean cave, 24
Ptous (Mt.), *370*; Temple of Apollo, 218
Pydna, Battle of, 326; tumulus, 328
Pylos (Messenian), *347*; Aegean settlement, 3; excavated, xxiv; Palace of Nestor, 21; shaft graves, 25
Pylos (Triphylian), Aegean settlement, 3; Tholos tombs, 29, 34

Rakhmani, Aegean settlement, 3; houses, 6, 7
Ramath Rahel (Judea), relief, 60
Rhamnus, *363*; Statue of Nemesis, 182–183; Temple of Nemesis (earlier), 88, fig. 34; (later), 148, 149, 169, *181–183, 339
Rhegium, *384*, colonised, 37, 123
Rhodes, *373*; Aegean settlement, 3; city plan, 214; colonised, 37; commercial supremacy, 323
Rini, Aegean settlement, 3; house, 6
Rome, Romans, 265–266; Acanthus, column, 253n; Arch of Titus, 277n, 311; Cancellaria Palace, 311n; Capitolium, 280; Chemaera capital, 311n; Portico of Octavius, 157n; Terme Museum, 159n; Theatre of Pompey, 308, 310; Villa Albani collection, 183n

Russia (Crimea), *371*

Sagalassus, Temple of Antoninus Pius, 283, 340; Temple of Apollo Clarius, 278; Theatre, 309, 315–317
Sakje-Gozu (Syria), reliefs, 60
Salamis (Attica), Battle of, xi, 69, 123
Salamis (Cyprus), bracket capital, 290n
Salonica, Arch of Galerius, 327n
Samaria, *380*; colonnaded streets, 336; ivories, 60; Proto-Ionic capitals, 60
Samos, *373*; altars (small), 141; Altars of Hera, 39–40, 65, 124, 134, 136, 140; Aqueduct of Polycrates, 118; excavated, xxii, 75n; house model, 41, 65; neolithic settlement, 4; Propylon, 65; sarcophagus, 145; school of sculpture, 123; South building, 142; Statue of Hera, 40, 46; stelae, 144, fig. 54; Stoas, 134, 142; Temple of Hera (primitive), 40, 45–46, 48; (earlier, Rhoecus), 75, *124–125, 127–129, 136, 224; (later, Polycrates), 91, 106, 126n, *134–137, 170, 193, 229n, 271, 275, 276, 339; Temples, Roman, 136
Samothrace, *373*; Arsinoeum, 284; excavated, xxi; Doric temple (?), 221n; Ionic anta capital, 144; Ptolemaeum, 286; Temple of the Cabiri (earlier), 221, 236; (later), 41n, 269; Victory, 327
Sardis, *378*; captured by Ionians, 226; captured by Persians, 123; chamber tombs, 66; excavated, xxii; Lydian building, 227n; Temple of Artemis-Cybele, 38, 170, *225–229, 231, 242n, 259, 271, 274, 275, 283, 337n, 340, fig. 82, Pl. LIII; tumuli, 66
Sarmatian Costobocs, xii, 233, 285
Segesta, *384*; studied, xx; Temple, 112, 169, 170, 173, 179, 339, Pl. XXVII; Theatre, 303, 304, 307, 313, 314, 317, 319
Selinus, *384*; Acropolis, 45, 78, 122n, 330; city plan, 122n, 330; colonised, xi, 37; destroyed, xii, 100, 112, 122n, 216, 330n; excavated and studied, xx; Megaron of Acropolis, 45, 100n, fig. 17; Megalon of Demeter Malaphorus, 78, 83–84, fig. 30; Propylon of Demeter, 284–285; quarries, 78, 100; Shrine of Zeus Meilichius, 271; Temple 'A,' 78, 83n, *110, 338, fig. 28; Temple 'B,' 78, *270, fig. 28; Temple 'C,' xxiii, 78, *80–83, 86, 93, 98, 105, 110, 177, 201, 337, figs. 28, 29, Pl. XXI; Temple 'D,' 57, 78, *98–99, 122n, 337, fig. 28; Temple 'ER' (Hera), 78, 81, *109, 110, 338, fig. 28, Pl. XX; Temple 'FS,' 78, 81, *98–99, 101, 105, 337, fig. 28, Pl. XX; Temple 'GT' (Apollo), 78, 91, 93n, 96, *99–101, 109, 144, 160, 169–171, 175, 242n, 274, 338, fig. 28, Pl. XX; Temple 'O,' 78, *110, fig. 28; Temple 'X,' 78; Temple 'Y,' 78n, 80, 81; votive capitals, 144, 270n
Seriphos, Aegean settlement, 3
Sermeda (Syria), bicolumnar monument, 327n
Sesklo *346*; Aegean settlement, 3; houses, 5, 8
Shornakh (Kurdistan), rock-cut tombs, 279n
Sicily, *381–384*; colonisation, 37; exploration, xix–xx, xxiii. *See also* list of Sicilian sites above (p. 399)
Sicinos, Temple of Apollo, 271, *373*

405

INDEX OF PLACES

Sicyon, *367*; Bouleuterion, 243–244; columnar tombs, 255; Theatre, 299, 300, 302–306, 308, 312–314, 316, 317
Side, Theatre, 316, 317, 319
Sidon, *380*; Alexander Sarcophagus, 262; commercial supremacy, 36; Lycian Sarcophagus, 68n, 145; Mourning Women Sarcophagus, 145, 262, Pl. LXIII; Sarcophagi, 261–262; Satrap Sarcophagus, 145
Silaris, The (near Paestum), excavated, xxii; Temple of Hera (earlier), ★85–86, 95, 144, fig. 32; (later), ★96, 274
Sinope, colonised, xvii
Siphnos, Aegean settlement, 3
Sippara, relief of Nabu-apal-iddina, 61
Sitiá, Aegean settlement, 3; house, 6
Siva, grave circle, 29n
Smyrna, colonised, 36; sima, 64; Tomb of Tantalus, 66
Soli, *372*; Theatre, 317
Spain, *385*
Sparta, 69, *367*; Aegean settlement, 3; Altar of Artemis Orthia, 39; eacavated, xxii; lack of monumental quality, 149; Scias, 119; stelae, 65–66; supremacy, 216; temple model, 51n; Temple of Artemis Orthia, 45, 49; Temple of Athena Chalkioikos, 41n; Theatre, 307–308, 309n, 310, 314–317; votive capitals, 121, 144
Spata, Aegean settlement, 3; chamber tombs, 7n, 27
Stobi, Theatre, 310, 318
Strasbourg Library, 158n
Stratos, *370*; Temple of Zeus, 169, 220, 339
Sunium, *363–364*; Propylon, 205; Temple of Athena, 158, ★184, 185n, 186n; Temple of Poseidon (earlier), 107, 169, 338; (later), xxiii, 148, ★181–182, 338, Pls. III, XLIII; temporary shrine, 151
Susa, Persian capitals, 61n, 62, 64, 290n; Persian column bases, 229
Suweida (Syria), Tomb of Hamrath, 330
Sybaris, baths, 121; colonised, xvii, 37; destruction, 121; opaion tile, 151n
Syra, Aegean settlement, 3
Syracuse, 69, *384*; Altar of Athena, 118, 292; Altar of Zeus Eleutherius, 287; Amphitheatre, 319; colonised, xi, xvii, 37; defeats Athens, xii, 75, 112, 116, 257; supremacy, 75, 216; Temple of Apollo, ★75–78, 80, 84, 108, 275, 292, 337, figs. 26, 27; Temple of Artemis, 75n; Temple of Athena (earlier), 44–45; (later), 83n, ★108, 111n, 338, fig. 43; Temple of Zeus Olympius, ★75–78, 299n, 337, fig. 26; Theatre, 120n, 208, 210, 211n, 299, 303, 304, 309n, 310, 312, 314, 316, 317, 319; votive capitals, 144
Syria, *379*; corbels on column shafts, 277

Talati de Dalt (Minorca), column, 13n
Tamassos, Proto-Ionic capital, 60, Pl. XVIII
Tanagra, Battle of, 151n
Taormina, Odeum, 319; Temple of Serapis, 104n, ·270; Theatre, 309n, 310
Tarentum, *384–385*; acanthus on column shafts, 277n; colonised, 37; Temple, 84

Tarsus, *378*; "Tomb of Sardanapalus," 283
Tartessus, *385*
Taxiarchi, *370*; Temple. 88–89
Tegea, *367*; excavated xxiii; Temple of Athena Alea (earlier), xii, 53; (later), 151n, 165, 186n, ★217–220, 236, 258, 339, fig. 79, Pl. LVIII; votive capitals, 121, 144
Tell Halaf, reliefs, 60
Tell Tainat, relief, 60
Telmessus, rock-cut tombs, 67, Pl. XIX
Tenea, funerary "Apollo," 122
Tenos, exedra and sundial, 289n
Teos, *379*; excavated, xxi; Stoa, 292; Temple of Dionysus, 273n, 274, 340
Termessus, Corinthian temple (hexastyle), 284; Corinthian temple (tetrastyle), 284; Ionic temple, 278; Theatre, 309, 311, 315–317, 319; Tomb of Alcestas, 328
Thasos, *373*; Bouleuterion, 296; simas, 64; Theatre, 303
Thebes, *346, 370*; Aegean settlement, 3; Palace of Cadmus, 21, 58; supremacy, 216; Temple of Apollo Ismenius, 169, 218; Temple of Demeter Thesmophorus, 58
Thera, *374*; Aegean settlement, 3; houses, 5; Temple of Thea Basileia, 271; Theatre, 303, 304n, 312, 317
Thermi (Lesbos), *346*; houses, 7
Thermopylae, Battle of (first), xi; (second), xii; Tomb of Leonidas, 212
Thermum, *346, 370*; Aegean settlement, 3; houses, 6, fig. 14; Megaron 'A,' 6n, 42, fig. 14; Megaron 'B,' 41n, 42, 47–48, 51, fig. 14; Temple of Apollo, 51–53, 56, figs. 14, 18, Pl. XVII
Thespiae, Lion monument, 212; Theatre, 316
Thessaly, *346, 370*
Thoricus, *364*; Aegean settlement, 3; Stoa (Telesterion), 170, 196; Theatre, 208n, 210, 211n; Tholos tomb, 29, 32, 34
Thurii, city plan, 214
Tiryns, *347, 367*; Aegean settlement, 2, 3; Beehive palace, 16; cist graves, 25; Doric capital, 73; excavated, xxiv, 18n; gallery in walls, 24, Pl. XIV; houses, 16; Megaron (later), 21; Mural painting, 24; Palace, 18–21, 73, fig. 9, Pls. X, XI; Tholos tomb, 34; walls of citadel, 24, Pls. XI, XIV
Tolmeta, Hellenistic house, 253n
Tralles, Agora for produce, 334; Theatre, 309, 314
Tripoli, Arch of Marcus Aurelius, 277n
Troad, Stele from the, 144, fig. 54
Troezen, *368*
Trojan War, 2; Metopes, 177; Pediments, 105, 107, 218
Troy, *346, 379*; Aegean settlement, 3; captured by Achaeans, xi, 2; excavated, vii, xxiv, 16n, 17n; houses, 7, 8n; Palace, 16–17, 267, fig. 7; Temple of Apollo (Homeric), 40; Temple of Athena (Homeric), 40; (Hellenistic), 267; walls of citadel, 23
Trypiti, Neolithic remains, 4n
Trysa (Gjölbaschi), *379*; Heroum, 46, 256; rock-cut tombs, 67
Tsangli, Aegean settlement, 3; houses, 5

406

INDEX OF PERSONS

Tylissos, *346*; Aegean settlement, 3; Palace, 15
Tyndaris, Theatre, 304, 307, 314, 315, 318
Tyre, commercial supremacy, 36

Ugarit (Syria), *347*; Royal tombs, 35n

Vathia, tumulus, 328
Velanideza, Statue pedestal of Phaedimus, 122; tumulus, 122
Velia (Elea), *385*; colonised, 37; Temple, 112n
Verona, Porta de' Borsari, 311n, 328n
Volo, gold temple plaque, 24
Vouni (Cyprus), *372*; Palace, 121
Vourva, tumulus, 122

Washington (D.C.), Lincoln Memorial, 239n

Xanthus, *379*; excavated, xxi; gabled tombs, 144; Harpy Tomb, 144; Lion Tomb, 144; Nereid Monument, 46, 88n, *256–257, 259, 260, fig. 95; Tomb of Payava, 68, 144, fig. 23

Yasili-kaya (Anatolia), reliefs, 60

Zakro, Aegean settlement, 3; bricks, 12n
Zancle, colonised, 37
Zarzi (Kurdistan), rock-cut tomb, 279n
Zygouries, *347*; Aegean settlement, 3; houses, 5

B. PERSONS

Names of divinities refer back to sites in Index A (Places); rulers distinguished by cities or countries in parentheses; other individuals lack ethnics except when required for distinction.

Aahmes (Amasis) II (of Egypt), xi, 123, 125
Achilles, 220
Ada (of Halicarnassus), 220n, 258
Aegisthus (of Mycenae), 29
Aelian cited, 47n
Aemilius Paullus, Lucius, 326
Aeschylus, 120n, 207, 208, 210; cited, 49n, 129
Agamedes, 71, 86
Agamemnon (of Mycenae), vii, 20n, 25n, 26, 30–32, 56
Agatharchus, 208
Agathocles (of Syracuse), 44
Agathon, 217
Agoracritus, 149, 182
Agrippa, Marcus Vipsanius, 119n, 285, 319, 326
Ahab (of Israel), 60
Ahiram (of Byblus), 60
Alaric (the Goth), xii
Alcaeus, 61
Alcamenes, 149, 152n, 179, 180n, 181, 182, 184, 209n
Alcestas, 328
Alcibiades, 211
Alcmaeonidae, 141
Alexander the Great (of Macedonia), xii, 127, 179, 216, 217, 221, 223, 224, 236, 253, 262, 265
Alyattes (of Lydia), 66
Amazons and Greeks, 158, 177, 218, 259, 275, 276
Amyntas (of Macedonia), 236
Anaxagoras, 208
Andronicus Cyrrhestes, 289
Androsthenes, 217
Angelion, 133
Antalcidas, Peace of, 216
Antigonus I (of Macedonia), 217
Antigonus II Gonatas (of Macedonia), 290n, 291, 292
Antimachides, 91
Antiochus II (of Syria), 329
Antiochus III the Great (of Syria), 266, 326
Antiochus IV Epiphanes (of Syria), xii, 154n, 268, 280, 287, 296, 297

Antiochus of Megalopolis, 249
Antiphanes, 122
Antistates, 91
Antoninus Pius (of Rome), 203, 289
Apellis, 298n
Apollo, 38, 154, 159n, 231
Apteros, epithet of Athena Nike (Athens), 387
Arcesius, 280
Archermus, 133n
Archilochus, 189
Ariobarzanes II (of Cappadocia), 265
Aristaeneta, 235n
Aristeides, 149, 211
Aristophanes cited, 209n
Arsinoe II (of Egypt), 269, 284
Artemis, 38, 131n, 159n, 254
Artemisia (of Halicarnassus), 220n, 257, 261
Asclepius, 38, 235, 240
Astarte, 38, 322
Athena 38, 177, 180n, 187n; Acroterion, 108; Pediments, 107, 177, 181
Athenaeus cited, 298n
Atreus (of Mycenae), 30, fig. 13
Attalids (of Pergamum), 265, 282
Attalus I (of Pergamum), 292, 326, 331
Attalus II (of Pergamum), 270, 273n, 278
Augustus (of Rome), xii, 181, 183n, 276, 281
Aurelius, Marcus (of Rome), 270, 277n, 283, 285, 310
Avidius Quietus, 278

Bathycles, 141
Berenice II (of Egypt), 268
Bryaxis, 258
Byzes, 132n

Cadmus (of Thebes), 3, 58
Caesar, Julius, xii, 289
Callaeschrus, 91
Callias, 211
Callicrates, 148, 159, 160, 183, 185
Callimachus of Athens, 149, 157, 159, 188, 236

407

INDEX OF PERSONS

Callimachus of Cyrene cited, 153n
Canachus, 233
Caracalla (of Rome), 273n
Carpion, 159
Cecrops (of Athens), 191, 192, figs, 70, 71
Celsus, 293, 332
Centaurs and Lapiths, 152, 158, 177, 259, 330
Charmylus, 329
Chersiphron, 47n, 59, 127, 131, 224
Choerilus, 120n
Cicero cited, 136
Cimon, 180n, 195
Claudius (of Rome), 285, 289, 332n
Claudius Pulcher, Appius, 286
Cleisthenes, 91, 119, 207, 244
Clement of Alexandria cited, 49n
Cleopatra, Pl. LXX
Cleosthenes (of Syracuse), 75
Clytemnestra (of Mycenae), 30–33, 34n
Colotes, 149, 154
Coroebus, 195, 196n, 295
Cossutius, 280, 281
Craterus, 253, 262
Croesus (of Lydia), xi, 47, 123, 127
Cyrus (of Persia), xi

Damocopus, 210
Damophon, 154n, 268, 269
Daochus, 253
Daphnis, 229, 336
Darius I (of Persia), xi, 62n, 64, 123, 133, 229
Deinocrates, 224
Demeter, 38, 287
Demetrius of Ephesus, 224
Demetrius of Phalerum, xii, 240, 254, 328
Demetrius I Poliorcetes (of Macedonia), xii, 217, 290n, 298n
Democritus, 208
Demosthes cited, 237n, 260n, 298n; "lantern" of, 237n
Dexileos, 255
Diodorus Siculus cited, 28, 101n, 104, 105, 214n
Dionysius of Athens, 254
Dionysius I (of Syracuse), 216
Dionysus, 38; Frieze, 238; Priest, 318
Duris of Samos cited, 298n

Epicles, 75
Eumenes II (of Pergamum), 231, 268n, 278, 287, 292–293, 307, 309n, 326, 331
Eupalinus, 118
Eupolemus, 53, 149, 183
Eurydice (of Macedonia), 236
Eusebius cited, 40
Eustathius cited, 120n

Frontinus, cited, 49n

Galerius (of Rome), 327n
Gelon (of Syracuse), xi, 108, 110
Glauce, 118
Gods and Giants, 90, 105, 177, 288

Gorgon (Medusa), 45, 51, 52, 71, 74, 81, 82, 86, 133, 144, 231, Pl. LV

Hadrian (of Rome), 270, 274n, 277, 281, 283, 289, 293, 309n, 321, 327n
Hamrath, 330
Harpalus, 255
Harpocration cited, 298n
Hazael (of Damascus), 60
Hegeso, 254
Helios, Metope, 267
Hephaestus, 38, 180n
Hera, 38, 240
Heracleidae, 36
Heracles, 39, 253. Metopes, 81, 86, 152; Pediments, 71, 72
Heracles-Melcarth, 322
Hermes, 39
Hermogenes, 222, 272–275, 288, 292
Herodes Atticus, 239n, 250, 288, 319, 320
Herodotus cited, 47n, 91n, 124, 125, 134, 135, 151
Herostratus, 127
Hesychius cited, 120n
Hieron I (of Syracuse), 108, 210, 299n
Hieron II (of Syracuse), 287, 299
Hippias (of Athens), 91
Hippodamus, 214
Homer, xi, 40; cited, 7n, 17n, 20–22, 30n, 40
Hyginus cited, 49n

Ictinus, 148, 153, 154, 156, 159, 160, 167n, 195, 196, 233
Idrieus (of Halicarnassus), 220n, 258
Isidore of Seville cited, 49n

Laodice (of Syria), 288
Leochares, 223, 236, 258
Leon, 329
Leonidas of Naxos, 251
Leonidas (of Sparta), 212
Libon, 149, 151, 152, 154, 183
Livia (of Rome), Temple, 183n
Lucian cited, 49n, 284n
Lycurgus, 208n, 209n, 211n, 240, 244, 246, 248n, 249n, 250
Lysander, 212
Lysicrates, 237
Lysimachus (of Thrace), 267, 331

Martial cited, 261, 330
Mausolus (of Halicarnassus), xii, 220n, 257, 261, 326n
Megacles, 122
Menander, 299
Menecrates, 122
Menesthes, 273n, 276
Metagenes of Athens, 195, 196
Metagenes of Cnossus, 47n, 59, 127, 131, 224
Micciades, 133n
Micon, 149
Midas (of Phrygia), 66

408

INDEX OF PERSONS

Miltiades, 211
Minos (of Cnossus), xxiv, 3, 28
Minotaur, 12
Minyas (of Orchomenus), 30, 32
Mithridates VI Eupator (of Pontus), 226, 327, 329
Mnesicles, 148, 188, 199, 203
Mummius, Lucius, 154n, 266
Myron (of Sicyon), 41n

Nabu-apal-iddina (of Babylon), 61
Nannion, 298n
Nebuchadnezzar (of Babylon), 61
Nereid, 88n, 231, 256, 257, 290n, fig. 95, Pl. LVI
Nereis (of Syracuse), 299n
Nero (of Rome), 179, 309
Nestor (of Pylos), 21
Nicanor, 330
Nicias (I), 184, 209n; Peace of, xi, 183, 188
Nicias (II), 185n, 238, 286, 309n
Nicomedes, 168n
Niobids, 159n

Octavius, Cneius, 157n
Odysseus (of Ithaca), 22
Oenomaus (of Elis), 53, 152
Olympias (of Macedonia), 236
Oribasius cited, 330–331
Orophernes (of Cappadocia), 222, 274n
Oxylus (of Elis), 53

Paeonius of Ephesus, 224, 229
Paeonius of Mende, 149, 152
Panaenus, 149, 179
Panionius, epithet of Apollo, 88
Pantaenus, 293
Pausanias cited, 26, 30, 40n, 41n, 47n, 53, 54, 55n, 114, 117, 119, 124, 132n, 135n, 141, 142n, 151, 152n, 153–156, 157n, 163, 177–179, 180n, 181, 184, 190, 193, 198, 203, 210n, 211, 217, 218, 220, 234–236, 243, 253n, 255, 264, 287, 307, *341*
Payava, 68
Peisistratids (of Athens), 90–91, 280
Peisistratus (of Athens), xi, 90, 91, 113, 118, 133, 142, 198n
Peisistratus the Younger, 141
Pelops (of Elis), 152
Pericles, xi, xxiv, 147, 149, 208n, 211, 214, 216, 248n
Perseus (of Macedonia), 326
Phaedimus, 122
Phaedrus, 293n, 309
Phalaris, 329
Phidias, xi, 88, 148–149, 153, 154, 160, 176, 177n, 178, 183, 236n, 268
Philetaerus (of Pergamum), 326
Philip II (of Macedonia), xii, 236, 265
Philip V (of Macedonia), 170, 264, 291, 292
Philistis (of Syracuse), 299n
Philocles, 189
Philon of Byzantium cited, 224n

Philon of Eleusis, 171n, 233, 241
Phormis, 208
Photius cited, 120n
Pindar cited, 43n
Pirene, 118, 157n, 288
Pliny cited, xviii, 43n, 49n, 53, 124n, 125, 127–130, 224, 225, 258–261, 326n, *341*, 395
Plutarch cited, 49n, 207, 211
Pollis (of Syracuse), 75–76
Pollux cited, 129
Polyaenus, cited, 47n
Polybius cited, 105
Polycleitus the Elder, 149, 183
Polycleitus the Younger, 120n, 235, 236, 244, 246
Polycrates (of Samos), 118, 127, 134, 135
Polygnotus, 149, 179
Pompey, Gnaeus, 308, 310
Porinus, 91
Poseidon, 38, 177, 187n
Poseidon (Semitic), 322
Pratinas, 120n
Praxias, 217
Praxiteles, 55n, 258n, 284n
Protomedes, 253n
Prusias (of Bithynia), 326
Psammetichus I (of Egypt), 37
Ptolemy I Soter (of Egypt), xii, 217, 290n
Ptolemy II Philadelphus (of Egypt), 269, 286, 289, 326
Ptolemy III Euergetes (of Egypt), 268
Pythionice, 255
Pythius, 221, 222, 258

Rhea, 24, 38
Rhoecus, 124, 134, 140, 142
Roma, Shrine, 322

Samsi-Adad IV (of Assyria), 61n
Sardanapalus (of Assyria), 283
Sargon II (of Assyria), 61
Satyr, 311
Satyrus, 258, 260
Sciron, 289
Scopas, 218–220, 235, 236, 258
Seleucidae (of Syria), 265
Seleucus I Nicator (of Syria), xii, 233, 280, 330
Sennacherib (of Assyria). 61
Septimius Marcellinus, Flavius, 286
Septimius Severus (of Rome), 277n, 288n
Silenus, 309, 311
Smilis, 124n
Solomon (of Israel), 60, 61
Sophocles, 208
Sostratus, 289
Spintharus, 217
Strabo cited, 124, 136, 151, 229, 232, 330
Suidas cited, 120n, 298n
Sulla, Lucius Cornelius, 211, 241, 266, 280, 314n

Tantalus (of Lydia), 66
Tectaeus, 133
Telephus, 220

409

INDEX OF PERSONS

Theagenes (of Megara), 118
Themistocles, 91, 195, 196n
Theodorus of Phocaea, 219, 234–236
Theodorus of Samos, 41, 119, 124, 125, 127, 134
Theodosius I the Great (of Constantinople), xii
Theodotus, 218
Theron (of Acragas), 330
"Theseum architect," 148, 180, 181
Theseus, 3, 39; Metopes, 180n
Thespis, 119, 120n
Thothmes III (of Egypt), 13n
Thrasyllus, 239, 247n
Thrasymedes, 218
Thucydides cited, 149, 251
Timotheus, 218, 223, 258
Titus (of Rome), 277n, 311
Trajan (of Rome), 311
Triton, 71, 72, 138, 289
Troilus, 71n
Trophonius, 71, 86

Vedius, Antininus, Publius, 333

Verulanus, Claudius, 331–332
Vespasian (of Rome), 310
Victory. Acroteria, 133n, 139, 152, 182, 187, fig. 50, Pls. XXXII, XXXIV; Parapet, 178, 187; Statues, 152n, 211–212, 327
Vitruvius cited, xviii, 7n, 49n, 50n, 56, 65, 74, 87, 106, 124n, 127, 129, 130, 148, 157, 165–167, 170, 171, 173n, 178, 184, 192, 206, 209, 211, 222, 229, 234, 242n, 258, 263, 267, 270, 271, 273–276, 279–281, 287, 289, 301, 302n, 303, 308, 309, 313–315, 317, 320, 323, 325, 326n, 336, *341*, 388, 390, 392, 393, figs, 114, 115
Vulcan. *See* Hephaestus

Xenocles, 195, 196
Xenodorus, 217
Xenvares, 122
Xerxes I (of Persia), 62n, 113, 127, 133, 233

Zenon, 310
Zephyrus, 289
Zeus, 24, 38

C. SUBJECTS

These subjects all stem from the key entries "Construction" and "Design" (thus making it possible to study Greek architecture by the analytical method) and from "Historical evidence."

Abacus, 387; Aegean, 13, 56; Aeolic, 140; Corinthian, 158, 281, 289; Doric, 56, 72–73, 162; (with mouldings), 121, 218, 271, 292; Ionic, 59, 94, 130–131, 156; (absent), 133, 136, 137, 143, 157
Abutment, 387
Acanthus, 157–159, 212, 219, 228, 231, 238, 253, 254, 276–277, 279, 281, 287, 290, *351*, 387, figs, 84, 100, 101, Pls. XLVII, LVIII, LX, LXV
Acroterion, *351–352*, 387; bronze (sculpture), 152, Pl. XXXIV; (tripod), 152, Pl. XXXIV; gold, 108, 182, 187; marble (floral, palmette, volute), 72, 107, 113, 122, 140, 162, 182, 183, 201, 212, 235, 254, 276, figs. 46, 51, 54, 76, Pl. XX; (sculpture), 72, 86, 90, 107, 108, 117, 138, ,139, 182, 187, 201, 257, 330, figs. 50, 76, Pls. XXXII, XLIII, LXVII; poros, 125, fig. 33; terracotta (painted), 44, 52, 55; (modelled) 45, 52, 98, 138
Adytum, 49, 76, 80, 83, 84, 92, 96–98, 100, 109, 110, 155, 156, 217, 220, 227, 387, figs, 26, 28, 36, 56; with interior columns, 84, 86, 227, figs. 82
Agora, Aegean, 9; Greek, vii, 212, 214, 263–264, 289, 292, 333–334, *356*, 387, figs. 96, 122–125
Aisle, 92, 241, 387
Alabaster, 20; green, 32–33
Altar, Aegean, 19; Greek, 38–40, 43, 49, 51n, 65, 90, 117–118, 120, 124, 133, 134, 136, 140–142, 186, 190, 231, 274, 287–288, 292, 295, 297, 314, 331, figs. 51, 52, 70–71, 74, 77, 108, 111, 121, Pls. LXVII, LXXI
Ambulatory. 162–164, 220, 245, 247, 312, 314, 315, figs, 57, 67, 81; with column on axis, 156, 163, 180, figs, 56, 57, 67
Amphidistyle in-antis, 387, 396; fronts (Doric), 205, 270n (error), 284

Amphiprostyle, 387, 396; hexastyle fronts (Doric), 183, 199, 285, fig. 75, Pls. XLIII, XLVIII, LI, LXVI; (Ionic), 286; tetrastyle fronts (Doric), 270, 285; (Ionic), 185, 190, 286, figs. 68, 71, Pl. XLIV
Amphitheatre, 310, 315, 319
Anactoron, 387
Anathyrosis, 173, 387
Ancones, 112, 170, 171, 173, 205, 387, figs. 33, 76, 87, 95
Andron, 253, 325, 387
Andronitis, 323, 325
Angle capital, Doric, 162; Ionic, 64, 131, 133, 187, 193, 222–223, 231, 258, fig. 69, Pl. XLIX
Angle contraction, Doric, 53, 55, 86, 89, 92, 99, 101n, 108–111, 128, 161, 165, Pls. XXXV, XXXVIII, XXXIX, XLII, XLIII; (absent), 74, 76, 80, 81, 86, 88, 93, 98, 99, 184n, 221; (double, gradation), 80n, 108–112
Annulets, 73, 74, 77, 94, 116, 178, 387, Pls. XL, XLII
Anta, 387; Aegean, 6n, 7, 8, 17, 21, 22, 24, Pl. X; Doric, 55, 58, 70, 75, 88, 109, 150, 152, figs. 18, 87, Pls. XX, XXIX, L, LI; double, 203, 205n, 280, Pl. LI; Ionic, 134, 140n, 222, Pls. XXXII, XLV, LVII; of stele, 254; wood casing, 21, 55
Anta base, Aegean, 17, 19, 21, 22; Doric, 150; Ionic, 276, fig. 50, Pls. XIX, XXXII, XLV, LIII
Anta capital, Corinthian, 276; Doric, 71, Pls. XX, XXIX; Doric of Ionic type, 86, 94–95, 100, fig. 32; Ionic, 133, 137, 138n, 140, 141, 144, 185, 193, figs, 49, 50, Pls. XIX, XXXI, XXXII, XLV, XLVII; Ionic of sofa type, 144, 286n (error)
Antechamber, 231, 232

410

INDEX OF SUBJECTS

Antefix, 387; marble, 75, 116, 133, 159, 179, Pl. XL; (false, not opposite cover-tiles), 162, 238, 254, Pl. LIX; (on ridge), 387, fig. 72; (on top of flank sima, rampant), 72, 194, 217, 219-221, 235, figs. 72, 86, Pl. LIX; terracotta, 44, 55, 125, 134, fig. 20; (human masks), 52, 84, 134, Pl. XVII; (lion heads); 52; (on top of flank and raking sima), 84, fig. 31
Anthemion (Lotus-and-palmette), 59, 72, 75, 81, 82, 86, 90, 94, 96, 98, 126, 127, 131, 134, 137-140, 142, 159, 178, 179, 185n, 188, 193, 223, 231, 233, 276, 282, 387, figs, 29, 32, 49, Pls. XXXI, XXXII, XLVII, XLIX; with birds, 183
Anthology (Palatine) cited, 279n
Antithema, 387
Apophyge, 387, figs, 48, 101, Pls. XXX, XXXVII, XL, XLIX, LX
Apse, 268, 271, 288, 311, 387; polygonal, 7; segmental, 7, 89, 269
Apsidal plan, 6, 41-42, 47-48, 65, 89, 118-119, 233-234, figs, 3, 14, 44
Aqueduct, 118
Araeostyle, 273, 388, 392
Arch, 264, 293-295, 311, 320, 324, 325, 328, 388, fig. 107, Pl. LII; triumphal arch, 327
Architrave, 388; Aegean, 32, 33; Corinthian, 282n; Doric, 51, 74, 77, 78n, 80, 81, 95, 97, 116, 239, figs. 29, 38, Pls. XX, XXII, XL, XLII, LIX; (in courses), 102, figs. 25, 41; (internal, with mouldings), 111; (internal, with regulae and guttae), 107; (sculptured), 88, 271, fig. 33; (with fascias), 279, 293; (with Ionic mouldings), 92, 95, 96-98, 111, 186, 182, 267; (wood), 115; (wooden origin), 51, 55, fig. 20; Ionic, 64, 131, 133, 138, 139, 158, 186-187, 193, 203, 225, 229, 231, 275, Pls. XLIX, LV, LIX, LXV; (internal), 186-187, 203, fig. 66, Pl. L; (sculptured), 133, 257, fig. 95; (with astragals), 138, 272, 273; (with rosettes), 139, 193, 194, figs. 50, 72, Pls. XXXII, XLVI; (without fascias), 133, 139, 158, 184, 185, fig. 50, Pls. XXXII, XXXVII, XLIV; (wood), 125, 131n, 135, 142, 241; (wooden origin), 64
Archivolt, 264, 311, 388
Arena, 315, 318
Arrephoros, 193
Arris, 388, 391; Doric, 168, 169, figs. 37, 61, Pls. XX, XL, LIX; Ionic, 94, 125, 126, 130, 140, 143, fig. 47, Pl. XXX; on axis, 88, figs. 33, 48 (error); with astragal, 116
Arsenal, 205, 241-242, 290, figs. 88, 121
Ashlar masonry, 23n, 28, 32, 35n, 101, 170, 241, 255, 388, figs. 8, 75, Pls. XI, XV, XLV, XLVI, LI; in column, 101
Astragal, 388; Aegean, 13, 33, Pl. VIII; Greek, 56, 59, 74, 75, 78, 80, 92, 94, 121, 126, 130-132, 141, 156, 193, 238, 279, figs. 30, 47-49, 69, 100, Pls. XXX, LVIII; (countersunk), 74, 81, 116, fig. 29, Pl. XXI
Atlas, 388. See Telamon
Atrium, 324, 388
Attic, 388; external, 239, 260-261, 330, Pl. LXIII; space in roof, 106, 109, 111, 151-152n, 153, 159, 219, 270

Auditorium (Cavea, *Koilon*, Theatron), in Bouleuterion, 242-244, 295-297, fig. 109; in Ecclesiasterion, 295, fig. 108; in Odeum, 319; in Pnyx, 244; in Theatre, 120, 208n, 209, 244-247, 249, 250, 389, figs. 77, 90, 110, 111, 113-115, Pls. LXI, LXII, LXIX
Awning, 295, 319

Balteus, 388. See Baluster side
Baluster side, 130, 137, 193, 203, 229, 272, 275, 388, figs. 48, 69, Pls. XXX, XLIX
Barrel vault, 388. See Vault
Base, 388; Aegean, 7, 8n, 12-13, 17n, 18-19, 21, 22, 24, figs. 4, 5, Pls. VIII, XIII; Asiatic, 132, 136, 140, 222, 224, 225, 227, 230, 256, 272, 273, 276, 277, 282, 388, fig. 48, Pl. LIII; Asiatic and Attic in same temple, 230-231, 277, 282; Asiatic-Attic mixed, 230-231, 273; Attic, 185, 186, 192, 231, 274-277, 282, 388, fig. 72, Pls. XIX, XLIV, XLV, XLVIII, LX; Doric, 77, 101n, 103, 268, 269, 271, fig. 41; nondescript, 42, 46, 48, 51, 63, 142, 143, 156, 236, 279, fig. 86, Pls. XXXVII, LVI; Persian, 132 See also Anta base, Plinth, Scotia, Torus, Trochilus, Wall base
Basement storey, 85, 189, 240, 255, 258, 290, 293-294, 297, 351, figs. 107, 125, Pls. XLVI, LXIII, LXXI
Basilica, 206, 294, 388. See also Paestum (A)
Bastion, 9, 23, 186, 187, 198, 285, fig. 11, Pl. LI
Bath, Aegean, 10n, 12, 18, 20, fig. 5; Greek, 121, 251, 321-322, Pl. II
Bead-and-reel, 62, 75, 78, 82-83, 92, 94, 126, 130, 132, 138-140, 144, 162, 193, 272, 388, figs. 48, 51, 84, Pls. XXX, XXXI, XXXII, XXXIII, XLVII
Beam (ceiling), Aegean, 5, 7, 8, 12; Greek (marble), 158, 194, 203, fig. 66, Pls. XLVIII, L; (diagonal), 330, Pl. LXXI; (hollow), 176; (wood), 45, 46, 63-64, 77, 100, 158, 164, 194, 241-242, figs. 75, 88
Bed-moulding, 90, 111n, 112, 126, 179, 184, 201, 223n, 231, 267, 271, 388
Beehive house, 6, fig. 2; palace, 16; tomb
Belt course, 103, 199, 203, 268, 271, 276, 278, fig. 41
Bema, 24, 119, 244, 279n, fig. 10
Bench, 46, 48, 234
Bevelled joint, 173, 175, 203n
Bible cited, 60, 61, 287
Bibliography, *341-386*
Bibliotheca, 388. See Library
Bicolumnar monument, 326-327
Boar (Calydonian), 220
Bombardment, 160n, 199n, 239n
Book-cases, 293
Books, Architectural (ancient), 47n, 124, 127, 148, 159, 221, 222, 224, 234, 235, 258, 273, 280, See also Error, Vitruvius (B)
Bouleuterion, 65, 118-119, 206, 242-244, 295-297, 334, *356*, 388, figs. 44, 108, 109
Brace, 388
Braced beam, 105, 164, 194, 296, 388
Breccia (conglomerate), 388; grey (hard), 28, 29, 32, 33; red (hard), 272; (soft), 182, 184, 208n, 209n, 210n, 246n, 248

411

INDEX OF SUBJECTS

Brick, 388; burnt, 12n (error), 66, 236 (error), 268n, 269, 304, 307, 325; mud, 5, 12, 13n, 16, 17, 21, 32, 42, 43, 45, 47, 55, 58, 86, 121, 198, 244, 249, 252, 255, 304, figs. 2, 20. *See also* Half-timber

Bridge, Aegean, 9; in theatre, 246, 312

Bronze, acroterion, 152, 236, 289; attachments of doors, 328; attachments of sculpture, 139, 222; capitals (and attachments), 33, 55, 59, 143-144, 157n, 193, 238; casing of beams, 25; Corinthian bronze, 157n; empolion, 171n; evolution of, 2; grille, 119; nails, 32; pins, 171n; relief sculpture, 153; revetment, 30, 32, 41; rosette, 194; statue, 39, 152, 211, 212, 289

Bucranium, 277, 284, 286, *351*, 389, Pl. LXVII

Bull, 12, 254, fig. 105; heads, 231, 290, 292, Pl. LV

Buttress, 5, 16, 47, 48, 55, 270, 293; figs. 19, 56, Pl. XXXVI; diagonal, 156, 157n, 233, fig. 56

Cabling, 389

Canalis, 389; concave, 136, 141, 143, 327, Pls. XXXIII, XLIX, LV, LXV; convex, 62, 94, 133, 135-137, 140, 327, figs. 21, 48, 49, 51, Pls. XVIII, XXX; flat, 62, fig. 53, Pls. XVIII, XXXVII

Cantilever, 176, 389

Capital 389; Aegean (bracket), 13, 35, 59, Pl. VII; (Proto-Doric), 13, 23, 33, 35, 56, Pls. VIII, IX, XII, XIII; Aeolic, 61n, 140, 157, 293, 387, Pl. XXXIII; (origin), 59-61; (two-tiered), 140n (error); bracket, 290, fig. 105; Caryatid, 139, 193, Pls. XXXII, XLVI; Composite, 277, 311, 389, fig. 100; Corinthian 149, 157-159, 178, 188, 219, 232, 234-238, 279-284, 287, 289, 329-330, *350*, 389, figs. 84, 101, Pls. XXXVII, LVIII-LX; (origin), 140, 157; simplified, 289-290, 311;

Doric, 54-55, 72-74, 76-77, 80, 84-90, 94, 96, 97, 99, 101, 103-105, 116, 121, 122, 152, 155, 162, 169, 173, 178, 218, 268n, 270, 271, 290, 292, 297, 334, figs. 24, 25, 27, 29, 33, 37, 38, 41, Pls. XX, XXII, XL, LIX; (origin), 56; (with console), 141, fig. 52, Pl. XXXIII; Egyptian (campaniform), 56n, 157n; (lily), 59-60; (lotus-bud), 56n; (palm), 59; (Proto-Doric), 56; hexagonal, 287, Pl. LXV;

Ionic 94, 125-126, 130-131, 133, 135-137, 142-144, 156-157, 159, 184, 185, 187, 193, 202-203, 225, 226n, 228-229, 236, 256-257, 272-277, figs. 47-49, 53, 66, 69, Pls. XXX, XXXIII, XXXVII, XLIX, LV, LXV; (origin), 58-60; Persian, 61n, 62-64, 290n; Proto-Ionic, 59-63, 142, 143, fig. 21, Pl. XVIII; sculptured, 139, 231, 287, 290, 311. fig. 105, Pls. XXXII, LV, LXV; triangular, 288, Pl. III

Carceres, 389

Caryatid, 138-139, 141, 188, 189, 192, 193, 254, 296-297, *350*, 389, 394, figs. 50, 52, 72, 93, Pls. XXXII, XLV, XLVI

Catacomb, 328

Cauliculus, 219, 232, 236, 280, 281, 287, 330, 389, Pl. LVIII

Cavea, 389. *See* Auditorium

Cavetto, 389; Aegean, 33, 56; Greek, 185, 218, 225, 279; (carved with anthemion), 276; (Egyptian type), 75, 83, 84, 96, 116, 122, 141, 267, 271, figs. 30, 32, 45

Ceiling, Aegean, 28, 30-31, Pl. XVI; Greek (absent, exposing roof), 133, 183-184, 204-205, 206, 290; (marble or stone), 158, 163, 194, 201, 203, 219, 254, 257, 267, fig. 75, Pl. L; (wood), 55, 57, 63, 64, 70, 103, 106, 111, 151n, 152, 153, 158, 164, 190, 194, 204

Cella, 42, 49, 57, 70, 76, 80, 88, 89, 96, 98, 222, 279, 389; double, 89, 90, 150, 163, 164, 187, 189-190, 227, figs. 35, 57, 70-71, 81, 82; hypaethral (*see* Hypaethral); sunken, 220, 231-232, 267; with absence of interior columns, 63, 105, 111, 180, 182, figs. 26, 28, 36, 43, 68, 70-71, 80, 97, 98; with buttresses or engaged columns (Corinthian in Doric temple), 219, fig. 79; (Corinthian in Ionic temple), 232, figs. 83-84; Doric, 55, 103, 270-271, figs. 19, 40; (Ionic in Doric temple), 156, fig. 56, Pl. XXXVI; (primitive), 47, 48; with one row of interior columns (Aegean), 7n, 24, fig. 10; (Doric), 51, 92-93, 97, 98n, figs. 18, 36, Pl. XXIII; (Ionic), 63, 64, 142, fig. 22; (primitive), 45-46, 84, fig. 17; with two rows of interior columns (Corinthian), 283, fig. 102; (Corinthian in Doric temple), 220; (Doric), 53, 74, 86, 90, 92, 100, 106, 111, 150, 152-153, 163, 180, 183, 269, figs. 28, 35, 36, 42, 55, 57, 67, Pls. XXV, XXXIV; (Ionic), 125, 132, 134, 227, 275, figs. 81, 82, 99; Ionic in Doric temples; 218, 221; (primitive), 142n

Centring, arch or vault, 389; device for column drums, 171-172, fig. 61

Chalcotheca, 198n, 205, fig. 74

Chamber tomb, Aegean, 26-28, fig. 12. *See also* Rock-cut

Change of order, Doric to Corinthian, 91, 280; Doric to Ionic, 267n, 273; Ionic to Doric, 184, 221

Channel, 389

Chequer, 20, 44, 72

Chevron, 33, 72, 74, 134, fig. 25

Chimaera, 311

Choragic monument, 236-240, 288, figs. 77, 87, Pls. III, LIX, LX, LXI

Chronological list of Greek temples, facing 340

Chronological memoranda, xi-xii

Church (temple transformed), 108n, 109n, 111n, 160n, 179n, 188n, 194n, 271n, 336

Circular plan, Aegean, 4-6, 8n, 15, 16, 26, 28-34, figs. 11, 13; Greek, 41, 65, 66, 117-121, 133, 205, 206, 211n (error), 234-238, 284, 289, 322, 326, figs. 44, 85, 103, 119

Citadel, Aegean, 16n, 22

City block (size), 213-214

City plan, 122, 212-214, 262-264, 330-336, *356*, figs, 78, 96, 121-123

Clamp, 389, fig. 64; iron, 174-175, 181, 192, 235; lead, 138n, 175; wood, 175

Clerestorey, 196, 206

Clock, 289, 332, 389

Clock-tower, 289-290, Pl. LXVIII

412

INDEX OF SUBJECTS

Club-house, 206
Coffer, 389; ceiling (marble or stone), 158, 179, 194, 234, 257, 261, 267, 330, figs. 63, 66; (painted), 179, 254, 257; (sculptured), 261, 330; (wood), 194; cornice, 96, 279
Coin (as evidence), 178, 225n, 288n, 289n
Colonnade, 389
Colossal stone, Aegean, 32, Pls. XI, XII, XV; Greek, 99–100, 127n, 131, 132, 144, 194, 203, 225, 244; Lycian, 65, fig. 23
Coloured stone, Aegean, 13, 32–33
Column (brick), 13n, 304, 325
Column (limestone or marble), Acanthus, 253–254, 276, fig. 93; Aegean, 13n, 23, 32–33 *344–345*; Aeolic, 140, fig. 50; breaking forward, 311; choragic, 288, Pl. III; Corinthian, 234–238, 279–284, 329–330, Pls. XXXVI, LX, LXIV, LXXI; (Roman), 88; coupled, 42, 328;

Doric, 54, 72–74, 76–77, 80, 84–90, 92–94, 98–101, 106–112, 117, 121–122, 152, 155, 160–163, 168–169, 171–173, 199, 218–221, 267–271, 290–297, 303, 324, 334, figs. 24, 27, 33, 38, 41, 76, Pls. XXI–XXVII, XXIX, XXXIV–XXXV, XXXVIII–XXXIX, XLI–XLIII, XLVIII, LIII, LVII, LIX, LXX; double or elliptical, 288, 292–293, 325, 330; dwarf (Doric), 290, 308; Egyptian, 13n, 56, engaged or semi-detached, 33, 47, 56, 98, 99, 102, 103, 104n, 156, 189, 192, 219, 221, 236, 237, 240, 257, 267–271, 279n, 283, 284, 288, 290, 293, 297, 303, 304, 308, 309, 328, 330, 390, figs. 28, 36, 40, 41, 56, 79, 83, 84, 97, 105, Pls. XXXVI, XLVI, LIX–LX; higher toward centre, 167, 201n; inside other buildings, 65, 118, 119, 142, 195–196, 201–202, 204–206, 211, 234–236, 240–244, 291–295, 284, figs. 44 (B), 73, 75, 85, 88, 105, 106, 109, 116, 119, 124, Pl. L;

Ionic, 90, 94, 124–126, 128–131, 134–137, 142–143, 156–157, 164, 184–186, 192–193, 201–204, 206, 218–219, 222–231, 236, 240–241, 243, 251, 255, 256–259, 272–277, 284, 286, 292, 295, 296, 303, 326, figs. 72, 86, 95, Pls. XIX, XXXVI, XLIV–XLV, XLVIII, L, LIII, LXVII (*see also* Capital and Proportion, Ionic); Ionic in Doric buildings, 90, 94, 134, 156–157, 164, 185, 201–202, 204, 206, 221; Ionic on sarcophagi, 145, 262; nondescript, 241, 303; octagonal, 115; on axis (front), 7, 9, 14, 17, 24, 45, 46, 48, 51, 71–72, 84, 89, 92, 97, 98, 101, 113, 118, 125, 128, 131n, 134, 136, 137, 203, 259, figs. 4, 10, 18, 36, 40, 44 (B), 81, Pl. LXIII; (inside cella), 156, 163, 180, figs. 56, 57, 67, Pl. XXXVI; sepulchral, 122; thicker at corners (Corinthian), 282; (Doric), 106, 150, 160, 165 (absent, 112, 152, 165); (Ionic), 274–275; thicker on fronts (Doric), 73, 80, 89, 99 (west front only), 110, 111, 152, 155 (north front only), 165; thicker toward centre (Ionic), 125, 128, 135n, votive, 121, 143, 219, 326
Column (wood), Aegean, 4, 5, 7, 8, 10, 12, 13, 16, 19, 20, 33, Pls. VIII, IX; Doric, 51–56, 118, 206: Ionic, 142n

Columnae caelatae, 129–130, 133, 223–225, 231, 389, fig. 48, Pls. LIV, LVI
Compass, centre points for volutes, 225, 286
Conchoid of Nicomedes, 168n
Concrete, 283n, 389
Console, 132, 139, 141, 194, 257, 306, 389, Pls. XXXII, XXXIII, XLVII
Construction, *352*
Coping, 84, 199
Copper, introduction of, 1, 3
Copying buildings, 285
Corbel, 104n, 277, 389
Cornice, 389; coffered, 96, 279, fig. 38; Doric, 51, 71, 72. 81, 88, 98, 105, 115, 116, 201, 218, 267, 269, 279, figs. 25, 29, 31, 33, 39, 41, Pls. XX–XXI, XLII, LIX; (origin of), 50, 57, fig. 20, Pl. XVII; interior, 163, 179; Ionic, 127, 141, 158, Pl. XXXI; nondescript, 83, 92, figs, 30, 39; omitted under pediment, 96; raking, 81, 83–84, 90, 92, 96, 99, 113, 270, 273, 395, figs, 25, 30, 31, 33, 45, Pls. XX, XXXII, XL; terracotta casing, 51, 78, 81, 82n, 84, 115, figs. 25, 29, 31, 45; with rosettes, Pl. XXXII
Corona, 389; rosettes on face, 279
Cover-tile, 43–44, 116, 159, 390, figs, 16, 20, 45, Pl. XVII
Crepidoma, 390; high without steps, 117, Pl. XXIX; lowest step of different colour, 150, 180, 182; number of steps, (1), 90; (2), 53, 124, 127, figs. 19, 33; (3, normal), 91, 106, 142, 150, 155n, 180, 184, figs. 28 (C, ER, FS), 38, 42, 55–57, 67, 68, 72, 79, Pls. XXXIV, XXXV, XXXIX, XLIV, XLV; (4), 199, figs. 26 (Apollo), 28 (A, D), 75, Pls. XLIII, L; (5), 103, 270, 282, figs, 40–41; (7), 230, 276, fig. 83; (8), 274, fig. 99; (10), 134, 136; (11), 272, fig. 98; (14), 224, fig. 81
Cresting, 75, 81, 238, 279, fig. 29, Pl. LIX
Crowbar, 395
Cruciform plan, 204, fig. 75
Crypt, 278, 283n, 329
Cuckoo, 183
Cuneus (*Kerkis*), 245–247, 249, 299n, 317, 390, figs, 77, 90, 109, 113–115, Pls. LXI, LXII
Curtain, 154n, 156, 268, 298n, 309, 310n
Curvature (upward), 90, 150, 164, 166–167, 173, 201, 230, 273n, figs. 58, 59, 62; absent, 110n, 155, 166, 167, 199–201
Curved joint, 132
Cyclopean masonry, 22–24, 390, Pls. XI, XIV
Cyma recta, 75, 92, 96, 141, 142, 159, 185n, 204, 221, 229, 272, 390
Cyma reversa, 112, 130, 140, 141, 155, 157, 169, 179, 184, 185, 193, 194, 201, 223, 260n, 314, 390, 391
Cymatium, 390

Dado, 12, 34, 199, 236, 249, 269, 278, 295, 390, fig. 86
Decastyle, 390, 394, 397; peripteral (Corinthian), 280n (error), 283; (Ionic), 229, fig. 83; semiperipteral (Ionic), 184
Decatetrastyle, prostyle (Doric), 243, 390, **397**, fig. 89

413

INDEX OF SUBJECTS

Dentellation, 44
Dentils, 64, 68, 131, 138, 193, 220, 221, 223, 225, 233, 236, 251, 256, 260n, 271–273, 281, 288, 290, 303, 327, 334, 390, fig. 86, Pls. XLVI, LIV–LV, LIX, LXIII; below Doric mutules, 279, 297; in Doric cornice instead of mutules, 297; in raking cornice, 273, 297; omitted in Ionic, 139, 140, 184, 185, 193, Pls. XXXII, XXXVII, XLIV–XLV, XLVIII; origin of, 64, 67–68, fig. 23, Pl. XIX; sculptured, 231, Pl. LV; with modillions, 284
Derrick, 112, 173
DESIGN. *See* Arch and Vault, Bench, Books (Architectural), Building types, Ceiling, Change of order, Copying, Dimensions, Faults, Floor, Foot unit, Geometrical diagram, Levels, Lighting, Model, Module, Moulding, Optical refinement, Order, Orientation, Painting, Patterns, Pedestal, Pediment, Pier, Plan (shape), Podium, Preliminary plan, Proportion, Ramp, Ratio, Roof, Sculpture, Seat, Specifications, Stairway, Step, Superposed, Wall
Destruction (ancient), 2, 3, 17, 36, 40, 78, 80, 90–91, 112, 113, 142, 149, 185, 186n, 194n, 195, 198, 199n, 205n, 212, 226, 229, 233, 238, 243; (modern), 17n, 110n, 126n, 157n (error), 158n
Diastyle, 273, 390, 392
Diaulos, 390
Diazoma, 245, 247, 249, 317, 390, figs. 77, 90, 113
Die, 390
Dimensions in ancient units, Doric feet, 54–55, 72n, 99, 106, 107, 112, 150, 152, 153, 161, 162, 163n, 178, 183, 199, 202, 219, 241, 244, 246, 247, 249, 251, 268n, 287, 312n; false feet, 137n, 161n, 163n, 222n, 241n, 275n; Ionic feet, 137, 222–224, 227–229, 258–261, 263, 274, 275, 312n; reproduced in other buildings, 161, 162, 182, 183, 186, 188, 219, 220, 227, 229, 268, 312; Roman feet, 301, 303, 309; stadium length, 250–251
Dimensions in modern units, English feet, *see* Chronological Table; metres, 337–340
Diminution of column shaft, 390
Dipteral, 390; Corinthian, 280–283, fig. 102, Pl. LXIV; Doric, 91; Ionic, 91n (error), 125, 128, 133, 134, 224, 229, 258–259 (error), figs. 81, 83, Pls. LIV, LVII; Proto-Ionic (front only), 64
Distyle in-antis, 390, 394, 396; front (Aegean), 8, 17, 19, 21, 24, 28, fig. 9, Pl. X; (Corinthian), 280; (Doric), 41, 52, 78, 89, 92, 109, 117, 205, 270, figs. 28, 34, 77, 97, Pl. XXIX; (Ionic), 134, 138–140, 142, 273, 278, fig. 50, Pl. XXXII; in-antis inner porch (Doric), 88, 90, 109, 110, 128, 132, 218, figs, 26, 28, 36, 42, 43, 55, 56, 67, 79; (Ionic), 185, 276, figs. 80, 81, 98, 99. *See also* Amphidistyle
Distyle prostyle, front (Corinthian), 286, fig. 104; (Doric), 269, 289, Pl. LXVIII; (primitive), 43, fig. 15
Dodecastyle, 390, 394, 397; prostyle front (Doric), 196, 233, fig. 73, Pl. LXVI
Dog, 255; head, 218, 221

Dolphin, 20, 238, 290n
Dome, 390; corbelled (Aegean), 5, 28–34, figs. 2, 13, Pl. XIV; (Greek), 257, 390; rock-cut (Aegean), 15; semi-dome, 288
Domestic architecture. *See* Hotel, House, Palace
Door, *351*, figs, 86, 87; chryselephantine, 108; stone, 190, 328–329; wood, 328
Doorway, Aegean, 5, 10–11, 15, 20, 21, 27, 29, 32–34, figs. 5, 8, 13, Pl. XV; Greek, 46, 55, 58, 70, 100, 103, 132, 139, 164, 185, 190, 194, 196, 201, 205, 210, 227, 229, 231, 232, 240–241, 243, 248, 261, 286–287, 293–294, 306n, *351*, figs. 76, 86, Pls. XXXII, XLVII–XLVIII, LVII, LXXI; in attic space, 111; in theatre, 303, 308, 309, 311; lateral (cella), 155, 156n, 189, 219, 269, 271, figs. 56, 79; rear (cella), 107, 189, 269, 271, 278, fig. 42. *See also* Console, Gate, Jamb, Lintel, Ogee, Threshold
Doric leaf, 44, 52, 72, 75, 90, 179, 391, figs. 29, 39
Doric order, *349–350*, 390
Double façade colonnade, peripteral (Corinthian), 283; (Doric), 75, 80, 98, 110, 124n, figs. 26, 28; (Ionic), 277n (error); prostyle (Doric), 269
Dowel, 390; iron, 172n, 174–175; lead, 138n. *See also* Brace, Pins
Drafted margin, decorative, 155, 184, 271, 276, 311, figs. 51, 86; preliminary, 173, fig. 61, Pl. XLIV
Dressing of masonry. *See* Anathyrosis, Bevelled joint, Curved joint, Drafted margin, Joint dressing, Protective, Relieving margin, Setting devices
Dromos, 390; Aegean, 27–29, 32, 35n, figs. 12, 13
Drum, 390; in conical roof, 234, 235, fig. 86; of column, 54, 80, 84, 100–101, 106, 150, 151, 160, 162, 171–173, 217, 253, 387, figs. 61–62; sculptured, *see* Columnae caelatae

Earthquake, 22n, 78, 99, 151n, 153n, 154n, 217, 226, 229n, 253n, 268
Eaves, 390
Eaves tile, 44, 75, 134, 390
Ecclesiasterion, 295–296, 390, fig. 108
Echinus, 390; Aegean, 13, 33, 35, 56; Doric, 54, 56, 72–73, 84, 86, 89, 90, 94, 97, 105, 162, 169, 271; (carved with egg-and-dart), 292, 297, 334; (replaced by mouldings), 270; Ionic 62, 94, 125–126, 130, 135, 142–143, 185, 228, 275, figs. 47–49, 53, Pls. XXX, XXXIII, XLIX, LV, LXV; (absence), 157, 184, 231, 236, Pls. XXXVII, LV
Egg-and-dart, 62, 92, 94–96, 103, 112, 125–126, 130–134, 136, 138n, 139n, 141, 142, 179, 184, 185n, 193, 194, 201, 211, 257, 260n, 272n, 274n, 282, 292, 297, 334, 390, figs, 47–49, 51, 53, 69, 84, 100, Pls. XXX–XXXIII, XLVII, LV; carved with superposed relief, 132, 228–229
Egyptian bead, 134, fig. 45; capital, *see* Capital; circular houses, 4n; column, *see* Column; hypostyle hall, *see* Hypostyle hall; temple, 124–125; throat moulding, 44 (*see also* Cavetto)

414

INDEX OF SUBJECTS

Elevator, 301n, 306n, 307
Eleusinian limestone. See Limestone
Ellipse, 169, 391
Elliptical plan, Aegean, 6, 8n; Greek, 8n, 41, 65, 205
Empolion, 390, fig. 61; bronze, 171n; wood, 171–172
Engaged column, 390. See Column
Engraved setting line, 164, 171, 172n, 179, 199n
Enneastyle, 390, 394, 397; dipteral (Ionic, rear only), 125, 128, 131n, 134, 224; peripteral (Doric), 92, 97, fig. 36; prostyle (Doric), 113; pseudo-dipteral (Ionic), 259
Entablature, 390–391; Corinthian, 235, 238, 281, 283–284, 286, Pl. LIX; Doric, 51, 55–57, 71, 72, 76–77, 80–81, 87, 95–96, 98, 180, 182, 235, 268, 269, figs. 20, 25, 27, 33, 38, 39, 41, Pls. XVII, XX, XXV–XXVII, XXIX, XXXIV, XXXV, XXXVIII, XL, XLII, XLIII, LIX; (friezeless), 92, 221; (with blank frieze), 204, 239, fig. 87, Pl. LI; Doric on Corinthian columns, 271, 279, 287; Doric on Ionic columns, 279, 293, 329, 330, 334;
  Ionic (friezeless), 64, 66–68, 130, 131, 133, 138, 139, 193, 223, 225, 251, 256, 262, 288, 289, 303, 327, 334, fig. 95, Pls. XLVI, LIV, LV, LXIII, LXVII; (with frieze and no dentils) 139, 140, 158, 184, 185, 193, figs. 50, 72, Pls. XXXII, XXXVI, XXXVII, XLIV, XLV, XLVIII; (with frieze and dentils), 221, 223, 229, 231, 233, 236, 259–260, 271–275, 303, 327, fig. 86, Pls. LV, LVII, LIX, LXIII; Ionic on Doric columns, 92, 271, 334; mixed Doric-Ionic, 233, Pl. LXVII; wood, 51–52, 54–57, 64, 84, 115, 126, 135, fig. 20, Pl. XVII. See also Architrave, Cornice, Dentils, Frieze, Proportion, Soffit
Entasis, in column, 94, 156, 164, 168–169, 176, 391, figs, 38, 60, Pl. XXIII; in pier, 169; omitted in column, 89, 168; omitted in wall and anta, 169
Ephebeum (Ephebic exedra), 320
Epicranitis, 111, 193, 391, Pls. XLV, XLVII
Epinaos. See Opisthodomus
Episcenium, 210n, 297, 299, 301n, 304–307, 391, figs. 111, 112
Epistyle, 391. See Architrave
Error (in ancient authors) of date, 40n, 53, 54n, 101n, 117, 142n, 151n, 152n, 154, 155; of description, 218, 236, 264, 320n; of dimension, 128, 258n, 260; of omission, 229, 234, 273n
Eustyle, 273, 391, 392
Euthynteria, 391
Exedra, 212, 253, 295, 320, 322, 326, 329, 331, 391, figs. 44, 106, 108; colonnaded, 212, 253, 327; semicircular, 212, 253, 261n
Expense accounts, 160n, 171, 175, 189n, 194–195, 199n, 217, 218, 236, 298n, 299, 300, 301n, 305, 341
Explosion, 160n, 199n
Eye (of volute), 94, 133, 136, 137, 193, 225, 286, 391; absent, 130, 136, 140, 143

Faience, 4–5, Pl. IV
Fascia, 132, 133, 391
Fastening devices. See Brace, Centring, Clamp, Dowel, Empolion, Nails, Pins, Pour-channel, Tenon
Faults of design, 180, 296–297. See also Diagonal displacement, Moulding with inappropriate pattern
Fence (wood), 318
Festival, Delia, xi, 184n; Demetrieia, 298n; Olympia, see Olympiad; Panathenaea, xi, 71, 150n, 159, 177; Pythia, 299
Fillet, 391; between flutes, 135–137, 142, figs. 49, 66, 84, 100, Pls. XLIX, LV, LVIII, LX, LXV; (on axis), 186n (error), fig. 49 (error); moulding, 229, 260n
Finial, 66, 236, 238, 284, 289, 391, fig. 86, Pls. LIX, LX, LXVIII. See also Acroterion
Fire, 2, 12n, 21, 22, 53, 91n, 105, 125, 127, 133, 135n, 150–151, 160, 183, 194, 198, 212, 220, 221, 223, 241, 284n, 310
Flat tile, 391. See Pan-tile
Fleuron, 158, 228, 391, fig. 101, Pls. LVIII, LX
Floor, painted (Aegean), 18, 20, Pl. X; pavement, 234, 235, 253, 316, fig. 67; wood, 290, 294. See also Gallery, Impluvium, Mosaic, Stage
Flutes on shaft, 391; Aegean, 32, 33, 35, Pl. XIII; Corinthian (20), 158, 219, 234, Pl. XXXVII; (24, normal), figs, 84, 100, Pls. LVIII, LX; Doric (16), 54, 72, 73, 77, 80, 88, 100, 111, 141, 182, figs. 24, 29, 33, Pl. XLIII; (18), 84–85, 88, 96: (20, normal), 54, 80, 111, etc., figs. 37, 38, 41, 61, 65, Pls. XX, XXII, XL, XLII, LIX; (24), 74, 84, 87, 111, fig. 25, Pl. XXV; (32), 116; (56?), 121; (spiral), 121; Ionic (16), 142; (18), 140; (20), 158, 218, Pl. XXXVII; (22), 140, 236; (24, normal), 135, 137, etc., figs. 49, 66, 69, Pls. XLIX, LV, LXV; (25), 126, fig. 47; (26), 59; (28), 94; (32), 136; (36), 143; (40), 125; 130, fig. 48, Pl. XXX; (44), 130, 143, Pl. XXXIII; (48), 130; Ionic on Doric shaft, 270, 271, 295; Ionic unfluted, 63, 277; lower third unfluted, 269, 280, 324, Pls. LXX, LXXI; profile, 169; tops with petals, 73, 74, 94, 96, 116, 121, 122, 141, 238, fig. 37, Pl. LX; tops with vases, 277. See also Arris, Fillet
Fluting, process, 77, 93, 94, 99–100, 112, 135, 170, 171, 173, 175–176, 182, fig. 65
Foot unit, 353; Doric, 54n, 72n, 161n, 163n, 195n, 199n, 241n, 247n, 257n, 275n; false, 73n, 124n, 137n, 161n, 163, 222n, 257n; Ionic, 55n, 94n, 137, 222n, 229n, 241n, 257n, 258n; stadium length, 250–251, 396
Fortification, Aegean, 22–26; absent in Crete, 9, 22; Greek, 357
Foundations, 52n, 53n, 63n, 71, 72n, 73, 89–91, 97, 98n, 101n, 110, 116n, 117, 120n, 124, 127, 128, 132n, 133, 134n, 135, 150, 160, 170, 182, 184, 185n, 196, 210n, 233, 248, 258–259, 280; charcoal, 127; sand, 267
Fountain-house, 65, 71n, 118, 288–289, 351, 356. See also Nymphaeum
Frieze, 391; Doric (triglyph), figs. 25, 29, 38, Pls. XX, XL, XLII, LIX; absent, 92, 271; cantilever construction, 176; without triglyphs, 204, 239, fig. 87, Pl. LI. See also Metope, Pentaglyph, Triglyph

415

INDEX OF SUBJECTS

Frieze (Ionic, continuous), absent, 64, 131, 133, 138, 139, 193, 223, 225, 251, 256, 259–260, 260 (error), 262, 272n (error), 288, 289, 303, 327, 334, fig. 95, Pls. XLVI, LIV, LV, LXIII, LXVII; cyma-profiled, 233, 235, 271, 286, 327; fluted vertically, 277; in Corinthian entablature, 235, 238, 281–284, 286, Pl. LIX; in Ionic entablature, 139, 140, 158, 184, 185, 192–193, 221, 223?, 229, 231, 233, 236, 259–260, 271–275, 277, 282, 286, 303, 327, figs, 50, 72, 86, Pls. XXXII, XXXVI, XXXVII, XLIV, XLV, XLVIII, LV, LVII, LIX, LXIII; pulvinated, 283–284; sculptured, 46–47, 51n?, 59, 74n?, 135n?, 139, 140, 144, 158, 185, 187, 192, 221n, 238, 259–260, 273–275, 282, 289, 326; sculptured in Doric temples, 90, 154n, 158, 163, 177, 178, 180, 182, Pl. XL; sculptured on podium, 68, 257, 259–260, 288, figs, 23, 95, Pls. LXIII, LXVII; sculptured on wall, 256, 257, 259; sima frieze, *see* Sima; with consoles, 277n; with floral borders, 231, 233; (on wall), 276, 278, 282, 283. *See also* Zophorus

Funerary architecture. *See* Sepulchral

Gable, 7, 19, 48, fig. 15, Pl. X. *See also* Pediment, Roof
Gallery, in arsenal, 241, fig. 88; in cella, 106, 153, 241, Pl. XXXIV; (omitted), 111, 156, 163; in house, 325, Pl. LXX; in stadium and hippodrome, 320; in theatre, 306, 317, fig. 113
Galley, 290; carved pedestal, 327
Gate, 23, 241; in grille, 48, 152, 153; parodos, 246n, 318–319. *See also* Propylaea
Geison, 51, 391
Geographical notes, xvii
Geometrical diagram, 193n, 161n, 234
Glass, beads, 193; paste, 20
Gneiss, 325
Goat, 254
Gold, 25, 131, 178, 182, 184n, 187. *See also* Chryselephantine
Grave, cist, 25; pit, 25, 31; shaft, 25–26, 65
Grave circle, 4, 26, 29, fig. 11
Greek foot. *See* Dimensions, Foot unit
Griffin, 10, 107, 182, 201, 232, 330, fig. 33, Pl. VII
Grille, 119, 152, 153, 163, 186, 189, 244, fig. 86
Groin, 391
Guildhall, 322
Guilloche, 44, 52, 58, 59, 78, 94, 193, 194, 227, 391, figs. 29, 45, Pl. XVII
Guttae, 50, 57, 71, 72, 74, 81, 84, 87, 117, 178, 391, figs, 25, 29, Pls. XXI, XL, XLII; absent, 88, 116, 117, 279, 293; continuous, 204, 239, fig. 87; on antefix and sima, 84, fig. 31; separately inserted, 159, 178, 221n. *See also* Trunnel
Gutter (in theatre), 208n, 244–246, 249, 250, 312–316; cover (wood), 249, 312
Gymnasium, 121, 251, 320–322, 391, fig. 44, Pl. II. *See also* Diaulos, Ephebeum, Palaestra, Xystus
Gynaeconitis, 323, 325, 391
Gypsum, 10, 12, 18, 28, 33

Hairpin plan. *See* Apsidal
Half-timber, 5, 45, 48, 198, fig. 8, Pls. IV, VIII, X

Hall of the Mysteries. *See* Telesterion
Harpy, 144
Hawksbeak, 71, 75, 90, 103, 141, 169, 179, 218, 390, 391
Heart-and-dart, 129–132, 134, 138, 140, 141, 179, 194, 391, fig. 48, Pls. XXXII, XLVII
Hearth, Aegean, 5, 7, 16, 18, 20, 22, figs. 3, 4, 7, 9, Pl. X; Greek, 43, 46, 49, 63, 253
Helix, 238, 391. *See* Volute
Hemicycle, 391
Henostyle in-antis, 391, 394, 396; front (Aegean), 7, 9, 14, 17, 24, figs. 4, 6, 10, Pl. V; (palace), 121; (primitive), 45, 46, inner porch (Doric), 51, fig. 18
Heptastyle, 392, 394, 396; peripteral (Doric), 84; (Ionic, rear only), 136, 137; (primitive), 48; pseudo-peripteral (Doric), 101, fig. 40
Heroum, 297, 329, figs. 44, 109
Hexastyle, 392, 394, 396; peripteral (Corinthian), 279, 280, 282, 283; (Doric), 53, 75, 78, 80, 86, 88–90, 92, 93, 97, 98, 105, 107–112, 150, 151, 155, 180, 182, 217–219, 267, 268, figs. 19, 26, 28, 33, 35, 36, 42, 43, 55, 56, 67, 79, Pls. XXV–XXVII, XXXIV, XXXV, XLI–XLII; (Ionic), 136, 137, 184, 222, 274, 276, 278; (primitive), 48, 49; (Proto-Ionic), 63?; prostyle front (Corinthian), 284; (Doric), 115, 221, 238, 269, 290 (*see also* Amphiprostyle); (Ionic), 133, 189, 190, 221n, figs. 70, 71, Pl. XLV; prostyle inner porch (Doric), 163, fig. 57; prostyle pavilion (Doric), 206, 248
Hieron, 113, 392
Hilani, 121
Hip roof, 392. *See* Roof (shape)
Hippodrome, 251, 320, 392. *See also* Carceres, Spina
HISTORICAL EVIDENCE. *See* Chronological list, Chronological memoranda, Coin, Destruction, Festival, Inscription, Olympiad, Potsherds, Vases: *see also* ancient authors cited (B)
Historical notes, xi–xii, 1–3, 36–38, 69, 123–124, 147, 216–217, 265–266
History of study of Greek architecture, xviii–xxiii
Horse, 45, 98, 330; se-horse, 138, 231, Pl. LVI; winged, 74, 231, 287. *See also* Centaurs (B), Quadriga, Statue (equestrian)
Horseshoe plan, in theatre, 245, 250, 316–317. *See also* Apsidal
Hotel, 251, figs, 44, 91
House, Aegean, 3–8, 17, 345, figs, 1–4, 14, Pl. IV; Greek, 41, 65, 121, 211, 252–253, 263, 322–325, 356, figs, 15, 92, 117, 118, Pl. LXX. *See also* Andron, Andronitis, Atrium, Gynaeconitis, Hearth, Megaron, Cecus, Palace, Pastas, Prodomus, Prostas, Prothyron, Reservoir, Thelamus
House tomb, Aegean, 4, 34
Hurricane, 189n, 280n
Hydra, 71
Hypaethral, 392; cella 106, 128?, 134, 229, 232; (erroneous), 100n, 106, 152n, 158n, 164, 220, 281, figs. 81?, 83; porch, 100?, 227, 242n
Hypaethron, 106. *See also* Hypaethral
Hyperbola, 162, 168n, 169

416

INDEX OF SUBJECTS

Hypostyle hall, Egyptian, 113, 125; Greek, 113, 211, 294–295, figs. 73, 89. *See also* Odeum, Telesterion
Hypotrachelium, 392. *See* Necking

Ikria (bleachers), 120, 209n, 249
Imbrex, 392. *See* Cover-tile
Impluvium, 128, 153, 235n (error), 290, 324, 325, 392, fig. 105
In-antis. *See* Amphidistyle, Distyle, Henostyle, Tetrastyle, Tristyle
Incision (necking), (1), 178, Pls. XL, XLII; (3) 80, 105, 155, fig. 29; (4) 90
Inclination, abacus, 166; absent in cross-wall, 166; anta, 166; column, 110, 150, 164–165, 172–173, fig. 62; door jamb, 21, 27, 32, 111, 166; volute plane, 131; wall, 165–166; window jamb, 166
Incrustation style, 325, 326
Inscription, 54, 55n, 68, 91n, 92, 117, 121, 127, 138n, 179, 180n, 184n, 185, 186n, 190n, 195n, 196n, 199n, 206, 219–220, 220n, 222, 226, 237n, 238n, 239, 240, 246, 253, 254, 258, 269, 273n, 274n, 276, 277, 278, 282, 297, 298n, 306n, 309n, 312n, 314n, 318n, 341, fig. 48, Pls. LIX, LXVII. *See also* Expense accounts, Numbers, Specifications
Interaxial, 392. *See* Intercolumniation
Intercolumniation, 392; perspective gradation, 212; unintentional irregularities, 80, 164; wider at centre (Corinthian), 282–284; (Doric), 75, 196, 199, 205, 285, 303, figs. 26, 27, 75, 76, Pls. XLVIII, LI; (Ionic), 124, 128, 135–137, 224, 227, 275–277, 303, figs. 81, 82, 99, 103, Pl. LIV; wider at corner (Ionic), 125, 128, 135n; wider on flanks (Doric), 73n, 93, 98, 99, 101, 109, 111; wider on fronts (Doric), 73n, 76, 77, 80, 89, 110, 150, 155; (Ionic), 125, 128, 224. *See also* Angle contraction, Araeostyle, Diastyle, Eustyle, Metriostyle, Pycnostyle, Systyle
Intrados, 392
Ionic foot. *See* Dimensions, Foot unit
Ionic influence on Doric, 73, 75, 86, 88, 90, 92, 94–98, 100, 103, 108, 122, 134, 141, 144, 147–148, 150, 156, 163, 164, 180, 201–202, 214–215, 221, 233, 270, 271
Ionic order, 350, 392. *See also* Base, Capital, Column, Entablature, Temple
Iron, beam, 104–105, 112, 176, 203, figs. 41, 66; brace, 388; clamp, 174–175, 181, 192, 235; dowel, 172n, 174–175; nails, 81, 84, 98, 115; pins, 75, 187
Ivory, relief, 13, 23n, 59, 60. *See also* Chryselephantine

Jamb (door), 23, 132, 139, 205n, 392; wood casing, 10, 21, 55, 201n (error)
Joint dressing, 138n, 172, 173

Katagogion, *See* Hotel
Kerkis, 299, 317. *See also* Cuneus
Koilon, 244, 316. *See also* Auditorium

Konistra, 315, 318. *See also* Arena
Kore (maiden) and Kouros (Apollo), 122, 124n, 138–139. *See also* Caryatid

L-shaped plan, 15, 21, 294
Labyrinth, 12, 124, 125, 235
Laconian tile. *See* Roof tile
Lacunaria, 392. *See* Coffer
Ladder, 106, 306
Lantern, *See* Opaion
Lathe, 125, 126n
Lead, clamp, 138n, 175; dowel, 138n; sealing, 174–175
Leaf, girdle (pendant), 60–62, 125–126, 140, 143, fig. 21, Pl. XVIII; laurel, 276; water-plant, 234, 238, 290; "wind-blown," 234. *See also* Acanthus, Doric leaf, Flutes
Leaf-and-dart. *See* Heart-and-dart
Lecythus, 254
Leopard (or Panther), 72, 75, 261
Lesche. *See* Club-house
Lesbian cyma, 129, 179, 392. *See also* Cyma reversa
Levels, adaptation to ground, 10–11, 18, 187, 189–191, 199, 201, 284–285, 295, figs. 70–72, 75, Pls. XLVI, L
Lewis, 174, 392, fig. 63
Library, 293, 325, 355–356, 388. *See also* Bibliotheca, Book-cases
Lifting devices, fig. 63. *See* Ancones, Derrick, Lewis, Loop cutting, Notch, Tongs
Light-court, 295, fig. 108. *See also* Light-well
Lighthouse, 289, Pl. LXVIII
Lighting, 151n, 158–159, 164, 353. *See also* Clerestorey, Doorway, Hypaethral, Light-court, Light-well, Opaion, Window
Light-well, 4, 10–12, 14, 15, fig. 5, Pl. VIII
Lily capital. *See* Capital (Egyptian)
Limestone, Acrocorinth, 315; black, 141, 142, 211, 212, 234, 329 (*see also* Eleusinian); common, 70, 78, 151, 153, 234, 236, 237 (*see also* Poros); Eleusinian, 179, 181, 192, 193, 199, 203, 233; hard (gray), 29, 154, 183, 217, 221; Kara, 90, 150
Lintel, 388, 392; nondescript, 303; frieze used as lintel, 306, fig. 112. *See also* Post-and-lintel
Lion, 33, 122, 212, 255, 257, 261, Pl. XII; head, 52, 90, 96, 98, 105, 109, 118, 132, 152, 178, 194, 217, 229n, 268n, 279, fig. 86, Pls. XVII, XXXI–XXXII, XXXIX–XL, LV, LIX; winged, 231
Lion Gate. *See* Mycenae (A)
Logeion, 299, 302n, 392
Loop cutting, 86, 174, fig. 63
Lotus, 122, 132, 134, 392, fig. 32
Lotus-and-bud, 58, 59, 126, fig. 46
Lotus-and-palmette. *See* Anthemion
Lotus-and-rosette, 94, fig. 36
Loutrophorus, 254
Louvre Museum, *See* Paris (A)
Lyre pattern, 223, 234

Maeander, 44, 74, 78, 86, 134, 178, 231, 234, 278, 392, figs. 25, 45

INDEX OF SUBJECTS

Magazine, Aegean, 9, 10, 15, 24, figs. 6, 9, Pls. VI, XIV; magazine hall, 104n

Marble, 70, 75, 89, 91, 109, 113, 116, 122, 127, 155, 158, 183, 198, 210, 217, 218, 220, 234, 236, 238, 269, 271, 300, 325, 326, 392; blue, 182; coloured (lack of evidence for), 326n; green, 6; Hymettian, 72, 237, 241, 311, 326; island, 90, 117, 212n; Naxian, 3, 39, 132n, 142; Parian, 3, 39, 91, 105, 110, 149, 151, 154n, 180, 182; Pentelic, 39, 149, 151, 153, 154n, 180, 185, 192, 199, 233, 237, 250, 268n, 320; red, 33; stucco, see Stucco

Margin. See Anathyrosis, Drafted, Relieving

Market-hall, 241, 293–294, figs. 107, 123, 125

Masonry. See Ashlar, Cyclopean, Dressing, Polygonal, Pseudo-isodomic, Rubble, Rusticated

Materials. See Brick, Concrete, Faience, Glass, Ivory, Metal, Mud, Papyrus, Plaster, Stone, Stucco, Terracotta, Wood.

Mausoleum, 257–261, 329–330, Pls. LXIII, LXXI

Medallion (with bust), 285, 327, 329

Megaron, 392; Aegean, 6n, 8, 11 (misnamed), 16, 17n, 18–22, 34, 58, 73n, 345, figs. 4, 7, 9, 14, Pl. X; Greek, 45, 78, 322–323, 325, fig. 17

Metal. See Bronze, Copper, Gold, Iron, Lead, Silver

Metope, 392, figs. 25, 39; carved with bucranium, 287, Pl. LXVII; carved with rosette, 235, 287, Pl. LXVII; horizontal oblong, 50. 51, 77–78, 80, 84, 117, 118, 292, fig. 27; marble in poros frieze, 71, 72, 178, 199n, 238, Pl. XX; narrow, 80, 81, fig. 29; origin of, 52, 57, 392; painted terracotta, 51–53, 57, fig. 20, Pl. XVII; sculptured, 51, 72, 80, 86, 88, 96, 99, 105n (error), 109, 117, 151, 152, 159, 177, 180–183, 218, 219, 234, 267, 279, 351, fig. 33, Pls. XXI, XXIX, XXXV, XXXVIII–XL, XLII, LVII, LIX; Vitruvian theory of corner half-metope, 271; widened at corner, 88, 90, 95, 96; wider towards centre (gradation), 162

Metriostyle, 273, 392

Metrology. See Foot unit

Metropolitan Museum. See New York (A)

Military architecture. See Arsenal, Bastion, Chalcotheca, Citadel, Fortification, Ship-shed

Model, 352; capital, 156, 235, Pl. LVIII; house or temple (Aegean), 4–6, 24, Pl. IV; (primitive), 41–43, 46, 51n, 63, 65, fig. 15; sculpture, 107n; temple, 185, 186

Modillion, 279, 284, 290, 392

Module, 393

Monolithic, 393; arch, 311; column (Corinthian), 280, 289; (Doric), 54, 75, 76, 80, 89, 100, 106, 186, 270; (Ionic), 142, 186; door jamb, 23, 132, 139; entablature, 271; pier, 186, 203; roof, 238

Monopteral, 393; circular, 284, fig. 103; rectangular, 116n (error?), 269

Mosaic (floor), 253, 325, 326, 332

Moulding, 351, 393; curves of, 169; with inappropriate pattern, 127, 140, 185n; with related pattern, 179

Mud, for roof, 7n, 159, 242, fig. 20. See also Brick, Half-timber, Wattle-and-daub

Mural painting, Aegean, 5, 9–13, 17, 20, 24; Greek, 179, 180, 198, 203, 210, 240

Museums (modern). See Alexandria, Athens, Berlin, Boston, Cambridge, Candia, Carlsruhe, Copenhagen, Delphi, Florence, Istanbul, London, Munich, Nauplia, New York, Oxford, Palermo, Paris, Rome (A)

Music hall. See Odeum

Mutule, 393; absence of, 115, 271, 297; alternating, 71, 81, 87, 99, 117, figs. 25, 29, Pls. XX, XXI; countersunk, 271; horizontal (non-sloping), 267, 279; in raking cornice, 270; miniature, 98, fig. 39; origin of, 50, 51, 57, fig. 20; regular, 88, 99, 100, 105, 117, 178, fig. 33, Pls. XL, LIX

Nails, bronze, 32; iron, 81, 84, 98, 115

Naos, Neos, 389, 393. See also Cella, Hecatompedon

Naxian marble. See Marble

Necking, 393; Doric, 74, 77, 80, 86, 94, 116, 141, 292, figs. 25, 29; Ionic, 126, 131, 135, 136n, 193, 223, 277, figs. 47, 49, Pl. XLIX. See also Trachelium

Niche, 47, 55, 84, 156, 187, 212, 254, 271, 277, 278, 287, 311, figs. 19, 56; semicircular, 212, 308. See also Exedra

Notch for lifting, fig. 39

Numbers (inscribed), 52, 181n, 229, 248n, 284, 304n

Nymphaeum, 288, 289, 332, 393

Octagonal plan, 289–290, Pl. LXVIII

Octastyle, 393, 394, 396; dipteral (Corinthian), 280, fig. 102, Pl. LXIV; (Doric), 91; (Ionic), 91n (error), 124–125, 128, 134, 224, fig. 81, Pl. LIV; peripteral (Doric), 86, 160, 267, fig. 57, Pls. XXXV, XXXVIII, LI; (Proto-Ionic), 64; prostyle (Corinthian), 289; (Doric), 269; pseudo-peripteral (Corinthian), 282, 283; (Doric), 73–74, 78, 96, 99, fig. 28; (Ionic), 226–227, 272, 274, 276, 277, figs. 82, 98, 99

Octopus, 20

Odeum, 211, 319, 393

Oecus, 252, 322, 325, 393

Ogee, door enframement, 111; moulding, 133, 294, 393

Ogival barrel vault. See Vault

Ogival roof. See Roof

Olympiad, first, xi, 47; 78th, 151; 238th, 54; 293rd (last), xii

Opaion, 106, 113, 158n, 190, 195, 196, 206, 211, 243, 295, 393. See also Hypaethral

Opaion tile, 106, 151n, 159, 219

Opisthodomus, 393; Doric, 49, 51, 53, 54, 100, 109, 110, 218, 219, figs. 18, 19, 28 (A, ER, GT, O), 35, 36, 42, 43, 55–57, 67, 79; Ionic, 128, 222, 225, 227, figs. 80–82, 98–99; omitted, 88, 92, 93, 134, 218, 220, 232, 268, figs, 36 (Demeter), 83; The Opisthodomus, see Athens (A)

INDEX OF SUBJECTS

Opisthonaos. *See* Opisthodomus
Optical refinement, xxi, 164–165, *352–353*. *See also* Angle contraction, Column (higher, thicker), Curvature, Curves, Entasis, Inclination, Intercolumniation, Perspective
Orchestra, in Bouleuterion, 295–297, figs. 108–109; in Theatre, 120, 208, 209, 244, 246–247, 249, 300n, 301, 302n, 305n, 306–308, 312–316, 393, figs. 77, 90, 111, 112, 114, 115, Pls. LXII, LXIX; rectangular or trapezoidal, 120n, 210, 314; The Orchestra, *see* Athens (A)
Order, *349–350*, 393. *See also* Column, Entablature
Orientation, 40, 42, 49, 52, 91, 113, 117, 127, 132, 133, 136, 137, 140, 150n, 155, 180n, 186, 198, 204, 207, 209n, 213, 214, 218, 224, 252, 274, 279n, 322–324, 330–331, *353*, figs. 28, 44, 56, 74, 77, 78
Ornament, *See* Pattern
Orthostate, 55, 58, 70, 86, 220, 234, 268n, 393, fig. 88, Pls. XXXIX, XLV, XLVI
Ovolo, 52, 90, 92, 94, 95, 121, 126, 127, 130, 133, 137, 152, 162, 179, 182–185, 187, 193, 201, 206, 218, 223, 225, 260n, 269, 295, 393

Painting (on flat surfaces), in Pinacotheca, 203; on coffer, 257, on floor, *see* Plaster; on metope, 51–52; on panel, 298n, 303, 308; on pediment, 71; on podium, 318; on stele, 121, 122, 328, fig. 46; on wall, *see* Mural painting. *See also* Mosaic, Polychromy, Vases
Palace, Aegean, 8–22, 58, *345*, figs. 5–9, Pls. V–X; Greek, 325–326, figs. 119, 121. *See also* Bath, House, Stairway, Theatral area, Toilet room
Palaestra, 251, 320, 393, figs. 44, 96, 116, Pl. II
Palmette, 45, 58, 59, 62, 100, 121, 122, 125, 130, 132, 144, 158, 159, 162, 179, 212, 222, 228, 229, 231, 232, 238, 257, 280, 393, figs. 21, 32, 33, 46, 51, 54, 84, Pls. XXXVII, LVIII; circumscribed, 116n, 133, Pl. XXXI
Panathenaic festival, *see* Festival; frieze, 90, 158, 163, 177, 178, Pl. XL
Panhellenic congress, xi
Pan-tile, 43–44, 116, 159, 393, fig. 16
Papyrus (paper), 153n
Parabola, 167, 169, 222
Parapet, 10, 26, 92, 246n, 284, 293–295, 318, 329, 393, Pl. LXI; sculptured, 131–132, 178, 187, Pl. LI; sima, 44, 47, 131–132
Parascenium, 208n, 209n, 210n, 246, 248, 249, 298, 299, 303–307, 309–310, 393, figs. 77, 90; oblique, 304, 307, 393
Parastade, 393
Parodos, 120n, 208n, 209n, 248, 306, 307, 318–319, 393, figs. 77, 90, 114, 115; gate, 246n, 318–319, figs. 111, 112, Pl. LXII
Parotid, 230, 329, fig. 83, Pl. LVII
Partition. *See* Curtain, Door, Fence, Gate, Grille, Parapet, Screen, Wall
Pastas, 121, 252, 322, 323, 325, 393
Patera, 277, 284, 286n, 393
Patterns, *351–352*; inappropriate for mouldings, 127, 140, 185n; related to mouldings, 179
Pavilion, 206, 291, 292, 311

Pedestal, circular, 139, 211; for column, 130, 225, 227, 278–279, 284, Pls. LIII–LIV; for statue, 49, 53n, 121–122, 138, 139, 153, 164, 178, 181–184, 205, 211–212, 236, 253, 260–261, 269, 285, 286n, 301, 326, 327, fig. 50, Pls. XXXII, L; sculptured, 130, 153, 164, 178, 181–183, 225, 227, 278–279, 327, Pls. XXXIV, LIV; segmental or semicircular, 183, 236, 253; triangular, 211–212. *See also* Die, Podium
Pediment, 41–43, 45, 46, 51, 64, 212, 233, 243, 255, 292, 394, figs. 33, 76, Pls. XXV–XXVII, XLI–XLII, LXVI; half, 204; painted, 71; sculptured, 50, 71–75, 90, 91, 105, 107, 110, 117, 139, 151, 152, 154n, 159, 177–178, 181–183, 217–218, 220, 225, 257, 268n, 269, 283n, *351*, figs. 25, 76, 95, Pls. XX, XXXII, XXXIV, XXXVIII, segmental, 311; terracotta, 81–82. *See also* Acroterion, Cornice (raking), Sima (raking), Tympanum
Pentaglyph, 98, fig. 39
Pentagonal plan, 251
Pentastyle, 394, 396–397; peripteral (Doric), 51, fig. 18
Pentelic marble. *See* Marble
Periaktoi, 394
Peribolus, 394
Peripteral, 394, 396–397. *See* Decastyle, Dipteral, Double façade colonnade, Enneastyle, Heptastyle, Hexastyle, Octastyle, Pentastyle, Pseudo-dipteral, Pseudo-peripteral, Tetrastyle, Tripteral
Peristasis, 394. *See* Peristyle
Peristyle, 394; Aegean, 11, 15, 20, figs. 5, 6, 9; Greek, 47–49, 219, 220, 233, 258–259, 267, fig. 14 (*see also* Peripteral); (court), 251–253, 320–322, 329, 331, figs. 44 (L), 91, 109, 116; (house), 323–326, figs. 92, 118
Persian capital. *See* Capital
Perspective, 208, *352*; allowance for, 109, 131, 156, 199, 237, 304, 307; illusion, 162, 165, 212, 253, 254. *See also* Inclination
Phylakes, 299
Pier, 394; Aegean, 4, 5, 10, 14, 28; Greek, capital, 252, 326, fig. 120, Pl. LVIII, compound (with semicolumns), 264, 267–269, 271, 284, 290, 293, 303, 304, 325, figs. 105, 109; corner of peristyle, 145, 262, 268, 269, Pl. LXIII; double anta, 203, 205n, 280, Pl. LI; L-shaped, 163n; nondescript, 89; octagonal, 118, 240, 294; rectangular, 169, 183, 186, 203–204, 220, 239, 241, 252, 253, 320, figs. 68, 75, 87, 88, 108; square, 103, 118, 243, 286n (error), 294, 295, 330, figs. 40, 112
Pilaster, 394; Aegean, 28, 33; Greek, 102, 183, 212, 232, 240, 241, 283, 286n (error), 294, 297, figs. 40, 41, 83; capital, 232, fig. 41, Pl. LVIII. *See also* Anta
Pillar, 23, 394
Pinacotheca, 198n, 203, 204, 325, 394
Pinax, 299, 301n, 303, 394
Pins, bronze, 171n; iron, 75, 187; wood (pegs), 21, 57, 171
Pit grave. *See* Grave
Plan (shape), *See* Apsidal, Circular, Cruciform, Elliptical, Horseshoe, L-shaped, Octagonal, Pentagonal, Square, T-shaped, U-shaped

INDEX OF SUBJECTS

Plaster (painted), Aegean, 5, 12, 18, 20, 27
Plinth, 394; base, 129, 202, 222, 224, 227, 229, 236, 273–275, 277, 281, 282, 388; circular, 202, 231, 279; dodecagonal, 231, Pl. LVI; omitted, 225, 271, 273; sculptured, 231, Pl. LVI
Pnyx. *See* Athens (A)
Podium, 134, 136, 150, 189, 232, 237, 245–246, 256–258, 261, 272n, 276–279, 287–288, 308, 329, 330, 394, figs. 72, 95, Pls. XLVI LX, LXIII, LXVII, LXXI. *See also* Basement, Pedestal, Socle
Polos, 394; centring pin, 171–172, fig. 61; cylindrical headdress, 139, fig. 50, Pl. XXXII
Polychromy, 70–72, 99, 118, 139, 151, 178–179, 218, 238, 261–262, 328, 352; fig. 25, Pls. XX, XL; natural (dark *vs.* light stone), 141, 142, 150, 153, 179–182, 192, 199, 203, 211, 234, 272, 326, Pls. XLV, XLVIII
Polygonal masonry, 23n, 89, 120n, 186, 249, 255, 394
Polytriglyphal, 394; (3), 199, 205, 206, 268–271, 279, 284, 291, Pls. XLVIII, LI; (4), 270, 279
Pomegranate, 98, fig. 39
Porch, 394; Corinthian in Ionic temple, 276, 277; Ionic in Doric temple, 90, 94, 134, 221. *See also* Distyle, Henostyle, Tristyle in-antis; Hexastyle, Tetrastyle prostyle; Pronaos, Opisthodomus
Poros, 29, 70, 71, 89–91, 113, 121, 122, 125, 135, 151, 164, 170, 198, 217, 218, 220, 238, 299–300n, 394; "Poros Temple," 133. *See also* Limestone (common)
Porphyry, 32
Portico, 394. *See* Hilani, Pavilion, Peripteral
Post, 42, 43, 45–49, 84, 210, 252
Post-and-lintel system, 47, 284, 336
Posticum, 394. *See* Opisthodomus
Potsherds (as evidence), 25, 28n, 46, 47n, 53n, 89n, 134n, 150n, 180n, 210n. *See also* Vases
Pour-channel, 394
Preliminary plan, 93n, 162, 180, 182, 184–186, 190–192, 195–196, 204–205, 221, figs. 71, 75, 76
Private house *See* House
Prodomus, 394; Aegean, 6, 7, figs. 3, 4, 7, 9, 14; Greek, 42, 322–323
Proedria, 244–247, 248n, 249, 312, 314, 317–318, fig. iii, Pls. LX, LXI, LXIX. *See also* Throne
Pronaos, 21, 49, 394; aligned with third flank column, 88, 180, 182, figs. 56, 67; Corinthian, 283; (in Ionic temple), 276, 277; Doric, 57, 58, 72, 76, 88, 93, 98, 100, 109, 152, 162–163, 179, 180, 182, 183, 218, 219, 267, 277, figs. 18, 19, 26, 28, 34–36, 42, 43, 55–57, 67, 79, 97; enclosed, 80, 83, 98, 142, fig. 28 (C, FS); Ionic, 125, 128, 134, 222, 225, 227, 229, 231, 275, figs. 80–83, 98–99; (in Doric temple), 90, 93, 94, 134, 221, figs. 36 (Demeter), 70–71; omitted, 51, 86, 89
Proportion, 353; column (Corinthian), 281, 283n; (Doric), 50n, 56, 72–73, 76–77, 80, 84, 87, 92, 99, 102, 109, 110, 117, 152, 161–163, 180, 181n, 182, 183, 199, 214, 219, 220, 234n, 268, 270, 271; (Ionic), 50n, 130, 140n, 142, 143, 186, 192, 201, 222–224, 227–229, 258–259, 273–275, 279; entablature (Doric), 80–81, 87, 92, 180, 182, 235, 236, 268–270; (Ionic), 139, 223, 225, 259–260; façade (Doric), 161, 165; plan, 53, 72n, 74–76, 80, 88, 92, 96, 98, 100, 109, 155, 161, 180, 182, 218–220, 222, 259, 268, 272, 274, 275, 278, 301, 309, 313, figs. 114, 115

Propylaea, xi, xxiii, 81, 114–115, 198–205, 284–287, 297, 320, 321, 333, 334, 394, figs. 74–76, 104, Pls. XLVIII, L–LI
Propylaeum, 394
Propylon, 394; Aegean, 9, 14, 17–21, figs. 7, 9, Pls. V–VI; Greek, 65, 198, 284, figs. 44, 104, 109, 116, Pl. LXVI
Proscenium, 208n, 210n, 246n, 248n (error), 297–304, 305n, 306–309, 312–316, 394, figs. 90, 111, 112, Pl. LXIX; wood, 298–301, 314
Prostas, 323, 325, 394
Prostyle, 394, 396–397. *See also* Amphiprostyle, Decatetrastyle, Distyle, Dodecastyle, Double façade colonnade, Ennaestyle, Hexastyle, Octastyle, Tetrastyle
Protective strips, 173, 175n; surface, 173, 175, 182, 205, 220, 394, figs. 61, 65
Prothyron, 395
Proto-Doric column (Egyptian), *See* Column
Proto-Ionic capital. *See* Capital
Pry-cutting, 395
Prytaneum, 205, 395
Pseudo-dipteral, 395; Corinthian, 282, 283; Doric, 74, 92–93, 96, 100, 103, 233, fig. 28; Ionic, 227, 261, 272, 274, 276, 277, figs. 82, 98, 99
Pseudo-isodomic masonry, 71, 138, 140, 141, 218, 223, 269, 271, 273, 297, 326, 395, figs. 50, 51, Pls. L, LXXI
Pseudo-peripteral, 395; Corinthian, 283; Doric, 101, 257, figs. 40, 41
Pteroma, 80, 100, 180–182, 218, 395
Pteron, 258, 330, 395
Pulvinus, 395. *See* Baluster side
Purlin, 241, 395
Pycnostyle, 273, 392, 395
Pyramid, 257–261, 330, Pls. LXIII, LXXI

Quadriga, 81, 258, 260, 261, 285, 326, 395, Pl. LXIII
Quarry, 78, 100, 149, 171

Rafter, 50, 51, 57, 132, 159, 183, 204, 236, 242, 395, figs. 20, 75, 88; hip, 93n, 395, fig. 75; valley, 292
Raking, 395. *See* Cornice, Sima
Ram, head, 90, 113
Ramp, 106, 152, 198, 199, 120n, 285, 289, 395, figs. 42, 55, 79, 85, Pls. L–LI; in theatre, 246n, 304, 306, 318–319, figs. 90, 112
Ratio, 54–55, 72n, 103n, 137, 152, 161, 183, 186, 199, 202, 219, 222, 241, 244, 246, 257, 259–261, 272–275, 278, 301, 309, 313
Rebuilding and alteration, classical, 80, 105, 153, 154, 198 (*see also* Preliminary plan); Hellenistic, 52, 84, 112, 134n, 135, 142, 153–154n, 179, 184, 205, 211, 221, 231–233, 239, 246n, 248n, 249n, 267, 268, 271, 279, 299–309, 312–315, 317–319; Roman, 46, 84, 88, 105,

420

INDEX OF SUBJECTS

136, 140, 154n, 163n, 179, 181, 183n, 188n, 189, 194, 196n, 198, 201, 206, 221, 226, 229, 231, 233, 236, 238–239, 246n, 250, 267, 273n, 274n, 279, 281, 284n, 285–287, 292n, 293n, 294, 299n, 309–311, 315–316, 318, 319; mediaeval, 108n, 109n, 111n, 128n, 133n, 160n, 179n, 188n, 194n, 199n, 336; Renaissance, 108n; modern, xxiii, 3n, 80n, 105n, 108n, 112n, 117n, 154n, 160n, 179n, 181n, 186n, 188n, 199n, 257n, 289n
Reeding, 16, 395
Refinements. *See* Optical refinement
Regula, 87, 117, 178, 395, figs. 25, 29, 41, Pls. XXI, XL, XLII; continuous (with guttae), 204, 239, fig. 87, Pl. LI; double (omitting guttae), 279; on antefix, 84, fig. 31; on cornice, 84, fig. 31; origin, 51, 57, fig. 20; replaced by mouldings, 270; without guttae, 88, fig. 33; without triglyph above, 107, 163, 182, 239
Relief (sculpture), Aegean, 23, 25, 33; Hittite, 60; on stage front, 309; on stele, 121–122, 254; on throne, 141, 318n. *See also* Antefix, Architrave, *Columnae caelatae*, Frieze, Ivory, Metope, Parapet, Pedestal, Pediment, Polos, Sima
Relieving lintel, 33
Relieving margin, 173n, 395
Relieving triangle, 23, 29, 33, 34, 395, fig. 13, Pls. XI, XV
Religion, 38–39. *See also* Divinities (B)
Religious structures. *See* Altar, Heroum, Hieron, Peribolus, Propylaea, Sanctuary, Shrine, Stoa, Telesterion, Temenos, Temple, Thymele, Treasury, Votive monument
Renaissance, Ionic. 216, 255
Repair. *See* Rebuilding
Reservoir (cistern), 28n, 118, 190, 205, 294, 322, 324, 325
Respond, 396
Retaining or terrace wall, 120n, 207, 208n, 309, 357
Revetment, 395; marble, 139, 198, 201, 326n; terracotta, 44, 51, 70, 78, 81, 84, 95, 98, 115, figs. 29, 31, 45
Rhyton, 13, 22, 395, Pl. VII
Ridge beam, 7, 42, 45, 205, 206, 242, figs. 75, 88
Ridge cover-tile, 44
Ridge tile, 44
Rinceau, 217, 219, 221, 223, 231, 235, 236, 272, 273, 276, 395, Pls. LV, LIX, LXV
Rock-cut tomb, Aegean, 7n, 26–28, fig. 12; Lycian, 66–68, Pl. XIX; Lydian, 66; Phrygian, 66
Roman foot. *See* Dimensions
Roman looting of Greek art, 34, 159, 182, 183n, 218, 266, 280
Roof (shape), "Chinese," 52n, 82n, 91, 96, 132, fig. 38; conical, 205, 234–236, 284, 289–290, 319, 390, fig. 86, Pl. LXVIII (*see also* Drum); domical, 238, Pl. LXIX; flat, 4, 5, 7n (error), 17n (error), 20n (error), 34, 43n, 46, 47, Pls. IV, IX; gable, 4, 6, 7, 17, 19, 27, 48, 323, figs. 15, 88, 105, Pls. X, XXXIV (*see also* Gable, Pediment); hip, 50, 51, 71, 93n, 132 (error), 196 (error), 203–205, 211, 240, 295, 323, 336, 395, figs. 75–76, Pls. L–LI; ogival, 68, 144, 145, fig. 23; pyramidal, *see* Pyramid; umbrella, 242; unfinished, 103, 105. *See also* Awning, Hypaethral, Opaion
Roof construction, 45, 70, 105, 159, 241–242, 319, figs. 20, 88, Pl. XXXIV. *See also* Attic (space), Braced beam, Mud, Purlin, Rafter, Ridge beam, Roof tile, Shingle, Thatch, Truss
Roof tile, Aegean, 7n; Corinthian, 43–44, 52, 125, 152, 390, 391, fig. 16, Pl. XVII; imitation, 238, 289, 290, fig. 105, Pl. LIX; Ionian, 44; Laconian, 43, 55, 65, 390, 391, figs. 16, 20; marble (Corinthian), 70, 72, 75, 110, 132n, 133, 151, 158–159, 268n, figs. 76, 86, Pls. L–LI; rhomboidal, 205; scale-shaped, 238, 284, Pl. LIX; Sicilian, 44, 78, 116, figs. 16, 45; terracotta, 43, 70, 75, 132, 135, 196, 290, 352 (*see also* Corinthian, Ionian, Laconian, rhomboidal, Sicilian).
Rope pattern, 59, 132
Rosette, 27, 33, 35, 51, 52, 58, 59, 86, 122, 131, 136, 193, 194, 235, 238, 254, 267, 279, 286, 311, 316, 328, 395, figs. 25, 32, 54, Pls. XVI, XXX, XLVII, LX. *See also* Lotus-and-rosette
Rotunda. *See* Tholos
Rubble masonry, 5, 12, 21, 29, 53, 58, 151, 252, 269, 303
Rusticated masonry, 294, 311, fig. 107

Samian foot, 124n, 137n, 257n. *See also* Foot unit (false)
Sanctuary, cave, 24; open, 24
Sandstone, 70, 86, 94–96
Sarcophagus, 32, 34, 60, 68, 144–145, 261–262, 329, Pl. LXIII
Sarcophagus tomb, Lycian, 68, 256, fig. 23
Saw (for stone), 29
Scaenae frons, 308–311, 315, 320, fig. 113
Scale pattern, 121, 132, 137, 229, 231, 238, 284, fig. 49, Pls. LVI, LIX
Scamilli impares, 167, 170, 173n, fig. 59
Scene, 395
Scene building, 206, 208, 209, 244, 246–250, 297–315, figs. 77, 90, 110–115, Pl. LXII; wood, 208n, 249, 299, 305, 307–308
Scenery (theatre), 208, 210, 248, 306
Schist, 30, 40n
Scotia, 395; Doric capital, 54n, 56, 77, 80, 84, 86, 94, 97, 99, 105, 121, figs. 27, 29, 37; Doric cornice, 178; Ionic base, 129, 136, 185, 230, 231, 236, 388, fig. 48, Pl. LX
Screen, column or pier, 118, 288, 320, 322; wall, 99, 101–103, 153, 241, fig. 28 (FS); wood, 307
Sculpture. *See* Acroterion, Animal, Pediment, Relief, Statue, Stele
Seat, Aegean, 10, 20, Pl. VII; Greek, in Bouleuterion, 119, 206, 243–244, 295–297, figs. 108–109; in odeum, 211; in Propylaea, 100, 201; in stadium, 250, 320, Pl. LXII; in Telesterion, 113, 196, fig. 73; in theatre, 208, 209, 245, 247, 250, 316–318, figs. 77, 90, 110–115, Pls. LXI, LXII, LXIX. *See also* Bench, Exedra, *Ikria*, *Proedria*, Throne
Second-hand material, 52n, 80, 116n, 117, 124,

421

INDEX OF SUBJECTS

125, 149–150, 160, 162, 199n, 205n, 217, 233n, 238n, 248n, 249n, 286, 304n, 309n, 310

Secular architecture, *355–356*. *See* Administrative, Civic, Commercial Cultural, etc., Domestic, Military

Sepulchral structures, Aegean, 25–35, *345*, figs. 11–13, Pls. XIV–XV; Greek, 65–66, 121–122, 144–145, 212, 254–262, 327–330, *354*, figs. 46, 54, 94, 95, Pls. LXIII, LXXI; Lycian, 66–68, fig. 23, Pl. XIX; Lydian, 66; Phrygian, 66

Sequence of erection, 91, 99, 106, 109, 112, 135, 162, 170

Serpentine pattern, 86, 96, fig. 32

Setting devices (masonry). *See* Engraved setting line, Lifting devices, Pry-cutting, Shift-cutting

Shaft, *395*; with console or corbel, 277, 324; with tablet, 54, 277, 282. *See also* Apophyge, Arris, Cabling, Flutes, Incision, Reeding, Tapering

Shaft grave. *See* Grave

Shield, bronze, 59, 151n, 154n, 179, Pl. XXXIV; gold, 108; marble, 297, 327; terracotta, 52

Shift-cutting, *395*

Shingle, 43n

Ship-shed, 242, 290. *See also* Galley

Shops, 240–241, 292–294, 322, 332, 333, 335, figs. 106, 123–124. *See also* Market-hall

Shrine, Aegean, 24, Pl. IX; Greek, 151, 232, figs. 28, 70, 71, 83

Shutter boards, 294

Sicilian tile. *See* Roof tile

Silver, 22, 30n, 59, 64

Sima, 351, *395*; limestone, 105, 109, 112, 138, 267, fig. 30; (parapet sima), 64; marble, 72, 90, 116, 139, 140, 141, 151, 182, 183, 185, 187, 194, 204, 217–221, 225, 234–236, 259n, 272, 281, Pls. XXXI, LV; (parapet sima), 131–132; (pierced interstices), 193–194, 201; (raking), 72, 75, 90, 113, 159, 162, 219, 272, Pls. XX, XXXII, XL; sandstone, 96; terracotta, 44, 52, 75, 78, 84, 85, 90, 96, 279, Pl. XVII; (horizontal under pediment), 45, 78, 81–82, 116, fig. 45; (parapet sima), 44, 64, 116n; (pierced interstices), 81, fig. 29; (raking), 44, 134, 184, 196, 279, figs. 25, 31, 45. *See also* Water-spout

Siren, 254, 255, fig. 94

Skene, 120

Skenotheke, 208n, 210n, 307

Slaves, 194

Socle, *395*

Soffit, *396*

Specifications, 185, 241, 268, *341*

Sphinx, 52, 80, 98, 139, 143–144, fig. 50, Pl. XXXII

Spina, *396*

Spiral, 13, 27, 32, 33, 35, 58, 59, 132, 144, 234, fig. 25, Pls. IV, XVI. *See also Rinceau*, Volute

Square plan, 113, 119, 195–196, 206, 211, 243–244, 251, 289, 295–296, 320, 329, 330, figs. 73, 91, 108, 116

Stadium, 121, 250–251, 319–320, *396*, figs. 44, 96, 122, Pl. LXII

Stage, 210n, 297–299, 301, 302, 307–310, 315, figs. 113, 115, Pl. LXIX; rolling, 303n, 307–308, 314

Stairway, Aegean, 4, 5, 9, 11, 12, 14, 15, 17, 18, 28, figs. 5, 6, 9, 10, Pls. V, VIII, IX; Greek, 189, 240, 285, 287–289, 321, 325, 329, fig. 74, Pls. L, LXVII; (before temple), 136, 227, 230, 279, figs, 26, 28, 82, 83; (in Bouleuterion and theatre), 245–250, 295–297, 301n, 306n, 307, 309, 310, 314, 316, 317, figs. 77, 90, 108–113; (in palace), 121; (inside temple), 109, 111, 220, 231, 232, 267, 270n, 278, figs. 28, 36, 83, 97; (wooden), 153, fig. 55. *See also* Parotid, Step

Star, 96, 179

Statue, 133, 183–184, 185–186n, 223; acrolithic, 156, 387; bronze, 46, 47n, 124n, 149, 156, 179, 180n, 181, 233, 326; chryselephantine, 39, 88, 149, 153, 154n, 160, 163, 178, 183, 184, 218, 236, 268, 269, 281, 389, Pl. XXXIV; Daedalid, 76; equestrian, 205, 326, 327; *korai* and *kouroi*, 122, 124n, 138–139; marble, 55n, 88, 132, 182–183, 239, 284n, 293, 311, 330; wood and bronze, 222; xoanon, 39–41, 46, 141, 187, 397, fig. 52. *See also* Caryatid, Pediment, Quadriga, Telamon

Stele, *396*; Aegean, 25, 26, fig. 11; Greek, 65–66, 122, 144, 212, 254, 328, *351*, figs. 46, 54, 94

Step, undercut, 246; with nosing, 283; with sunken margin, 155, 184, figs. 41, 86, Pl. XLIV. *See also* Crepidoma, Ladder, Stairway, Stereobate, Stylobate

Stereobate, *396*

Stoa, 118, 134, 142, 196, 240–241, 247, 263, 264, 290–295, 333–334, *396*, figs. 44, 74, 77, 106, 123–125, Pl. XXVIII

Stone, earliest examples of temples in, 54, 63–64, 70–84; Greek timidity in use of, 77, 176

Storeroom. *See* Arsenal, Chalcotheca, Magazine, *Skenotheke*

Street, 212–214, 236, 262–263, 320, 332–333; colonnaded, 331–336

String course, 294

Stucco, 70, 78, 80, 100, 105, 122, 151, 178, 183, 198, 217, 244, 269, 271, 324, 325, 328, *396*; painted, 236. *See also* Incrustation style

Stylobate, 52–54, 75, 90, 103, 112, 117, 124, 127, 134, 150, 161–162, 176, 199, 221, 224, 227, 268n, *396*, figs. 33, 38, 41, 61, Pls. XXVI, XXXIX, XLII–XLV; absence, 51, 85, 227; curvature, *see* Curvature; internal, 156, 164, figs. 42, 56, 57, 67, Pl. XXXVI; interrupted by road, 166, 199. figs. 75–76, Pls. L–LI; jointing, 161–162, 184, 221, figs. 61, 67; sloping, 242

Sundial. *See* Clock

Superposed columns, external (both Doric), 240, 290, fig. 125; (Doric and Ionic), 288, 292; internal, 86, 100, 106, 111, 152, 153, 163, 180 183, 220, 236, Pls. XXV, XXXIV

Superposed storeys, Aegean, 4–5, 9, 10, 12, 14, 15, 18, 20, fig. 8, Pl. IV; Greek, 251, 290, 292–294, 310–311, *351*, figs. 113, 125, Pls. LXX, LXXI. *See also* Basement, Podium

Swag (Festoon), 277, *351*, 389, *396*

422

INDEX OF SUBJECTS

Synedrion, 297
Systyle, 273, 392, 396

T-shaped, plan, 184, 199, 238, 270, 329
Table monument, 122, 254
Tablet on column. *See* Shaft
Taenia, 51, 74, 81, 109, 178, 396, figs. 25, 29, 41, Pls. XL, XLII; moulded, 206, 269; replaced by mouldings, 218, 267
Tank, 10n, 241
Tapering, column shaft, 390; (downward), 13, 16, 19, 23, 32, 33, Pls. VIII-X, XII-XIII; (upward), 13, 56, 63, 72-73, 94, 115, figs. 24, 27, 33, 38, 41, 62, Pls. III, VII, XXII-XXVII, XXXIII-XXXV, XXXVII-XXXIX, XLI-XLIII, XLVIII, LIX-LX, LXIV; stele, fig. 46, Pl. XVIII; superposed columns, 106-107, 111; triglyph, 86; wall thickness, 165-166. *See also* Inclination (door, window)
Tegula, 396. *See* Pan-tile
Telamon, 101n, 103, 287, 388, 396, fig. 41
Telesterion, 113, 195-196, 233, 396, fig. 73
Temenos, 113, 197-198, 396, figs. 10, 44, 74, 77, Pls. XXVIII, LXVI
Template, 186
Temple, *354*; Aegean, 7n (error), 24, fig. 10; Corinthian, 279-284; Doric, 50-58, 70-113, 149-184, 217-221, 267-271: Ionic, 58-64, 124-138, 184-195, 221-233, 271-279; nondescript, 40-49, 88-89, 271; origin of, 20-21, 34-35, 40-49
Temple plan (external), 396. *See* In-antis, Monopteral, Peripteral, Peristyle, Prostyle, Pteroma, Pteron
Temple plan (internal). *See* Adytum, Aisle, Ambulatory, Antechamber, Cella, Opisthodomus, Porch, Pronaos, Stairway
Temple plan (irregular), 184, 187-192
Tenon, 158, 326
Terracotta, model, 41-43, 46, 51n, 65, fig. 15; pediment, 81-82; revetment, *see* Revetment; roof tile, *see* Roof tile; water-pipe, 118
Tetrastyle, 394, 396; in-antis front (Doric), 71, 198, 270, 322; in-antis inner porch (Doric), 283; (Ionic), fig. 83; peripteral (Doric), 269; (Ionic), 256, 278, fig. 95; (Proto-Ionic), 63; prostyle front (Corinthian), 279, 282, 284; (Doric), 72n, 85, 116, 142, 184, 270, figs. 77, 105 (error); (Ionic), 142, 189-191, 223, 232, 273, figs. 70, 71, 83, Pl. XLVIII; prostyle inner porch (Doric), 93, 100, 150, fig. 28 (GT); (Ionic), 90, 94, 227, 276, figs. 36 (Demeter), 70-71, 82
Thalamus, 6, 20, 325, 397
Thatch, 27n, 42, 48
Theatral area, 12, 14, fig. 6, Pls. VI, IX
Theatre, 119-120, 207-211, 244-250, 297-319, *344-345*, figs. 77, 90, 96, 110-115, 121, 122, Pls. XXVIII, LXI-LXII, LXIX, LXXI; used as amphitheatre, 310, 315, 318
Theatron, 120, 397. *See also* Auditorium
Thersilion. *See* Megalopolis (A)
Tholos, 117, 205, 234-236, 284, *356*, 397, figs. 44, 74, 85, 86, Pls. XXIX, LVII, LIX; tomb, 28-34, 65, fig. 13, Pls. xiv-xv; vault, 15, 257. *See also* Beehive

Threshold, 11, 29, 32, 132, 139, 199, 231, 269
Throne, 10, 141, 247, 314, 318, 329, figs. 111, 112, Pls. VII, LX; throne room, 9, 10, 15, 17, 20, 61
Thymele, 397
Thyromata, 210n, 301n, 304n, 306-308, 310, 397, figs. 111, 112
Tile, 397. *See* Roof tile
Timber. *See* Half-timber, Roof construction, Wood
Toilet room, 12, 121, fig. 5
Tomb, *See* Sepulchral structures
Tongs, 173-174, fig. 63
Tools. *See* Compass, Crowbar, Lathe, Lewis, Saw, *Scamilli impares*, Template, Tongs, Toothed chisel
Toothed chisel, 72, 138n
Torus, 126-129, 140, 185, 186, 192-193, 236, 245, 312, 388, 397; fluted, 126, 192, 222, 230, fig. 48; with guilloche, 183, 227; with leaves, 227, 231, 276, Pl. LVI
Tower, 22, 121, 285, 289-290, 299n, 304
Trachelium, 397
Transportation of stone, 160-161, 171
Treasury, Aeolic, 139-140, fig. 50; Doric, 71, 89, 91, 115-117, 205, 233, fig. 44, Pls. XXVIII-XXIX; Ionic, 138-139, fig. 50, Pl. XXXII. *See also* Mycenae, Orchomenus (A)
Triglyph, 397, figs. 25, 29, 33, 38, 41, Pls. XXI, XL, XLII, LIX; Aegean, 13, 19, 33, Pl. VII; always flush with architrave, 271; moulded, 81, 95, 97, 98, 116, 162, 183, 201, 218, 269; narrow on corner return, 116, 152; off-centred from column, 162; omitted between columns, 77, 84, 117, fig. 27; omitted in Doric entablature, 204, 239, fig. 87, Pl. LI; on altar or terrace, 117-118; origin, 50, 56, fig. 20; sculptured, 287, Pl. LXVII; spacing, *see* Intercolumniation, Metope, Polytriglyphal; tapering, 86; terracotta, 51-53; unrelated to column, 117, Pl. XXIX; wider at corner, 81; wider on front, 72, 73. *See also* Pentaglyph
Tripod, 152, 211, 236-238, 253-254, 277, 327, figs. 87, 93, Pls. XXXIV, LIX
Tripteral front, 397; Corinthian, 280, fig. 102; Ionic, 128, 134, 224, fig. 81
Tristyle in-antis, 394, 396, 397; front (Doric). 45, 71-72, 89, 98, 119, 203, fig. 75, Pl. L; inner porch (Doric), 88, 92, 128, fig. 36; (Ionic), 128, fig. 81
Trochilus, 126, 128-129, 136, 137, 140, 231, 397, fig. 48
Trunnel, 57, 397. *See* Guttae
Truss, 242, 295, 296; cantilever, 311, 319
Tumulus, Aegean, 28, 34; Greek, 65, 122, 212, 328; Lydian, 66
Tunnel (in theatre), 299, 300, 309, 314, 318, 319, fig. 110
Tympanum, 74, 225, 397, figs. 33, 38, Pls. XXV-XXVII, XXXVIII, XLII, XLVIII; poros behind marble sculpture, 90; recessed for sculpture, 92, 162

U-shaped plan, stadium, 250, 320; theatre, 247, 249, 317. *See also* Apsidal

423

INDEX OF SUBJECTS

Unfinished building, 91–92, 99–100, 103, 105, 107, 111, 112, 125, 132, 134–136, 150, 169–170, 182–184, 194–196, 199, 201, 203–205, 220–222, 225, 227–229, 231, 233, 244, 268, 273n, 280, 281, 283, 286, figs. 61, 76, Pls. XXVII, LIII, LVII–LVIII, LXVI: column or entablature (back), 234, 286n

Vases, *351*; black-figured (amphorae, hydriae), 118; François, 73, Laconian, 142n, lecythus, loutrophorus, 254; marble, 254, 255, 330; pattern in fluting, 277; red-figured, 286n; Rhodian, 116n, rhyton, 13, 22, 395, Pl. VII; Samian, 116n; silver, 22; South Italian, 210; steatite, 13. *See also* Potsherds
Vault, 397; barrel, 250, 288, 300n, 305n, 319, 320, 328, 329, 388, fig. 110; (intersecting), 328; (sloping), 231, 320, 321; corbelled (Aegean), 6, 24, 28, 35n, 66, Pl. XIV; (Greek), 42; (Lydian), 66; ogival, 66, 261n (error); rock-cut segmental, 118. *See also* Arch and Vault
Via, 81, 178, 397
Volcanic eruption, 5, 22n
Volute, 58–61, 122, 125, 134, 139–143, 156, 158, 193, 223, 225, 232, 234, 238, 286, 397, figs. 48, 49, 51, 53, 54, 84, 100, 101, Pls. XXX–XXXI, XXXVII, XLIX, LVIII, LX, LXV; canted, 156, 276, 277, 279, 292, 295, 303, 330, Pls. XXXVII, XLIX, LVIII, LX; cushion (sagging), 193, 222, 273, 275, figs. 48, 49, 53, 66, Pls. XXX, XXXVII, XLIX, LV; inclined, 131; uncarved, 142, 187, 295; vertical, 60–63, 142, 232, figs. 21, 53, 120, Pls. XVIII, LVIII; watch-spring, 279. *See also* Angle capital, *Canalis*, Eye, Helix
Votive monument, 121, 142–144, 211–212, 253–254, 285, 326–327, *354*, figs. 44, 93, Pls. XXXIII, L. *See also* Column (votive), Commemorative
Voussoir, 30, 294, 295, 328, 395

Wages, salaries, 194
Wall, base, 139, 140, 150, 170, 180, 234, 273n, 276, Pls. XLV, XLVI, LIII; capital, *see* Epicranitis; tapering, 165–166; wooden, 198, 208, 241, 290
War memorial, 91, 107, 150–151, 198. *See also* Commemorative
Water-basin. *See* Reservoir, Tank
Water-spout, dog head, 218, 221; lion head, 52, 90, 96, 105, 109, 118, 132, 152, 194, 217, 259n, 268n, 279, fig. 86, Pls. XVII, XXXI–XXXII, LV, LIX; (false), 98, 178, Pls. XXXIX–XL; ram head, 90; (false), 113; replaced by pierced interstices, 81, 193–194, 201, fig. 29; trumpet, 44, 72, 78, 90
Wattle-and-daub, 4, 5
Wave pattern, 27, 238, Pl. LIX
Window, Aegean, 5, 11, 20, fig. 8, Pl. IV; Greek, 42, 113, 183, 189, 194, 195, 235, 236, 241, 252, 278, 284, 290, 291, 293–294, 297, *351*, figs. 72, 76, 86, 88, Pls. XLVI, L; in pediment, 42, 132n, 225, 276, 277, fig. 15
Wood. *See* Anta (casing), Architrave (internal), Beam, Braced beam, Ceiling, Clamp, Column, Coffer, Empolion, Entablature, Fence, Floor, Gutter (cover), Half-timber, *Ikria*, Jamb (casing), Ladder, Parodos (gate), *Pinax*, Pins, Post, Proscenium, Ridge beam, Roof construction, Scene building, Shingle, Shutter boards, Stairway, Statue (chryselephantine, wood), Wall (wood)
Workmen, 194
Wreath, 239

Xoanon. *See* Statue
Xystus, 397

Zig-zag pattern, 18, Pl. XIII
Zophorus, 132, 139, 397. *See also* Frieze